D0848990

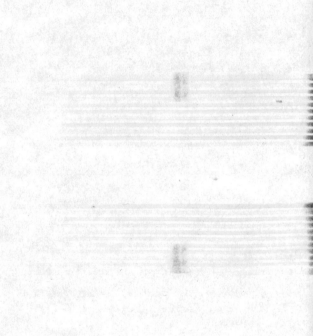

THE
CAMBRIDGE EDITION OF
THE LETTERS AND WORKS OF
D.H. LAWRENCE

THE LETTERS OF D.H. LAWRENCE

*Vol. I: September 1901 – May 1913
James T. Boulton

*Vol. II: June 1913 – October 1916
George J. Zytaruk and James T. Boulton

Vol. III: October 1916 – June 1921
James T. Boulton and Andrew Robertson

Vol. IV: 1921 – 1924
Warren Roberts and Elizabeth Mansfield

Vol. V: 1924 – 1927
David Farmer, James T. Boulton and Lindeth Vasey

Vol. VI: 1927 – 1928
Gerald M. Lacy and James T. Boulton

Vol. VII: 1928 – 1930
Keith Sagar and James T. Boulton

* Already published

THE LETTERS OF D. H. LAWRENCE

THE LETTERS OF
D. H. LAWRENCE

VOLUME III
October 1916 – June 1921

EDITED BY

JAMES T. BOULTON

AND

ANDREW ROBERTSON

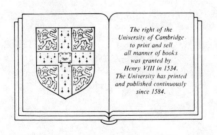

The right of the
University of Cambridge
to print and sell
all manner of books
was granted by
Henry VIII in 1534.
The University has printed
and published continuously
since 1584.

CAMBRIDGE UNIVERSITY PRESS

CAMBRIDGE

LONDON · NEW YORK · NEW ROCHELLE
MELBOURNE · SYDNEY

Published by the Press Syndicate of the University of Cambridge
The Pitt Building, Trumpington Street, Cambridge CB2 1RP
32 East 57th Street, New York, NY 10022, USA
296 Beaconsfield Parade, Middle Park, Melbourne 3206, Australia

First published 1984

Printed in Great Britain at
the University Press, Cambridge

Library of Congress Catalogue card number: 78–7531

British Library Cataloguing in Publication Data
Lawrence, D. H.
The Letters of D. H. Lawrence.
Vol. 3: October 1916 – June 1921 (The Cambridge
edition of the letters and works of D. H. Lawrence)
1. Lawrence, D. H. – Correspondence
2. Authors, English – 20th century – Correspondence
I. Title   II. Boulton, James T.
III. Robertson, Andrew
ISBN 0 521 23112 4

SE

CONTENTS

ILLUSTRATIONS

Between pages 322 and 323

ACKNOWLEDGEMENTS

The Editorial Board continue to be deeply grateful for the generosity displayed by all holders of Lawrence manuscripts. The list of cue-titles of manuscript locations shows the particular owners to whom the present editors are indebted.

The volume editors have benefitted from the critical, but kindly, advice given them by other members of the Editorial Board. They have also been sustained in their work by the unflagging interest of Mr Michael Black and his staff at Cambridge University Press. A notable debt of gratitude is owed to Dr Lindeth Vasey: her meticulous editing for the Press has been of incalculable service.

A variety of people have kindly put their time and knowledge at the editors' disposal. Those to whom thanks are especially due include the following: Dr Colin Bailey; Dr Ben Benedikz; Dr Neville Birdsall; Mr Giovanni Cacópardo; Mr John P. Carswell; Mr W. H. Clarke; Mr Guy Collings; Dr Philip Crumpton; Mr Jim Davies; Mr Tony Davies; the Director of the Uffizi Gallery, Florence; Mrs Diana Farr; Mr L. Foreman; Dr Nigel Fortune; Mr Salvatore Galeano; Miss Jenny Gill; Mrs Chloë Green; Mr Ian Greenlees; Professor James Hepburn; Dr Jürgen Hess; Mrs Enid Hilton; Dr A. V. M. Hubrecht; Professor Philip McNair; Mr Salvatore Martorana; Professor Hamish Miles; Mr Cyril Noall; Miss Daphne Phelps; Mr Piers Plowman; Mr Gerald Pollinger; Miss Marjory Rigby; Mrs Rachel Robertson; Dr Janice Robinson; Mr Anthony Rota; Professor Harold Shapiro; Mr G. S. Slowey; Mrs Norah Smallwood; Dr Robert Smallwood; Professor Robert Smith; Dr Bruce Steele; Professor Arrigo Subiotto; Rev. D. N. Swain; Mr Ron Swift; Mr Adam Thorpe; Mr Julian Trevelyan; Mrs Julian Vinogradoff; Mr Nicholas Welchman; Dr Paul Werkman; Dr John Worthen; Mr Carlo Zuccaro.

Special thanks are due to Dr Frank K. Robinson who has again been responsible for translating the letters Lawrence wrote in German, to Mrs Anne Buckley whose secretarial assistance has been quite invaluable, and to Mrs Alma Forbes who compiled the final index. And finally, the editors are deeply indebted to Mrs Margaret Boulton who typed the text of the entire volume, prepared most of the index and read proof.

For permission to use copyright material in the annotation, gratitude is expressed to: Messrs Chatto and Windus (for letters relating to the publication of *Look! We Have Come Through!*); Mrs Sylvia Secker (for letters written by Martin Secker); University of Illinois (for use of the Secker Letter-Book).

Illustrations in the volume have been made available through the kindness of: the Beinecke Rare Book and Manuscript Library, Yale University; Mrs Joan Curtis Brown; Mr John P. Carswell; Mrs Diana Farr; Mrs Chloë Green; Mrs Olive Hopkin; Dr A. V. M. Hubrecht; Mrs Alexandra Lee Levin; the National Portrait Gallery; Mrs Margaret Needham; Mr Piers Plowman; Mrs Jay Harold Russell; Mr Richard Sadler; the late Mr Charles H. Smith; the University of Birmingham.

NOTE ON THE TEXT

A full statement of the 'Rules of Transcription' and an explanation of the 'Editorial Apparatus' are provided in Volume I, pp. xviii–xx. The reader may, however, like to be reminded that the following symbols are used:

[   ] indicates a defect in the MS making it impossible even to conjecture what Lawrence had written. Where a reconstruction can be hazarded or a fault corrected, the conjecture or correction is shown within the square brackets.

[. . .] indicates a deletion which cannot be deciphered or a postmark which is wholly or partly illegible.

TMS= typed manuscript

TMSC= typed manuscript copy

TSCC= typescript carbon copy

Maps are provided to show the location of places which Lawrence visited for the first time during the period covered by this volume. No attempt has been made fully to repeat information given on the maps in Volumes I and II.

CUE-TITLES

Cue-titles are employed both for manuscript locations and for printed works. The following appear in this volume.

A. Manuscript locations

BL	British Library
BosU	Boston University
BucU	Bucknell University
Carswell	Mr John Carswell
Clarke	Mr W. H. Clarke
ColU	Columbia University
CorU	Cornell University
Cotterell	Mrs Hilda Cotterell
Davis	Mr A. R. Davis
DC	Dartmouth College
Dunlop	Mr John Dunlop
Forster	Mr W. Forster
GSArchiv	Goethe–und Schiller-Archiv, Weimar
HL	Henry E. Huntington Library and Art Gallery

HU	Harvard University
Hubrecht	Dr A. V. M. Hubrecht
IEduc	Iowa State Education Association
Jeffrey	Mr Frederick Jeffrey
KCC	King's College, Cambridge
Lazarus	Mr George Lazarus
LC	Library of Congress
NCL	Nottinghamshire County Libraries
Needham	Mrs Margaret Needham
NL	Newberry Library
NWU	Northwestern University
NYPL	New York Public Library
NZNL	National Library of New Zealand
Plowman	Mr Piers Plowman
RLFund	Royal Literary Fund
Sagar	Dr Keith Sagar
Simpson	Mr Robert L. Simpson
SIU	Southern Illinois University
Smith	the late Mr Charles H. Smith
StaU	Stanford University
UB	University of Birmingham
UCB	University of California at Berkeley
UChi	University of Chicago
UCin	University of Cincinnati
UCLA	University of California at Los Angeles
UInd	University of Indiana
UN	University of Nottingham
UNCCH	University of North Carolina at Chapel Hill
UNM	University of New Mexico
UNYB	State University of New York at Buffalo
UP	University of Pennsylvania
UT	University of Texas at Austin
UTul	University of Tulsa
UV	University of Virginia
Young	Mr K. M. Young
YU	Yale University

B. Printed works

(The place of publication, here and throughout, is London unless otherwise stated.)

Asquith, *Diaries*	Lady Cynthia Asquith. *Diaries: 1915–1918.* Hutchinson, 1968
Carswell, *Adelphi*	Catherine Carswell, 'Reminiscences of D. H. Lawrence', *Adelphi*, iii (November 1931–March 1932), 77–85, 162–70, 210–18, 283–93, 387–96
Carswell	Catherine Carswell. *The Savage Pilgrimage: A Narrative of D. H. Lawrence*. Chatto and Windus, 1932
Damon	S. Foster Damon. *Amy Lowell: A Chronicle*. New York: Houghton Mifflin, 1935
Delany	Paul Delany. *D. H. Lawrence's Nightmare*. Hassocks, Sussex: The Harvester Press, 1979
DHL Review	James C. Cowan, ed. *The D. H. Lawrence Review*. Fayetteville: University of Arkansas, 1968–
Gransden	K. W. Gransden, 'Rananim: D. H. Lawrence's Letters to S. S. Koteliansky', *Twentieth Century*, clix (January–June, 1955), 22–32
Huxley	Aldous Huxley, ed. *The Letters of D. H. Lawrence.* Heinemann, 1932
Lacy, *Seltzer*	Gerald M. Lacy, ed. *D. H. Lawrence: Letters to Thomas and Adele Seltzer*. Santa Barbara: Black Sparrow Press, 1976
Lawrence–Gelder	Ada Lawrence and G. Stuart Gelder. *Young Lorenzo: Early Life of D. H. Lawrence.* Florence: G. Orioli [1931]
Letters, i.	James T. Boulton, ed. *The Letters of D. H. Lawrence*, Volume I, September 1901–May 1913. Cambridge: Cambridge University Press, 1979
Letters, ii.	George J. Zytaruk and James T. Boulton, eds. *The Letters of D. H. Lawrence*, Volume II, June 1913–October 1916. Cambridge: Cambridge University Press, 1981
Mackenzie	Compton Mackenzie. *My Life and Times: Octave Five 1915–1923*. Chatto and Windus, 1966
Moore, *Intelligent Heart*	Harry T. Moore. *The Intelligent Heart: The Story of D. H. Lawrence.* New York: Farrar, Straus, and Young, 1954

Moore, *Poste Restante*	Harry T. Moore. *Poste Restante: A Lawrence Travel Calendar*. Berkeley and Los Angeles: University of California Press, 1956
Moore	Harry T. Moore, ed. *The Collected Letters of D. H. Lawrence*. 2 volumes. Heinemann, 1962
Nehls	Edward Nehls, ed. *D. H. Lawrence: A Composite Biography*. 3 volumes. Madison: University of Wisconsin Press, 1957–9
Roberts	Warren Roberts. *A Bibliography of D. H. Lawrence*, 2nd edition. Cambridge: Cambridge University Press, 1982.
Secker	Martin Secker, ed. *Letters from D. H. Lawrence to Martin Secker 1911–1930*. [Bridgefoot, Iver] 1970
Tedlock, *Lawrence MSS*	E. W. Tedlock. *The Frieda Lawrence Collection of D. H. Lawrence Manuscripts: A Descriptive Bibliography*. Albuquerque: University of New Mexico, 1948
Zytaruk	George J. Zytaruk, ed. *The Quest for Rananim: D. H. Lawrence's Letters to S. S. Koteliansky 1914 to 1930*. Montreal: McGill–Queen's University Press, 1970

MONETARY TERMS

tanner = sixpence (6d) = $2\frac{1}{2}$p.
bob = one shilling (1/–) = 5p.
half-a-crown = 2/6 = $12\frac{1}{2}$p.
quid = £1.
guinea = £1/1/– = £1.05.

17 March 1916– 15 October 1917	At Higher Tregerthen, Zennor, St Ives, Cornwall
c. 7 November 1916	Visited by Robert Mountsier and Esther Andrews
21 November 1916	Returns typescript of *Women in Love* to Pinker
22 November 1916	St Ives
Christmas 1916	Visited by Mountsier and Esther Andrews; she stays till c. 12 January 1917
January 1917	'Street Lamps' in *The Egoist*
c. 4 January 1917	Reading for *Studies in Classic American* *Literature*
February 1917	'Autumn Rain' in *The Egoist*
12 February 1917	Refused fresh passports for America
March 1917	'Samson and Delilah' in *English Review*; 'The Thimble' in *Seven Arts*
April 1917	'England, My England' in *Metropolitan*
6 April 1917	USA declares war on Germany
11 April–11 May 1917	Esther Andrews at Higher Tregerthen
14 April 1917	'Terra Nuova' in *Some Imagist Poets*; Ripley, Derbyshire (at Ada Clarke's)
19 April 1917	Nottingham
19–25 April 1917	London (at Koteliansky's in St John's Wood)
25–7 April 1917	Chapel Farm Cottage, Hermitage, Berkshire
27 April 1917	Returns to Higher Tregerthen
4 May 1917	Penzance
30 May 1917	St Ives
May–August 1917	'The Reality of Peace I' – 'IV' in *English* *Review*
June 1917	'Resurrection' in *Poetry*
8 June 1917	Penzance
c. 16–19 June 1917	London to see specialist (stays at Dollie Radford's in Hampstead)
23 June 1917	Bodmin (for Army medical re-examination)
July 1917	'The Mortal Coil' in *Seven Arts*
from August 1917	Lawrence and Frieda under surveillance by the authorities

25 August 1917	Receives TS of *Women in Love* from Cecil Palmer
29 August 1917	Bosigran Castle (staying with Cecil Gray)
September 1917	'The Sea', 'Constancy of a Sort' and 'Frost Flowers' in *English Review*
12 October 1917	Police raid Higher Tregerthen; Lawrences ordered out of Cornwall by 15 October
15 October 1917	London (at Dollie Radford's)
c. 20 October– 30 November 1917	44 Mecklenburgh Square (Hilda Aldington's flat); begins writing *Aaron's Rod*
c. 22 October 1917	Meets Arabella Yorke
31 October – post 6 November 1917	Visited by Ada Clarke
2 November 1917	Seeks permission from War Office to return to Cornwall (refused c. 15 November)
16 November 1917	Meets John Galsworthy
18 November 1917	Offers *Women in Love* to Maunsel & Co., Dublin (rejected c. 29 November)
26 November 1917	*Look! We Have Come Through!* published in England by Chatto and Windus (in USA by Huebsch in 1918)
30 November– 18 December 1917	13B Earls Court Square (at Mrs Gray's)
11 December 1917	Visited by C.I.D.; asks Lady Cynthia Asquith to intervene via contacts in Scotland Yard
c. 13 December 1917	Sends *Women in Love* to Fisher Unwin (returned January 1918)
18 December 1917– 2 May 1918	Chapel Farm Cottage, Hermitage, Newbury, Berkshire
28 December 1917– 11 January 1918	Ripley (at Clarkes')
January 1918	'Love' in *English Review*
4? January 1918	London (at Kot's)
12 January 1918	Hermitage
February 1918	'Life' in *English Review*
19 February 1918	Sends *Women in Love* to Cyril Beaumont
26 February 1918	Temporarily lodges with Bessie Lowe in Hermitage
5–6 March 1918	London (at Kot's)
6 March 1918	Hermitage

5–12 April 1918	Ripley
18 April 1918	Completes collection of poems for *Bay*; selects poems for *New Poems*
19 April 1918	Decides to keep lease of Higher Tregerthen (relinquished 28 December)
c. 24 April 1918	Receives TS of *Women in Love* from Lady Cynthia Asquith
May 1918	'Labour Battalion' and 'No News' in *New Paths*
2 May 1918– 24 April 1919	Mountain Cottage, Middleton-by-Wirksworth, Derbyshire
June 1918	'War-Baby', 'Town' and 'After the Opera' in *English Review*
14 June 1918	Visits Eastwood; applies for assistance from Royal Literary Fund
30 June 1918	Ripley
12 July 1918	Receives £50 from Royal Literary Fund
26 July 1918	Completes first three chapters of *Movements in European History*
12–16 August 1918	London (at Kot's)
17–20 August 1918	Mersea, Essex (staying with Barbara Low and Edith Eder)
20–2 August 1918	London (at Kot's)
22–6 August 1918	Hermitage (at Margaret Radford's)
26–31 August 1918	Ross-on-Wye, Herefordshire (with Carswells)
31 August 1918	Returns to Middleton-by-Wirksworth
11 September 1918	Called for Army medical re-examination at Derby; graded 'for secondary work' by military authorities (26 September)
October 1918	*New Poems* published in England by Martin Secker (in USA by Huebsch on 11 June 1920); writes *Touch and Go*
7 October 1918	London (at Dollie Radford's); visits the Murrys
c. 14 October 1918	Visits G. S. Freeman, editor of *The Times Educational Supplement*, who requests articles
22 October– 19? November 1918	Hermitage
November 1918	'Spirit of Place' in *English Review*
11 November 1918	Armistice

12 November 1918	London for Armistice party (at Montague Shearman's)
19? November 1918	London (at Kot's); visits Catherine Carswell, Katherine Mansfield, Richard and Hilda Aldington
28 November 1918	Returns to Middleton-by-Wirksworth (Frieda returns 14 December)
30 November– 1 December 1918	Ripley; Eastwood
December 1918	'Benjamin Franklin' in *English Review*
5 December 1918	Completes first essays of 'Education of the People' for *Times Educational Supplement* (rejected 1 January 1919)
10 December 1918	Finishes 'The Fox'
19 December 1918	Matlock
25–7 December 1918	Ripley
January 1919	'Henry St John Crèvecœur' in *English Review*
29 January 1919	Matlock
February 1919	Six poems in *Poetry*; 'Fenimore Cooper's Anglo-American Novels' in *English Review*
3 February 1919	Completes *Movements in European History*
c. 15 February– 17 March 1919	Ripley; Lawrence collapsed with influenza
6 March 1919	Middleton Murry, editor of *Athenæum*, asks for contributions
17 March 1919	Returns to Middleton-by-Wirksworth with Ada and Jackie Clarke
April 1919	'Edgar Allan Poe' in *English Review*; 'Tickets Please' in *Strand*
11 April 1919	'Whistling of Birds' in *Athenæum*
23 April 1919	Finishes revision of *Movements in European History*
24 April 1919	Leaves Middleton; in Birmingham
25 April– 28 July 1919	Returns to Hermitage (staying with Margaret Radford)
May 1919	'Nathaniel Hawthorne' in *English Review*
June 1919	'The Two Principles' in *English Review*
8 June 1919	Resumes writing *Aaron's Rod*
July 1919	'The Little Town at Evening' in *Monthly Chapbook*; 'War Films' in *Poetry*; three poems in *Voices*

3–4 July 1919	London (at Barbara Low's and then Kot's) to obtain passports; visits Clifford Bax and Edward Marsh
5–6 July 1919	To the Foye House, Otford, Kent, with Vere Collins (at Helen Thomas's)
7 July 1919	London
8 July 1919	Returns to Hermitage
22 July 1919	London (at Kot's); sees Edward Marsh, meets Edward Moult
28 July– 29 August 1919	Myrtle Cottage, Pangbourne, Berkshire (at Rosalind Baynes's)
August 1919	Second edition of *New Poems* (Secker)
c. 6–29? August 1919	Editing Kot's translation of Shestov's *All Things Are Possible*
13 August 1919	Visits Margaret Radford at Hermitage; visits Cecily Lambert and Violet Monk
15 August 1919	Joined by Rosalind Baynes, and by Godwin Baynes on 21st
22 August 1919	Mapledurham
28 August 1919	Writes preface for American edition of *New Poems*
29 August– 12 September 1919	Grimsbury Farm, Long Lane, Newbury, Berkshire (staying with Cecily Lambert and Violet Monk)
7 September 1919	Corrects proofs of *Bay*. Introduced to Thomas Seltzer through Goldring; sends him *Women in Love*, further revised; Secker offers to publish novel in England
12 September– 4 November 1919	Hermitage
30 September 1919	Completes *Studies in Classic American Literature* (sends MS to Huebsch, 10 October)
October 1919	'Verse Free and Unfree' in *Voices*
14 October 1919	London (at Catherine Carswell's in Hampstead)
15 October 1919	Frieda departs for Germany
16 October 1919	Visits Douglas Goldring
17 October 1919	Returns to Hermitage
18 October 1919	'The Average' in *The Word* (first of three essays later published as 'Democracy')
c. 20–5 October 1919	Ripley

25 October 1919	'Identity' in *The Word*
4–14 November 1919	London (at Kot's); visits Goldring and Thomas Dunlop, meets Max Plowman
14 November 1919	Paris, en route for Italy
15–17 November 1919	Modane; Turin; Val Salice (staying with Sir Walter and Lady Becker)
17–19 November 1919	Genoa; Lerici
19 November– 10 December 1919	Florence; sees Norman Douglas, meets Maurice Magnus
20 November 1919	*Bay* published in England by Cyril Beaumont
December 1919	Writes 'David'; 'Seven Seals' in *Georgian Poetry 1918–1919*
3 December 1919	Frieda arrives from Baden-Baden
6 December 1919	'Personality ' in *The Word*
10–13 December 1919	Rome
13–22 December 1919	Picinisco (staying with Orazio Cervi)
22 December 1919	Naples, via Atino and Cassino
23 December 1919	Capri; meets Francis and Jessica Brett Young
25 December 1919– 26 February 1920	Palazzo Ferraro, Capri; friendship with Compton Mackenzie
27 December 1919	Breaks with Pinker
20 January 1920	Gilbert Cannan's 'A Defense of Lawrence' in *New York Tribune*
27–9 January 1920	Amalfi
29 January 1920	Completes *Psychoanalysis and the Unconscious*
30 January 1920	Breaks with Middleton Murry, and with Katherine Mansfield on 8 February
early February 1920	Ill with 'flu'
12 February 1920	Arrival of MS of 'The Insurrection of Miss Houghton' from Germany; begins rewriting as *The Lost Girl*
16 February 1920	Asks Mountsier to act as his American agent (accepted on 26 March)
26 February 1920	Sicily
6 March 1920	Giardini
8 March–2 August 1920	Fontana Vecchia, Taormina, Sicily
9 March 1920	Confirms Seltzer as American publisher
10–13 March 1920	*The Widowing of Mrs Holroyd* produced by Altrincham Stage Society, Cheshire
28 March 1920	Secker offers to publish *The Rainbow* and *Women in Love*

April 1920	*All Things Are Possible* published in England by Secker
7 April 1920	Shestov extracts in *Freeman*
8 April 1920	Visited by Gilbert Cannan
9 April 1920	Offers Secker rights to half-completed *The Lost Girl*
ante 18 April 1920	Catania
24–7 April 1920	Randazzo with Jan Juta, Réné Hansard and Alan Insole; Maniace (visits the Duca di Bronte, 25 April); Syracuse (staying with Alan Insole)
29 April 1920	'You Touched Me' in *Land and Water*
May 1920	*Touch and Go* published in England by Daniel (in USA by Seltzer on 5 June)
5 May 1920	Finishes *The Lost Girl*; sends first half to Rome for typing
17–28 May 1920	Malta with Mary Cannan; visits Maurice Magnus
ante 29 May 1920	Lawrence sketched by Juta
11 June 1920	Sends typescripts of *The Lost Girl* to USA via Ciccio Cacópardo and to England via Mackenzie
16 June 1920	Finishes revising *Studies in Classic American Literature*
19 June 1920	'Poetry of the Present' in *New York Evening Post Book Review*
24 June 1920	Finishes 'Education of the People'; final revisions of *The Lost Girl* sent to Secker
July 1920	'The Blind Man' in *English Review*
c. 7 July 1920	Curtis Brown approaches Lawrence to act as agent
2–5? August 1930	Montecassino
6–7 August 1920	In Rome with Juta
7 August 1920	'The Blind Man' in *Living Age*
8–12 August 1920	'San Filippo', Anticoli Corrado, near Rome (staying with Juta and Insole)
12–15 August 1920	Florence
16–18 August 1920	Milan
17 August– 1 September 1920	With Percy and Irene Whittley on walking-tour to Lakes Como, Iseo and Garda, Verona, Venice; Frieda to Baden-Baden

30 August 1920	Sends corrected proofs of *The Lost Girl* to Seltzer and Secker
September 1920	'Adolf' in *Dial*
2 September 1920	Florence
3–28 September 1920	Villa Canovaia, San Gervasio (borrowed from Rosalind Baynes); visits Reginald Turner and Anna di Chiara; writes 'Fruits'
8 September 1920	Settignano; visits Herbert Trench
16 September 1920	Anton Kippenberg granted German translation rights for one year (in November 1920 extended till 1924)
ante 24 September 1920	Meets Carlota Thrasher
28 September– 14 October 1920	Venice; sees Juta and Insole
30 September 1920	Finishes 'Tortoises'
Autumn 1920	*Foreword to Women in Love* published in USA by Seltzer
7 October 1920	Frieda returns from Germany
14 October 1920	Florence
18 October 1920– 9 April 1921	Fontana Vecchia
25 October 1920	Receives advance copy of *The Lost Girl*
4 November 1920	MS of *Birds, Beasts and Flowers* sent to typist
8 November 1920	'The Fox' in *Hutchinson's Story Magazine*
9 November 1920	*Women in Love* published in USA by Seltzer (in England by Secker, June 1921)
25 November 1920	*The Lost Girl* published in England by Secker (in USA by Seltzer, January 1921)
c. 28 November 1920	Begins *Mr Noon*
29 November 1920	Letojanni
December 1920	'America, Listen to Your Own' in *New Republic*
1 December 1920	'Tropic' and 'Slopes of Etna' sent to Professor John Metcalf for *The Enchanted Years* (published in USA, June 1921)
c. 12 December 1920	Resumes writing *Mr Noon* after 'sudden stop'
31 December 1920	Completes two thirds of *Mr Noon*
4–5 January 1921	Palermo
5–13 January 1921	Sardinia; visits Cagliari, Mandas, Sorgono, Nuoro, Terranova; returns to Sicily (Fontana Vecchia) via Rome and Naples

5 January 1921	'Medlars and Sorb Apples' in *New Republic*
19 January 1921	'The Revolutionary' in *New Republic*
from 21 January 1921	Writing 'Diary of a Trip to Sardinia' (later *Sea and Sardinia*)
c. 27 January 1921	Visited by Juta and Insole; Juta paints Lawrence's portrait
February 1921	*Movements in European History* published in England by Oxford University Press; 'Rex' in *Dial*; *The Widowing of Mrs Holroyd* reissued by Seltzer
4 February 1921	Amends *Women in Love* for Secker
22 February 1921	Sends TS of *Mr Noon* Part 1 (to be three parts) to Mountsier
22 February 1921	Finishes 'Diary of a Trip to Sardinia'
March 1921	'Pomegranate' in *Dial*
c. 5–20 March 1921	Millicent Beveridge paints Lawrence's portrait
11–14 March 1921	Palermo; sees Frieda off to Baden-Baden
22 March 1921	Sends TSS of *Birds, Beasts and Flowers* and *Mr Noon* Part 1 to Barbara Low, who agrees to act as Lawrence's English agent
28 March 1921	Sends TS of *Sea and Sardinia* to Mountsier
April 1921	'Apostolic Beasts' in *Dial*
4 April 1921	Asks Curtis Brown to be his English agent
9 April 1921	Palermo
15–19 April 1921	Capri; meets Earl and Achsah Brewster
19–20 April 1921	Rome
21 April 1921	Florence; sees Rebecca West
23 April 1921	In Switzerland
26 April 1921	Baden-Baden
27 April–10 July 1921	Hôtel Krone, Ebersteinburg, Baden-Baden
May 1921	Juta in Sardinia painting illustrations for *Sea and Sardinia*
from 2 May 1921	Resumes writing *Aaron's Rod*
10 May 1921	*Psychoanalysis and the Unconscious* published in USA by Seltzer (in England by Secker, July 1923)
11 May 1921	'Humming-Bird' in *New Republic*
1 June 1921	Finishes *Aaron's Rod*; begins *Fantasia and the Unconscious*
c. 10 June 1921	*Women in Love* published in England by Secker

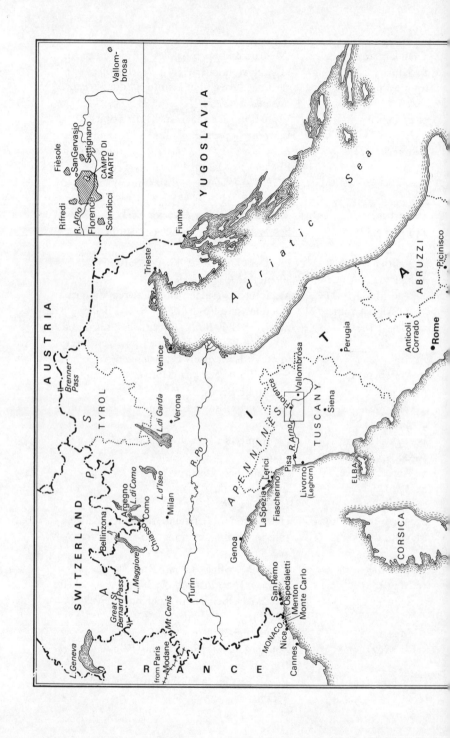

Taranto

CALABRIA

Ionian Sea

Naples

Salerno

Straits of Messina

Letojanni
Taormina
Giardini
Naxos

CAPRI

Randazzo

Bronte · Mt Etna

Catania

Syracusa

MALTA
Valetta

Città Vecchia

Palermo

SICILY

Girgenti
(Agrigento)

Trapani

MEDITERRANEAN SEA

Naples

Mt Vesuvius

Pompeii

Castellammare

Vietri Salerno

Amalfi

Gulf of Salerno

Sorrento

Bay of Naples

Massalubreuse

Anacapri Capri Il Farraglione

CAPRI Mt Solaro

Marina Piccola

ISCHIA

SARDINIA

Nuoro

Mt Gennargentu

Mandas

Cagliari

N

AFRICA

Tunis

0   5   100 miles

0   100   200 km

Italy (c. 1919)

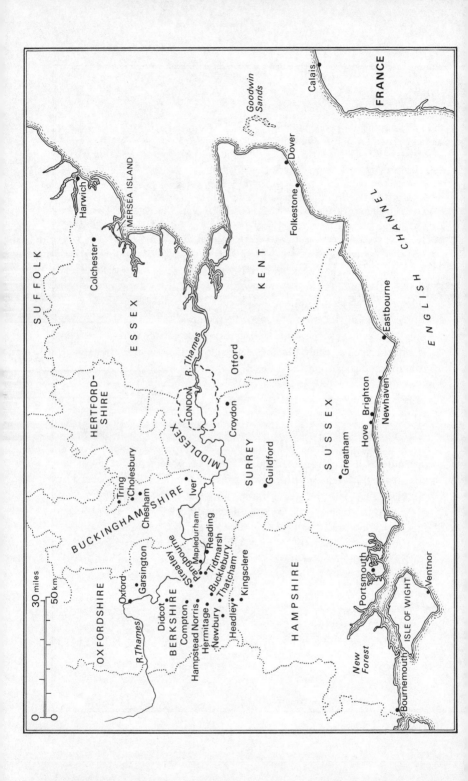

INTRODUCTION

In England during the period of the war – pretty well isolated. In 1915 *The Rainbow* was suppressed for immorality – and the sense of detachment from the bourgeois world, the world which controls press, publication and all, became almost complete. He had no interest in it, no desire to be at one with it. Anyhow the suppression of *The Rainbow* had proved it impossible. Henceforth he put away any idea of 'success', of succeeding with the British bourgeois public, and stayed apart.

Left England in 1919, for Italy – had a house for two years in Taormina, Sicily. In 1920 was published in America *Women in Love* which every publisher for four years had refused to accept, because of *The Rainbow* scandal. In Taormina wrote *The Lost Girl, Sea and Sardinia*, and most of *Aaron's Rod*.[1]

So Lawrence – looking back from 1928 – surveyed in his brief 'Auto-biography' the period covered by this volume. Noticeably he scarcely provides even a skeletal outline of private or public events: his emphasis is elsewhere. It is on the effects of the war, isolation, detachment from the seemingly malevolent society which punished and frustrated him as a writer. America is glanced at; Italy becomes central; and finally comes the flow of major publications, each of them in varying degrees significantly associated with Mediterranean lands. In the letters there are, it is true, other important themes; but Lawrence accurately points to those which are especially prominent.

Letters early in the volume, to Forster or Lady Cynthia Asquith, for example, recall comparable outbursts about the war to the same and other correspondents in Volume 2. Flood imagery, also found in the previous volume, recurs. Lawrence's virulence and misanthropy are still to be seen. He is in a black fury with the world; humanity is rat-like; he prophesies that man's self-destructiveness will continue for many generations; and the war itself is stupid, monstrous and contemptible.[2] Koteliansky learns that, if he is clear-sighted and willing to accept reality, he must acknowledge man's essential evil; Catherine Carswell is congratulated because she is 'beginning to reject people'; and Lawrence himself is overwhelmed by evidence of 'fiendishness triumphant over the earth'.[3] The war was for Lawrence, as Compton Mackenzie later put it, 'a period of continuous mental torment'.[4] Inevitably the anguish was exacerbated by his hatred of the army medical examinations at Bodmin and Derby, and by his expulsion from Cornwall in October 1917; these gave an extra dimension to his loathing of militarism; but

---

[1] Nehls, iii. 234.
[2] See Letters 1303 and 1311.
[3] Letters 1305, 1306, 1370.
[4] Nehls, ii. 24–5.

I

they also strengthened his conviction that the world as a whole was a 'Slough of Despond'.[5]

It would be wrong to infer, however, that the dominant characteristics of the war-time letters here are railing and savage indignation. Many letters in 1917–18 contain no reference to the war. What Lawrence called his 'suspended fury' makes its presence felt through allusions to 'Ypres and Mount Kemmels', or metaphors – 'gangrened inertia' – clearly prompted by his imaginative response to trench-warfare;[6] but the anger so often evident in Volume 2 is generally replaced by a numb, horrified acceptance, an exhausted resentment. 'We are tired in body and soul'; 'one's heart gets very dry and weary with the day after day of this life – all suspense and tension and nullity and humiliation'; 'these months and years of slow execution'.[7] Yet, though Lawrence once proclaimed his 'genuine indifference to public questions',[8] his underlying bitterness cannot always be contained. It breaks through, for example, in an ironic re-phrasing of a line from one of his own poems written before the expulsion from Cornwall. The poem, 'Craving for Spring' (written by April 1917), celebrates the season's actual and symbolic vitality as well as the poet's intense longing for universal rejuvenation; its penultimate line in manuscript read: 'do not let me die on the brink of so much hope!'. Writing to his friend and neighbour in Cornwall, Cecil Gray, Lawrence says: 'What shall we do, how shall we get out of this Inferno? "Pray not to die on the brink of so much horror"', to parody myself.[9] Naturally, as the war gradually drew to a close, he sensed 'a curious nascent quality in the world'; he rejoiced in 'sweet peace' when the Treaty of Paris was eventually signed in June 1919;[10] but the conviction that this represented the passing of winter and coming of spring is absent. That theme is more confidently present in his essay, 'Whistling of Birds' (published in April 1919 though written two years earlier), than in the letters.

'Only the human warmth, when one can get it, makes the heart rich.'[11] This belief, of course, is frequently apparent; it is particularly evident during the late years of the war. 'In a world where most of the human influence is now destructive and horribly humiliating',[12] the very process of recalling,

[5]   Letter 1655.
[6]   Letter 1565.
[7]   Letters 1454 (translation), 1591, 1605.
[8]   Letter 1574.
[9]   Letter 1466 and n.2. (When published in *Look! We Have Come Through!*, in December 1917, the line of the poem read: 'Ah, do not let me die on the brink of such anticipation!')
[10] Letters 1624, 1752.
[11] Letter 1590.
[12] Ibid.

recording or reinforcing satisfying human relationships was both pleasurable and therapeutic. It took various forms. There is a generous warmth in his occasional letters to the Hopkins, maintaining his links with Eastwood; in his expression of sympathy with Amy Lowell's illness and bereavement; in his readiness to help Nancy Henry get her husband's poems published; even in a couple of tolerably good-natured letters to Middleton Murry.[13] To give vicarious pleasure to his correspondents, to stir their imagination or provide amusement, was to engage their sympathy and secure their affection. Hence his report of the local Zennor gossip about Meredith and Lady Starr for Lady Cynthia (which incidentally marks Lawrence out as a reader of newspapers, here the local *St Ives Times*); or the justly famous descriptive letters to Katherine Mansfield, particularly the brilliant account of animal marks in the snow close to his Derbyshire cottage.[14] Other features of Lawrence's letters demand our attention, but these remain important and always memorable.

Highly as he valued close human attachment, Lawrence also needed separateness, independence. 'I can't be jammed in among people any more . . . we suffer badly at being cooped up with other folk.'[15] This reaction was on the personal level; the corollary – a determination to achieve autonomy – had what must be described as a political dimension. The resolution to break free is similarly present in a remark to Lady Cynthia in September 1918. Writing from Wirksworth Lawrence proclaimed: 'I've been shut up long enough . . . I want to burst this sort of coccoon that I'm in – it is likely to prove a shroud, if I don't.'[16] Again the immediate impulse was to break out of the isolation of Derbyshire, to be disentangled from his family; but the remark had wider implications. To achieve freedom and independence on the larger scale impelled Lawrence into political thought since it called into question his attitude to 'the bourgeois world' mentioned at the outset.

'The principle of life is after all stronger than the principle of death', he had told Lady Cynthia in April 1917, 'and I spit on your London and your government and your armies. Pah, what are they, Lloyd Georges and Haigs and such-like canaille?'[17] Frequently in later works – in *Kangaroo* and the 1924 Epilogue for *Movements in European History*, for example – Lloyd George was identified, as here, with an oppressive, bullying mob-spirit which was anathema to Lawrence both in personal and in social terms. 'Liberty, ones own proud liberty, is worth everything else on earth.'[18] The conflict is plain; so is the cause of his disaffection from a society presided over by the 'clever

[13] See Letters 1326, 1412, 1417, 1596. [16] Letter 1635.
[14] Letters 1452, 1698. [17] Letter 1407.
[15] Letter 1541. [18] Letter 1933.

little Welsh *rat*' and symbolised by 'that bloated ignominy, *John Bull*', the child of Lawrence's *bête-noir*, Horatio Bottomley.[19] A political stance was inevitable particularly when society, whether in the shape of General Western, who signed the expulsion order from Cornwall, or the Special Branch which kept him under surveillance, curtailed his freedom. It is therefore scarcely surprising to find significant evidence in the letters of Lawrence's inclination towards the radical Left (though there were also times of disenchantment with 'Socialism'[20]).

Precisely how Lawrence hoped to bring about 'a new world' is unclear from his correspondence, but his determination to smash the cocoon and to engage in purposive action is not. It intensified from 1917 onwards. 'I feel like starting something somewhere: but hardly know yet where to begin', he told Catherine Carswell.[21] In fact he was making a beginning on some of the essays on 'Classic American Literature' in which he deplored American democracy for its encouraging a mass identity and its opposition to individualism. The 'Reality of Peace' articles (published in the *English Review*, May–August 1917) were also significant: indeed Lawrence described them as 'a new beginning'.[22] In them he declared his contempt for the 'egoism of the flock' as well as his quest for 'a few men who are distinct and at ease in themselves like stars'.[23] Thus, long before what are classed as the 'leadership novels', Lawrence was advocating a form of democracy which would allow individuals to maintain their separateness and freedom while contentedly accepting the authority of a leader. There may be a degree of political naiveté here, but what cannot be doubted is Lawrence's commitment – his determination to participate in the formation of a society which would safeguard the 'creative spirit'.[24]

At first he was uncertain how to direct his energies. In early 1917 he was prepared to make contact with the National Council for Civil Liberty.[25] Then Russia became significant – 'our chiefest hope for the future . . . When I think of the young new country there, I love it inordinately.'[26] (Three years later, in May 1920, Lawrence declared in his preface to Koteliansky's translation of Shestov's *All Things are Possible*: 'Russia will certainly inherit

---

[19] Letter 1326; *Kangaroo*, chap. XII.
[20] See Letters 1328, 1329, 1945, 2031.
[21] Letter 1391.
[22] Letter 1384.
[23] *Phoenix*, ed. Edward D. McDonald (1936), pp. 685, 687.
[24] Letter 1381.
[25] See Letter 1400.
[26] Letter 1411.

the future.'[27]) Through his friend Ernest Collings he even came to the fringe of Slav politics and was gratified to learn that the Serbian Dimitrije Mitrinović had responded to the 'Reality of Peace' essays.[28] And, in September 1918, desperate to be active – 'if I don't do something I shall burst or go cracked'[29] – Lawrence told Kot that he wanted to meet Robert Smillie, Philip Snowden, Mary Macarther and Margaret Bondfield, all leading figures in the Independent Labour Party. 'One cannot wait for things to happen', he wrote in the same letter. 'One must actually move . . . So now I shall move actively, personally, do what I can. I am a desperado.'

Here it is opportune to introduce a correspondent who appears for the first time in this volume, Douglas Goldring; he was to exert a curiously effective, though evanescent, influence on Lawrence's development and publications. Before the two men met, Goldring had spent the last years of the war in Dublin where his closest friend was Philip Heseltine, Lawrence's former intimate, who 'spent many hours expounding . . . the "message" contained in . . . *Look! We Have Come Through!*'[30] Goldring described himself at this time as 'an uncompromising anti-war propagandist, rapidly turning into a Socialist revolutionary'; and, as if to prove it, he wrote his 'revolutionary left-wing play', *The Fight for Freedom*, a German translation of which was published in the Berlin Communist monthly, *Die weissen Blätter*.[31] Lawrence first met him, through Kot, in mid-1919. By then Goldring was a member of the '1917 Club' founded in honour of the Russian revolution; the London representative of 'an "advanced" New York publisher named Thomas Seltzer';[32] and the secretary of the English branch of 'Clarté', an international leftist movement (with Henri Barbusse as a founder-member) later to be revealed as a Communist front-organisation. Obviously Goldring was not prepared to 'wait for things to happen'. That the two men met at the very time when Lawrence was seeking an outlet for his political energies was of considerable consequence.

The importance of Seltzer, Lawrence's future American publisher, will be touched on later. Three other matters must take precedence. The first was Goldring's founding 'The People's Theatre Society' (an offshoot of 'Clarté') specifically 'to secure the production of one of Lawrence's plays'.[33] The play

---

[27] *Phoenix*, ed. McDonald, p. 215.
[28] Letter 1429.
[29] Letter 1637.
[30] Douglas Goldring, *Odd Man Out* (1935), p. 182.
[31] Ibid, pp. 177, 242.
[32] Ibid, p. 247.
[33] Ibid, p. 248.

was to be *Touch and Go* which had been completed by November 1918. At first sight it is not a play wholly to commend itself to revolutionaries. Though the mine-owner (the Gerald Crich of *Women in Love*) is portrayed as insensitive, assertive and determined to exercise power, the striking miners appear as unintelligent, brutal and exclusively concerned with money. The play is inconclusive but Lawrence's position is clear: a new system, involving mutual understanding and sympathy, is essential if 'living' is to triumph over mere industrial efficiency and the greed which industrialism engenders in both masters and men. The end of the play is ambiguous: some catharsis seems envisaged as necessary to resolve the strike; it might be provided by violent political action.

Lawrence's enthusiasm for Goldring's 'People's Theatre' cannot be doubted. *Touch and Go* was published (in May 1920) in C. W. Daniel's series, 'Plays for a People's Theatre'; it was rejected by James Fagan for the Royal Court Theatre; but Lawrence's support for Goldring's venture did not waver. From its inception he was keen. 'It is so very, very rarely I feel in sympathy with a new attempt. Now I do . . .' 'I should so like a People's Theatre to materialise.'[34] Four months later, in November 1919, he read plays in manuscript by the journalist and poet Max Plowman to advise him on whether they were suitable for Daniel's series. And in May 1920, while in Malta, he encouraged Maurice Magnus to offer translations of European plays; one of them was included in the series. This was not, then, a project which merely excited Lawrence's superficial interest.

Goldring directly influenced Lawrence in a second way. It followed from his visit to The Hague and the 'group of enigmatic and highly improbable Germans' who edited a journal (printed in English, French, German and occasionally in Dutch) entitled *The Word*.[35] This is the publication to which Somers refers in *Kangaroo* as one 'run absolutely by spies and shady people',[36] but perhaps a more trustworthy insight into its management is obtained through knowledge of the paper's English co-editor, Wilfred Wellock (1879–1972). The son of a textile worker, he was a Christian Socialist and pacifist; he was imprisoned in 1917–19 as a member of the No-Conscription Fellowship; he joined the ILP and was subsequently Labour M. P. for Stourbridge, 1927–31. Such details, as well as the contents of *The Word*, establish its political principles as strongly pacifist and Socialist. Goldring encouraged Lawrence to write for the journal, and its editors to

---

[34] Letters 1675, 1766.   [36] *Kangaroo*, chap. XII.
[35] *Odd Man Out*, p. 243.

accept his essay, 'Democracy', in four parts.[37] Lawrence was unequivocal in his handling of the subject. 'Democracy and Socialism rest upon the Equality of Man', he announced, and this equality in turn depends on 'the fatal little hypothesis of the Average'; the state, nation, democracy and Socialism are therefore 'dead ideals'; 'the highest Collectivity has for its true goal the purest individualism, pure individual spontaneity.'[38] His analysis was consonant with the views expressed in his essays on American literature and the 'Reality of Peace' articles; it may not have been wholly to the taste of *The Word*'s editorial board.

Goldring's meeting in Germany with Dr Anton Kippenberg, the head of the publishers Insel Verlag, resulted in the third contribution he made to Lawrence's career as a writer. Goldring claimed to have suggested that Kippenberg should consider publishing some of Lawrence's work in translation.[39] It was a profitable idea. Beginning with *The Rainbow* in 1922, Insel Verlag published translations of five works during Lawrence's lifetime.

It is, of course, possible to get the relationship between the two men out of perspective; Goldring's personal role in the letters themselves is relatively slight; but, at least for a time, Lawrence's high regard for him is manifest.[40] Goldring and his wife stayed at Chapel Farm Cottage for the last weekend before Frieda left for Germany in October 1919; he was one of the people Lawrence hoped to see before his own departure for Italy in November; and it was to him that Lawrence turned for advice about a new London agent in 1921. Their accord was disturbed early in 1920 when Lawrence discovered that Goldring's *Fight for Freedom* had preceded his *Touch and Go* in Daniel's series. Lawrence flared up; Goldring became 'such a shit';[41] but other irritations had contributed to his passing anger and their friendship was quickly restored. For his part Goldring dedicated to Lawrence his novel, *The Black Curtain* (March 1920), which he considered 'the most violently anti-war and revolutionary work of fiction to appear in England in 1920 and for some years afterwards'.[42]

---

[37] Three sections have recently been discovered, published in issues dated 18 and 25 October, and 6 December 1919. It is presumed that the fourth also appeared unless *The Word* abruptly ceased publication. It was in financial difficulties at the end of 1919.

[38] *Phoenix*, ed. McDonald, pp. 699, 701–2.

[39] *Odd Man Out*, p. 245.

[40] Goldring's regard for Lawrence as a writer is clear from his early critical essay, 'An Appreciation of D. H. Lawrence', in *Art and Letters*, ed. Herbert Read and Osbert Sitwell, ii (Spring 1919), 89–99. (It was reprinted in Goldring's *Reputations*, 1920.)

[41] Letter 1923.

[42] *Odd Man Out*, p. 277.

That Lawrence did not think highly of the novel is little to the purpose; more significant is his willingness to be publicly associated with Goldring's political radicalism. Admittedly his belief in Socialism was declining 'more and more as the time goes by'; he came to 'hate Labour and Capitalism and all that frowsty duality in nothingness'; but he remained confident that the old order was collapsing and deserved to.[43] Lawrence's radical inclinations continued strong. He told Eleanor Farjeon in January 1921: 'If I knew how to, I'd really join myself to the revolutionary socialists now. I think the time has come for a real struggle . . . I don't care for politics. But I know there *must* and *should* be a deadly revolution very soon, and I would take part in it if I knew how.'[44] A few months later Kot was assured that, in Europe, 'only some sort of Bolshevism is inevitable, later'.[45] In broad outline, events were confirming the prognostications of a doomed European civilisation implicit in *Women in Love*.

Lawrence was certain about the political and moral decline of England: the famous 'Nightmare' chapter in *Kangaroo* is evidence enough. We learn there that 'England had lost its meaning for him' (Somers); the letters testify to Lawrence's determination to leave. The letter which opens the volume expresses his 'longing' for Rome; in the fifth he tells Catherine Carswell:

I *know* now, finally:
a. that I want to go away from England for ever.
b. That I want *ultimately* to go to a country of which I have hope, in which I feel the new unknown.
In short, I want, immediately or at length, to transfer all my life to America.

Subsequently he considered visiting Palestine with David Eder; less seriously he even pondered the unlikely possibility of a trip to Zululand.[46] In January 1917 California seemed an appropriate site for 'Rananim'; in October, it was the Andes; in February 1918 the Abruzzi took precedence. But, though it was eventually to Italy that he went, in the early part of the volume his desire to go to America is insistent and repeated. 'It is not indecision which prevents my coming to America', he assured Harriet Monroe in February 1919, 'but damnable circumstance.'[47] The New York publisher Benjamin Huebsch, offered to sponsor a lecture-tour; Lawrence drew back with distaste from 'the overweening mechanical civilisation' and anxiety about lecturing: 'I am not a public man . . . always have a "Strictly Private" notice in my hat.'[48] Amy Lowell warned him against false expec-

---

[43]   Letters 1945, 2031, 2036.   [46]   Letters 1729, 1899.
[44]   Letter 2155.   [47]   Letter 1694.
[45]   Letter 2236.   [48]   Letter 1734.

tations of America; she was certain that a lecture-tour would be a failure.[49] And by mid-August 1919 Lawrence had abandoned the idea. America was a very potent symbol for him; the great store he placed on the quality of his essays on 'Classic American Literature' – 'They contain a whole Weltan-schauung'[50] – is clear proof; yet it was to his beloved Italy that (like Birkin, Ursula, Aaron and Somers) Lawrence went on 14 November. Frieda had gone to see her mother in Germany; they met in Florence in December.

Lawrence's emotions on leaving England were acknowledged through his fiction. They are reflected in Alvina's in *The Lost Girl* when she and Ciccio depart for Italy:

there behind, behind all the sunshine, was England. England, beyond the water, rising with ash-grey, corpse-grey cliffs, and streaks of snow on the downs above. England, like a long, ash-grey coffin slowly submerging. She watched it, fascinated and terrified. It seemed to repudiate the sunshine, to remain unilluminated, long and ash-grey and dead, with streaks of snow like cerements. That was England![51]

For Richard Somers, too, as he crossed the Channel and looked back towards Folkestone, England was 'a grey, dreary-grey coffin'; it was also the country 'he had loved so bitterly, bitterly'.

[Somers] felt broken off from the England he had belonged to. The ties were gone. He was loose like a single timber of some wrecked ship, drifting over the face of the earth. Without a people, without a land. So be it. He was broken apart, apart he would remain.[52]

It can scarcely be doubted that here Lawrence was drawing on his own vivid memories of 14 November 1919.

He travelled south with unmitigated eagerness. The Mediterranean represented freedom, liberation from the horrors and restrictions of war-time England, discovery of new places and people, and the sun.[53] The tone of his letters about Italy, Capri and especially Sicily wholly vindicates his choice for the first stage of his 'journey . . . away from England'.[54] He delighted in the 'nice carelessness' of Florence; sent vivid accounts of Capri to Catherine Carswell, Cecily Lambert and the Hopkins; met Compton Mackenzie, 'a man one can trust and like', and wrote relaxed, witty letters to him; and discovered

---

[49]   P. 369 n. 1.
[50]   Letter 1812.
[51]   *The Lost Girl*, ed. John Worthen (Cambridge, 1981), p. 294.
[52]   *Kangaroo*, chap. XII.
[53]   For the significance of the Mediterranean for Lawrence and many others, see Paul Fussell, *Abroad: British Literary Traveling Between the Wars* (Oxford, 1980).
[54]   Letter 1726.

Sicily with manifest relief.[55] 'I like this place . . . It seems so peaceful and still
– and the earth is sappy . . . It is where Europe ends: finally.'[56] In that letter
Lawrence insists (to some extent, rightly) on the non-European features of
Sicily; but there were in fact many reminders of a past European civilisation
in Taormina – the Teatro Greco, 14th- and 15th-century churches and
palazzos in the town, or the site of the Acropolis a few hundred feet above it at
Castel Mola. Moreover there was a sizeable group of mainly European
residents with whom Lawrence regularly associated. Among them were his
old friend Mary Cannan, now estranged from her second husband Gilbert; an
English water-colourist and photographer Robert Kitson (whose house, Casa
Cuseni, contained a splendid dining-room designed in 1910 by his friend
Frank Brangwyn); another English painter, John J. Wright; the homosexual
Baron Stempel from Baltic Russia; Rosalie Bull, a theosophist; Mabel Hill,
who worked tirelessly on behalf of poor children in Taormina (and is still
remembered for her philanthropic endeavours); the eccentric Duke of
Brontë, a descendant of the Nelson family; together with the wealthy
American Bowdwin and his impoverished compatriot, Wood. They were not
all to Lawrence's taste. Kitson's public-school background and his having
graduated from Trinity College, Cambridge (Bertrand Russell's college) did
not wholly endear him to Lawrence; Mabel Hill's earnest piety was perhaps
sometimes disagreeable; and Lawrence was inclined to mock what he
regarded as the pretensions of the 'Duca'. Yet Lawrence and Frieda accepted
the Duke's hospitality at the remote but impressively large Castello di
Maniace, founded in the 12th century; there is a relish about Lawrence's
account for Jessica Brett Young of the vivid pageant of cosmopolitans at the
Timeo hotel when he lunched there with Mary Cannan;[57] and partly at
Kitson's instigation the Lawrences took part in social activities (even a fancy
dress ball) generated by the well-educated and generally affluent expatriate
community. The recently-discovered letters to Marie Hubrecht (whose
Dutch forbears had built Fontana Vecchia where the Lawrences lived) also
reveal Lawrence's appetite for local gossip and 'parish-pump' affairs. And he
patently admired the elegant library and furnishing of Rocca Bella, once the
home of Marie Hubrecht and subsequently bought by Bowdwin. Inevitably
there were occasional furores; inevitably, too, Lawrence eventually became
restive and eager to move on; but for the most part, over – for him – a long
period, contentment and relative tranquillity characterise the letters from

[55] Letters 1849, 1929.   [57] Letter 1957.
[56] Letter 1948.

Sicily. The contrast with the tension and torment of the preceding years in England is sharp.

Sharp indeed. Gone was the tortured apprehension of feeling – as he felt in February 1917 – 'like a fox that is cornered by a pack of hounds and boors who don't perhaps know he's there, but are closing in unconsciously'.[58] As happened to Somers in *Kangaroo*, Italy dispelled Lawrence's fear of 'the malignant power of the mob-like authorities'.[59] The consequences are apparent in a new crop of publications. Lawrence himself underlines it in the autobiographical extract quoted at the beginning. In each of the years 1917–19 he had published only one book of poems: *Look! We Have Come Through!*; *New Poems* (mistitled, apparently by Secker, since the contents were largely from his earlier years); and *Bay*. Between November 1919, when the last appeared, and the end of this volume in June 1921 – leaving aside numerous contributions to books and periodicals – Lawrence published Shestov's *All Things Are Possible* (translated with Kot), *Touch and Go*, *Women in Love*, *The Lost Girl*, *Movements in European History* and *Psychoanalysis and the Unconscious*. *Sea and Sardinia* was finished and he had virtually completed *Aaron's Rod*. Remarkable though it is, this achievement should not be allowed to obscure the serious obstacles Lawrence had to overcome. The liability of the *Rainbow* prosecution remained. Though he could rejoice in his personal freedom, his freedom to publish when and what he wanted continued to be circumscribed. Publishers were understandably anxious to avoid prosecution; moreover, as Martin Secker bluntly put it in January 1920, Lawrence's works were 'not worth competing for from a money making point of view'.[60] Lawrence himself took a quite different viewpoint and summed up his general attitude to publishers in a remark to his American agent, Robert Mountsier: 'One must fight the little swine all the time.'[61]

His struggle to issue *Women in Love* – to take the most prominent example – is a recurring theme throughout this volume. The penultimate letter in Volume 2, 25 October 1916, contains the ominous prophecy: 'nobody will publish it'.[62] In the event it was four years before the American edition appeared; Secker's first English edition was not published until June 1921. 'Everybody will hate [it] *completely*', Lawrence told Margaret Dunlop on 31 October 1916 and though this proved untrue, most publishers feared it.[63]

Lawrence and his friends anticipated resistance from English publishers.

[58] Letter 1369.
[59] *Kangaroo*, chap. XII.
[60] P. 460 n. 1.
[61] Letter 2148.
[62] *Letters*, ii. 669.
[63] Letter 1302.

Kot suggested that he should try to bring the book out in Russia; Lawrence responded positively; but the proposal came to nothing. Lawrence toyed with the idea of dedicating the novel 'in the old-fashioned way' to some influential person who would afford it 'his, or her, protection':[64] Lady Cynthia Asquith was sounded, but unsuccessfully. (Meanwhile Lady Ottoline Morrell threatened legal action, alleging that she was libelled as Hermione.) Eveleigh Nash appeared as a possible publisher in April 1917, Cecil Palmer over the next few months.[65] Concurrently Pinker was trying to place the book with an American publisher; Little, Brown & Co. in Boston rejected it on 11 July, with the explanation: 'We feel that it is not as good as SONS AND LOVERS, and that Mr Lawrence has not made as good a presentation of his theme as we expected'.[66] The Dublin publishing house, Maunsel (contacted through Douglas Goldring) was the next to refuse. Fisher Unwin expressed an interest but did not pursue it.[67] Cyril Beaumont (later to publish *Bay*) declined in March 1918. He suggested publication by subscription at a guinea a copy; Lady Cynthia and Prince Bibesco (soon to be her brother-in-law) were alarmed at the prospect of being associated with such a venture.[68] It soon evaporated. Not until eighteen months later did Thomas Seltzer – through the agency of Goldring – make an approach; eventually this led to private publication but only after tortuous, often acrimonious, negotiations involving the American Benjamin Huebsch (who wanted *Women in Love* but claimed that Pinker had not shown him the manuscript) and Secker in London. Lawrence received the first proofs in early August 1920; the first copy reached him on 11 December whereupon he assured Seltzer that it 'has made us friends for life'.[69] For his part Martin Secker rarely ceased to be apprehensive. He expressed anxiety about the novel's title in April 1920, wanting Lawrence to be as unprovocative as possible; in January–February 1921 (after the book had appeared in America) he requested five amendments to the text.[70] He also hoped to release the book quietly through booksellers, preferring to avoid the publicity which would follow the normal distribution of review-copies.

In late 1916 Frieda had confessed to Mark Gertler that she had lived 'several lifetimes' during the writing of *Women in Love*;[71] she could not have guessed that what must have seemed several more would elapse before the first edition appeared, privately, about four years later. There was some

[64] Letter 1335.   [68] Letter 1537 and n. 3.
[65] Letters 1395, 1419, 1441.   [69] Letter 2139.
[66] TMSC NYPL.   [70] Letters 2152, 2166 and n. 1.
[67] Letters 1494, 1491.   [71] MS HU.

consolation for Lawrence in its reception. Seltzer assured him by letter that it was 'not only your best novel but one of the best ever written'.[72] Publicly the critic John Macy, writing in the *New York Evening Post Literary Review*, referred to him as 'one of the finest artists using the English language' and concluded his review of the novel: 'No writer of this generation is more singular, more unmistakably individual, than Mr. Lawrence, and none is endowed with his unfairly great variety of gifts.'[73]

In Lawrence's experience so far, the publishing history of *Women in Love* was *sui generis*; yet there were parallels in the resistance he encountered with some of his other writings of this period. This does not apply to his contributions to periodicals and anthologies: he was much sought after by editors of those publications. The American *Seven Arts* magazine asked him to submit short stories; Wilbur Cross, editor of the *Yale Review*, invited him to respond to an article on contemporary British novelists, and their exchange of letters shows not only Lawrence's toughness but also the standing he had acquired on both sides of the Atlantic; two of his poems appeared in *New Paths*, in May 1918, alongside contributions from Aldington, the Sitwells, Augustus John, Mestrović and Ernest Collings; Hutchinsons bought 'The Fox' for £30; the editor of *The Dial* requested permission to print 'Rex' as a companion piece to 'Adolf'; Lawrence was invited to submit poems to *New Republic*; and from the University of Virginia came an invitation to contribute to a book celebrating the University's centenary.[74] All such approaches – and there were others – acknowledged Lawrence's distinction. But editors of magazines and anthologies were not exposed to some of the anxieties endured by book-publishers. That fraternity were far more hesitant in their dealings with Lawrence. Chatto and Windus, for instance, who published *Look! We Have Come Through!* were concerned about 'the continuously sexual tone of the volume'; they pressed Lawrence into omitting two poems and altering specific lines elsewhere.[75] Again, his efforts to re-issue *The Rainbow* led to persistent frustration. Secker offered an outright payment of £200; Lawrence rejected it and asked Duckworth to make an offer; he requested the dropping of a whole chapter; Lawrence broke off negotiations, reverted to Secker and agreed with him the novel's publication on a royalty

72 Pp. 635–6 n. 2.
73 R. P. Draper, ed., *D. H. Lawrence: The Critical Heritage* (London and Boston, 1970), pp. 157–60.
74 Letters 1309 and n. 3, 1461, 2003 and n. 1, 2083 and n. 2, and 2133 and n. 1.
75 Letters 1437 and n. 1, 1439 and n. 1.

basis.[76] Secker was the focus of other irritation, this time over the issuing of *The Lost Girl*. He warned Lawrence that the lending libraries had refused to handle the book unless the account of the sexual encounter between Ciccio and Alvina were re-written. Since the sale of at least 2000 copies was at stake, Secker urged Lawrence to comply. He did so and substituted a muted version.[77] Lawrence could not know, however, that Secker had also omitted another doubtful sentence elsewhere without his permission. And, finally, there was the timidity of Oxford University Press in refusing to publish *Movements in European History*, a school textbook, under Lawrence's name: 'Lawrence H. Davison' became the author.

Lawrence's relations with the publishing world provide a recurring theme in the letters. In view of the prosecution of *The Rainbow*, the fear of publishers that they might suffer the same fate with *Women in Love*, and the censoring influence of lending libraries, it is not surprising that those relations were often tense and acerbic. Not surprising, either, was Lawrence's feeling that publishing was 'like throwing one's treasures in a bog'.[78] Exacerbating both that disgust and his dealings with publishers were two other factors: constant poverty and a gradual withering of confidence in his agent J. B. Pinker.

This volume opens and closes with Lawrence's finances 'at a low ebb',[79] with the very lowest point following shortly after his expulsion from Cornwall. In February 1918 he had 'exactly six pounds nineteen shillings in the world: and not a penny due'.[80] At about the same time Frieda summed up their situation in an undated letter to Kot: 'no money, no house, nothing'.[81] Their plight is brought into sharp focus in Lawrence's declaration of income connected with his application for a grant from the Royal Literary Fund: his earnings in the year ending August 1914 had been '£450 or £500', but from August 1917 to June 1918 he earned 'considerably less than £100'.[82] Indeed had it not been for his friends, the 'very dark cloud of penury' might have engulfed him.[83] Amy Lowell was three times a benefactor, Kot twice; others included Montague Shearman, Lady Cynthia, Catherine Carswell, Edward Marsh, J. D. Beresford and his sister Ada. There was also the 'miserable £50' from the Literary Fund.[84] There was, too, considerable bitterness at the lack of generosity on the part of Bennett, Wells and Prince Bibesco.[85] When Lawrence's fortunes improved in the first half of 1920 his own kind of open-

[76] Letters 1908, 1952, 1951, 1960.   [81] MS BL.
[77] Letter 2121 and n. 1.   [82] Letter 1580.
[78] Letter 1722.   [83] Letter 1513.
[79] Letter 2217.   [84] Letter 1598.
[80] Letter 1517.   [85] Letter 1681.

handedness revealed itself: he returned £10 to Kot, gave £2 to his father and burned a cheque for £50 sent by Catherine Carswell out of the proceeds of her first novel.[86] But for a professional writer to be sustained by friendly beneficence when he had achieved sufficient prominence to become the subject of lectures and articles, had been approached by a publisher with a view to printing his collected poems and by an agent for the film rights on his fiction, as well as by editors as described above[87] – to say nothing of the critical attention given to his every major publication: this anomaly was galling in the extreme. To be a 'charity-boy of literature' was a rôle Lawrence understandably detested.[88]

His resentment was aggravated by the belief that Pinker and the publishers were treating him like 'an aimiable imbecile'.[89] Letters in Volume 2 show a trust and confidence in Pinker's judgment which, while not unwavering, generally characterised their relationship. Early even in this volume Lawrence readily admits, 'you have been good to me'.[90] But this soon changed. Corrosive suspicions – perhaps on both sides – gradually destroyed what remained of their accord. When the break finally came Lawrence conceded, in January 1920, that he had been 'an unpleasant handful' for Pinker.[91] And there is some truth in the remark; the evidence in the letters of Lawrence's readiness to steal a march on his agent cannot be denied. In early 1917, for example, he wrote to Austin Harrison to interest him in publishing the 'Reality of Peace' articles in the *English Review*; only then did he ask Pinker to negotiate with Harrison; and later Pinker was rather curtly informed by Harrison that the financial arrangements were a 'purely personal matter' between Lawrence and himself.[92] In January 1919 Lawrence told Kot with some relish that he had received from the *English Review* (for the first two essays on American literature) £10 'which I circumvented from Pinker's clutches'.[93] He clearly tried to cut Pinker out of the negotiations with Huebsch over the publication of *New Poems*: 'make the arrangements with me – and if Pinker has to come in, he can come in after'.[94] Or again, in September 1919, assuring Secker that he could publish *Women in Love*, Lawrence added: 'don't speak yet to Pinker, wait a bit till I let you hear about America'.[95] Such evidence, isolated from the context of Lawrence's evident distrust of and contempt for Pinker – 'that little parvenu snob of a procureur

---

[86] Letters 1892, 1932, 2004.
[87] Letters 1585, 2081, 1775, 2012.
[88] Letter 1929.
[89] Letter 1916.
[90] Letter 1368.
[91] Letter 1902.
[92] Letter 1388; TMS NYPL.
[93] Letter 1681.
[94] Letter 1792.
[95] Letter 1799.

of books '[96] – seems to place all the odium on Lawrence. That would be unjust. Pinker's efficiency as an agent is frequently in question; the honesty of his dealing between his client and publishers is sometimes in doubt. He appears to have misled Lawrence – deliberately, Lawrence believed – over negotiations with Huebsch to publish *Women in Love*. As Lawrence explained to Huebsch in January 1920: 'it never occurred to me that Pinker could have had that MS. for almost two years, all the while assuring me that he was doing everything possible, without ever even mentioning it to you.'[97] He was convinced that Pinker had lied to him. Wherever, then, lay the principal blame – and it was doubtless shared – the relationship between author and agent had deteriorated beyond repair; trust between them had vanished. 'I think, there is not much point in our remaining bound to one another', Lawrence told Pinker in December 1919. 'I wish [our agreement] should be broken now.'[98]

'Whatever mess I make in the future, I'll make myself, not through an agent.'[99] Lawrence's reaction is easy to understand but it was impractical. For him to deal efficiently with publishers and editors in England and America, while he was in Sicily, was not possible. An agent was essential. To avoid a professional agency he briefly considered employing Barbara Low in London; finally, in April 1921 (on Goldring's advice), he accepted Curtis Brown as his agent there. A year earlier Robert Mountsier had agreed to act for him in America; as a result Mountsier became a highly significant correspondent. The recently-discovered letters to him are among the most important in this volume.

Mountsier was more than a literary agent to Lawrence; he was first of all a friend. He had visited the Lawrences in Cornwall and had himself come under suspicion from the police; indeed, if the treatment of 'Mr Monsell' in *Kangaroo* exactly reflects Mountsier's experience, he was arrested in London, 'conveyed to Scotland Yard: there examined, stripped naked, his clothes taken away'.[100] As a letter of December 1920 illustrates, the harassment from oppressive authority suffered by both Lawrence and Mountsier cemented the bond between them.[101] It was a link shared also by Frieda; she too wrote to Mountsier in a tone of established friendship.[102] The relationship was therefore quite unlike that between Lawrence and Pinker; in tone it is more reminiscent of that between Lawrence and Edward Garnett several years earlier.

[96]   Letter 1428.   [100]   *Kangaroo*, chap. XII.
[97]   Letter 1916.   [101]   Letter 2137.
[98]   Letter 1888.   [102]   See Letter 2042.
[99]   Letter 1916.

The letters to Mountsier contain an interesting mixture of frank, full discussion of business matters – with much more detailed information and directives than to either Garnett or Pinker – and exchanges about personal affairs: whether Lawrence should accept the offer of a farm in Connecticut or invest in buying a boat. Lawrence had obviously learned from his experience with Pinker: though he invariably took Mountsier's commercial advice seriously, he was determined to retain the overall direction of his publishing ventures. That he should answer Mountsier's letters by return is one sign of his resolve.[103] What Lawrence expected (as he told Huebsch) was 'precise dealing with one another';[104] Mountsier appears to have agreed. In his rôle as agent, Mountsier seems to have been energetic and meticulous; as friend he was both co-operative and generous, though quite prepared to express irritation when (as over Mrs Thrasher's Connecticut farm) his efforts were frustrated by an abrupt change of mind on Lawrence's part. But at this stage their friendship withstood such temporary strains, their mutual regard was unimpaired.

Mountsier became deeply involved in Lawrence's (doubtless bewildering) plans for future travel. Consequently it was to him more explicitly than to anyone else that Lawrence expressed his growing disenchantment with Sicily. Though Lawrence did not finally leave the island until early 1922, his visits to Malta in May 1920, to northern Italy in August–October 1920, and to Sardinia in January 1921 were clear signs of his restlessness. 'I am feeling absolutely at an end with the civilised world,' he told Mountsier in March 1921. 'It makes me sick at the stomach . . . I can't quite find my direction: can't quite make up my mind in which direction to turn my nose, to try a flight.'[105] Nearly a year before he had written to Catherine Carswell: 'one's instinct is to go south, south – and away, away from Europe'.[106] Now, in March 1921, Mountsier heard – 'This is a sort of crisis for me. I've got to come unstuck from the old life and Europe.'[107] Acquiring a farm in America or becoming part-owner of a boat, though temporarily and superficially attractive, would have curtailed his choice, limited his freedom of action. But it was becoming impossible for him to sit still. And as he looked south and east from his balcony at Fontana Vecchia some 600 feet above the sea, Lawrence wrote at the beginning of *Sea and Sardinia*: 'Comes over one an absolute necessity to move.' The visits to Italy and Baden-Baden which come at the end of this volume, and then to Austria, were merely precursors of the far more strenuous journeying soon to follow.

---

[103] See Letter 2177.
[104] Letter 1906.
[105] Letter 2189.
[106] Letter 1987.
[107] Letter 2194.

THE LETTERS

1302. To Margaret Dunlop, 31 October 1916
Text: MS Dunlop; Huxley 373–4.

Higher Tregerthen, Zennor, St. Ives. Cornwall.

31 Oct. 1916

My dear Mrs Dunlop,[1]

I was glad to have your card from Leghorn, telling us you were joyfully in Italy again with Dunlop. I wonder where you are now – back again in Milan? – and enjoying everything, I hope. But what about the children?[2] – though for my part, I think husbands and wives more important than children, so long as the latter are well looked after.

Here we are, still sitting lonelily over the sea like a couple of motionless cormorants. I have just finished a novel, which everybody will hate *completely*.[3] But if I can only get a little money for it, I shall come to Italy. My health is miserable, damnable. I seem half my time, and more, to be laid up in bed. I think the terrible moisture of England does it: it has rained every day now for nine weeks. I think in Italy I should be better. So I shall try to come. What do you think?

I should not go back to Fiascherino – I couldn't bear it. It is always lacerating to go back to the past: and then to find our beloved old Felice more old, and unhappy for the death of poor Elide[4] – no, I couldn't stand it, I should be a fountain of tears.[5] I should like to go to Rome. I don't know why, but one seems drawn to the great historic past, now the present has become so lamentably historic. So I want to go to Rome, and see if I should be better and happier there. – Then we should spend a day or two in Milan *en passant*, to see you and Dunlop again: which would be a *great* pleasure.

I don't know that there is any news I can tell you. Ivy Low is expecting an

---

[1] Margaret Annie Jessie ('Madge'), née Morris (1888–1970), wife of (Sir) Thomas Dacre Dunlop (1883–1964). Dunlop was British Consul at Spezia where DHL first knew him; he typed 'The Wedding Ring'. See *Letters*, ii. 152.

[2] Maurice Hamilton (1912–32), Margaret Dorothea Leda (b. 1913), and John Dacre Dunlop (b. 1915). See *Letters*, ii. 191–2, 628.

[3] *Women in Love* (Privately printed, New York, 1920).

[4] Elide Fiori and her mother Felice (1853–c. 1930) were DHL's servants at Lerici, near Fiascherino, October 1913–June 1914.

[5] Jeremiah ix. 1.

infant: everybody says 'poor infant'.[1] But Ivy is happy and important at last.
I think she feels no woman ever had a child before, and she is the inventress of
the human race: which no doubt is quite the right spirit.

   Of ourselves there is no news. Barring poverty and a few jolts, we are very
happy together. Frieda is allowed interviews with her children occasionally:[2]
which makes things easier. I, you will not forget, have a beard: purplish red,
people say. I must keep you reminded so you should not be shocked, when we
arrive in Milan. How do you find Italy? Still pretty nonchalant and happy in
itself, I hope. I should hate to come to a tragic country.

   Dunlop very nobly offered to lend me money: which, for some reason,
scared me. I should feel a monster, taking money from a man with a wife and
three children, and only his salary to keep them on. No, when I am forced to
beg for a[3] penny to throw between the teeth of the wolf at the door, I shall
ask rich people for it: they will give it me: I don't let myself be worried.

   I shall address this letter to Dunlop, so that if you are come back to
England, he will read it and write to me.

   Do you like Milan? I didn't. But I've got a longing to go to Rome.

   All good greetings from Frieda and me to both,

                                                                    Yours   D. H. Lawrence

1303. To E. M. Forster, 6 November 1916
Text: MS KCC; Delany 263–4.

                                            Higher Tregerthen, Zennor, St. Ives, Cornwall
                                                                                    6 Nov 1916

Dear E.M.[4]

   Your letter came today: I was glad to have it: you are much better and more
positive, from the sound of it: which is a blessing. I haven't sent you the
Amores yet, but will tell Duckworths to post it on to you.[5] Also I will lend you
the *Rainbow* if possible. I get sick of giving people my books, or even of
writing. People today want their senses gratified in art, but their *will* remains
static all the time with the old, and they would rather die than face a
conclusion out from the senses to the mind. There ought to be a flood to

[1] Ivy Teresa Low (1889–1977), novelist; she had known DHL since spring 1914. m. 1916,
     Maxim Litvinov (1876–1951), later Soviet foreign commissar; see *Letters*, ii. 160. Her son,
     Michael, b. 1917.
[2] Charles Montague (1900–82), Elsa Agnes Frieda (b. 1902), and Barbara Joy Weekley (b. 1904).
[3] MS reads 'beg for penny'.
[4] Edward Morgan Forster (1879–1970), novelist, whom DHL had known since January 1915.
     See *Letters*, ii. 262.
[5] Duckworth had published DHL's book of poems in July 1916.

drown mankind, for there is no health in it, and certainly no *proud* courage:
Plenty of the slave courage of death, but no proud courage of life, no
independent soul anywhere. Lord, let there be a flood to drown them all. –
But there, it rains bombs etc. by their own contrivance: they will annihilate
themselves in the end. I am sure, that even if *this* war ends in our lifetime, war
in the same sort will go on. The process of violent death will possess humanity
for many a generation yet, till there are only a few remaining of all these
hordes: a slow, slow flood of death will drown them all. I am glad, for they are
too corrupt and cowardly.

I believe in *bonheur*, when people feel *bon*. But to pretend bonheur when
you only feel malice and spite – à la Butler,[1] and à la everybody nowadays – no
thank you. I *do* believe in a man's standing on his own legs and spitting on the
flood of the world. And I *do* believe in straightforward *decency*: simple,
instinctive honorableness. I feel a bit shy even of Stendhal's bonheur. I look
for it in vain in *Rouge et le Noir*, and *L'Amour*, and *Chartreuse*.[2] A man may
believe in that which he in himself *is* not. But I don't give much for such a
belief. It is a belief of negation. Let a man go to the bottom of what he *is*, and
believe in that. And Stendhal was not *bon*: he was méchant to a high degree.
So he should have believed in his own wickedness, not kept a ticket to heaven
up his sleeve, called bonheur.

I am in a black fury with the world, as usual. One writes, one works, one
gives ones hand to people. And the swine are rats, they bite one's hand. They
are rats, sewer-rats, with all the foul courage of death and corruption,
darkness and sewers. But of openness and singleness – ah well – I am weary to
death of my fellow men. I think it would be good to die, because death would
be a clean land with no people in it: not even the people of myself. Where to
go, where to go away from them! They are like rats, they slither and bite one's
hands: anywhere, anywhere out of the world. But not yet to die in the body. *I*
believe in a free, proud happiness. But how can one be happy with rats biting
one. How to get away from them? They are everywhere, they cling on to one,
they carry one down with their weight. Perhaps Bishop Hatto had only
burned rats, after all.[3] How to escape, how to get out, where to find a clean
land? – Oh God above.

As for news: I have not a friend in the world, nor an acquaintance, I have
the honor to say. Neither have I any money at all, I have the dishonor to say.

[1] Most likely Samuel Butler (1835–1902), author of *Erewhon*.
[2] Works (published 1831, 1822 and 1839 respectively) by Stendhal (Henri Beyle) (1783–1842).
[3] According to legend, Hatto II (d. 970?) Archbishop of Mainz, was eaten alive by mice as a
    punishment for burning down a barn full of people caught stealing grain in a famine and whose
    dying shrieks he compared to the piping of mice.

Neither have I much in the way of health: I seem to have spent a great deal of my time in bed, lately. Really, one looks through the window into the land of death, and it *does* seem a clean good unknown, all that is left to one. But it is so *sure*, death, that one is always strong in it. It is so sure, one is free to live, whatever the world may be, having death as a certainty, a free, honorable land, inevitable.

I have finished the sequel to the *Rainbow* – rather wonderful and terrible. I don't suppose anybody will publish it. – But I am going to write saleable short stories now, so that I may have a little money, and may not be trapped in by the rats of the world. Money is the only mail they won't bite through. Then I think I shall go to Italy. I am so weary of mankind. If it speaks a foreign language, I don't notice it so much.

You are only like Christ because of a certain purity of spirit – You are unlike Christ in that you are one of the last products of Christianity.

D. H. Lawrence

1304. To J. B. Pinker, 6 November 1916
Text: MS UNYB; cited in Charles L. Ross, *DHL Review*, viii (1975), 201.

Higher Tregerthen – Zennor – St Ives, Cornwall.
6 Nov 1916

Dear Pinker[1]

First batch of typed MS. come today: many thanks.[2] How quickly it is done – and well.

I send a story which *may* be a *Strand* story: *sure* to be accepted by *some* magazine.[3]

Yrs   D. H. Lawrence

Send me typed MS. of stories as well as novel, so I can just run through them.[4]

---

[1] James Brand Pinker (1863–1922), DHL's literary agent from July 1914 to December 1919. See *Letters*, ii. 31 n. 1.

[2] On 25 and 31 October (see *Letters*, ii. 669) DHL had sent to Pinker the final third of *Women in Love* written in exercise books. Pinker had offered to have the typing done in his office, free.

[3] Perhaps 'Samson and Delilah' (published in *English Review*, xxiv, March 1917, 209–24). The MS of the story is entitled 'The Prodigal Husband': see Letter 1313.

[4] DHL had sent 'The Mortal Coil' (published in *Seven Arts*, ii, July 1917, 280–305) to Pinker on 31 October for typing (see *Letters*, ii. 669).

1305. To S. S. Koteliansky, 7 November 1916
Text: MS BL; Postmark, Zennor 9- NOV. 16; cited in Gransden 26.

Higher Tregerthen, Zennor, St. Ives, Cornwall
7 Nov. 1916

My dear Kot,[1]

I must tell you we laugh at you when you are in your bad moods, and see the world with a clear eye, and try to rebuke yourself that the eye which sees is wrong, not the world that is seen. My dear Kot, if only you would accept what your eye tells you; that people and the world *are* foul and obscene, that their life *is* a complication of ghastly trickery, then you would be free: because that is the *truth*. The world is quite as bad as you have ever seen it in your worst and most lucid moments; and *even worse*. Accept the fact baldly and callously, and you are a free man. Say 'no – no, men are good creatures, 'tis I who am bad,' – and you are the slave to a coward's self-delusion. The world *is* bad, bad beyond bearing. So reject it, spit it out, trample on it, and have done with it in your soul. Then you will be strong and free. Meanwhile, making these false efforts to see good in all, you become imprisoned in a lie.

Though everybody says the war will go on for ever, yet I think that this particular war will not last *very* much longer. While it lasts, we are more or less trapped. When it is over, we can clear out of *this* world, for ever. I tell you my Rananim, my Florida idea, was the true one.[2] Only the *people* were wrong. But to go to Rananim *without* the people is right, for me, and ultimately, I hope, for you.

I have done with the Murries, both, for ever[3] – so help me god. So I have with Lady Ottoline and all the rest.[4] And now I am glad and free.

Now we must wait for the wheel of events to turn on a little, so that we can escape out into the open, to the Rananim. That is all.

Yours   D. H. Lawrence

[Frieda Lawrence begins]

Your picture of your terrible visitors was most vivid.

---

[1] Samuel Solomonovich Koteliansky ('Kot') (1880–1955), Russian-born; he was a naturalised British subject. He translated over thirty Russian publications, some of them with DHL acting as 'editor'; a close friend and correspondent of DHL's 1914–30. See *Letters*, ii. 205 n. 4.

[2] In late 1915 DHL had contemplated the possibility of establishing his ideal society comprising a small, dedicated group of friends, in Florida. See *Letters*, ii. 252, 449–50.

[3] John Middleton Murry (1889–1957), journalist and critic; and Katherine Mansfield (1888–1923), short-story writer. They married on 3 May 1918. See *Letters*, ii. 31 nn. 5, 6.

[4] Lady Ottoline Violet Anne Morrell (1873–1938), well known as the hostess, at Garsington Manor near Oxford, to a distinguished group of artists and writers. DHL had known her since August 1914. See *Letters*, ii. 253 n. 3. m. 1902, Philip Edward Morrell (1870–1943), Liberal M.P. for S. Oxon. (1906–10) and Burnley (1910–18).

1306. To Catherine Carswell, 7 November 1916
Text: MS YU; Postmark, Zennor 9- NOV. 16; cited in Carswell, *Adelphi* 288–9, 389, 390.

Higher Tregerthen, Zennor, St. Ives, Cornwall.
7 Nov. 1916

My dear Catherine[1]

We never thanked you for the half-cheese – and we like it so much, it is so welcome in this wilderness. Of course we roared over the greasy pans and Ivy. But it is true 'a path there is where no man thought.'[2] Only I wonder what you had been thinking, that this appealed to you so strongly for the moment. – There is a difference, too, between 'you never can tell what will happen' and 'you never can tell *how* it will happen.' One *can* tell what will happen, more or less. Some things one knows inwardly, and infallibly. But the how and the why are left to the conjunction of circumstance.

I am glad you are beginning to reject people. They *are* separaters. They *are* a destructive force. They are like acid, which can only corrode and dissolve. One *must* shun them. The spirit they live by is the spirit of destruction and of putting apart. They bring this spirit into the house along with them, and it overcomes one. It is like a poison-gas they live in. And one is so few and so fragile, in one's own small, subtle air of life. *How* one must cherish the frail, precious buds of the unknown life in one's soul. They are the unborn children of ones hope and living happiness, and one is so frail to bring them forth. Shelter yourself above all from the world, save yourself, screen and hide yourself, go subtly in a secret retreat, where no-one knows you, only Carswell and your own soul, hiding like a bird, and living busily the other, creative life, like a bird building a nest. Be sure to keep this bush that burns with the presence of God,[3] where you build your nest, this world of worlds, hidden from mankind: or they will drag your nest and desecrate all. Do not admit them, do not acknowledge any kinship with any of them, at all. You are not kin with them, any more than a bird is kin to a cat. They *prey* on one, that is all.

We have had here two Americans.[4] Americans are as a rule rather dreadful,

---

[1] Catherine Carswell, née MacFarlane (1879–1946), reviewer, novelist, and subsequently the author of *The Savage Pilgrimage: A Narrative of D.H. Lawrence* (1932; reprinted Cambridge University Press, 1981). m. 1915, Donald Carswell (1882–1940), barrister. They had known DHL since June 1914. See *Letters*, ii. 187 n. 5.

[2] Euripides, *The Medea*, trans. Gilbert Murray (1906), p. 80 ['a path is there where . . .'].

[3] Exodus iii. 2–4.

[4] Robert Mountsier (1888–1972), journalist and subsequently DHL's literary agent in USA. He graduated B.A. (1909) and Ph.D. from the University of Michigan; he joined the *New York Sun* as literary editor in 1910; he served with the Red Cross during World War I after which he returned to the *Sun*, remaining till 1950. He published *Our Eleven Billion Dollars: Europe's Debt*

I think. They are *not* younger than we, but older: a second childhood. But being so old, in senile decay and second childishness, perhaps they are nearer to the end, and the new beginning.

I *know* now, finally:

a. that I want to go away from England for ever.
b. That I want *ultimately* to go to a country of which I have hope, in which I feel the new unknown.

In short, I want, immediately or at length, to transfer all my life to America. Because there, I know, the *skies* are not so old, the air is newer, the earth is not tired. Don't think I have any illusions about the people, the life. The people and the life are monstrous. I want, at length, to get a place in the far west mountains, from which one can see the distant Pacific Ocean, and there live facing the bright west. – But I also think that America, being so much *worse*, falser, further gone than England, is nearer to freedom. England has a long and awful process of corruption and death to go through. America has dry-rotted to a point where the final *seed* of the new is almost left ready to sprout. When I can, I shall go to America, and find a place. Then later you and Carswell will come. – I *know* my Florida idea was right: it was quite right, all save the people. It is wrong to seek adherents. One must be single.

Don't tell *anybody* what I say here. I don't tell anybody but you. Frieda is quite with me, we two will move in silence. Then when you and Carswell feel the day has come, you will come also. – Of course one must always wait for circumstance.

But don't be cast down, don't get used up. Above all, conserve yourself, and live only in marriage, not elsewhere.

If you would like to see the two Americans – they are really nice, gentle – he a journalist, Robert Mountsier – she also doing some journalism – a Miss Andrews – I will send them to you in London. I knew Mountsier last year also. They are living together – a queer, gentle couple, so old-old, that they are more innocent than children. They will be in London next week.

I finished my novel – save the last chapter, which, a sort of epilogue, I shall add on later.[1] – I *hated* the typing, so took to scribbling in pencil. Then there was a lot of the original draft that I *couldn't* have bettered. Pinkers are typing it out for me. When it is done, I shall send it on to you. I shall keep the title *Women in Love*. – The book frightens me: it is so end-of-the-world. But it is, it

---

to the United States (Seltzer, 1922). (See obituary, *New York Times*, 25 November 1972.) Esther Andrews was a part-time journalist and artist.

[1] It was probably never written. The draft printed in Keith Sagar, *D. H. Lawrence: A Calendar of His Works* (Manchester, 1979), p. 74 is a fragment of the last chapter as written in MS (Roberts E441c).

must be, the beginning of a new world too. So must your book. How is it getting on?[1]

Love from us both to you both.

                                                          D. H. Lawrence

1307. To Lady Cynthia Asquith, 11 November 1916
Text: MS UT; Huxley 376–7.

                                    Higher Tregerthen, Zennor, St. Ives, Cornwall
                                                         Saturday 11 Nov. 1916

My dear Lady Cynthia,[2]

We have been wondering about you for some time now. Did my last letter, that I sent to you to the hotel in Brighton, along with my book of poems, put you off from answering, or have things gone more amiss with you?[3] I have often wondered if you got the book of poems. As for the letter: that is how one feels, at a crisis.

Nothing is changed, outwardly, here. Frieda went to London and saw her children: and began to realise, I believe, that the mother-child relation is not so all-important; indeed, not profoundly important at all, touching the quick of being. It is, in real truth, one of the temporal, almost accidental connections, the connection between parent and children. But I suppose you will not agree to this at all. – Then, we still hear from Germany: Frieda's mother, being old and feeling the twilight of death in the air, very sad and wanting only comfort and reassurance, but Frieda's sisters still resistant and rather ugly in spirit.[4] I must say, judging from these, I can't feel that Germany wants peace yet, any more than England does. Their fulfilment is still in this ugly contending. But I think both countries are getting tired, emotionally tired. They won't be able to work up the fine frenzy of war much longer. – The whole show is too nasty and contemptible, essentially.

I have been seedy a good deal this autumn: seem to have spent a great deal of my time in bed. But I feel better now. Perhaps soon I shall come to London to consult a good doctor – if there *is* such a thing – and learn how to make the best of this bad job of health. Nevertheless, I feel much stronger and more established in my soul – really strong and single. – I have finished a novel,

---

[1] Her novel, at this time called 'Joanna' (Letter 1323), was published in 1920 as *Open the Door!*

[2] Lady Cynthia Asquith, née Charteris (1887–1960), m. Herbert ('Beb') Asquith (1881–1947), barrister and son of Herbert Henry Asquith, the Prime Minister. He was on active service in France. See *Letters*, ii. 41 n. 4.

[3] DHL wrote and sent a copy of *Amores* on 1 September 1916 (*Letters*, ii. 649). Lady Cynthia received it: see Asquith, *Diaries* 213.

[4] Frieda's mother was the Baroness Anna von Richthofen (1851–1930); Else Jaffe (1874–1973) and Johanna ('Nusch') von Schreibershofen (1882–1971), were Frieda's sisters. See *Letters*, i. 391, 409.

sequel to the *Rainbow*. *I* think very highly of it, but I don't suppose anybody will publish it – at least for some years to come. We are hopelessly badly off as far as money goes, though it never troubles me, so long as one is strong in one's soul. Still, I suppose I shall have to make some sort of move about it – what, I don't know. I think I would prefer to go to America – but it doesn't seem very possible just now. As far as material things go, one can drift as necessity impels one.

We had two American journalists here this week – at least, the man was a real journalist. He is called Robert Mountsier: very nice and gentle and decent in every way, a man one likes to know. I knew him last year. He wants to interview Lady Diana Manners, if it were possible.[1] He is over here to interview the leading authors. But he thinks Lady Diana's photograph so beautiful, he would probably forfeit Arnold Bennett and H G Wells put together to be able to write a long article about *her*. He represents the leading New York papers. – When you see Diana Manners, would you mind asking her if she would consent to be interviewed, and then tell me, and I will tell Mountsier. – The woman is a Miss Andrews: we liked her very much: she is not really a journalist: very understanding: she has a letter to your mother, I believe.

Write and tell us your news. If I ever get to London again, I hope we shall see you. What is Herbert Asquith doing? How does he feel now about the war etc? What was his book of poems like?[2] Why didn't you send me one? At least one can see something of what the man is like, apart from the literature itself. The whole crux of life now lies in the relation between man and woman, between Adam and Eve. In this relation we live or die. – The soldier-spirit is fatal, fatal: it means an endless process of death. A man who has a living connection with a woman is, ipso facto, not a soldier, not an essential destroyer, but an essential creator.

D. H. Lawrence

1308. To Mark Gertler, 13 November 1916
Text: MS SIU; cited in Moore, *Intelligent Heart* 225.

Higher Tregerthen, Zennor, St. Ives, Cornwall
13 Nov. 1916

Dear Gertler,[3]

Kot told me you had done your first Sculpture – *The acrobats*. I wonder

---

[1] Lady Diana (b. 1892) was the daughter of the 8th Duke of Rutland. m. 1919, Alfred Duff Cooper (1890–1954), later Viscount Norwich.

[2] *The Volunteer and Other Poems* had been published in December 1915.

[3] Mark Gertler (1892–1939), painter. He had been a friend of DHL's since autumn 1914 and one of his correspondents since January 1916. See *Letters*, ii. 214.

how you like it, what you think of it. We had an American woman here the other day, an artist. She admired the Roundabout – the *Merry-go-Round* – immensely.[1] We liked her very much. Do you think you might ask her up to see the picture one day? I wish you would. She is Miss Esther Andrews, 131 Cheyne Walk, Chelsea, S.W. Ask her and Mr Mountsier together, will you? He is a journalist for the New York papers. He wants to interview Gilbert.[2] I am sure Gilbert would be delighted. So you might arrange things. Miss Andrews and Mountsier were staying in Penzance and in St. Ives last week. They came up here several times. I think you will like them. Have Kot with you when they come.

Oh, and do send me Gilbert's address, will you? I will surely write him. Thank heaven I shall not be expected to condole with him for the loss of Sammy and Loofie[3] – not at this late hour.

I think the Murries must have heard what Frieda said to you and Kot when she was in London, for they have utterly dropped communication. This is just as well, for I don't want it to go on. One gets too sick of all these twists and falsities.

Tell me the news of everybody when you write – I like to hear it. Of ourselves there is nothing to say, it is so quiet and remote down here, there is nobody to quarrel with. I hope the accursed army still ignores you.

My health is not particularly good just now: and we are very hard up: all of which isn't worth the telling.

Frieda sends her greetings.

                                              Yours   D. H. Lawrence

1309. To J. B. Pinker, 13 November 1916
Text: MS Forster; cited in Carswell 49.

                         Higher Tregerthen, Zennor, St. Ives. Cornwall.
                                                          13 Nov. 1916
Dear Pinker
    I return the type-script of the story 'The Mortal Coil'. The novel I will

---

[1] *The Acrobats*, a sculpture in bronze, was exhibited at the London Group's gallery, April–May 1917; it is now in the Tate Gallery (Mary Chamot *et al.*, *The Modern British Paintings, Drawings and Sculpture*, 1964, i. 218). An undated letter (though certainly written c. November 1916) from Frieda to Gertler (MS HU) leads to the conclusion that the sculpture was finished by this date and that in Letter 1394 DHL is recollecting a piece first seen some months earlier. As for Gertler's famous painting, *The Merry-Go-Round* (1916), DHL had responded vividly to it on 9 October 1916: see *Letters*, ii. 660–1. See also Letter 1325 and n. 2.
[2] Gilbert Cannan (1884–1955), novelist and dramatist. m. 1910, Mary Ansell (formerly married to Sir James Barrie). See *Letters*, ii. 208. It was through Cannan that Gertler first met DHL. See also Letter 1314 and n. 3.
[3] Cannan's favourite dogs, Sammy and Luath, which had both died.

send on in a week's time: not longer. Then I will send a batch of poems, for the American magazines.[1] Then I have another short story on hand,[2] which I shall finish when I've sent off the novel. The novel is really rather wonderful: something quite new on the face of the earth, I think. I wonder what it will seem to you.

I *do* hope, now, we can begin to make a little money, on stories etc. in America. I am sure, if your American agent pushed them a little, he could place the stories.[3] I am so tired of being always pinched and penniless and in bad health. When it is possible, I shall go to a warmer climate – to Italy. I feel so wretched as the winter comes on. – Oh, and do send me a little more money. I am at the end of all I have.

The novel will have an epilogue – a small last chapter. But that, I don't wan̴ to write until the whole is sent in to the printer: and heaven knows when that will be. But again, I don't think this book is likely to be suppressed for *immorality*, like the *Rainbow*. God knows how it will go.

Yours   D. H. Lawrence

1310. To Amy Lowell, 14 November 1916
Text: MS HU; Damon 386–9.

Higher Tregerthen, Zennor, St. Ives, Cornwall.

14 Novem. 1916

My dear Amy[4]

I was infinitely touched when there came this morning a cheque for £60, sent by you through the bankers. One is so moved by the kindness: the money, after all, is necessity, but the kindness is given. This I shall always treasure up, the kindness, even if I can pay you back the money. Because after all, there is not much real generosity in the world.

I was rather sorry Frieda wrote and asked you for money: how do we know

---

[1] Only three poems appeared in American journals in the next year: 'Street Lamps' and 'Autumn Rain' in *Egoist*, iv (January and February 1917) and 'Resurrection' in *Poetry*, x (June 1917).

[2] Possibly 'The Horse Dealer's Daughter' later sent to Pinker under its original title, 'The Miracle', on 12 January 1917 (Letter 1354).

[3] Pinker's American agent was probably Paul Revere Reynolds (1864–1944), senior partner in a literary agency (under his own name) which was initially established to represent English publishers. Reynolds had written to DHL on 22 August 1916 (TSC NWU) offering to place his work in USA and specifically conveying a request from 'a new magazine . . . called the Seven Arts' for some short stories. 'They would pay a very low price, a cent a word.' Cf. *Letters*, ii. 670.

[4] Amy Lowell (1874–1925), American poet prominent in the 'Imagist' movement. She and DHL first met on 30 July 1914 (see *Letters*, ii. 203). Among her publications are *Sword Blades and Poppy Seed* (New York, 1914) – discussed by DHL in earlier letters (see *Letters*, ii. 234–5) – and *Men, Women and Ghosts* (New York, 1916), discussed here.

what you have to do with your money. But it is wearying, to be so much unwell, and penniless. I shall begin at once to move towards Italy: though heaven knows when we shall really get away. And I hope, from Italy, to come on to America, next year, when I am better and the winter has gone.

Why don't you come to Rome for a while? Think how jolly that would be, if we were all in Rome at the same time. Perhaps you would like it better, in these times, than London.

Your book, *Men Women and Ghosts*, came two days ago. We have both read all the poems. I like this book better than *Sword Blades*. I think 'The Cremona Violin' is both a lovely story and lovely verse: an exquisite picture into the bargain. Then I like 'The Fruit Shop', the sense of youngness and all the gorgeous fruitfulness in store, then the sudden destructiveness of Bonaparte, a smash of irony. I like that. Some of the movements of the 'Hammers' really startle one's heart – one listens, and hears, and lives, it is almost frightening. Only I don't care for the Ship.[1] 'Reaping' seems to me one of the very best – a real straight jet of a story – but of course there isn't the newness of sensation one gets in 'Hoops'[2] – it belongs to the old knowledge[3] – but it is *very* good. I always liked 'Spring Day' – sometimes the prose is best of all, better than any verse-form. – And then,[4] after all, I like 'Towns in Colour' more than anything in the book: and of these 'Opera' and 'Aquarium' most.

It is very surprising to me, now I have come to understand you Americans a little, to realise how much older you are than us, how much further you and your art are[5] really, developed, outstripping us by far in decadence and non-emotional aestheticism, how much beyond us you are in the last stages of human[6] apprehension of the physico-sensational world, apprehension of things non-human, not conceptual. We still see with concepts. But you, in the last stages of return, have gone beyond tragedy and emotion, even beyond irony, and have come to the pure mechanical stage of physical apprehension, the *human* unit almost lost, the primary elemental forces, kinetic, dynamic – prismatic, tonic, the great, massive, active, *inorganic* world, elemental, never softened by life, that hard universe of Matter and Force where life is not yet known, come to pass again. It is strange and wonderful. I find it only in you

---

[1] By 'the Ship' DHL means the first of the five parts of 'The Hammers'.
[2] Part I of 'A Roxbury Garden'.
[3] knowledge] school
[4] And then] Perhaps
[5] are] is
[6] human] non-human

and H[ilda] D[oolittle], in English:[1] in your 'Bath', and the fire of the lacquer music-stands, and 'Acquarium', and some 'Stravinsky',[2] and here and there in 'Roxbury Garden' – which, to my mind, is not quite chemical and crystollographical *enough*. Of course, it seems to me this is a real *cul de sac* of art. You can't get any further than

> 'Streaks of green and yellow iridescence
> Silver shiftings
> Rings veering out of rings
> Silver – gold –
> Grey-green opaqueness sliding down'[3]

You see it is uttering pure sensation *without concepts*, which is what this futuristic art tries to do. One step further and it passes into *mere noises*, as the Italian futurismo poems have done, or mere jags and zig-zags, as the futuristic paintings.[4] Then it ceases to be[5] art, and is pure accident, mindless. – But there is this to fulfil, this last and most primary state of our being, where we are shocked into form like crystals that take place from the fluid chaos. And it is this primary state of being which you carry into art, in

> 'Gold clusters
> Flash in soft explosions
> On the blue darkness
> Suck back to a point
> And disappear – –.'[6]

– for example. You might have called your book 'Rockets and Sighs'. It would have been better than *Men Women and Ghosts*.

If ever I come to America I will write about these things. But won't you try to come to Rome. Think of the Naples aquarium, and the Naples museum – and Rome itself. We might enjoy it so much.

---

[1] Though best known as 'H. D.', Hilda Doolittle (1886–1961), had become the wife of Richard Aldington (1892–1962) in 1913. (They separated in 1919 and divorced in 1938). She had published Imagist poems in anthologies and journals since 1913; *Sea Garden* and *Choruses from the Iphigeneia in Aulis* appeared in 1916. She also became literary editor of the *Egoist* in 1916. DHL had known her since 1914. See *Letters*, ii. 203.

[2] 'Bath' is the title of the first passage in 'Spring Day'; 'An Aquarium' is the title of part V of 'Towns in Colour'; and 'Stravinsky' refers to 'Stravinsky's Three Pieces "Grotesques", for String Quartet'.

[3] 'An Aquarium', ll. 1–5.

[4] For DHL's interest in the Italian Futurists see *Letters*, ii. 180–4.

[5] be] become

[6] 'An Opera House', ll. 9–13.

Thank you once more, dear Amy. Remember me to Mrs Russell.[1] My wife is writing to you. – I have just finished a novel, of which I am proud. – Did you get my *Amores* and *Twilight in Italy*?[2] Do let us have a letter.

Yours ever   D. H. Lawrence

These things are your best, by far, I think: 'Spring Day', 'Towns in Colour', 'Hammers', p. 344, some p. 346, and p. 347 of the 'Stravinsky'. The shock and clipping of the physico-mechanical world are your finest expression.

Do write a book called Fire Rockets.

1311. To Lady Cynthia Asquith, 15 November 1916
Text: MS UT; Huxley 378–80.

Higher Tregerthen, Zennor, St. Ives, Cornwall.
15 Nov. 1916

Both your letters come this morning: the second very cross.[3] – I will not speak of the war in the abstract any more. I will only say, in the particular, that for *me* the war is utterly wrong, stupid, monstrous and contemptible, and nothing, neither life nor death, makes it any different, for *me*. For me, it is better to die than to do something which is utterly a violation to my soul. Death is no violation nor ignominy, and can be thought of with sweetness and satisfaction. On the other hand, war cannot be thought of, for me, without the utmost repulsion and desecration of one's being. For me, the war is wrong, and nothing, neither life nor death, can make it right. – But – here I submit – I am only myself. At last I submit that I have no right to speak for anybody else, but only for my single self. War is for the rest of men, what it is. Of this I can say nothing. I can only speak of myself.

And it comes to this, that the *oneness* of mankind is destroyed in me. I am I and you are you, and all heaven and hell lies in the chasm between. – Believe me I am infinitely hurt by being thus torn off from the body of mankind, but so it is, and it is right. And believe me that I have wept tears enough, over the dead men and the unhappy women who were once one with me. Now, one can only submit, they are they, you are you, I am I – there is a separation, a

---

[1] Ada (Dwyer) Russell (b. 1863), Amy Lowell's travelling companion and life-long friend. See *Letters*, ii. 207.

[2] An enquiry first made on 12 October 1916; see *Letters*, ii. 665.

[3] Lady Cynthis recorded in her diary, 13 November 1916: 'Oddly enough, just as I had sent my letter, one arrived from him [Letter 1307] – very pip-pip – still accusing humanity of fighting as an end in itself, implying that the thing was an orgy rather than a sacrifice. I wrote again, expostulating with this view as eloquently as I could' (Asquith, *Diaries* 234).

separate, isolated fate. – And never again will I say, generally, 'the war': only 'the war to me'. For to every man, the war is himself, and I cannot dictate what the war is or should be to any other being than myself. Therefore I am sorry for all my generalities, which must be falsities to another man, and almost insults. Even Rupert Brooke's sonnet,[1] which I repudiate for myself, I know now it is true for him, for them. But for me it is *not* true, and nothing will ever make it so: least of all death, for death is a great reality and seal of truth: my truth, his truth. It is terrible to think there are opposing truths – but so it is. And I am mine, you are yours, it is so, in eternity as well as in time.

About money, suddenly Amy Lowell sends me £60 from America, which is enough. I shall begin to move towards Italy now – if they will let me go. Do you think they will let us go? But at any rate, we[2] shall be in London for a few days, before very long, and I want to see you then. I shall try to go to Italy very soon, because, especially now I feel torn off, it is hard to live here; and, if I can help it, I *will* not die, in spite of all. There is another life to live, here on earth, a different life.

I shall be glad to have Herbert Asquith's poems.[3] I feel a vivid little sympathy with him just now, also something new: though probably I shall hate some of his poems, as I'm sure he hates some of mine. But perhaps, when the war is over, and we come out of it, we can meet in a new way, and have a new unison, a happiness. Speriamo.

D. H. Lawrence

I dreamed of your mother-in-law last night![4] Absit omen.[5]

1312. To Catherine Carswell, 17 November 1916
Text: MS Carswell; Unpublished.

Zennor, St. Ives, Cornwall
17 Nov. 1916

My dear Catherine

I am so sorry you are feeling so done. Never mind – lie low – lie in bed and be still. Lie still as much as possible. – The novel will only come in your rising tides of strength – in the ebbs you should even *forget* it, and only, in your soul, sleep. Lie still, give way, don't bear up any more – just lapse and be still, like a sleep of death. So life comes, when one dies and has died.

---

[1] Presumably 'The Soldier'.   [4] Margaret ('Margot') Asquith (1868–1945).
[2] we] I   [5] 'May there be no (ill) omen'.
[3] See p. 27 n. 2.

I write to Miss Andrews to ring you up, or to write to you. I'm *sure* she is nice.

I agree about Jerusalem – it makes too little *fight*. It is a decked sepulchre, really.[1]

Loathsome about Don. But mark, the war won't go on much longer – do not be afraid. Keep him always with you, innerly – and a little soldiering won't really matter – it can be borne. There will be no disaster – don't be in the least afraid. There will be no disaster between you.

I don't know *when* we shall leave the country – when they will let us. But we shall only be fore runners – don't forget. – The war won't hold out much longer – it will end before next autumn – then we can all move.

I shall send you my novel in a few days' time.

D. H. Lawrence

Amy Lowell sent us £60 from America.

1313. To J. B. Pinker, 17 November 1916
Text: MS Forster; cited in Ross, *DHL Review*, viii. 202.

Higher Tregerthen, Zennor, St. Ives, Cornwall
17 Nov. 1916

My dear Pinker

Thank you for the cheque for £50 which has come today.

Will you tell me what stories you have by you: 'Once', 'Witch à la Mode', 'Primrose Path' – anything else? If any of these is missing I will send you another copy. Did you ever have a story 'Love among the Haystacks'?[2] I believe, careless as I am, I lost that entirely. If I could find it I should like to write it up again. – I will post the novel on Monday, or thereabouts. Revising it, I do admire it. But I am not everybody.

Yours   D. H. Lawrence

I sent the other story 'Prodigal Husband', off today. I rechristened it.[3] If you like the old title better, take it back.

[Frieda Lawrence begins]

L– has enough of very beautiful poems (different and *better* than the two

---

[1] Cf. Matthew xxiii. 27, 29. The specific reference to 'Jerusalem' is obscure.
[2] Douglas Clayton typed this early story and, on 2 July 1914, DHL asked him for the MS (see *Letters*, ii. 190).
[3] See Letter 1304 and n. 3.

first vol.) for a book. Also I think a number of short stories – that might soon make another vol –

I hope your son is well –[1]

With very kind regards   Frieda Lawrence

1314. To S. S. Koteliansky, [20 November 1916]
Text: MS BL; cited in Gransden 26.

Higher Tregerthen, Zennor, St. Ives, Cornwall
Monday 21 Nov. 1916[2]

My dear Kot,

Mendel and the *Baedeker* came this morning: many thanks for them. I looked into *Mendel*. It is, as Gertler says, journalism: statement, without creation. This is very sickening. If Gilbert had taken Gertler's story and *re-created* it into art, *good*. But to set down all these statements is a vulgarising of life itself.[3]

The *Baedeker* is *very* nice: I love its plans and maps and panoramas. We have been such Romans today, on the strength of it. Would God we were all in Italy, or somewhere sunny and war-less.

I think I shall come up to London for a few days before Christmas, to see a doctor, and to get my eyes re-tested, and so on. I shall be glad to see you again.

Today I have sent off the MS. of my new novel *Women in Love*. Can I tell you how thankful I am to have the thing done, and out of the house! – But I have a great respect for this new book. I think it is a great book – though no doubt I shall share the opinion with nobody. – Whether the book will ever get published, I do not know – and don't greatly care. It seems such a desecration of oneself to give it to the extant world.

You must let me pay you for the *Baedeker* – please tell me how much it cost. I too have got a little money again, so, as far as *that* goes, am a free man. Please tell me how much the *Baedeker* cost. A thousand thanks for getting it.

I think I am the opposite of Gertler – my work nearly kills me. I feel I shall be a new man now this book is done, strong and adventurous. – Say to Gertler I will write to him in a day or two. – Oh, I *don't* like *Mendel*.

---

[1] Eric Pinker.
[2] 'Monday' was 20 November 1916.
[3] Cannan's novel, *Mendel: A Story of Youth* (published in October 1916 and already in November in a second impression) presented the fictionalised story of Gertler including his time at the 'Detmold Art School' (Slade), his love for a fellow student 'Greta Morrison' (Dora Carrington) and his attraction towards a fellow artist, 'Logan' (John Currie, 1884–1914, the portrait painter).

I hope you will like Miss Andrews – the American – if Gertler forgets the address, it is 131 Cheyne Walk, Chelsea – and Mountsier is a *very nice fellow*.

Yrs   D. H. Lawrence

1315. To Catherine Carswell, 21 November 1916
Text: MS YU; cited in Moore, *Intelligent Heart* 219.

Higher Tregerthen – Zennor – St. Ives – Cwl.
21 Nov 1916

My dear Catherine

Here is the novel – at last. Thank God I have got it out of the house. – I have sent the other copy to Pinker. Will you forward this on to him at Talbot House, Arundel St, Strand, W.C. when you have done with it.

I want you and Carswell to read it, and *please* make any corrections necessary, and tell me any discrepancy. *Don't let anybody else read it.* I want to know what both of you think of it. *I* think it a great book, whatever anybody else says. – Ask Don if he thinks any part libellous – e.g. Halliday is Heseltine, The Pussum is a model called the Puma, and they are taken from life –[1] nobody else at all lifelike.

How is your book? – have infinite patience with it, and wait for it to come. I was like that with the *White Peacock* – it took me over two years to write it – One must get one's hand in.

Shall we let Miss Andrews read the MS., she being America for the moment? We will think about it.

Love from both of us   D. H. Lawrence

I shall probably come to London for a few days before Christmas, to see a doctor and have my eyes (spectacles changed) tested. Can you put me up then – I don't know if Frieda will come, it is so *dear*.

I write this during a great hail-storm – that is the storm of abuse and persecution. Now the sun shines sweetly on the MS. – that is the light of victory. I will hastily make up the parcel with the sun in it.

Of course there is a last chapter, an epilogue, yet to be written: but that must wait for the wheel of time to turn.

---

[1] Philip Arnold Heseltine (1894–1930), the composer 'Peter Warlock', and 'Minnie' Lucie Channing (b. 1894), a Soho artist's model, whom he married in December 1916. See *Letters*, ii. 442, 481. (Heseltine later threatened DHL with a libel suit over the portrait of him as Halliday.)

1316. To Dollie Radford, [22 November 1916]
Text: MS UN; Postmark, St. Ives 22 NO 16; Nehls, i. 405–6.

Higher Tregerthen – Zennor – St. Ives – Cornwall
23 Nov 1916

My dear Dollie[1]

How long is it since we heard from each other? – it seems ages. But I have felt seedy and all gone but my cap and beard – but now I am better. I have finished and sent in my novel *Women in Love*. I don't know whether it will get published: and it is rather terrible. But I think it is a masterpiece.

We drove to St. Ives yesterday for the first time for 9 weeks – I have not been down for so long. It was most beautiful – the sea blue and the air over the sea clear as crystal, only wonderful clouds poised as if in thought, casting an iridescence on the far sea. It was all gold, the West, when we drove home, all pure gold, with the rosy-purple host of the afterglow hovering above glistening. Far beneath we could see the tiny lights of the Scillies, glinting *so* tinily. – And today is beautiful too, beyond words blue and crystal.

Hilda Aldington is in town – 44 Mecklenburg Square W.C., if you want to see her.[2] There is also a *very nice* American – man and woman – Miss Esther Andrews, 131 Cheyne Walk, and Robert Mountsier, same address. They came here, and we liked them *very* much. Write to them Dollie, if you would like to see them.

What are you doing for christmas? Aren't we going to have our party? – But perhaps I shall come to town soon for a few days. Shall I? I should like to see everybody before the year goes out.

I believe, Dollie, we shall have peace (end of war) before six months are out. Let us gather our souls and bring it to pass, by prayer or whatever it is. – I firmly believe that the pure desire of the strong creates the great events, without any action: like the prayer of the Saints. I firmly believe that.

With much love from us both.

D. H. Lawrence

---

[1] Dollie Radford, née Maitland (1864?–1920), poet. m. Ernest Radford. DHL had known her since early 1915; he had stayed in her cottage at Hermitage and at her London home in Hampstead. See *Letters*, ii. 316 n. 2.
[2] MS reads 'here'.

1317. To Catherine Carswell, [23 November 1916]
Text: MS YU; Postmark, St. Ives 23 NO 16; Unpublished.

Zennor – St. Ives – Cwl.
Thursday

Do send me (lend me) one or two books to read. I should like Zola *Nana*, *Assommoir* (I've only read *Germinal*)¹ – or any odd books – perhaps *Pendennis* or *The Virginians* – or some of Don's out of the way books: just 2 or 3 vols: or a *Cousin Pons* – anything you *have*.²

DHL

I should very much like Jean Paul Richters *Flower Fruit and Thorn Pieces*,³ if you had it. Hope you're better.

1318. To Lady Cynthia Asquith, 25 November 1916
Text: MS UT; Huxley 380–2.

Higher Tregerthen, Zennor, St. Ives, Cornwall
Saturday 25 Nov. 1916

My dear Lady Cynthia

Thank you for your husband's poems. I was glad to read them. At any rate he is not a deader, like Rupert Brooke: one can smell death in Rupert: thank heaven, not really here: only the sniff of curiosity, not the great inhalation of desire. (You won't mind what I say). I think Herbert Asquith is a poet – which is after all the most valuable thing on earth. But he is not writing *himself* at all, here – not his own realities. Most of this is vieux jeu. Still, it is the writing of a poet, thank God. Only let him burst through the dry dead old self that is on him, like a snake, come out his fresh real self: and he is a poet and a leader. But it needs the death of an old world in him, and the inception of a new. – Not Ares, not Aphrodite – these too are old hat, and not real in us (neither him nor you nor me). No gods but truth – that's the motto. I hope we shall be friends, one day, he and I – fighting together quite another kind of fight: the fight of that which is to come, not the fight of that which is passing away.

When are we going to have a shot at preparing this nation for peace? Peace

---

¹ This appears to conflict with DHL's offer, in April 1911, to give Zola's *La Débâcle* (1892) and *L'Assommoir* (1876) to Louie Burrows; one assumes he had read them (*Letters*, i. 258). *Nana* (1880) and *Germinal* (1885) had not been previously mentioned.

² The reference to Balzac (*Le Cousin Pons*, 1847) and to Thackeray's novels (*The History of Pendennis*, 1848–50 and *The Virginians*, 1857–9) recalls DHL's early marked preference for the former (see *Letters*, i. 98).

³ Translated in 1845 from the original (*Blumen-, Frucht- und Dornenstücke*, Berlin, 1818), by E. H. Noel.

and war lie in the heart, in the *desire*, of the people – say what you will. Germany, nations – are external material facts. The reality of peace, the reality of war, lies in the hearts of the people: you, me, all the rest.

We should say 'enough of war' while yet we are alive. We should say enough of war, because the desire for something else is strong and most living in us. It is foolish to drop down at last in inertia, and let the war end so – in inertia. While we have the vitality to create, we ought to stop the fighting – otherwise, when the end comes, we are spiritually bankrupt. Which is final disaster.

I think that Germany – peace terms – allies – etc – *do not matter*. What matters is the power in our own hearts, to create the new. Keep that, and all is saved. Say that to your husband – he will probably accept it sooner than you.

Oh, and *do not think* I blame the government, or howl at it.[1] The fools who howl at the government make my blood boil. I respect the Prime Minister because I believe in his real *decency* – and I think Lloyd Georges are toads. – I must here assert again, that the war is, and continues, because of the lust for hate and war, chiefly hate of each other – 'hate thy neighbour as thyself'[2] – not hate of Germany at all which is in the hearts of people; and their worship of Ares and Aphrodite – ('But a bitter goddess was born, of blood and the salt sea foam –')[3] – both gods of destruction and burning down. But in many hearts, now, I fully believe that Ares and Aphrodite have ceased to be gods. We want something else: it is fulfilled in us, this Ares–Aphrodite business: let us have something else, let us *make* something else out of our own hearts. – Germany, peace terms etc don't matter. It is a question of the living heart – that only.

I wish to heaven it might be allowed to discuss peace with the country this winter. I *am sure* we could still save the life and hope. But let the Prime Minister be changed, let the Lloyd George and Carson fools come in, and one can only leave the country (when it *is* possible) for ever, having left it in one's heart already. If it were possible to speak in the country this winter, we could

[1] The Prime Minister, H. H. Asquith, had increasingly become the target for violent newspaper attacks (particularly following the slaughter of the Somme offensive), their purpose being to drive him out of office. David Lloyd George (1863–1945) had long been urging 'a change in the direction of the war'. In late November and early December 1916 the Ulster leader Sir Edward Carson (1854–1935), Sir Max Aitken (1879–1964) – later Lord Beaverbrook – and Andrew Bonar Law (1858–1923) persuaded unionist members of the Cabinet to shift their allegiance from Asquith to Lloyd George. Asquith resigned on 5 December. Lloyd George succeeded him as Prime Minister. See *Letters*, ii. 379.

[2] Cf. Mark xii. 33.

[3] Swinburne, *Atalanta in Calydon* (1865), ll. 729–30, 742 ['For an evil blossom was born/Of sea-foam and the frothing of blood . . . A perilous goddess was born'].

save the living germ, I am sure. But it is our last chance. Failing this, one can only flee from the chaos and the orgy of ugly disintegration, which is to come.

Don't think of me as a raving impractical vain individual. *To be material at this juncture is hopeless, hopeless – and worse than impractical.* Only the living heart and the creative spirit matters – *nothing else.* Is one to be allowed to say so – or not? And do you believe it – or don't you?

Yours   D. H. Lawrence

1319. To S. S. Koteliansky, [25 November 1916]
Text: MS BL; Postmark, Zennor 27 NOV 16; Moore 485–6.

Higher Tregerthen – Zennor – St. Ives – Cwl.
Saturday 23 Nov. 1916

My dear Kot,

We sent the *Mendel* back straight to Gertler, as no doubt he told you. I only looked it through: could not read it.

Now I am not doing any work, we need books to read. I enclose ten shillings, with which will you pay yourself for all I owe you, *including postage*. With what remains, will you get me any of these books I put down: Zola: *L'Assommoir* or *Nana*: Fennimore Cooper: *Last of the Mohicans* and *Pathfinder*: Hermann Melville: *Omoo* or *Typee* (preferably *Typee*). Captain Marryatt: *Peter Simple* or *Jacob Faithful* or *Poor Jack*. D'Annunzio: *L'Innocente* (in Italian) – also an Italian dictionary. My dear Kot, some of these books are done at sixpence or sevenpence, some are in *Everyman*, some you might find second hand – Zola at 1/-, for sure.[1] Buy them as cheap as you can – and send me just a couple at a time – and keep a *strict* account for yourself, postage as well, and tell me when my ten shillings is spent.

This is a kind of interval in my life, like a sleep. One only wanders through the dim short days, and reads, and cooks, and looks across at the sea. I feel as if I also were hibernating, like the snakes and the dormice. – I saw a most beautiful brindled adder, in the spring, coiled up asleep with her head on her shoulder. She did not hear me till I was very near. Then she must have felt my motion, for she lifted her head like a queen to look, then turned and moved slowly and with delicate pride into the bushes. She often comes into my mind again, and I think I see her asleep in the sun, like a Princess of the fairy world. It is queer, the intimation of other worlds, which one catches.

---

[1] The novels by Cooper, Melville and Marryat (with the exception of *Poor Jack*) were all available in Everyman's Library.

I shall come to London when the energy comes upon me. We shall meet like exiles returned – it seems so long since we saw each other.

D. H. Lawrence

1320. To Catherine Carswell, 27 November 1916
Text: MS Carswell; Moore, *Intelligent Heart* 219–20.

Zennor – St. Ives – Cornwall
27 Nov 1916

My dear Catherine

I heard from Ottoline Morrell this morning, saying she hears she is the villainess of the new book.[1] It is very strange, how rumours go round. – So I have offered to send her the MS. – So don't send it to Pinker till I let you know.

I got *Sportsmans Sketches* and have read them.[2] No, I don't like Turgenev very much: he seems so very critical, like Katharine Mansfield, and also a sort of male old maid. It amazes me that we have bowed down and worshipped these foreigners as we have. Their art is clumsy, really, and clayey, compared with our own. I read *Deerslayer* just before the Turgenev. And can I tell you what a come-down it was, from the pure and exquisite art of Fennimore Cooper – whom we count nobody – to the journalistic bludgeonings of Turgenev. They are all – Turgenev, Tolstoi, Dostoevsky, Maupassant, Flaubert – so very *obvious* and coarse, beside the lovely mature and sensitive art of Fennimore Cooper or Hardy. It seems to me that our English art, at its best, is by far the subtlest and loveliest and most perfect in the world. But it is characteristic of a highly-developed nation to bow down to that which is more gross and raw and affected. Take even D'Annunzio and my *Trespasser* – how much cruder and stupider DAnnunzio is, really. No, enough of this silly worship of foreigners. The most exquisite literature in the world is written in the English language.

Don't talk much about my novel, will you? And above all, don't give it to anybody to read, but Don. I feel it won't be published yet, so I would rather nobody read it. I hope Ottoline Morrell won't want the MS. – And if you can prevent Aunt Barbara from knowing you have the book by you, *do* – because, having read the beginning, she is sure to claim her right to read the rest.[3]

---

[1] i.e. she had heard of her portrayal as Hermione Roddice in *Women in Love.*
[2] Turgenev, *A Sportsman's Sketches,* trans. Constance Garnett, 2 vols (1895).
[3] Barbara Low (1877–1955), the aunt of Catherine Carswell's friend Ivy (Low) Litvinov; she was herself a pioneer of psychoanalysis in England. In August 1916 she stayed with the Lawrences and began her reading of the *Women in Love* MS. See *Letters,* ii. 279.

How are you feeling? – better, I hope. And how is your work going now?
Let it go as slowly as it likes.

It is a sunny cold morning – I shall go out now.

D. H. Lawrence

1321. To Barbara Low, 28 November 1916
Text: MS UT; Postmark, St. Ives 28 NO 16; Nehls, i. 406.

Higher Tregerthen, Zennor, St. Ives. Cornwall
28 Nov 1916

My dear Barbara

The sweets came yesterday, and we have eaten them all up. They were very good. Such is life.

The weather is better, one feels a little less delugious and more like a higher mammal. I am wondering if one cannot now begin to work for peace. The time has come, I am sure. Can you tell me if anything is being done in London or anywhere. You might send me any newspaper or such that shows any interesting attitude towards the war. One might write and speak, now, for peace, if it were in any way possible.

I can quite understand you are indifferent about going back to the suburb. One feels that everything is so suspended, that any movement of any sort is vain. I feel, for the moment, it is even vain to have my hair cut. – But the moment is coming for us to rise up in a fight. We can fight for peace, at any rate – that is a definite object – very soon.

For heaven's sake dont be analysing Spiers[1] or anybody else. The longer I live the less I like psychoanalysis. Depart from evil and do good[2] – I think analysis is evil.

What are the Eders doing? – have they moved yet into their new house.[3] When they have unpacked the books, steal for me Friedas volume of Swinburne, that I may read him in a loud and declamatory voice – it gives me great satisfaction. I have read your volume loudly from cover to cover.

Ugh! – I feel the time drawing near when I must issue out of my little lair

---

[1] A man whom Barbara Low had met on her visit to the Lawrences in August; he was alleged to doubt DHL's sanity (see *Letters*, ii. 642, 648).

[2] Psalms xxxiv. 14.

[3] Dr Montagu David Eder (1865–1936), an early Freudian psychoanalyst; he had strong socialist sympathies and was intimately involved with the Labour Party in London; he became a prominent leader of the Zionist movement. (See *Letters*, ii. 258 n. 2.) m. Edith Low, sister of Barbara. The Lawrences had known the Eders for nearly two years and had stayed with them in Hampstead Garden Suburb.

and howl in the teeth of the world. Till that time comes, one seems nothing but a seed that is shoving at its integument.

D. H. Lawrence

1322. To S. S. Koteliansky, 1 December 1916
Text: MS BL; Postmark, St. Ives 1 DE 16; Moore 489.

Higher Tregerthen – Zennor – St. Ives. Cwl
1 Dec 1916

My dear Kot.

We got the letter with the photograph, also the second letter about books. The portrait has really something of you – quite true. But it has indeed none of your good looks. It makes you uglier. It is you in your bad and hopeless moods. I don't really like it. But don't tell Gertler.[1] There is still a youthful and foolish warmth about you, which is perhaps the nicest part, and this is left out on the photo. You are here the old old old *Jew*, who ought to hasten into oblivion. But there is a young and clumsy uncouth human being, not a Jew at all, a sort of heavy colt, which I should paint if *I* painted your portrait.

About books – it grieves me to have to pay 6/- for a dictionary – yet one needs a decent one. But I *can't* pay 5/- for *L'Innocente*. – There is a shop in Charing Cross Rd, rather far up, which is a Libreria Italiana and Espagnol – it only has Italian and Spanish books do see what they can do for you. If there is no cheap *Innocente*, buy some other book – D'Annunzio or Matilde Serao or Grazia Deledda[2] – I have read *Fuoco*, *Vergine Delle Rocche*, and *Trionfo della Morte* – of D'Annunzio.[3]

It will be a great boon if S[latkowsky] goes to Russia – We might have a very free and simple time at 212.[4] – But I suppose the old landlord will *never* clear out. And he is impossible.

I know you don't mind looking for the books. Find that Italian shop.

Post – rush   DHL

---

[1] For Gertler's portrait of Kot (dated 1917), see *Letters*, ii. where it is reproduced.

[2] Matilde Serao (1856–1927) was an Italian novelist who concentrated her attention on Neapolitan and Roman subjects; Grazia Cosima Deledda (1871–1936) chose Sardinia (her birthplace) as the setting for most of her novels and tales.

[3] *Il Fuoco* (Milan, 1900), trans. as *Flame of Life* (1900); *Vergine Della Roche* (Rome, 1895), trans. as *Virgins of the Rocks* (1899); and *Trionfo della Morte* (Milan, 1894), trans. as *The Triumph of Death* (1898).

[4] R. S. Slatkowsky, (d. 1918?), a Russian who ran the Russian Law Bureau at 212 High Holborn where Kot was employed as secretary and translator. DHL had displayed his dislike of Slatkowsky on earlier occasions, e.g. *Letters*, ii. 623.

1323. To Catherine Carswell, 2 December 1916

Text: MS YU; Postmark, St. Ives 2 DE 16; cited in Carswell, *Adelphi* 389.

Zennor, St. Ives, Cornwall
Sat 2 Dec 1916

My dear Catherine

I am glad you liked the novel – thanks for the suggestions. Gudrun's coat was supposed to be that pale and lovely bluish green which is a painter's emerald green – really a beautiful shade.[1] Is that still common? You might just put Thomas Bannerman instead of Sholto – or Balfour – any ordinary Scotch name.[2] Gerald and his 'as usual' is sarcastic if anything – *I* can't understand his persistence in 'dressing'. But good to cross him out. I am very glad you make these suggestions. – About Miss Andrews – she says she read the first chapter, so I suppose it is only fair to give her the whole. Let her have it when you and Carswell have done with it, will you. – Your books just come – *many* thanks. They are all interesting.

I am so afraid to come to London – my state seems so shaky. I am sure I should be ill by the time the train was at Plymouth. I keep on saying to myself 'next week – next week' – and whenever the next week comes I am still incapable of starting. It is almost impossible, I find, for me to go further than Penzance: and even then I want to run back like lightning. It is a curious moral and physical incapacity to move towards the world. Yet I want to come to London: I must wait for the tide to turn in me.

I think I shall have to give Ottoline Morrell the novel to read. Do you think it would really hurt her – the Hermione? Would you be hurt, if there was some of you in Hermione? You see it isn't really her at all – only suggested by her. It is probable she will think Hermione has nothing to do with her.

We had *Mendel* – Gertler lent us his copy. It is a bad book – statement without creation – really journalism. Gertler, Jew-like, has told every detail of his life to Gilbert – Gilbert has a lawyer's memory, and has put it all down – and so ridiculously, when it comes to the love affair. We never recognised ourselves – or Frieda – but now I remember she must be Mrs Lupton – or whatever it was – wife of an artist.[3] I only glanced through the book.

---

[1] In the revised typescript of *Women in Love* (Roberts E441f), Gudrun was described as having an 'emerald velvet coat'; in the published version (chap. XXIX) it is a 'dark glossy coat, with grey fur'.

[2] Sholto Bannerman appears as a name in the revised typescript of DHL's novel; it became Donald Gilchrist in the published work (chap. XXIX). (John Sholto Bannerman was also the name of Joanna's father in Catherine Carswell's novel.)

[3] As p. 52 n. 1 makes clear, Frieda had recognised herself in the character, Nelly Oliver, the mistress of the painter, Logan (who eventually murders her). Nelly's tempestuous, sensual, jealous and possessive nature confirms this perception.

It is beautiful weather these last days, still and soft. What a nuisance your in-laws are hovering round you again. But you will take them coolly, I know. – As for Joanna, she seems to be coming on. I feel that when she is 'out', when you have finished her, that will be an epoch closed in your life, and an epoch to begin.

I do want to come to London for spectacles and things – and to hear about the country, what everybody is saying and feeling. It seems to me a change is taking place again. I should like to come and talk – very much. The spirit is willing, but the flesh is so weak.[1] Do you know, when I think of getting into a big train to come a long distance, I feel I should faint. Either one is bewitched, or something. But this seems like a magic country with invisible walls, and one is kept in it by enchantment.

I shall be glad to hear what Don has to say – and am very grateful for his suggestions. I *must* come and talk to him, also, about the extant world, – before he is conscripted or anything vile like that.

I feel you are better, on your legs again and ready to forge ahead. Good!

Oh, don't think I would belittle the Russians. They have meant an enormous amount to me, Turgenev, Tolstoi, Dostoevsky – mattered almost more than anything, and I thought them the greatest writers of all time. And now, with something of a shock, I realise a certain crudity and thick, uncivilised, insensitive stupidity about them, I realise how much finer and purer and more ultimate our own stuff is.

Auf wiedersehen –   D. H. Lawrence

1324. To S. S. Koteliansky, [4 December 1916]
Text: MS BL; Postmark, St. Ives 5 DE 16; Zytaruk 101.

Zennor, St. Ives, Cornwall
Monday

My dear Kot,

The books came today – a great pleasure. The dictionary is one of the 'faithful friend' sort. Do borrow me an Italian book, if you can. But you spent all the money, and now I owe you for the *Baedeker and* the postage. Never mind, when I have read these books, I will send money for more. For the present we sail on gaily. With many thanks.

D. H. Lawrence

---

[1] Cliché deriving from Matthew xxvi. 41.

1325. To Mark Gertler, 5 December 1916
Text: MS SIU; Huxley 384–5.

Zennor, St. Ives, Cornwall
5 Dec 1916

My dear Gertler,

I have owed you a letter for some time – but there is nothing to say, that we don't know already. Like you, we have got £60 – which solves the money difficulty for the time being. – Thank you very much for offering to lend us. But it is a principle with me, to borrow from the rich as long as I can, not from the poor. Always spoil the Egyptians as far as possible.[1] I am better in health now, because I don't work and don't bother any more. One ought, like the fields, to lie fallow during the winter and neither work nor think, but only, in one's soul, sleep. Can't you put your soul to sleep, and remain just superficially awake, drifting and taking no real notice, just amuse yourself like a child with some sort of play work. I have just made a 'pouffe' – a sort of floor cushion, square, and like a mound – and on the black cover, all round I have stitched a green field, then house, barns, haystacks, animals, man and woman, all in bright coloured stuffs – it looks very jolly and bright. That is a kind of play, which makes one busy and happy while one's soul of contention sleeps. I wish you could take some of your sculpture rather like that.

Looking in a[2] dictionary the other day I saw '– *Sculpture*: the lowest of the arts' – That surprised me very much – but I think perhaps it is true. Sculpture, it seems to me, is truly a part of architecture. In my novel there is a man – not you, I reassure you – who does a great granite frieze for the top of a factory, and the frieze is a fair, of which your whirligig, for example, is part. – (We knew a man, a german, who did these big reliefs for great, fine factories in Cologne)[3] – Painting is so much subtler than sculpture, that I am sure it is a finer medium. But one wants the unsubtle, the obvious, like sculpture, as well as the subtle.

The war is beyond weariness, it has reached the stage of stony oppression. And though I think Asquith is by far a more decent man than Lloyd George or any of the other striving toads, yet I wish he would clear out, and leave them to it.[4] The débacle would come the quicker. It is bound to come, the great smash-up in this country – and oh, oh God, if it would only come

[1] i.e. despoil the oppressor (cf. Exodus iii. 22).   [2] a] the
[3] The real-life German sculptor has not been identified. The sculptor in *Women in Love*, Loerke, was so named in a draft version of 'The Sisters' (Roberts E441a) dating from 1913, before DHL knew Gertler. However, after seeing Gertler's *Merry-Go-Round*, he altered the description of the frieze from a scene of wolves and peasants to one of a fair.
[4] See Letter 1318 and n. 1.

quickly. But it will never take place while Asquith holds the Premiership. He is too much the old, stable, measured, *decent* England. Alas and alack that such an England must collapse and be trodden under the feet of swine and dogs. But so it is, by the decree of inalterable fate. And therefore, the longer the old decency remains standing, the longer the tops of our heads will tickle, expecting it to come crashing down on us. It is this Sword of Damocles business which one cannot bear. – But sleep – sleep in your soul – everything will come, and will go, in the end.

I can't come to London, for some reason or other. I am like a ship becalmed, down here in this offing, waiting for some wind to blow me back to town, and into the world. I look like Elijah, or Elisha, whichever it was, for a cloud as big as a man's hand – but see nothing.[1] I can conceive myself down here, still waiting, an old, hook-nosed, benevolent old man, living on crusts and charity.[2] So be it – it's very nice down here, much nicer than anywhere else. – But when you write, tell me all the *world-news* you can.

D. H. Lawrence

1326. To Amy Lowell, 7 December 1916
Text: MS HU; cited in Moore, *Intelligent Heart* 226.

Higher Tregerthen – Zennor, St. Ives, Cornwall
7 Dec. 1916

My dear Amy

We were very sorry to hear, from Mrs Russell's letters, that you were so ill. It must have been lacerating, and just at the time of your brother's death![3] I do hope you are better. I shall be glad to hear from you yourself, when you are well.

I am reviving quite a lot – even going out for walks again, and looking at the world. I think of going to London for a few days soon, to see everybody, for I have not left Cornwall for a whole twelve months. Heaven knows, the outer world does not look very inviting to me. But I must see people, and hear what they have to say.

There have been so many restrictions put on travelling, I don't know even now whether they will let us go to Italy – most probably not. I was disappointed – but there, one must be thankful if one can live in any kind of

---

[1] See 1 Kings xviii. 44.
[2] Cf. Elijah who was fed with 'bread and flesh' by the ravens: 1 Kings xvii. 4–6.
[3] Amy Lowell had been so ill (latterly from jaundice) that she could not be told at once of her brother Percival's death on 13 November 1916.

freedom at all, nowadays. I am thankful to be better in health, to be walking about and facing life again, so I won't grumble.

We have got Lloyd George for Prime Minister. That is a bad look-out for England. There was in Asquith the old English *decency*, and the lingering love of liberty. But Lloyd George is a clever little Welsh *rat*, absolutely dead at the core, sterile, barren, mechanical, capable only of rapid and acute mechanical movements. God alone knows where he will land us: there will be a very big mess. But the country at large wanted him. 'Quem Deus vult perdere –'. All the time, when I look at my countrymen, my mind exclaims in amazement 'Whom the Gods wish to destroy, they first make mad.'[1]

I was glad to hear that your book was going so well:[2] that will cheer you up. Yesterday I saw it advertised in the *Times*, but have not seen any reviews. I hope it will do well in England too.

We both wish you a peaceful and happy Christmas. Kindest greetings to Mrs Russell.

D. H. Lawrence

1327. To Gordon Campbell, 7 December 1916
Text: MS UCin; Peter L. Irvine and Anne Kiley, *DHL Review*, vi (1973), 7–8.

Higher Tregerthen – Zennor – St. Ives, Cornwall
7 Dec. 1916

Dear Campbell[3]

I think of coming up to town some time during the next few weeks, and I should like to see you if you are in London. Write and tell me what you are doing, will you, and what you think of the world by now.

I have been in Cornwall for twelve months now, never out of it, so I feel a stranger to the world. I find myself divested of all my friends, and much more confident and free, having no connections anywhere. Why should one seek intimacies – they are only a net about one. It is one's business to stand quite apart and single, in one's soul.

But the world (England) seems to be smashing up pretty fast, so I should

---

[1] James Duport, *Homeri Gnomologia* (1660) ['Quem Jupiter vult perdere, dementat prius': 'Whom God would destroy, he first sends mad'].

[2] *Men, Women and Ghosts*, published in London in December 1916, was about to go into a third edition in America.

[3] Charles Henry Gordon Campbell (1885–1963), later 2nd Baron Glenavy of Milltown. He was educated at Charterhouse and the Royal Military Academy. By profession a barrister, he was now serving in the Ministry of Munitions (1915–18). Murry had introduced him to DHL in July 1913. See *Letters*, ii. 50–1.

like to have a look round me, to see what one might make out of the confusion. You must tell me about things.

Warm regards to you all from Frieda and me.

D. H. Lawrence

1328. To Lady Cynthia Asquith, 11 December 1916
Text: MS UT; Huxley 385–6.

Zennor, St. Ives, Cornwall.
Monday 11 Dec. 1916

Here's a pretty state of affairs – Messrs Lloyd George and Lord Derby[1] – funny – pretty! This is the last stage of all, that ends our sad eventful history.[2] So be it. It is what the countryful of swine wanted, now let them have it. All we have to do is wait for the débâcle.

Over Cornwall, last Wednesday and Thursday, went a terrible wave of depression. In Penzance market, farmers went about with wonderstruck faces, saying 'We're beaten – I'm afraid we're beaten. Them germans are a wonderful nation, I'm afraid they're more than a match for us.' That is Cornwall at the present time. – I must say, I too expect a national disaster before very long. But I don't care very much. They want it, the people in this country. They want, in their vile underneath way of working, to scuttle the old ship and pitch everybody into the water. Well, let them. Perhaps when we've all had a ducking in the sea of fearful disaster, we shall be more wholesome and truthful. At any rate, then I feel we shall be able to do something, something new. – It is no use adhering to that old 'advanced' crowd – Cambridge, Lowes Dickinson, Bertie Russell,[3] young reformers, socialists, Fabians – they are our disease, not our hope. We want a clean sweep, and a new start. And we will have it. Wait only a little longer. Fusty, fuzzy peace-cranks and lovers of humanity are the devil. We must get on a new track altogether. Damn humanity, let us have a bit of inhuman, or non-human truth, that our fuzzy human emotions can't alter.

I send you MS. of a tiny book of poems, to see if you like them.[4] If you do, and if they find a publisher, I think they might be a real success – and I would

---

[1] Edward George Stanley (1865–1948), 17th Earl of Derby, was appointed Secretary of State for War in the new administration under Lloyd George. See *Letters*, ii. 495.

[2] Cf. *As You Like It*, II. vii. 163–4.

[3] Goldsworthy ('Goldie') Lowes Dickinson (1862–1932) and Bertrand Arthur William Russell (1872–1970) were both Cambridge Fellows; both were also leading pacifists and reformers during and after the First World War. See *Letters*, ii. 273, 286.

[4] The collection called 'All of Us' (later 'Bits').

like to inscribe them to you – 'To Cynthia Asquith' – damn initials. But that is just as you like.

We keep putting off our coming to London. But it is bound to be within a month's time now – probably in early January. Then we must see where we are, how we stand, all of us, what we feel and what we are ready for.

D. H. Lawrence

The story 'The Thimble' is being published in an American magazine called *The Seven Arts*.[1]

1329. To Barbara Low, [11 December 1916]
Text: MS UT; Nehls, i. 407.

Zennor – St. Ives – Cornwall
Monday

My dear Barbara

Many thanks for the papers. They make me sick. I am convinced, if one is to do anything real in this country, one must eschew all connection with Fabianism, socialism, Cambridgism, and advancedism of all sorts, like poison. It is a nasty form of dry rot in the human species. One must go out on one's own, *unadhering*. I would rather, myself, appear in the *Morning Post* than anywhere: but of course it is unthinkable. – I have not read Bertie Russell's book, but I can assure you it is no good.[2] – As for *Mendel* – I looked it through – disliked it: it is a piece of journalism, absolutely without spark of creative fire. Gertler, in true Jewish manner, would relate his life in minutest detail, to anybody, at one time. Gilbert has a prodigious memory, and has got it all down word for word: journalism. Now Gertler is very sick about it: serve him right. But then I think Gilberts attitude is slimy to the last degree.

The visit to my sister is not quite definite for Christmas, because my elder sister talks of coming down from Glasgow the 2nd week in January, so of course I should have to meet her.[3] At any rate, I shall go to Ripley between now and the end of January. And so I shall be in London in a week or two – we both shall. I want to find a decent bed-sitting room where we can stay, perhaps for a week or a fortnight, somewhere down in town: I had rather,

[1] Vol. i (March 1917), 435–48.
[2] Russell's *Principles of Social Reconstruction* had appeared in November 1916. DHL already knew the gist of Russell's argument since the book consisted of lectures – discussed at length between the two men – Russell had delivered January–March 1916 in Caxton Hall. See *Letters*, ii. 505 and n. 1.
[3] DHL's younger sister, Lettice Ada Clarke (1887–1948), lived at Ripley, Derbyshire; see *Letters*, i. 27. His elder sister, Emily Una ('Pamela') King (1882–1962), had lived in Glasgow since June 1912; see *Letters*, i. 36, 416.

really, be in town, and on my own. Of course it would not have to be an expensive room. Tell me if you know of anything.

I shall send you the MS. of my novel, so that you can finish reading it, in a very short time: some time next week, I expect. I want to know what you will think of it as a whole.

It is queer you feel Germany must win. Last Wednesday and Thursday the most terrible wave of depression went over Cornwall. In Penzance the farmers went saying 'We're beaten, we're beaten.' Really, I don't care either way, now. It is when this affair is over we must do something.

Katie Berryman says someone else wants the cottage, and will you let her know at once.[1]

Love from both   D. H. Lawrence

Send a p.c. to Miss Esther Andrews, 131 Cheyne Walk, Chelsea – she is an American who came to see us here: I am going to lend her the MS: go and see her, or ask her to tea one day.

1330. To J. B. Pinker, 11 December 1916
Text: MS Forster; Unpublished.

Zennor, St. Ives, Cornwall.
11 Dec 1916

Dear Pinker

I send you the MS. of a tiny book of poems of the present day.[2] I am not sure they are not tours de force – and I wouldn't mind if they were published anonymously – if they are published at all. Properly done, by the right man, they might have a real popular success. Give it the people as the 'war *literature*' they are looking for: they will find themselves in it: good, a popular success. For myself, as I say, I doubt the poems are tours de force – but, for *people*, so much the better.

Have you any news of the novel or anything? Will the *Seven Arts* send me a copy containing my story? I wish they would.

D. H. Lawrence

---

[1] Katie Berryman – regarded with affection by the Lawrences – was a shopkeeper in Zennor. See *Letters*, ii. 624.
[2] Presumably DHL would send the ribbon copy of the poems to Lady Cynthia (see Letter 1328 and n. 3); this then would be a carbon copy for Pinker. DHL requested its return on 5 March 1918 (Letter 1534).

1331. To S. S. Koteliansky, [12 December 1916]
Text: MS BL; Postmark, St Ives 12 DE 16; Zytaruk 102.

[Frieda Lawrence begins]
                                   [Higher Tregerthen, Zennor, St. Ives, Cornwall]
                                                                          12th of Dec
Dear Kot,
    I found this letter in a pocket I thought you had it – It is *very* dirty! but I ll
send it!¹ We are very pleased because some well to-do Americani are lending
us a house near *Guildford*,² it is'nt settled so dont say *anything*, but you must
come as it is not far –

                                                             In a hurry   Frieda
    We shall come early in January –

[Lawrence begins]

---

¹ Frieda's letter (conjecturally dated 5 December 1916 from her reference to Asquith's speech)
  reads as follows (MS BL):
                                                                              Zennor
  Dear Kot,
      It was nice of you to ask Shearman for those Italian books – L[awrence] will read them aloud
  to me – I never thanked you for your *nice* letter – but I was very glad to get it – I always knew we
  ought to be friends – and it grieved me that we were not, but now we are. Anyhow I hold that as
  a fact and a very pleasant one – I heard a day or two ago from Mrs Carswell that there was a
  portrait of me in *Mendel* – I suppose I am the murdered woman – We live and learn, I never
  recognised myself! Except some of L's speeches I recognised – I was sorry that Gilbert made
  me quite so horrid – so vulgar – But there – We are coming to London after the new year – L.
  wants to – I am afraid it will be very depressing, even Cornwall feels the war at last – Poor
  Asquith, his speech to-day seemed to me the 'oraison funèbre' of the great old England – But I
  being German cannot help feeling that now at last a better spirit may blossom in Germany, it
  was time – what do you feel about Russia? Did you ever really believe in it? I thought not – You
  put your hope into England – And personally I have had a lot from England – But now it is sad
  – I just read *Peter Simple*, it is so jolly and proud, then it hurts one that it all should be a thing of
  the past – God help us all! When we come to London we shall take a room for a week or two –
  Murry wrote to L. after a long time, but it's no good – I do wish L. and I could go to America,
  but I know L. cant, somehow he belongs to England till the war is over. He does not feel *free*.
  And I feel like *bursting* – But I am getting used to it – I want you to read L.s new novel – It is so
  good and to my satisfaction I am a nicer person there than Gilbert made me – Gertler writes you
  are sad – I wish you would come and make me laugh – I do *so* want to be happy. But with the
  new year we shall meet –
                                                                 Yours ever   Frieda
      Forgive pencil!

  (For Shearman see p. 103 n. 5)

² Unidentified.

My Dear Kot

   Thank you very much for the Italian books – I will not keep them too long.
– Frieda rushes in, as usual – It is the merest chance we might go to Guildford
for a week or two. But it is quite near London, we should see you. I am sure
Sl[atkowsky] won't go to Russia. We shall certainly come to London in
January. – I wonder if this new government will worry you. All is vile.

                                                                                                                          DHL

1332. To S. S. Koteliansky, [15 December 1916]
Text: MS BL.; Postmark, Zennor 15 DEC 16; Moore 492.

                                                                          Zennor, St. Ives, Cornwall
                                                                                                                    Friday

My dear Kot

   Thank you for the little Dostoevsky book.[1] I have only read Murry's
Introduction, and Dostoevsky's 'Dream of a Queer Fellow'. Both stink in my
nostrils. I call it offal, putrid stuff. Dostoevsky is big and putrid, here, Murry
is a small stinker, emitting the same kind of stink. How is it that these foul-
living people ooze with such loving words. 'Love thy neighbour as thyself'[2]
– well and good, if you'll hate thy neighbour as thyself. I can't do with this
creed based on self-love, even when the self-love is extended to cover the
whole of humanity. – No, when he was *preaching*, Dostoevsky was a rotten
little stinker. In his art he is bound to confess himself lusting in hate and
torture. But his 'credo' – ! – my God, what filth!

   And Murry, *not being an artist*, but only a little ego, is a little muckspout,
and there is an end of it. I never said he was honest: I said we *had* liked him
and therefore we still liked him. But one can mend one's ways. I have liked
him and I don't like him any more. Basta! As for his novel – I read it in MS.
and thought it merely words, words.[3] It is the kind of wriggling self-abuse
which I can't make head or tail of. But then, as Murry says, I am not clever
enough. – Enough enough – I have had filth in my mouth. Now I spit it out.

   We have read the *Cavalleria Rusticana*: a veritable blood-pudding of
passion![4] It is not at all good, only, in some odd way, comical, as the
portentous tragic Italian is always comical.

---

[1] Dostoievsky's *Pages from the Journal of an Author*, trans. by Kot and Murry, was published in
   December 1916.
[2] Leviticus xix. 18.
[3] Murry's (wholly unsuccessful) novel, *Still Life* (December 1916). But see *Letters*, ii. 548.
[4] Giovanni Verga's *Cavalleria Rusticana* (1880). DHL's translation was published (by Cape) in
   1928 under the title *Cavalleria Rusticana and Other Stories*.

I don't want too much Varvara when we are in town.[1]

I heard from Campbell. It's about time he made a fresh start somewhere. He's worn his legs to stumps trotting in an old round. Basta! That's a great word.

I have just read *Deerslayer*. What an exquisite novel. Oh, English novels, at their best, are the best in the world.

I don't want to hear you talk for a fortnight about Murry. Five minutes, then not a moment more. Stink bores me, as well as oppresses me.

Yours   D. H. Lawrence

1333. To J. B. Pinker, 18 December 1916
Text: MS Forster; cited in Vivian de Sola Pinto, ed., *D. H. Lawrence after Thirty Years* (Nottingham, 1960), p. 27.

Higher Tregerthen – Zennor, St. Ives, Cornwall
18 Dec 1916

Dear Pinker

My friend S. Koteliansky, of the Russian Law Bureau, 212 High Holborn, writes that he thinks he could get the new novel *Women in Love* placed and *paid for* in Russia, if it could appear in Russian simultaneously with, or even before the English edition. It only means making another typed copy. But you might see Koteliansky, ring him up at the Russian Law Bureau, and speak with him about it.

I hope to send off duplicate MS of novel in a few days.

D. H. Lawrence

1334. To S. S. Koteliansky, 18 December 1916
Text: MS BL; Postmark, St. Ives 18 DE 16; Zytaruk 104.

Zennor, St. Ives, Cornwall
18 Dec. 1916

My dear Kot,

Many thanks for thinking about publishing my book in Russia. I should like it to be done. Unfortunately there is no spare MS. – one must go to America – but one might be made. I have written to Pinker about it, and asked him to ring you up. He is my literary agent: J.B. Pinker, Talbot House, Arundel St, Strand, W.C. He would arrange with you, and get a type-copy made. He has the MS. now. I hope this will come off: it would be a real pleasure.

With many thanks, and greetings   D. H. Lawrence

---

[1] 'Varvara' is the Russian equivalent of 'Barbara'; Barbara Low is the person in question here.

1335. To Lady Cynthia Asquith, 19 December 1916
Text: MS UT; Huxley 386–7.

Zennor, St. Ives, Cornwall
19 Dec 1916

I wonder if you could help me in another little matter. I have finished and sent in the novel *Women in Love*, which is more or less a sequel to the *Rainbow*. It is a very fine piece of work, and I will stand by it for ever. But there is the same danger ahead as ever: it is, perhaps, almost as likely to be suppressed as was the *Rainbow*: which seems to me monstrous, a serious and profound piece of work like that. I wondered if I could dedicate it to some patron, in the old-fashioned way, and so secure it some patronage which would save it from the barkings of the little newspaper curs.[1] Do you know anybody of any weight or importance, who would take it under his, or her, protection, so far as to accept a serious dedication? It is a much finer book than the *Rainbow*, and I would rather it were never published at all than insulted by petty dogs as that was. However, in your mad scurry of train catching, you might think it over for me.

Really, when the Almighty asked you what you did on earth, to justify your existence, shall you breathlessly answer: I just caught the Last Post.

D. H. Lawrence

Shall I write to Eddie about this?[2]

1336. To Barbara Low, 20 December 1916
Text: MS SIU; Unpublished.

Higher Tregerthen – Zennor – St. Ives, Cornwall
20 Dec 1916

My dear Barbara,

We are staying here for Christmas after all. There was a plan for us to have a little house in Surrey, very nice, and to come up immediately. But the American woman who had let it to some people this[3] autumn suddenly is hauled up, as the people prove to be *Germans*, and there is a row altogether: so this little plan falls through. Now I shall merely wait: for I hear that London is so foul, one would die in it in a fortnight. I shall go to Ripley as soon as my

---

[1] In 1920 *Women in Love* was published without any dedication.

[2] (Sir) Edward Howard Marsh (1872–1953), a close friend of Lady Cynthia's, was assistant private secretary to the Prime Minister, Herbert Asquith, 1915–16; from 1917–22 he was private secretary to (Sir) Winston Churchill. More important for DHL, Marsh was an influential patron of the arts. (See DHL's letters to him, *Letters*, i and ii.)

[3] this] last

elder sister comes down from Glasgow: which is fixed at present for the first or second week in January: though nothing is certain on the face of the earth. As for a room in town – what's the good of saying anything. Miss Andrews talks of going to France directly after the New Year: we *might* have her studio place for a bit: I don't know. It seems not worth while moving from anywhere to anywhere nowadays.

I didn't like the Peace pamphlets you sent: oh dear, too squashy altogether. Today I have read Lloyd George's first Prime Minister speech. The man means nothing: he has no more inside to him than an empty tin: or perhaps he has a certain amount of clockwork, but absolutely nothing more. It is really funny. I only hope he will do all he says, and go on in just the same key for three little months. He will by that time have steered the ship of the State on to such a wonderful Goodwin Shoal of submerged opposition, that she will split in two like a walnut, and the waters will be over our heads.[1] Good! – so be it. If there is no other way to get rid of their folly, drown it. But we are running rapidly into the jaws of hell, as a country. I am glad. I want now to see the jaws of hell crack our little island like a nut: God knows what sweetness they will extract, and where we shall be. But it will be an end, and this torture of suspense will be over. When I think of the house of Commons cheering away at little Lloyd George's remarks, my blood curdles into a cynical whey. Three months – three little months – and then, voyons!

We intend to go to St. Ives tomorrow, if it isn't a blizzard, and we shall send you some little thing from the Cornish Stone Shop, for Christmas.

Probably Miss Andrews will let you have the novel some time this week. If so, read it quickly, my dear Barbara, and hand it on to Mrs Hilda Aldington, 44 Mecklenburg Square, W.C. That must be fairly near you. Then she must send it to Lady Ottoline.

I feel we *shall* come to London very soon. But as I tell you, having a bellyful of the Welsh rabbit out of this morning's paper, I am suffering from social indigestion, and feel I wouldn't take the trouble to walk to Zennor to be crowned with King George's crown. But, as you will have holidays immediately, do you write to me and tell me what you think of the state of things, and what you hear other people say.

There is no Zennor news. There is a concert by the remains of the Church Choir in the schoolroom on Boxing Day, 'Mixed Entertainment', it is called: and a Public Tea on the Saturday following, where you pay tenpence, eat, and come away. That is the whole. But the farce of Christmas is too sickening this year.

[1] i.e. the Goodwin Sands, off the eastern tip of Kent.

Let me know if you get the novel all right: and read it quickly, and tell me if you like it. Frieda sends her love, and says she will write too. – I feel something *must* happen in the world before I can leave Zennor: I feel scotched, as if my movement were locked. Attendons.

D. H. Lawrence

1337. To Catherine Carswell, 20 December 1916
Text: MS YU; cited in Carswell, *Adelphi* 285, 387.

Zennor, St. Ives, Cornwall.
20 Dec. 1916.

My dear Catherine

No, we shan't come to town for a fortnight now, at least. It sounds too horrible. And the Lloyd-George speech in this morning's paper is such an unsavoury dollop, that one wants to hide one's head in a gorse-bush and pretend one is hidden. It is too disgusting. The man means nothing, stands for nothing, is nothing: and he mechanically does what Germany does, and the nation vociferously cries Hear Hear! Do tell me what you think of it, and what the people are saying, and what Don and the *Times* people say.[1] I feel I want to know the current opinion. I think, of course, that we are now just curving into the final Maelström: in a few more months there will *be* no English nation, there will be a vast horde of self-interested mad brutes padding round seeking their own ends: a chaos, a horror. How long will it be before Ll.G. and the War Council have the Conservatives, the Liberals, and the Laborites tearing them into three morsels? Not long, I think. So hurrah for the débâcle: let it be soon, for suspense is intolerable.

What an ugly farce Christmas is this year. Will anybody *dare* to sing carols etc. Pah, it all stinks. What a pity you cannot poison your belle soeur.[2] What a *blind mouth* devouring your life.[3] Schoo her off – schoo!

I am glad Don likes the novel. About the Gerald-Work part:[4] I want it to come where it does: you meet a man, you get an impression of him, you find out *afterwards* what he has done. If you have, in your arrogance, writ him down a nobody, then there is a slap in the eye for you when you find he has done more than you have done. Voilà. (I don't mean *you*, Catherine Carswell, of course.)

[1] Before Carswell was called to the Bar (on 26 January 1916), he had worked on the *Times*; he continued to have many friends on the newspaper's staff.
[2] Isabel Macquarie Carswell (1887–1974). See *Letters*, ii. 617.
[3] Cf. Milton, *Lycidas*, l. 119.
[4] The reference is imprecise but DHL appears to be alluding to 'The Industrial Magnate' chapter in *Women in Love*.

Don't hate Joanna:[1] she is young: she will grow up: I hate nobody who will grow up. But the hideous wasters who will only rot in the bud, how I hate them. So Joanna is all right. She goes through her bad phases, as she ought. She is a kind of dead-nettle who looks a pure weed, and comes out with very quaint and happy bunchy flowers at the last minute. Patience! But I wish you got along with her: I am anxious to see her to the end. I feel she will gather up her skirts and fly like the wind to her conclusions, as the New Year comes in.

I believe Pinker will have some difficulty in getting the novel *Women in Love* published. Methuen, having had the MS., agrees to cancel the agreement. I am glad not to be thrown any more under the snout of *that* particular swine.[2] But it shows what the market value of the book is likely to be at the moment: the moment being from now onwards, indefinitely. For I believe that England, in spite of your woman friend,[3] is capable of not seeing anything but badness in me, for ever and ever. I believe America is my Virgin soil: truly. But patience, always patience. – What a pity your Australian millionaire[4] wasn't one of the heavenly babes who see and speak wisdom without understanding it.[5] He might have given us £1000 to publish our novels with. But I have no hopes of millionaires. – I want to know what Don thinks of the latter half of the book. I must see his notes too. Are they pencilled on the MS?

I wonder when we shall see you. Everything seems in a state of unstable solution, ready to precipitate out at the least shock. It is a blessing, there are one or two people in the world one can feel pretty safe with: for I have a horror of all the other trillions.

I feel we shall all be meeting is a *very little while*. Hush! – one feels quite portentous.

D. H. Lawrence

I was wondering if it would be wise to try to get some well-known and important person to take the novel under his protection; that is, if I could dedicate it with a proper inscription, in the 18th century fashion, to some patron whose name would be likely to save it from the yelping of the small newspaper curs. What do you think?

[1] See pp. 26 n. 1 and 44 n. 2.
[2] DHL is bitterly recalling what he regarded as Methuen's treacherous acquiescence in the suppression of the *Rainbow*. See *Letters*, ii. 430 n. 1, 457 and n. 2.
[3] Unidentified.
[4] Unidentified.
[5] Cf. Luke x. 21.

1338. To Dollie Radford, 20 December 1916
Text: MS UN; Postmark, St. Ives 21 DE 16; Nehls, i. 408–9.

Zennor, St. Ives, Cornwall.
20 Dec. 1916

My dear Dollie

We send you this pendant of lapis lazuli, and this little chain, with great joy. We have talked of it ever since you were here, always saying: 'At Christmas we will send Dollie that pendant, it is her own true blue.' And now Christmas has come, and we actually do what we said we would do. There always seems to me something wonderful, when one fulfils an intention, after many days. But I am glad. I feel that this bit of blue smooth stone really belongs to you, and it is a pleasure to send it to its living home.

One hasn't the heart to make Christmas wishes. We *always* wish that better days would come: perhaps they will soon. If not, one has the strength to go on as long as is necessary.

We are staying down here still a little longer. You know I keep saying I will come to London for a while. But something inside me won't let me. I am much better in health: much. But when I think of coming to London, a pressure comes on my heart, and I know it is impossible. I suppose it is the finger of the Lord.[1] – I will come when I can come: why violate oneself.

The days of the world – not of Zennor – are dreary, too dreary to talk of in a Christmas letter. I think there will come a big smash, an internal smash, before long. Till it has come, we are in suspense. I think Lloyd George stands for nothing, and *is* nothing. He is a thing of the moment. We shall see him pass like a straw on the wind.

I send you back Trotter also.[2] I didn't like him very much. Oh, I *cannot* stand this scientific talk of instincts and bee communities and wolf packs and such like, as if everything worked from a mechanical basis. It is a great lie. They think a living being is a thing that can be wound up in the head, and made to go through its proper motions. It is just like anatomy: it examines every bit of the dog, but, the dog is all *dead dog*. So they do with the human being: it is all dead humanity, that which is material to life, never that which is life itself. It irritates me exceedingly. I think all science, but particularly the sciences of psychology and sociology, are loud-mouthed impertinence: impertinent, that is what they are.

I agree with you, we need a republic. But heavens, not a republic based on the idea of Equality and Fraternity. We want a republic based on the idea of

[1] Cf. Exodus viii. 19.
[2] Wilfred Trotter, *Instincts of the Herd in Peace and War* (1916).

extrinsic equality, and intrinsic inequality. When we can give precedence to our betters in spirit, and take precedence of our inferiors in spirit, we are true people. We are only equal in so far as that every man should have equal opportunity to come to his own fulfilment. But that every man should come to the same fulfilment is mere rubbish, and that every fulfilment is equal to every other is mere meaningless words. – What the world needs to learn, today, is to give due honor to those who are finer in spirit, and to know the inferiority of those who are mean and paltry in spirit. At once we have an end of the Horatio Bottomley[1] Lloyd George world. – But people want equality, and if nothing must be better than anything else, and no man better than another, then we must all come down to the level of the lowest, there is no bedrock of humanity but the bottom dog. And this is our actual aim now. – Oh dear, it makes my arms ache with weariness, even to write it. – *When* will people cease from this mongrel, currish desire?

We both send our love, and wish you inward peace for the Christmas.

D. H. Lawrence

1339. To Arthur McLeod, 21 December 1916
Text: MS UT; cited in Moore, *Intelligent Heart* 226.

Higher Tregerthen – Zennor, – St. Ives. Cornwall.
21 Dec. 1916

My dear Mac,[2]

Your book and letter came today: I was glad. It isn't that one forgets, it is that the events of this ugly world make one live so from moment to moment, that one feels isolated within the immediate present. But I was glad to hear from you, to know you are out of the army.

They gave me complete exemption on the score of health, so I am in peace for the moment, as regards compulsion. What that Welsh rarebit of a Lloyd George intends to inflict on us in the future, God above knows. He is an empty activity, and soon we shall find ourselves sheering giddily into chaos. What will happen when the waters actually close over us – nay, who knows!

After shifting restlessly from place to place, we got a house here, under the moors and over the sea, towards Lands End. It is beautiful, wild, and open: the big open space of the sky over the sea, blue and western-clear is my only

[1] Horatio William Bottomley (1860–1933), journalist and fraudulent financier currently enjoying political prominence and a 'patriotic' reputation; editor of *John Bull*. DHL frequently expressed contempt for him (see *Letters*, ii. 371).
[2] Arthur William McLeod (1885–1956), DHL's close friend and colleague on the staff of Davidson Road School, Croydon, 1908–11. See *Letters*, i. 10, 136.

consolation: though when I see the inflated sausage of an airship edging through the blue heavens, and submarine destroyers nosing like swimming rats up the coast, I feel the universal sickness. Oh I am so sick and nauseated of this general state of ugliness and base foulness. One wishes the Flood might come, to sweep away the festering excess of ugly-spirited people.

I have written a novel, called *Women in Love*. It is a sequel to the *Rainbow*, but very different. But whether, after the *Rainbow* affair, being also what Dr Horton would call a pernicious book, it will find a publisher, I don't know, and don't very much care.[1] It is a very good piece of work: in fact, a masterpiece. So it will keep. What is the good of its coming out into the orgy of baseness which is today.

I send you my copy of the Imagiste Anthology from America, for the sake of the 'Errinyes' poem, which I hope you will like.[2] I think H[ilda] D[oolittle] is good: none of the others worth anything. Amy Lowell is James Russell Lowell's daughter.[3] She is not a good poetess, I think. But she is a very good friend. – I almost wept when I put together the *Amores* poems. It all seems so strange and far-off, unreal, and yet, in another mood, so near and *navrant*.[4] You are the only person who brings it near, really: the old Davidson Road past. And that is because we have a stand in books we read together: I remember so many odd books you lent me: Trelawney's *Shelley* and Mallocks *New Republic*.[5] And I was so anxious for you to read the bits of MS., so anxious to hear what you had to say.

Tell me if you have read anything lately which has interested you. Poor Aylwin, is he happy as a Lieutenant?[6] And Humphreys, what of him?[7] Do you mean that Philip Smith is not teaching? – I can't believe it.[8] And Miss

---

[1] Robert Forman Horton (1855–1934), a prominent Congregational minister whom DHL associated with the 'National Purity League' which he believed instigated the suppression of *The Rainbow* (see *Letters*, ii. 477). The belief has not been substantiated.

[2] DHL's poem appeared in *Some Imagist Poets 1916: An Annual Anthology* (Boston and New York, 1916), ed. Amy Lowell. Hilda Doolittle also contributed to the volume.

[3] James Russell Lowell (1819–91), American poet, essayist and diplomat.

[4] 'heart-rending, distressing'.

[5] DHL's letters do not mention his having borrowed from McLeod either Edward John Trelawny's *Recollections of the Last Days of Shelley and Byron* (1858; ed. E. Dowden, 1906) or the satire, *The New Republic* (1877) by William Hurrell Mallock (1849–1923). (For the first see *Letters*, ii. 625.)

[6] Robert Henry Aylwin (1885–1931), another former colleague at Davidson Road School. He had been recently commissioned (on 25 October 1916) in the Royal West Surrey Regiment and was – on 22 December – to go overseas until February 1919. See *Letters*, i. 194.

[7] Ernest Arthur Humphreys (b. 1882), another teaching colleague who was also in the army 1916–19. See *Letters*, i. 194.

[8] Philip Frank Turner Smith (1866–1961) had been headmaster of Davidson Road School when DHL taught there (see *Letters*, i. 84); he too was by now in the army.

Mason,[1] any news of her? And the Jones family?[2] And little Byrne?[3] And that feather-brained Robertson,[4] and all the rest of Croydon? Glean me a little news, will you.

We may come up to London for a time, in January. If so, we must arrange a meeting. I feel we are all like drowning men, who remember the past vividly in a flash. And this is our flash. `

But out of the chaos we must rescue a future, that is all. We will do it. With affection from me, and kindest regards from Frieda.

D. H. Lawrence

1340. To S. S. Koteliansky, 23 December 1916
Text: MS BL; Zytaruk 105.

Zennor, St. Ives, Cornwall
23 Dec 1916

My dear Kot

Thank you so much for thinking about the Russian translation of the novel. I hope it will come off.

I send you a tiny little paper-knife of blue agate. It is a curious stone that loses colour when exposed to light. It is a fragment of Cornwall itself, as the stone is found here.

One doesn't feel very Christmassy. For some reason, I am sad at heart, and very heavy-spirited. But next Christmas we shall be happy, really doing something and happy.

With love from both of us   D. H. Lawrence

1341. To Gordon Campbell, 23 December 1916
Text: MS UCin; cited in Moore, *Intelligent Heart* 226.

Zennor, St. Ives, Cornwall.
23 Dec. 1916

My dear Campbell,

I was glad to hear from you, but your letter was not a happy one. I read

---

[1] Agnes Louise Eliza Mason (1871– c. 1950), senior mistress in the Croydon school. See *Letters*, i. 194.

[2] John William Jones (1868–1956) and his wife Marie (1869–1950): DHL lodged with them in Colworth Road, Addiscombe, Croydon. See *Letters*, i. 82.

[3] Algernon M. Byrne (1889–1928), another teaching colleague in Croydon. See *Letters*, i. 194.

[4] Stewart A. Robertson (1866–1933), an Inspector of Schools in Croydon who took a particular interest in DHL. See *Letters*. i. 202; Nehls, i. 92–5.

Murry's novel in MS, and thought it just wasn't a book at all: statement, not created. I am afraid he is not a creative artist in any sense. Where it looks like creation, it is replica. – I am glad you didn't write your novel, really, if it was going to be at all like Murry's. What I can't stand about him is his central conceit. He wants to be, in his own idea, equal with the best and greatest of men: Tolstoi or Dostoevsky or whosoever it may be: he is utterly unwilling to take himself for what he is, a clever, but non-original, non-creative individual. He never has a *new* thought: he is a very clever arranger of given thoughts, making new combinations of given terms. He can never create a new term. – I dislike him that he must assume himself the equal of the highest. That is the very essence of his malady, and all his twist and struggle is to make this falsehood appear a truth to himself.

I saw in a paper that your father is a Baronet – and Lord Chief Justice of Ireland.[1] I am glad, because now probably you will be at ease in your own soul, ambitionally. Your father will be sure to manage that there will be enough money to enable you and Paddy to keep up the title. Perhaps you will really feel free of something now.

There is a ghastly feeling in the country. I never felt so sick as I do now, with the ugly spirit that pervades everything. It is loathsome that this is Christmas. But the coming year will see the collapse of a great deal of us, and I hope we shall be able to begin something new. One always hopes and hopes for this.

I am afraid after all we can't come to London. Now that the fare is raised, it costs £3.15.0 return from St. Ives to London, and we have no money at all. I don't know what will happen to us – it doesn't seem to matter much. I feel all right in myself: it is the social part of me that feels dragged down. My individual self is all right, but it seems quite cut off and isolated, as if it had no connection and no relation with anybody, beyond Frieda. It is all right for myself: that side of myself which is single is fulfilled and happy. But there *is* a gnawing craving in oneself, to move and live not only as a single, satisfied individual, but as a real representative of the whole race. I am a pure self, and fulfilled in that. But I have *no connection* with the rest of people, I am only at war with them, at war with the whole body of mankind. And to be isolated in

[1] James Henry Mussen Campbell (1851–1931) was a distinguished Irish lawyer-politician. KC, 1906; Solicitor-General for Ireland, 1901–5; made Lord Chief Justice of Ireland in December 1916 and created a baronet, 1917; 1918–21 Lord Chancellor of Ireland. He was created 1st Baron Glenavy in 1921. (His son, DHL's correspondent, succeeded his father as 2nd Baron Glenavy; he was in turn succeeded by his own son, Patrick Gordon Campbell, 3rd Baron, on his death in 1963.)

resistance against the whole body of mankind isn't right. But it will alter, when the existing frame smashes, as it must smash directly.

I hope one day we shall be in accord, you and I, and do some sort of work together. Kindest regards to you all from Frieda and me.

Yours   D. H. Lawrence

1342. To Catherine Carswell, 26 December 1916
Text: MS YU; Postmark, St. Ives 27 DEC 16; cited in Carswell, *Adelphi* 387.

Zennor – St. Ives – Cornwall
26 Dec. 1916

My dear Catherine

Christmas, thank goodness, is over. I hated its coming this year: I nearly hated even presents. I feel awfully downhearted – down altogether. God alone knows what is upon us. I feel smothered and weary, and buried alive in the world, horribly buried alive. And when will the graves open? Oh dear!

Miss Andrews and Robert Mountsier have come up and are staying till the end of the week. They are very nice, really. Yesterday we had a party with the Hockings, which was jolly.[1] But my heart never felt so down in the dirt, as it does now. What is going to happen, what can we do, how can we move? It is worse than any *Laocoon* with the snake round him:[2] such a weight on one's arms and limbs and heart: an utter imprisonment in the tightening folds of this heavy serpent, and oneself impotent. How long will it go on?

I am afraid we shall not be able to come to London. Now they have put up the fare, it would cost the two of us £7.12.6, to come and go. And we shall never have any more money, I verily believe. So we may as well stay down here and spend our poverty in peace.

What is going to happen to Carswell? – do you know yet? I wonder if you feel as heartsick as I do with life.

I shall rouse up and send you some of your books back tomorrow.

Tell me if there is any news.

D. H. Lawrence

The rush mat looks so nice upstairs: Frieda very pleased.

---

[1] The Hocking family – farmers and neighbours of DHL – consisted of William Henry (DHL's particular friend), Stanley, Mary, Mabel and their mother. For a brief description of the party, see Nehls, i. 409–10.
[2] The famous statue (in the Vatican) had been known to DHL for many years: see *Letters*, i. 136–7; ii. 137.

1343. To Robert Mountsier, 4 January 1917
Text: MS UT; cited in Delany 280.

Zennor, St Ives, Cornwall
4 Jan 1917

My dear Montygue

What a nasty jar for you to be dropped into Scotland Yard like that! You say you are glad now of the experience, but I can't for my life see why you should be. It only seems to me disagreeable. It's a pity one can't just say to the fools 'Yes, I am the cleverest spy in the universe', and set them ransacking nothingness to its farthest corners.[1] My dear Montygue, I think it is vile for you. And poor Hadaffah,[2] who yesterday was the female rampant because there was no post from you, today is a wind-blown straw broken among the stones of adversity. For some reason this event casts her down painfully. – We are used to suspicions and Scotland Yard foolery and police busybodiness by now, and put out our tongues at the whole mystery-play. Integer vitae scelerisque purus of course is the motto.[3] Pah, but one is sick of the show. I think the best thing would be for us all to go to America in February, if it were possible. I have *finally* decided that it is only possible to live out of the world – make a sort of Garden of Eden of blameless but fulfilled souls, in some sufficiently remote spot – the Marquesas Islands, Nukuheva.[4] Let us do that. I am sick to death of the world of man – had enough. Why should one go on, beyond the nausea.

I make a list of the books.[5]

Herman Melville – *Moby Dick*
– *Omoo*
Fennimore Cooper – *Pioneers*
– *Prairie*
– *Deerslayer*
Whitman – *Leaves of Grass* etc

---

[1] This suggests that Mountsier had been questioned by the police, perhaps by the Special Branch. The records of the Metropolitan Police have failed to reveal any trace of Mountsier or any reference to a Special Branch investigation. Cf. *Kangaroo*, chap. XII where Monsell (Mountsier) was questioned at Scotland Yard.

[2] i.e. Esther Andrews.

[3] Horace, *Odes* I. xxii. 1 ['Integer . . . purus/ Non eget': 'The man whose life is pure and untouched by crime'].

[4] Nuku Hiva is the largest of the Marquesas Islands in the Pacific.

[5] The list is the clearest indication so far that DHL had conceived the project which eventually led to *Studies in Classic American Literature* (New York, 1923). There had been earlier signs of a growing interest – several references to Melville and Cooper (e.g. *Letters*, ii. 614, 615, 645), admiration for Jean de Crèvecœur's *Letters from an American Farmer* (1782) (ibid., ii. 645), for example – but this list includes almost every writer whose work was to be discussed in *Studies*.

Crévecœur – *Letters from an American Farmer*
Hawthorne – *Twice Told Tales*
               – *Scarlet Letter*
               – *Blithedale Romance*
Rousseau – *Emile*
Lincoln's – *Speeches*
Emerson – Essays, 3 vols
               – *Society and Solitude,*
               – *Nature,*
               – *Conduct of Life.*
B. Franklins – Autobiography
Hamilton – *The Federalist*
Poe's – *Tales of Mystery and Imagination*
    Frieda isn't very well – in bed with pains in the back. I hope you are all right. Wouldn't it be nice if we all set off from Falmouth to New York next month!

                                        saluti di cuore   D. H. Lawrence

[Frieda Lawrence begins]

                                                            Higher Tregerthen
Dear Mountsy,
    Well you are a hero and martyr since you left with egg sandwiches and an apple – The policeman here that you birped at St Ives must have telegraphed to those shining lights in London – Henceforth I am an *Americano*, I am beginning to stitch an American trousseau!! In Typee we shant want much – Ester looks very well, in fact she *is* Hadaffah to-day with her hair done in a most bewitching outlandish way – She has also worked and done some clever stitches, now she is making a Russian blouse and cuts it about in an alarming manner – If you want anybody to hear your praises sung high and low send them to Katie Berryman 'Oh, what a *nice* gentleman, you would do anything for *him*,' in fact Zennor wishes you well, in spite of all the . . . . . . I am so keen to go to America,
                                        in fact I am
                                        Yours   Columbina
[Lawrence interjects: (f[eminine] of Columbus (Christopher) *joke*)]

1344. To Edward Marsh, 5 January 1917
Text: MS NYPL; Edward Marsh, *A Number of People* (1939), pp. 230–1.

Higher Tregerthen, Zennor, St. Ives, Cornwall.

5 Jan. 1917

Dear Eddie,

It now behoves me to bestir myself, lest I find myself an ignominious dependent, so I come to you for advice. You know I finished a novel, *Women in Love*, which I know is a masterpiece; – but it seems it will not find a publisher. It is no good, I cannot get a single thing I write published in England. There is no sale of the books that *are* published. So I am dished.

I know it is no good writing for England any more. England wants soothing pap, and nothing else, for its literature: sweet innocent babe of a Britannia! Therefore I have got to get out some way or other.

Do you think they would let me go to New York? I know I could make a living there. And I want only to get a little connection, and then go away right west, to the Pacific, and live with my back to mankind, for I am sick of it. I want to get people to publish stories, and my novels, and to write literary stuff. As for the War, I don't want even to mention it, it is such a nausea in my soul. We both want something new, not to have to do with this old mess at all.

I have got enough money to take us to America, if we could go fairly soon. – You know they gave me total exemption from military service on score of health.

Or do you think I might get some little job, away off in one of the Pacific islands, where we could both live in peace. I don't want to have anything to do whatsoever with quarrelling nations. If I could have some little peaceful job to do, I would do it and be thankful. But not in England – I couldn't stand it.

Perhaps you will think this all vague and foolish. I merely want you to tell me if you think I could carry it out at all.

Yours   D. H. Lawrence

1345. To Robert Mountsier, [6 January 1917]
Text: MS UT; Postmark, St. Ives 6 JA 17; Unpublished.

Zennor, St. Ives, Cornwall
Saturday

My dear Montague

The twelve books have just come: thank you very much. In the invoice it says 16 books, so perhaps four more are on the way.

I wrote to you immediately on receipt of the Scotland Yard letter – Hadaffah has written two or more letters since. I expect you will have got these by now. We are in a black fury at the insolent pawing of these officials.

The booksellers are *Wm. Glaisher Ltd, 265 High Holborn, W.C.* and *Hy J. Glaisher, 55 Wigmore St, Cavendish Square, W.* The Holborn shop is the best. If you go in to the booksellers, ask them for *Moby Dick* for me: there is sure to be one knocking about, and I want a copy.

We were very upset by your affair – and indignant fit to burst. If I can, I shall go to America immediately.

Love from all   D. H. Lawrence

1346. To Robert Mountsier, [6 January 1917]
Text: MS UT; Postmark, St. Ives 6 JA 17; Unpublished.

Zennor, St. Ives, Cornwall
Saturday

My dear Montague

Twelve books have come this morning: very many thanks for them.[1] The invoice says 16 vols, so perhaps four more are on the way: I got the letter and handed to Hadaffah the one enclosed to her.

I wrote you immediately on receipt of your letter telling about the insolent and abominable behaviour of the Scotland Yard fools. E[sther] A[ndrews] has since written[2] two or three – two letters and a piece of MS.

The booksellers are Wm. Glaisher Ltd, 265 High Holborn, W.C. – and Hy Glaisher, 55 Wigmore St. The first is best. Ask for a *Moby Dick* whenever you are in the booksellers, will you.

There is a storm of rage in my heart.

With love from all   D. H. Lawrence
package for E. not arrived – only laundry.[3]

1347. To S. S. Koteliansky, 8 January 1917
Text: MS BL; cited in Gransden 26.

Zennor, St. Ives, Cornwall
8 Jan. 1917

My dear Kot

I ought to have written to you before. I got your letter, and the little money order from America – which I have lost: not that it matters, it wasn't much.

---

[1] The reason for DHL's having written two almost identical letters appears to be his intention to ensure that Mountsier received his instructions either at his office (at John Lane Ltd, Vigo Street) or at his residence (131 Cheyne Walk, Chelsea).

[2] MS reads 'write'.

[3] The postscript is written on the verso of the envelope.

There isn't any news, except that I feel perfectly hopeless and disgusted with the world here. My dear Kot, when we can but set sail for our Rananim, we shall have our first day of happiness. But it will come one day – before very long. I shall go to America when I can – and try to find a place – and you will come on. That is the living dream. We will have our Rananim yet.

I think my novel won't get published in England: it is just as well it shouldn't. Perhaps I shall be able to lend you another copy of the MS – but you will read the one Pinker sends you for Russia. Has it come yet.

There is no hope here, my dear Kot – there is no hope in Europe, the sky is too old. But we will find a new sky, and pitch our tents under that.

D. H. Lawrence

1348. To Lady Cynthia Asquith, 8 January 1917
Text: MS UT; Huxley 391–2.

Zennor, St. Ives, Cornwall
8 Jan. 1917

I didn't answer your letter about *Women in Love*, because it seems the book will not find a publisher in England at all. Indeed, nobody will print me nowadays, the public taste is averse from me. It is a nasty quandary. The books I have don't sell, so it's a bad look-out.

I wrote to Eddie asking him if he thought we could get pass-ports to U.S.A. Of course we have the passports of Nov. 1915 – but they won't do, I believe. We have some friends going over to New York in March, and I should like to go with them.[1] I am pretty sure of selling my stuff if I am in America. I don't want to write or talk about the war *at all* – only stories and literary stuff: because I think the war will end this year, and even if it doesn't, I can't help it any more. I feel there is disaster impending for England. Not that I want to run away – only I feel useless, it is quite useless my trying to live and write here. I shall only starve in ignominy: should be starving now if an American hadn't given me £60.[2]

After the Cornwallis-West affair[3] – and how disgusting that is, how

---

[1] See letter following.
[2] Amy Lowell was the benefactor (Letter 1310).
[3] DHL's awkwardness about asking Lady Cynthia's assistance in a way which would involve her using 'influence' in a Government department (via Edward Marsh) relates to the case of Mrs Beatrice Stella Cornwallis-West (formerly Mrs Patrick Campbell) which had recently been given considerable publicity. A military Court of Inquiry had exposed her unscrupulous exercise of such influence first to secure a commission for a Sgt Patrick Barrett and then, when he rejected her advances, to have him transferred to another battalion without appeal or explanation. Mrs Cornwallis-West's behaviour was condemned as 'highly discreditable' (*Times*, 4 January 1917).

loathsome the attitude of the papers, how indecent the whole publicity – I know one ought not to ask for anything from you. But I believe it is quite legal for us to go to America: I am medically exempt, we are not spies, and I will neither write nor talk about the war to the Americans – they have nothing to do with it, it is our affair, alas. So just confer a little with Eddie about it, will you. I shall have just enough money to take us to New York if we can go on the first of March, with our friends. And I *can't* go on living here on a miserable pittance which Pinker, my literary agent, will allow me. I can't take a pittance from Pinker: it is too insulting. And it is worse than useless my living in England any more.

I don't think America is a paradise. But I know I can sell my stories there, and get a connection with publishers. And what I want is for us to have sufficient to go far west, to California or the South Seas, and live apart, away from the world. It is really my old Florida idea – but one must go further west. I hope in the end other people will come, and we can be a little community, a monastery, a school – a little Hesperides[1] of the soul and body. That is what I will do, finally.

Don't be worried, thinking I am always asking of you something you can't do. If this is at all troublesome, merely talk it over with Eddie, if ever you have an opportunity, and tell me what seems best to you.

But in the end, I will go far away and make a little new world, like a seed which drops in a fertile soil, and germinates with a new earth and a new heaven.[2] I don't believe in practical life, nor this materialism, nor in submitting to falsity because there is nothing else to do.

D. H. Lawrence

I hope we shall always be friends.

1349. To Robert Mountsier, 8 January 1917
Text: MS UT; Postmark, St. Ives 8 JA 17; cited in Delany 280.

Zennor, St. Ives, Cornwall
8 Jan 1917

My dear Montague,

I am glad the British lion, which you have always held such an admirable beast, has pawed you about a bit in its bestial and ugly fashion: now you will know the enemy, and where he lies. These ancient nationalities are foul in the extreme.

---

[1] The name of the sisters who guarded the golden apples received by Hera, wife of Zeus, as a wedding-gift. DHL uses the term to apply to the garden where the apples grew and therefore suggests a place of rich creativity and contentment.
[2] Cf. Revelation xxi. 1 ['a new heaven and a new earth'].

I have written to a man to ask him to help me to get passports renewed for America.[1] If he doesn't turn up trumps I shall try elsewhere. I *very much* want to go with you on the first of March – I will try every way to get out. Can you think of anything?

I don't think Diana[2] Manners wants to be interviewed. The Hon. Bertrand Russell might be useful. Of course he's *very* anti-war. He is 34 Russell Chambers, Bury St., W.C. – just near British Museum. I hear Gilbert Cannan is near Tring – or somewhere in Herts, not far from London, doing work of national importance, farming. Write him c/o Mark Gertler, Penn Studio, Rudall Crescent, Hampstead, N.W. – with 'please forward' –

If you see Bertrand Russell, he would give you addresses of all the Union of Democratic Control people[3] – Lowes Dickinson, Gilbert Murray probably. I think if you mention my name to Bertie Russell he will be all right – though we have quarrelled. Find John Masefield[4] – I don't know him – but if he is still in Hampstead, I'm sure he'd see you.

Very many thanks for the books[5] – the extra six came today – I shall do those essays on American literature. Get me *Moby Dick* if you can – and enquire about a little handbook of American literature.

I only hope and trust we can all sail away on the 1st. March.

D. H. Lawrence

1350. To Catherine Carswell, 8 January 1917
Text: MS YU; cited in Carswell, *Adelphi* 387.

Zennor, St. Ives, Cornwall
8 Jan. 1917

Do you really feel more hopeful about the world? No, I don't. I feel quite hopeless. But why should oneself be dragged down. That is the wrongness. One should have courage, and stand clear.

I feel there is nothing to do but wait, and when it is possible, go right away. The only way is the way of my far-off wilderness place which shall become a

---

[1] See Letter 1344.
[2] Diana] Cynthia
[3] The U.D.C. was a pacifist organisation: Lowes Dickinson was the first president and Russell a founder-member. See *Letters*, ii. 309 n. 5. Though Gilbert Murray (1866–1957), the eminent classical scholar, currently argued that Germany's power-lust had to be resisted with force, he was firmly committed to the belief that future wars should be prevented by concerted international action.
[4] Despite this suggestion, DHL was not an admirer of works by John Masefield (1878–1967): see *Letters*, i. 523; ii. 254.
[5] See Letter 1343.

school and a monastery and an Eden and a Hesperides – a seed of a new heaven, and a new earth. That is the only way.

I can't come to London now because I have no belief in London. London must come to me – I can move itwards no more. I shall wait to go away, that is all. And I must economise my mere pittance of money.

It seems my novel won't find a publisher over here. I don't wonder, seeing the state of the newspapers. I don't even want it to be published – better not. How is Joanna going?

Esther Andrews is still here. She makes me feel that America is really the next move. Not but what the Americans are *awful*. But the future can take place there – and it seems it can't here.

Nevertheless I wish we could see you. *Essentially*, I don't want to see a soul in London, except you two and perhaps Hilda Aldington – and Robert Mountsier, who has gone back. But we must – and shall – have a meeting before long.

with love from both   D. H. Lawrence

1351. To Robert Mountsier, 9 January 1917
Text: MS UT; Postmark, St. Ives 9 JA 17; Unpublished.

Zennor, St. Ives, Cornwall
9 Jan. 1917

My dear Montague

I have a letter from my friend Eddie Marsh, saying he thinks I could quite easily get over to America if I could state a definite work that took me over. I *very much want* to go with you on the first March – does a Dutch boat sail then? We must try and get some sort of an appointment for me in New York. Can you suggest anything? I am writing to Pinker, and telling him I want his help as far as possible. I feel I *must* leave England now, or I shall burst – my cup is full.[1] There is no reason for their detaining me, it seems: only the trial of Frieda's birth. I feel I shall be able to manage: only we must all lay our heads together.

I don't think Hadaffah is in a particularly good humor: but that is as it is. I try my best to bring them both to reason – Frieda and Hadaf – but in vain. It is a duel without pistols for all of us.

saluti cari   D. H. Lawrence

---

[1] Cf. Matthew xx. 22; xxvi. 39.

1352. To J. B. Pinker, 9 January 1917
Text: MS Forster; cited in Carswell 81.

Zennor – St. Ives – Cornwall
9 Jan. 1917

My dear Pinker,

I suppose there is no news concerning any of my MSS. I don't wonder at it, if no one will publish the novel. When I read the newspapers, I see it would be vain. It does not matter very much – later will be better. It is a book that will laugh last.

I want to go to America. It is necessary now for me to address a new public. You must see that. It is no use my writing in England for the English any more. I want to go to New York and write a set of essays on American literature, and perhaps lecture. It is no use my sitting cooped up here any longer. I feel I shall burst.

I can go to America if I can state definite work to do there. I am sure you can help me. I don't want to talk about the war, or peace, or have anything to do with that concern. I only want to be able to write and publish my own literary stuff, and to be in connection with some sort of public. It is useless here.

I have two friends going over to New York on the 1st. March, and I should be very glad if my wife and I could go with them.

My dear Pinker, I know you can help me. I hope you don't feel uneasy about my work. I tell you it is true and unlying, and will last out all the other stuff. It is really necessary for me now to move under a new sky – it is a violation to be shut up here any longer.

I have got in my head a set of essays, or lectures, on Classic American literature.[1] But I can't write for America here in England. I must transfer myself.

Yrs   D. H. Lawrence

1353. To S. S. Koteliansky, [12 January 1917]
Text: MS BL; Postmark, St. Ives 12 J[. . .]; Zytaruk 107.

Zennor, St. Ives, Cornwall
Friday

My dear Kot,

Thank you very much for the offer of the £10.[2] If I need it, I shall ask you

---

[1] Cf. Letter 1343 and n. 5.
[2] According to Catherine Carswell (Carswell 80 n. 1), Kot offered the money as if it were an advance on the hoped-for Russian translation of *Women in Love* (mentioned in Letter 1334): 'He knew that only so . . . would Lawrence feel able to accept it from one who was himself not well off.'

for it. Meanwhile, if my plans come off, I shall make Pinker supply me, if I can.

It is true, I must go away. At the present moment, I am trying to get passports for America. If these come all right, then we shall sail for New York next month, I hope. I shall say goodbye to England, for ever, and set off in quest of our Rananim. Thither, later, you must come. For the present I only want to get to the USA.

It seems nobody will publish the novel *Women in Love*. It is just as well – why cast the pearls before irredeemable swine.[1]

Don't tell anybody about the American project. It is, like so many of our plans, a secret. But I hope we can go – I do hope so. We should see you first.

Love from both   D. H. Lawrence

1354. To J. B. Pinker, [12 January 1917]
Text: TMSC NWU; Huxley 380.

Zennor, St. Ives, Cornwall.
Friday.

Dear Pinker,

I send you the MS. of another story – 'The Miracle', which is beautiful and ends happily, so the swine of people ought to be very thankful for it.[2]

I am glad there is no more Methuen. You will do as you think best about the novel. I don't suppose anybody will be dying to publish it, though it is a chef d'oeuvre. Perhaps the faithful Duckworth will rise up and be noble: though I very much doubt his paying. The duplicate MS. shall come to you very soon. I lent it.

I shall be rather glad if nobody wants those little poems.[3] Then I shall put them in the fire.

It would be a good thing if Mitchell Kennerley sold *all* the rights to my things. He has swindled me unscrupulously. For everything of mine he has ever done, he has paid me only £10 – sent me a bad cheque for £25, which I couldn't cash, so I sent it back to him for correcting, and have never heard from him since. I am sure the American rights of *Sons and Lovers* are worth more than £10 – to say nothing of the other things.[4]

---

[1] Matthew vii. 6 (R.V.) ['neither cast your pearls before the swine'].
[2] The story – possibly referred to on 13 November (Letter 1309) – was eventually re-titled 'The Horse Dealer's Daughter' (see Tedlock, *Lawrence MSS* 93) and published in *English Review*, xxxiv (April 1922), 308–25.
[3] Cf. Letter 1330.
[4] Mitchell Kennerley (1878–1950) had become DHL's American publisher with the publication of *The Trespasser* (1912). DHL's complaints about Kennerley's failure to meet his financial

I am determined that I will have some money before long. I am sick of poking about in a corner, up to the neck in poverty. It is enough. I think America is my untilled field.

Yrs. D. H. Lawrence

1355. To Catherine Carswell, 13 January 1917
Text: MS YU; cited in Moore, *Intelligent Heart* 227.

Zennor, St. Ives, Cornwall.
Saturday 13 Jan. 1917

My dear Catherine

I am sending back your books. Thank you very much for lending them to me. *The Unknown Sea* is one of your lapses – even one worse than the *Babe Unborn* (you have strange weaknesses for these 'un-' novels).[1] Mallock is clever, so is George Moore:[2] but neither is very sympatico to me.

What are you doing just now? It is time you wrote again. I still feel very end-of-the-tetherish, and don't know what the next move will be. I feel there will have to be a move very soon. Things seem to have come to an end here. Perhaps we can go to America. I still dream of that far-off retreat, which is the future to me.

Esther Andrews has gone back to 131 Cheyne Walk, so I expect you will see her. Do let us have news of you and Don.

D. H. Lawrence

1356. To J. B. Pinker, 16 January 1917
Text: MS YU; Huxley 394–5.

Zennor, St. Ives, Cornwall.
16 Jan. 1917

My dear Pinker

Thank you for promising to help me to go to New York. I must go soon. One's psychic health is more important than the physical.

I think I can get passports for us if I can state definite business reasons for my going to America. It is here I want you to help me. You can give me some

---

obligations began as early as October 1913 (*Letters*, ii. 99); Amy Lowell agreed to intervene on DHL's behalf, in New York (ibid., ii. 210, 217); but he was still plainly dissatisfied in February 1915 (ibid., ii. 279). Now, nearly two years later, the complaint – interestingly different in detail – reappears.

[1] *The Unknown Sea* (1898), a novel by Clemence Housman; *A Babe Unborn* (1911), a novel by Ernest James Oldmeadow (b. 1867).

[2] DHL had read several novels by George Moore (see *Letters*, i. 154). See also p. 191 n. 1.

sort of credentials that it is necessary for me to be in New York for the publishing of the *Twilight in Italy* and the *Rainbow* and the *Women in Love*. I think that would be enough. Do you know of anything else. You see I feel I must be under a new sky. All the oxygen seems gone out of the vital atmosphere here, and one gutters like a suffocated candle. I want to get into contact with something new – not to talk or write about the war, nothing of that – but to start somehow afresh.

Tell me if you know anything else necessary for me to do.

D. H. Lawrence

I expect the MS of the novel every day – when it comes I will send it to you post haste.

1357. To Edward Marsh, 16 January 1917
Text: MS NYPL; Marsh, *A Number of People*, pp. 231–2.

Zennor, St. Ives, Cornwall.
16 Jan. 1917

My dear Eddie

Thank you for your letter. Pinker is giving me a note stating that it is necessary for me to be in America for the publication of *Twilight in Italy* and the new novel. Do you think this will be enough? We have passports issued a year ago last October. Could I get them renewed, do you think, without coming to London? It is so far, and costs so much. If we can go to America, I shall take a Dutch boat from Falmouth. I wish you would tell me, if you can, how to go about the passport business, and if there is anything else necessary before I can be permitted to leave.

About the new novel, I am sure it is no good trying to get it done in England. It is not that it is so 'improper', but that it is too directly in antagonism with the existing state of squilch. If you like, I will lend it you for a while – the duplicate MS. – though Pinker urges me for it; and I am afraid, to use your phrase, wouldn't be able to follow it – which means, I know, that you feel entirely out of sympathy with it. Still, you can read it if you like. Whether it is unsympatisch or not, whether it finds a publisher over here or whether it doesn't, it is a masterpiece and a great book, and I care no more. I have *written* it, and that is enough for me.

Be so good as to advise me if you can about this matter of our getting permission to go to America. I can't live here any more. The vital principle seems gone out of the air, and one feels one's soul gradually sinking down, like a lamp-flame in an exhausted atmosphere. I deeply respect Rupert, that he died.[1] But shall we all die?

D. H. Lawrence

Heinemann and Sidgwick both hold me abhorrent.[2] J.M. Barrie[3] knows I lived near the Cannans – he would not look in my direction. I never heard of Russell Louis; who is he?[4]

1358. To Robert Mountsier, 16 January 1917
Text: MS UT; Unpublished.

Zennor, St. Ives, Cornwall.
16 Jan 1917

My dear Montague

I have written Pinker as you suggest: also again to the man friend, since the Lady has not answered.[5] I am sure we shall get away.

Why don't you send a little news of yourself? When are you sailing – and where from? I am glad you feel all right.

Here, wonderful to relate, deep snow. When we got up this morning, Esther Andrews' cottage muffled in white, the door drifted up right to the knob. We should have had to dig her out. The sun shines now, and it is very beautiful. I wish you were both here, and we could be happy. But patience!

Tell Esther Andrews to find me a *Moby Dick*.

Ah, how glad I shall be when we can all gather round a glass of gin in the New World, and feel heart free. It is a great weariness, this old world.

Warm greetings from both   D. H. Lawrence

1359. To S. S. Koteliansky, 19 January 1917
Text: MS BL; Zytaruk 108.

Zennor, St. Ives, Cornwall.
19 Jan. 1917

My dear Kot,

It is a trying and difficult life. But I shall see that Pinker gets the MS. next

---

[1] Rupert Brooke; see *Letters*, ii. 330 and n. 5.

[2] William Heinemann (1863–1920), the publisher of DHL's first novel, *The White Peacock* (1911); he had refused to publish *The Trespasser* and *Sons and Lovers*. Frank Sidgwick (1879–1939) refused the offer to publish *Amores* (*Letters*, ii. 535 n. 2) and annoyed DHL with his 'very impertinent criticism of the MS.' (ibid., ii. 558).

[3] DHL had had slight contact with Sir James Barrie (1860–1937), dramatist and novelist (see *Letters*, ii. 120), but his friendship with Gilbert Cannan who was married to Barrie's former wife, Mary, would be enough to rupture the acquaintance.

[4] Unidentified.

[5] Edward Marsh (Letter 1357); Lady Cynthia Asquith.

Tuesday or *Wednesday*, and then I shall ask him to type off two or more copies, so that I can keep one by me. You shall have yours for Russia very shortly: about a week's time. Just be patient for one moment.

I don't seem to get any nearer to passports for America. If you see Campbell, you might ask him, if he can tell me what it is necessary for me to do to get these passports renewed now. I want to go to New York as soon as ever I can, and I am afraid it will be rather difficult. I wonder if Campbell could help me. Shall I write to him.

It has been snowy all the week here, very cold. I don't like it. And I can't live in England any more. It oppresses one's lungs, one cannot breathe. Wait, only wait for our Rananim. It shall come quite soon now.

Yes, I have decided I shall ask you for the £10 as soon as ever I need it.[1] I count it a reserve store, to fall back on in any moment of urgency. It is very nice to feel it behind me.

What is all this that happens in Russia now: about the Duma and the resignations?[2] Is there anything behind it, do you know?

Now I *do want* something nice to happen.

It doesnt seem much good offering the novel to the English public: really.

D. H. Lawrence

1360. To Robert Mountsier, 20 January 1917
Text: MS UT; cited in Delany 281–2.

Zennor – St. Ives – Cornwall.
20 Jan. 1917

My dear Montague

So you are really going on Wednesday! Well, it is best, it is a good move. Remember, one should move *westwards*, never eastwards. Eastwards is retrogression. We should move west and southwards – that is the living direction. Before very long, we will all see the Pacific Ocean. Do not doubt it.

My dear Montague, I can't write about women and the war, and labour. I haven't the guts. All I can say is, that in the tearing asunder of the sexes lies the universal death, in the assuming of the male activities by the female, there takes place the horrid swallowing of her own young, by the women. Ask Gilbert Cannan for a copy of his *Windmills*.[3] I am sure woman will destroy

---

[1] See Letter 1353.

[2] It was announced in Russia on 18 January that the opening of the Duma, due on 25 January, was to be postponed until 27 February. The official explanation was that the delay was required in view of recent changes in Government.

[3] *Windmills: A Book of Fables* (1915); the volume was dedicated to DHL. It is conceivable that some of DHL's remarks which follow (though not the classical allusions) were prompted or at

man, intrinsically, in this country. But there is something in me, which stops still and becomes dark, when I think of it. It is all dark in front, when I think, I cannot see anything, because it is not my fate, I don't belong here any more. But I am sure there is some ghastly Clytemnestra victory ahead, for the women: and heaven help Orestes, what is he ever but a rambling dotty.

I don't want to think about it any more. It hasn't anything to do with me any more. It is over and vorbei.[1] My way is elsewhere. It is not I who will stay to see Medea borne up on a chariot in heaven. That belongs to the tearing asunder, of which I have had enough. I am going now out of this Sodom.

You think it will be hard for us to get permission to leave this country? Probably – but we will get it somehow. Wait only a little while.

Tell Esther Andrews the orange coat has not come, but it will be perfectly satisfactory, and she is not to trouble about a pink one. We will write to her on Monday.

I may be able to send you some news of our coming, on Monday, I hope so. So I won't put any valedictions here. I feel sure of the bella ventura.[2]

                          With love from both   D. H. Lawrence
Don't forget to write to Wm. Henry.

1361. To J. B. Pinker, 20 January 1917
Text: MS Forster; cited in Pinto, ed., *D. H. Lawrence after Thirty Years*, p. 27.

                                   Zennor, St. Ives, Cornwall
                                           20 Jan. 1917

My dear Pinker
   I am glad the *English Review* took a story.[3]

I think I can assure you, the duplicate MS. of the novel will be in your hands by next Tuesday. You are going to type[4] from it a copy for Russia? – Don't you think it would be well to have a duplicate, or even two duplicate copies made at the same time? It is rather doubtful when the novel will be printed. And I have no written MS, because I recomposed all the first part on the typewriter. So I should be very glad if you would make for me a fair typed copy, at the same time as the one is being made, for Koteliansky, for Russia. Please do this for me.

---

least sharpened by one of Cannan's poems, 'Gynecologia', in which women tyrannise over men.
[1] 'past'.
[2] 'I feel sure that it will turn out well'.
[3] 'Samson and Delilah'. See Letter 1304 and n. 3.
[4] type] print

I shall let you know as soon as I have any news about my movements.

D. H. Lawrence

Tell me the history of the *Women in Love* up to now, will you? What did Duckworth say when he refused it? – And Methuen? – And to whom else will you offer it?

1362. To Gordon Campbell, 22 January 1917
Text: MS UCin; cited in Moore, *Intelligent Heart* 227.

Zennor, St. Ives, Cornwall.
Monday 22 Jan. 1917

My dear Campbell,

Could you tell me how I could best get passports for America? Could I send these I got in 1915 – you remember – and have them renewed? – do you think they would let me go? Tell me what is the procedure for going away now, will you, if you can.

I want to go clean away, for ever. I feel it is finished in me, with this side of the globe. Now one is like a seed that needs to fall into new soil, under new skies. One needs a new earth and a new heaven. I want to go to New York first, as the first step to an ultimate somewhere, somewhere on the Pacific Ocean, where the air one breathes nourishes the new things in one's soul, and the soil is good and vivid. You said to me once that a man could be free in prison. I think of that so often – and so often, I know it is terribly untrue. One needs to be free body, soul, and spirit – there is no chopping about with freedom. One must cast off the old – absolutely cast it off, as a seed casts off the parent-tree. I admit the parentage – gladly. But the homogeneity, never. Christ was right, when he said 'Leave all and follow me.'[1] Only now one must leave all and follow the deepest spirit, and the deepest instinct, within one. But I *know* the first condition, is to leave all: as the first motion of a seed is to leave the parent organism. And there is no departing in spirit, and remaining in body. That old sophistry won't do. Here, the very physical atmosphere, consisting of hydrogen and oxygen and nitrogen and God knows what, hurts, starves, injures my spirit by being breathed into my lungs and blood. It is as near as that, the relation is *immediate*. I want to go away *as soon as I can*, under a new sky.

I hope, in the long run, to find a place where one can live simply, apart from this civilisation, on the Pacific, and have a few other people who are also at

[1] Cf. Luke v. 11 (R.V.): 'they left all and followed him.'

peace and happy, and live, and understand, and be *free*. To be really free to live and grow – that is all one wants. Here one is thwarted, cribbed, stunted, body, soul, and spirit, there is no peace of being. – One cannot leave any heritage, here, even to one's children, except this same course of inward *want* and *nullity*. One should take one's children away.

Don't mind my previous censures. You are a man who *can* understand – but you don't want to sacrifice the world. I hope you will one day. One can have patience, and wait, so long as one knows one's course.

Have you heard of Murry lately? You seem to be the only man left in England, to whom I can say even so much as is in this letter. Remember us both to Beatrice.[1]

D. H. Lawrence

1363. To Edward Marsh, 25 January 1917
Text: MS NYPL; Unpublished.

Zennor, St. Ives, Cornwall
25 Jan 1917

Dear Eddie,

You didn't answer my last letter: I don't know if it importuned you too much.

I am trying to get my passports renewed in the ordinary way. If I need to, may I give your name as a reference? I give you my word that I won't do anything at all, or say anything, to injure the cause of England in the war. I don't want even to think of the war. One must move on to something new.

If you do not answer this, I shall know you would rather not be concerned; so that will be quite definite.

Excuse the pencil. I am in bed with a cold, for the moment.

D. H. Lawrence

1364. To Gordon Campbell, 25 January 1917
Text: MS UCin; cited in Moore, *Intelligent Heart* 227.

Zennor, St. Ives, Cornwall.
Thursday 25 Jan 1917

My dear Campbell

Your letter came this morning. *Do please* find out all you can for me, about pass-ports: and if I can get them without coming up to London: get these

---

[1] Campbell's wife, née Elvery (d. 1970).

renewed, that is. Yes, I must go. Even if the voice of Bowden rings from San Francisco to San Diego, still I must go. It is written inside me. And I should like to meet Bowden.[1]

I shall have a duplicate MS. of my novel very soon: perhaps at the end of next week. Then I will send it to you. But I shall send it with a heavy heart and a slow pulse, because your negative opposition is far worse than my bellowings. And you are pretty sure to be opposed.

Your letter made me laugh. I think you feel it is your duty to play Fool to the Lear in you. But both Lear and his Fool are *vieux jeu* by now. It is all very true and very clever, what you say, it makes a most entertaining joke. But after all, it is only a joke. Don't imagine for a moment you take me in with your white shoulders and washed necks. I know a thing or two as well. Murry says I'm not 'clever' enough: too unsubtle are my bellowings, in short. But I'm old bird enough, if it comes to that. No, my dear Campbell, it is no good coming forth in motley and leaving Lear in the ruined cottage. I've had some of that motley: and some of that Lear. Perhaps I prefer the motley to the Lear: he's the jam in the tart: but it's a stale tart by now. – Your prison argument is simple lawyer's sophistry, very nice too. Real thinking is not a game: it is a fulfilment. Twiddley intellectualism is a game. – But one cannot have any real sensuous experience, any new and developing sensuous experience, without a correspondingly increasing understanding. As for your sensationalism, it is a repetition ad nauseam, and *very boring*. Sensuous experience unfolds in two ways, into understanding and into sleep; and a failure to understand, an incapacity to think to a conclusion, only means arrested, thwarted activity in the Sensuous Soul, a chronic indigestion. One can see that in the Cornish, who have never thought one new thought for 1300 years, and have kept up a perpetual sensationalism, very subtle and serpent-like. But they are all of them just horrible, all, they have got a hole inside them, a ghastly gap in their being, they are only half there. Don't talk to me about simple people. The only simple people are those who are most fully and directly conscious. I don't see anything that is[2] so terribly complicated[3] and knotted-up inextricably and torturously in themselves as these cattle, horses and bulls, in the field round the house: to say nothing of the farmers.

The thought of Murry makes me unhappy also. I would write to him, but it seems no good. He must work out his own fate. So must everybody.

I think myself I ought to be *made* (sic) to laugh. Nevertheless, I am not like

[1] Presumably George Bowden, first husband of Katherine Mansfield, though DHL's meaning is obscure. See *Letters*, ii. 32.
[2] that is] so very
[3] complicated] wasted and

the public, I don't want anybody to tickle me in the ribs to bring it about. Neither, having a toothache in my social soul, do I think it incumbent upon me to laugh. I can grin hard enough. But one wants space to laugh in. Here, the waistcoat is too tight. That's why I will go to the Pacific (though it wasn't California at all, I aimed at, it was the *Marquesas Islands*). So, my dear Campbell, do use your courage, sincerity, and faith to help me get out of this vinegary fly-trap: I ask you sincerely, courageously, and faithfully.

Excuse the pencil – I've got a cold and am in bed. And *don't* think I'm antagonistic. You resent me too much. Why should I not bellow, if I am of the bellowing sort. You exasperate me almost to contempt, still the liking doesn't change. Murry fills me with loathing: still, somewhere, I am fond of him. Kot wearies me to extinction, and yet I wouldn't forego him.

Have you read anything lately? I have found Fennimore Cooper and Herman Melville such a treasure – and Dana's *Two Years Before the Mast*.[1] They are so mature – even beyond us: au delà de tout ceci.[2]

Remember the Marquesas Islands. I must go before the skies fall over here: you will never come till they have tumbled.

D. H. Lawrence

1365. To Robert Mountsier, 25 January 1917
Text: MS UT; Postmark, St. Ives 25 JA 17; Unpublished.

Zennor, St. Ives, Cornwall.
Thursday 25 Jan 1917

My dear Montague

I had a letter from a man today, saying he would help me what he can with passports. So I think we shall most probably get off by the First of March. Prepare for me a little in New York.

I've got a cold and am in bed for a day: this is the low-water mark with us. Tide turns tomorrow.

It is still *very* cold. I tremble for you on your journey, and wish you Godspeed. I am quite sure we shall see you again before many weeks.

Here's my blessing upon you

D. H. Lawrence

[1] DHL had read Richard Henry Dana's *Two Years Before the Mast* (1840) at least eight months before (*Letters*, ii. 614) and had remarked to Amy Lowell on its maturity (ibid., ii. 645). This is clearly a re-discovery arising out of his reading in preparation for the essays on American literature.
[2] 'beyond all that'.

1366. To Edward Marsh, 29 January 1917
Text: MS NYPL; Marsh, *A Number of People*, p. 232.

Zennor, St. Ives, Cornwall.
Monday. 29 Jan. 1917

Dear Eddie

Thank you very much for your note and the green form. I do hope they will let us go away.

Have I showed any public pacifist activity? – do you mean the *Signature?*[1] – At any rate, I am not a pacifist. I have come to the conclusion that mankind is not one web and fabric, with one common being. That veil is rent for me.[2] I know that for those who make war, war is undeniably right, it is even their vindication of their being. I know also, that for me, war, at least this war, is utterly wrong, a ghastly and unthinkable falsity. And there it is. One's old great belief in the oneness and wholeness of humanity is torn clean across, for ever.

So how should I be a pacifist. I can only feel, that every man must fulfil his own activity, however contrary and nullifying it may be to mine.

Duckworth refused[3] the novel: said he could not publish it. But no matter.

I am getting ready another book of poems: my last and best. Perhaps I shall never have another book of poems to publish: or at least, for many years. Would you like to see this MS., when I have done it? Then, if there should happen to be anything you would like for *Georgian Poetry*, ever, you can take it.[4]

Thank you very much for sending the passport form. I shall send it in immediately I have got one for Frieda too.

If I go to America, and can make any money, I shall give you back what you lent me. I do not forget it.

D. H. Lawrence

P.S. Don't you think H[ilda] D[oolittle] – Mrs Aldington – writes some good poetry? I do – really very good. I send you an *Egoist* for this month. It is nothing of a paper – but H.D. is good, without doubt.[5]

[1] The magazine of which only three numbers were published (4 and 18 October, 4 November 1915) and to which DHL contributed three essays under the title of 'The Crown'. See *Letters*, ii. 385 n. 2. (Murry, who was involved in *Signature* along with DHL, Kot and Katherine Mansfield, claimed that DHL's purpose for the magazine was 'to prepare the way for a moral and spiritual "revolution"'; Nehls, i. 323.)

[2] Cf. Matthew xxvii. 51 ['the veil of the temple was rent in twain'].

[3] refused] received

[4] The collection of poems DHL was preparing eventually appeared in December 1917 as *Look! We Have Come Through!* (Letter 1368 refers to it under the title 'Poems of a Married Man'; Letter 1375 introduces the title 'Man and Woman'.) Marsh did not accept DHL's invitation to select from it for publication in *Georgian Poetry*.

[5] Two poems by H. D. were printed in the January issue of the *Egoist*: 'The God' and 'Adonis'.

1367. To Robert Mountsier, 29 January 1917
Text: MS UT; Postmark, St. Iv[es] 29 JA 17; Unpublished.

Zennor, St. Ives, Cornwall
Monday 29 Jan. 1917

My dear Montague

The book,[1] and your letter, came this morning. I am glad you are staying on. We thought of you every hour, on Saturday and Sunday, sailing in a gale most awful. – I believe sympathy is always misplaced on you.

This morning I heard from Eddie Marsh about passports. He thinks it will be all right if I produce strong enough evidence of necessity for my going. Frieda's birth is a difficulty.

He only sent me one form, Male British Subject. I want another, Female Subject, for Frieda. Could you or E[sther] Andrews send me one on – they will give it you at the Passport Office, Downing St. Then I must state date of sailing proposed, and route. Confer with E.A. about *that*. It saves us £4. to go from Falmouth – which is a lot: and Frieda flatly refuses to go English boat.

So confer with Hadaffah, and send me a definite date for sailing – Dutch boat preferred.

Can you think of any other definite reason to give for going, besides publication of novels?

Shall we see you again down here? What are you doing.

We will move quickly now about these passports for us.

D. H. Lawrence

1368. To J. B. Pinker, 29 January 1917
Text: MS Forster; Huxley 395–6.

Zennor, St. Ives, Cornwall.
29 Jan. 1917

My dear Pinker,

I am going to apply immediately for my passports for America. Now as to definite reasons for my going: I hear they must be as convincing as possible. I shall give

1. Ill-health
2. Failure to make any money at all over here.
3. Necessity to place short stories, and literary articles, and poems, and to arrange with a publisher the publication of *The Rainbow*, which is ready for press but has been deferred, and of the novel *Women in Love*.

Then I shall refer to you for corroboration, if it is necessary.

---

[1] Perhaps *Moby Dick* as requested in Letter 1358.

Do you think this is all right? Tell me at once if there is anything you disagree to. I don't want to do anything at all without your knowledge. You have been good to me, and I am grateful.

Only I do want to go to America now – not so much for business – but I feel I can't breathe here. There is an oppression on one's breathing.

I expect you have that duplicate MS. by now.[1] I am sorry it is so late.

I am doing out a last book of poems: real poems: my chief poems, and best. This will be the last book of poems I shall have, for years to come. I have reaped everything out of my old notebooks now. I think I shall call this: 'Poems of a Married Man'.[2] Would that do, do you think?

I shall send you the MS. in a week or so. But there is no hurry at all about publishing it.

There is no news of the novel?

D. H. Lawrence

1369. To Catherine Carswell, [5 February 1917]
Text: MS YU; Postmark, St. Ives 5 FE 17; cited in Carswell, *Adelphi* 292, 387, 388.

Zennor, St. Ives, Cornwall
Monday Jan 5. 1917

My dear Catherine

I never answered your last letter. We seem all to be pretty downed, floored. I feel myself awfully like a fox that is cornered by a pack of hounds and boors who don't perhaps know he's there, but are closing in unconsciously. It seems to me to be a crucial situation now: whether we are nabbed by the old vile world, and destroyed, or whether we manage, with the help of the unseen, to make good our escape. I am applying for re indorsement of my passports to New York. If I can but get it done, and if no other horror, like American exclusion, intervenes, I shall be off at once: this month, I hope. I feel it is really a question of to be or not to be. If we are to be, then we must move at once out of this into another world. Otherwise it is not to be.

My dear Catherine, for me the hour is crucial. But everything has its season. Perhaps your times are a little different. Perhaps – this in answer to your last letter – it is necessary for you and Don to have another bout, another round, to try another fall with this old world. Every man has his own times and his own destiny apart and single. It only remains for us to fulfil that which is *really* in us. For me, it is time to go

[1] i.e. *Women in Love.*   [2] See p. 84 n. 4.

'Time for us to go
Time for us to go –' as the song is.[1]

I don't know why I go to America – except that I feel all right in going there. One instinctively takes ones way, and it is all right. I feel we shall get off. I am not beaten yet. – But don't say anything about our going will you?

Everybody refuses to publish the novel. It will not get done over here. I don't care.

As a sort of last work, I have gathered and shaped my last poems into a book. It is a sort of final conclusion of the old life in me – 'And now farewell' is really the motto.[2] I don't much want to submit the MS. for publication. It is very intimate and vital to me. But I have got it *very nearly* ready. Would you like to see it? I will send it you if you would.

How is Joanna? My heart aches a bit for her: it is so wintry for her to come forth. Have patience and courage. *Write for America* if you can't write. I find I am unable to write for England any more – the response has gone quite dead and dumb. A certain hope rises in my heart, quite hot, and I can go on. But it is not England. It seems to me it is America. If I am kept here I am beaten for ever.

How are you yourself, and Don? The weeks go by very bitterly, don't you find? They are hardly bearable. By the way Ottoline Morrell was in a frenzy over the novel: I told her it was her own fault, there was nothing to be in a frenzy over. So now I expect we are enemies for ever. I don't care. I don't care if every English person is my enemy – if they wish it, so be it. I keep a reserve for the Scotch.[3]

The weather is cold down here also: but sometimes very sunny, as today. We live on tenterhooks, hoping for departure. You too will move away, when your time comes.

Do you see Esther Andrews? And how is she? We want her to go with us to America, and to the ultimate place we call Typee or Rananim. There is indeed such an ultimate place.

Don't treat me as I have treated you, and make me wait a long time for an answer. Write soon.

D. H. Lawrence

---

[1] Unidentified.
[2] Translation of 'Jamque Vale', Eurydice's final words to her husband, Orpheus, as she is taken back to Hell (Virgil, *Georgics*, iv. 497). Cf. *Letters*, ii. 330.
[3] The remark pleased DHL's Scottish correspondent: see Carswell 62.

1370. To Robert Mountsier, 7 February 1917
Text: MS UT; cited in Delany 283.

Zennor, St. Ives, Cornwall.
7 Feb. 1917

What a state we are in. The world is one slab of horror. It can't go on: this is really breaking-point. America won't declare war, credimi.[1] This is all diplomacy. I feel very hopeful about that. If American declares war, I think I shall die outright. But she won't, believe me. Heaven helping us, we will sail off at the end of this month.

It is all fearful and ghastly. Yesterday two ships were submarined just off here: luckily we didn't see them: but Stanley[2] watched one go down, and the coastwatchers saw the crew of the other struggling in the water after the ship had gone: all drowned: Norwegians, I believe. My sister writes a ghastly story from Glasgow, of a new and splendid submarine on her trial trip in the Clyde: she dived and never came up, all watching expecting her. But I cannot bear it, it makes me tremble. It can't go on, it is the maximum of evil.

The days are most wonderfully beautiful, with a bell-like clear blue sky and a powerful sun, a sea like a blue flower. I sat in a sheltered nook in the cliffs yesterday, warm as summer. But the wind is very cold, and the birds, of which there are great numbers come south for shelter, are dying rapidly in the frost: one finds them everywhere. There is a kind of fiendishness triumphant over the earth. – Heaven help us! But we are not beaten yet. We shall last it out. We shall still go to Typee. – But meantime, one groans with torture and horror.

Wouldn't you like to come back to your little cottage? There it waits for you, and I am sure you will be better here than in London. We must wait out this last phase: it will not be very long, and we shall come out all right. *We* shall win, not they, who are all the rest. Do come down if you want to at all.

D. H. Lawrence

1371. To Mark Gertler, 9 February 1917
Text: MS SIU; Huxley 396–7.

Zennor, St. Ives, Cornwall.
Friday 9 Feb. 1917

My dear Gertler,
    It was bad news to hear from Kot that your father is dead. Not that death

---

[1] 'believe me'. (Virtually every day the *Times* carried reports of the increasing pressure on President Wilson for the USA to declare war on Germany.)
[2] Stanley Hocking.

itself seems to me a calamity. It seems very much like going to sleep when one is thoroughly done up. But there is your mother left, and the others.[1] It is a blessing you have your work. Take care not to be knocked up. These things do one a good deal of damage inside. To think of oneself, and cherish one's flame of life, is very necessary.

I feel as if we were all just up to the chin in the flood of things. Let it rise a little higher, and we are swamped, suffocated, done for. All the time, the foul world of mud is rising and trying to envelope us, to destroy the quick of independence and singleness which is in us. It is time for me to pray for the help of the unseen, for I don't know how much longer I can keep my head up.

You know we have applied for passports to America. Yet what is America, now? Nevertheless, if they will give us the passports, we shall sail directly, in an American ship. I believe that, barring mines, that it[2] is quite safe. But I don't feel very hopeful, now, about the passports. At any rate, we ought to know in a few days time.

If we have to stay here, I too shall become a farmer. I shall help the man just below,[3] whom I like. But I still hope to go away. In America, if we get there, I can make ready for you, if you want to come when the war is over.

My novel does not find a publisher. I don't mind. What is the good of its coming out in a world like this? The Ott. was angry with it: let her be so: what does it matter? All that side of the old show is dead for me.

I hear you are doing a big wood sculpture.[4] I wonder if I shall ever see it. I should like to.

Frieda sends her love, and sympathy, with mine.

D. H. Lawrence

1372. To S. S. Koteliansky, 9 February 1917
Text: MS BL; George J. Zytaruk, ed., *Malahat Review*, i (January 1967), 30–1.

Zennor, St. Ives, Cornwall.
Friday 9 Feb 1917

My dear Kot,
Your letter to Frieda came today. I meant to have written you before. Pinker has got the MS, and has put it out to be typed. He is having two copies

[1] Mark Gertler was the son of Louis Gertler (of Przemysl) by his wife, Kate Berenbaum.
[2] MS reads 'is'.
[3] William Henry Hocking.
[4] It is said to have disappeared (*Mark Gertler: Selected Letters*, ed. Noel Carrington, 1965, pp. 136, 138).

made, one for you, one for me, so that I can always keep by me a spare MS. I should think it ought to be done very soon.

We have not heard yet about passports. Everything seems to have gone to pot in the world. And still I hope – hope to get away, hope that America won't come in, hope we can find our Rananim, hope they won't conscript you in any way. Hope is a great thing. We are not beaten yet, in spirit, but it is a critical moment. We must pray to the good unknown. I think we shall come out all right, even against so many millions.

Campbell wrote today: yes, he is quite friendly. I have written to Gertler. I would write to poor Gilbert and Mary, but I feel I could do no good.[1] As for the rest, they are gone, like the leaves of last autumn. The Ott., the Murries – they are gone into the ground. Only for poor Katharine and her lies I feel rather sorry. They are such self-responsible lies. But then, pity is worse than useless. I move no more upon the basis of feeling sorry for anybody.

I should like the novel to be published in Russia. Certainly it won't come out here – not as long as the war lasts: but I am just as well content. I have got together my final book of poems. It seems like my last work for the old world. The next must be for something new. – I want you to read the novel.

I am pretty well in health – so is Frieda – though the weather is most devilish cold. We shall all come to our Rananim before many years are out – only believe me – an Isle of the Blest, here on earth. But the first thing is to cut clear of the old world – burn one's boats: if only one could.

I shall let you know as soon as there is any news of us: and you do likewise for yourself. They will not conscript you.

The world is at an end.

D. H. Lawrence

1373. To Lady Cynthia Asquith, 12 February 1917
Text: MS UT; Huxley 397–8.

Zennor, St. Ives, Cornwall.
12 Feb. 1917

They have refused to indorse my passport. It is a bitter blow, because I must go to America. But I will try again in a little time.

How are you, and what are you doing? For me, the skies have fallen, here in England, and there is an end. I must go to America as soon as I can, because to

---

[1] Gilbert Cannan suffered a nervous breakdown and faced the disintegration of his marriage. He had by this time met Gwen Wilson who became his mistress; in addition, Mary Cannan's maid was pregnant by him.

remain here now, after the end, is like remaining on one's death bed. It is necessary to begin a new life.

You mustn't think I haven't cared about England. I have cared deeply and bitterly. But something is broken. There *is not* any England. One must look now for another world. This is only a tomb.

I must wait, and try again in a little time. I don't want to bother you with woes or troubles. Only I feel there is some sort of connection between our fates – yours and your children's and your husband's, and Frieda's and mine. I know that, sometime or other, and somehow or other, I shall pull through. And then, when I can help you, or your husband and the children, that will be well. Because, don't hide away the knowledge, real life is finished here, it is over. The skies have already fallen. There are no heavens above us, no hope. It needs a beginning elsewhere. That will be more true, perhaps, of Herbert Asquith and of John the Son,[1] than of you. But it is a bit of knowledge not to be evaded even whilst one struggles through with the present.

I feel the war won't be so very much longer. The skies have *really* fallen. There is no need of any more pulling at the pillars. – New earth, new heaven, that is what one must find. I don't think America is a new world. But there is a living sky above. America I know is shocking. But there is a new sky above it. I must go to America as soon as ever I can. Do you think I don't know what it is to be an Englishman.

I have often thought you find my letters something ridiculous, to be rather ashamed of. But if you only remember what you were before the war, and what you are now, you will see that there is another reality, besides Brighton and momentary sensation.[2] Having children, you *must* know this. Having children, you *must* stand firm by the inner reality, and have some hold on a *future*.

There is one thing, America won't come in to the war. If she does, that will be a most fearful blow, which I don't know how I shall recover from.

There is no news here, we seem as in a lost world. My health is fair. It is this old collapsing misery that kills one.

Frieda sends her love.

D. H. Lawrence

---

[1] On Lady Cynthia's son, John (1911–37), see *Letters*, ii. 335–8. (She also had a son Michael, 1914–60.)

[2] Herbert Asquith was stationed at an army camp near Brighton; his wife had seized the opportunity to live in an inn nearby so that they could spend as much time together as possible before he went to France (on 26th February).

1374. To Robert Mountsier, [12 February 1917]
Text: MS UT; Postmark, St. Ives 12 FE 17; Unpublished.

Zennor, St. Ives, Cornwall.
Monday

My dear Montague

They won't indorse my passport: a bitter blow. We can't go to America yet.

But I don't feel hopeless or downcast. I shall try again in a little while, and it will be all right. We shall come to America before the summer.

I feel America won't declare war – heaven be praised. I should really despair if she did. But she won't. – There's a good time coming.

I hope you are not sailing on the accursed *Baltic*, or whatever she is called. Wait a little while for an American ship, and don't be so abominably recusant. Do for heaven's sake give up the old old world, and go in for a new one.

D. H. Lawrence

1375. To Catherine Carswell, [13 February 1917]
Text: MS YU; cited in Carswell, *Adelphi* 387.

Zennor, St. Ives, Cornwall
Tuesday

My dear Catherine

We got your letter this morning. What a bother and a misery everywhere. Whatever root or connection or vital ligament there is, the devils will try to snap. I curse my country with my soul and body, it is a country accursed physically and spiritually. Let it be accursed forever, accursed and blasted. Let the seas swallow it, let the waters cover it, so that it is no more.[1] And let it be known as accursed England, the country of the damned. I curse it, I curse England, I curse the English, man, woman, and child, in their nationality let them be accursed and hated and never forgiven.

Perhaps you will like being a sort of camp-follower for a little while. God above knows.

They will not give me a passport for America: and only, if you please 'in the interests of National Service'. A new deviltry, this National Service. The Foreign Office would give me the passport.

I can't live in England. I can't stop any more. I shall die of foul inward poison. The vital atmosphere of the country is poisonous to an incredible degree: to me at least. I shall die in the fumes of their stench. But I *must* get out.

---

[1] DHL's execrations recall those of the psalmist: cf. Psalms lxix. 14–28.

I shall send you the MS. of the poems directly.[1] I wanted to type off a fair copy. You shall have them, I hope, by the end of the week. I shall not send them yet to Pinker. I couldn't bear them to be published yet. You must tell me what you think of them.

I like the verse from Hezekiah, but I don't care for the Heart of Flesh as a title for Joanna.[2] Joanna is still better.

I have called the book of poems 'Man and Woman', but I am not satisfied. You must suggest something else, or some modification of this, when you have the MS.

Poor Joanna, I wish it were not *such* winter for her.

My dear Catherine, the present time is the limit, the ne plus ultra. One cannot stand any greater pressure of foulness. Cry aloud to the good spirit now, for we are in a bad way.

Sometimes I feel as if you had been right, when you said the war would be over in a month. At moments, I feel that it is over, the war, that the tide is turning, that the good spirit is beginning to triumph. At moments I feel so happy, as if the quick of the foulness was quenched, and the good was coming into being. But oh dear, the torment when this happiness goes again, and one is once more gasping in the acid fumes of a world's accumulated evil. Really, one cries Return, Oh Lord, how long![3]

Esther Andrews is very miserable about Mountsier. There is something very nice and lovable in him. But also underneath is the old worldly male, that is bent on this evil destructive process, and which battens on the ugliness of the war. There is a great ugliness and vultureness underneath, quite American. But I hope for the good to triumph in him also.

With love.   D. H. Lawrence

1376. To Catherine Carswell, 18 February 1917
Text: MS YU; cited in Carswell 83.

Zennor, St. Ives, Cornwall.
Sunday 18 Feb. 1917

My dear Catherine

I am sending you the book of poems today. I have put the title as you see. I

---

[1] See Letter 1366 and n. 4.

[2] The quotation, 'the Heart of Flesh', is from Ezekiel xi. 19 or xxxvi. 26. It appears that either DHL or Catherine Carswell had confused Hezekiah with Ezekiel. (She had a predilection for titles deriving from the Old Testament: *Open the Door!* – her final choice for her novel – originates in 2 Kings ix. 3.)

[3] Psalms xc. 13.

have finished it today. It has meant a great deal to me. And I feel more inclined to burst into tears than any thing. I can't send this MS. to Pinker yet. I loathe him to have it. I loathe it to go to a publisher. I feel for the moment most passionately and bitterly tender about it. I wonder what it will seem to you – this book of poems. It will either seem much, or very little. I want you to tell me what effect it has on you. Because, perhaps I shall not send it to Pinker, perhaps I shall keep it by me, this MS, for some time to come. I must see how I feel about it later, and how it strikes you.[1]

You must be in an upset, getting ready to leave your house.[2] It must seem like the end of the world to you. Let us hope it is the beginning of a new world rather. But the breaking off with the old is bitter.

Did we thank you for the Chinese coat come back, and, the very good shortbread? But aren't you robbing Peter to pay Paul, sending us your good food.

It is a curious interval with me now. Now the poems are done, I feel I don't know what next, or where next, or anything. I wish we were going to America.

The weather is most overwhelmingly lovely. I lay on the cliffs and watched the gulls and hawks in the perfect sky. Already the pigeons were cooing, and it was warm as summer. I feel I don't know where I am, nor what I am. This is somnambulism, or a trance.

Don't forget, if ever you feel homeless, we shall be *very* glad to have you in the other cottage here. Count it as a place of your own, for you both.

This is the only complete MS. of the poems – so don't lose it, will you. I want Hilda Aldington to have it next: she is 44 Mecklenburg Square, W.C. But I will write you again. I hope everything is going well with you and Carswell.

With love from us both   D. H. Lawrence

---

[1] Catherine Carswell recorded her reaction to DHL's 'book of poems':

> I shall never forget reading those poems in the author's neat handwriting in the tiny room over a garage to which we had moved upon Donald's being called up. We had let our house, had found these two rooms . . . and ourselves carried along enough of our furniture after nightfall to make them habitable . . .
> By the light of a candle I read the poems through. I confess that no other poet except Hardy (and Shakespeare in his sonnets) has so deeply conveyed to me the wistfulness of humanity as distilled in a noble heart – a heart the nobler for its perfect admission of imperfections . . . In the case of [this MS] I advised him to expunge a love letter – beautiful and interesting, but a real, sent letter, in prose, which he had included with the poems. He did not at first agree about this, but came round later (pp. 84–5).

[2] They were moving from 9 Golden Square to Hollybush House, Holly Hill, Hampstead.

1377. To J. B. Pinker, 20 February 1917
Text: MS YU; cited in Carswell 81.

Zennor, St. Ives, Cornwall
20 Feb. 1917

My dear Pinker

Really, the world has gone completely dotty! Hermione is not much more like Ottoline Morrell than Queen Victoria, the house they claim as theirs is a Georgian house in Derbyshire I know very well – etc. Ottoline flatters herself. – There *is* a hint of her in the character of Hermione: but so there is a hint of a million women, if it comes to that.[1]

Anyway, they could make libel cases for ever, they haven't half a leg to stand on.

But it doesn't matter. It is no use trying to publish the novel in England in this state of affairs. There must come a change first. So it can all lie by. The world is mad, and has got a violent rabies which makes it turn on anything true, with frenzy. The novel can lie by till there is an end of the war and a change of feeling over the world. And poor vindictive old Ottoline can be left to her vanity of identifying herself with Hermione. What does it all matter!

D. H. Lawrence

1378. To J. B. Pinker, 22 February 1917
Text: MS Forster; Unpublished.

Zennor, St. Ives, Cornwall.
22 Feb. 1917

My dear Pinker

I send you this letter of Augusta de Wit. Will you arrange with her any charges for copyright for translating *The Widowing of Mrs Holroyd*.[2] One doesn't charge much, if anything, does one?

D. H. Lawrence

---

[1] Cf. Letter 1320 and n. 1.
[2] Nothing further is known about this offer to translate DHL's play (published in 1914) by Anna Augusta Henrietta de Wit (1864–1939). She had already published a number of works: *Verborgen Bronnen* (Amsterdam, 1900); *De Godin die Wacht* (Amsterdam, 1904); *Java: Facts and Fancies* (1905). She also contributed to the *Yale Review* (see Letter 1461).

1379. To Gordon Campbell, 23 February 1917
Text: MS UCin; cited in Moore, *Intelligent Heart* 229.

Zennor, St. Ives, Cornwall.
Friday 23 Feb. 1917

Dear Campbell

No, I don't think you are cross with the book: how can you be, when you haven't seen it. I always feel you dislike my letters – but that is different.

I don't suppose Mills and Boon will publish:[1] don't care whether they do or not: this is no season for it. Besides, it only hurts one to have things come out. And I don't want to be hurt. I would rather it lay by for some time, so I needn't have any more trouble of it.

They refused to reindorse my passport at present. It makes me angry, because I do want to go. But I shall go a little later. Enough of England.

I heard of Gilbert from Gertler. It seems only nasty and messy.

Dollie Radford wants us to fulfil a promise to go and stay with her. I don't know whether I could come up to London at present. If I can bring myself, I shall.

It is spring coming here: already the birds singing and the silveriness in the air. I wish to God it was spring in the world of people. One is almost dead with the foulness of mankind.

I'll send you the MS. of the novel when at length it comes, a duplicate MS., from Pinker. He is *very* long winded.

Do you find any signs of a change coming over people, a newness, for a new start?

D. H. Lawrence

1380. To Dollie Radford, 23 February 1917
Text: MS UN; Postmark, St. Ives 23 FE 17; Nehls, i. 411–12.

Zennor, St. Ives, Cornwall.
23 Feb. 1917

My dear Dollie

If only I can come to the cottage.[2] I want to, but there seems a sort of spell on me. What is the invisible force that won't let one move from Zennor? I don't know. But as soon as it is lifted, I shall come to London and the cottage. Only it is not in my control.

[1] A publishing firm (at 49 Rupert Street, London, W.1) specialising in popular fiction, particularly that addressed to female readers (Campbell may have been deceived by the title *Women in Love*).
[2] Chapel Farm Cottage, Hermitage, Berkshire, owned by Dollie Radford. The Lawrences lived there intermittently between 14 December 1917 and 2 May 1918.

The spring is coming also. Yesterday the lambs were dancing, and the birds whistled, the doves cooed all day down at the farm. The world of nature is wonderful in its revivifying spontaneity. But oh god, the world of man – who can bear any more? I can't bear any more of mankind. One can only lapse. At any rate, the cooing of the doves is very real, and the blithe impertinence of the lambs as they peep round their mothers. They affect me like the Rainbow, as a sign that life will never be destroyed, or turn bad altogether.

I keep hoping now for an intimation of spring in the heart of mankind, new world to come. Do you catch any signs? As soon as I do, I shall come forth. One waits in a strange expectancy. I suppose we have our hour for coming out, like everything else.

We have sat motionless in Zennor for a long time: scarcely ever been to St. Ives or to Penzance. So there is not any news.

I shall try every day to come to London. And when I know I can, I shall write you at once. I would rather come to the Hermitage first. You must tell me the address, and, if ever it is easy to you, look out a train for us from here. I feel we shall be coming soon. Frieda at any rate intends to come in March. I shall come with her if I can.

Give my love to Margaret.[1]

with love to you from us both   D. H. Lawrence

1381. To Catherine Carswell, [24 February 1917]
Text: MS YU; cited in Carswell 87.

Zennor, St. Ives, Cornwall
Saturday

My dear Catherine

I don't know what to say about you and Carswell. It is misery, and there it is. It has got to be borne, and nothing from outside can help.

But there is this, it won't *really* hurt you, in the long run. Nothing bad will happen *inside* you and Don. Be sure of that. And only misery will hurt outside: not vital damage. One has to make up one's mind to endure, and not lose any faith, or even any triumph. Though the enemy seizes my body for a time, I shall subtly adjust myself so that he pinches me nowhere vitally, and when he is forced to release me again, I am the stronger.

Even, I hope Don will learn the great lesson, really to reject the world of man, as it now is. I hope he will learn the bitter lesson of repudiating this death. 'Except a seed fall into the ground and perish –'[2] And this is the

---

[1] Younger daughter of Dollie and Ernest Radford.
[2] John xii. 24 (A.V.) ['. . . a corn of wheat fall . . . and die'].

perishing. But you have all the while the faith of the new life. Never relinquish that, however beset you are. It matters *more* than love, the faith in the creative spirit. One must have a citadel in one's soul, where one *never* gives in to anything but the supreme faith: not even to love. You have that inside yourself: and he must have it inside himself. He has stood with one foot on each side the Rubicon. Now he will be dragged back into the old world, so his soul will cross over entirely into the new.

Don't be *innerly* downcast: it will come out as I say. *You* cannot bear him again out of *your* womb. He must be born of himself out of his own unknown. And your sheltering of him would only *frustrate* his death and re-birth. Your cherishing of him in sleep would only deny his oneness with the rest. You won't be happy with him till then. So be of good courage,[1] and, instead of wishing to shelter him, send him forth to find out which side he really belongs to.

You see, he must not wish to be successful at the law: it is Dead Sea Fruit.[2] So let him taste the fare of the world of which his law is part. Let him eat the crust, since he desires the crumb. Harden your heart in faith against his suffering, and love him sternly, with hope of a new life and a new world. Love the great spirit of the new even more than you love him – it is the *only* way.

There is the great act of rejection necessary on his part. You are much nearer to it than he. And you can never do it for him: every man must reject himself from himself, he must perish in the old self, and there is no vicarious perishing. So harden your heart for the last extremity, and you will see what new life comes forth out of him his right to real existence. Your desire to foster him and shelter him is *too strong*. It is an enclosing him in an old womb, like a woman who grips her child inside her and won't let it be born.

He must be born of himself, without your ordaining. He must die *his own death* – you can never die it for him – and to attempt to spare him is to take away his great opportunity; as if Mary the mother of Jesus had snatched him up and saved him from the crucifixion. Here you have no power. He must go down into a separate grave and rise again in pure singleness. *Then* you will be happy together, you and he.

It only needs to have a faith which is unshakeable against everything, a faith in the creative unknown.

D. H. Lawrence

---

[1] A command occurring frequently in the Old Testament, e.g. 2 Samuel x. 12, 1 Chronicles xix. 13.

[2] i.e. apples of Sodom, or a fruit that is beautiful to look at but when touched turns to ashes.

1382. To Harriet Monroe, 28 February 1917
Text: MS UChi; Huxley 399.

Higher Tregerthen, Zennor, St. Ives. Cornwall.
28 Feb. 1917

Dear Harriet Monroe,[1]

The copy of *Poetry* came today, with the notice of *Amores*. Thank you very much. I am sorry I forgot to inscribe my thanks to your magazine.

We can't come to America yet, I am sorry to say. But we shall come.

Do you think you might ask Josephine Preston Peabody to give me a copy of her *Harvest Moon*?[2] I will gladly send her a copy of either of my books of poetry in return. The bits you quote of her seem to me very real and valid. I should be glad to read the rest. Most of your American verse I find ungenuine: it isn't valid. Most of the people show off – something empty and noisy, as if they want to attract attention. It is all so blatant.

I have got together the MS. of a new book of verse: by far the best. I will not forget to mention *Poetry* in front.

Ask Josephine Preston Peabody about her book, for me, if you can, will you?

Yours very sincerely   D. H. Lawrence

1383. To Ernest Collings, 3 March 1917
Text: MS UT; Huxley 400.

Higher Tregerthen, Zennor, St. Ives. Cornwall
Sat. 3 March 1917

Dear Collings[3]

I was very sorry to hear of you laid up in hospital.[4] But heaven knows, one wonders that anybody of any sensitiveness is left alive.

We have been here just a year, in a very nice cottage above the sea. I like this place very much. I was completely rejected from military service, thank God – for health – I know I should have died in a month. As it is, it is a

[1] Harriet Monroe (1860–1936), American poet and editor; she founded *Poetry: A Magazine of Verse* (Chicago) in 1912. See *Letters*, ii. 167. DHL's poems had already appeared in two issues of the magazine (in January and December 1914).
[2] *Harvest Moon*, a collection of war poems by the American poet and playwright Josephine Preston Peabody (1874–1922), was published in USA in 1916 and by Longmans in London in March 1917.
[3] Ernest Henry Roberts Collings (1882–1932), artist and illustrator, to whom DHL first wrote in November 1912 (*Letters*, i. 468); they exchanged letters with fair regularity until September 1915 since which time there had been an unexplained silence. Collings had enlisted in the Artists' Rifles in January 1917 and was to be discharged unfit in April 1917.
[4] MS reads 'hospitable'.

struggle to go on living. The world is too foul, it poisons us. I dont know what will become of us all. If only a better spirit, a new spirit, would come into men, and make them begin to make life real and fine, instead of only death. The tension of trying to keep a spirit of life and hope against such masses of foulness wears one right out.

No, there is nothing published of mine lately – save a story in this month's *English Review* which I don't much care for.[1] I have done a novel, which nobody will print, after the *Rainbow* experience. It has been the round of publishers by now, and rejected by all. I don't care. One might as well make roses bloom in January, as bring out living work into this present world of man.

I wish there could be a new spring of hope and reality in mankind: I do wish a few people could change, and stand for a fresh and happier world. I suppose it will come, and we shall live through. That is our business, at any rate. We must live through, for the hope of the new summer of the world.

At any rate, don't lose all your strength in illness. Save enough for when the change comes, the time to work for real happiness.

D. H. Lawrence

1384. To Catherine Carswell, [7 March 1917]
Text: MS YU; PC; Postmark, St. Ives 7 MR 17; Huxley 401.

Zennor –
Wed.

I have seven short articles – little essays – called 'The Reality of Peace'.[2] They are very beautiful, and I think, very important. Something *must* be done with them. They are a new beginning. Shall I send them along to you, to see what you and Don think, and about publishing? Or shall I send them straight to Pinker? How much time have you? – But they are *very* short.

What is happening to you?

Reply at once, will you.

DHL

---

[1] 'Samson and Delilah'.
[2] Four of these essays were published in *English Review*, May, June, July and August 1917; of the remaining three, 'Whistling of Birds' appeared in the *Athenaeum* (11 April 1919), but the other two are lost. The book which DHL intended should follow (see Letter 1388) did not materialise; see also p. 143 n. 3.

1385. To Dollie Radford, 9 March 1917
Text: MS UN; Postmark, St. Ives 9 MR 17; Nehls, i. 412–13.

Zennor, St. Ives, Cornwall

Friday 9 March 1917

My dear Dollie

The news of Herbert is a great shock, one cannot bear it.[1] And one has no tears to weep, only a dry aching heart that aches harder. Now he is dead, I don't mind. But the death I cannot cannot cannot cannot ever bear, cannot live and think of it. My dear Dollie, after all, he had a real religious side to him. *How much* greater is the living spirit, than the world of man's activity. Well, at any rate, he will have peace. That he is dead, I can bear. The dead seem to be real and beloved, they have reached reality. But the death will never be forgiven to mankind – But we will have him in our hearts, dead and pure now. And we will forget, we will forget the death. Let us forget the death, let us keep the pure dead with us, unspoiled.

My dear Dollie, it is a lovely spring morning, and in spite of all, the dead do not darken it: only the evil ones, the death-makers. The blue sea and the west wind and the full sunshine give me no sorrow for Herbert, now he is dead. Rather he is with us now, in spirit, to strengthen us.

My dear Dollie, we must now begin, with our deepest souls, to bring peace and life into the world. I have written my first articles 'The Reality of Peace'. I shall send them to you next week. These must be published, we must begin. It shall begin to end now, this horror and evil. We will come in, now, Dollie, we will be strong for life and perfection. Let us rouse ourselves now.

I won't write to Margaret – perhaps you will tell her what I say. I am sending her a little plaque, which I think is rather beautiful.[2]

You shall have my seven little essays 'The Reality of Peace' next week. Then we must consider hard how best to publish them.

With much love from us both   D. H. Lawrence

---

[1] Herbert Watson, a close friend of the Radfords, had died of war-wounds in France; he was called up c. April 1916 (*Letters*, ii. 596). It is clear that when the Lawrences left their flat, 1 Byron Villas in Hampstead (on 21 December 1915), Watson bought some pieces of furniture to help them raise money (see *Letters*, ii. 577). He had also been a subscriber to *Signature* (*Letters*, ii. 413).

[2] The plaque is thought to have been 'a copy of warriors in the Parthenon frieze' (Nehls, i. 588 n. 374).

1386. To Catherine Carswell, [9 March 1917]
Text: MS YU; Huxley 401.

Zennor, St. Ives, Cornwall.
Friday

I send you the 'Seven' today. – I have promised them to Dollie Radford next. You won't keep them long, because they are so short.

We must think *hard* about their publication. *We must begin now to work for a new world, a creative peace.*

Only Esther Andrews and Hilda Aldington have had the poems. Esther Andrews seems to feel very much with you about them – for which I am glad. Hilda Aldington says they won't do at all; they are not *eternal*, not sublimated: too much body and emotions.

You will be having a bad time just now. Never mind, it is near to a new beginning.

Warn me again before you leave your house. The news of Herbert Watson made me feel ill.

D. H. Lawrence

I wrote to Austin Harrison to ask if he would like to see the Seven for the *English Review*.[1] Do you think that all right?

1387. To S. S. Koteliansky, 12 March 1917
Text: MS BL; Moore 506–7.

Zennor, St. Ives, Cornwall
12 March 1917

My dear Kot,

I believe it was your turn to write. At any rate I have been expecting a letter from you this long while. What is happening to you now? What is happening in Russia? Is the world coming to an end?

They wouldn't let me go to America. I will go one day. Meanwhile I content myself at Zennor. I have done some peace articles – called 'The Reality of Peace'. I wonder if anybody will publish them. They are very good, and beautiful. I have heard nothing from Pinker about the MS. of the novel. What about your copy?[2] – But everything seems to have gone to pot.

Now I am going to garden. I believe we are really going to be pinched for food. But we are going to see the end of the war soon. Anything to have that. I

---

[1] See p. 100 n. 2. Austin Harrison (1873–1928) had been editor of the *English Review* since Ford Madox Hueffer was dismissed in December 1909. See *Letters*, i. 152 n. 4.

[2] This relates to Kot's suggestion that *Women in Love* might be published in Russia; see Letters 1333 and 1334.

will become even a little thinner than I am, if only the war will end. – It will end soon. It is *virtually* over. We are coming out of it all. We will be happy before long.

I send you back the Italian books.[1] Alas, I have wearied of passion and eroticism and sex perversions, so that though we have read through these books, I end with a feeling of weariness and a slight nausea against things Italian.

I *do* wish peace would come quickly. You might then come down here and help me to dig gardens. You would be happy here. I only want the war to end now.

Have you got any news? I have none. I was seedy these last weeks, but I feel better again, and am sure we shall soon have peace and some happiness, even if there is not quite enough for us to eat.

Tell me news of yourself, and of other people. I *do* hope Gertler is better. His letter was so painful I couldn't write about it.[2] And the news of Gilbert was nasty – something sordid and putrid.[3] We want to get into something new. But very soon now, we will. Is there any news of Murry? I have not heard from either of them for many months, which is as it should be. I have really a disillusion from them.

Oh, do get me a gardening book *Culture of Profitable vegetables in Small Gardens* by Sutton and Sons – 6d.

You will think I only write when I want something. But it isn't so.

The spring is coming quickly, the birds whistle their best, the lambs are full of spirits, they hold a Panatheneia under the windows of the house. They are *very* jolly when the sun shines. It shone so beautifully today. I have been painting a picture of the death of Procris,[4] which fills me with great delight. – I wish you could come down for a time – do you think you might manage it? If only the war stopped, you would certainly come.

What do you do with yourself nowadays, tell me that.

I should think you could get the little sixpenny gardening book anywhere.

Thank Mr Shearman very heartily on my account, for the books.[5]

---

[1] The only certainty among these books is *Cavalleria Rusticana* (see Letter 1332); others which may have been included are mentioned in Letters 1319 and 1322.

[2] Gertler was made desperately unhappy by the realisation that Dora Carrington could no longer return his intense love and was about to desert him for Lytton Strachey.

[3] See Letter 1372 and n. 1.

[4] She was accidentally killed by her husband Cephalus.

[5] See p. 52 n. 1. Montague Shearman, barrister (1886–1940), son of the judge Sir Montague Shearman (1857–1930). He was a friend of Campbell, Kot, St John Hutchinson, Dora Carrington, and Gertler (whose paintings he collected as well as those of Duncan Grant). He was also a keen book-collector. Shearman was employed at the Foreign Office, having been rejected for military service at the outbreak of war. (See *Times* obituary, 6 February 1940.)

I wish you could come here for a few weeks. Warm greetings from Frieda.

D. H. Lawrence

I send you *Moby Dick*, because I have two copies, and it is a book I like *very* much.

1388. To J. B. Pinker, 19 March 1917
Text: MS Forster; Huxley 402.

Zennor, St. Ives, Cornwall.

19 March 1917

My dear Pinker

I am sending you seven little Articles called 'The Reality of Peace'. I wrote to Austin Harrison about them: will you send them to him, to see if he will put them in the *English Review*. They are very beautiful and dear to me, I feel very delicate and sensitive about them. I intend to follow them up with more such chapters, to make a book.[1] Perhaps in America the *Yale Review* would print them.[2]

I have done my new book of poems and got it ready. That also is very precious to me. But it *could* not come out just now, the world is far too vile and horrific. Let there be just a little sign of a new dawn.

Are you really doing the copies of the novel, – or having them done – the one for Koteliansky and the one for me?[3] *I wish I could have a copy.* I would like to look at Ottoline Morrells imaginary portrait again. I feel weary, and wish something better would come.

D. H. Lawrence

Harrison must not cut the articles without letting me know first – if he takes them.

1389. To Amy Lowell, 23 March 1917
Text: MS HU; Damon 405.

Higher Tregerthen, Zennor, St. Ives. Cornwall

23 March 1917

My dear Amy

I received the other day your letter with cheque for £5, for the anthology,[4] and was *very* glad to hear of you better in health, and busy.

---

[1] See p. 100 n. 2.
[2] There is no record of the essays having been printed elsewhere than in *English Review* (before they were collected in *Phoenix*, ed. Edward D. McDonald, 1936, pp. 669–94).
[3] See Letter 1333.
[4] DHL had contributed (and was now being paid for) his poem 'Terra Nuova' to *Some Imagist Poets: An Annual Anthology* (Boston and New York) which was to be published on 14 April 1917. (The poem was later retitled 'New Heaven and Earth'.) See *Letters*, ii. 664.

Hilda Aldington sent me your Japanese poems, for the new anthology.[1] I don't like them *nearly* so well as your other things, and I do wish you hadn't put them in. *Don't* do Japanese things, Amy, if you love us. I would a million times rather have a fragment of 'Aquarium'[2] than all the Japanese poems put together. I am so disappointed with this batch you have decided to put in, it isn't you at *all*, it has nothing to do with you, and it is not real. Alas and alas, why have you done this thing?

Hilda Aldington seems very sad and suppressed, everything is wrong. I *wish* things would get better. I have done a set of little essays called 'The Reality of Peace', very important to me. I wish they would come out in America. They may appear in the *English Review*, in which case I shall send them to you. Oh dear, it is a real struggle to get any further, we seem really stuck in a bog of wrongness. I wish above all things the tide would turn in the hearts of people, and make for creation and happiness: for we are almost lost. But we will hope on, and struggle.

Do write from your *real* self, Amy, don't make up things from the outside, it is so saddening.

With love from both   D. H. Lawrence

1390. To J. B. Pinker, 28 March 1917
Text: MS Forster; Unpublished.

Zennor, St. Ives, Cornwall
28 Mar 1917

My Dear Pinker

The MS of the novel has come – thank you very much. Is there any news of the 'Peace' Articles? They seem the most important for the moment.

D. H. Lawrence

1391. To Catherine Carswell, [31 March 1917]
Text: MS YU; Postmark, St. Ives 31 MR 17; Huxley 402–3.

Zennor, St. Ives, Cornwall
1 April 1917

My dear Catherine

What is happening to you by now – and to Don? Frieda told us all about

---

[1] Amy Lowell's contribution to the Imagist anthology (pp. 79–86) was the group of poems, 'Lacquer Prints': they were the only poems in the volume 'wholly untouched by the war' (Damon 407–8). (Hilda Doolittle herself contributed 'The God', 'Adonis', 'Pygmalion' and 'Eurydice'.)

[2] See p. 31 and n. 2.

you in your little rooms.[1] I sincerely hope you are feeling better in health. It is all a question of hope, and peace of spirit. If one could have a real fresh hopeful spirit, one would be well in health.

There is this new Military Service Act, which makes me liable to more re-examinations.[2] But my soul is made up now: I will go to prison rather than be compelled to anything. I have had enough. I will *not* be compelled by these foul dogs, not to anything.

Austin Harrison will probably publish the 'Reality of Peace': at least some of them: for which I was very glad. I was sorry they did not mean much to you: disappointed. Because still, to me, they are very important. I still feel, if they are published, they will be effective. It is time something was done. It is time something new appeared on the face of the earth. It is time we abandoned our old selves and our old concerns, to come out into something clear and new, beyond humanity. We must establish ourselves in the absolute truth, and scorn this filthily contemptible world of actuality. We must do something – it is time to move away from our little selves into the flood of a real living and effective truth. We *must* have done entirely with the half-truths of actual lies. They are leeches hanging on our souls. I feel like starting something somewhere: but hardly know yet where to begin. I believe there are peace demonstrations every Sunday in the Victoria Park. I think I am almost ready to set out preaching also, now: not only cessation of war, but the beginning of a new world. My dear Catherine, it is time to begin something like this. I feel on the brink of coming to London, but wait still a little while, for the definite impulse. It is really time for us to rouse ourselves now, to set out on the new journey.

Write and tell me what you think, how you are and how you feel. Frieda sends her love. She is very happy with the terra cotta statuette, but I do not find it *very* good.

D. H. Lawrence

[Frieda Lawrence begins]

I was so glad to have seen you, you were an oasis in the London desert – Yes, I think our time will come – it will be fighting still and misery, but in the end we shall come through – Yes, I love the little statue –

The sun is shining and we are gardening. Is'nt it marvellous that the

---

[1] See Letter 1376 and n. 1.
[2] The terms of the new bill were published on 29 March. The Government was given powers to call up for examination (among other classes of men) 'men who have previously been rejected on any ground' (*Times*, 29 March 1917).

English Review wants to do the peace articles – Harrison said they were extraordinarily suggestive – and new – I wish you were here, tell us Don's news –

Yours with love   Frieda

Tell Joy, I will write to her –[1]

1392. To Dollie Radford, [31 March 1917]
Text: MS UN; Postmark, St. Ives 31 MR 17; Nehls, i. 413–14.

Zennor, St. Ives, Cornwall
1 April 1917

My dear Dollie

I want to thank you very much for looking after Frieda. You are a very great tower of strength for us there in London: the place would be a howling waste of terrors but for you and your sheltering roof.

I was glad to hear of Maitland so happy.[2] I must write to him. The little cloth with stripes is *very* nice, so fresh and cheerful. We have not spread it yet, till everything is spring.

Have you read the 'Reality of Peace'? Do read them, Dollie, they are quite short. I think Austin Harrison will publish some or all of them in the *English Review*. I do hope so. It may be the initiation of a new state of feeling, or the nucleus of a new hope. Do read them, and tell me what you think of them. I should like Maitland and Margaret to read them, if they would care to: particularly Maitland. But they wouldn't keep them long, because I should like the MS. back, to make another copy. Pinker wants the copy you have, for America. I must certainly get another copy made. I do feel, Dollie, that those articles might make a new start. I hope you can have a moment's quiet, to read them.

I really think, Dollie, it is time something new and good came to pass: therefore we must bring it to pass. It is time now to begin. If one only knew where to lay hold! But if we all watch out, we shall see the opening. Let us really be alert now – and get Maitland and his promessa sposa to help also. Let us watch and be ready for the new sign.

There must be a new spirit – and then a new world. This old Parliament, which is so disgusting, must be turned out. We *must* have a real, living

---

[1] Unidentified.

[2] Dr Maitland Radford (1884–1944), Dollie's son; after serving with the Royal Medical Corps he had been appointed to a post at Queen Mary's Hospital, Carshalton, Surrey (*Letters*, ii. 540 n. 3), and had just announced his engagement to Muriel Lloyd. They were married in September 1917.

representative government. This can be brought to pass, if only we will begin.

I hope you are not very worn out with burdens at home. Let them slide, the immediate burdens, let us go for a more permanent happiness.

I will write to Maitland. With much love to you from us both.

D. H. Lawrence

1393. To S. S. Koteliansky, 1 April 1917
Text: MS BL; Zytaruk 112–13.

Zennor, St. Ives, Cornwall.
1 April 1917

My dear Kot

You saw Frieda on her visit – otherwise I should have written sooner to thank you for the gardening book.[1] Your elation over Russia, has it come back, or do you feel still despondent?[2] I am very sick with the state here. The new Military Service Bill makes me liable to be pestered again. But I am resolved this time. If they bother me, I will go to prison. I *will not be compelled*: that is the whole of my feeling. I should very much like to do something to get a better government. This Parliament must be kicked out: it is a disgusting fraud. It is time we had a living representative government here. How can we tolerate such a grunting Schweinerei?[3] I think I must come to London soon and see a few people.

I believe Austin Harrison is going to publish some essays of mine, called 'The Reality of Peace', in the *English Review*. I hope he will. It may start a new feeling among people. It is time now that there was something new. It is quite time.

You will have got the complete MS. of the novel by now. I want you to tell me if you like it to the end. Don't hurry about Russia. I always believe in giving things time. If Gertler likes to read the MS, lend it to him: or to Campbell, if you are keeping it long enough.

I am busy gardening: breaking up a little field to set vegetables. It is hard work, and I wish I had you here to utilise some of your spare force. But we drive slowly ahead. I wish I could feel real occasion for my coming to London.

[1] See Letter 1387.
[2] DHL's question must relate to the developing political situation in Russia where the Duma had carried through a *coup d'état* on 12 March 1917; the Emperor Nicholas II had abdicated; and the Russian Revolution had begun. A provisional government under Prince George Lvoff had been set up.
[3] 'pigsty'.

But I don't see that it is any use contemplating it, for the moment.

Frieda greets you   D. H. Lawrence

[Frieda Lawrence begins]

How is your poor suicide Russian?[1] Has your new hat recovered from the snowstorm on the bus? I was *disgusted* to find that Ernst[2] who poses as the tragic figure to the children, takes Gladys[3] (she is a handsome, coarse girl) out to dinner, flirts with her, but keeps of course the last respectability – Lord, I was so furious – but then he *is* both things, but the children are different, thank God!

My love to you   Frieda

1394. To Mark Gertler, 1 April 1917
Text: MS SIU; Huxley 403–4.

Zennor, St. Ives, Cornwall.
1 April 1917

My dear Gertler

I was glad to hear from Frieda that you are well and happier. She sees a change in you, a newness and a certain peace which are everything. Also she thinks the bathing scene wonderful. – I think the wrestlers interesting: but sculpture never quite satisfies me.[4] It is not sufficiently abstracted. One resents the bulk, it frustrates the clarity of conception.

Kot has the whole MS. of my novel by now, and will have read it. If you care to, borrow it from him, and read it through: though probably you will find it laborious. And then, please tell me how much likeness you can see between Hermione and the Ott. The Ott. is really too disgusting, with her threats of legal proceedings etc. She is really contemptible. We have flattered her above all bounds, in attending to her at all.

There is now this new Military Service Act, which makes me liable to be

---

[1] The reference is obscure.
[2] Ernest Weekley (1865–1954), University Professor and etymologist; first husband of Frieda. See *Letters*, i. 374 n. 5.
[3] Perhaps Gladys Bradley who had been a close friend of Ernest and Frieda in their Nottingham days. She (and her sister Madge) had actively encouraged the relationship between Frieda and DHL. See *Letters*, i. 388 n. 2.
[4] Gertler's picture of 'the bathing scene' was almost certainly the 'good old-fashioned "Cézannish" bathing scene' of which he told Carrington in January 1917 (*Gertler: Selected Letters*, ed. Carrington, p. 136). It was subsequently entitled *Bathers*. The sculpture of 'the wrestlers' was probably *The Acrobats*: see p. 28 n. 1.

called up again. But I am so nauseated with the whole affair, that if they do bother me, I will go to prison rather than comply in the least. I will not be compelled – that is quite definite in me: I will not be compelled to anything. I am sick of the whole ignominious show.

We are busy gardening, and I am writing short essays on philosophy. The pure abstract thought interests me now at this juncture more than art. I am tired of emotions and squirmings of sensation. Let us have a little pure thought, a little perfect and detached understanding. That is how I feel now. It may be Austin Harrison will put some essays of mine 'The Reality of Peace', in the *English Review*. I hope he will. If so, you must read them. I am very weary of this world of ugly chaos. I am sick to death of struggling in a cauldron of foul feelings, with no mind, no thought, no understanding; no clarity of being anywhere, only a stinking welter of sensations. One must get out of it somehow.

The weather is very cold: I wish it would turn warmer. I wish one could *do* something: I wish one could see where to lay hold, to effect something fresh and clear, just to begin a new state. You say 'it is life, life is like it.' But that is mere sophistry. Life is what one wants in one's soul, and in[1] my soul I do not want this wretched conglomerate messing, therefore I deny that it is life at all, it is only baseness and extraneous, sporadic, meaningless sensationalism.

Still I hover on the brink of moving from Zennor towards London, and still I do not get away. But all in good time. Let me know what you *think* by now.

                                                                        D. H. Lawrence

[Frieda Lawrence begins]

You would have laughed to see me draw your new picture for L– to g⁞ him an idea – It's good to be here! –

1395. To J. B. Pinker, 2 April 1917
Text: MS UNYB; cited in Moore, *Intelligent Heart* 230.

                                                                Zennor, St. Ives, Cornwall
                                                                2 April 1917
My dear Pinker
    Harrison wrote me about the 'Reality of Peace' articles, saying he will do the last three in[2] three consecutive months. I hoped he would have done them all, or at least six of them, two at a time, but he says he can't. So I suppose we

---

¹ in] I   ² in] as

shall have to swallow this. Perhaps we might place the first four elsewhere – only I do want them to come together, not to be scattered. I hope we shall be able to get them published at the end of the summer, with several other little essays of the same kind, in a small book. I will send you the duplicate as soon as I can.

D. H. Lawrence

Eveleigh Nash says he would like to see *Women in Love*.[1] Somehow I don't want it published, even if it were possible, just yet. What do you think about the poems? I think I will send the MS to you, and we will see how we feel about it. I will send the MS. tomorrow – or when I hear from you.

DHL

1396. To J. B. Pinker, 3 April 1917
Text: MS Forster; Unpublished.

Zennor, St. Ives, Cornwall.
3 April 1917

My dear Pinker

I have decided to send you the MS. of poems.[2] This is the best of my poetry, and I feel very unwilling to let it go. Will you tell me what you think of it, and what you think about offering it for publication. Will you please tell me also who is your representative in America.[3] I feel there is no haste to get this MS. published. The 'Reality of Peace' seems to me much more important now. Perhaps you will have heard from Harrison.

I got a copy of the *Seven Arts*, with the 'Thimble' story, from America: also the *Metropolitan Magazine*, with 'England, My England'.[4]

The world feels cold and horrible. Have you any hopeful news of any sort?

D. H. Lawrence

---

[1] J. Eveleigh Nash (1873–1956) had founded his own publishing house in 1902; he directed it until 1929. He had published works by Kipling and Hardy among others.
[2] Those published (in December 1917) as *Look! We Have Come Through!*
[3] See p. 29 n. 3.
[4] 'The Thimble': see p. 50 n. 1; 'England, My England' in *Metropolitan*, April 1917 (after its first publication in *English Review*, xxi, October 1915, 238–52).

1397. To S. S. Koteliansky, 4 April 1917
Text: MS BL; Zytaruk, ed., *Malahat Review*, i. 31–2.

Zennor, St. Ives, Cornwall.
4[1] April 1917

My dear Kot

I was out when Carrington's telegram came, and Frieda answered it.[2] I don't really want anybody else to read the MS. – I don't very much want even Carrington to have it. But it is all right, since Frieda wired yes. Let her have it on the stipulation she shows *nobody else*: and if Campbell and Gertler have read it, then *don't let it go any further*. You know that the Ottoline threatens me with law-suits: I feel she would go any length to do me damage in this affair. I feel that these people, all the Ott. crowd, are full of malice against me. Altogether I feel bad about that novel, and I will not publish it now. I *know* it is a good book. But my god, to have all these canaille already grunting over it is more than I can bear. I feel awfully raw against the whole show. I will show the *MS* to *nobody* absolutely any more: so please help to protect me in this.

Don't say anything to hurt Carrington's feelings: don't tell her I would rather she *hadn't* seen the MS., since things have happened as they have.

I cannot cannot cannot bear the feeling of all these canaille yapping and snapping at me – they are too disgusting and insufferable. *Why* did I give myself away to them – Otts and Murries etc! –

D. H. Lawrence

1398. To Catherine Carswell, 11 April 1917
Text: MS YU; Postmark, Zennor 12 APR. 17; cited in Moore, *Poste Restante* 46.

Zennor, St. Ives, Cornwall
11 April 1917

My dear Catherine

You have not written for so long – is anything amiss?

I have promised to go up to Derbyshire to meet my Sisters on Saturday. I shall stay a few days, then propose to come on to London. I hope I shall see you then. Answer me

c/o Mrs Clarke, Grosvenor Rd, *Ripley*, nr Derby.

---

[1] 4] 3
[2] Dora de Houghton Carrington (1893–1932) – always known by her surname – had been a student at the Slade with Dorothy Brett and Mark Gertler. Though Carrington was not herself a member of the inner circle at Garsington, DHL was justified in associating her with it: Gertler had introduced her to Lady Ottoline's gatherings (*Ottoline: The Early Memoirs of Lady Ottoline Morrell*, ed. Robert Gathorne-Hardy, 1963, pp. 277–8) and her increasingly intimate relationship with Lytton Strachey linked her with one of the Morrells' close friends.

I shall probably be in London this day week – 18th or 19th.
Frieda sends her love – she will stay in Zennor.

D. H. Lawrence

1399. To John Middleton Murry, 13 April 1917
Text: MS NYPL; Unpublished.

Zennor, St. Ives, Cornwall
13 April 1917

I am going up to Ripley tomorrow, and shall probably be in London next week, Wednesday or Thursday. If you like we will have a meeting. I shall probably stay with Dollie Radford. But send me a line
c/o Mrs Clarke, Grosvenor Rd. *Ripley*, nr. Derby.
I hope you are all right.

D. H. Lawrence

1400. To J. B. Pinker, 13 April 1917
Text: MS NYPL; Unpublished.

Zennor, St. Ives, Cornwall
13 April 1917

My dear Pinker
Have you received the two MSS. of the poems, which I sent ten days ago to your office? I wonder I have had no acknowledgment.

I am going up to the Midlands for a few days, and shall come back via London. Then I shall come and see you. That will be about Thursday or Friday of next week. Will you let me know if you will be at Talbot House. Please write me
c/o Mrs Clarke, Grosvenor Rd. *Ripley*, nr. Derby.
I shall be there from tomorrow to Wednesday, I suppose.

I have sent back the corrected proof of the first instalment of the 'Peace' essays to the *English Review*. I am rather surprised, and very pleased, that he is printing the thing untouched. I feel that soon one can begin to work for a new feeling. I shall go when I am in London to the National Council for Civil Liberty – they sent me Norman Angell's book today.[1] Perhaps they will print

---

[1] (Sir) Norman Angell (1874–1967) was a lifelong apologist for peace and liberty (he won the Nobel Peace Prize in 1933). He had recently published *Why Freedom Matters* (1916), probably the book referred to here.

the 'Reality of Peace' in full, when Harrison has done his three. Have you got anybody to consider those four which Harrison didn't want? –

I hope to hear from you at once.

D. H. Lawrence

1401. To S. S. Koteliansky, [16 April 1917]
Text: MS BL; Zytaruk 115.

c/o Mrs Clarke, Grosvenor Rd, *Ripley*, nr. Derby
Monday

My dear Kot

I shall come down to London from Nottingham on Thursday, arrive Marylebone at 1.12 – so that I should be at Acacia Rd at about 1.30. I do hope I shan't be a nuisance to Mrs Farbman.[1] My regards to her, and I am very sensible of her kindness in letting me stay in her house. Don't bother about lunch on Thursday, for me. – I stay here till Wednesday – stay Wed. night in Nottingham – then come on.

Dollie Radford is getting copies made, of the 'Peace' Articles. I hate the Midlands.

D. H. Lawrence

1402. To Catherine Carswell, [16 April 1917]
Text: MS YU; Postmark, Ripley 16 AP 17; cited in Moore, *Poste Restante* 46.

c/o Mrs Clarke. Grosvenor Rd, *Ripley*, nr Derby
Monday

My dear Catherine

I was glad to hear from you – I was afraid you were not well.

I shall come to London on Thursday – and shall stay with Koteliansky, in *5 Acacia Road, St. Johns Wood*. I have written to Dollie Radford saying I will come to Hampstead on Friday.[2] Will you be at home? – and what part of the day? I very much want to have a talk.

D. H. Lawrence

---

[1] Michael S. Farbman (1880?–1933), a Russian journalist, and his wife Sonia (née Issayevna), took over the house at 5 Acacia Road, St John's Wood, London, from Katherine Mansfield on 18 November 1915; Kot went to live with them. Later Kot himself owned the house; he lived there till his death. See *Letters*, ii. 570 n. 3.

[2] The letter has not been found.

1403. To J. B. Pinker, [19 April 1917]
Text: MS UNYB; PC; Postmark, Nottingham 19 APR 17; Unpublished.

Nottingham –
Thursday

I will call in tomorrow about 11.30.

D. H. Lawrence

1404. To J. B. Pinker, 21 April 1917
Text: MS UNYB; Unpublished.

5, Acacia Road, St John's Wood, N.W.
21 Apr 1917

My dear Pinker

Harrison asked me if I could let him have some poetry. You might send him, either the whole MS. and let him take what he wants, or these things
'Moonrise'
'The Sea'
'Constancy of a Sort'
'Rabbit Snared in the Dark'
'Frost Flowers'
'Craving for Spring'.[1]
On the whole, I would rather he *didn't* have the MS, but only a selection of the more impersonal poems. If you haven't the MS. by you, let me know, and I will copy some things out for him, when I get back to Cornwall, which will be on Tuesday or Wednesday next.

D. H. Lawrence

1405. To Sallie Hopkin, 22 April 1917
Text: MS NCL; Postmark, St. John's Wood 23 APR 17; Huxley 404–5.

5 Acacia Rd, St. Johns Wood, London, N.W.
Sunday 22 April 1917

My dear Sallie[2]

I hope you are feeling a bit better and a bit happier. When you rise fully

---

[1] All the poems were published in *Look! We Have Come Through!* Harrison accepted three for publication in *English Review*, xxv (September 1917), 193–7: 'The Sea', 'Constancy of a Sort' and 'Frost Flowers'.

[2] Sarah ('Sallie') Annie, née Potter (1867–1922), m. William Edward Hopkin (1862–1951); they had one daughter, Enid (b. 1896). The Hopkins were among DHL's closest friends in Eastwood where they played a prominent part in political and intellectual life. See *Letters*, i. 3, 176 n. 2.

into your new life, beware of seeing as the world sees, and thinking as the world thinks. 'Not as the world giveth, give I unto you.'[1] Christ was right in all those things. It is necessary to go beyond the outer life, to the life of death and creation, and take ones stand there, and let the world which intervenes have its own, merely secondary place. Even you, it is *not* really money which you need, to satisfy your unsatisfaction: it is the peace and fulfilment of the spirit, that which is *ultimate*, and beyond interference. Now that it is time for your resurrection, don't drag the grave clothes of the old state with you. The world doesn't matter: you have died sufficiently to know that: the world doesn't matter, ultimately. Ultimately, only the otherworld of pure being matters. One has to be strong enough to have the just sense of values. One sees it in the old sometimes. Old Madame Stepniak was here yesterday.[2] I find in her a beauty infinitely lovelier than the beauty of the young women I know. She has lived, and suffered, and taken her place in the realities. Now, neither riches nor rank nor violence matter to her, she *knows* what life consists in, and she never fails her knowledge.

London is a bit chastened and helpless. There is no *real* intention of peace in the govt. Yet most people think that peace will come soon. The strikes in Germany are *really* serious. And Austria is really trying to separate herself. She wants to act independently of Germany. Russia also really wants peace, and Italy is very unsatisfied. So that, in spite of the English govt and the English higher military, peace will be thrust upon us, I believe, this summer.

I feel less hopeful about England. It seems as if there are bound to be labour insurrections, *purely selfish* on the part of labour, caring *not* for life, but only for labour. Which is wearying. It seems to me there is bound to be a smash-up. One can only stand far aside, and wait till there is a showing of a good spirit, a resurrection in the hearts of people. But they have the last stages of death to go through yet: and it will not be a lovely process.

Come and stay with us *as soon* as you feel able. I shall leave London on Tuesday: stay perhaps a few days in Berks: then home to Cornwall. I hope you will get stronger.

Warm regards to Willie and Enid.   D. H. Lawrence

---

[1] .John xiv. 27.
[2] Fanny Markovna Stepniak-Kravchinskaya (1855–1945), the widow of Serge Michaelovitch Kravchinsky (1852–95), a leading Russian revolutionary who wrote under the name of Stepniak. She was a close friend of Kot's.

1406. To S. S. Koteliansky, [26 April 1917]
Text: MS BL; Zytaruk 116.

Hermitage –
Thursday[1]

– My dear Kot

I got here all right last night: am feeling almost quite well. Tomorrow I am going back to Cornwall.

I shall think about the Russian question when I am at home. But for the time, I feel I can't bother about anything. It is spring, let us not worry at all about anything whatsoever.

I was very glad to stay with you. I feel that everything is working itself out, and we will all have a happy time, in the end. As for the others, vile ones, Campbells and Murrys etc, they are being carried their own separate way to their own separate end. It is as if the current of life was dividing now, and carrying some definitely one way, others definitely in a quite different direction. And the Murrys Campbells etc, the whole crew, are being borne off away from me, but you and I, we bob about tipsily like two vessels in the same stream. But we shall get our clear direction soon.

D. H. Lawrence

1407. To Lady Cynthia Asquith, [26 April 1917]
Text: MS UT; Huxley 405–6.

Hermitage – Berks.
Thursday.

My dear Lady Cynthia

I didn't ring you up, because on Sunday suddenly I collapsed with sickness and diarrhœa,[2] and was quite seedy. Then just as suddenly, on Tuesday, my soul inspired itself, and I got well. So yesterday I came on here. Tomorrow I am going back to Cornwall, thank God.

It was the evil influence of aggregate London made me ill: suddenly I start to be sick. It is all very vile.

It is much best for you to go down to Stanway.[3] The spring is here, the cuckoo is heard, primroses and daffodils are out in the woods, it is very lovely.

---

[1] As Letter 1408 makes clear, DHL arrived at Dollie Radford's Chapel Farm Cottage, Hermitage, on Wednesday 25 April. He wrote to Kot the next day.
[2] 'and diarrhœa' are crossed out in MS, probably by Huxley.
[3] Stanway House, Gloucestershire, where Lady Cynthia grew up. For a description see Asquith, *Diaries* xiv–xv. (She had probably told DHL of her intention to go to Stanway on 28 April; see *Diaries* 299.)

I feel that the buds as they unfold, and the primroses come out, are really stronger than all the armies and all the war. I feel as if the young grass growing would upset all the cannon on the face of the earth, and that man with his evil stupidity is after all nothing, the leaves just brush him aside. The principle of life is after all stronger than the principle of death, and I spit on your London and your government and your armies. Pah, what are they, Lloyd Georges and Haigs[1] and such-like canaille? Canaille, canaille, all the lot of them – also Balfour,[2] old poodle that he is.[3]

Then the son John. He is a direct outcome of repression and falsification of the living spirit, in many generations of Charterises and Asquiths.[4] He is possessed by an evil spirit, but it is a spirit that *you* have kept safely inside yourself, cynic and unbelieving. Now the spirit is one too strong for the race, and we find ourselves scotched. – But don't worry, life and the power of creation is stronger even than you. John will come all right. If ever there is an opportunity, I will help with him.

Come and see us whenever you are near enough, and feel like it. The state of your desperation is really a thing to be ashamed of. It all comes of submitting and acquiescing in things one *does not vitally believe in*. If you learned flatly to reject things which are false to you, you wouldn't sell yourself to such deadness. One should stick by ones own soul, and by nothing else. In one's soul, one knows the truth from the untruth, and life from death. And if one betrays one's own soul-knowledge, one is the worst of traitors. I am out of all patience with this submitting to the things that be, however foul they are, just because they happen to be. – But there will fall a big fire on the city before long, as on Sodom and Gomorrah,[5] and will burn us clean of a few F.E. Smiths etc,[6] and some of our own flunkeying to mere current baseness. – I feel angry with you, the way you have betrayed everything that is real, by admitting the superiority of that which is merely temporal and foul and external upon us. If all the aristocrats have sold the vital principle of life to the mere current of foul affairs, what good are the aristocrats? As for the people,

[1] Sir Douglas Haig (1861–1928), cr. 1st Earl Haig, 1919. He had been Commander-in-Chief of Allied Forces since 1915.

[2] Arthur James Balfour (1848–1930), cr. 1st Earl of Balfour, 1922, statesman and author. He was Prime Minister, 1902–5; at this time he was Foreign Secretary.

[3] Lady Cynthia recorded this paragraph – 'a wonderful passage' – in her diary; she added at the end: 'I like the poodle climax' (Asquith, *Diaries* 299).

[4] John suffered from autism.

[5] Cf. Genesis xix. 24.

[6] Frederick Elwin Smith (1872–1930), cr. 1st Earl of Birkenhead, 1922; now the Attorney-General. He was a personal friend of Lady Cynthia's. Cf. *Letters*, ii. 593.

they will serve to make a real bust-up, quite purposeless and aimless. But when the bust-up is made, and the place more or less destroyed, we can have a new start.

It is a very lovely day. Hope you are well.

D. H. Lawrence

1408. To Catherine Carswell, 28 April 1917
Text: MS YU; Postmark, St. Ives 28 AP 17; Carswell 86.

Zennor, St. Ives. Cornwall
Sat. 28 April 1917

My dear Catherine

I didn't come to see you again, because on the Sunday, after I saw you on the Friday, I collapsed with sickness and diarrhoea, and was quite laid up. That was at Kots. However, on Wednesday I managed to scramble out to Hermitage, to Dollie Radford's cottage, and was better. Last night I got back here: Frieda not at all well: Esther Andrews well.

You were very sad when I saw you: and there seemed nothing that could be said. Things must work themselves out. It is a great weariness. I felt, that, as far as peace work, or *any* work for betterment goes, it is useless. One can only gather the single flower of one's own intrinsic happiness, apart and separate. It is the only faithful fulfilment. I feel that people *choose* the war, somehow, even those who hate it, *choose* it, choose the state of war, and in their souls provoke more war, even in hating war. So the only thing that can be done is to leave them to it, and to bring forth the flower of one's own happiness, single and apart.

It is so lovely here, now, my seeds have come up, there is a strange joyfulness in the air. For those of us who can become single and alone, all will become perfectly right.

You were queer and sad as the train went off at Leicester Square Station. But don't be sad. In the innermost soul there is happiness, apart from everything.

Come and stay here if ever you can, and if you feel like it.

Frieda sends her love, Esther Andrews wishes to be remembered. I think Frieda has some inflammation of the bowels. I have sent for the doctor. It is rather a worry.

Write and let me know how you are.

With love   D. H. Lawrence

1409. To Dollie Radford, 28 April 1917
Text: MS UN; Nehls, i. 414–15.

Zennor, St. Ives, Cornwall.
28 April 1917

My dear Dollie

I got down here all right last evening: not too tired. But I find Frieda unwell: it seems to me she has a bit of inflammation of the bowels, colitis, or what not. I have written for the doctor. I hope she will soon be better.

It is wonderful weather, and in the very middle of one's heart, one is happy, apart from all the world of man. That is the only way: to turn to the essential world of the creative spirit, ignoring the chaos of humanity. Beyond man and all his works, is the primroses.

My white violets arrived so fresh and lovely, also Mrs Brown's crimson carnation.[1] I am going to set the roots. – *All* my seeds are up: the cress and mustard are *ready to cut*. I think it is wonderful.

I send you a couple of books, for the cottage: and you can keep them or give them to Maitland, as you like.

Send me the 'Reality of Peace' as soon as you can, will you? I want to get it ready for America. And tell me if you liked it.

I think your woods are so lovely, I shall never forget them, that first evening, when the primroses were glamorous lights on the dusk of the ground, and again, in the morning, when the tall larch-trees swung in imperceptible magic. One is really very happy, having all this.

I shall send you some furniture as soon as there is a sale. – Tell Margaret I will write to her.

Much love from us both   D. H. Lawrence

1410. To J. B. Pinker, [28? April 1917]
Text: MS Forster; Unpublished.

Zennor, St. Ives, Cornwall
Saturday[2]

My dear Pinker

Will you tell me if you sent any poems to Harrison – and what – or whether

---

[1] Dollie Radford's Chapel Farm Cottage was semi-detached; Mr and Mrs Brown, and their daughter Hilda, lived next door. See Nehls, i. 454–7.
[2] The date appears to fall shortly after that of Letter 1404: DHL, having arrived back in Cornwall, is repeating his offer to copy out poems for Austin Harrison.

I shall copy him some out now. Also if there is any news of Collins and publishing the poems.[1]

Yrs   D. H. Lawrence

1411. To S. S. Koteliansky, [1 May 1917]
Text: MS BL; cited in Gransden 27.

Zennor, St. Ives
Tuesday[2]

My dear Kot

I got your telegram yesterday about Gorki's paper. Write and tell me what it means exactly – I shall be only too glad to contribute anything I can.[3]

I feel that our chiefest hope for the future is Russia. When I think of the young new country there, I love it inordinately. It is the place of hope. We must go, sooner or a little later. But let us go gently. I feel a violent change would be the death of me. Toujours doucement,[4] as the nuns say. – I am working in the garden. – We will go to Russia. Send me a Berlitz grammar book, I will begin to learn the language – religiously. And when Farbman comes back, we will scheme – and perhaps you will come down here for a few weeks. Nuova speranza – la Russia.[5] – *Please send me a grammar book.*

Greet Mrs Farbman from me – *di cuore*.[6] I must learn her real name – Sonia – what else? I hate the word '*Mrs*' – and '*Mr*'.

It is most beautiful weather – and gardening makes me happy.

DHL

---

[1] Letter 1426 confirms that DHL is referring to the publishers, William Collins, Sons & Co., and not to Vere Collins of Oxford University Press.
[2] This letter clearly precedes that written to Kot on 11 May: in the latter he sends greetings to 'Sonia Issayevna' whereas here he specifically asks for her 'real name'. It must therefore be presumed that the envelope (postmarked 15 MY 17), attached to the MS in BL, belonged to a missing letter and not to this one.
[3] Maxim Gorky, pseudonym of Aleksey Peshkov (1868–1936), Russian novelist and playwright. The paper to which DHL refers, the daily, *Novaya Zhizn* ('New Life'), had been launched on 18 April 1917; Gorky was on the editorial board. His aim was to offer some protection to writers and intellectuals during the revolutionary turmoil.
[4] 'Always gently'.
[5] 'New hope – Russia'.
[6] 'from the bottom of my heart'.

1412. To John Middleton Murry, 5 May 1917
Text: MS NYPL; cited in John Middleton Murry, 'Reminiscences of D. H. Lawrence,
I–VII', *New Adelphi*, iii (June–August 1930 – March 1931), 200.

Zennor, St. Ives, Cornwall
5 May 1917

Yes, I did think you preferred not to answer my note. How rotten that nobody forwarded your letters.

There is no real *news*. Frieda had ptomaine poisoning, and has now progressed to *colitis*, and is quite seedy. The doctor makes her drink fermented milk – koumiss. I think she is rather better. – I had a little collapse in London: the foulness of the spirit of the place: but am better.

I have been gardening very hard: made a new garden just above the little one, and planted also a large corner of a potato field – not with potatoes, but carrots peas spinach etc. We are very quiet here – the Shorts have been away all the time.[1] Heseltine, however, has turned up at Tinners,[2] to my chagrin – and taken that 'Trewey Consolidated' bungalow, by the roadside, on the moors, on the way to Penzance. But I don't like him any more, it can't come back, the liking.

There is no change at the farm[3] – little domestic upheavals which are too long to write. Annie Thomas, the washerwoman, had a son of sixteen years, illegitimate son of Willie Berryman. This self same son went and fell off the cliffs on Sunday, getting gulls' eggs, and is quite lost.[4] – I was in Penzance yesterday: very hot and sunny. The primroses and blackthorn are out. All the Cornish farmers are filled with the sense of inevitable disaster: talk freely of the end of the world. – I give it all up. One can only stand far off, and watch – or not watch. Heaven knows what the end will be. At any rate, it is no use talking or saying anything at all.

Really, I give up feeling either love or hate – it seems to me a bit of kindness is worth all the love of mankind. – But I give it all up, it is beyond me.

If we are left alive, I think we shall all recover. It is just plain sink or swim.

D. H. Lawrence

[1] Captain John Tregerthen Short (1894–1930), formerly ship's captain and shipowner, and his wife Lucy owned the Higher Tregerthen cottage where the Lawrences had lived since 17 March 1916. See *Letters*, ii. 575.
[2] The Tinner's Arms, Zennor, where the Lawrences stayed 29 February–17 March 1916.
[3] i.e. the farm occupied by the Hocking family.
[4] William Berryman Thomas (aged 17) died in the way DHL describes, on 29 April; the 'Cornish Cliff Fatality' was reported, together with the inquest, in the *St Ives Times*, 11 May 1917.

1413. To Sallie Hopkin, 7 May 1917
Text: MS NCL; Postmark, St. Ives 7 MY [. . .]; Huxley 406–7.

Zennor, St. Ives, Cornwall.
Monday 7 May 1917

My dear Sallie

I should have written you before, but waited to see if Frieda would be well, so you could come at once and stay a few weeks. I got back here about ten days ago, after having collapsed in London with the same sickness and diarrhœa that Emily had in Ripley. And I find Frieda, having progressed from her ptomaine poisoning to colitis – some sort of inflammation in the bowels – laid up quite ill. Nor does she seem to get much better. The doctor sent her medicine, and ordered her koumiss – fermented milk – but it doesn't seem to do much good. Everything in the world is wrong just now. Myself, I still feel shaky.

But I suppose we shall all quite suddenly recover, and then we really want you to come and stay. I will write again in a few days, to say how Frieda is. I hope you yourself are keeping moderately well.

There was no hope of anything good, in London: everybody seemed weary, and helpless, drifting along in the worst kind of laissez aller. The government is quite quite incompetent, yet determined to prosecute the war indefinitely. The military authorities are in the filthiest state of bloodthirstiness, it is all a just hopeless mess. As for the people, nowhere do I find them wanting anything good. They want to go on from bad to worse. It is impossible to believe in any existing body, they are all part of the same evil game, labour, capital, aristocrat, they are the trunk, limbs, and head of one body of destructive evil. How can one say, the head is to blame, but the trunk is blameless? They are all one thing.

Yet I feel that peace, that is, the end of the war, will come quite soon. I feel that it is a question only of weeks, now. There will be an end soon, though how it is to come to pass, I don't know. Certainly not because *England* will bring it about.

Ah well, we can only hang on till there is an end. At any rate, I will let you know as soon as Frieda is well enough, and then I hope you will come down at once. The flowers are all out, but the earth is *very* dry. The bluebells won't be here for another fortnight. I hope you will catch them at their best.

With very warm regards to you all from us both.

D. H. Lawrence

1414. To S. S. Koteliansky, 11 May 1917
Text: MS BL; Postmark, St. Iv[es] 12 My [. . .]; cited in Gransden 26.

Zennor, St. Ives, Cornwall.
Friday 11 May 1917

My dear Kot

I read unfathomable depths of gloom in your last letter, and concluded, alas, that the wrong things were happening in Russia. Was that what cast you down so deep? Never mind, Russia is bound to run wrong at the first, but she will pull out all right. – As for me, I sincerely hope she will conclude a separate peace.[1] Anything to end the war. – But tell me what news there really is, from Petrograd.[2] – In the meantime, I keep my belief in Russia intact, until such time as I am forced to relinquish it: for it is the only country where I can plant my hopes. America is a stink-pot in my nostrils, after having been the land of the future for me.[3]

Frieda is a good deal better at last. She has been quite seedy. I am pretty well. I felt the effects of my London upset – still feel them a bit. – We are alone in Tregerthen. Esther Andrews has gone back to London. Philip Heseltine has taken a bungalow about two miles away, but we see little or nothing of him. I sit looking towards the North West, and wondering what next. This is the interregnum in my kingdom.

The weather is very hot and lovely. I go about in a silky shirt you gave me, and a pair of trousers, and nothing else. Today I have been cutting blackthorn and gorse to make a fence to keep the lambs out of my garden. I loathe lambs, those symbols of Christian meekness. They are the stupidest, most persistent, greediest little beasts in the whole animal kingdom. Really, I suspect Jesus of having had *very little* to do with sheep, that he could call himself the Lamb of God.[4] I would truly rather be the little pig of God, the little pigs are infinitely gayer and more delicate in soul. – My garden is very beautiful, in rows. But the filthy lambs have eaten off my broad beans. The salads are all grown, and the scarlet runners are just ready for the sprint.

Remember me in the nicest possible way to Sonia Issayevna, also to Gita.[5] Tell me what news there is. I cannot write or do anything, but wait for a new

---

[1]   There were signs that this might be done. The Council of Workmen's and Soldiers' Delegates had declared their peace proposals on 10 April and reiterated them on 4 May.
[2]   Petrograd (formerly St Petersburg and, in 1924, to become Leningrad) was in some turmoil: bread rationing had been introduced, and strikes were threatened (they occurred in early June 1917).
[3]   USA had declared war on Germany on 6 April 1917.
[4]   At no time is Christ recorded as referring to himself as 'the Lamb of God' though the term was often used of him (e.g. in Revelation), most memorably by John the Baptist (John i. 29).
[5]   The daughter ('Ghita') of Kot's landlord, Michael Farbman.

start from somewhere. – If only the war would end! But don't be downcast –
nothing in the outer world is worth being downcast about. – Remember me to
Madame Stepniak. – I have heard nothing of Campbell or Fottrell – – but tell
me about Biddie the child.[1]

affectionately   D. H. Lawrence

1415. To Catherine Carswell, 11 May 1917
Text: MS YU; Huxley 408.

Zennor, St. Ives, Cornwall.
11 May 1917

My dear Catherine

There isn't any news, either about the 'Reality of Peace' or anything else.
Only Esther Andrews has gone back to London, so I expect you will be seeing
her soon.

We are having very beautiful weather, so hot and bright. I have never seen
anything so beautiful as the gorse this year, and the blackthorn. The gorse
blazes in sheets of yellow fire, and the blackthorn is like white smoke, filling
the valley bed. Primroses and violets are full out, and the bluebells are just
coming. It is very magnificent and royal. – The sun is just sinking in a flood of
gold. One would not be astonished to see the Cherubim flashing their wings
and coming towards us, from the west. All the time, one seems to be expecting
an arrival from the beyond, from the heavenly world. The sense of something,
someone magnificent approaching, is so strong, it is a wonder one does not see
visions in the heavens.

I was glad to hear that the novel was going. When it is done, you will send it
me, won't you? It will be really something overcome, a phase surpassed in
you, when the book is finished.

I am not doing anything, except garden, just now. Yesterday I began to
type out the 'Peace' articles – I want another copy – and I was recasting the
second one. But suddenly I felt as if I was going dotty, straight out of my
mind, so I left off. One can only wait and let the crisis come and go.

My gardens are so lovely, everything growing in rows, and so fast – such
nice green rows of all kinds of young things. It looks like a triumph of life in
itself. But there needs rain, we are very dry on these slopes.

Frieda is much better in health these last two days. She sends her love. I
hope the eggs won't get broken. Send the box back, and you can have some

[1] Netty Fottrell, a beautiful young woman, had developed an infatuation for Campbell (Zytaruk 119); 'Biddie' was Campbell's youngest child, Brigid Columbine (1914–44), who had been ill.

more. I'm glad Don is all right. I'm sure the war will end soon. I wonder if I *am* a bit dotty.

D. H. Lawrence

No news yet of the desk. Please send me the bill for packing – you are poor now.

1416. To Sallie Hopkin, 15 May 1917
Text: MS NCL; Postmark, St. Ives 15 MY [. . .]; Unpublished.

Zennor, St. Ives, Cornwall
15 May 1917

My dear Sallie,

Frieda is really a good deal better now, and we are ready for you to come any day. There is a train leaves Derby at 9.5 in the morning, and gets to St. Ives at 7.30, or to Penzance 7.20: I think those are the correct times. It is quite an easy journey. – Derby to Bristol, where you will probably have to wait twenty minutes; Bristol to Plymouth, where I expect you must change, and then Plymouth to St. Ives, changing at St. Erth, which is only six miles from St. Ives, and where I would meet you.

I think you will find this right:

Nottingham	8.15
Derby	9.5
Bristol arr.	1.2
„ dep.	1.15
Plymouth (North Road)	4.4
„ „ dep.	4.11
St. Erth	7.6
St. Ives	7.32

There may be no change at Plymouth, only at Bristol. If you come on a Thursday, you might come to Penzance instead of St. Ives: it is only about 3 miles further to drive, and there is no change at St Erth.

Let me know in time what day you think of coming, and I will meet you either at St. Erth, or at Penzance. I hope you are really feeling better. The weather is very fine, I am sure you would be happy here.

You may have no change at Plymouth. And no doubt you can get the Bristol express at Trent,[1] at about 8.45. The journey is very long, I do hope you could stand it. But it is very simple.

Greetings to Enid and Willie   D. H. Lawrence

---

[1] A railway junction mid-way between Nottingham and Derby.

1417. To John Middleton Murry, 23 May 1917
Text: MS NYPL; cited in Murry, *New Adelphi*, 'Reminiscences', pp. 200, 202.

Zennor, St. Ives, Cornwall.
23 May 1917

I was wondering if you will be going to Mylor this summer.[1] If you are, you must come over and see us. What are your holidays? And what are you doing, save the office[2] and living in Redcliffe Rd. Tell me anything interesting, will you?

It is very quiet here: Frieda and I alone now. Frieda was very seedy with colitis, but is better: I am in bed for a few days, but reviving like a plant after rain. This spring has been very different from last: so dry and bright: no rain for weeks, always sunshine and dryness: no fog. Last Saturday is a year since the *Manu* came in.[3] Yet all is so different. The gorse is out in masses this year, and the blackthorn a great white smoke. I have three gardens: the little one, which is a gem: pansies and colombines and fuchsia as well as veg.: then the little field at the back of the red room, is half garden: broad beans, etc., spinach, many beautiful rows: then in the field below, peas beans etc. I have worked hard. We *should* have mounds of vegetables. But it has been so dry, the little seeds in the field are backward.

There is no writing and publishing news. Philosophy interests me most now – not novels or stories. I find people ultimately boring: and you can't have fiction without people. So fiction does not, at the bottom, interest me any more. I am weary of humanity and human things. One is happy in the thoughts only that transcend humanity.

I don't know how I am going to earn money now: but I can't care. I try to think of it, but can't. The Lord will have to provide.

Write and tell me your news, and what you are thinking and doing apart from office. I don't know why you have been in my mind lately.

You shouldn't say you love me. You disliked me intensely when you were here, and also at Mylor. – But why should we hate or love? We are two separate beings, representing what we represent separately. Yet even if we are opposites, even if at the root we are hostile – I don't say we are – there is no reason why we shouldn't meet somewhere.

D. H. Lawrence

---

[1] When Murry and Katherine Mansfield abandoned the Lawrences at Higher Tregerthen in June 1916 they moved to a cottage at Mylor near Falmouth. See *Letters*, ii 608 n. 1.
[2] Murry was working at the War Office. See *Letters*, ii. 647 n. 1.
[3] This Spanish ship was wrecked off St Ives on 20 May 1916. See *Letters*, ii. 606 n. 2.

Send me any catalogues of cheap books you might have, will you? I have read all my books here, being laid up awhile. – What are you doing with the Mylor house?

1418. To Cecil Gray, 31 May 1917
Text: MS StaU; cited in Mark Schorer, *London Magazine*, iii (February 1956), 57.

Zennor, St. Ives, Cornwall
31 May 1917

Dear Grey,[1]

I got your letter yesterday: have asked a farmer to enquire in Penzance if your goods have arrived: I shall know today. Then, if they are there, I will go over and see them sent to Bosigran.[2] I was in St. Ives yesterday, called in the second-hand dealers. There was a one-leaf mahogany table, seat six comfortably, for 10/-: do well for a smallish dining table. I'll get that if you think it big enough. Also a good strong round table – 4 ft. diam – would do for big room, not for kitchen – 7/6. But you might think it ugly. There was a pleasant dark 2-leaf square table, 12/6. – Of beds, there was only a 3 ft 6., spring and wool mattress all complete £2. But 3 ft. 6 is big for a single bed, and not quite big enough for a double. I got you one nice chair – 3/6. There is plenty of time: we can get the things bit by bit. Send me a post card *by return*, and say what you think you would like. I said I would say definitely on Saturday, what I would have. – What news of Heseltine?

Yours   D. H. Lawrence

I missed the post, so shall expect your reply Monday. Your goods have come to Penzance, and some of them at least will be carted over to Bosigran tomorrow – Friday.[3]

1419. To Ernest Collings, 31 May 1917
Text: MS UT; Unpublished.

Zennor, St. Ives, Cornwall.
31 May 1917

Dear Collings

Mitchell Kennerley, a New York publisher, published my first books:

[1] Cecil Gray (1895–1951), composer and music critic. He was a close friend and eventually the biographer of Philip Heseltine through whom he met DHL. For a fortnight in early December 1917 the Lawrences lived in his mother's flat in Earls Court Square. Gray was the music critic for *Nation and Athenæum* (1925–30) and the *Manchester Guardian* (1931–2). He published an autobiography, *Musical Chairs* (1948). (See *Times* 19 and 26 September 1951.)

[2] Gray had decided to take a house in Cornwall and chose to live at Bosigran Castle, Morvah, near Pendeen.

[3] There is further writing on the verso of DHL's letter, but it is not in his hand.

Trespasser and *Sons and Lovers*, *Love Poems*, I know; W. B. Huebsch has published *Prussian Officer*, *Twilight in Italy*, *Amores*: also in New York. He has got the *Rainbow* all ready, but daren't bring it out.[1] Kennerley published the *Widowing of Mrs Holroyd*, but has sold it to Little Brown and Co of Boston. That is all I know about my American publications.

There was no news of Palmer and the novel, any further, was there?[2] Thank you so much for writing me about it.

I am glad you are out of the army – though the city is dreary enough. I feel *very* weary and sick of the state of things. Do you think it is ever going to alter? Shall we ever have peace, and a modicum of decency in the world. Or shall we all just fizzle out whilst the war fizzles on and on?

I wish there was a little comfort somewhere – one stares into a ghastly blank, ahead. I feel that people have gone so wrong, they will just go on getting wronger, till a gradual collapse falls on humanity.

Not that I care about humanity. I wish it *was* wiped out, it is a foul verminous breed.

What are you doing, besides going back to the City?[3]

D. H. Lawrence

1420. To Cecil Gray, 9 June 1917
Text: MS StaU; cited in Schorer, *London Magazine*, iii. 58.

Zennor, St. Ives, Cornwall.
9 June 1917

Dear Grey,

Your things from London are all safely in Bosigran – taken over last Monday, a week ago. The workmen are in the house. I saw Thomas[4] in

---

[1] Benjamin W. Huebsch (1876–1964) was a New York publisher (*Letters*, ii. 426 n. 3). In fact he had published an expurgated edition of *The Rainbow* on 30 November 1915 (*Letters*, ii. 420 n. 2) and a more expensive version in 1916; DHL told Pinker of the extent of the expurgations on 18 December 1915 (*Letters*, ii. 480 and n. 3); and he presented a copy of that edition to the Hopkins in January 1916 (*Letters*, ii. 514). Therefore what DHL is referring to is Huebsch's reluctance to publicise the availability of the book; he allowed the novel to sell quietly, on demand.

[2] As subsequent letters show, Cecil Palmer appears to have shown a keen interest in being the publisher of *Women in Love*. Collings had acted as intermediary between DHL and the publisher, Palmer & Hayward. (In 1929 Palmer published Collings's *Modern European Art*.)

[3] After being discharged from the Artists' Rifles as unfit, on 27 April 1917, Collings was employed both by the Hand in Hand Insurance Co. and by the *Westminster Gazette*. In addition he covered all the main London art exhibitions and wrote of them in such periodicals as *Studio*, *Art News* and *New Age*. This writing of art criticism, together with his own painting, designing and exhibiting, was always his principal concern.

[4] Unidentified.

Penzance. He asked me about distemper colors for upstairs. I said, white would be all right for the small bedrooms, but for the bigger rooms, he must ask you. Let him know, will you. Also he doesn't want to take down the end bit of the passage partition. You remember it is like this.

[sketch][1]

He doesn't want to make the two end bedrooms depend on one another. You must decide this and write to him. He is very reluctant to have it down.

We are going over on Wednesday, to see him at the house. If you reply by return, I will tell him what you say. – I have got you 2 tables, 2 chairs, and a bed with *new* wool mattress. Other things I will get as they turn up. Have you any idea at all when you might be coming down.

I got papers to go up to be medically reexamined at Bodmin on the 23rd:[2] sent them back with a certificate from doctor here to say I was unfit.[3] Don't know what will happen.

The Starrs are at the bungalow all the time.[4] What news of H[eseltine]. If you have any idea of coming down soon to Bosigran, I will get more chairs and cooking utensils etc quickly – if not, I will wait till things turn up. There is a nice old small fender, 8/-. Do you want it? And a rather lovely long big old bench, £4.

[sketch]

– plain oak. But that no doubt is too dear.

D. H. Lawrence

1421. To Catherine Carswell, 10 June 1917
Text: MS YU; Postmark, Zennor 10 JUN 17; cited in Carswell 89.

Zennor, St. Ives, Cornwall
Sunday 10 June 1917

My dear Catherine

What are you doing now, and how are you going on? I heard from Esther Andrews that she had been to see you, but she didn't say much, except that you hardly think of the war. Which shows the war has passed out of you, which is a blessing. If only it would pass out of more people, be fulfilled and exhausted in them, so that they don't partake of it any more, *what* a blessing it

---

[1] A sketch of the layout of the bedrooms in Gray's house.
[2] DHL was first examined at Bodmin on 28–9 June 1916 (see *Letters*, ii. 618); he was being summoned for a second examination in accordance with the new Military Service Act (see Letter 1391 and n. 2).
[3] See Letter 1422.
[4] Meredith Starr and his bride (m. 1 March 1917), Lady Mary, née Grey (1881–1945), daughter of 8th Earl of Stamford; they were living at The Cottage, Treveal, St Ives. Starr later wrote *The Future of the Novel* (1921) in which DHL was quite ignored.

would be! Poor Esther Andrews is still too much in it, and too much out of it. The nervous fire of irritable opposition has not yet burnt itself out of her. I wish it had.

We are the same: have got Mrs Tarry here, from 2 Byron Villas.[1] She will only stay a week now. That is really a week too long, for me. But I grow philosophic to the minor evils. How *very* rich it is to be alone, without these other human beings. People are poverty and negation – to be alone is wealth uncountable. I shall be so glad when Frieda and I have got room again. What an obstruction one little being is.

What would be nice, would be if the few, very few people one liked could have the cottages round about, far enough away, and near enough. I wish you and Don had a cottage about 1½ miles from here.

How is he, and what is he doing? Is he in the fish's belly, or out of it?[2] This monstrous whale of a Mammon, it gulps 'em down. What a big belly the militarism has!

They sent me my papers to be medically re-examined. I got an 'unfit' note from a doctor here, and sent it back: don't know what the developments will be. War, and militarism, and the whole whale of authority, seems to have swum off from me and left me alone on a small peaceful island. But it is an island exposed to *bad* storms.

How is Joanna? She ought to be grown up enough to be coming out soon. Have you nearly done? – and are you thrilled?

I am doing philosophy only: very good, I think, but a slow job.[3] Still, I beat it out. I feel like the chorus in *Great Expectations*

> 'Beat it out, beat it out, old Clem
> With a clink for the stout, old Clem.'[4]

But I feel as if you weren't interested in philosophy just now. – No news of anything being published, from me. Novel and poems lie by.[5] What of Joanna?

I feel the war will end soon. But I have no plans. What are yours. I sit, a very tender nursling, on the knees of the Gods.

What about Greifenhagen?[6] One cannot go back to old loves: I think it is a mistake. Better have none.

---

[1] The Lawrences' neighbour when they lived at 1 Byron Villas in Hampstead, 4 August–21 December 1915.
[2] Cf. Jonah i. 17. (MS reads 'fishe's'.)
[3] See Letter 1435.
[4] Dickens, *Great Expectations* (1861), chap. XII. ('Old Clem' was regarded as 'a patron saint' by blacksmiths.)
[5] i.e. *Women in Love* and what would be *Look! We Have Come Through!*
[6] Catherine Carswell had been in love with Maurice Greiffenhagen (1862–1931), the painter whose *Idyll* is frequently a subject of comment in DHL's early letters. See *Letters*, i. 103, 234 n. 5; ii. 627.

The weather, and the country, is very lovely. I only want to be peaceful.
Do send the egg box, so I can let Esther Andrews have some eggs.

D. H. Lawrence

1422. To John Middleton Murry, 11 June 1917
Text: MS NYPL; Unpublished.

Zennor, St. Ives, Cornwall.

11 June 1917

Dear Jack,

The military are bothering me again. They called me up for re-examination on the 23rd. inst. I got a certif. from Dr. Rice here,[1] to say I was unfit, but they sent it back saying they could not accept it. I don't intend to go to Bodmin again if I can help it. I have a bad feeling about Bodmin. So I shall probably come up to London this week, and see a specialist, or see if I can do anything about being examined. It is a sickening wearying business, but I suppose one will pull through everything. If I come to London we must meet. I will let you know. I suppose you don't know anything I could do in the matter.

I shall probably stay with Dollie Radford – you can ring up there for me.

D. H. Lawrence

1423. To Lady Cynthia Asquith, 11 June 1917
Text: MS UT; Unpublished.

Zennor, St. Ives, Cornwall.

Monday 11 June 1917

I shall probably be in London again this week. If you are in town, you might send me a note, or ring up Dollie Radford, 32 Well Walk, Hampstead, on Thursday. Then we might arrange a meeting.

I am coming because of the military. They have called me to be re-examined at Bodmin on the 23rd. I got a certif from doctor here, saying I was unfit, but they returned it, saying they couldn't accept it. I think I shall come to see a specialist in London, and get another certif. I feel it would be fatal to go to Bodmin again: one is so spent with all this misery, it is always touch and go. And somehow, I *can't* go to Bodmin again, after that last year's experience.

[1] Dr John Dyer Rice (b. 1870?).

I expect I shall come up on Wednesday, or Thursday at latest. So let us meet if possible.

God, though, what a weariness this life is.

D. H. Lawrence

1424. To Cecil Gray, [14 June 1917]
Text: MS StaU; cited in Schorer, *London Magazine*, iii. 57–8.

Zennor, St. Ives, Cornwall
Thursday[1]

Dear Gray

I wonder how you have gone on today. I hope you have written to tell us. It is raining in wild torrents here, the air is full of dark omens, and surcharged with Starr's destructive electricity. I feel as if bad things were on the wing, a doom, huge and dark, flying towards us. But it isn't our doom – not of us individuals, but of the pernicious multitude. We must still be the chosen few, who smear our doorposts with hyssop and blood.[2] I feel as if bad things were abroad, and hide in my cottage as if it were a refuge.

I went to St. Ives this morning, and got you some things – 6 chairs, 3 small tables, 2 fenders, 2 kitchen chairs, mirror, chest of drawers, pillows, lamp, stair-rods etc. I have spent for you in all £10,,12,,6½: I hope you won't be disappointed that it is so much. Still a fair number of things remains to be got: but nothing expensive, save floor-covering – only saucepans, kettle, oil-stove, and small things that you can buy at odd times and carry home – no more cartage.

If it is fine tomorrow all the furniture will be taken to Bosigran. I hope the workmen will be there. We shall go over and see it installed. I think, with all this furniture, you will be able to move in immediately, and be quite decent.

I bought a big chest of drawers, 32/6. That is dearer than you want. Our chest is small, cost 17/6. Frieda would like the big one, so we will send you on this small one. That takes 15/- off your bill. So now, I have spent for you £9,,17,,6½. I have a crown in hand for you, and everything is paid, all carting and everything. – You would not have cared about the big chest of drawers, as it has a varnished surface, which is bad. – The other things I am sure you will like; and our chest is a nice one.

Of course the chief matter is the militarism: if that is all right, these things are pleasantly interesting, these furniture details. I shall be glad if you can

---

[1] It is assumed that this letter follows Gray's reply to Letter 1420.
[2] Cf. Exodus xii. 22.

come down again immediately, and we can install you. If you are detained, which God forbid, I will see the place as straight as possible.

Let me know how it is: also tell me about Heseltine. I am feeling kindly about him again.

Greetings from both   D. H. Lawrence

I have kept all the bills for you to see. Have you got the key to Bosigran? – Remember the revolution.

1425. To Dollie Radford, 20 June 1917
Text: MS UN; Postmark, St. Ives 20 JU 17; Nehls, i. 418–19.

Zennor, St. Ives, Cornwall.
20 June 1917

My dear Dollie

I got home safely, found Cornwall all wet with rain, grass long and green, and foxgloves very red. The lunch was most wonderful and complete: I almost wept over it, you had done it so nicely. But I ate it instead of weeping, and was thankful. Although I don't think I got much good out of the doctors, still something in the visit made me happier, a new, freer, happier feeling between us, growing like leaves. I felt there was something of new[1] being in us, which made us happier together. The old day is over. It is like the psalm: Say unto her that her warfare is accomplished, and that her iniquity is pardoned[2] – We will have a new day now.

Bodmin hardly troubles me at all. It will come out all right.

Frieda was so pleased with her little pot. She stands the glass of daisies and orchids inside it, and it looks so nice. She says she will write to you this afternoon, and sends warm love.

I was glad we went to the Davis':[3] it made an impression on me, I don't know quite what, but something I learned from seeing them. – I shall send the chairs this week, and the bellows. They are not very good. Perhaps I can get other things later.

I feel now we have only to wait for peace, and a new start in happiness: it is on the way.

With love from me   D. H. Lawrence

[1] new] a new
[2] Isaiah xl. 2 ['cry unto her . . . accomplished, that . . .'].
[3] Unidentified.

1426. To J. B. Pinker, 25 June 1917
Text: MS Forster; Moore 515–16.

Zennor, St. Ives, Cornwall.
25 June 1917.

My dear Pinker

I am afraid I am coming to the end of my resources. I don't like asking you for advances, when prospects are no brighter than mine at the moment. But you must tell me when you think I have had enough.

Is there any news of the poems? Have you tried them with anybody else, since the Collins people?[1] – I heard that a publisher called Cecil Palmer would very much like to see the novel, would like to publish it. So a mutual friend told me.[2] You do as you like about sending it him.

I have been having some bother about medical re-examination, but have got rejected again. I wouldn't do anything for the army, any way.

I think the tide of affairs is turning: soon we shall look up: soon I shall be moving forward. The old order is coming to an end. How do you feel about this?

Ezra Pound wants to publish that short story 'Once', which I believe we have lost between us.[3] It seems he has a copy of the MS. How and where he will bring it out I don't know, his letter is so foolish – as usual. Shall I let him do it?

Yrs   D. H. Lawrence

1427. To Edward Marsh, 26 June 1917
Text: MS NYPL; Huxley 411.

Zennor, St. Ives, Cornwall.
26 June 1917

Dear Eddie

Thank you very much for the cheque for £7.15. It is a nice sum, and *Georgian Poetry* is a good goose, her egg is much appreciated, and I hope she will live for ever.[4]

[1] See p. 121 and n. 1.   [2] The mutual friend was Ernest Collings.
[3] DHL's typist, Douglas Clayton, was asked on 25 July 1914 to send a typed copy of 'Once—!' to Pinker (*Letters*, ii. 201), and DHL enquired of Pinker about it on 17 November 1916 (Letter 1313). There had been several earlier attempts to publish it, in *Smart Set* and *English Review*, for example (*Letters*, ii. 82). In December 1913 Ezra Pound (1885–1972) had offered to try to place it with the *Egoist* with which he was closely associated (*Letters*, ii. 131–2), but to no avail. Indeed 'Once—!' remained unpublished until it was included in the posthumous collection, *Love Among the Haystacks* (1930).
[4] Contributors to the *Georgian Poetry* volumes each received a proportion of the royalties earned (see *Letters*, ii. 35, 39, 211, 565). Since DHL felt indebted to Marsh, he requested in November 1915 that he should not receive any further royalties (*Letters*, ii. 429); but Marsh persisted.

I got myself rejected again at Bodmin on Saturday: cursed the loathsome performance. As for flourishing, I should like to flourish a pistol under the nose of the fools that govern us. They make one spit with disgust. Only let the skies break, and we will flourish on top of the 'times', and the time-keepers and the time-servers.

Yrs   D. H. Lawrence

1428. To S. S. Koteliansky, 3 July 1917
Text: MS BL; Postmark, St. Ives 3 JY 17; Moore 516–17.

Zennor, St. Ives, Cornwall.
3 July 1917

My dear Kot,

I was glad to hear of Farbman's safe return, and to have hopeful news of Russia. Russia seems to me now the positive pole of the world's spiritual energy, and America the negative pole. But we shall see how things work out. Meanwhile everything looks dreary enough, and I do not feel at all happy. But ça passera.

How can I write for any Russian audience! – the contact is not established.[1] How can the current flow when there is no connection? As for England, it is quite hopeless.

I wrote and told Pinker I must soon have more money. He does not answer. Probably he does not want to advance any more. Tant pis pour lui[2] – I am just as well satisfied. My relations with that little parvenu snob of a procureur of books were always strained, best have them broken. – As for money, I have got plenty to go on with, and more will come.

There is no actual news at all. I feel you in a bad mood. I am not in a good one. I would read Béranger if I had got a copy of him.[3]

'O Richard, O mon roi
Tout le monde t'abandonne –'

though who Richard is, is a puzzle.[4]

Why humanity has hated Jews, I have come to the conclusion, is that the Jews have always taken religion – since the great days, that is – and used it for their own personal and private gratification, as if it were a thing administered

[1] See Letter 1411.
[2] 'So much the worse for him'.
[3] Pierre-Jean de Béranger (1780–1857), a prolific French author of light, popular verse.
[4] The lines are from the play, *Richard Coeur de Lion* (1784) by Michel-Jean Sedaine (1719–97) ['. . . roi/ L'univers t'abandonne']. They were made more famous by being set to music by André-Ernest-Modeste Grétry (1741–1813).

to their own importance and well-being and conceit. This is the slave trick of the Jews – they use the great religious consciousness as a trick of personal conceit. This is abominable. With them, the conscious ego is the absolute, and God is a name they flatter themselves with. – When they have learned again pure reverence to the Holy Spirit, then they will be free, and not slaves before men. Now, a Jew cringes before men, and takes God as a christian takes whiskey, for his own self-indulgence.

This is the conclusion to the last conversation – an exhortation to the unflinching adherence to the Spirit. I am preaching at you, Kot, because you are 'near the mark'. – But let us trust to the invisible spirit, not to ourselves and our own ridiculous universality of knowledge.

At any rate, don't be cross.

D. H. Lawrence

1429. To Ernest Collings, 9 July 1917
Text: MS UT; Unpublished.

Zennor, St. Ives, Cornwall
9 July 1917

Dear Collings

I got your letter this morning. I have written to Cecil Palmer,[1] telling him I will send him the MS. of the novel this week: I want just to look it through once more. Thanks *very much* for your help.

I thought those 'Reality of Peace' articles had had no effect whatsoever, so am very glad to hear of the Serbian.[2] What is he really like? – I am very chary, nowadays, of new people: one has been so badly let down, so often.

I wonder when I shall be next in London: I don't know. At any rate, I will certainly let you know when I do come up. We will see what Palmer decides. Tell me about Mitrinović: age, appearance, profession, history etc.

Yrs   D. H. Lawrence

---

[1] The letter is missing.
[2] Collings had been keenly interested in Serbian politics and culture for a considerable time; he had, for example, included 'Homage to Ivan Mĕstrović' in *Outlines*, the book of drawings he dedicated to DHL (see *Letters*, ii. 157–8); and a drawing with the same title had been exhibited at Burlington House in January 1917. (In 1919 the Serbian Crown Prince conferred on Collings the Order of St Sava in recognition of his service to the country.) The art of the sculptor Ivan Mĕstrović (1883–1962) was a subject of great importance also to the Serbian Dimitrije Mitrinović; he had lectured on it at the Leeds City Art Gallery (see *Yorkshire Post* and *Manchester Guardian*, 6 October 1915); and doubtless this shared interest cemented the friendship between him and Collings. Mitrinović and Mĕstrović, furthermore, were intimately involved in the political endeavours which eventually led to an independent Yugoslavia. This would give them and Collings's link with them additional significance for DHL.

What is the news of the air raid, which is officially concealed from us provincials?[1]

1430. To Cecil Gray, [11 July 1917]

Text: MS StaU; PC; Postmark, St. Ives 11 JY 17; Unpublished.

Tregerthen
– Wed.

I feel pledged to help with the hay while the weather lasts, so will postpone coming to Bosigran for a day or two. You and Krustchoff come over here[2] – come to tea and supper any day: and we will come out to you on Sunday, if that is all right for you.

D. H. Lawrence

1431. To Catherine Carswell, [20 July 1917]

Text: MS YU; PC; Postmark, St. Ives 20 JY 17; cited in Carswell, *Adelphi* 293.

Zennor
– Friday

Was glad to hear of you happily installed in Bournemouth[3] – no, am not particularly depressed – somewhat nauseated. – Thanks for address of Samuel George[4] – I shall write to him at once – he may be amusing, if no more. – I haven't got any news of any sort. There is to be the fourth 'Reality of Peace' in next month's *English Review* – really the seventh of the seven. I think one understands best without explanations. Aunt Barbara does not *want* to understand – her sort never does.[5] They want a lot of words to chew over: it all *means* nothing to them, but a certain mental conceit.

I too still believe the end of the war is not far off – but – what then?

D. H. Lawrence

---

[1] The *Times*, 9 July 1917, carried a full account of a heavy German air-raid on London on 7 July; 37 people were killed and 141 injured; and four (out of 20) German planes were destroyed.
[2] Boris de Croustchoff, Russian bibliographer, whom DHL knew through Philip Heseltine (*Letters*, ii. 448).
[3] They were at Bournemouth while Carswell was 'at a cadet school' (Carswell 88).
[4] Little can be established about Samuel George. He was a prolific author, publishing largely through the Power Book Co. (then at 52 High Holborn); he also edited a periodical entitled *Spiritual Power*.
[5] Barbara Low.

1432. To Eunice Tietjens, 21 July 1917
Text: TMSC NWU; Huxley 412–13.

Higher Tregerthen, Zennor, St. Ives, Cornwall.

21 July 1917

Dear Eunice Tietjens[1]

Your book of *Profiles from China* came today. I have just read it. At least it is actual, thank God, true as far as it goes. But an inward boredness with all the phenomena of humanity and the humanized cosmos, revealed flatly, is the best. Only the Proem smacks slightly of the Brummagem[2] quality of high faluten and priggish self-seriousness, which makes Yankee things so detestable. The rest is quite honest. The Americans usually take themselves and their twaddle au si grand serieux. I am really thankful to see a book that is flat and honest and bored and rather disgusted.

One thing – the truth of evolution is *not* true. There is no evolving, only unfolding. The lily is in the bit of dust which is its beginning, lily and nothing but lily: and the lily in blossom is a ne plus ultra: there is no evolving beyond. This is the greatest truth. A lily is a ne plus ultra: so also, a pure Chinaman: there is *no* evolving beyond, only a slipping back, or rather rotting back, through all the coloured phases of retrogression and corruption, back to nought. This is the real truth. Man was man in eternity, has been man since the beginnings of time, and is man in the resultant eternity, no evolution, only unfolding of what *is* man. And the same with the Chinaman: no evolution beyond the Chinaman, none, none, none. But, I don't pretend to define what *is* the Chinaman. (This in reference to your ricksha boy with the ears that suggest a horse's ears.)[3] There are animal *principles* in man, which totemism recognises, but these have nothing evolutionary.

But humanity is a bad egg: there is no more meat in it. As for republics, they are the imaginary chickens of an addled egg. Nothing will save us now: we must lapse sheer away from the extant world, reject it all, become indifferent, and listen beyond. It is no good balking at the given issues. The

---

[1] Eunice Strong Tietjens, née Hammond (1884–1944), American poet and novelist. She was a friend of Harriet Monroe and closely associated with *Poetry* of which she became advisory editor. (For her comments on poems DHL submitted for publication in *Poetry*, in 1914, see *Letters*, ii. 203 n. 4.) *Profiles from China: Sketches in Verse of People & Things Seen in the Interior* (Chicago, 1917) was her first major publication.

[2] i.e. worthless, showy. (The 'Proem' is Eunice Tietjens' poem 'The H⎯⎯⎯' to which DHL returns in Letter 1434.)

[3] DHL is alluding to 'Reflections in a Ricksha' in which the poet speaks of the rickshaw boy: 'What interests me chiefly is the back of his/ ears . . . I find them smaller than/ those of a horse, but undoubtedly near/ of kin' (ll. 21–6).

given issues are all old, old hat, bad egg. One must get beyond, and try for sheer understanding, inhuman.

I think the war will end soon: then I want to come to America, with my wife: not for the American people, not for any Uncle Sam, but for the strange salt which must be in the American soil, and the different ether which is in the sky, which may feed a new mind in one. I hope, then, that we may come to Chicago.

D. H. Lawrence

1433. To J. B. Pinker, 24 July 1917
Text: MS NYPL; Unpublished.

Zennor, St. Ives, Cornwall.
24 July 1917

Dear Pinker

I heard from a woman in Paris,[1] who is collecting material for the *Seven Arts* magazine, that New York periodical which published 'The Thimble'. She particularly wants fiction of mine, and seems very anxious to have some. The magazine does not pay very well, but is perfectly honest, and sound as far as it goes.

Will you send MS. either to her, or to the New York office: –

Miss Esther Andrews,
c/o American Express Co., Rue Scribe, Paris.

The woman is going back to New York *immediately*. I believe you have several stories that *The Seven Arts* would publish.

Yrs   D. H. Lawrence

1434. To Eunice Tietjens, 27 July 1917
Text: MS NL; cited in Harry T. Moore, ed., *A D. H. Lawrence Miscellany* (Carbondale, 1959), p. 342.

Zennor, St. Ives, Cornwall.
27 July 1917

Dear Miss Tietjens

This in answer to your letter received yesterday. There is all the difference in the world between *understanding* the extreme and awful workings of sex, or even fulfilling them, responsibly; and abnormal sex. Abnormal sex comes from the fulfilling of violent or extreme desires, *against the will*. It is not the

---

[1] See Letter 1435.

desires which are wrong, nor the fulfilment, *per se*; but the fixed will in ourselves, which asserts that these things *should not be*, that only a holy love should be. – You see it is impious for us to assert so flatly what *should be*, in face of what *is*. It is our responsibility to know how to accept and live through that which *is*. It is the labouring under the burden of self-repudiation and shame which makes abnormality. And repudiation and shame come from the false doctrines we hold. Desire is from the unknown which is the Creator and the Destroyer, beyond us, that which precedes us and brings us into being. Therefore Desire is holy, belonging to the mystic unknown, no matter *what* the desire. – Abnormality and insanity comes from the split in the self, the repudiation and the condemning of the desire, and the furtive fulfilment at the same time. This makes madness.

I dont want to abuse. Art itself doesn't interest me, only the spirit content. I hate Yankee 'art' because it contains the spirit of puerile self-magnification, the magnification of a second-hand self, affected and ape-like. – But in some Americans there is a sense of truth which is to be found in no European: and this is what matters. And I liked your book because of the spirit of responsible truth in it, the will-to-understand, cost what it might. Nothing matters but the sheer truth, and again, truth beyond truth. I believe in America there is the courage of ultimate truth – which in Europe there *is not* – But your Sandburgs and Untermeyers, even your Edgar Lee Masters or Robert Frosts – the vanity ticklers – no, they are not to be borne.[1] The mass of America is too too disgusting – But the remnant matters. And in Europe there is no remnant.

Remember me to Harriet Monroe –

D. H. Lawrence

When I [. . .] abuse the 'Hand' poem, it is because you do not feel so strongly about the boneless hand as you say.[2] You feel a real *mental* irritable curiosity, and a certain angry contempt, which is not quite contempt because you can't understand. But you should address the hand with irritable

---

[1] Carl Sandburg (1878–1967) had been encouraged by Harriet Monroe, and some of his poems were published by her in *Poetry*. He had also published *Chicago Poems* (1915) and was later to be well known as the biographer of Lincoln. Louis Untermeyer (1885–1977) was the contributing editor of *Seven Arts*; he published *Challenge* (1914), *These Times* (1917), etc. and edited anthologies. Edgar Lee Masters (1868–1950) had published a much-praised collection of poems, *Spoon River Anthology* (1915); DHL found it 'good, but too static . . . not really art' (*Letters*, ii. 503). Robert Frost (1874–1963), the distinguished American poet – later awarded the Pulitzer prize on three occasions – had lived in England 1912–15 and been considerably influenced by Brooke, Abercrombie, Gibson and Edward Thomas, all of whom were known to DHL.

[2] See Letter 1432 and n. 2. DHL is alluding to 'The Hand', ll. 10–12: 'It is supple and boneless as the hands/ wrought in pigment by a fashionable/ portrait painter.'

curiosity, rather than with false reverence and not quite genuine desire.

Persuade Harriet Monroe to publish a bit of my verse, so I can have a little money, will you. I enclose a sea poem – don't know if I sent it before.

I had better write her direct, and send her the poem – I won't enclose it.[1]

1435. To Waldo Frank, 27 July 1917
Text: MS UP; Moore 518–20.

Higher Tregerthen, Zennor, St. Ives, Cornwall.

27 July 1917

Dear Mr Frank[2]

Thank you for your letter. I wish you wrote a better hand, for I don't know how much I have invented out of your squiggles, which you never intended.

I heard from Esther Andrews from Paris, a day or two ago, asking for stories for the *Seven Arts*, on behalf of her friend Louise, who was collecting for your magazine, and was returning immediately to New York. I wrote at once to Pinker, my agent, – who is a rather tiresome tyrant to me, as far as America goes – I am afraid I am in his debt for money – bidding him send stories at once, either straight to you in New York, or to the Louise in Paris via Esther Andrews. – I hope you will get several MS.

You say you have published two of my stories. I only know of one 'The Thimble'.[3] I had a copy of *Seven Arts* containing this. –

About the *Rainbow*: it was all written before the war, though revised during Sept. and Oct. of 1914. I don't think the war had much to do with it – I don't think the war altered it, from its pre-war statement. I only clarified a little, in revision. I knew I was writing a destructive work, otherwise I couldn't have called it *The Rainbow* – in reference to the Flood. – And the book was written and named in Italy, by the Mediterranean, before there was any thought of war. – And I knew, as I revised the book, that it was a kind of working up to the dark sensual or Dionysic or Aphrodisic ecstasy, which does actually burst the world, burst the world-consciousness in every individual. – What I did through individuals, the world has done through the war. But alas, in the world of Europe I see no Rainbow. I believe the deluge of iron rain will

---

[1] The poem was probably 'The Sea'; see p. 115 n. 1.

[2] Waldo David Frank (1889–1967), American novelist and essayist. He was a founder and editor of *Seven Arts*. He published his first novel, *The Unwelcome Man*, in 1917.

[3] 'The Thimble' had appeared in *Seven Arts*, March 1917; the second story, 'The Mortal Coil' was published in the current issue of July 1917 (ii. 280–305). This story, considered by DHL one of his 'purest creations', had been refused by Austin Harrison for *English Review* in March 1917 (see *Letters*, ii. 669, 670 n. 2).

destroy the world here, utterly: no Ararat will rise above the subsiding iron waters.[1] There is a great *consummation* in death, or sensual ecstasy, as in the *Rainbow*. But there is also death which is the rushing of the Gadarene swine down the slope of extinction.[2] And this is the war in Europe. We have chosen our extinction in death, rather than our consummation. So be it: it is not my fault.

There is another novel, sequel to the *Rainbow*, called *Women in Love*. I don't know if Huebsch has got the MS. yet. I don't think anybody will publish this, either. This actually does contain the results in one's soul of the war: it is purely destructive, not like the *Rainbow*, destructive-consummating. It is very wonderful and terrifying, even to me who have written it. I dare hardly read it again. – I suppose, however, it will lie a long time without being printed – if ever it is printed.

You say you hope I shall come over to you, spiritually, well on the other side – What are you, spiritually? – Theosophist? – I am not a theosophist, though the esoteric doctrines are marvellously illuminating, historically. I hate the esoteric forms. Magic also has interested me a good deal. But it is all part of the past, and part of a past self in us: and it is no good going back, even to the wonderful things. They are ultimately vieux jeu.

I have just written a tiny book of philosophy – called philosophy because I don't know what else to call it.[3] It might be called mysticism or metaphysic, though unjustly. If ever it is published, I hope you will read it.

I think there ought to be some system of private publication and private circulation. I disbelieve *utterly* in the public, in humanity, in the mass. There should be again a body of esoteric doctrine, defended from the herd. The herd will destroy everything. Pure thought, pure understanding, this alone matters – the impure herd is a herd of Gadarene swine, rushing possessed to extinction. But oh, the sheer essence of man, the sheer supreme understanding, cannot we save this to mankind? We must. And it needs a detachment from the masses, it needs a body of pure thought, kept sacred and clean from the herd. It needs *this*, before ever there can be any new earth and new heaven. It needs the sanctity of a mystery, the mystery of the initiation into pure being. And this must needs be purely private, preserved inviolate.

I want to come to America, bodily, as soon as the war stops and the gates are opened. I believe America is the New World. Europe is a lost name, like

[1] Genesis viii. 4.
[2] Matthew viii. 28–32.
[3] The book was to be called 'At the Gates' (a title which may derive from the remark, '. . . and the gates are opened', later in this letter). Developed out of the 'Reality of Peace' articles, it never appeared.

Ninevah or Palenque.[1] There is no more Europe, only a mass of ruins from the past.

I shall come to America. I don't believe in Uncle Samdom, of course. But if the rainbow hangs in the heavens, it hangs over the western continent. I very very very much want to leave Europe, oh, to leave England for ever, and come over to America.

I hear Huebsch is a Jew. Are you a Jew also? The best of Jews is, that they *know* truth from untruth. The worst of them is, that they are rather slave-like, and that almost inevitably, in action, they betray the truth they know, and fawn to the powers that be. But they *know* the truth. Only they must cringe their legs and betray it. The material world dominates them with a base kind of fetish domination. Yet they *know* the truth all the while. Yet they cringe their buttocks to the fetish of Mammon, peeping over their shoulders to see if the truth is watching them, observing their betrayal. – I have got Jewish friends, whom I am on the point of forswearing for ever.

                                    tutti saluti buoni   D. H. Lawrence
Tell Huebsch, if he gets the MS of the new novel, *Women in Love*, that this MS. needs correcting from the English copy, and needs a tiny foreword, which this other has.[2]

1436. To J. B. Pinker, 28 July 1917
Text: MS Forster; cited in Carswell 85.

                                            Zennor, St. Ives, Cornwall
                                                      28 July 1917
Dear Pinker
    Thank you for sending the MS. to Miss Andrews.
    I shall reluctantly consider making any fair alterations in the poems, if you will say what the publishers want, and will send me the MS.
                                                    D. H. Lawrence
The thought of Chatto and Windus rather pleases me.[3] They seem such nice old-flavoured people. Not that I know anything of them today.

[1] Nineveh was an Assyrian city; Palenque a modern name for a Mayan city in Chiapas, Mexico.
[2] Neither the English nor the American edition of *Women in Love* was published with a foreword. A 'Foreword' was published independently in 1920; it had been designed for the American edition. (See Roberts A14.5.)
[3] Chatto & Windus were to publish *Look! We Have Come Through!*

1437. To J. B. Pinker, 3 August 1917
Text: MS Forster; Huxley 413–14.

Zennor, St. Ives, Cornwall.
3 Aug 1917

Dear Pinker

Your letter and the poems came today. Truly the ways and the taste of publishers is mysterious and beyond finding out.[1]

The only thing I feel strongly about is the 'Song of a Man who is Loved'. *Can* you or anybody tell me why they want it omitted? I'm sure Alice Meynell might print it without reproach.[2] I dont want to omit it. I send a copy of it. Please convince them they are absurd on this point.

---

[1] Partly through an allusion to Romans xi. 33 (A.V.), DHL is referring to a letter from Chatto & Windus to Pinker, 18 July 1917 (TMS Chatto & Windus). It read as follows:

CHATTO AND WINDUS, III ST MARTIN'S LANE, LONDON W.C.
July Eighteenth Nineteen Seventeen

Dear Mr. Pinker,

We have now been able to give very careful consideration to the volume of poems by Mr. D. H. Lawrence, entitled 'Look! We have Come Through', which you recently submitted to us. We appreciate to the full the quality of Mr. Lawrence's work, and it would give us great pleasure to be associated with the publication of this volume of poems. At the same time we consider that some justifiable exception might be taken to certain passages appearing in the MS. as it stands. It is not our desire to suggest an emasculated version of Mr. Lawrence's poems, but in view of the general character of the work, we feel that the number of passages referring to purely physical phenomena should be slightly reduced. We have accordingly prepared a short list of deletions which we regard as essential if we are to publish 'Look! We have Come Through'. If the author could see his way to acceptance of our proposed modifications, we should be glad to include the book among our Autumn publications; and in that event we would suggest as a preliminary basis of agreement the payment to Mr. Lawrence of a royalty of 15% on all English sales, with an advance of twenty guineas.

The list to which we have referred is as follows:

pp. 59–60 'Song of a Man who is loved'   Omit
63–65 'Meeting among the Mountains'   Omit
121   line 13 omission or modification
126   omission of lines 17–21
'Even then . . .
. . . they pretty!'" plus the words in last line 'for them'.
128   omission of line 9, 'plunging . . . obscenely'.

In addition we venture to question the good taste of the titles 'Candlemas' and 'Eve's Mass' as applied to poems of an amorous character.

We hope Mr. Lawrence may accept the above suggestions, as we have great admiration for the book and do not feel that its quality or its integrity would be in any way impaired by such a process of refinement as we have proposed.

Yours very faithfully,   Chatto & Windus

Jas. B. Pinker, Esq.

[2] Alice Meynell (1847–1922), poet and essayist, is cited as an example of a religious and somewhat ethereal writer free of the slightest suspicion of sensuality. (The Lawrences had

I will omit 'Meeting Among the Mountains', if they want it. But *do* ask them why they wish it. It has already been printed in the *English Review*, and in *Georgian Poetry*.[1] The *Georgian Poetry* public is a very big one, according to sales, and they are sure to be glad to come upon something they know already. – The lines I will alter, though for some of them it is a great pity, spoiling the clarity and precision of the expression. I will look after my bad taste in Eves Mass and Candlemas.[2] Strange are the ways of man, strangest of all, of publishers.

Do convince them that the 'Song of A man who is Loved' is beautiful, necessary, and innocuous as a sprig of mignonette. If they still persist, make them say *what* they object to. For I cannot believe that this poem shall be omitted.

Yrs   D. H. Lawrence

Do you think anybody would care to publish as a little book or pamphlet, the 'Reality of Peace', four numbers of which (out of Seven) came in the *English Review*.

– If Chattos leave out the 'Meeting Among the Mountains', I must leave out all reference to *Georgian Poetry*, which is a name which I am sure gives a good deal of sanction among a certain class.

P.P.S. I have already changed all the lines and the two titles. There remain only the two poems to be decided on. – 'Meeting –' I don't feel strongly about – but the other I do.

1438. To Catherine Carswell, 13 August 1917
Text: MS YU; Unpublished.

Zennor, St. Ives, Cornwall.
Monday 13 Aug 1917

My dear Catherine

How *very* abominable to have such a motor-accident![3] I always detested motor-cars and all that pertains to them. I hope you are really better. Don't ride again with your brother Gordon, or with anybody home from France.[4] They are an ill star.

stayed at Greatham on the Meynell estate 23 January–30 July 1915.) DHL omitted the poem from *Look! We Have Come Through!*

[1] *English Review*, xvi (February 1914), 306–7; *Georgian Poetry 1913–1915*, ed. E. Marsh (1915), pp. 154–5. DHL omitted the poem from *Look! We Have Come Through!*

[2] DHL changed the titles of these two poems to 'Birth Night' and 'Valentine's Night' respectively.

[3] Catherine Carswell recalled: 'I met with a slight motoring accident which kept me a fortnight in bed, and Lawrence wrote scolding and giving me good advice. Again he was full of suggestions for titles for my novel, which was only now nearing an end of its re-writing' (Carswell 88).

[4] George Gordon MacFarlane (1885–1949), Catherine's younger brother, studied as an

Frieda, who has been so exuberantly well for a month or two, is smitten low with neuritis in her leg: very bad pain. She has been in bed this last week, utterly crippled. But I must see that she gets well soon.

I am pretty well. There is talk of Chatto and Windus' publishing the *poems*. But they want me to leave out several things. One poem they want removed I want to keep. Pinker is negotiating. I will let you know what comes out. – I thought, when I had the MS., you were right about the 'Love Letter'.[1] I took it out. Chattos want the 'Song of a Man Who is Loved', and 'Meeting Among the Mountains' to be omitted. This is what I don't want. The other things they mention I don't mind.

Good news about Joanna. I shall be *very glad* to see the end. Let me know as soon as it is done. Alas for a title. I like Fear and Trembling very much, but it is *not* true of Joanna, and it tastes a little of Turgenev. Has anybody used 'Birds of Passage'. The word 'Passage' in this sense seems truer of your people. But Fear and Trembling is good – perhaps as good as you can get. It is only a bit – I don't know – too fixed. I like rather open phrases – 'They That Pass By.' – 'How Far Is It?'[2] 'Whither Do We Go?' 'Whence Come They, and Where Go They?' 'Whither Go They, and Whence Come They?' One gets impatient of the cliché label. Send me the MS. as soon as you can. – Constable rejected my poems, hence I despise him: I *believe* Pinker said he had sent them to Constable.[3]

I wrote to your mad publisher man, but never had an answer.[4] – My[5] novel is at the present with Cecil Palmer. – It would be folly, I think, to publish it in the ordinary way, so exposed.

I begin to wonder where I am, as in a dream.

Frieda sends her love, and is *very* sorry about the accursed motor car.

D. H. Lawrence

I only got your letter today, Monday – and it is dated 9th.[6]

---

architect and then served in the army. Later published a vivid war-novel, *The Natural Man* (1924) – pseudonym Patrick Miller – among other works. m. Nannie Niemeyer (d. 1942). (See *Times* obituary, 13 January 1949.)

[1] See Letter 1376 and n. 1.
[2] Is It?] Shall We Go?
[3] He had certainly offered the MS of *Amores* (1916), but Constable rejected it (*Letters*, ii. 535 n. 1).
[4] Possibly Samuel George (Letter 1431).
[5] My] The
[6] Catherine Carswell was convinced that the Lawrences were already suspected of pro-German sympathies, even of spying. 'By August [1917] Lawrence's letters were being held back and examined. I posted him one from Bournemouth on the 9th which did not reach him till the 13th. Nor was this a single occurrence' (Carswell 91).

1439. To J. B. Pinker, 14 August 1917
Text: MS UNYB; Unpublished.

Zennor, St. Ives, Cornwall.
14 Aug. 1917

My dear Pinker

I send you the MS. of the poems. I have taken out the two poems.
Publishers are fools, one wants to spit on them. – But it is not worth while
making a real breach.

I return you their letter.[1]

I have heard nothing from Cecil Palmer since the card to say they had
received MS. of novel. Soon I must wake him up.

Tell me whenever there is any news.

D. H. Lawrence

---

[1] Pinker had evidently conveyed to Chatto & Windus the sentiments expressed by DHL in
Letter 1437. The publishers replied to Pinker on 13 August 1917; their letter had presumably
reached him the same day; he sent it at once to DHL. It read (MS Chatto & Windus):

Dear Mr. Pinker,
  As you know, Mr. Spalding is away from town, but we have today received a letter from him
in which he gives his views on the question of retaining, in Mr. D. H. Lawrence's proposed
volume of poems, a set of verses which we had previously mentioned as non-admissable.
  Mr. Spalding fully appreciates the kindness with which Mr. Lawrence has met our other
suggestions for the omission of various poems. But he regrets that he does not feel disposed to
alter his opinion in regard to the 'Song of a man who is loved'.
  We believe that you are aware that the list of poems to be omitted, as given to you, by no
means represents the total of those which appeared to us and to our Readers to be questionable.
But it has never been our intention to emasculate the volume of all such poems. Only, in view of
past history, it has seemed desirable from the firm's standpoint, that the continuously sexual
tone of the volume should be modified. The list as first presented to you represents the
minimum of omissions which we believe could safely insure this result, and to that list we are
afraid that we must stand.
  We believe that on the whole our suggestions have been reasonable, and even if some of our
objections appear arbitrary in the Author's eyes, we trust that he will realize that the objections
are made less to certain of the poems as such, than with a view to insuring a wide and favourable
reception to the volume as a whole.
  We greatly hope that you may be able to inform us that we may add the book to our Autumn
list, so that we may put it in hand without delay for early publication.
                                                    Yours faithfully,   Chatto & Windus.
J. B. Pinker Esq.
Talbot House, Arundel St. Strand.

Percy Spalding (1854–1930) was a partner in Chatto & Windus, 1876–1926. (See *Times*
obituary, 19 August 1930.) The writer of the letter was Geoffrey Whitworth; he joined the firm
in 1905 and was Art Editor and reader. A letter from him to Spalding, also on 13 August 1917,
makes it clear that both men held identical views on the need to omit particular poems from
DHL's volume (MS Chatto & Windus).

1440. To Katherine Mansfield, [15? August 1917]
Text: The Letters of Katherine Mansfield, ed. John Middleton Murry (1928), i. 79.

[Zennor, St. Ives, Cornwall]
[15? August 1917][1]

[Katherine Mansfield records reading 'a long letter from Lawrence – He has begun to write to me again and quite in the old way – all about the leaves of the melon plant'] speckled like a newt ['and all about'] the social egg which must collapse into nothingness, into *non-being*.

1441. To J. B. Pinker, [21 August 1917]
Text: MS UNYB; Unpublished.

Zennor, St. Ives, Cornwall.
Tuesday

My dear Pinker

I send you copies of the two omitted poems, for you to insert in the American set.[2]

I heard from Cecil Palmer, who is returning the MS. of the novel. He says it is his only regret that he is not rich enough to publish it privately, for his pleasure. – I think the only thing at present would be to publish privately, – or else to leave it. – I was wondering about Blackwell of Oxford.[3] They are rich, and have an enormous clientèle, and I have some reputation in Oxford.

But we can see what the poems do.

D. H. Lawrence

1442. To Dr David Eder, [24 August 1917]
Text: J. B. Hobman, ed., *David Eder: Memoirs of a Modern Pioneer* (1945), p. 119.

Zennor, St. Ives, Cornwall.
Friday, 25th Aug., 1917.

Dear Eder,[4]

I was sorry you didn't come to Zennor – I have thought about you often

---

[1] Katherine Mansfield's own letter, from which the extract is taken, is dated 15 August 1917, but, immediately before her reference to DHL she indicates that 'a whole day has gone by' since she began. If, as seems highly likely, she had received DHL's letter in the interval, he probably wrote on 15 August.

[2] Huebsch published the first American issue of *Look! We Have Come Through!* in 1918; he published from sheets supplied by Chatto & Windus; consequently the two poems to which the English publishers objected (see Letter 1437) were not included by Huebsch.

[3] DHL's first publication with Basil Blackwell was his translation of Verga's *Little Novels of Sicily* (1925).

[4] See p. 42 n. 3.

since I saw you in London, and we could have talked and perhaps got somewhere – because life seemed at a crisis with you – as it is with me – and with most folks, probably. Barbara says you think of going to Palestine with the Jewish Contingent.[1] One must go somewhere, I suppose – it is abominable to keep still in nothingness. Yet it is no good running about either. One has got to live through, or die through, this crisis. Why do you go with the Jews? They will only be a mill-stone round your neck. Best cease to be a Jew, and let Jewry disappear – much best . . . Have you read Blavatsky's *Secret Doctrine?*[2] In many ways a bore, and not quite real. Yet one can glean a marvellous lot from it, enlarge the understanding immensely. Do you know the physical – physiological – interpretations of the esoteric doctrine? – the *chakras* and dualism in experience? The devils won't tell one anything, fully. Perhaps they don't understand themselves – the occultists – what they are talking about, or what their esotericism really means. But probably, in the physiological interpretation, they do – and won't tell. Yet one can gather enough. Did you get Pryce's *Apocalypse Unsealed*?[3]

    . . . I should like to talk to you also about the lunar myth – the lunar trinity – father – mother – son, with the son as consort of the mother, the *magna* Mater. It seems to me your whole psycho-analysis rests on this myth, and the physical application. And it seems to me this myth is the mill-stone of mill-stones round all our necks.

    I have written a little book of philosophy. Tell me if you would like to see it.

---

[1] The 'Jewish Contingent' was to become the Palestine Zionist Commission led by Dr Chaim Weizmann which went to Palestine to advise the military authorities administering the occupied territory. Eder was attracted by a proposal that he should join the Commission. He became political head of the Zionist Executive in Jerusalem, 1918–23. See *Letters*, ii. 258 n. 2.

[2] *The Secret Doctrine* (1888), by the renowned spiritualist and theosophist Helena Petrovna Blavatsky (1831–91), claims to incorporate the 'Book of Dzyau', a work supposed to expound the occult origins of the earth; the 'Book' has never been identified. (See also Letters 1661, 1988.)

[3] James Morgan Pryse, *The Apocalypse Unsealed* (1910). Pryse was a friend of Helena Blavatsky; he had introduced George Russell ('A.E.') and W. B. Yeats to magic and initiation rites. On the contribution of Blavatsky and Pryse to providing a background of ideas for DHL's views on apocalyptic writings, see *Apocalypse and the Writings on Revelation*, ed. Mara Kalnins (Cambridge, 1980), pp. 4–6. DHL had learned about 'chakras' from Pryse who believed that 'a latent power . . . could be liberated through the controlled awakening of the seven principal nerve centres or "chakras" along the spine' (Kalnins, p. 5).

1443. To Cecil Gray, [25 August 1917]
Text: MS StaU; PC; Schorer 58.

Tregerthen –
Sabato

E venuto il manoscritto del mio romanzo – se vuole leggerlo prima della partenza per Londra, venga trovarlo.

    Ho comminciato La Litteratura Americana – povero di me!

    La Frieda sta poco megliore. – Non dimenticare quelli libri promessi.

DHL

[The manuscript of my novel has come – if you want to read it before your departure for London, come and collect it.

    I have begun The American Literature – poor me!

    Frieda is a little bit better. – Don't forget those books you promised.

DHL]

1444. To Cecil Gray, [27 August 1917]
Text: MS StaU; Unpublished.

Tregerthen
Monday[1]

Dear Gray

    At last we are coming – unless you put us off on account of some other Russian,[2] as you did before. Frieda is a good deal better – will be *quite* able to get over on Wednesday – so expect us that day, in the afternoon. Let me know by return if you have enough blankets for us – I believe you have not sufficient for three beds. If not, we will bring a couple.

a rivederci   D. H. Lawrence

1445. To Cecil Palmer, 27 August 1917
Text: MS SIU; Unpublished.

Zennor, St. Ives, Cornwall.
27 Aug. 1917.

Dear Mr Palmer

    Thank you for the MS. of the novel, which I received safely on Saturday.

---

[1] Dated with reference to DHL's report on Frieda's health in Letters 1447 and 1449.
[2] Possibly Boris de Croustchoff: see Letter 1430.

I will send you on the MS. of 'At the Gates' in a little while.[1] I want to go through it again.

Do you publish a list of your publications? Would you send me one, if so. I should very much like to see what you are doing, and what books are going. I believe, myself, that there will arise a certain demand for sheer thought and truth, now, soon, almost immediately.

Yours Sincerely   D. H. Lawrence

1446. To J. B. Pinker, 27 August 1917
Text: MS Forster; Unpublished.

Zennor, St. Ives, Cornwall.
27 August 1917.

My dear Pinker

I send you here all the poems you ask for, including those deleted for Chatto.[2] Do you know what they intend to do with the book? Will they put it on the autumn list, as the man suggested?[3] – and what are the terms of the agreement? – What sort of book will they make of it? – and at what price will they sell it? – And these three poems, 'Rabbit Snared in the Night' etc, do you want them for an American periodical?[4]

I have got finished a little book of philosophy called 'At the Gates' – will make about 140 pp. I spoke to Cecil Palmer about it, and he said he would like to see it, with a view to publishing it in the spring. Shall I send it him, or would you rather see it first? I don't suppose publishers are dying to publish such a book, yet it just *might* be well received. Tell me what you think. Cecil Palmer seems rather nice. He is a friend of a friend of mine.[5]

Yrs   D. H. Lawrence

1447. To Catherine Carswell, [27 August 1917]
Text: MS YU; PC; Postmark, Zennor 28 AUG 17; cited in Carswell, *Adelphi* 392.

Zennor –
Monday

I should have written before, but lost your address. – So sorry you are laid up

[1] See p. 143 n. 3.
[2] See Letter 1437 and n. 1.
[3] See p. 148 n. 1.
[4] For 'Rabbit Snared in the Night' (formerly '. . . the Dark'), see Letter 1404 and n. 1. The other two poems are unidentified.
[5] See Letter 1426 and n. 2.

– why aren't you more careful. You know how much on the verge we all are, we can take few risks of that sort – at least, you can.

Frieda is a good deal better, though not by any means right. However, she comes downstairs about midday, and gets about a bit.

Never mind about Constable. I don't think he is up to much – too timid and niggardly. – When are you going to send me the last half of your book?

It pours with rain – wet as the bottom of the ocean.

DHL

Did I tell you we've got a piano – old, red silk front – five guineas – nice old musty twang with it.

1448. To Ernest Collings, 29 August 1917
Text: MS UT; Unpublished.

Zennor, St. Ives, Cornwall.
29 Aug 1917

Dear Collings

Never mind about the publishing of the novel. It is probably just as well that it should wait a while longer: and perhaps one day we can evolve some scheme of private publication. Heseltine's attempt fell through – but it was not made very seriously.[1] And now he is just military-dodging, I believe – don't know really what he is about.

Did I tell you Chatto and Windus are doing a vol. of my poems – whether they will get them out this autumn I can't say. – And perhaps Cecil Palmer will do something else of mine. I like the idea of him, somehow. He might do a little book of philosophy I have got. I shall send it on to him directly.

I hope things are all right with you.

D. H. Lawrence

1449. To Dollie Radford, 29 August 1917
Text: MS UN; Postmark, Zennor 30 AUG 17; Nehls, i. 419–20.

Zennor, St. Ives, Cornwall.
29 Aug. 1917

My dear Dollie

I have been intending for a long while to write to you – nothingness is the only reason why one doesn't. And there seems a blight of nothingness in the air.

---

[1] A reference to the abortive attempts made jointly by DHL and Heseltine to launch a private publishing venture, in February 1916, called 'The Rainbow Books and Music'. For the circular issued to potential subscribers see *Letters*, ii. 542n.

Frieda has been seedy: in bed with neuritis in her leg, for nearly a month. But now she is up again and about better. It is astonishing how these illnesses come and go, in meaningless visitings. We haven't had anybody to see us, not to stay – and nothing very nice has happened, at all. It is a bad time with everybody, I believe. But we shall get through with it.

It rains, and the corn is cut and can't be taken in, and is getting damaged: the rain has smashed my marvellous garden to bits, the rain and the masses of wind we have had. – My garden *was* so splendid, thirty nice marrows sprawling and rolling abroad under the leaves, festoons of beans and peas, and myriads of sweet-peas and nasturtiums climbing, to say nothing of endive and beet and spinach and kohl rabi and all the rest. – The little gourd plants I brought from Pinner are travelling post-haste, with little fruits, and on the speckled *melon* plant there is a big green melon, lovely. If there were sun, it would ripen. Alas, there is no sun, only wind and rain, mountainous seas, and wetness. The blackberries are ripe – big and fat and many – but no sugar. Categories of badness.

Chatto and Windus are going to publish a new book of poems of mine – but whether this autumn or not, I don't know. When it comes I will send it you, and I hope you may like it. What about Margaret's book? – has she got that ready yet?[1] She has never told me any more about it.

So Maitland is getting married![2] – I rather wish he wasn't – why, I don't know. Still, I suppose he knows best. – I must write to him pleasantly. Is it really the 9th. of next month?

There is a man here called Gray – has taken a house about four miles west, on the coast – young – musician: he comes fairly often. Then there is Meredith Starr, and his wife Lady Mary, the Earl of Stamford's daughter, and a half-caste, half negro. I don't like them very much. – Gray is nice. This is all our visitors. The Starrs have a cottage down at Treveal, where we went one evening, when you were here.

Oh, I *do* wish this tension would go out of the air, and leave us free to breathe and live. It is too ghastly that it continues so long.

Frieda sends her love: she is very glad to be able to get about again. Yes, I wish we could meet. But let there come a bit of inward sunshine and newness first. As we are, we can but keep isolated.

With love to you and Margaret   D. H. Lawrence

---

[1] Her next book was *Pomegranate Flower*, published in 1929.
[2] See Letter 1392 and n. 2.

1450. To J. B. Pinker, 30 August 1917
Text: TMSC Lazarus; Huxley 414.

Zennor, St. Ives, Cornwall.
30 Aug. 1917.

My dear Pinker,

I return Chattos agreement, signed and initialled. Don't you think we might have had 20% after the first 1000 or 2000? – I always have hopes of the future. And I wish you could bring them to give me twelve instead of six presentation copies.[1] Let me know when they fix the price, and the format.

I will send you on the MS. of 'At the Gates' in a day or two. On second thought, I send it at once. You will see it is based upon the more superficial 'Reality of Peace'. But *this* is pure metaphysics, especially later on: and perfectly sound metaphysic, that will stand all the attacks of technical philosophers. Bits of it that might be very unpopular, I might leave out.

I am doing, in the hopes of relieving my ominous financial prospects, a set of essays on 'The Transcendental Element in American Literature'.[2] You may marvel at such a subject, but it interests me. I was thinking of speaking to Amy Lowell about it. Her brother is Principal of Harvard,[3] and she can touch the pulse of the *Yale Review* and things like that. We might get the essays into a periodical here in England – seems my only hope – I won't and can't write *Strand* stories.

D. H. Lawrence

1451. To Amy Lowell, 30 August 1917
Text: MS HU; Damon 421–3.

Higher Tregerthen, Zennor, St. Ives, Cornwall.
30 Aug. 1917

My dear Amy

How are you, and what are you doing? It is ages since I have heard of or from you. How is your health, and what are you writing?

I am all right in health. Frieda has been laid low with neuritis in her leg: very bad for a month, but righting now. I think she'll soon be sound.

---

[1] Chatto & Windus had offered 15% on 'all English sales' (p. 145 n. 1). On the extra author's copies see p. 165 n. 1. The publishers signed and returned the agreement to Pinker on 4 September 1917 (TMS Chatto & Windus). At the same time Percy Spalding sent DHL's advance of 20 guineas even though it was not due until the day of publication. He also sought DHL's agreement to a publication price of 5/-.

[2] These were to be the essays entitled *Studies in Classic American Literature*, eight of which would be published in *English Review* between November 1918 and June 1919.

[3] Abbott Lawrence Lowell (1856–1943) was President of Harvard 1909–33.

Here the community seriously thinks of building an ark, for the cataclysmic deluge has certainly set in. It rains and rains, and it blows the sea up on to the land, in volleys and masses of wind. We are all being finely and subtly sea-pickled, sea-changed, sure enough, 'into something new and strange'.[1] I shouldn't be a bit surprised to find one morning that fine webs had grown between my toes, and that my legs were slippery with sea-weedy scales. I feel quite spray-blind, like any fish, and my brain is turning nacreous. I verily believe I am metamorphosed – feel as if I daren't look to see.

The corn is cut, and being washed back again to the bowels of the earth. I made a wonderful garden: but the pea-rows are already beaten and smashed and dissolved to nauseous glue, and the leaves are blown to bits from off the marrow vines, leaving the voluptuous smooth-skinned marrows naked like Virgins in the hands of the heathen. All's wrong with the world, in contradiction to Browning.[2] But I don't care – why should I!

Nobody will publish my novel *Women in Love* – my best bit of work. The publishers say 'it is too strong for an English public'. Poor darling English public, when will it go in for a little spiritual athletics. Are these Tommies, so tough and brown on the outside, are they really so pappy and unbaked inside, that they would faint and fall under a mere dose of *Women in Love*? – Let me mix my metaphors thoroughly, let me put gravy-salt into the pudding, and pour vanilla essence over the beef, for the world is mad, yet won't cry 'Willow, Willow,' and drown itself like Ophelia.[3]

Chatto and Windus are this autumn bringing out a new book of verse of mine *Look, We Have Come Through*. They are actually going to give me 20 guineas in advance of royalties. – I will send you a copy as soon as I can (not of the guineas). – This is a one bright beam in my publishing sky. – But I shall have to go and look for daylight with a lantern.

This is to say, with an eye to material things as well as spiritual: at last I am learning to squint: – I am doing a set of essays on 'The Transcendental Element in American (Classic) Literature.' It sounds very fine and large, but in reality is rather a thrilling blood-and-thunder, your-money-or-your-life kind of thing: hands-up, America! – No, but they are very keen essays in criticism – cut your fingers if you don't handle them carefully. – Are you going to help me to hold up the *Yale Review* or the *New Republic* or some such old fat coach, with this ten-barrelled pistol[4] of essays of mine, held right in the

---

[1] *The Tempest* I. ii. 398–9 ['. . . suffer a sea-change/ Into something rich and strange'].
[2] Robert Browning, 'Pippa Passes' (1841), i. 227–8 ['God's in his heaven –/ All's right with the world'].
[3] *Hamlet* IV. vii. 167–84. (See also *Othello* IV. iii. 41–8.)
[4] this . . . pistol] those . . . pistols

eye of America?[1] Answer me that, Donna Americana. Will you try to suborn for me the conductor of one of these coaches? – Never say nay. – Tis a chef-d'œuvre of soul-searching criticism. – Shall I inscribe it to you? Say the word!

> To
> Amy Lowell
> Who buttered my bread
> These few fair words.
> For[2] she can butter her own parsnips.
> Being well-to-do
> She gave to the thankless
> Because she thought it was worth it.

Frieda says you will be offended. Jamais de la vie![3] cry I. – But please yourself.

Ah me – it's a long way to Tipperary, if Tipperary means a place of peacefulness. – I shall come to America directly the war is over. No doubt you don't want me – but it will be one of the moments of my life when I can say 'Farewell and Adieu' to Europe; the 'It is finished' of my Golgotha.[4] As for Uncle Sam, I put my fingers to my nose, at him.

D. H. Lawrence

1452. To Lady Cynthia Asquith, 3 September 1917
Text: MS UT; Huxley 415–16.

Zennor, St. Ives, Cornwall.
3 Sept. 1917

After all, neither have you written to us. – There seems nothing but futility in writing, nowadays.

I guessed Herbert Asquith was all right, or we should have heard from one source or another: all right in health, I mean, nobody can be all right in mind, nowadays.

I am pretty well. Frieda has had bad neuritis in her leg: in bed a month with it, a complete cripple. Today she seems quite well again, good as ever.

For the rest, what is there to say? – I made wonderful gardens, where

---

[1] If Amy Lowell acceded to DHL's request, she was unsuccessful; the essays were not published in America.
[2] words./ For] words of appreciation/ Because
[3] 'Never! out of the question!'
[4] John xix. 17, 30.

things grew by magic: fat marrows, on plants that seemed as if they were going to roam till they encircled the earth; long, flat beans in festoons among red flowers, and a harvest of peas, myriads of rich full pods – and kohl rabi, and salsify, and scorzonera, and leeks, and spinach, – everything in the world, it seems. But we have had massive storms that have smashed my pea-rows back into the earth. Sic transit.

We have been very quiet. There are near some herb-eating occultists, a Meredith Starr and a Lady Mary ditto: she a half caste, daughter of Earl of Stamford. They fast, or eat nettles: they descend naked into old mine-shafts, and there meditate for hours and hours, upon their own transcendent infinitude: they descend on us like a swarm of locusts, and devour all the food on shelf or board: they even gave a concert, and made most dreadful fools of themselves, in St. Ives: violent correspondence in the *St. Ives Times*.[1] – I believe his mother is a Mrs Wauchope, has a house in Hyde Park. You might even know her.

At present I am writing essays on 'The Transcendent Element in Classic American Literature'. This is snuff to make Uncle Sam sneeze. But I severely hope to get a few dollars by it. My last shilling is singing 'Larboard Watch Ahoy!' to my last ha'penny, as usual. But I forget. Chatto and Windus are going to bring out a book of verse of mine this autumn, and I am to have 20 guineas in advance of royalties. A little seed, you see, out of Chattos' Lotus, scattered on my doorstep. Still I persevere with the American essays.

Frieda has discovered a genius in herself for making embroidered caps. If you sent her a band that just fits nicely round your head, she might make you one. These caps are her Wunderstück.[2]

I am busy in the harvest, binding corn. Heaven and earth have passed away,[3] apocalyptically I bind corn in the fields above the sea, and know the distance. There is no more England – only a beyond. As for me, I look round and cannot find myself, hereabouts. But I have a whereabouts, elsewhere. Où donc?

I hope the children are good and well.

Addio!   D. H. Lawrence

[1] Letters to the *St Ives Times*, 24 and 31 August 1917 make clear the intense irritation caused to local residents by the Starrs' 'buffoonery' at their concert in aid of the Red Cross on 22 August. Meredith Starr felt obliged first to apologise (24 August), and then with considerable pomposity to justify the buffoonery (31 August). In his second letter he names Aleister Crowley as 'by far the greatest living artist in England'; he also cites Augustus John, Jacob Epstein and 'D. H. Lawrence, the celebrated Author' as believing that 'ninety-nine percent of British art is worse than buffoonery'.

[2] 'supreme achievement'.

[3] Matthew xxiv. 35 ['. . . shall pass away'].

1453. To J. B. Pinker, 7 September 1917
Text: MS Forster; Unpublished.

Zennor, St. Ives, Cornwall.
7 Sept. 1917

My dear Pinker

The enclosed letter came today. – These people are rather cool. – I shan't answer them[1] – you will do that, won't you.

Ask[2] Harrison if he will give me the rest of the money he owes me – £15 in all – I shall be glad. It is low water again on my shores.

D. H. Lawrence

1454. To Catherine Carswell, [15 September 1917]
Text: MS YU; PC; Postmark, St. Ives 17 SP 17; Unpublished.

Zennor –
Saturday

Sorry things go badly – ma è lo stesso nel tutto il mondo: anche qui, pōcó da dire del buono.[3]

Esther Andrews still in Paris – *very depressed*: talks of going back to New York, but doesn't seem as if she can bring it off. She has no particular news – her address is c/o American Express Co. Rue Scribe, Paris. Write to her.

Frieda is, I think, quite better – touch wood! – How are you?

Here the autumn has come – the bracken is more dead than it was last year in November: many blackberries. – Ma siamo stanchi in corpo ed in anima.[4]

D. H. Lawrence

1455. To Waldo Frank, 15 September 1917
Text: MS UP; Moore 524–5.

Zennor, St. Ives, Cornwall.
15 Sept. 1917

Dear Mr Frank,

Your book came yesterday,[5] your letter today. Thank you very much for both. The former I have only looked at as yet – I will write about it later. The latter I have safely read.

[1] Unidentified.
[2] Ask] Tell
[3] 'it's the same throughout the world: here too, nothing good to say.'
[4] 'We are tired in body and soul.'
[5] Possibly a copy of Frank's novel, *The Unwelcome Man.*

I would come to America tomorrow, if they would let me. But they won't give passports. And my wife is German. I have tried once or twice to get a passport. – Perhaps in the winter I shall try again – when this National Service bubble is again burst.

It seems to me, the trouble with you Americans is that you have studied the European Word too much and your own word too little. As for us Europeans, I know our attitude 'those Americans are such *children*'. – But, since I have known some Americans pretty intimately, and since I have *really* read your literature, I am inclined to think 'those Americans are so *old*, they are the very painted vivacity of age'. – 'Pourrie avant d'être mûri' some Frenchman said seventy years ago,[1] about America – U.S.A., that is. – You *have been* perfectly articulate.

I am writing a set of essays on 'The Transcendental Element in Classic American Literature' – beginning with Crèvecœur. I hope America will publish it and read it and pay for it – for there is a damnable hard-uppedness over here, and damnable vacuums over there.

When you say 'Beresford' do you mean J.D.?[2] – He is sane enough, if you mean tolerant: awfully nice, and tolerant to the last degree. – But since I am not tolerant, and since I *loathe* humanity, and see the Spirit of Man a sort of aureoled cash-register, and am bored to death by humanism and the human-being altogether, I don't have much in common with J.D., much as I esteem him in one way. – No, what I should like would be another Deluge, so long as I could sit in the ark and float to the subsidence. –To me, the thought of the earth all *grass* and trees – grass, and no works-of-man *at all* – just a hare listening to the inaudible – that is Paradise. Do you think I imagine your Yankee-land Paradisal? – The last word of obscene rottenness contained within an entity of mechanical egoistic *will* – that is what Uncle Sam is to me. – But there is a quality in your sky, a salt in your earth, that will, without the agency of man, *destroy you all*, and procreate new beings – not men, in our sense of the word. – Oh, for a non-human race of man!

So Judas was a Super-Christian! And Jews are super-christian lovers of mankind! No doubt it is true. It makes me dislike Judas and Jews very much. – To learn plainly to hate mankind, to detest the spawning human-being, that is the only cleanliness now.

We shall disagree too much. – I believe in Paradise and Paradisal beings: but humanity, mankind – *crotte*![3] We shall disagree too much, from the root.

---

[1] 'Rotten before being ripe' (the author is unknown).
[2] John Davys Beresford (1873–1947), novelist and architect. See *Letters*, ii. 484 n. 2. He had lent DHL his house at St Merryn, near Padstow, Cornwall, from 30 December 1915 until 29 February 1916.
[3] 'dung'.

Better let it be an Ave atque Vale – jamque Vale.[1] – God, I *don't want* to be
sane, as men are counted sane. It all stinks.

D. H. Lawrence

What is a voodoo?

1456. To Catherine Carswell, [17? September 1917]
Text: MS YU; Unpublished.

[Frieda Lawrence begins]

[Zennor, St. Ives, Cornwall]
Monday

Dear Catherine,

Yes, do come; I have hoped before now, that you would. Your news made
me very glad for you – It will make you happy and I want it to be a little girl,
another little girl, it's time one was happy, one has been so terribly through
the mill – It's already a little wintry but there are still some blackberries – and
you might have some fine autumn days still – What *is* happening to Don?[2] It's
most mysterious. The people 'seem no longer to exsist any more for me', I am
not frightened of anything anymore, I *know* new things will be – I am sure and
damn the rest – So come and we'll have some peaceful days –

Yours with love   Frieda

[Lawrence begins]

If you can lay hold of the Eders or Aunt Barbara, you might tell them I
asked you to hand on to you the MS. of the Philosophy as soon as they have
done with it – if you want it.

What is this about Don?

DHL

1457. To J. B. Pinker, 22 September 1917
Text: MS Forster; Unpublished.

Zennor, St. Ives, Cornwall.
22 Sept. 1917

My dear Pinker

Thank you for the *English Review* money – £13-10-0, which I got today.[3]

---

[1] Catallus, *Carmina* ci. 10 ['ave atque vale']; Virgil, *Georgics* iv. 497 ['jamque vale']: 'Hail and
farewell – and now farewell'.

[2] Donald Carswell had been admitted to a military hospital (see p. 169 n. 1).

[3] See Letter 1453.

I am getting on with proofs of the poems, so expect the book wont be long.[1]
Did you venture to cajole or squeeze the extra six presentation copies out of
Chattos?

D. H. Lawrence

1458. To S. S. Koteliansky, 23 September 1917
Text: MS BL; Postmark, Zennor 25 SEP 17; cited in Gransden 27.

Zennor, St. Ives, Cornwall
23 Sept. 1917

My dear Kot

I was thinking about you several times these last few days. – You should
never mind my onslaughts: go on as if they hadn't taken place: why answer
them, they're no better for it.

Please unlearn all the social lessons. I have learnt to be unsocial entirely, a
single thing to myself. I hate being squashed into humanity, like a strawberry
boiled with all the other strawberries into jam. God above, leave me single and
separate and unthinkably distinguished from all the rest: let me be a paradisal
being, but *never* a human being: let it be true when I say 'homo sum, humani
omnis a me alienum puto'.[2] Henceforth I deal in single, sheer beings –
nothing human, only the star-singleness of paradisal souls.

This is the latest sort of swank: also true.

The summer has gone quickly. We have been all the time here. Frieda had
a bad attack of neuritis in her leg, in July. She is well again now. I am pretty
well. We have had nobody to see us since Esther Andrews was here in the
spring: that is, nobody to stay. There is a young fellow – Gray, once friend of

---

[1] DHL had evidently returned the first batch of proofs to Chatto & Windus, expressing his
displeasure at the setting of the 'Ballad of a Wilful Woman'. His letter is missing; the
publishers replied courteously on 19 September 1917 (MS Chatto & Windus):

Dear Sir
    We are much obliged to you for the letter which accompanies corrected proofs of pp 1–32 of
Look! We have come through. We are writing to the printers instructing them to do as you wish
regarding the 'Ballad of a Wilful Woman'. This involves over-running the whole volume; but
we appreciate the importance of this alteration. The printers, we think, should at least have
queried the style. Unfortunately at this time they are so short-handed, and in such confusion,
that they are tempted to be arbitrary in such things, and we have no real hope that they will
admit a fault.

Yours very truly   Chatto & Windus
D. H. Lawrence Esq
Zennor, St. Ives, Cornwall.

[2] Terence, *Heauton Timorumenos*, I. i. 25 ['. . . humani nil a me . . .']: 'I am a man, I count
everything [Terence: nothing] human indifferent to me'.

Heseltine, has taken a house about four miles further on, down the coast. He comes occasionally, occasionally we go to him. I like him. He is music. Then there is a rather dreadful Starr, with a Lady Mary Starr, half-caste she. We try to get out of seeing them. – Murry wrote me once or twice – but it fell off again. Katharine wrote once or twice – that too falls off again. The past is past. So little of it has survived into the present. – I am fond of the people at the farm.

I am finishing correcting proofs of a book of poems which Chatto and Windus are bringing out next month. I have written into its final form that philosophy which you once painfully and laboriously typed out, when we were in Bucks, and you were in the Bureau.[1] I always remember you said 'Yes, but you will write it again'. – I have written it four times since then. Now it is done: even it is in the hands of my friend Pinker. But I have no fear that anybody will publish it. – Now I am doing a set of Essays on The Mystic Import of American Literature. I hope the title doesn't seem ludicrous: perhaps I shall find a better. – These were begun in the hopes of making money: for money is a shy bird. – But I am afraid they have already passed beyond all price. It is a pity.

I think this is all the news, as news goes. We have had fine gardens full of vegetables: I have worked like a laborer through corn and hay harvest: corn yet remains to be carried in. There has been a curious subtle mystic invisibleness in the days, a beauty that is not in the eyes. – Mystically, the world does not exist to me any more: nor wars nor publishings nor Gertlers nor Ottolines: I have lost it all, somehow. There is another world of reality, actual and mystical at once, not the world of the Whole, but the world of the essential now, here, immediate, a strange actual hereabouts, and no before and after to strive with: not worth it.

I wonder when we shall see you again. Everything seems strange, as having passed beyond. – Remember me very kindly to Mrs Farbman and Gita, also to Mr Farbman. Where did they go to, for the seaside? – Frieda will write to you.

D. H. Lawrence

---

[1] DHL is clearly relating the evolution of 'At the Gates' to his 'Study of Thomas Hardy' which was written when the Lawrences were staying in a cottage at Bellingdon Lane, Chesham, Bucks (August 1914–January 1915) and typed by Kot (*Letters*, ii. 220; see also ii. 295 n. 1).

1459. Catherine Carswell, [26? September 1917]
Text: MS YU; Huxley 416–17.

Zennor, St. Ives, Cornwall
Wednesday[1]

My dear Catherine

Here are the two essays you asked for. I had forgotten all about them. I shall send them on to the *English Review*: no doubt Harrison will print them[2] – and it will mean a little money, which is the chief consideration now. Not that I am short, for the moment. But I believe the war is going to end soon, and I shall need some money then, if only for Frieda's going to see her people.

I am very glad you are feeling so well, and happy in the thought of a child. If you are happy in the anticipation, that is all that matters. There is no need to let a child make you less free – and it might make you much more so – sarà come sarà.[3]

I have done the proofs of the poems. Chattos are making quite a nice book of it. I suppose it will be out soon – next month. I am sorry they left out 'Song of a Man Who Is Loved'.[4] Fools. They do these things for sheer bullying. The other things I didn't mind so much.

I feel changes coming to pass in the world. I really think the war will end soon. Pah, *people* will be just the same. I hope to be able to go away afterwards.

The weather has been pretty bad. Do you remember how it rained when you were here this time last year! It has rained a good deal the same lately. – I wonder where you will go after Bournemouth. We might meet then, when you leave.

I told you I took out the 'Love Letter' from the poems.[5]

We've got an old piano – did I tell you that? – and some very fine Hebridean songs – marvellous. Gray lent them us.[6]

---

[1] Dated with respect to DHL's reference to Catherine Carswell's having stayed at Higher Tregerthen 'this time last year' (her visit began on 28 September 1916); she was also early in her pregnancy (cf. Letter 1456); and DHL's remarks about 'the two essays' and the proofs of *Look! We Have Come Through!* place this letter close to but before the one to Pinker which follows.

[2] The two essays were 'Love' and 'Life' (probably written in mid-1916). Harrison printed them in *English Review*, xxvi (January 1918), 29–35, and (February 1918), 122–6, respectively.

[3] 'it will be as it will be'.

[4] See Letter 1437 and n. 1.

[5] See Letter 1438.

[6] Catherine Carswell recalled: 'Through Cecil Gray, Lawrence had recently become acquainted with the researches of Mrs. Kennedy Fraser. And he had some Hebridean numbers which he howled in what he ingenuously supposed to be the Gaelic, at the same time endeavouring to imitate the noise made by a seal!' (Carswell 90–1). Marjorie Kennedy-Fraser (1857–1930) had published *Songs of the Hebrides* (with English and Gaelic texts), in 1909; it was reissued in 1917.

Frieda is well, so am I. There is not any news. – I will lend you more philosophy later.

D. H. Lawrence

1460. To J. B. Pinker, [3 October 1917]
Text: MS UT; Unpublished.

Zennor, St. Ives, Cornwall.
Wed.

My dear Pinker
    I send you a couple of essays – on 'Love' and 'Life', which I have just turned up. No doubt Harrison would publish them in the *English Review*, as they are quite magazinable. – And they might help to prepare the way for the philosophy. – All the proofs of poems are returned to Chattos. It will be a nice book – nice print and page, very. – They ought not to charge me anything for proof corrections – I made very little on my own account – the only two serious ones came from the printer's not having followed the MS. – So if I am charged, I shall be mad.[1]

D. H. Lawrence

[1] The justification for DHL's attitude is clear from a letter of 25 September 1917 in which the publishers wrote (MS Chatto & Windus):

Dear Sir
    The extraordinary omissions from 'Rabbit Snared in the Night' are quite certainly due to some mistake of the printers; and we are taking the matter up with them. We had wished, in order to save delay, to avoid sending you a revised proof, but with this second blunder in view we think it necessary to send you another proof of the whole book. No doubt you will be good enough to return it as soon as possible. The revise will not reach you for some days. We think 'The Ballad of a Wilful Woman' will be found to have been set right. We are very sorry that you should have been given so much trouble by the printers' carelessness.
                                                              Yours sincerely   Chatto & Windus
D. H. Lawrence
Higher Tregerthen, Zennor, St Ives, Cornwall

    A second letter, on 28 September 1917 (MS Chatto & Windus), informed DHL that one set of revised proofs had been dispatched to him; two sets had gone to Pinker 'to send to America'. The publishers added: 'Mr Pinker tells us that you wish the number of author's copies to be increased to twelve. We shall have much pleasure in forwarding them in due course.'

1461. To Wilbur Cross, 8 October 1917
Text: MS YU; Moore 526–7.

Higher Tregerthen, Zennor, St. Ives, Cornwall
8 Oct. 1917

Wilbur Cross Esq – *The Yale Review.*[1]

Dear Sir

I have got your letter through the *English Review*, but not, as yet, the copy of the *Yale Review* you speak of.[2] – God knows whether I shall find in my heart to write 40 or 50 MS. pages about contemporary English novelists; which I suppose means Wells Bennett Galsworthy Compton Mackenzie and Gilbert Cannan.[3] They all bore me, both in print and in the flesh. By this time, they are such vieux jeu that all the game's gone out of it. And why should I answer some preposterous American female with a tit for tat?

I see the *Yale Review* sometimes: 'Gusta de Wit' sent me a copy too,

---

[1] Wilbur Lucius Cross (1862–1948), editor of the *Yale Review*. He was also currently Dean of the Graduate School at Yale (1916–30) and became Sterling Professor of English, 1921–30. Later he served four terms as Governor of Connecticut, 1931–9. Author of *The Life and Times of Laurence Sterne* (1909), *The History of Henry Fielding* (1918), etc.

2 Cross had written as follows on 22 September 1917 (TCC YU):

Dear Sir: –
    Not having your address, I am writing you in care of The English Review. To the same address I am also sending you a copy of The Yale Review which contains an article on The Contemporary British novelist. You are, I see, treated very cavalierly by the woman who writes it.
    I wish that I could obtain from you an article on the contemporary British novelist from a different point of view. The articles in The Yale Review usually run from four thousand and five hundred to six thousand words, and the honorarium would be ten guineas. Will you not consider the proposal and write to me, giving me your address.

Believe me, Yours very truly

The article to which DHL was invited to react was entitled 'British Novelists, Ltd.' (*Yale Review*, 1917, pp. 161–85); its author, Katharine Fullerton Gerould (1879–1944), Reader in English at Bryn Mawr College, 1901–10, had published *Vain Oblations* (1914), *The Great Tradition* (1915), etc. Her main purpose in the article was to compare older novelists like Wells, Bennett and Galsworthy with younger such as Walpole, Beresford and Mackenzie, to the disadvantage of the latter. Mrs Gerould admitted and flippantly reiterated that she had read nothing by DHL.; she expected him to be no better than his disappointing contemporaries.

3 H. G. Wells had sunk in DHL's estimation: in 1909 DHL thought *Tono Bungay* a great book and urged Blanche Jennings to read it along with *Kipps* and *Love and Mr Lewisham* (*Letters*, i. 127), though even then he felt Wells lacked 'the subtle soul of sympathy of a true artist' (ibid., i. 119); but by March 1916 he believed that 'the old stars, Wells and Co., are setting' (ibid., ii. 560). Bennett had never stood so high in DHL's assessment: he hated the 'resignation' he sensed in *Anna of the Five Towns* (ibid., i. 459) and was disparaging about Bennett's novels constructed as 'copies of other novels' (ibid., ii. 479). John Galsworthy had been, so far, largely disregarded; as for Compton Mackenzie DHL felt (in December 1914) that 'the times are too serious to bother about his *Sinister Street* frippery' (ibid., ii. 240); and he had been scathing about Cannan's *Young Earnest* (ibid., ii. 284–5) and about *Mendel*.

containing her 'Hunter'.[1] It is a good stout periodical, and if you let me say what I liked, which you wouldn't, I should like to write for it. – I will see if I can get up any feeling about contemporary English novelists – I don't care a rush for any of them, save Thomas Hardy, and he's not contemporary, and the *early* Conrad,[2] which is also looming into distance.

D. H. Lawrence[3]

1462. To Cecil Gray, 12 October 1917
Text: StaU; Huxley 418.

Zennor, St. Ives, Cornwall.
12 Oct 1917

Great trouble in the land – police raiding the house this morning – searching for God knows what – and we must leave the area of Cornwall by *Monday*, and not enter any prohibited area. – Come and see us at once. – I have not the faintest idea what it is all about – Curse them all.[4]

D. H. Lawrence

---

[1] See Letter 1378 n. 2.

[2] Presumably DHL had in mind Joseph Conrad's novels such as *Almayer's Folly* (1895), *The Nigger of the 'Narcissus'* (1897), or *Lord Jim* (1900). He declared in 1912 that *Under Western Eyes* (1911) 'bored' him (*Letters*, i. 456).

[3] In reply to this letter Cross wrote:

October 24th, 1917.

D. H. Lawrence, Esq.,
    Higher Tregerthen, Zennor,
      St. Ives, Cornwall, England.

Dear Sir,
   I trust that you have received by this time the copy of The Yale Review. The author of the article on the British novelists in that number apparently classes you with the men whose work you really dislike, as if you were one of the company. I do not care for a reply to that clever female; but if you felt disposed to write of the present novelists in the light of Thomas Hardy, that would be first-rate. I should like about five thousand words. I doubt whether you would say in literary criticism anything that I would not publish. If you were writing a novel, that would be another question – not that I do not like to read you; but you might be too erotic for a staid quarterly. I can, however, take something hot in the way of criticism.

Very truly yours

[4] If, as is likely, DHL's letters were intercepted by security personnel, his writing to Gray would perhaps further arouse suspicions. A mere few days earlier Gray was himself fined £20 by local magistrates 'for permitting an unobscured light in [his] house which was visible from the sea' (*St. Ives Times*, 5 October 1917). Numerous complaints about his failure to observe regulations about lights were reported and the chairman of the Bench pointed out that Gray's house 'was so situated that the light would be a guide to hostile submarines'.

1463. To Lady Cynthia Asquith, 12 October 1917
Text: MS UT; Huxley 417.

Zennor, St. Ives, Cornwall
12 Oct. 1917

My dear Lady Cynthia

You asked me for a letter, then never answered it. – Now comes another nasty blow. The police have suddenly descended on the house, searched it, and delivered us a notice to leave the area of Cornwall by Monday next. So on Monday we shall be in London, staying, if possible c/o Mrs Radford, 32 Well Walk, Hampstead, N.W.

This bolt from the blue has fallen this morning: why, I know not, any more than you do. I cannot even conceive how I have incurred suspicion – have not the faintest notion. We are as innocent even of pacifist activities, let alone spying in any sort, as the rabbits of the field outside. – And we must leave Cornwall, and live in an unprohibited area, and report to the police. – It is *very* vile. – We have practically no money at all – I don't know what we shall do.

At any rate we shall be in London Monday evening. You can see us if you feel like it, during the week.

This order comes from W. Western, Major-General.[1] i/c Administration, Southern Command, Salisbury. – They have taken away some of my papers – I don't know what. It is all very sickening, and makes me very weary.

I hope things are all right with you.

D. H. Lawrence

1464. To J. B. Pinker, 12 October 1917
Text: MS Forster; Unpublished.

Zennor, St. Ives, Cornwall.
12 Oct. 1917

My dear Pinker

Sudden blow! we are served with notice to leave the area of Cornwall by Monday next, by the military. – It is a complete mystery to me – complete.

However, we shall have to move. We shall come to London – address for

---

[1] Major-General (Sir) William George Balfour Western (1861–1936); KCMG 1919. He had served in Egypt, India and South Africa before 1914; he was at Gallipoli and served at Mudros until appointed Major-General in charge of Administration, Southern Command in October 1916. (See *Times* obituary, 10 January 1936.)

the moment c/o Mrs Radford, 32 Well Walk, Hampstead, N.W.

I shall come and see you.

D. H. Lawrence

1465. To Catherine Carswell, 16 October 1917
Text: MS YU; cited in Carswell 92.

32 Well Walk, Hampstead, N W.
16 Oct. 1917

My dear Catherine

We are here with Dollie Radford – called to see you – found you gone to Edinburgh.[1] What is all your bother about? Why haven't you told us?

On us too the skies have suddenly fallen. – Last Friday, police raid and search the house, and we are ordered to leave Cornwall, to enter none of the areas in Class 2[2] – report ourselves to police etc. It is all a nasty blow, and I have no idea what it can be about, or how it has come to pass. It comes from the *military*, but they refuse to say one word as to why this extraordinary thing has taken place.

It is very foul – I hate London – God knows how it will all work out. But I am going to try hard to get back to Cornwall.

London seems in a bad state – everybody lost their souls – sickening.

Write and let us know about you.

We shall stay in London a bit – try and get a flat – perhaps Gray's mother would lend us one. She is in Edinburgh – lives at the Caledonian Hotel – has a nice little flat in Earl's Court. You might meet her – Mrs Gray.[3] They are rich. We of course are the fag end of poverty.

But send us your news – we have not heard from you at all lately.

Love from us   D. H. Lawrence

1466. To Cecil Gray, 17 October 1917
Text: MS StaU; Huxley 418–19.

32 Well Walk, Hampstead, N.W.
Wed. 17 Oct. 1917

Caro mio Grigio,

Got your card this morning – shall be thankful if we hear from your mother

[1] 'I had gone to Edinburgh where Donald was ill in a military hospital' (Carswell 93).
[2] The order (made under Section 14B of the Defence of the Realm regulations) prohibited the Lawrences from entering any coastal region or major ports.
[3] Catherine Carswell did meet her and arranged with Mrs Gray for the Lawrences to occupy her flat at 13B Earls Court Square at the end of November (Carswell 93).

and can move in to the flat on Friday: for it is prison and misery to be in other people's houses. Failing the flat, Hilda Aldington offers us her room 44 Mecklenburgh Square, so we shall go there.

London is not to be thought of. – We reported to police here – they had heard nothing about us, and were not in the least interested – couldn't quite see why we report at all. It is evident they work none too smoothly with the military. – Saw Cynthia Asquith last night – she will do what she can for us, she says.[1]

But oh, the sickness that is in my belly. London is really very bad: gone mad, in fact. It thinks and breathes and lives air-raids, nothing else. People are not people any more: they are factors, really ghastly, like Lemures, evil spirits of the dead. What shall we do, how shall we get out of this Inferno? 'Pray not to die on the brink of so much horror', to parody myself.[2]

I hope, if we have to stay in town, you will come up before long, to be a strength and a stay for us. One grasps for support.

> 'To every brave cometh test of fire
> Blacker fate to be left behind –'

you know your Diarmad's Lay, or whatever it is.[3] – It's like that – only should be 'cometh test of mud'. It is like being slowly suffocated in mud.

Nevertheless, we will come out somehow. But I have never known my heart so pressed with weight of mud.

Write and let us know everything. Frieda sends her love.

D. H. Lawrence

1467. To Enid Hopkin, [19 October 1917]
Text: MS UCLA; Unpublished.

32 Well Walk, Hampstead, N.W.
Friday

Dear Enid

Frieda's cold is keeping her in bed a day or two, I'm afraid. She is fast abed

---

[1] Lady Cynthia lamented in her diary that DHL was poor, that his health would be adversely affected by London, and then added: 'People should be either left in peace *or* interned at the country's expense. I promised to do what I could in the matter, but doubt whether it will be much – after all, the woman *is* a German and [the banning order] doesn't seem unreasonable' (Asquith, *Diaries* 356).

[2] In MS the penultimate line of DHL's poem 'Craving for Spring' (published in *Look! We Have Come Through!*) read: 'Ah, do not let me die on the brink of so much hope!'; the final three words were changed in proof to 'such anticipation' (*The Complete Poems of D. H. Lawrence*, ed. Vivian de Sola Pinto and Warren Roberts, 1964, p. 1012).

[3] The lines are from 'The Lay of Diarmad' in *Songs of the Hebrides*, ed. Kennedy-Fraser, p. 113 ['To each brave . . .']. (The love story of Diarmad and Grainne corresponds to that of Lancelot and Guinevere.) Cf. Letter 1459 and n. 6.

now. Also Dollie is very seedy and weak. So we shall have to put off tomorrow. Oh, if only it was a sound free world – not just one huge mess.

I'll write you again in a day or two. Love to your mother.

D. H. Lawrence

1468. To Cecil Gray, [19 October 1917]
Text: MS StaU; PC; Postmark, Hampstead 19 OCT 17; cited in Moore, *Poste Restante* 47.

Hampstead –
Friday

No news from Edinburgh as yet. Unless we hear tomorrow, we shall move in to 44 Mecklenburgh Square, W.C. – that will be the address after today, failing a letter about the flat tomorrow.

D. H. Lawrence

1469. To J. B. Pinker, 22 October 1917
Text: MS Forster; Unpublished.

44 Mecklenburgh Square. W.C.
22 Oct. 1917

Dear Pinker

Did you get my letter, telling you how we were kicked out of Cornwall? We are fixed up here for the present, but I hope to go back soon.

Let me know when you are in, and I will come and see you.

D. H. Lawrence

1470. To Catherine Carswell, [22 October 1917]
Text: MS YU; cited in Moore, *Intelligent Heart* 236.

44 Mecklenburgh Square, London, W.C.
Monday

My dear Catherine

Hilda Aldington has lent us her room here for the time – a very nice room. So as far as housing goes, we are safe and sound for the moment Many thanks for going to Mrs Gray for me.

I have got your MS safe, and am starting to read it today.[1] We've been too much hustled about before. I will write you all about it in a day or two – and shall I send you back the MS to Edinburgh?

[1] The MS of the novel still called 'Joanna' (eventually *Open the Door!*).

I know nothing further about my 'case', so far, but Cynthia Asquith is making enquiries, and I hope to get it settled. I want to go back to Cornwall before Christmas. I want to very much, though I am content to stay in London for a few weeks.

When shall you be back? – And how is Don? What a blessing it would be if he could be free. And what a weariness things are, as it is! – I get very tired.

Love from both   D. H. Lawrence

1471. To Cecil Gray, [23 October 1917]
Text: MS StaU; PC; Postmark, London 23 OCT 17; Unpublished.

44 Mecklenburgh Sq. WC
Tuesday

Your letter was forwarded.

The 'Americans' are at a standstill.[1]

London is very bad.

I know no more now, about a return, that I did a week ago. – But I *will* return. Before Christmas I will return.

Don't send anything of ours as yet.

I don't want to see Crustchoff.[2]

We shall stay in London for the time being.

Life is difficult, but there is not, alas, any *vital* difference between here and Zennor. Perhaps, innerly, it is even a little easier here – less stressed.

I will let you know about the poems when I hear from Chatto.[3]

DHL

1472. To J. B. Pinker, [25 October 1917]
Text: MS Forster; Unpublished.

44 Mecklenburgh Square, W.C.
Thursday

My dear Pinker

I should have come round to Arundel St. today, but London as usual has

---

[1] Most likely a reference to the essays which formed *Studies in Classic American Literature*.
[2] See p. 138 n. 2.
[3] A letter from Chatto & Windus to DHL., 23 October 1917 (MS Chatto & Windus) makes it clear that he had written to them giving his new address. His letter is missing. He had obviously taken the opportunity to enquire about the publication-date for *Look! We Have Come Through!* The publishers assured him that 'if the printers keep their promise' the date would be 'about November 15'.

given me a cold in my throat and chest, which keeps me indoors for the moment. Perhaps next week I can see you – though I have no news about anything.

> Yrs   D. H. Lawrence

1473. To Catherine Carswell, [27 October 1917]
Text: MS YU; Postmark, London OCT 27 17; cited in Carswell, *Adelphi* 167.

> 44 Mecklenburgh Square – W.C.1.
> Saturday

My dear Catherine

I have just finished the novel. Yes, I think it is very good. The part re-written is very much improved. – But it shakes me badly – with a kind of nerve-racking pain. Of course the one character you have not really drawn – not conceived even – is Lawrence Urquhart. You haven't got it in. It wasn't to be got in, in this book. The book ends strictly, with Louis and Aunt Perdy. Lawrence, in this end, is ex machina.[1] But the book is good – and a complete whole. It only doesn't really state the other problem – the problem of what Urquhart really means to Joanna. But that is a dark problem, not to be written now. We will talk some things when we meet.

There is no news of my affairs. We live quietly here. I am kept indoors for the time being by a bad cold – Frieda also has a cold. It is London. I wish we could soon go[2] back to Cornwall. But I can't get any news of any sort.

We have got a much more definite plan of going away. There will be Frieda and I, and Eder and Mrs Eder, and William Henry and Gray, and probably Hilda Aldington and maybe Kot and Dorothy Yorke.[3] We shall go to the east slope of the Andes, back of Paraguay or Colombia. Eder knows the country *well*. Gray can find £1000. The war will end this winter. In that case we set off in the spring – say March. How do you feel? – what about your coming with Don? – how do you feel? The coming of a baby is a complication.

---

[1] Joanna's Aunt Perdy has ceased to be a significant character long before the end of the novel and her final appearance could have been omitted without loss. Louis Pender, a painter, betrays Joanna's intense love for him and fades away as a central figure. Lawrence Urquhart, who is briefly engaged to Joanna, is rejected by her because of her passion for Pender; his final reunion with Joanna is contrived but not altogether surprising.

[2] go] come

[3] Dorothy Yorke (b. 1892), generally known as 'Arabella', was an American who had lived for several years in England and Europe; she too had a flat at 44 Mecklenburgh Square. She had had an affair with John Cournos (who presents her as Winifred in his novel, *Miranda Masters*, 1926); she had just begun a long relationship with Richard Aldington. DHL presents her as Josephine Ford in *Aaron's Rod* (1922).

But this plan at last *will come off.* We shall go. And we shall be happy. – What about you and Don?

When shall you be in town. I fully hope to go back to Cornwall in a week or two. We ought to have a talk soon. I feel the crisis and the end is very near – we are breaking free – at last our plan materialises, really – we shall sail away to our Island – at present in the Andes – before long.

Let us know about you and Don, how you are and what you do, and what prospects there are.

With love from both of us   D. H. Lawrence

Call the book after the poem 'Frost Flowers'.[1]

1474. To Cecil Gray, [29 October 1917]
Text: MS StaU; Huxley 421–2.

44 Mecklenburgh Square. W.C.1
Monday

We are a *little* nearer to definiteness, but not much. These govt. people are the devil, with their importance and their 'expediency' and their tyranny. But I believe we shall get back to Zennor next month.

I am not anxious to come back just now. One seems to be, in some queer way, vitally active here. And then people, one or two, seem to give a strange new response. – The Andes become real and near. Dr Eder will come – something *right* in him. And he knows all that – Brazil Paraguay Colombia. He has relatives who have big estates in Colombia. We can get as far as these estates – rest there – then move on to find our own place. The Eder plantations are in the Cauca Valley, Colombia – towards the old Spanish town of Popayan, which is inhabited now only by Indians. – I am convinced the war will end this winter. – Italy France and Russia will make it be so. In the spring we will sail off.

I hope this appeals to you as much as it does to me. I have been expecting to hear from you. You are so queer and evanescent, one feels one loses you a bit.

London is better – since there are no air-raids, they are getting over their insanity. It seems to be going to pieces. It seems to be going all to pieces – everybody on the verge of disappearance from any stable reality whatsoever. – But I don't do any work – none at all – only read and see people. Yet in some queer way I feel we are getting along – by we I mean Frieda and you and me and William Henry. – I should like you to meet one or two people. – Do write

[1] See p. 115 n. 1.

and say how you are feeling – if you really feel like the Andes. It has become so concrete and real, the Andes plan, it seems to occupy my heart. I shall be bitterly disappointed if it doesn't mean much to you.

I wonder when you will come up. I feel we shall be here for a week or two more. – The world feels as if *anything* might happen at any moment. – And somehow I don't want to be in Cornwall for the present.

Chattos said November 14 was fixed for publication of poems.

Excuse this incoherent letter – I am keeping up a running conversation meanwhile.

Why dont you write?

Love from both   D. H. Lawrence

1475. To Montague Shearman, [29 October 1917]
Text: MS UT; Huxley 419–20.

44 Mecklenburgh Square – W.C.1.
Monday

Dear Mr Shearman.

We shall be glad to see you at your rooms, having heard of you so often from Gertler and Koteliansky. But I want you to help me if you will – and can. A fortnight ago the police suddenly descended on us in Cornwall, searched the house, and left us the notice to leave the area of Cornwall in three days, and not to enter any prohibited area, and to report ourselves to the police. We don't know in the least why this has taken place. Of course my wife was corresponding with her people in Germany, through a friend in Switzerland – but through the ordinary post. – When the house was searched, the detective dogs took away, as far as I can tell, only a few old letters in German from my mother-in-law, and such trifles – nothing at all. It is all ridiculous and boring and a nuisance. – The order came from the competent Military Authority at Salisbury. – I am told that the only way to find out why this has taken place, is to write to the Secretary for the War Office. But Campbell suggested first asking you if you could find out more directly, perhaps through Hutchinson.[1] I want to know *why* this action has been taken against

[1] St John ('Jack') Hutchinson (1884–1942), barrister. He was a friend of Gertler. See *Letters*, ii. 591n. In April 1916 DHL had warned Kot against the Hutchinsons: 'they are bad people' (ibid.); he may now have felt that Hutchinson could be of service not only because he might be sympathetic (having been associated with 'the No-Conscription league', ibid., ii. 612), but also through his new post (1917) as Assistant Legal Adviser to the Ministry of Reconstruction.

my wife and me. As far as I am aware, there cannot be any reason whatsoever for their attacking us. We are as innocuous as it is possible for anybody to be. – I very much want to be allowed to go back to Cornwall. We have got the house there, and are rooted there. – Perhaps you could ask Hutchinson if he could tell me what person or persons in the War Office Intelligence Department it would be possible or profitable to approach.

I hope this is not a nuisance to you. Take no notice if it is. I look forward to a meeting on Wednesday, anyhow.

Yours   D. H. Lawrence

1476. To Cecil Gray, [2 November 1917]
Text: MS StaU; PC; Postmark, London. W.C. NOV 2 17; Unpublished.

44 Mecklenburgh
Friday

If you go to Tregerthen on Sunday, take the remainder of the bottle of Hollands out of the cupboard.

And don't be a Didymus.[1]

Frieda has written to Mrs Van Dieren.[2]

It will be hard lines on you if your chimney-smoke drives you out of Cornwall.

DHL

1477. To Lady Cynthia Asquith, [2 November 1917]
Text: MS UT; cited in Delany 338.

44 Mecklenburgh Square – W.C.1.
Friday

We will come on Sunday at one – though if it is any bother to you, don't mind leaving it till later.

I promised to sit to John for a portrait-sketch: one sitting.[3] It would be better if I hadn't. I only feel about it: 'What the devil am I doing that for?' – I liked John – but he is a drowned corpse. I'm afraid $\frac{3}{4}$ hour is the limit.

---

[1] i.e. a doubter. 'Doubting Thomas' was also called Didymus (John xx. 24–9).

[2] Frida Kindler, the pianist, wife of the Dutch composer Bernard van Dieren (1884–1936); they were friends of Gray and Heseltine. In February 1917 Gray gave a concert in the Wigmore Hall devoted entirely to van Dieren's music (Nehls, i. 590 n. 417).

[3] The Lawrences had visited Augustus John's studio the previous day when Lady Cynthia was sitting for her portrait. John had asked DHL to sit for him (Asquith, *Diaries* 361); but, unfortunately, 'this plan never came off' (Nehls, i. 440).

I can't get any nearer my Cornwall. Everybody seems to go into a state of blue funk at the mere mention of the War Office. It is very sickening – and so knock-kneed everywhere. Do wring out of your Bingham man if there is anything one can possibly do.[1] If one could get an interview with the responsible man, I should think that would be enough: though there never *is* a responsible man. God!

I feel I should like to see Catherine Asquith again, if she would care to see me.[2] If she perceives a certain likeness in our faces, she is realer than I thought. But one is a bit frightened of the misery of her. – But ask her one day if she would like to see me again: also your Marie Herbert.[3] There is a dusty unused corner of gentleness somewhere in me, which might come into use.

John can't paint you – very boring, his attempts.

D. H. Lawrence

1478. To Wilbur Cross, 5 November 1917
Text: MS YU; Moore 531.

44 Mecklenburgh Square, W.C.1

Wilbur Cross Esq

5 Nov. 1917

Dear Sir,

I have written the article you asked me for, for the *Yale Review*, in answer to 'British Novelists Ltd.' J.B. Pinker, my agent, will forward it on to you: it is called 'The Limit to the British Novelist'. I hope you will get it in time, and will print it. Let me know please.[4]

Yrs Sincerely   D. H. Lawrence

[1] Probably the barrister, Hon. Frank Bigham (1876–1954) who was Assistant Commissioner of the Metropolitan Police, 1914–31.

[2] Katharine Asquith, the former Prime Minister's daughter-in-law, had met DHL on 20 July 1915 and 'loved him' (Asquith, *Diaries* 56). For his part DHL thought he would like her '*very* much' (*Letters*, ii. 368). Her husband, Raymond, had been killed in action in September 1916.

[3] Presumably Mary Herbert (b. 1889) (wife of Hon. Aubrey Herbert) whom Lady Cynthia considered one of the 'great contemporary beauties' (Asquith, *Diaries* 507).

[4] Cross replied as follows (TMSC YU):

D. H. Lawrence, Esq.,   December 4, 1917.
   Higher Tregerthen, Zennor,
     St. Ives, Cornwall, England.

Dear Mr. Lawrence:
   Your article came too late for the December number of The Yale Review. Being a quarterly, the next number appears in March. As you devote so much space to a direct comment upon Mrs. Gerould, what you have to say would be ineffective at that late date. Once, I published a reply of this kind to an article, and it failed. I am particularly sorry that this is so, for I have read your article with very great enjoyment.

Very truly yours

All trace of the article itself has disappeared.

1479. To J. B. Pinker, [5 November 1917]
Text: TMSC NWU; Unpublished.

44, Mecklenburgh Square, W.C.1.
Monday.

My dear Pinker,

I send you an essay which the editor of the *Yale Review* asked me for, in reply to an article which appeared in his periodical. I got his letter through the *English Review*. Will you send the Article on at once, so that it may perhaps come in time for the January issue. They will pay only ten guineas, which is little. The address is *Wilbur Cross Esq, 'Yale Review'*, *Yale Station, New Haven, Connecticut.*[1]

Shall I come and see you this week? Some friends want to get *Women in Love* published by subscription. But I must ask you first about it, I don't feel particularly keen myself.

Shall I come in on Wednesday or Thursday afternoon?

D. H. Lawrence

1480. To Cecil Gray, [6 November 1917]
Text: MS StaU; Schorer, *London Magazine*, iii. 58.

44 Mecklenburgh Square, W.C.1.
Tuesday[2]

I don't care what you accept or don't accept, either: it bores me a bit. But don't go throwing about accusations and calling me a liar gratuitously. Look, we have come through – whether you can see it or not. – Perhaps you are right to resent the impertinence of the 'Look!'. None the less, we have come through. – But enough of this – we can leave it alone henceforth, and abstain, me from underworlds etc,[3] you from calling me a liar.

I send you £5., of which I owe you £4. I intended to send it. Eder gave me some money, so it is your due. I don't send it thinking you hinted at it. I know when you gave me the £4 you gave them completely. Now you are short and I am not, so we'll equalise again.

---

[1] To Pinker, Cross replied on 4 December 1917 (TMSC YU):

Dear Sir:
    As I have explained in a letter to Mr. Lawrence. It has been necessary to my very great regret to return to you the article which you sent from him to The Yale Review.
                                                                Very truly yours

[2] The date is provided through DHL's reference to seeing Puccini's *Madame Butterfly* 'last Wednesday' and Moussorgsky's *Khovántchina* 'tonight'; both refer to performances directed by Sir Thomas Beecham at Drury Lane (on 31 October and 6 November 1917 respectively).

[3] See Letter 1482; see also Delany 333–4 for a discussion of DHL's relationship with Hilda Aldington, and her use of underworld symbolism in a poem she was currently writing.

I believe it is true, Mrs Hocking misses us most. As for William Henry, sarà come sarà: he does as he likes, either Popayan-wards or otherwards.

We went to *Butterfly* last Wednesday with my sister,[1] and all wept bitterly. Tonight I think we are going to *Kovantchina*, though I have got a cold, one of my usuals.

I have written direct to the War Office to be allowed to come back to Cornwall. If we can, we shall come: though there is no immediate hurry. I get irritated here, because I cannot read, not anything at all – nor write. But I have begun to learn Greek – faintly and fitfully.

D. H. Lawrence

1481. To Catherine Carswell, [6 November 1917]
Text: MS YU; PC; Postmark, London. W.C. NOV 6 17; Unpublished.

44 Mecklenburgh Sq. – W.C.1.
Tuesday

I wonder why we haven't heard from you. Hope everything is all right with you and Don.

Mrs Eder wants the novel MS. Shall I give it her before I send it back? I should like to talk to you about it. When will you be in London.

DHL

1482. To Cecil Gray, [7 November 1917]
Text: MS StaU; Huxley 422–3.

44 Mecklenburgh Square – W.C.1.
Wednesday

You are only half-right about the disciples and the alabaster box.[2] If Jesus had paid more attention to Magdalene, and less to his disciples, it would have been better. It was not the ointment-pouring which was so devastating, but the discipleship of the twelve.[3]

As for me and my 'women', I know what they are and aren't, and though there is a certain messiness, there is a further reality. Take away the

---

[1] Most likely Ada Clarke.

[2] Gray later recalled the substance of his own letter which provoked this reply from DHL: 'I accused him, in point of fact, of allowing himself to become the object of a kind of esoteric female cult, an Adonis, Atthis, Dionysos religion of which he was the central figure, a Jesus Christ to a regiment of Mary Magdalenes' (Nehls, i. 432).

[3] There are three accounts of the incident to which DHL refers; he takes details from Mark xiv. 3–9 and Luke vii. 36–50.

subservience and feet-washing, and the pure understanding between the Magdalen and Jesus went deeper than the understanding between the disciples and Jesus, or Jesus and the Bethany women. But Jesus himself was frightened of the knowledge which subsisted between the Magdalen and him, a knowledge deeper than the knowledge of Christianity and 'good', deeper than love, anyhow.

And both you and Frieda need to go one world deeper in knowledge.[1] – As for Spikenard, if I chance to luxuriate in it, it is by the way: not so very Philippically filthy either. Not that it matters.

I don't a bit mind being told where I am wrong – not by you or anybody I respect. Only you don't seem to be going for me in anything where I am really wrong: a bit Pharisaic, both you and Frieda: external.

It seems to me there is a whole world of knowledge to forsake, a new, deeper, lower one to *entamer*.[2] And your hatred of me, like Frieda's hatred of me, is your cleavage to a world of knowledge and being which you ought to forsake, which, by organic law, you must depart from or die. And my 'women', Esther Andrews, Hilda Aldington etc, represent, in an impure and unproud, subservient, cringing, bad fashion, I admit, – but represent none the less the threshold of a new world, or underworld, of knowledge and being. – And the Hebridean Songs, which represent you and Frieda in this, are songs of the damned:[3] that is, songs of those who inhabit an underworld which is forever an underworld, never to be made open and whole. And you would like us all to inhabit a suggestive underworld which is never revealed or opened, only intimated, only *felt* between the initiated. – I won't have it. The old world must burst, the underworld must be open and whole, new world. – You want an emotional sensuous underworld, like Frieda and the Hebrideans: my 'women' want an ecstatic subtly-intellectual underworld, like the Greeks – Orphicism – like Magdalen at her feet-washing – and there you are.

D. H. Lawrence

1483. To Cecil Gray, [9 November 1917]
Text: MS StaU; PC; Postmark, London. W.C. NOV 9 17; Unpublished.

44 Mecklenburgh
Friday

Will meet you Paddington on Monday 5.30, unless something untoward prevents it.

---

[1] There is some likelihood that Frieda and Gray had a brief affair (Delany surveys the evidence, pp. 311, 331–3); whether DHL's linking of their names indicates his knowledge of it cannot now be known.

[2] 'to start upon, open up'.   [3] See Letter 1459 and n. 6.

If you get this in time, bring me a pound of butter from Katie[1] or anywhere.

W[illia]m H[enr]y had talked of coming to London soon: did he mention it to you?

DHL

Van Dieren gone to hospital again, so we couldn't go to see them.

1484. To J. B. Pinker, [11? November 1917]
Text: TMSC NWU; Unpublished.

44, Mecklenburgh Square, W.C.1.
Sunday.[2]

My dear Pinker,

I will come to the Arts Club on thursday at one – thanks very much.

If Mrs. Eder comes to see you about the publishing of the novel, be nice to her.

D. H. Lawrence

1485. To Montague Shearman, [11 November 1917]
Text: MS UTul; Unpublished.

44 Mecklenburgh Square, W.C.1.
Sunday[3]

Dear Shearman

I wrote you a letter a week ago, thanking you for yours – but could not post it because I did not know your number.

I am sorry we couldn't come on Friday evening – hope we can all be free one evening of this week, so that we can come together – Gertler as well. Shall we keep Thursday or Friday open? We are booked for Tuesday and Wednesday – at least I want to go to the *Magic Flute* on Wednesday – I think it is then.

We will arrange with Kot and Gertler.

Yrs   D. H. Lawrence

---

[1] Katie Berryman.

[2] It is presumed that the meeting with Pinker, tentatively mentioned in Letter 1479, had been postponed and would now occur on 15 November.

[3] Dated by DHL's reference to 'the *Magic Flute* on Wednesday'; Mozart's opera was performed on 14 November (cf. Letter 1480 and n. 2).

1486. To Chatto & Windus, [c. 11 November 1917]
Text: MS Chatto & Windus; Unpublished.

[44 Mecklenburgh Square, London, W.C.1.]
[c. 11 November 1917]

[Lawrence responded to the publishers' request that he should provide the
names of newspapers beyond the principal dailies and weeklies to which
review copies of *Look! We Have Come Through!* might be sent. He proposed
the *Nottingham Guardian* and asked for two copies to be posted to private
friends.][1]

1487. To Lady Cynthia Asquith, [17 November 1917]
Text: MS Lazarus; Unpublished.

44 Mecklenburgh Square, W.C.1.
Saturday.[2]

Sorry you can't come tomorrow: we had actually sported a cold chicken,
because I know you like that dead bird. Never mind, we'll get somebody else
to come in and eat that with us, and we'll make another start on Tuesday. – *Do*
come in for a scrap. But come *early*: come at seven, so we can go easily along.
If you take 18 bus, it will put you down at the Grays Inn end of Guilford St,
and then in one minute you are in Mecklenburgh Sq.

[sketch][3]

The dots are your footsteps from the Russell Sq. tube station, the crosses are
the same from the 18 bus stoppage on Grays Inn Rd.

I got a letter from the War Office 'Sorry we cannot permit you to return to
Cornwall.'[4] I am very mad, but not shaken. I *will* go back, voilà.

How many people have you asked for Tuesday? How mad is Nicholls?[5]

If you've not asked much other people, could we take with us Miss Yorke –

---

[1] Information about this missing letter is derived from a copy of the publishers' reply dated 13
November 1917. Their initial request for information is dated 8 November. (One of the friends
to whom the publishers sent a copy of the book was Amy Lowell: see Letter 1497.)

[2] Lady Cynthia 'dined with the Lawrences for the opera' on Tuesday, 20 November (Asquith,
·*Diaries* 369), thus confirming the date of this letter as 17 November.

[3] A map showing the route described for Lady Cynthia.

[4] See Letter 1480.

[5] Lady Cynthia's diary-entry makes it clear that the theatre-party to see Mozart's *Seraglio*
included 'Miss [Dorothy] York[e] – a chic poor American, like a drawing in *Vogue*, with
straight whiskers – . . . and Nicholls and Ivo Grenfell' (Asquith, *Diaries* 369). DHL had met
the poet Robert Nichols (1893–1944) two years earlier when he was in hospital suffering from
shell-shock (*Letters*, ii. 442–9). Grenfell (1889–1926), a close friend of the Asquiths, was the
son of Lord Desborough.

American girl – elegant but poor – lives in this house – usually lives in Paris – like her very much. – But only if there's plenty plenty of room, as we've said nothing to her.

I lunched with John Galsworthy yesterday – sawdust bore.[1]

I feel the possibility of some happiness for us all near ahead. Do you feel the same? I feel a certain jolliness creeping up from the unknown.

Don't be late on Tuesday – I'll get a taxi if I can.

D. H. Lawrence

Frieda is making an evening dress.

1488. To Joseph Hone, 18 November 1917
Text: MS UT; Huxley 423–4.

44 Mecklenburgh Square, W.C.1.
18 Nov. 1917

Dear Hone[2]

Campbell suggests my writing to you about my novel. There is a serious scheme for publishing it here privately by subscription, under the auspices of Arnold Bennett and John Galsworthy. Campbell however, and Koteliansky, say that probably Maunsell would do it in Dublin, which would be better.[3] – The English publishers daren't do it, although they would like to, because they fear it would meet the same fate as the *Rainbow* – which, I suppose you remember, was suppressed for its immorality.

Do please tell me at once if you think Maunsel would be likely to publish such a book of unlucky antecedents. If he would *seriously* consider it, I will send the MS. But otherwise, I would rather keep it and get on with the scheme of private publication by subscription over here. The novel is more or less a sequel to *The Rainbow*, and I think I'll call it 'Noah's Ark'.

Let me know as soon as you can.

Do you remember me from the Selwood Terrace days?[4] I remember you a sad and silent visitor. Hope things go well with you now.

D. H. Lawrence

[1] Galsworthy's account of the meeting (which he misdated 13 November 1917) was as follows: 'Lunched with Pinker to meet D. H. Lawrence, that provincial genius. Interesting, but a type I could not get on with. Obsessed with self. Dead eyes, and a red beard, long narrow pale face. A strange bird' (Nehls, i. 447).

[2] Joseph Maunsel Hone (1882–1959), Irish writer and – as Letter 1490 makes clear – literary editor for the Dublin publishing house, Maunsel and Co. Author of *Bishop Berkeley* (1932), *Swift* (1935), *Life of W. B. Yeats* (1943), etc.

[3] Kot, with Murry, had prepared translations of Chekhov's *The Bet and Other Stories* (1915) and Dostoievsky's *Pages from the Journal of an Author* (1916): Maunsel had published both.

[4] DHL is alluding to the period 24 June–15 August 1914 when he and Frieda stayed at 9 Selwood Terrace, South Kensington, the home of Hone's fellow Irishman, Gordon Campbell.

1489. To Chatto & Windus, [c. 18 November 1917]
Text: TMSC Chatto & Windus; Unpublished.

[44 Mecklenburgh Square, London, W.C.1.]
[c. 18 November 1917]

[Lawrence wrote a postcard to the publishers asking when he could expect to receive copies of *Look! We Have Come Through!*]¹

1490. To J. B. Pinker, [24 November 1917]
Text: MS Sagar; cited in Carswell 81.

44, Mecklenburgh Sq. W.C.1.
Saturday²

Some friends of mine insist that Maunsel would be glad to do the novel in Ireland. They insist on my writing to Joe Hone – Maunsels literary manager – whom I know. I have done so and will let you know what he says. Also I enclose letter from Fisher Unwin.³

My copies of poems have *not* come from Chatto, though I look for them all the while.

Let me know what dear old out-of-date Galsworthy says.

D. H. Lawrence

What does Fisher Unwin want? Shall I write him or see him?

---

¹ The information about this missing postcard comes from the reply sent by Chatto & Windus on 20 November 1917 (TMSC Chatto & Windus). The publishers assured DHL that copies would be dispatched within the week. They continued:

We believe that the cover will create some interest, and we hope that you will like this rather curious and artistic design. The artist, Mr. Kauffer, says that it is based on the idea of two figures walking briskly; and it struck us as likely to attract the eye to the book, which is the main purpose of a cover of this kind.

Yours very faithfully,   Chatto & Windus

The cover-designer was Edward McKnight Kauffer (1890–1954), a member of the Cumberland Market Group of artists and later (1920) of the short-lived Group X.

For DHL's reaction to the cover (which is reproduced in Roberts 255) see Letter 1494.

² It is assumed that the letter would be written on the first Saturday after the previous letter to Hone.

³ The contents of the letter are not precisely known, but (from the letter following) they appear to have raised the possibility of publishing *Women in Love*. Thomas Fisher Unwin (1848–1935) had been interested in publishing DHL's work since 1912 (see *Letters*, i. 458. n. 4).

1491. To J. B. Pinker, [28 November 1917]
Text: MS Sagar; Unpublished.

44 Mecklenburgh Square, W.C.1.
Wednesday

I heard from Hone – he asks me to send on the MS. of novel – but I am working at it, so shan't send it till I hear something more definite. – Perhaps we might let Fisher Unwin see it. I wrote him about it, and he said he would like to see the MS. But I feel very doubtful. – However, we'll keep it for a few days, while I go over my copy.

The thing Hone really would like to see, he says, is the philosophy – the essays 'At the Gates.'[1] You might send him off this at once.

         J.M.Hone, Palermo, Killinly, Co. Dublin.
I think you have a copy by you, have you not?[2]

Revising the novel, I think of poor John Galsworthy's sufferings as he reads it. He will *never* risk his name to it, poor darling.

My copies of the poems are very slow: they haven't yet come from Chattos.

                                 D. H. Lawrence

---

[1] See pp. 100 n. 2 and 143 n. 3. In a letter to Robert Nichols, Philip Heseltine asserted that Maunsel's interest in 'At the Gates' was instigated by him; in his opinion the book was 'the supreme utterance of all modern philosophy'; and he had encouraged 'several well-known people – writers and others – who know Lawrence and know the value of his work, [to] write letters to the firm expressing a hope that the work be speedily published' (Nehls, i. 452). Nichols, then on active service, responded to Heseltine's prompting and wrote to Joseph Hone as follows (MS NYPL):

                   Office of Deputy Engineer in Chief, G.H.Q., B.E.F., France
                                  Jan. 26th 1918
Dear Sir,
    It has come to my knowledge that you are thinking of publishing D. H. Lawrences great philosophic work which has appeared in parts of the *English Review*. As a writer of I believe a certain following and reputation I desire to congratulate you if you carry it through.
    D. H. Lawrence possesses in my opinion nothing short of genius. As a prose writer he possesses an unexampled expressiveness of phrase, a command of colour no other present writer can equal. The depth of his speculation is beyond the common public I admit but time brings its reward and I think that not only will the publication be a boon to real thinking persons but later will become a paying proposition with the public . . .

[2] DHL expected that Pinker had the copy of 'At the Gates' which Chatto & Windus returned to him on 8 October 1917 when they politely declined to publish the book (TMSC Chatto & Windus). In fact, as Pinker's note on this letter – 'write Secker' – confirms, he had sent the copy to Secker (see also Letter 1494).

1492. To Chatto & Windus, [29 November 1917]
Text: MS Chatto & Windus; Unpublished.

[44 Mecklenburgh Square, London, W.C.1]
[29 November 1917]

[Lawrence wrote to Chatto & Windus to acknowledge receipt of his copies of *Look! We Have Come Through!*, to express his pleasure at the volume's appearance and to dismiss the *Times* review as of little permanent significance.][1]

1493. To Lady Cynthia Asquith, [30 November 1917]
Text: MS UT; cited in Delany 343.

13 Earls Court Square. SW
Friday

We have moved here today.[2] It is a bourgeois little flat with a retired Admiral downstairs. I must say, at the first blow, I loathe it. The middle classes, and the whitewashed devil of middle class-dom sends me mad. I suppose we shall be here for a fortnight or so.

When will you come and see us – at tea lunch or supper – fix your own time, and we will stay in for it. If you would like an evening next week we will have one or two people, and sing songs and play a bit – if you feel like it.

But I hate this milieu. It makes Cornwall seem *very* desirable. I suppose there is nothing else one could do to the War Office to make them let us go back? – If there is nothing, in bitterness of spirit one will have to think of another place in the country.

---

[1] Chatto & Windus, acknowledging DHL's (missing) letter, wrote to him on 30 November 1917 (MSC Chatto & Windus):

Dear Sir
   We are very glad indeed that you are so pleased with the appearance of your book; and we hope it may be possible to obtain a sale for it. *The Times* notice was certainly very pained, and we are sorry for this as we had taken trouble in sending a specially early copy. But, as you say, no Muse will be able to do the book any damage; and, so long as you have the appreciation of those who can recognise literature when they see it, you will be able to dispense with muses and the precarious support they lend.
   With all good wishes for the book
                                        We are   Yours sincerely Chatto & Windus

For *The Times Literary Supplement* review see p. 187 n. 4.

[2] Letter 1465 and n. 3.

I liked Charles Whibley – but he is a generation beyond me.[1] But he has gute Augen.[2]

No ink – excuse pencil.

D. H. Lawrence

1494. To J. B. Pinker, [30 November 1917]
Text: TMSC NWU; Unpublished.

13, Earls Court Square. S.W.
Friday.

My dear Pinker,

We are staying here for a fortnight or so – then whither, I don't know.

I had a letter from Hone – he had discussed with Maunsels – they don't want to publish any English books during the war – but still they will consider the *essays* – he wants to see them as soon as possible. So if you get them from Secker[3] will you send them him – either to 50, Lower Baggot St., Dublin – or to Palermo, Killinly, Co. Dublin.

Shall I send to Fisher Unwin the MS. of the novel, next week, or shall I not? I feel he wouldn't publish it. And if he wouldn't, then I am not anxious for him to read it.

I know John Galsworthy must have *loathed* it. Do tell me what he discreetly said.

D. H. Lawrence

My poems have come – on the whole I like them very much – the get-up. I *love* the red, now I see it plainly – and the wrapper isn't so bad, really – though a bit *criant*.

I saw the dainty Timesey Muse averting her eyes.[4] Have there been any more notices?

DHL

---

[1] Charles Whibley (1859–1930), critic, editor and journalist. He wrote for the *Pall Mall Gazette*, was a member of Whistler's circle in Paris and knew Mallarmé and Valéry, and influenced T. S. Eliot through his essays in *Blackwood's Magazine*. His latest book, *Political Portraits*, had just been published (November 1917). (See *Times* obituary, 5 March 1930.)

[2] 'he is perceptive'.

[3] Martin Secker (1882–1978) had offered to publish a volume of DHL's short stories as early as 1911 (see *Letters*, i. 275); he published *New Poems* in 1918 and continued as DHL's publisher until after DHL's death.

[4] *Look! We Have Come Through!* was reviewed in *TLS*, 22 November 1917: '. . . we need hardly say that he has much of the art of writing and avoids banality. By no means, however, does he avoid verbiage . . . varied by orgies of extreme eroticism . . .' The reviewer quotes from 'She Looks Back' and concludes with this comment: 'And so on, an excited morbid babble about one's own emotions which the Muse of poetry surely can only turn from with a pained distaste.'

1495. To Lady Cynthia Asquith, [11 December 1917]
Text: MS UT; Huxley 424–5.

13B Earls Court Square, S.W.
Tuesday[1]

It is a pity you couldn't come this evening – and you didn't write and say why, after all.[2]

We are leaving here on Friday – going, I think, to Dollie Radford's cottage in the country near Newbury.

But it seems we are never going to have any peace. Today there has been a man from the Criminal Investigation Department inquiring about us – from Gray.[3] It is quite evident that somebody from Cornwall – somebody we don't know, probably – is writing letters to these various departments – and we are followed everywhere by the persecution. It is just like the Cornish to do such a thing. But it is *very* maddening. The detective pretended to Gray that I was a foreigner – but what has the Criminal Investigation Department to do with that? Altogether it is too sickening.

Ask your man at Scotland Yard[4] if he can tell me how I can put a stop to it – if there is any way of putting a stop to it. – I hate bothering you – but really, this is getting a bit too thick. I shall soon have every department in the country on my heels – for no reason whatever. Surely I can find out from the Criminal Dept. what the persecution is about?

Just write a letter to your man at Scotland Yard, will you? At least this last vileness against me I ought to be able to quash.

Address me at

44 Mecklenburgh Square, W.C.1.

will you, unless you hear from me. That address will always find me. I hate worrying you – but perhaps you will forgive me.

Frieda sends her love.

D. H. Lawrence

---

[1] Dated with reference to the Lawrences' planned departure for Chapel Farm Cottage at Hermitage, on Friday, 14 December 1917.

[2] She was engaged at a family party and a theatre-visit to see Barrie's *Dear Brutus* (Asquith, *Diaries* 379).

[3] Gray confirmed this allegation: 'On visiting [the Lawrences] on one occasion I was intercepted outside the door by a gentleman of the C.I.D. and subjected to a mild form of third-degree examination concerning the Lawrences and my relations with them, which eventually reached such a pitch of impertinence and offensiveness that I told him to clear out or I would throw him out' (Nehls, i. 429).

[4] See p. 177 and n. 1.

1496. To Montague Shearman, [11 December 1917]
Text: MS UT; Huxley 424.

13B Earls Court Square, S.W.

Tuesday

Dear Shearman,

It doesn't look as if we were going to finish our talk very quickly, after all. The people who own this flat want to come in directly – and as we have nowhere else to go, we think of going to the country – Hermitage, near Newbury – on Friday. And Wednesday evening and Thursday we are full up. Perhaps we shall have to snatch an odd evening later on. – But I will let you know if we can manage to stay in town over this Friday – that was to be our evening.

I am very mad because today a detective has been round enquiring all about me – from the Criminal Investigation Dept, if you please – asking for all information. Now this is *impossible*. I¹ should like to get at the bottom of this. Perhaps you might help me this time² – because I am infuriated at being followed and persecuted. The man said there had been³ a letter from Cornwall, and that was what he was come about. Now this is nothing to do with War Office – so do help me if you can to get at the bottom of it.

Yrs   D. H. Lawrence

1497. To Amy Lowell, 13 December 1917
Text: MS HU; Damon 437–8.

44 Mecklenburgh Square, W.C.1.

13 Dec. 1917

My dear Amy,

Your letter reached me yesterday: your book came a little earlier.⁴ This latter I had not acknowledged. But I had thanked you for the cheque for the *Anthology*, which I received some weeks back. – My publishers have sent you my new book of poems. I hope you will get it all right.

Since writing my last letter, everything has gone wrong with us. The police and military came and searched our house and turned us out of Cornwall – for no reason under the sun, except of course that Frieda is German by birth, and I am not warlike. So here we are cast upon a rather disagreeable world. Hilda

¹ *impossible*. I] *impossible*. It is evident somebody is writing accusations somewhere – probably from Cornwall. I
² Shearman was working in the Foreign Office (p. 103 n. 5).
³ said there had been] said he had had
⁴ *Tendencies in Modern American Poetry*, published on 10 October 1917.

like an angel came to the rescue and lent us her room. But now she and Richard are come back, we must yield it up and go down to the country to a cottage that can be lent us by another friend. When one has no money to pay for lodgings, it is no joke to be kicked out of one's house and home at random, and given nowhere to go. However, we shall get over it all.

My book *Look, we have Come Through* is out about a fortnight: as usual the critics fall on me: the *Times* says 'the Muse can only turn away her face in pained distaste.'[1] Poor Muse, I feel as if I had affronted a white-haired old spinster with weak eyes. But I don't really care what critics say, so long as I myself could personally be left in peace. This, it seems, cannot be. People write letters of accusation, because one has a beard and looks not quite the usual thing: and then one has detectives at one's heels like stray dogs, not to be got rid of. It is very hateful and humiliating and degrading. It makes me mad in my blood: so stupid and unnecessary. I want to be in quiet retreat in my own place in Cornwall – but they haul me out and then follow me round: really, is too maddening. One would think they did it to amuse themselves.

I met Fletcher for the first time the other day.[2] It surprised me to find him so nervously hyper-sensitive and fretted. I thought he was a rather hearty American type, from his poems. I was mistaken. But I liked him.

The Aldingtons are in London – Richard has another fortnight or so: and then heaven knows where he will be sent: let us hope, somewhere in England. They seem pretty happy, as far as it is possible under the circumstances. We have had some good hours with them in Mecklenburgh Square – really jolly, notwithstanding everything: remembering that evening at the Berkeley with you, when we all met for the first time, and laughing at ourselves.[3] Oh my dear Amy, I do wish to heaven we could all meet again in peace and freedom, to laugh together and be decent and happy with each other. This is a more wintry winter of discontent than I had ever conceived. – Never mind, the devil won't rampage in triumph for ever.

Frieda sends her love. We both hope that nice things will happen to you for Christmas: and we look forward to a meeting again – soon.

                                                        D. H. Lawrence

---

[1] See p. 187 n. 4.

[2] In *Tendencies* Amy Lowell substantiated her thesis about the change from Victorian poetry to modern by reference to the writings of specific poets: John Gould Fletcher (1886–1950) – together with H. D. – illustrated her case that Imagism represented the full achievement of the contemporary period. Fletcher lived in London for a number of years from 1916 when he married Florence Emily Arbuthnot. He was introduced to DHL by John Cournos; for Fletcher's recollection of the meeting see Nehls, i. 448.

[3] DHL first met Amy Lowell on 30 July 1914 (see *Letters*, ii. 203), but the occasion he probably had in mind took place at the Berkeley Hotel on 13 August 1914 (ibid., ii. 207 n. 3).

1498. To J. B. Pinker, 18 December 1917
Text: MS Forster; cited in Carswell 80, 95.

Chapel Farm Cottage, Hermitage, nr. Newbury. Berks.
18 Dec. 1917

My dear Pinker

We have come down here for a fortnight or so.

I heard indirectly that George Moore had read the MS. of the novel, and praised it highly.[1] Who gave him the MS? Did you, or Fisher Unwin? I sent it to Fisher Unwin last week.

Let me know about that, will you.

I have also a letter from Hone, who is very smitten with the 'At the Gates' essays, and thinks, if I can only get a letter to back him up, he can make Maunsels do them. He suggests Bertrand Russell – who used to be a fairly intimate friend of mine – but whom I don't agree with. I wonder if I shall ask him for a letter.

Why did Secker not want them? – did he say?

Harrison is publishing two essays of mine next month – I suppose you knew.[2]

D. H. Lawrence

1499. To S. S. Koteliansky, [19 December 1917]
Text: MS BL; PC; Postmark, Hermitage 19 DE [. . .]; Zytaruk 124.

Chapel Farm Cottage, Hermitage, nr Newbury. Berks
Wed.

We got here yesterday – snow everywhere, and sharp frost: very cold but very pretty. The cottage is nice. – I want to hear from my sister – perhaps she will write direct to you.

Greet the Farbman's kindly from me.

D. H. Lawrence

---

[1] George Moore (1852–1933), Irish novelist and playwright who, since 1911, had lived in London. As well as Moore's novels, DHL had read his volume of autobiography *Salve* which he did not consider 'up to much' and about which Frieda was scathing (*Letters*, i. 512, 524). Fisher Unwin published four of Moore's works.

2 See Letters 1459 and n. 2 and 1460.

1500. To S. S. Koteliansky, [20 December 1917]
Text: MS BL; Zytaruk, ed., *Malahat Review*, i. 32.

Chapel Farm Cottage, Hermitage, nr Newbury, Berks.
Thursday

My dear Kot,

My sister says she arrives at Marylebone Great Central at 5.40 on Sunday, in the evening. She wants to go straight on to Waterloo to catch the 6.40 train to Portsmouth. According to my time table however, there *is* no 6.40 on Sunday to Portsmouth, only a 7.0 oclock train. I have written her to this effect. If my time table is right, she will take the seven train.

You will go straight across by the Bakerloo, I suppose.

She says you are to look for a tallish thin woman with dark furs, in a pale bluey-grey long coat. – I'm sure you will know each other. I described to her your villainous appearance.[1]

Thank you very much for meeting her.

It is *very* cold here. I wish the world were nicer.

D. H. Lawrence

1501. To Catherine Carswell, 22 December 1917
Text: MS YU; cited in Carswell 95.

Chapel Farm Cottage – Hermitage, nr Newbury, Berks.
Saturday 22 Dec 1917

My dear Catherine

I must write you just a line for Christmas. We are here in the cottage – Margaret Radford has been here a day or two – is going back to Hampstead on Monday. There is still snow on the ground here. It has been bitterly cold. But there is a half thaw today. – We are staying till Thursday – 27th – when we come to London to meet my sister on her way from Portsmouth – then we shall go with her to the Midlands for a week or so: after that, probably here again. God knows. – I am not in a good mood in any way whatsoever.

I hope you are all right. One has a sort of buried-alive feeling which is very disagreeable. Frieda sends her love – I hope you and Don are happy.

D. H. Lawrence

[1] If this description was contained in a letter to Ada Clarke, the letter has disappeared.

1502. To S. S. Koteliansky, [26 December 1917]
Text: MS BL; PC; Postmark, [. . .]6 DE 17; Zytaruk 126.

Hermitage –
Wednesday

Thanks so much for going to Marylebone to my sister. She told me you were there.

We are going to the Midlands on *Friday* – address there c/o Mrs Clarke, Grosvenor Rd. Ripley, nr. Derby. We shall stay about a week, then come back here, I think. But we will see you as we cross London on our return. Let me hear from you. – No news from Gertler. – When do the Farbman's return?

DHL

1503. To S. S. Koteliansky, [29 December 1917]
Text: MS BL; Zytaruk 127.

c/o Mrs Clarke, Grosvenor Rd. – Ripley, nr. Derby.
Saturday

My dear Kot,

Here we are in the snowy midlands – very queer. I think we shall stay till next Thursday. We are going to look for a cottage near here. Derbyshire is beautiful – and it will be near my sister. – She made us laugh very much about your one eye-glass, your pseudo-monocle, and your serious outgaze, and the relief you evidenced in fleeing. –

We shall look for a cottage, and have our goods sent from Cornwall. That will take five or six weeks. We shall return to Hermitage, I think, for the meantime. – The war will end by the summer. Then we will really go to Russia, and leave our cottage to my sister. It is a good arrangement.

When do the Farbman's return? If they are not back on Thursday, could we stay one night with you? If they are returning before then, dont mention it to them.

See you next week.

D. H. Lawrence

1504. To Mark Gertler, 29 December 1917
Text: MS SIU; Huxley 425–6.

c/o Mrs Clarke, Grosvenor Rd, *Ripley*, nr Derby.
Saturday 29 Dec· 17

My dear Gertler,

I got your letter today here – we are staying in the Midlands with my sister a few days. I think we shall be in London next Thursday – stay the night perhaps with Kot, then go on to Hermitage. I find I'm better and happier in the country. I don't feel the cold very much – don't mind it. We might see you on Thursday evening – Kot will know. Carrington talked of coming to see us in Hermitage.

We must have some talks. For the last nine months nothing has interested me but thinking about 'deep subjects', as you call them. – But I find myself becoming more unsociable. As soon as I have promised to meet people, I want to take to my heels in the opposite direction. It is only at rare sympathetic moments that I feel like talking.

I think the old way of life has come to an end, and none of us will be able to go on with it. We must either get out into a new life, altogether new – a life based neither on work or love – or else we shall die. This is the end of us, in one self: and unless we can start right new, it is the end of us altogether: So it behoves us to lay fresh hold, – no work or running away will help us. It is a hard job too – very hard. But we have no choice. – The war will end before summer, and then, unless we have got some foothold on some new world of our own, we are dished. – Yes, we will try to meet and talk. But my heart shuts up against people – practically everybody – nowadays. One has been so much insulted and let down.

I'm afraid I can't believe any more in Murry.

If it turns warmer, you might come and stay at Hermitage.

D. H. Lawrence

1505. To S. S. Koteliansky, 1 January 1918
Text: MS BL; Zytaruk 128.

c/o Mrs Clarke, Grosvenor Rd., Ripley, nr Derby.
1 Jan. 1918.

My dear Kot

If the Farbmans are back, we shall not trouble you. Perhaps we shall not stay in London: perhaps we shall stay a couple of nights in the room of a man called Collins.[1]

We shan't come to London before Friday, and it may be not till Saturday. I shall let you know. We will have an evening meeting.

---

[1] Vere Henry Gratz Collins (1872–1966), Educational Books Manager of Oxford University Press until he retired in 1935. He encouraged DHL to write *Movements in European History* (1921). The Lawrences had briefly stayed with Collins at 2 Hurst Close, Hampstead Garden Suburb, in December 1915 (*Letters*, ii. 482–3).

I heard from Gertler – peu de chose. We'll all meet if I am in town. May the New Year make us all happier.

D. H. Lawrence

All good greetings to Mr and Mrs Farbman.

1506. To Lady Cynthia Asquith, 12 January 1918
Text: MS UT; Huxley 426–7.

Chapel Farm Cottage, Hermitage, nr Newbury, Berks
12 Jan. 1918

Where are you now, and what are you doing? – We are back here from the Midlands – where I got just the wrong kind of chill.

There is no news. – I was dreaming of you two nights in succession, so must write. I dreamed you were a sort of prima ballerina – which is a translation of cinema star, I suppose. How is that? – the cinema? – You were very pleased with yourself, in my dream. Hope it isn't a case of contraries. – But also you were troubled by what, in dream language, was called your 'fat little boy.' – Hope that *is* a contrary.

This cottage is not an ideal – cold, a little comfortless. I suppose we must be casting our eye round, for a flight again, before long.

Frieda sends her love.

D. H. Lawrence

1507. To Joseph Hone, 12 January 1918
Text: MS UT; Unpublished.

Chapel Farm Cottage, Hermitage, nr Newbury, Berks
12 Jan. 1918

Dear Hone

I have received your letter here. I shall be so pleased if Maunsel does the philosophy. Fisher Unwin just wrote to me, asking if I would let him see it.

There is, of course, the [   ]¹ write him. Is he in Ireland or London, I wonder. – You might send me his address, if you have it. I should like him to back me up in the novel – which we shall get printed privately, if no publisher can be found for it.

¹ The disappearance of pp. 2 and 4 of the letter cannot be explained.

Let me know the news. – If you see Philip Heseltine, tell him I got the Book of Kells, and think it very lovely[1] – am much touched by his[2]

1508. To George Moore, [c. 14 January 1918]
Text: Letters of George Moore (1942), p. 42.

[Chapel Farm Cottage, Hermitage, nr Newbury, Berks]

[c. 14 January 1918][3]

[Lawrence wrote to George Moore 'telling that he had heard from several sources that [Moore] liked his novels, and would [he] read some MSS. that were going begging'.][4]

[1] Heseltine, in Ireland from summer 1917 for about a year, had presumably sent DHL a reproduction of some feature from the illuminated copy of the Gospels preserved in Trinity College, Dublin.

[2] The following is part of the note later made by Hone (MS UT) about the 'portion' of this letter which remains:

> My hopes that the 'philosophy' spoken of in this letter might be brought out by the Dublin publisher, Maunsel, were not fulfilled. The m.s. subsequently passed into the hands of Philip Heseltine ('Peter Warlock', the musician) who in revenge for being caricatured by Lawrence in *Women in Love* put the pages to the base uses of the water-closet. To Arland Ussher, then a very young man, the work came as a revelation, and he made a transcript of the whole which unhappily was destroyed or lost in the course of a moving from house to house.

[3] It is presumed that in the missing portion of the previous letter, DHL urged Hone (and therefore Maunsel) to interest himself in publishing *Women in Love*. It is conjectured that the person whose address DHL requests (also in the previous letter) was George Moore: an Irishman normally resident in London, a friend of Hone's and an obvious choice for a writer to support an argument for publishing DHL's novel. These hypotheses lead to a date for this letter which allows DHL to have received a reply from Hone and in time for Moore to write to John Eglinton on 22 January 1918 (as quoted in the next note).

[4] Moore sent his friend and adviser John Eglinton (W. K. Magee), a copy of his reply to DHL; it is reproduced in *Letters of George Moore*, pp. 42–3. He expressed marked admiration for *Sons and Lovers*, somewhat less for *The White Peacock*, and the following observations on DHL's 'later writings':

> . . . I believe that some part of your difficulties may be attributed to your abandonment of the description of human persons with human fortunes for vague animal abstractions. If we look back into the literature of the past we find that men have always been interested in the concrete. The poetry that attracts us in middle life is a poetry about things rather than ideas. Return then to your dahlias: I remember them much better than your ideas.
>
> In *The White Peacock* you describe some dying dahlias with so much insight and feeling that I doubt if I shall ever forget them.
>
> If I may venture to criticise your writings in detail, I would say, for I believe the criticism may be of use to you, that I should like you to keep the classes separate. It is possible that miners' sons may retire into corners, while their mother is laying the kitchen table for supper, to discuss Shelley's poetry and Sarah Bernhardt. But it does not seem to me wise to introduce these incongruities into prose narrative. I doubt very much if Shelley's poetry and Sarah Bernhardt's French accent should ever find their way into English prose narrative, and if I feel certain about anything in this world, it is that reapers from the corn fields should not indulge in aesthetics.
>
> Thanking you for the pleasure your novels have given me, I remain, etc.

1509. To Cecil Gray, [17 January 1918]
Text: MS StaU; Huxley 428–9.

Chapel Farm Cottage, Hermitage. nr Newbury. Berks.
Thursday.

Dear Gray

I heard from Katie that Mrs Fisher¹ had come to Zennor, and that you were expected. How queer it will be for you to be back in Bosigran! It is queer even to think of it. – On some sunny, gentle spring day when celandines are out, I should like to come back to Zennor, to Tregerthen. But it would only be an Ave atque Vale, I think. I have left Cornwall, as an abiding place, for ever, I am sure. But I shall come back to see it.

Having been seedy this week, I have sat in bed, my usual style, and looked out of the window in front. There is a field – the thatched roof of a cottage – then trees and other roofs. As the evening falls, and it is snowy, there is a clear yellow light, an evening star, and a moon. The trees get dark. Those without leaves seem to thrill their twigs above – the firs and pines slant heavy with snow – and I think of looking out of the Tregerthen window at the sea. And I no longer want the sea, the space, the abstraction. There is something living and rather splendid² about trees. They stand up so proud, and are alive.

I'm not writing anything – only sit learning songs, which I find a great amusement. I can read well enough to learn a song nicely in about a quarter of an hour – so I have already got off twenty or thirty. I don't know why it amuses me so much more than reading or writing. – So perhaps your opera will amuse you.³

I had a letter from Richard Aldington. But I didn't like it. 'These human relationships which now seem so important', he says, 'will I know soon become trivial, almost nothing. For soon I go to my Father. That is to say, in a short time I shall inevitably be sent to France, to that great holocaust of atonement for the wrongs of mankind.' – which, to *me*, is a bit thick.

I am afraid I'm not very friendly lately. But ones self seems to contract more and more away from everything, and especially from people. It is a kind of wintering. The only thing to do is to let it *be* winter.

Remember me to Tregerthen, if you go there. Hope Bosigran will be good to you. Frieda sends greetings.

D. H. Lawrence

¹ Unidentified.
² MS reads 'plendid'.
³ Gray wrote three operas: *Deirdre*, *The Temptation of St Anthony* (after Flaubert) and *The Trojan Women*. It is likely that DHL is here alluding to the early stages in the genesis of the second; Gray had discovered the subject, resolved to set it to music, but did not complete it until 20 years later (see Gray, *Musical Chairs*, pp. 124, 303–13).

1510. To S. S. Koteliansky, [20 January 1918]
Text: MS BL; Postmark, Hermitage 21 JA 18; Moore 536–7.

Chapel Farm Cottage. Hermitage, nr. Newbury.
Sunday

My dear Kot

I alas am seedy, and Frieda not very well. – But this will pass.

About the money, I shall be glad to ask for it when the hour comes – but not yet.

About the cottage in Cornwall – I think the Woolfs might have it.[1] For how long a time do they want it? And do they share the house in Richmond? I wonder if they would care to change houses. – Gray said he would like to go to Tregerthen instead of to his Bosigran – which is some 4 miles further on. If he persists, the Woolfs might have his Bosigran, a much better house. – Do they want to take a servant, do you know? And when do they want to go?

I am afraid peace won't come without the great Bacchanalia you mention. And god knows when the people will be worked up to this. – But it *will* come. It is en route.

As for myself, I sit in bed and look at the trees and learn songs from a book and wait for the Judgment Day – there is not much more to be said for me.

Perhaps we shall be in town again soon – everything is in flux like a pot that is vigorously stirred. – It might be possible for us to stay awhile in the Woolfs house – I think Frieda wants to be nearer London.

Hope I shall be out again soon. Remember me very kindly to Sonya Issayevna, and to Grisha the Odessa villain[2] – why has he always got his villain face on now, even when he is not acting?

D. H. Lawrence

1511. To Cecil Gray, [20 January 1918]
Text: MS StaU; cited in Schorer, *London Magazine*, iii. 59.

Hermitage.
Sunday

Just got your letter. – I am not particularly unhappy – not at all – but still a bit seedy.

About Tregerthen – Virginia and Leonard Woolff – novelists, perhaps you

---

[1] See letter following. Leonard Woolf (1880–1969), historian, novelist and critic. m. 1912, Virginia Stephen (1882–1941), novelist and essayist. Kot provided the link between the Woolfs and DHL.

[2] Michael Farbman.

know – had asked us through Kot if we would sublet to them. I hadn't definitely answered. – Do you think the Fisher would be content there? If you lived in our cottage, and she in Esther Andrews', she would have to carry all your meals across in all weathers – and I don't see how you're going to get over that difficulty. – The trouble about the tower is that the stove there will only go when the wind suits it.

But if you really solidly want Tregerthen, we could either tell the Woolfs no, or else, if *your* sublet does not come off, they could go to Bosigran. You must let me know as soon as you can about this.

I don't think I shall come to London. Frieda might perhaps like to come for a week. But we have nowhere to go, and can't afford hiring London rooms. – And I really don't want to be in London.

If you would like to come down here, do so. We are expecting Arabella. You might like to come at the same time – or when she returns – as you prefer. See her and ask her what day she thinks of coming.

If you would like to communicate with the Woolfs, they are Hogarth House, Paradise Rd. Richmond, Surrey – or with Kot, the intermediary, he is S. Koteliansky, 5 Acacia Rd., St. Johns Wood. – It might be that we could change houses with the Woolfs. I'll ask them.

DHL

1512. To Leonard Woolf, [20 January 1918]
Text: MS NYPL; cited in *The Question of Things Happening*, ed. Nigel Nicolson (1976), ii. 340.

Chapel Farm Cottage, Hermitage, nr Newbury, Berks
Sunday

Dear Mr Woolf

Koteliansky says you would like to go to my cottage at Tregerthen. Another man, Gray, says he would like to go. But he has got a house four miles further down the coast – a better house than mine – so perhaps if he insists on Tregerthen, you will be better pleased with his Bosigran.

How many of you would go? And when would you like to go? And how long do you think you might stay?

My sister very much wants to find us a house in Derbyshire, near her – and have our furniture up from Cornwall. But as it is not very easy to find a house just now, I suppose that needn't bother you for five or six weeks, at least.

You see, I'm not sure you will like it – it is very cottagey. And it isn't one house – it's two, and separate – like this

[sketch]

that is, it is an isolated little settlement of two buildings, of which I have $1\frac{1}{2}$. The other half is the landlords summer cottage – usually shut up. But my wife and I live entirely in this little cottage, adjoining the landlords – and we put visitors in the big cottage. For two people, I think my little cottage is perfect. It has a downstairs sitting-room – a rather lovely bedroom upstairs – and a back scullery – no more: tight, compact, handy, easy – a mere stone cottage.

The other big cottage is only half furnished. It has six rooms – seven, counting the little room upstairs. Of these are furnished, at the bottom end, a little kitchen-sitting-room (one room), a bedroom above, and a small room next the bedroom, for washing in. – besides this, a sitting room at the other end, with great windows – called the tower. All the rooms are *small* – but pleasant. There are three empty rooms.

Two people can live quite comfortably in my tiny cottage – there is a good little cooking stove in the back scullery. – The tower-room is a beautiful room for a study, but the coke-stove will only burn in certain winds.

There is a decent bed, big enough for two, in my cottage – in the other house, a single bed – and in the tower room, a camp bed, a decent one, used as a sofa.

There is coal in – I think the place has been kept aired by the people at the farm below – the Hockings – they are two fields below – the only neighbours.

In Zennor is a good little inn, The Tinners Arms, where you can sleep the first night, if you like – or I could probably have everything got ready for you. – A woman fetches the washing – Annie Thomas – and she will perhaps come twice a week to clean for you, if you take no servant.

The rent I pay is £21, plus £2. taxes a year. If you like the place you can pay the rent – and a little more if it is easy for you, for the coal and furniture and vegetables, as you will. There should be a nice bit of coal, and there should be potatoes in the house, and roots in the garden. You can get milk and butter at the farm, and everything else except meat[1] and fruit at Mrs Berryman's, at the post office, in Zennor Churchtown – $\frac{3}{4}$ mile away. The Hockings at the farm, and Katie Berryman at the post office, are our very good friends. You can get a trap from Mrs[2] Berryman, to drive you out: the cottage is 4 miles from St. Ives:

Higher Tregerthen, Zennor, nr. St. Ives.

There is everything you will want, bedding linen etc, I think, for three people – but it is all rough, common.

Tell me what you are wanting – whether just a holiday change or a long stay.

Yrs   D. H. Lawrence

---

[1] meat] milk   [2] Mrs] Kate

The houses are plonked on the hill side, slap above the sea – which is about ten minutes, down the fields. It is beautiful, I think – and as lonely as necessary.

Tell me how many bedrooms you think to require, and I will say how much bedding you might take with you, if any.

What are you doing with your own house, while you are away?[1]

1513. To Lady Cynthia Asquith, 28 January 1918
Text: MS UT; Huxley 429–30.

Chapel Farm Cottage, Hermitage, nr. Newbury, Berks
Monday 28 Jan. 1918

I'm glad Herbert Asquith is physically safe so far, at least. I believe he's charmed to come out whole.

We are here – perfectly uneventful. I am writing a set of essays for America, in the hopes that they *may* get published by the ninnies and blockheads of the public world.

One day, we might talk really about your boy John. I'm sure he only needs proper psychic influence. Something has got locked in his psychic mechanism. Perhaps we might see him and be with him for a bit, one day – and then, perhaps, if we felt it might be any good, Frieda and I might have him with us for a time. I'm certain there is nothing primarily wrong – only something locked in the running. – I have not liked to speak of it, for fear of intruding on your feelings. But I think I might be, in some sort, a psychic physician – not doing anything direct, but merely as a presence – especially Frieda and me together. – Though of course it may be a conceit and a fallacy. But – I would help if I could.

I am looking with an anxious eye on the world and on Providence. It is time the latter showed a little silver over the edge of this present very dark cloud of penury. If the war were only over, Frieda could get something from her people. Meanwhile I fix an anxious eye on Providence. – But there, it's no use bothering.

I wonder if the opera will really come again in February – and if we shall go. What will happen to us all next, I wonder.

It has been very warm – but almost more like autumn than spring: like

---

[1] On 23 January 1918 Virginia Woolf recorded in her diary: 'we're in treaty with D. H. Lawrence for his house at Zennor. It's very distant & improbable at present though sufficiently tempting to make me think of that sea & those cliffs several times a day' (*Diary of Virginia Woolf*, ed. A. O. Bell, 1977, i. 112). For the Woolfs' subsequent correspondence with Captain Short see ibid., i. 258ff.

early October, so still and languid. – 'There's nae luck aboot the hoose – '.
Only one doesn't mind any more. – Certain snowdrops are out in the garden
and in the woods, and the birds sing very loudly at evening. One almost feels
like a bird oneself, whistling out of the invisible.

a rivederci   D. H. Lawrence

1514. To Michael Sadleir, [31 January 1918]
Text: MS UNCCH; Unpublished.

Chapel Farm Cottage, Hermitage, Nr. Newbury, Berks
31 Jan. 1917

Dear Mr Sadler[1]

I send you a couple of poems, as you asked me.[2] If you don't like them,
please send them back. – I hope you don't expect me to share the expenses of
publication, because I can't. I am up a very high tree of poverty just now.

Yours truly   D. H. Lawrence

Change the titles if you like.

Labour Battalion
(by D. H. Lawrence)

I.

The town grows fiercer with heat!
It does not shrivel like big herbage,
But it makes the sunlight beat
Backward and forward from wall to wall
And exults in its bitter usage
       Of us all.

Our hands, our breasts rebel against us,
Our eyes darken, and impotence hurts
Our soul. Nothing but the mad monotonous

---

[1] Michael Thomas Harvey Sadleir (1888–1957) adopted this spelling of his surname in 1919 to
avoid confusion with his father, Sir Michael Sadler, Master of University College, Oxford.
Sadleir was a novelist, bibliographer and bibliophile ('the most accomplished book collector of
our time', *Times*, 20 December 1957). He had joined the publishing firm, Constable & Co., in
1912 and became a very influential director in 1920; meanwhile, 1915–18, he served in the War
Trade Intelligence Department. He was the author of many works on Victorian fiction and
bibliography (particularly on Trollope), and novels (including *Fanny by Gaslight*, 1940). (See
Times obituary, 16 December 1957.)
[2] The two poems which follow were published in *New Paths: Verse, Prose, Pictures, 1917–1918*
(May 1918) which Sadleir edited with Cyril Beaumont (see p. 212 n. 1). (Beaumont also acted
as publisher for the volume.)

Stress of compulsion remains, and a band that girts
The heart – heart that beat
Once free as the running of angels' feet.

II.

Oh, and I wish that I
Was at Mablethorpe,
Where the long fawn foreshores lie
Taut as a wetted warp,
And the long waves rush and ply
Like a shuttle that carries the weft,
Like a harpist that strikes his deft
    Fingers across the harp.

Oh, to see the long waves rush,
Like the woof the shuttle carries,
Along the coast; to hear the hush
    Of the waves that wash
To the distance, the wave that tarries
Far down the coast, then comes up flush.

III

The cool, the cleanness of the sea,
    The sea all wet
Would wash away this ignominy:
    And better yet,
To hear the long waves strike the coast
As a harpist running along the strings,
Would take away the sickening fret
Of nerves that grind and a soul that stings
    And shame that hurts most.

For Oh, to feel the rhythm set
    In me again,
The substance tangled in the net
Of this days ignominy and sweat
    Set free again.
For the sound of the sea as it furls and unfurls
To sing in the shell of my heart the lull and increase;
For a rhythm to compel me back, for peace
    In the whispering whorls.

IV.

But I'll never reach the long sweet shore
    Of Lincolnshire.

Only the waste night lies in store.
Already I see the shelled moon lie
Like a shed white husk on the torrid sky,
         A thing of fear.

For the moon like a Fata Morgana will lean
         Out of the sky tonight.
The town will cluster her herbage then,
And sinister beings will beckon between
The thick rank streets; and a stark white light
         Envelop our den.

And we shall be sealed and stowed away
         And not like men.
We shall strip to the Fata Morgana, betray
And disown ourselves; and then when the light
Of morning is back, we shall change again
         And disown the night.[1]

No News

Ah heaven, send
Her letter somehow
To tell me
How she fares at her end
Of this journey,
So terrible now.

Rain, and a falling world
And never a word
To my silenced heart.
Explosions have whirled,
And a silence that stirred
Saw my last hope start
In vain –

She has sent me a letter.
The skies fall
The unseen cloud
Rains heavy: to me
Nothing again.
Nothing yet.

[1] l. 30 better] sweeter l. 33 sickening] sickness and l. 35 And] But l. 44 the] my l. 55 streets]
leaves

Were it better
To forget?
Forget all?
Is death so proud
That he dares demand
Everything from me
Thus beforehand?

Am I lost?
Has death set me apart
Beforehand?
Have I crossed
That border?
Have I nothing in this dark land,
Even no pain of heart
To afford her?

1515. To J. B. Pinker, 2 February 1918
Text: MS UT; cited in Carswell 96.

Chapel Farm Cottage – Hermitage, nr Newbury, Berks.
2 Feb. 1918

My dear Pinker

I am sorry to tell you that I am coming to the last end of all my resources, as far as money goes. Do you think that Arnold Bennett or somebody like that, who is quite rich out of literature, would give me something to get along with.[1] It is no use my trying to delude myself that I can make money in this world that is. – But there is coming a big smash-up, after which my day will begin. And as the smash up is not far off, so I am not very far off from a walk-in. – Meanwhile I am finally going through a set of *Studies in Classic American*

[1] Pinker sent DHL's letter to Bennett on 5 February 1918; Bennett replied on the 6th:
What a characteristic letter, and how unpromising for the future! I am not prepared to keep Lawrence, nor to give him a lump sum, as I doubt if the latter would help him very much. As to the vast fall in my income, I need only point out to you that it is about half what it was, & that I am keeping a number of people. I would willingly subscribe something towards a regular fund for Lawrence, say £1 a week for at least a year, if you think this would help and if you could get other subscriptions. So far as I am concerned there is no reason why he should know the names of the donors (*The Letters of Arnold Bennett 1916–1931*, ed. James Hepburn, 1970, i. 260).
It is probable that DHL's letter to Pinker, and Bennett's quoted above, together represent the source of Frieda's claim: 'I remember [DHL's] writing to Arnold Bennett and saying "I hear you think highly of me and my genius, give me some work." Arnold Bennett wrote back: "Yes, I do think highly of your genius, but that is no reason why I should give you work"' (Frieda Lawrence, *"Not I, But the Wind . . .",* Santa Fe, 1934, p. 105).

Literature, which of course rejoice my soul, but which no doubt would give the Americans – or the English – fits and convulsions of wrathful disgust if ever they went so far as to read them. I shall send you these essays in a little while. They are really very good – for the world that will come after this poor, weak-stomached show. You will see how you like them, and if you think you can do anything with them.

Do try and tempt a little money out of some rich good-natured author for me, will you – or I don't know what I shall do. And really, you know, one can't begin taking one's hat off to money, at this late hour of the day. I'd rather play a tin whistle in the street. – What a lively world!

Yours   D. H. Lawrence

I don't think the American essays will be so impossible for the editors, if we let the poor puppies chop them up for puppy-meat, and take out all the bone and gristle.

1516. To Michael Sadleir, 4 February 1918
Text: MS UNCCH; Unpublished.

Chapel Farm Cottage – Hermitage – Newbury, Berks.
4 Feb. 1918

Dear Mr Sadler

I am much obliged to you for speaking to Beaumont about *Women in Love*. I was having some correspondence with Maunsel about publication – not very satisfactory. Yes, I should be glad for Beaumont to see the MS., if he really thinks he might get the book out. I hate having it lie by. I have the MS. here with me, and will send it to Beaumont if I hear from him – then we could come to an agreement, I hope. The idea of a man like Beaumont pleases me – and the book, I know, is first rate. – Of course Pinker is my agent. But I could, I hope, come to an agreement with Beaumont myself, and just tell Pinker. He is very decent.

Thanks again.

Yours   D. H. Lawrence

1517. To Lady Cynthia Asquith, 12 February 1918
Text: MS UT; Huxley 430.

Chapel Farm Cottage – Hermitage – nr Newbury. Berks.
Tuesday. 12 Feb./18

We may be coming up to London in about a fortnight's time. Dollie Radford wants this cottage again. So we are once more on the streets. – As you infer, it doesn't bother me much, the poverty – perhaps it ought to bother me more, and I should provide better. For the time has come when I shall have to turn beggar, or something. I find we have got exactly six pounds nineteen shillings in the world: and not a penny due. I have written to Pinker, my agent – he might advance me something – probably will, one day – £20, I expect – but at present I can get no answer from him. An American woman said she was going to send – but that is months ago.[1] It is more a bore than anything else. But what to do, in ten days time when Mrs Radford will come here, I don't quite know. You don't think the War Office would now consider letting us return to Cornwall? – I could bleed my sister once more to get down there. – How stupid everything is. Gaudeamus igitur –[2]

I don't know why I should bother you with this. But if you know anybody that would be likely to patronise me – at a distance – I am very happy to be patronised – at a distance – why not. – I dreamed last night we had just arrived in Italy. So much for it, I am a great dreamer. It is time I found my Pharaoh – but the connection would have to be distant.[3]

Probably we shall be seeing you in a fortnight's time – if you stay in London. What about those February operas?

D. H. Lawrence

1518. To Michael Sadleir, 13 February 1918
Text: MS UNCCH; Unpublished.

Chapel Farm Cottage – Hermitage, nr Newbury. Berks.
13 Feb. 1918

Dear Mr Sadler

I had hoped to have a line from Beaumont about the novel *Women in Love* – but have heard nothing. Can you tell me if he would really consider publishing the book? – and if so, would you at least send me the address. I can't forward the MS. till I have that – and I should like to be assured that Beaumont is serious also.

I hope the anthology is coming together nicely.[4] – I should be grateful if you would just fix for me this matter of sending or not sending the MS. to Beaumont.

Yours Sincerely   D. H. Lawrence

---

[1] Perhaps Amy Lowell; at any rate on 12 March 1918 she sent DHL $200 in addition to royalties on the *Imagist* anthologies (Damon 443). See Letter 1585 for DHL's acknowledgement.

[2] A medieval students' song ['Let us live then and be glad'].

[3] An allusion to Genesis xli which relates Pharaoh's dream, Joseph's interpretation of it, his elevation to the rank of ruler subordinate only to Pharaoh, and his success in husbanding resources during fruitful years in preparation for the lean.

[4] i.e. *New Paths*.

1519. To S. S. Koteliansky, 16 February 1918
Text: MS BL; Postmark, Hermitage 17 FE [. . .]; cited in Gransden 27.

Chapel Farm Cottage – Hermitage – nr Newbury, Berks.
Sat. 16 Feb. 1918

My dear Kot,

Your last was a very desperate letter, in a quiet way. Its a good deal how I feel myself. The damned show goes on and on, grinding like a coffee-mill, till one feels one will burst with the madness of it. But do you know I believe it will go on for quite a long while yet. Only a cataclysm will stop it – and a cataclysm is quite a long way off, I believe.

We are rather in a tight corner just now, what with money and houselessness. But nothing serious. We shan't come to London. Probably we shall get rooms in this village, for such time as Dollie Radford is here. It doesn't seem much to matter, so long as one gets through the days.

I wish you had got a type-writing machine now, I should ask you again to do some typing for me, as before in those fatal first months of the war, when most wearily you pegged through a hundred pages of philosophy.[1] Alas, the bureau – alas, Slatkowsky. Alas, that one cannot hang a wreath of thin cheap sausages over the mantel-piece of his room in 212, in memoriam.[2] Well, one blot is under the earth instead of upon it – which is a blessing.

So you and Farbman are setting up another Russian Lawless Bureau at No. 5. I see it coming – another bureau – history repeating itself. – Why this break-up of the family circle? Alas, and nothing but alas, everywhere.

I have had a sore throat for such a long time now, that I am getting thoroughly tired of it. Oh my dear, dear Kot, why didn't we go to our Rananim! What a weak-kneed lot we were, not to bring it off. I do so want something nice – a bit of a pleasant world somewhere – nothing but the corner of a cemetery seems to offer – and I might find a Slat. there first.

You grumble at me for not writing, but you never answered my last letter – Even now it is your turn to write to me.

Remember me to the grim and grizzly Grisha.

D. H. Lawrence

---

[1] See Letter 792, *Letters*, ii. 220. [2] See p. 43 n. 4.

1520. To Mark Gertler, 16 February 1918
Text: MS SIU; cited in Moore, *Intelligent Heart* 239-40.

Chapel Farm Cottage – Hermitage – nr Newbury, Berks.
Saturday. 16 Feb. 1918

Dear Gertler,

How are you by now? I didn't like your last letter about women – viz. prostitutes. I have an aesthetical or physical aversion from prostitutes – they smell in my inward nostrils. – Are you still painting? I am doing a set of very nice (to me) essays on[1] America – philosophic – but I doubt if they will ever be published while this world stands. True, it seems cracking. But curse the old show, it will go on cracking for another century, without tumbling down.

I find things, both in general and in particular, very exasperating. In the first place, I am at the dead end of my money, and can't raise the wind in any direction. Do you think you might know of somebody who would give us something to keep us going a bit. It makes me swear – such a damned, mean, narrow-gutted, pitiful, crawling, mongrel world, that daren't have a man's work and won't even allow him to live. – Then, in this state of blankness, Dollie Radford wants this cottage, so I suppose we are to camp out like babes in the wood, and ask the robins to cover us with warm leaves. We shall clear out of here in about a week's time – where to, God knows. Probably we shall get a room in the village – like Mrs Gommes, minus Gilbert and Mary.[2] – Then I've had the very devil of a bad throat for three weeks, which gives me a queer feeling as if I was blind – why, I don't know. – and makes me talk in a senile fluty squeak very ignoble.

But nothing is so boring as woes. – But if you could cast over in your mind some individual who might give me a little money on my merits – why – we will go on a little longer. – Poor Kot. offers me his remaining ten pounds. He might as well offer me his nose.

Still I wait for the day when this foul tension of war and pot-bellied world will break, when we can meet in something like freedom and enjoy each other's company in something like decency. Nowadays one can do nothing but glance behind to see who now is creeping up to do something horrible to the back of one's neck.

Whatever else you do, write and say you are still alive, and ready to have the last laugh of all these fleas and bugs of righteous militarism. Tell me any news, if there is any.

D. H. Lawrence

---

[1] on] of
[2] For part of the time Gilbert and Mary Cannan were living in Mill House at Cholesbury Common (near Bellingdon where the Lawrences lived from August 1914 until January 1915), Gertler was housed in 'wretched and uncomfortable rooms' in the village (Diana Farr, *Gilbert Cannan*, 1978, p. 114). His landlady was Mrs Gomm.

1521. To Catherine Carswell, 16 February 1918
Text: MS YU; Postmark, Hermitage 17 FE 18; cited in Moore, *Intelligent Heart* 239.

Chapel Farm Cottage – Hermitage – nr. Newbury, Berks.

16 Feb. 1918

My dear Catherine

How are you by now? Are you well, both of you? Will Duckworth take the novel? – If not, who is it that has a 'First Novel Series'?[1] Either John Lane[2] or Fisher Unwin. Try that. Are you in Holly Bush House? Have you any prosperity?

With us things are tiresome. I've had the devil of a sore throat for three weeks – sort of blinding effect. – Then money is coming to a dead end – don't know quite how to raise the wind. – Then Dollie Radford wants this cottage next week – I don't know where we shall go – probably get rooms in this village. Tiresome altogether, nothing good: except a day of beautiful sunshine today.

The world seems to crack a bit, but I believe it'll go on crackling and fizzing a long time before there is any break. We've got a good bit more of this old sort to go on with, if nothing worse. Well, it's a good thing we are as well as we are.

I suppose food is tiresome in Hampstead – here meat is the most difficult. But I'd put up with the food if there were a little relief in life.

Barbara Low says she saw you and you seemed happy. It is the only thing to do – save oneself and be happy apart. They are chopping down much timber here: we go and get wood: it is strange and sort of other-world – the fires in the clearings.

If you see Ivy, tell her from me I'm so glad Litvinov has got this office: I hope she'll become a full-blooded ambassadress, I do.[3] It pleases me immensely. I sit here and say bravo. I almost feel like asking Litvinov if I can't help – but I don't suppose I'm of much use at this point. Tell Ivy, if there is anything interesting, I do wish she'd write.

Frieda is pretty well – wondering what is to become of us. – There are primroses in the wood – and avenues of yellow hazel catkins, hanging like curtains.

Love from us to you both   D. H. Lawrence

---

[1] Fisher Unwin had launched the series 'First Novel Library: First Novels of New Authors'.

[2] John Lane (1854–1925), publisher, who, with Elkin Mathews, had founded the Bodley Head publishing firm in 1887.

[3] On 2 January 1918 Maxim Litvinov was appointed 'provisional Plenipotentiary in London of the People's Commissariat for Foreign Affairs' (*Times*, 3 January 1918). The Russian Government, in the expectation that their request would be refused, had not so far asked that Litvinov be accredited as Ambassador.

1522. To J. B. Pinker, 16 February 1918
Text: MS UT; Moore 541–2.

Chapel Farm Cottage – Hermitage – nr Newbury. Berks.

Saturday 16 Feb. 1918

My Dear Pinker

Two weeks ago I wrote to you that my affairs are very low, and asked for help, if you could give it. But you have not answered at all.

I am afraid in another fortnight I shall not have a penny to buy bread and margarine. Would you be so good as to ask Austin Harrison to let me have something. He owes me, I suppose, for the last two essays – in this month's, and last months issues.[1] – Did Chattos pay you the £20 all right, on publication of the poems?[2] I suppose I am a fair amount in your debt. How much?

I am afraid I am an infernal nuisance – seems my fate to be such.

D. H. Lawrence

1523. To Lady Cynthia Asquith, [18 February 1918]
Text: MS UT; Unpublished.

Chapel Farm Cottage – *Hermitage*, nr. *Newbury. Berks.*

Monday

Thanks for your letter. Yes, it will be nice if you can send me a little money from somebody. At first I had a bit of a revulsion, from mixing up my friendships and money matters. But one is really too tired for these squeamishnesses – they are false. I would give you money, if I'd got any.

We have taken a room in the village here: can't afford to come to London, just now – nothing has come for us: and we have nowhere to go in London. Then there are raids. It is nice enough here.

DHL

[1] See p. 164 n. 2.   [2] See p. 155 n. 1.

1524. To Cyril Beaumont, 19 February 1918
Text: MS UCin; Unpublished.

Chapel Farm Cottage – *Hermitage*. nr. Newbury. Berks
19 Feb. 1918

Dear Sir,[1]

I am sending you the MS of my novel *Women in Love*, according to Mr Sadler's suggestion. It would please me very much to have it done by you, away from such people as Methuen.[2] And I am sure we can easily come to terms, if you would care to do the book. I know it is a big thing. And though I am hopelessly hard up, yet I would dearly like to see this book in print, to have it off my hands, and safe. While it remains in manuscript, and myself always in such a state of jeopardy, I feel it may get lost.

Some friends already asked me to let them start a scheme for private publication. And probably that would be best. You will see what you think. We could bring you the list of subscribers, and you might do the book privately under your name. If you liked, after you have read the MS., and thought about it, I could come to London to see you. But don't keep the thing hanging about, will you? If you don't care to undertake the publication, I should like to get on with the private scheme, quickly – so let me know fairly soon. – I have no qualms about the merit of the book – but shall be interested to hear what you think.

Yours Sincerely   D. H. Lawrence

1525. To S. S. Koteliansky, [20 February 1918]
Text: MS BL; Postmark, Hermitage 20 FE 18; Moore 542.

Hermitage –
Wednesday[3]

My dear Kot,

Will you be good, and get for me Edgar Allan Poe's *Tales of Mystery and*

---

[1] Cyril William Beaumont (1891–1976), bookseller and publisher (at 75 Charing Cross Road). He was the author of several books on the theatre and classical ballet; he was regarded as the scholar of the post-Diaghilev ballet revival in England. From 1917–31 he ran the Beaumont Press specialising in the work of contemporary writers; in addition to publishing DHL's *Bay* (1919), he published work by Drinkwater, Nichols, Flecker, Blunden, etc. Though Beaumont had been a friend of Lady Cynthia Asquith's brother, Hon. Yvo Charteris (1896–1915), his link with DHL was initiated by Michael Sadleir. Beaumont and Sadleir jointly edited *New Paths* (see p. 202 n. 2). See *Times* obituary, 25 May 1976.

[2] DHL had felt betrayed by his publisher Methuen who offered no defence against the police prosecution of *The Rainbow* (*Letters*, ii. 441).

[3] Wednesday] Tuesday

Imagination, out of the Everyman's Library, and send the book[1] to me by return – I think it is 1/6 now. I am in the middle of an essay on Edgar Allan, and have lost my copy.[2]

I got your letter. Yes, I know the Ot. is very nice, somewhere. I once was *very* fond of her – and I am still, in a way. But she is like someone who has died: and I cannot wish to call her from the grave. She is good and, in a way, I love her, as I love someone who is dead. But not for life.

I too am sick of world builders – à la Lansbury.[3] I want their world smashed up, not set up – all the world smashed-up. These Lansbury and Bertie Russell world-builders are only *preventers* of everything, the negators of life. – I'm afraid there will be noise for a long while yet.

DHL

1526. To J. B. Pinker, 20 February 1918
Text: MS UT; cited in Delany 345.

Chapel Farm Cottage – Hermitage – nr. Newbury, Berks
Wed. 20 Feb. 1918

My dear Pinker

Thank you for your letter of this morning. If Arnold Bennett will help, why the devil must he wait for others to keep him in countenance.[4] And if he won't, why then, so be it.

As for the Authors Society, I very much doubt if they would give me anything. I had from them £50, I believe, in the first months of the war.[5] But I am not a member of their society – and I can guess what their opinion of me is. If they would be any use, well and good. But I don't much like the thought of them.

I suppose Austin Harrison will let me have some of what is owing. Thank you for letting my debt to you stand aside.

Yours   D. H. Lawrence

---

[1] the book] them
[2] 'Edgar Allan Poe' (eventually to be included in *Studies in Classic American Literature*) appeared in *English Review*, xxviii (April 1919), 278–91.
[3] George Lansbury (1859–1940), Christian Socialist, and Labour politician. He earned a reputation as an idealist and internationalist; during the war he was closely identified with the pacifist section of the Labour party. He edited the *Weekly Herald* up to 1918 and the *Daily Herald*, 1919–22.
[4] See p. 205 n. 1.
[5] DHL appears to be confusing the Society of Authors (to which he had been elected on 6 December 1915, see *Letters*, ii. 433 n. 1) with the Royal Literary Fund which awarded him £50 on 14 October 1914. There were some grounds for his confusion: see *Letters*, ii. 226 n. 1.

1527. To S. S. Koteliansky, [21 February 1918]
Text: MS BL; Postmark, [Herm] itage 21 FE [. . .]; cited in Gransden 27.

Hermitage – nr Newbury. – Berks.
Thursday

My dear Kot

I didn't tell you about the pennilessness because

1. You are a gentleman of strictly limited means,

and 2. – much too ready to dissipate those limited means

in which case 3 – you are a stranger in a strange and not very friendly land,[1] with no prospect but to bay the moon.[2]

But thank you very much, though it is really a blow to me, to diminish your capital.[3] We will bay the moon together, when it comes to that.

If I came to London for a few days, in a week or a fortnight's time, could you put me up? I would bring food – what I could. – Beaumont, in Charing Cross Rd., *might* be doing the novel – in which case I should have to discuss with him.

Spy round, and see if there isn't a type-writer anywhere. It would be good for you to do something, and a great blessing for me. Out of these Essays on American Classic Literature I might even make some money – if you typed them for me – in which case we could all say Pfui! to the moon.

I have such a desire, that after the war, we should all go together to some nice place, and be really happy for a bit – insouciant, sans souci, and all that – perhaps in Italy – Gertler and Shearman and Campbell and Frieda and you and me – and anybody else that seemed particularly nice – and Gertler to be weaned from the paint brush – and we'll cook for ourselves, and row in a boat, and make excursions, and talk, and be quite happy for a while: in the Abruzzi, for example. – Shearman sent me £10., in a very decent way. – I told him about this post-war plan. Let us have our Rananim for a month or two, if we can't for ever. – One must have something to look forward to. And the only way is to get out of the world.

Eder is going with a Commission in a fortnight to prospect Palestine for Zion.[4] I wish they'd give *me* palestine – I'd Zionise it into a Rananim. Zion might be *so* good – save for the Zionists.

Have you sent me the Poe? I hope it'll come tomorrow.

Mila saluti cari[5]   D. H. Lawrence

---

[1] Exodus ii. 22 (A.V.) ['a stranger in a strange land'].
[2] *Julius Caesar* IV. iii. 27.
[3] Kot had sent £10: see letter following.
[4] See p. 150 n. 1.
[5] 'Very many (literally, a thousand, 'mille') affectionate greetings'.

1528. To Mark Gertler, 21 February 1918
Text: MS SIU; Huxley 431–2.

Chapel Farm Cottage – Hermitage – nr. Newbury, Berks.
21 Feb. 1918

Dear Gertler,

Thanks very much for your letter and the help from Shearman. I must say Shearman is very decent – much better than Eddie. – But Kot. went and sent me also £10. when you told him, though really I don't want to take his money, when he has *no* prospects. But perhaps things will clear up.

As for my feelings – they won't interest you very much. About the world, I feel that nothing but a quite bloody, merciless, almost anarchistic revolution will be any good for this country, a fearful chaos of smashing up. And I think it will come sooner or later: and I wish it would come soon. And yet, somehow, I don't want to be in it. I know it *should* come, and must come; yet I would like to go away, not to see it. – But if I tried to go, I suppose some whale or other would snap me up and carry me back like a gudgeon in its mouth, and cast me back on Britannia's miserable shores.

Then, as to work, I *don't* think that to work is to live. Work is all right in proportion: but one wants to have a certain richness and satisfaction in oneself, which is more than anything produced. One wants to *be*. I think we need, not to paint or write, but to have a liberation from ourselves, to become quite careless and free. And we need to go away, as soon as we can, right to a new scene, and at least for a bit, live a new life – you and Campbell and Kot and Shearman and Frieda and me – and whosoever else you want – and in some queer way, by *forgetting* everything, to start afresh. We live now in such a state of tension against everything – *you* are always wound up in a dreadful state of resistant tension. Now I think, that between a few of us, this tension ought to go, we ought to be able to relax altogether, to be perfectly confident with each other, and free. As it is, if you meet me, at once there is a sort of tension between us, you holding out hard against me, I holding hard against you. I believe it wants only just a little change, and this tension of resistance could disappear, and we could be at peace with one another, at peace, and free, and spontaneous, no need to hold our own each against the other in a tension of self-conscious self-insistence. I believe this could be so between Shearman and Kot and Campbell and you and Frieda and me – a kind of fulfilment, as if we were all complete beings, and therefore all free by being together, as in a new world.

So I always want to have a plan of going away after the war – anywhere that is not England – perhaps Italy – going away and living in one place, all of us, at least for a while. – But it is no good, if work, or love either, seems to you the be-all and the end-all. Work and love are subsidiary. What one wants is a free, spontaneous, harmonious relation amongst ourselves, each of us being in some way a complete fulfilled being. – Whatever you think of this plan, we might try it for a holiday.

I should beware of Garsington. I believe there is something exhaustive in the air there, not so very restful.

I am doing some philosophic essays, also, very spasmodically, another daft novel.[1] It goes slowly – very slowly and fitfully. But I don't care.

Don't wear yourself down to the last thread, without hope or relaxing – that's all.

I may come to London for a little while, in a fortnight, perhaps.

D. H. Lawrence

1529. To Montague Shearman, 21 February 1918
Text: MS UT; Huxley 432–3.

Chapel Farm Cottage – Hermitage, nr Newbury. Berks.
21 Feb. 1918

My dear Shearman

Thank you very much for the £10. Now we need not worry any more; for the moment, at least. I have never been so tight put – for money and everything else – damnable. But I don't mind taking from you: no, I am glad to have the money from your hand. But I hate depriving you of it. One man's gain is another man's loss. But I can't help it. – It is damnable people like Pinker, my agent, who dangle a prospective fish on the end of a line, with grinning patronage, and just jerk it away every letter, that make me see red. I've got quite a lot of murder in my soul: heaven knows how I shall ever get it out.

I may come to London for a bit, soon. That man Beaumont, in Charing Cross Rd., *might* do my novel. If I am in town, then we must have a quiet talk – perhaps without Marcus,[2] who is a terrible young egoist, and breaks all the eggs into *his* batter.

I always imagine what a lovely time we will all have together, for a bit, when the war is over: perhaps in Italy, it is so cheap. Let us make a plan of this, shall we? You and Gertler and Kot and Frieda and me and Campbell and anybody else you like, go to Italy and have a house by the sea, and row and bathe and talk and be as happy as birds for a bit. It is owing to us. I shall have some money when the war ends.

D. H. Lawrence

[1] The first reference to the novel eventually (in April 1922) published as *Aaron's Rod*.
[2] Unidentified.

1530. To J. B. Pinker, 22 February 1918
Text: MS UNYB; Unpublished.

Chapel Farm Cottage – Hermitage – Newbury, Berks
22 Feb. 1918

My dear Pinker

Thank you for the cheque for nine guineas, received from you today, for the *English Review* essays.

Yrs   D. H. Lawrence

1531. To Lady Cynthia Asquith, [22 February 1918]
Text: MS UT; Unpublished.

Chapel Farm Cottage – Hermitage, nr Newbury – Berks
Friday

Thank you for the £5., which came this morning. I'm sure you must hate asking people for money – dont do it any more – I got from Pinker £9. which was owing me from the *English Review*.

DHL

You only put half the address on your letter – or was it you who added the other half, or the post office?

1532. To S. S. Koteliansky, [25 February 1918]
Text: MS BL; Moore 594–5.

c/o Mrs Lowe[1] – Hermitage, nr Newbury, Berks
Monday[2]

My dear Kot

I send you the first part of the essays. I am afraid there is much more to follow.

It troubles me that I have made so many alterations, you will have difficulty in reading.

In the first essay, I have made little marginal headings. Don't type these. We must consider whether to write them small in the margin of your typed MS. when it is done: – so that it should be printed in small fount marginal headings. Decide that for me – help me.

Oh, my dear Kot, these essays are a weariness to me. I know they are really very good. You may not be in tune for them, so they may bore you. But do

---

[1] c/o Mrs Lowe] Chapel Farm Cottage.
[2] Dated with reference to Kot's typing the essays on American literature and the possibility of DHL's visiting London, both of which are mentioned in Letter 1527.

read them through *very* carefully for me, before you type them. And then, if you see anything that would be best left out, from the publishing point of view, do leave it out. I very much want to sell these essays. I know how good they are in substance. Yet I know it will be difficult to get them accepted. I want to make them acceptable to a publisher, if it is in any way possible. So go through them carefully as if you were an editor, will you.

I send you type-paper. Do me *two* copies will you – one carbon.

Tomorrow Dollie Radford comes here with the madman,[1] so we go to rooms in the village: c/o Mrs. Lowe.

I *might* come to London at the week-end – Friday or Saturday. Could you do with me for a brief day or two.

I'm so grateful to you for this typing work. We *must* sell these essays if we can.

DHL

I underlined the little marginal headings in the first essay. Don't type them.

1533. To Cyril Beaumont, 26 February 1918
Text: MS SIU; Unpublished.

c/o Mrs Lowe, Hermitage, nr. Newbury, Berks.
26 Feb. 1918

Dear Mr Beaumont

I return proofs of the two poems.[2] Let me know about the novel soon, what you think – I might come up to town to see you in a few days time.

Yrs   D. H. Lawrence

1534. To J. B. Pinker, [5 March 1918]
Text: MS UNYB; PC; Postmark, London, W.C. MAR 5 18; Unpublished.

5. Acacia Rd. – St. John's Wood, N.W.
Tuesday

My dear Pinker,

I am here in London for a couple of days.[3] – Could you send me the little manuscript of a book of tiny poems I sent you quite a long time ago – short little pieces which refer more or less to the war – I think I sent it a year ago last

---

[1] Her husband, Ernest Radford, was mentally unstable towards the end of his life (he died in 1919).
[2] See Letter 1514 and n. 2.
[3] DHL was staying with Kot.

Christmas.[1] – Do let me have the MS. by return if you can, as I think of leaving London on Thursday.

Yrs.   D. H. Lawrence

1535. To Lady Cynthia Asquith, [6 March 1918]
Text: MS UT; Unpublished.

[5 Acacia Rd, St John's Wood, London, N.W.]
Wednesday[2]

I am just off back to Hermitage. – Saw Beaumont – he says he is not to come in at all (mind this) – that we are to proceed delicately – that the cost of printing will be £365 – that there will have to be a sum advanced before anything can begin – that it will be sold a guinea a copy. – But go and see him and ask him about it – but say you *know* he has nothing to do with it.

This is all about the novel I am speaking.

C.W. Beaumont, 75 Charing Cross Rd.
D. H. Lawrence

1536. To S. S. Koteliansky, [7 March 1918]
Text: MS BL; Zytaruk 136.

Chapel Farm Cottage, Hermitage, nr Newbury, Berks.
Thursday.

My dear Kot

I got back here last night – very tired. I had your telephone message from Collins[3] – saw Beaumont. He says he himself would not have anything to do with the publishing – but gave me estimates from another man. It would cost about £375 to do the book – an enormous sum. He suggests selling at a guinea a copy, by subscription – says it could be made to pay. I am bored.

I have a kind of belief we shall make some money with the American essays. And when I have money, if ever I do, you will have money too. We'll take courage.

I like being at Acacia Rd. without Mrs Donald[4] – it is fun. Thank you very much for doing for me so well.

<hr>

[1] The typescript of 'All of Us' was sent to Pinker on 11 December 1916 (see Letter 1330).

[2] The date is confirmed as 6 March 1918 by Lady Cynthia's record of a conversation with DHL about Beaumont and *Women in Love* (though she calls it 'Goats and Compasses') on the previous evening, 5 March (Asquith, *Diaries* 417). Presumably the letter formed a 'postscript' to the conversation. (On 'Goats and Compasses' see *Letters*, ii. 558 n. 4.)

[3] Vere Collins.

[4] Presumably the domestic 'help'. He had discussed the matter of household help with Lady Cynthia Asquith only two days earlier and said 'he really preferred living without servants' (Asquith, *Diaries* 417).

Don't get despairing – I really think we have come to the bottom of things.
We'll start to rise up just now, see if we don't.

Let me hear from you. Remind Gertler to ask Ottoline about the book.

DHL

1537. To Lady Cynthia Asquith, [7 March 1918]
Text: MS UT; cited in Ross, *DHL Review*, viii. 208.

Chapel Farm Cottage – Hermitage, nr Newbury, Berks
Thursday

The full story of the novel is that Beaumont does not want his name to come
in at all, as it is not too good a name in the Purity ears already.[1] It would all be
done in my name. – Cost of printing and binding would be about £375 – which
seems to me excessive. A certain sum – say £150 – would have to be put down,
the printing would then begin, and we should issue little order-forms, saying
the work was in hand, and subscriptions of a guinea were invited. Everything
would go first to pay the £375 – after that, everything would be mine: i.e. the
rest of the 1000 copies, which would be the whole edition. It depends a good
deal what Antoine B[ibesco] would think fit to fob out. If he is a £20. touch,
he is not much good. – But if he is more – why, he can have the book inscribed
to him, if he likes – 'To Prince Antoine Bibesco, whose liberality has enabled
this book to appear' – Work your sister-in-law, and see what is possible. – But
if Antoine is going to help, he must put the money right down – promises are
no good. If he would help a good deal with the initial cost, very nice of him –
If not, this thing can wait. – If anything comes of it we might come to London
for a month or two, to do the business – a friend offers us a house in the
Hampstead Garden Suburb.[2] – If it came off, it might even make me £200 or
£300 – or more trouble. – A friend is approaching Ottoline to know how she
feels. I know she would like the thing to appear, for self-advertisement – and
her sheep-faced fool of a husband would like to denounce it, for further self-
advertisement. Pah, people make one sick.

Write and tell me if there is anything to tell. Don't do anything you don't
want to do – 'tisnt worth it.[3]

DHL

[1] See p. 61 n. 1.
[2] Probably Vere Collins; see p. 194 n. 1.
[3] Lady Cynthia approached Beaumont on DHL's behalf and had clearly discussed *Women in
Love* with the Roumanian diplomat, Prince Antoine Bibesco (1878–1951) who was to marry
her sister-in-law, Elizabeth Asquith (1897–1945) in 1919. (At this time he was trying to initiate

1538. To Lady Cynthia Asquith, 8 March 1918
Text: MS UT; Huxley 433.

Chapel Farm Cottage, Hermitage, Newbury
Friday 8 March 1918

Long ago I put these little poems together, and asked you if you would like me to inscribe them to you.[1] Then I held them back, because they are ironical and a bit wicked. But Beaumont asked me particularly for a book exactly this length – so I send it you, to see if you would care to have it inscribed to you after all. – Tell me what you think of the poems. If they make a bad impression on you, I will still hold them back, I think. But in their own way – to me they are bitterly ironical – they are quite good, I think. If you like them, send them on to Beaumont – 75 Charing Cross Rd – or take them to him, and I will write to him. – But write to me quickly about them, as I promised Beaumont to let him have the MS at once.[2]

DHL

But Beaumont wants only to give me £8. or £9. for them – I think it is too little – not worth having them published for so little.

1539. To Captain John Short, 8 March 1918
Text: MS UT; Unpublished.

Chapel Farm Cottage, Hermitage, nr. Newbury, Berks.
Friday 8 March 1918

Dear Captain Short,

I am afraid I shall have to give up the cottages – things don't change in London, and there is no immediate hope of our coming back. It makes me very angry – but it's no use wasting oneself.

I think the little cottage is taken from March 21st, and the others from May

---

an affair with Lady Cynthia herself.) She recorded in her diary, 9 March 1918 (following the receipt of Letter 1538): 'I bicycled off to Charing Cross Road to find Beaumont . . . We then discussed the book: he had only just seen Lawrence for the first time and was full of amazement at him. He is emphatic that his name must not appear in connection with Lawrence's book in the event of its being published – so is Bibesco! – and so am I . . . *commercially* Beaumont's opinion was that it would be a success . . . It would have to be done without any name of printer as it might mean prison. We agreed that the only course was to get the manuscript and let Bibesco read it for himself and make up his mind whether he wishes to proceed in the matter or not. Personally I don't feel very keen about it' (Asquith, *Diaries* 419).

[1] 'All of Us'; see Letter 1328.
[2] Lady Cynthia took the poems to Beaumont when she received them, on 9 March. She was relieved that the poems were 'mainly (thank Heaven)! *not* erotic – ironical glimpses at aspects of the war – with very little rhyme or rhythm about them' (Asquith, *Diaries* 419).

1st. I owe you £5. or so on the big house. I will send it before long. Meanwhile I am not quite sure whether to sell up the furniture altogether, or to bring it up to Derbyshire, where my sister would store it for me till she finds us a place in the country near her. I must decide in a day or two, and then I will let you know. There are several pieces of yours in the two houses.

If I decide to take the things away, I will get Benney to pack them off for me, if he will do so.[1] Of course I should be glad to have any help from you that you could give.

I am so sorry things have turned out so stupidly and miserably. Never mind, there will be a big change one day. – Perhaps you will be able to let the cottages again quite quickly – this is the favorable time of the year.

I hope you and Mrs Short are well. My wife and I are all right – but sick of things, and very short of money. It is a cursed life.

Best greetings from us both   D. H. Lawrence

1540. To J. B. Pinker, 9 March 1918
Text: MS UNYB; PC; Postmark, Hermitage 9 MR 18; Unpublished.

Chapel Farm Cottage – Hermitage, nr. Newbury.
9 Mar. 1918

My dear Pinker

Thank you for the MS. of poems which I have received safely.

D. H. Lawrence

1541. To William Hopkin, 12 March 1918
Text: MS NCL; Postmark, Hermitage 12 MR 18; Huxley 436–7.

Chapel Farm Cottage – *Hermitage*, nr Newbury, Berks.
12 March. 1918

Dear Willie

Ada told me you would write to Mr Marsden about the house at[2] Bole Hill.[3] I wonder if you did so. It is a very pleasant little house, and I should love to have it – if only it might be empty. I should really like to come back now, and be not far away from all the old people. How nice it would be if we had the house at Bole Hill – I used to stay there when Miss Marsden was alive

---

[1] Benny appears to have had a furniture shop (or perhaps auctioneer's rooms) in St Ives (see *Letters*, ii. 585, 590, 631).
[2] MS reads 'it'.
[3] Bole Hill is close to Derby. (The Marsdens are unidentified.)

– and you could come and see us, you and Mrs Hopkin. – But any little place, nice and separate, would do. I can't be jammed in among people any more. Frieda and I have lived so much alone, and in isolated places, that we suffer badly at being cooped up with other folk. Ada takes it very much amiss that we don't go and stay with her, to look round. But it is real purgatory to be in her little house, with everybody and everything whirling round. If she had really cared, surely she would have got someone to look out for a place for us. It is very nice here – Hardy country – like *Woodlanders* – all woods and hazel-copses, and tiny little villages that will sleep forever. There are two such charming cottages we could have here – one in the village, under the church, with fields slanting down, and a hazel copse almost touching the little garden wall: the other on top of a hill against a big wood. I am *very* tempted to take one of these places, they are so still and secure and peaceful for ever, as only the West country can be. But still I will wait, and see if something won't turn up in Derbyshire or Notts. – wait till after Easter, perhaps.

We are very quiet here – with no particular news – nothing at least that one can write. I should be glad to see you and Sallie again, to have a talk. I should be really glad to live within reach. There are lots of things to say, nowadays.

Let me hear how you are. Remember us *very* warmly to Sallie. – Do you see me returning to the Midlands, or do you not?

D. H. Lawrence

1542. To Cecil Gray, 12 March 1918
Text: MS StaU; Huxley 434–6.

Chapel Farm Cottage – Hermitage – nr Newbury, Berks.
12 March 1918

How are you finding Bosigran? – if you have got back there. I hope it is nice, now the weather is soft and sunny. I wrote to Capt. Short to say I would not keep on the cottages at Tregerthen – also I wrote to William Henry, to tell him the same news. But I have not yet quite decided what to do about the furniture. My sister gets furious if I say we may not go near her. Yet she does not find us a house. On the other hand there are two charming cottages here – one down in a little village, fast asleep for ever: a cottage just under the hill, under the hazel-woods, with its little garden backing to the old church-yard, where the sunny, grey, square-towered church dozes on without rousing: the other on the hill touching the wood. Frieda of course is *dying* for one of these. And when we were down in Hampstead Norris yesterday, I quite shook with panic, lest we should actually go and take the cottage under the hill by the church.[1] A real panic comes over me, when I feel I am on the brink of taking another house. I truly wish I were a fox or a bird – but my ideal now is to have a caravan and a horse, and move on for ever, and never have a neighbour. This is a real after-the-war ideal. There is a gipsy camp near here – and how I envy them – down a sandy lane under some pine trees.

I find here one is soothed with trees. I never knew how soothing trees are – many trees, and patches of open sunlight, and tree-presences – it is almost like having another being. At the moment the thought of the sea makes me verily shudder.

I ebb along with the American essays, which are in their last and final form. In them, I have got it all off my chest. I shall never write another page of philosophy – or whatever it is – when these are done. Thank God for that. Yet it is absolutely necessary to get it out, fix it, and have a definite foot hold, to be *sure*. Of course I think the world ought to hold up its hands in marvelling thankfulness for such profound and relieving exposition. And of course I see the world doing it.

It is very spring-like. In spite of the fact that I *think* the war will last forever, I believe this particular war with Germany wont last so very much longer, on our part. Not that it matters all the world, – people won't alter: and they won't die in sufficient quantities to matter. I have come to think that it is enough to lapse along pleasantly with the days. It is very nice. That is why the cottage in the village fills me with such panic. I believe I could go into a soft sort of Hardy-sleep, hearing the church chime from hour to hour, watching the horses at the farm drink at the pond, writing pages that *seemed* beautifully important, and having visits from people who *seemed* all wrong, as coming from the inferior outer world.

– But no doubt some new sword of Damocles is just spinning to drop on one's head.

I don't know why you and I don't get on very well when we are together. But it seems we don't. It seems we are best apart. You seem to go winding on in some sort of process that just winds me in the other direction. You might just tell me when you think your process is ended, and we'll look at each other again. Meanwhile you dance on in some sort of sensuous dervish dance that winds my brain up like a ticking bomb. God save us, what a business it is even to be acquainted with another creature. But I suppose one day we might hit it off. Be quick and wind yourself to the end. The one thing I don't seem to be able to stand is the presence of anybody else – barring Frieda, sometimes. Perhaps I shall get over it.

[1] Hampstead Norris is a village two miles n.e. of Hermitage.

I shall ask you if I want any help at Tregerthen, in the removing. Meanwhile adieu. Frieda greets you.

D. H. Lawrence

But I do loathe possessing things, and having another house. If only one could be an animal, with a thick warm hide, and never a stitch or rag besides. Nobody ought to own houses or furniture – any more than they own the stones of the high-road.

1543. To Captain John Short, [13 March 1918]
Text: MS UT; Unpublished.

Chapel Farm Cottage – Hermitage, nr Newbury. Berks.
Wed

Dear Capt Short.

I have received your second letter this morning. – Tiresome about the cottages. – Frankly, I *cannot afford* £21. for another years rent for Tregerthen, as things are. See if you can't arrange something. In the first place, won't you definitely reduce the rent for the bigger place, for the coming year? It is not worth £16., as it stands now – I asked you last year to make it lower for me, but you would give me no definite answer, so I paid all. – Then perhaps Mrs Kennedy[1] would take the place, *furnished* – tower as well – and we would leave the furniture as it is, at her convenience. If she would do this, and pay as much for 4 or 6 months as would cover the rent for the year – not £21., to be sure, but about as much rent as you would require – that would be very good.

See if you can't arrange this, or something like it. Then, if you can't, and you think it would be better for you not to let me have the little cottage, I will just sell my furniture to Benney and leave you quite free. – In the meantime I will have sent only just the sheets and clothes and silver and a few books.

I am sorry there is this bother. I know it is tiresome for you. – But I hope we will manage something all right.

– Kindest regards   D. H. Lawrence

[1] Unidentified.

1544. To Mark Gertler, [16 March 1918]
Text: MS SIU; Huxley 434.

Chapel Farm Cottage – Hermitage – Newbury, Berks
Saturday

I'm glad *that* dirty business is settled, at least.[1] I knew you would be all right. There is some mystic quality inside a few of us, which puts them off at once, these military mongrel-sniffers. One would say it was a guardian angel – but it is rather an influence within the very being.

As for the Ott. – why should I bother about the old carrion?[2] If I can publish, I shall publish. But ten to one I can't, and I don't care a straw either way. – Money is a conundrum, and will have to remain so. It is a sphinx riddle I shan't attempt to solve. The sphinx can go hungry for ever, if it is going to wait for me to solve its problem. Je m'en fiche of everything.[3]

I don't feel like you about work. I go on working, because it is the one activity allowed to one, not because I care. I feel like a wild cat in a cage – I long to get out into some sort of free, lawless life – at any rate, a life where one can move about and take no notice of anything. I feel horribly mewed up. I don't want to act in concert with any body of people. I want to go by myself – or with Frieda – something in the manner of a gipsy, and be houseless and placeless and homeless and landless, just move apart. I *hate* and *abhor* being stuck on to any form of society.

I wish you would come down here. Kot said you and he might come at Easter. But then the impossible Margaret Radford will impose herself on us – and I shall go away, the day after Easter Monday, to the Midlands, to look for a house there. Can't you come before Easter – any time. Mrs Eder will probably be here from 22nd. to 25th. – but you wouldn't mind being here at the same time with her, I am sure. – But come on Monday, if you like – and send me a wire. There is a train leaves Paddington 1.40 – change at Reading and Newbury – get here 4.10. Come by that. Or if you come Tuesday, I will meet you in Newbury. – Ask Kot too. But I know he won't be here while Mrs

---

[1] Gertler had received his call-up on 27 February and had at once appealed against it on grounds of his Austrian parentage and of conscience. He had agreed to do 'work of national importance', preferably farm-work at Garsington. See *Gertler: Selected Letters*, ed. Carrington, p. 158.

2 As Letter 1536 shows, Gertler had undertaken to discover what Lady Ottoline's reaction might be to the publication of *Women in Love*. As recently as 28 February 1918 Lady Cynthia understood that 'the Morrells actually threaten a libel action in the case of publication' (Asquith, *Diaries* 416).

3 'I don't give a rap for anything'.

Eder is here. – I feel we shan't be here much longer – and the Midlands is farther off.

Frieda greets you.

D. H. Lawrence

1545. To Lady Cynthia Asquith, [17 March 1918]
Text: MS UT; Huxley 427.

Chapel Farm Cottage – Hermitage – nr Newbury, Berks
Sunday

Got your letter today – glad you like the poems – I myself think they are highly amusing and interesting – they might have quite a run – so why should I sell them out for £9?[1] Why, America gives me £9 for three or four poems – Beaumont must make a different sort of agreement with me. I shall tell him. – Would you have preferred to be inscribed with your title, not only your bare name? It is as you like.

I don't know if I've had anything from the Literary Fund. The only thing I've ever had from any fund or body was £50, which I had two months after the war began, and which came from the Authors Society, I believe, though whether they drew it out of the Literary Fund I don't know.[2] I believe Alfred Sutro got it me.[3] – I am very willing to have £100 from any fund whatsoever – as for obligation, I shall certainly go on writing, and I am not married to the censor. I have begun a novel now – done 150 pages – which is as blameless as *Cranford*.[4] It shall not have one garment disarranged, but shall be buttoned up like a member of Parliament. Still, I wouldn't vouch that it is like *Sons and Lovers*: it is funny. It amuses me terribly.

Tell my well-wisher to get me the £100, which will be a great boon to me, as being a mere necessity, and not to mind about any obligation, which is surely infra dig. on the part of a[5] gentleman.[6] Why has the world become so

---

[1] See Letter 1538.
[2] See Letter 1526 and n. 5.
[3] Alfred Sutro (1863–1933), dramatist and translator, sent £10 privately to DHL in September 1914 and was active in promoting DHL's case to the Royal Literary Fund (*Letters*, ii. 213, 224–5 n. 4).
[4] The novel which DHL compares with Elizabeth Gaskell's *Cranford* (1853) is *Aaron's Rod*, though the published work does not bear out DHL's observations on it here.
[5] a] any
[6] The person in question was Charles Whibley; he was a very close friend of Lady Cynthia's. Whibley was already well known to committee-members of the Royal Literary Fund; indeed from 1919 until his death he was himself an active member of the Fund's general committee

ambidextrous, that the left hand must always be implicated in what the right hand does! Pah – people – pfui!

Tell me about 'notre prince'.[1] It seems to me we are a vaudeville to ourselves, in this money-publishing plot of ours.

D. H. Lawrence

1546. To Cyril Beaumont, 18 March 1918
Text: MS DC; Unpublished.

Chapel Farm Cottage, Hermitage, nr. Newbury. Berks
18 March 1918

Dear Mr Beaumont,

I suppose Lady Cynthia Asquith left with you the MS. of the little book of poems. Let me know what you think of it. Send it me back here if you don't want it.

I haven't any more news about the novel at present – perhaps shall have no more at all – in which case I shall ask you for the MS., with many regrets for having bothered you, and many thanks for your kindness.

Yrs   D. H. Lawrence

1547. To S. S. Koteliansky, 20 March 1918
Text: MS BL; Zytaruk 137.

Chapel Farm Cottage – Hermitage, nr Newbury, Berks
20 Mar. 1918

My dear Kot

Thank you very much for the MS. which has come today.[2] I know you hate typing. Tell me the moment you have had enough – don't for the Lord's sake go on when you're sick of it.

We're going to Derbyshire after Easter to look for a house. Gertler says you will come and see us there – as he is off to Garsington. Margaret Radford is coming here – so we shan't stay. The midlands is the place where we will *really* meet – as we first met in the North.[3] London and the south is wrong for us.

(*Times*, 13 March 1930). He had told Lady Cynthia on 6 March that 'he could probably get [DHL] £100 from the Literary Fund, only he thought there should in that case be a tacit understanding that [DHL] should write something – and that, not inevitably censorable' (Asquith, *Diaries* 418).

[1]   Prince Bibesco.

[2]   Some of the essays on American literature.

[3]   The two men first met on a walking-tour near Barrow-in-Furness in August 1914 (see *Letters*, ii. 268 and n. 2).

Why don't you write, you owe me a letter.

Ask Gertler if he would ask Ottoline if she would be so good as to have posted to me here the bundle of MS. she kept for me.[1] A man worries me to give him some poems[2] – and I might root out a few from the old books – and make a trifle of money.

Rien de nouveau, in our world. Write to me. And if you would like to run down for a few days before Easter, *do*.

DHL

I dont believe Mrs Eder will come *this* week-end. Won't you come?

1548. To S. S. Koteliansky, [21 March 1918]
Text: MS BL; Zytaruk 138.

Hermitage –
Thursday[3]

My dear Kot

We've had a wire from Mrs Eder and she's *not* coming. I've got a feeling that I wish you'd come for a day or two. We've got *plenty* of *food* for the moment – a haul.

Come Saturday – 1.40 Paddington – change at Reading and Newbury. I will meet you at *Hermitage* station at 4.5.

Let me have a line by return, that you will come.

DHL

1549. To Cecil Gray, [21 March 1918]
Text: MS StaU; Huxley 429.

Hermitage – Newbury.
Thursday

Do look among my books in the cottage for my two MS. poetry books: one a German 'Tagebuch', brown, not little, hard covers[4] – one a little fat common

---

[1] The MSS cannot be identified.

[2] The man was Cyril Beaumont: see Letter 1549.

[3] In the BL collection an envelope bearing the postmark 'Herm[itage] 1 OC 19', with an additional frank on the verso, 'Lond[on] OC 1 19', is erroneously attached to this letter. There can be little doubt that DHL's reference to Mrs Eder's cancelled visit should be associated with corresponding remarks in Letters 1544 and 1547, and that this letter should therefore be dated 21 March 1918.

[4] This 'brown Tagebuch of Frieda's' had already been inadvertently left behind in Italy when the Lawrences departed from Fiascherino in June 1914; it was recovered by Thomas Dunlop and sent to DHL; he received it at Porthcothan, Cornwall, on 22 January 1916 (*Letters*, ii. 478, 511).

cheap account book – like a milkman's book, but fat – with black shiny wash-
leather down the back, and mottled boards. Beaumont worries me for a
pretty-pretty book of verse – I might rake one out and make a little money.

We got your postcard – feel waves of Cornish malaise coming from the west
– [. . .] – Don't you stay very long down there, if it worries you. It is a bit
mystic-disintegrating, perhaps.

I think we shall go to the Midlands about April 3rd.

Let us have real news of you.

DHL

Take any books of your own – or anything you want.

1550. To S. S. Koteliansky, [30 March 1918]
Text: MS BL; Zytaruk 139.

Hermitage –
Saturday

My dear Kot

Please don't have any qualms about the MS. I am very grateful for what
you have done, and only sorry to think of your having slaved at it. The rest I
will do myself one day. What you have done will be a good lift to start with.

Don't think about it again – and don't curse me for having let you in for the
unpleasant job, in the first place.

I shall be thankful if you get telegrams again from Russia, and are a man of
business. You will be much happier.

We are staying on here till a week or so after Easter – Margaret Radford will
be here; and then, I think we shall go to the Midlands, where I hope you will
be able to come.

I will tell you if there is any change in this. Let me know about your
telegrams.

D. H. Lawrence

1551. To Lady Ottoline Morrell, [1 April 1918]
Text: MS UT; Sandra Darroch, *Ottoline: The Life of Lady Ottoline Morrell* (New York,
1975), pp. 196–7.

Chapel Farm Cottage. Hermitage. Newbury. Berks
Easter Monday 1918

My dear Ottoline

Thank you for the two bundles of MS. which came this morning – I am
sorry to have troubled you – but I wanted to hunt up a few old things that
might possibly meet a publisher in these days of leanness.

I am awfully sick of the world that is – I wish to heaven there would be an end of it. Meanwhile one persists in one's own way against it all.

Perhaps we shall meet in some sort of Afterwards, when the laugh is on a new side.

D. H. Lawrence

1552. To Catherine Carswell, [1 April 1918]
Text: MS YU; cited in Carswell, *Adelphi* 390–1.

Hermitage – nr Newbury – Berks
Easter Monday 1918

My dear Catherine

I meant to have written you before. It is absurd of Duckworth to expect you to cut down the novel so ridiculously. But of course they shy at the cost of production. You know it would *really* cost £350 to bring it out now – as against £130 before the war. For this reason the publishers like little slight things.

We have no news – same poverty and incertitude. Barbara Low has been here since Thursday – leaves today. – I shall go to the Midlands next week; but whether to stay for some time, or only for a few days, I don't know. – I feel horribly sick and surfeited of things.

Barbara said you were tired of the long wait. I am sure you are. I know exactly how it feels. I feel as if I had a child of black fury curled up inside my bowels. I'm sure I can feel exactly what it is to be pregnant, because of the weary bowel-burden of a kind of contained murder which I can't bring forth. We will both pray to be safely delivered.

Write to us and say how you are. My regards to Don. Frieda sends her love, with mine.

DHL

1553. To S. S. Koteliansky, [3 April 1918]
Text: MS BL; PC; Postmark, Hermitage 3 AP 18; Zytaruk 139.

Hermitage –
Wed

Thanks for the MS. which came today. – I am going to the Midlands on Saturday, but shall probably be back in a week – going to look at a place – shall let you know what turns up.

DHL

1554. To Catherine Carswell, [3 April 1918]
Text: MS YU; cited in Carswell, *Adelphi* 391.

Chapel Farm Cottage, Hermitage, nr Newbury, Berks
Wednesday

My dear Catherine

We are going up to the Midlands Friday instead of Thursday – and shall only have time in London just to catch trains. But we shall only be away a week – then we'll see you on the return. The address is c/o Mrs Clarke, Grosvenor Rd, Ripley, nr Derby.

Oh God, the bombs! One fell in the garden of 42 Mecklenburgh Sq. – all back windows smashed in 44. Thankful we weren't there.

Did I tell you George Moore read *Women in Love*, and says it is a great book, and that I am a better writer than himself.[1] That is really astounding.

No further news.

Love from both   D. H. Lawrence

1555. To Cecil Gray, 18 April 1918
Text: MS StaU; Huxley 438–9.

Chapel Farm Cottage, Hermitage – nr Newbury, Berks.
18 April 1918

My dear Grigio,

I was up in the midlands for a week last week – my sister negotiating for a little place for us – a bungalow, on the brow of the steep valley at Via Gellia – near Cromford. We should have it furnished, for a year, – my sister would pay for it – if the people agree to let. It is a nice place – with pleasant little grounds, and two rough fields. We should hear in a day or two about it. And then, if the people let it us, we shall go in a week or ten days' time. It is quite open and free – you would have to come and see us there.

Frieda went to London and saw her children and it all went off quite pleasantly and simply, apparently. – I feel unsettled here now, as if we must move soon. And we *must* move – the Radfords want to come here in May.

I have made a little book of poems that Beaumont asked me for – all smallish, lyrical pieces. I have been doing poetry for a few weeks now – I want to make a second little book. But it is exhausting to keep it up. – The first book has 18 poems, it more or less refers to the war, and is called *Bay*. I don't know

---

[1] Catherine Carswell remarked: 'Who sent George Moore the MS. I do not know . . . Nor do I know how the pleasing verdict was conveyed' (Carswell 94–5).

if Beaumont will really do it. – The second would be different – I would call it 'Chorus of Women', or something like that.[1]

That's all the news – except that yesterday there was deep snow, though the trees are in bloom. Plum trees and cherry trees full of blossom look so queer in a snow landscape. Their lovely foamy fulness goes a sort of pinky drab, and the snow looks fiendish in its cold incandescence. I hated it violently.

I hope we shan't be bothered by the military. I believe as a matter of fact they have too bad an opinion of us – let us hope so. I don't believe, moreover, that they will have the *energy* to comb out those things that stick at all tight. There is a great exhaustedness coming.

Richard sent me a line to say he was off to France.[2] I believe he was glad to go. It is harder to bear the pressure of the vacuum over here than the stress of conjestion over there.

I am reading Gibbon.[3] I am quite happy with those old Roman Emperors – they were so out-and-out, they just did as they liked, and vogue la galère,[4] till they were strangled. I can do with them. – I also read two ponderous tomes on Africa, by a German called Frobenius.[5] He says there was a great West African – Yoruban – civilisation, which preceded Egypt and Carthage, and gave rise to the Atlantis myth. But he is a tiresome writer.

Greetings [. . .] Let us hear from you.

DHL

1556. To Cyril Beaumont, 18 April 1918
Text: MS UCin; Cyril W. Beaumont, *The First Score* (1927), p. 35.

Chapel Farm Cottage, Hermitage, nr. Newbury – Berks
18 April 1918

Dear Beaumont

I have now got a little book of 18 poems – à propos of the war – called *Bay*. Let me know if you are still alive and still publishing and still wanting the MS. – and I'll send it along. Also tell me if there is any other news. – Also *do* you think it is worth while to give you these poems outright, for £10[6] – in my present state of hopeless poverty?

Yrs   D. H. Lawrence

---

[1] The volume was published as *New Poems*.   [2] See Letter 1509.
[3] In Letter 1565 DHL identifies the edition of Gibbon's *The History of the Decline and Fall of the Roman Empire* which he was reading.
[4] 'let come what may',
[5] Leo Frobenius (1873–1938), *The Voice of Africa*, trans. Rudolph Blind, 2 vols (1913).
[6] The amount is almost illegible since an attempt has been made to cross it out, but it is confirmed in Letters 1557 and 1567.

1557. To J. B. Pinker, 18 April 1918
Text: MS UT; Unpublished.

Chapel Farm Cottage, Hermitage, nr. Newbury. Berks.

18 April. 1918

My dear Pinker

This is a little book of poems more or less on one note which C.W. Beaumont, 75 Charing Cross Rd, asked me to do for him, some time back. – But he proposed paying £10. for the rights for six months – £10. would clear him altogether, that is – and after six months we could do as we like. – It is a queer arrangement. I have not yet sent him the MS. – I can't type it because I have no type-writer here – but I kept another copy. – Some of the poems – like 'On the March', might appear, perhaps, in the *English Review* or *Westminster*[1] – I should be glad if they made a few pounds. – Such a little book would not take long to come out, however.

Let me know what you think.

Yrs   D. H. Lawrence

1558. To Lady Cynthia Asquith, 18 April 1918
Text: TMSC NWU; Unpublished.

Chapel Farm Cottage, Hermitage, Nr. Newbury, Berks.

18th April 1918

This is a long silence of yours. Won't you let us know how things are – I suppose the Literary Fund, or whatever it is, shied at my name . . . And . . . Novel? and you, what about you? Beaumont shied at those little poems – he found them too doubtful little pills – it's a shy world – I have made another little book of Impeccable Poems – *I* think – which I will still inscribe to you, if you will.[2] Let me know about the Novel – who has the MS. I don't want it to be lost, as it is the only complete copy.

We are middling. Probably we shall go to Derbyshire – my sister is negotiating a little house for us – as this only lasts till May.

I *hope* you've got some good news of yourself to tell.

DHL

---

[1] The poem, included in *Bay*, was not published in any periodical.
[2] The 'doubtful little pills' were 'All Of Us' which Beaumont refused to publish; the 'Impeccable Poems' constituted *Bay* which he did publish.

1559. To S. S. Koteliansky, 19 April 1918
Text: MS BL; Zytaruk 140.

Chapel Farm Cottage, Hermitage, nr Newbury. Berks.

19 April 1918

My dear Kot

I heard from my sister today that she has taken a house for us in Derbyshire, furnished, and we can go in on May 1st. So I suppose we shall be soon moving from here. – I saw the place last week – it is a very nice situation – and a very pleasant little bungalow, with grounds – a croquet lawn: we can play croquet. It looks over a steep valley – something like the memorable Westmoreland where we first met.

There is no news other than this – except it is very nastily cold. You have promised to come and see us in Derbyshire – when we get settled down you must keep your promise.

Let me know how you are, and the Farbmans.

Greetings from both   DHL

Tell Gertler I'll write him directly.

1560. To Captain John Short, 19 April 1918
Text: MS UT; Unpublished.

Chapel Farm Cottage, Hermitage – nr. Newbury. Berks.

19 April 1918

Dear Captain Short,

I have been a long time writing to you – but I have been waiting to see what we should do. My sister has now taken for us a furnished house in Derbyshire, for a year. We shall be going there in a fortnight's time.

About the cottages, I should like, if I may, to keep the little one, my first cottage, for £5. a year, and give up the others. Then if I come back, and the big house hasn't let, I can take it again. I should like to keep the little cottage furnished just as it is, and let it to friends in the summer, and have it for myself, ready, when this accursed business is over. Will you tell me if this would be agreeable to you? I enclose cheque for £6., which makes up all the rent for last year, I believe.

About the bit of furniture in the other house – Mr. Gray wants some – Mrs Hocking some – some is *yours*. I should like sent the big *rug* from the tower floor – and my *desk* from the tower. I believe *all* the packing for the desk, in which it came from London, is in the coal-place of the end cottage. Then the camp bed in the tower I should like kept in the little[1] cottage – with its

---

[1] little] other

mattress: also what books and bits of china there are – also the smaller of the two wooden arm-chairs – these would go in the little cottage I want to keep. – You have the bit of coco-matting from the floor and stairs of the far cottage, if you want it. The rest of the things over there we will leave, to see what Mr Gray and Mrs Hocking want.

I shall have only one small case of books sent – the rest I shall leave. There is a packing case over in the other coal-place – two, I believe. I should like clothes, boots, sheets, the coloured woollen bed-spread, towels, table-cloths put in another packing case and sent – also knives, forks, and spoons – but this little job I'll ask Mary Hocking to do, as she knows the things. I should like also the little Dutch clock from across – also the two brass candlesticks, leaving two[1] – that is about all.

If you would do the desk for me, I should be very much obliged indeed. – I hope you will let me keep my little cottage. – I shall write again soon. Let me hear from you as soon as possible.

Our very kind remembrances to Mrs Short. Send us news of the Whitleys – we have been wondering about Mrs Whitley lately.[2] Greetings to yourself.

Yours   D. H. Lawrence

1561. To Cecil Gray, 19 April 1918

Text: MS StaU; cited in Schorer, *London Magazine*, iii. 59.

Hermitage – nr Newbury. Berks.

19 Apr. 1918

Dear Grigio

I heard from my sister this morning that we have got the place at Via Gellia – to go in May 1st.

I have written to Capt. Short to ask him to let me *keep* my own little cottage, and give up the others. – So if you want the bed and mirror – or chairs or anything from the other house, go over and see about it, will you. I have written the Hockings to say what I want to keep.[3]

And will you pack me a few books – chiefly books of reference – like classical dictionary, and other dictionaries, atlases, bible, and so on: also all remaining MS. – all remaining books to be left in my own cottage – also the *paints* and the drawing-board, if it will go in. And do you think my type-writer

---

[1] the two . . . two] the brass and copper candlesticks. (Those which DHL wished to have sent were probably the pair originally owned by his mother. See *Letters*, ii. 584.)

[2] Irene Tregerthen Whittley (b. 1887) and Percy Whittley were Captain Short's daughter and son-in-law (see *Letters*, ii. 590 n. 1).

[3] The letter has not been found.

will be all right sent as it is? Send me any books you think I should like to have by me.

I am only having my desk sent – and the big rug – and linen, the few books, and the type-writer.

DHL

1562. To Cyril Beaumont, 21 April 1918
Text: MS Lazarus; Unpublished.

Chapel Farm Cottage, Hermitage – nr Newbury, Berks
21 April 1918

Dear Beaumont

I send you the MS. of poems.[1] Since it was made for you, will you tell me if there is anything you would like left out or altered. You may as well have it as you want it – if you want it.

I suppose you will send me a copy of *New Paths* – or shall I have to pay for one?[2]

I told Pinker I was sending you this MS.

D. H. Lawrence

1563. To Lady Cynthia Asquith, [27 April 1918]
Text: MS UT; Unpublished.

Chapel Farm Cottage – Hermitage, nr Newbury. Berks
Sat.[3]

I got the MS. of the novel from Cadogan Square[4] a few days ago – thanks for returning it. – et M. le Prince?

Beaumont wants to do the little book *Bay*, which I inscribed to you. He will only give me £10 – *tanto poco!*[5] – I can't let you see the MS., because I haven't got a copy. Ask him to show you his copy. – There is nothing in it to scare you in the least – impeccable. Even the *Daily News* could swallow it and not know but what it was drinking water.

---

[1] See Letter 1556.
[2] See p. 202 n. 2.
[3] It is clear that Lady Cynthia did not receive Letter 1558 until 20 April 1918; she obviously then responded from Pixton Park where she was staying; and this is DHL's reply to her letter. The reference to 2 May in this letter therefore confirms Saturday 27 April as the date.
[4] 62 Cadogan Square was the London house of Lady Cynthia's father, Hugo, 11th Earl of Wemyss (1857–1937).
[5] 'so little'.

We are going from here next week – on May 2nd., I suppose – to
    Mountain Cottage, *Middleton* by *Wirksworth*, Derbyshire.
Will you come and see us there? Yes do.

I hope that Literary Fund isn't an addled egg.

You sounded very jubilant in your letter from Pixton Park. What was it
put you in such good feather?

Frieda greets you.

DHL

1564. To J. B. Pinker, [27 April 1918]
Text: MS UT; Unpublished.

Chapel Farm Cottage, Hermitage – nr Newbury

Sat.

My dear Pinker

I enclose the letter from Beaumont about the poems. When he says
'complete English Rights', does he mean for ever? That seems a bit much, for
£10. Will you tell me what you think about this? – tell me what you would
settle with him. – 'Labour Battalion' is a poem I gave him for his anthology
New Paths – He is quite welcome to put it in this book[1] – and to have my
signature for his Edition de Luxe.[2] But before you settle with him, tell me
what you think to agree to, will you? – I suppose we shall get the ordinary 6
author's copies. I wish it were 12.

Did *Look We Have Come Through* appear in America?[3] Will it do so? – Will
you try this for America?[4] – I shall make other little books of poems like these.
It strikes me as the best thing to do.

Yrs   D. H. Lawrence

[1] Beaumont did not include it.
[2] The most expensive edition of *Bay* – 30 copies on vellum – included the signatures both of
DHL and of Anne Estelle Rice, the artist responsible for the cover and decorations. On Rice
see p. 331 n. 3.
[3] Huebsch published an American edition, using sheets supplied by Chatto & Windus, in 1918.
Pinker had asked the English publishers (on 20 February 1918) whether they would supply
Huebsch with sheets of their edition; they agreed on 26 February to sell Huebsch '500 copies in
flat sheets' (TMS Chatto & Windus). On 8 April Percy Spalding wrote to Pinker: '. . . if Mr
Huebsch likes to begin with a smaller number of Mr. Lawrence's poems, let him take 300
instead of 500 . . .' (TMS Chatto & Windus). He agreed to send three copies of the volume at
once to Huebsch.
[4] There was no American edition of *Bay*.

1565. To Mark Gertler, [28 April 1918]
Text: MS SIU; Huxley 439–40.

Chapel Farm Cottage, Hermitage – nr Newbury, Berks
Sunday

Dear Gertler,

We are going to Derbyshire this week – Thursday, I think – address
Mountain Cottage, Middleton, *Wirksworth*, Derby.

It is quite a pleasant little place – about 2 miles only from Wirksworth station
– so when we get settled you must come, with or without the immovable
elephant.[1]

What is happening to you. I am getting through day after day – and
becoming very weary. One seems to go through all the Ypres and Mount
Kemmels and God knows what.[2] In some blind and hypnotic fashion I do a
few bits of poetry – beyond that, I am incapable of everything – except I dig
and set potatoes, and go walks with Frieda – who is actually forbearing to
demonstrate her impertinent happiness, and daring to know her monstrous
angry unhappiness. I don't pretend to be 'happy' – and for the moment don't
want to be. I am much too angry. My soul, or whatever it is, feels charged and
surcharged with the blackest and most monstrous 'temper', a sort of hellish
electricity – and I hope soon it will either dissipate or break into some sort of
thunder and lightning, for I am no more a man, but a walking phenomenon of
suspended fury. I found a great satisfaction in reading Gibbons *Decline and
Fall of the Roman Empire* – the emperors are all so indiscriminately bad. But
unfortunately I only had the first vol. in the *Oxford Classics* – and there are
seven such vols. – I must borrow the work from somewhere.

Also I have been reading another book on Occultism. Do you know
anybody who cares for this – magic, astrology, anything of that sort. It is very
interesting, and important – though antipathetic to me. Certainly magic is a
reality – not by any means the nonsense Bertie Russell says it is. – By the way,
is he in gaol?[3]

Money is a great curse. But why not go on borrowing from your brother, if

---

[1] i.e. Kot.
[2] Ypres (close to the river Yser and channel ports) was the scene of a series of battles; the
penultimate major engagement was taking place at the time of DHL's letter. Kemmel Hill, s.w.
of Ypres, had been taken by German forces on 25 April 1918.
[3] On 10 February 1918 Bertrand Russell was sentenced at Bow Street to six months
imprisonment in the Second Division for 'having in a printed publication made certain
statements likely to prejudice His Majesty's relations with the United States of America'
(Ronald W. Clark, *The Life of Bertrand Russell*, 1975, p. 339). His appeal was heard on 2 May;
the sentence was amended to the less rigorous régime of the First Division; but he was gaoled
from May till 18 September.

you can? I got about £20 out of my sister – and she is paying £65 for the years rent of the place we're going to. One rather hates taking money from ones hard-worked people. But this is a peculiar and crucial time, and one must get through it somehow – it doesn't seem to matter how much.

We went for a walk this evening through the woods – and I found a dead owl, a lovely big warm-brown soft creature, lying in the grass at my feet, in the path, its throat eaten by weasels. It sticks in my mind curiously – as if something important had died this week-end – though what it can be I don't know.

I hope soon we shall get out of the state we are in, and have a jolly reunion somewhere, breathing free. Let us know how you are. – And stick pins or something into Kot – I believe he's getting into a state of gangrened inertia.

Frieda greets you. –

D. H. Lawrence

1566. To Catherine Carswell, [28 April 1918]
Text: MS YU; Huxley 440–1.

Hermitage –
Sunday

My dear Catherine,

We are going away, I think on Thursday, to the new place
Mountain Cottage, Middleton by *Wirksworth*, Derby.
I think it will be nice. It is in the darkish Midlands, on the rim of a steep deep valley, looking over darkish, folded hills – exactly the navel of England, and feels exactly that. – It is a smallish bungalow – with rather pretty little grounds – croquet lawn – and a field attached. Later, you must come with Don and the baby and stay there. Wouldn't it be queer, the baby!

I am sure you must be tired to death. We feel the same, fairly hit right in the middle. One keeps some sort of a superficial wits, but I think it would be wrong to assume that one is quite sane just now. But I think it is a crisis – the storm is at its height – it will break soon. But the afterwards even one can't contemplate. There seems no afterwards, in known terms. – What will be will be, however, and I don't care. We'll come through by a gap in the hedge, if not by the gate. – Your business is just to look after yourself – which is not so very easy, even that.

This evening we went through the woods – and I found a dead owl at my feet, a lovely soft warm-brown thing. It seems a sort of symbol of something – but I don't know of what. – Also we found some very lovely big cowslips, whose scent is really a communication direct from the source of creation – like the breath of God breathed into Adam. It breathes into the Adam in me. – Let us know how you are – our love to you both.

DHL

1567. To Cyril Beaumont, 29 April 1918
Text: MS UCin; Unpublished.

Chapel Farm Cottage, Hermitage – nr Newbury, Berks
29 April 1918

Dear Beaumont,

Certainly include 'Labour Battalion', if you wish to: also I will sign your Edition de luxe. I wrote to Pinker – and he will settle with you, for the £10 for six months, as you said. Will you go ahead with him?

I am leaving the address on Thursday, to go to

Mountain Cottage, Middleton by *Wirksworth*, Derby.

Will you write to me there.

Yrs   D. H. Lawrence

Have you got any other books for the series? – or thought of a name?

1568. To J. B. Pinker, 29 April 1918
Text: MS UT; cited in Moore, *Poste Restante* 48.

Chapel Farm Cottage – Hermitage, nr Newbury. Berks.
29 April 1918

My dear Pinker

I wrote to Beaumont to settle with you.

I am leaving this address on Thursday, and going to

Mountain Cottage, Middleton by *Wirksworth*, Derby.

Probably we shall be there all the summer, so will you write to me there.

Yrs etc   D. H. Lawrence

1569. To Lady Cynthia Asquith, 7 May 1918
Text: MS UT; Huxley 441–2.

Mountain Cottage, Middleton by *Wirksworth*, Derby.
Tuesday – 7 May 1918

We are here, feeling very lost and queer and exiled. The place is beautiful, but one feels like Ovid in Thrace, or something like that.[1] I wish we could have gone back to Cornwall.

I wrote to you last week – but I suppose you were busy, weddings and so on – to ask you about B[i]b[esc]o and the novel – and to tell you I received the MS safely from Cadogan Sq. Tell me what he – Bbo – had to say – what fatuity, no doubt unpleasant.

I should think Beaumont will be signing the agreement with Pinker for the poems – does it matter to you whether you see the MS. or not?

I wish there was some good news on the face of the earth.

DHL

1570. To Edith Eder, [7 May 1918]
Text: MS SIU; cited in Hobman, ed., *David Eder*, p. 120.

Mountain Cottage, Middleton by *Wirksworth*, Derby
Tuesday.[2]

Dear Edith Eder

I have meant to write to you a long time. Any news of Eder? I dreamed he quite suddenly came back, and like a strange angry ghost. What's the 'contrairy' of that?

We are here, feeling queer and lost and exiled. The place is beautiful – and the house quite nice. But oh, one feels queer and dépaysé.[3] Would you care to come and see us a bit later. At Whitsun there will be a lot of my sister's people here. I might walk for a day or two in the hills with Vere Collins – to escape the crowd, for one thing.

I feel queer and desolate in my soul – like Ovid in Thrace. And the world is such a useless place. But I set potatoes and mow the grass and write my never-to-be-finished *Studies in Classic American Literature*. I am reading Gibbon. He says the Jews are the great *haters* of the human race – and the great *anti-social* principle.[4] – Strikes me that is true – for the last 2,500 years, at least. – I

---

[1] The Roman poet Ovid suffered exile in Thrace. (Cf. *The Lost Girl*, ed. John Worthen, Cambridge, 1981, p. 314.)

[2] This must be dated after 2 May (when DHL moved to Mountain Cottage) and before 19 May (Whit Sunday mentioned in the letter). The two possible dates are Tuesday 7 or 14 May; the similarity of feeling and phrasing to Letter 1569 suggests the former.

[3] 'out of one's element'.

[4] Gibbon asserts that the Jews are 'a distinct species of men, who boldly professed, or who faintly disguised, their implacable hatred to the rest of mankind' (*The History of the Decline and Fall of the Roman Empire*, ed. J. B. Bury, 1896, ii. 3).

feel such profound hatred myself, of the human race, I almost know what it is to be a Jew.

Could you lend me or borrow for me anywhere a book which describes the human nervous system, and gives a sort of map of the nerves of the human body? Do try and find a book to lend me – I want to see this. Ask Jones[1] or somebody.

Write and tell us how you are – and if there is any news of Eder – real news, I mean.

I can understand now the strong and elemental *anger*, which is your ruling principle – a fixed, congenital, immutable anger. I wish it could find expression.

Frieda greets you. Don't blankly abstain from writing.

DHL

1571. To Sallie Hopkin, [16 May 1918]
Text: MS NCL; Unpublished.

Middleton-by-Wirksworth
Thursday[2]

My dear Sallie

Glad you are both all right. We shall be expecting you, then, on Tuesday, and Willie on Thursday.

Let me know your train, and I'll meet you at Cromford – or Wirksworth.

It is disgusting weather – but by Tuesday it will have thrown off this fit.

DHL

1572. To J. B. Pinker, 22 May 1918
Text: MS UT; Unpublished.

Mountain Cottage, Middleton by Wirksworth, Derby
22 May 1918

My dear Pinker

I return to you the *Bay* agreement, which I think is very good, and for which many thanks.

Yrs   D. H. Lawrence

---

[1] Dr Ernest Jones (1879–1958), physician and psychoanalyst; he was a colleague and close friend of Dr David Eder (see *Letters*, ii. 258 n. 2, 623 n. 3). m. Katherine Jokl, 1919. See *Times* obituary, 12 February 1958.

[2] In Letter 1576 DHL refers to 'those two days' at Whitsuntide; it is presumed that he was remembering Tuesday 21 and Thursday 23 May, both in Whit week; and the date of this letter would therefore be 16 May 1918.

I have got a similar small book of poems called 'Choir of Women', which perhaps you would like to see.[1]

1573. To Lucy Short, 23 May 1918
Text: MS UT; Unpublished.

Mountain Cottage, *Middleton*-by-Wirksworth, Derby
Thursday 23 May 1918

Dear Mrs Short

Thank you for your letter, which came the other day. I should have answered before, but was waiting to hear if the Odles were settled to come.[2]

I should be glad to have the other house, for the £5., as you said, just for the year ending next March. I offered the Odles the place furnished for 30/- a month – calendar. I suppose they would stay about four months. Then at the end of that time we should probably be able to come back, and have our other little cottage, and I will give Capt. Short the £5. for that, if it is available: which would make £10, from me, for this broken year. I hope this would be agreeable. If we could not come back, the Odles might stay on, even through the winter. Any way, I hope they'll come to Tregerthen.

I heard from Mrs Odle, saying she had not seen[3] Capt. Short.

We need to patch up some sort of arrangement for this year, then next March we can make a proper agreement.

It has been terribly hot here – crowds of people to see us – and violent thunder-storms. I feel limp and stupid.

We didn't get a letter from Mrs Whitley, – not since she sent the little painted bag at Christmas.

No, for Heaven's sake, don't let us disagree. One has not even sufficient energy: and life is tiresome enough.

Warm greetings from us both to you and Captain Short.

D. H. Lawrence

Yes, leave the bed and wardrobe where it is – as you like.

1574. To Edith Eder, 28 May 1918
Text: MS SIU; cited in Hobman, ed., *David Eder*, p. 120.

Mountain Cottage – Middleton by Wirksworth, Derby
Tuesday 28 May 1918

Dear Edith Eder

I got the pages of the medical book – many thanks. Certain things I was

---

[1] See p. 233 n. 1.   [2] Unidentified.   [3] seen] heard from

able to find from it: but it was repulsive with diagnoses, and not very plain for me – I wanted of course a book of physiology rather than medicine. But it managed. I send it you back now.

Is there any news of Eder? He ought to be thinking of coming home now. I hope he'll come and see us here. At the moment I have no feelings about Palestine – not much feeling about anything, I'm afraid.

We have got my father here – also my elder sister, whose husband has had to join up – and her little girl; also my younger sister's little boy of three: a very charming boy indeed.[1] It is queer – and a bit irritating, to be en famille again. I am no worshipper of family. But it is very different from being alone. I can understand that people who live a number together in a house never think or understand – they make a kind of swamp, in which meals are islands. I have almost a passion for being alone – sometimes the thought of a hut in the Thebaid, inaccessible to all but lions or monkeys, is the desirable. Nevertheless, I feel it is good for me for some time to be with people, and en famille. It is a kind of drug, or soporific, a sort of fatness; it saves one. For the days of the world are just frictional and null.

You said you would come in June – do. It is rather lovely. And we might *walk* – you and Frieda and me – for a day or two. Would you like it? – I should.

I am not inclined to argue and discuss – so I shan't provoke you. I feel a genuine indifference to public questions – even my strenuous repudiation of psycoanalysis is gone. It's one of the ways, as you say – and where it leads to isn't my affair. – The chief point is that I am utterly callous to people and their ailments or complexes, even their foulnesses.

auf Wiedersehen   D. H. Lawrence

1575. To Catherine Carswell, 1 June 1918
Text: MS YU; Huxley 442.

Mountain Cottage, Middleton-by-Wirksworth, Derby
1 June 1918.

My dear Catherine

We had Don's card this morning – so glad the boy has come, and you are safe.[2] We were thinking so hard of you on Wednesday – I nearly wrote, but thought silence is best. – Blessings on the infant – and may it be blest. Also I hope you'll soon be well. – Will you really come here for a bit, in a little while?

---

[1] DHL's father John Arthur Lawrence (1846–1924); his elder sister Emily, her husband Samuel Taylor King (1880–1965) and daughter Margaret Emily ('Peggy') (b. 1909); and John ('Jack') Lawrence Clarke (1915–42), the son of DHL's younger sister Ada.

[2] John Patrick Carswell, b. 30 May 1918.

– all three of you? Yes do. – Frieda is making a gaudy little cover, for the child's cot. – What shall you call him? – In the *English Review* today there'll be a little 'War Baby' poem, which I wrote for you – at least, with you in my mind – and the infant, of course.[1] – I wonder if you'll like it. – Beaumont is doing a little book of my poems – called *Bay* – with this piece in it – at least, I have signed the agreement. If you like the poem, when I get the proofs, I shall initial it to the infant. – (To Little T.C.)[2] – Shall I? But what will the initial be? – Give him a Celtic name – like Geraint – or Gawain – which is Gavin in English.

I believe this month of June will see a turn in the tide of affairs, in the world: for the better. Let us hope we can all start off fresh.

It seems ages since we saw you – a real interval. It will be really on another shore, mystically, that we shall meet – we shall be new beings.

Tell Don to be sure to let us know how you are – another post card on Monday.

With love from Frieda and me   Lawrence

1576. To Sallie Hopkin, 3 June 1918
Text: MS NCL; Huxley 444.

Mountain Cottage, Middleton by Wirksworth, Derby
Monday June 3rd 1918

My dear Sallie

Ada came yesterday, and brought your things in a box. That was very good of you to send us these things – but too good, and extravagant. The salad dressing and cheese are a godsend in this heat – *good* salad dressing – and such nice little cakes.

Emily is still here, with her child, and with Jackie.[3] She is staying another week, I believe. The children may stay another fortnight – and Ada would send Lily, her girl, in that case. When can you come again and see us? Come both as soon as you can, we can *always* put you up. And one has such a sense of uncertainty and fleetingness, it is certainly best to seize the very first opportunity.

Perhaps I shall come over to Eastwood one day before long – we might both come.

---

[1] The poem was the first in 'Three Poems', *English Review*, xxvi (June 1918), 473. It was reprinted in *Poetry*, February 1919, as well as in *Bay*.
[2] Cf. 'The Picture of Little T.C. in a Prospect of Flowers' (1681) by Andrew Marvell (1621–78).
[3] Ada's son.

The very dry days have rushed the flowers through – but all our rhododendrons and peonies are out, and rock-roses very lovely on the fields.

I think with such regret of Whitsuntide, that those two days were so short. I feel a bit of the real mystic hatred of 'business' – destructive hatred – when its power nips one as close as that. One's soul is a pure sheathed weapon, nowadays. Ah, if one could unsheathe it, and stick it through a few million gullets – there might be no need of 'business' then.

I am writing a last essay on Whitman[1] – then I have done my book of American essays – salt on America's tail, if only America would stay long enough to have her tail sprinkled. The Whitman essay reminds me of Willie.

Is there going to be a crisis this month?

DHL

1577. To Lady Cynthia Asquith, 3 June 1918
Text: MS UT; Huxley 443–4.

Mountain Cottage, Middleton by Wirksworth, Derby.
3 June 1918

I dreamed of you so hard a few days ago, so must write, though there is no news to send. We are here with my sister, and two children – a very delightful boy of three, and a girl of seven. I am surprised how children are like barometers to their parents' feelings. There is some sort of queer, magnetic psychic connection – something a bit fatal, I believe. I feel I am all the time rescuing my nephew and my niece from their respective mothers, my two sisters: who have jaguars of wrath in their souls, however they purr to their offspring. The phenomenon of motherhood, in these days, is a strange and rather frightening phenomenon.

I dreamed also such a funny dream. When I had been to some big, crowded fair somewhere – where[2] things were to sell, on booths and on the floor – as I was coming back down an open road, I heard such a strange crying overhead, in front, and looking up, I saw, not very high in the air above me, but higher than I could throw, two pale spotted dogs, crouching in the air, and mauling a bird that was crying loudly. I ran fast forwards and clapped my hands and the dogs started back. The bird came falling to earth. It was a young peacock, blue all over like a peacock's neck, very lovely. It still kept crying. But it was

---

[1] The essay on Whitman, the last written of those included in *Studies in Classic American Literature*, was first published in *Nation and Athenæum*, xxix (July 1921), 616–18.
[2] where] with

not much hurt. A woman came running out of a cottage not far off, and took the bird, saying it would be all right. So I went my way. – That dream in some oblique way or other is connected with your 'aura' – but I can't interpret it.

Would you really like to come here – it's a nice place, really – you'd like it. – But I feel as if I were on a sort of ledge half way down a precipice, and didn't know how to get up or down: and it is a queer kind of place to ask visitors to see you, such a ledge.

I signed the agreement¹ for the poems. When proofs come I'll send them and you can tell me at once if there's anything you'd like different. But they're all right.

Poor Whibley, he is so good trying to get that money for me. Will it come off? I hope so – but if not, never bother.

Mr Billing is the last word in canaille.²

DHL

1578. To Catherine Carswell, 3 June 1918
Text: MS YU; cited in Carswell 100.

Mountain Cottage, Middleton by Wirksworth, Derby
Monday 3 June 1918

My dear Catherine

I hope you won't think Frieda's cover too wild and scaring for the poor infant.

I got you such a lot of flowers – but am *so* afraid they will die this hot weather. I *love* the yellow rock-roses: but they are so frail, I wonder if you'll ever see them as they really are. I'm afraid they'll be all withered. They are pure flowers of light – and they cover the dry, limey hills. The little blue and red bunch is milkworts: the wild columbines are wood-avens, I believe: the yellow pansies are mountain violets – they grow sprinkled close all over the tiny meadow just under the house, and so glittery standing on the close turf – like a Fra Angelico meadow. – There is a bit of wood-ruff with a few forgetmenots. We call it new-mown-hay. It smells like that if you crush it.

I do hope you are well as possible, also the infant.

Love   Lawrence

---

¹ agreement] proofs
² Noel Pemberton Billing (1880–1948), M.P. for East Hertfordshire, 1916–21. According to a *Times* report of a libel action, 5 June 1918, Billing had deliberately defamed individuals by name in a Hertford newspaper: 'a whole series of promiscuous innuendoes in which pro-Germanism was united with every sort of unnatural vice, against many thousands of men and women, some few of whom were actually named in Court'. The Asquith family had been so named on 31 May as being among 47,000 people in Billing's 'Black Book' of alleged German sympathisers.

1579. To J. B. Pinker, 14 June 1918
Text: MS UT; Unpublished.

Mountain Cottage, Middleton by Wirksworth, Derby.
14 June 1918

My dear Pinker

I got application-forms from the Royal Literary Fund, to fill in, for a grant. I filled them in. Llewelyn Roberts[1] said I should get two friends to write. Will you write for me?[2] You know all my literary affairs. – Curse the money and the Funds. – I am very tired of the business. But do write for me.

I shall send you the MS. of a little book of poems, next week.[3] What about Beaumont? – I have seen nothing of proofs or anything from him.

Yrs ever   D. H. Lawrence

1580. To Arthur Llewelyn Roberts, 14 June 1918
Text: MS RLFund; cited in Delany 365.

Mountain Cottage, Middleton by Wirksworth, Derby
14 June 1918

Dear Sir

I received your letter here yesterday – for which many thanks. I enclose the application forms, which I have filled in.

I have written to Mr. Pinker, to ask him to send you a letter. He knows all about my literary affairs. It is true I have no money save what comes from my books – and that is exceedingly little now. In the year which ended August 1914, I suppose I earned £450 or £500. Since last August I have had considerably less than £100. There is no prospect of my receiving anything worth mention, in the future as I see it now. So I am at a loss. Nevertheless it

---

[1] Arthur Llewelyn Roberts (1855–1919), Secretary of the Royal Literary Fund, 1884–1919. See *Letters*, ii. 244 n. 3.

[2] Pinker wrote to Roberts on 19 June 1918 (TMS RLFund) urging DHL's claim on the Fund: '. . . I know how difficult his situation is. His work is not of the character that makes a popular appeal, and as it is not possible for a man of his artistic temperament to adapt his work to the general taste he has for some time past been dangerously near to penury, in spite of the fact that his habits are of the most frugal.'

The second friend whose help DHL sought was the novelist, J. D. Beresford. He wrote to Roberts on 18 June (MS RLFund): '. . . I cannot imagine that there is any man in the British Isles more deserving of your support than D. H. Lawrence. His great misfortune is that his genius appeals to a very small public; and every lover of letters must applaud his courage in refusing to write anything less than his best. He is, at present, in great financial difficulties, although he has been living on absurdly little for the past three years.'

[3] Presumably *New Poems*. (The proofs expected from Beaumont relate to *Bay*.)

is with considerable chagrin that I fill in forms of application for help. I don't want to importune the Royal Literary Fund.

Yours faithfully   D. H. Lawrence

P.S. I am medically rejected from military service.

A. Llewelyn Roberts Esq.

1581. To Mark Gertler, 14 June 1918
Text: MS SIU; Moore, *Intelligent Heart* 241–2.

Mountain Cottage, Middleton by Wirksworth, Derby.

14 June 1918

Dear Gertler

I got your letter yesterday – bloody, things are. I have just filled in forms of application for money – help from the Royal Literary Fund – but I was not very polite and cringing, so probably shall get nothing. Curse them, that's all – curse them once more, fat fleas of literature that they are.

I got military papers from Cornwall to be medically re-examined – sent them back – but expect any day to have more from Derby. Again curse them. – I will not be made to do any serving of any sort, however. Your 'commission' is another rope for roping you in. Blast it all. There is no hope on earth – not the slightest hope from the people up here, I assure you.

I don't know about coming to London – dont know what I shall or can do – don't know anything – am awfully fed. Tell Kot I may flee down and hide with him – God knows. How is he? Is he metamorphosing into some sort of unnatural ichthyosaurus now – some black-crested lizard – in his No. 5 isolation.[1] The house is like a cave. – I thought you were coming to see us – can't you manage it? – Oh God!

We are spending a day in the place where I was born – Eastwood. For the first time in my life I feel quite aimiably towards it – I have always hated it. Now I don't.

I haven't got any news. We are both well. I am not working at the moment – don't want to.

Would you send this letter to Mary Cannan?[2] She helped me last time, in getting money from the Royal Literary Fund – perhaps she would again.

I'll write again, let us hope in better form.

Yrs   DHL

[1] i.e. Kot's house at 5 Acacia Road, St John's Wood.
2 See the letter following.

1582. To Mary Cannan, 14 June 1918
Text: MS Lazarus; Moore 557–8.

Mountain Cottage, Middleton by Wirksworth, Derby
14 June 1918

My dear Mary

I haven't seen you since you came to us at Greatham, have I? – nor written to you hardly.[1] I heard all about Gilbert – *very* wretched for you. Frieda wanted to write to you – but I said, no, don't rush in: we can only upset Mary more. I must say, you had my sympathy entirely – not Gilbert.[2] But it was most miserable. – We had some jolly times at Cholesbury, which I shall never forget. But I could never think of the mill now, without pain – just pain. – But I should like to know what Binky[3] said to you – did he stick to you.

We have our ups and downs – as far as the world goes, all *downs*. You know the police came on us in Cornwall, and raided our house, and turned us out of the county – for nothing at all. We remain all the while under police suspicion – for nothing at all. I don't make hardly any money at all. My sister has taken this cottage for us, furnished, for a year – near to my native place. But the place is very beautiful. Would you care ever to come and see us? You know we have both a place of affection for you – and always shall have. I know I shall. – We live practically on my sister – and that is very painful, too. Charles Whibley got the Secretary of the Royal Literary Society – or Royal Literary Fund – to send me application forms to fill in, – for help.[4] With a black and angry heart I fill them in. Do you remember in that autumn afternoon, on Cholesbury Common, when we were picking blackberries – only you and I – it was before lunch, really – you told me about Sutro, and how he would get me £50 from the Fund – which he did.[5] Could you speak to him again, do you think, Mary? – or any other members of the Fund – to vote or speak for me when the occasion of a grant on my behalf comes up? Do if you can. For months and months and months, now, we have lived from shilling to shilling – and a £10. from Sherman[6] – and so on. I am very tired of it, and *irritated* by it – terribly irritated. And it is not the slightest use my trying to write selling stuff, in this state of affairs.

[1] Mary Cannan stayed with the Lawrences at Greatham in March 1915 (see *Letters*, ii. 310); she had also stayed with them in Hampstead in October and visited them there on 23 November 1915 (ibid., ii. 412, 451). This is DHL's first letter to her since 24 December 1915.
[2] In February 1918 Mary Cannan had decided to break with Gilbert because of his adulterous relationship with Gwen Wilson.
[3] Gilbert's youngest brother, Felix.
[4] Whibley wrote to Roberts on 10 June (MS RLFund) proposing consideration of DHL's case and citing the names of Edmund Gosse and W. P. Ker in his support.
[5] See Letter 1545 and n. 3.　　　　[6] See Letter 1529.

I can't tell you with what pain I think of that autumn at Cholesbury – the yellow leaves – and the wet nights when you came to us, and Gilbert and the dogs – and I had got pork chops – and our cottage was hot and full of the smell of sage and onions – then the times we came to you, and had your wine – those pretty wine-glasses on your long table. Something inside one weeps and won't be comforted. But it's no good grieving. – But there was *something* in those still days, before the war had gone into us, which was beautiful and generous – a sense of flowers rich in the garden, and sunny tea-times when one was at peace – when we were happy with one another, really – even if we said spiteful things afterwards. I was happy, anyway. There *was* a kindliness in us, even a certain fragrance in our meeting – something very good, and poignant to remember, now the whole world of it is lost.

Perhaps we shall be happy again. I *do* think Gilbert let you down unpardonably. But perhaps we can get right – though differently. I am terribly weary in my soul of all things, in the world of man. Do you remember our 'island' scheme?[1]

Frieda sends her love – I mine.

D. H. Lawrence

1583. To Lady Cynthia Asquith, 17 June 1918
Text: MS UT; Huxley 445–6.

Mountain Cottage, Middleton by Wirksworth, Derby
17 June 1918

Are you as busy as all that, in your hospital? – and does it make you happy?[2]

If you come by the Gloucester – Birmingham – Edinburgh express, on the Midland Railway, you pass through Derby: and Derby is only 12 miles from Wirksworth. So you see how near we are. Therefore you can come for a few days on your way. – When do you think of going to Scotland?

I have had various forms of application, and letters of enquiry, from the Sec. of the Literary Fund – which I have filled in or answered, as the case may be, with considerable impatience. I long to send the impertinent impudent questioners to hell and further.

We have no news. I am very cross and disagreeable, even with myself, these days: don't like it at all.

---

[1] i.e. Rananim.
[2] Lady Cynthia was a Voluntary Aid Detachment nurse and, according to her diary, was particularly hard-pressed (see Asquith, *Diaries* 449–51).

We will meet you at the station, either Wirksworth or Cromford or Matlock – they are all near – when you come. Perhaps you will come to the one that is easiest for you.

Frieda is very well, and sends her love.

DHL

The Sec. of the Literary Fund will lay my application before his Committee on July 10th. – curse him.

1584. To Arthur Llewelyn Roberts, 17 June 1918

Text: MS RLFund; cited in Delany 365.

Mountain Cottage, Middleton by Wirksworth, Derby
17 June 1918

Dear Sir

In reply to your letter of this morning – I have not tried to obtain work in any Government department, because my health does not allow me to undertake any regular employment. – I have not applied for assistance from any other quarter, save the Royal Literary Fund.

Thanking you for your courtesy.

Yours faithfully   D. H. Lawrence

A Llewelyn Roberts Esq.

1585. To Amy Lowell, 18 June 1918

Text: MS HU; Damon 462–3.

Mountain Cottage, Middleton by Wirksworth, Derby. – England
18 June 1918

My dear Amy

I have just read your lectures – the one on me[1] – which I got from Hilda. Thanks for the nice things you say about me. I don't mind what people think of my work, so long as their attitude is *passionately* honest – which I believe yours is. As for intellectual honesty, I care nothing for it, for it may rest on the most utterly false *a priori*.

[1] On 20 and 27 March 1918 Amy Lowell had given two lectures at the Brooklyn Institute, New York, on 'Imagism Past and Present'. The second was on the work of Richard Aldington, the Imagist poet F. S. Flint (1885–1960) and DHL. She spoke highly but not uncritically of DHL: 'I do not hesitate to declare Mr. Lawrence to be a man of genius. He does not quite get his genius into harness; the cart of his work frequently overturns or goes awry; but it is no less Pegasus who draws it, even if Mr. Lawrence is not yet an entirely proficient charioteer . . . [His] last volume of poems, *Look! We Have Come Through!* is an amazing book . . . It is terrible in its intensity. It is sorrow made flesh. It is courage "coming through"' (Damon 443–7).

I never thanked you for the dollars, either:[1] not because I was not grateful, but because sometimes one's soul is a dumb rock, and won't be either coaxed or struck into utterance. We were very glad of the help – it is always a case of touch and go, with us, financially.

I have just heard also that Huebsch is bringing out an edition of *Look We Have Come Through*, in New York.[2] I am glad of that. Perhaps America will like it better than England does. Nothing but shams go down here, just now. I suppose it is inevitable.

I have not seen Hilda for some time – but believe she is happy in Cornwall – as far as it is possible to be happy, with the world as it is.

I have just gathered a new MS. of a book of poems – 'Coming Awake' – so named after the first poem.[3] I have worked at some of them for a long time – many years – but many are new, made this spring. I have just inscribed the MS. to you: simply put 'to Amy Lowell'. You must let me know if you would like this to stand. I finished the book, and made its list of contents, this very day – and I shall send it off today to Pinker. It is all different kinds of poems – nothing for anybody to take exception to, I believe. I hope you will like it.

We are here in Derbyshire, just near my native place – come home, in these last wretched days – not to die, I hope. Life is very wretched, really, in the outer world – and in the immediate world too, such a ghastly stress, a horrid pressure on one, all the time – and gnawing anxiety. The future seems utterly impenetrable, and as fathomless as the Bottomless Pit, and about as desperate. – But no doubt the world will sail out again, out of the Maelström. Perhaps even now it is moving clear from the Vortex.

I still want to come to America, to see you and the New World, when everything quiets down.

Frieda sends her love. Just let me know about the inscription.

Yours very Sincerely   D. H. Lawrence

1586. To J. B. Pinker, 18 June 1918
Text: MS UT; cited in Delany 354.

Mountain Cottage, Middleton by Wirksworth, Derby
18 June 1918

My dear Pinker

Thanks for the Hübsch agreement, which I return signed. Thanks also

---

[1] Amy Lowell sent the Lawrences $200 on 12 March 1918; Frieda had thanked her on 15 April (Damon 443, 449).

[2] Huebsch had written to Pinker on 24 May 1918 (TMS NYPL) to confirm the arrangement (cf. p. 238 n. 3).

[3] Another reference to *New Poems*. 'Coming Awake' was displaced by 'Apprehension' as the opening poem. The volume was dedicated to Amy Lowell.

for saying you will write for me to the Royal Literary Fund.[1] The Man is A. Llewelyn Roberts, Secretary to the Royal Literary Fund,

40 Denison House, (241?) Vauxhall Bridge Rd, S.W.1.

I forget the numbers of the street. Could you look up the Fund in the telephone book, do you think, and make sure of the address. I'm sorry if I'm a nuisance.

I am sending you MS. of a book of poems. I think there is nothing in it to offend anybody – tell me if you think there is: or if you think there is anything that would be better left out. I am sorry I haven't got a type writer here, so I can't type them out. Don't let this MS. get lost, will you, because it is the only one that is at all complete. At first I had it in two little separate books, one called 'In London', the other 'Choir of Women'.[2] I can split it up again if you think publishers would rather have it that way. But it were best left all together, I think. But you will tell me what you think about these things, won't you.

I shall send you shortly my Essays on Classic American Literature – which I don't think I dare offer to publishers in the present state of opinion and tyranny.

Do write to those Literary Fund people. I am in a painful way about money, as usual: so if they will help, I shall have to be helped by them – application forms and all.

I am glad *Look We Have Come Through* is being done in America. One day – God knows how late a day, however – the Americans will read me. But be damned to them – it is the same to me, so long as I can go on by myself: which isn't so easy, after all.

Tell me if you have any suggestions for alterations in the poems.

Yrs   D. H. Lawrence

1587. To Captain John Short, 18 June 1918
Text: MS UT; Unpublished.

Mountain Cottage, Middleton by Wirksworth, Derby.

18 June 1918

Dear Capt. Short,

Mrs Odle seemed very uncertain – so I have said to Miss Taylor she can have the cottage.[3] I enclose her letter to you. She will pay 30/- a month till the end of Sept., then she can have it cheaper, if we can't come back. If we

---

[1] See p. 249 n. 2.
[2] 'Choir of Women' ('Chorus of Women', Letter 1555) had been an earlier suggestion (Letter 1572) for the title of what was to become *New Poems*; this is the first mention of 'In London'.
[3] An acquaintance of Arabella Yorke's mother; see Letter 1672.

came back, she could still stay on, if she liked – if we had our own little cottage. – I don't know her – she is a friend of some friends: they say she is very nice. You will help her in what you can, won't you? If she wants to come at once, she will write to you, and also to Mary Hocking.

I have got a cold this last week, and feel dismal. Whenever shall we be able to meet again, and be cheerful.

Miss Taylor can at least pay the first three months rent to you – till the end of Sept – when we can make a more definite arrangement.

Greetings from us both to Mrs Short and you. Where is Mrs Whitley – and Whitley?[1]

Yrs.   D. H. Lawrence

1588. To S. S. Koteliansky, [20 June 1818]
Text: MS BL; cited in Gransden 27.

Mountain Cottage, Middleton by Wirksworth, Derby
Thursday

My dear Kot,

Many thanks for the cheque[2] – I shan't use it if I can help it – because what if your bank broke, what should we all do?

No, I haven't any news. It is true my cursing *mood* isn't my only mood: but my cursing *news* is my only news. I have finished up all the things I am writing at present – have a complete blank in front of me – feel very desperate, and ready for anything, good or bad. I think something critical will happen this month – finally critical. If it doesn't I shall bust.

Arabella is here – been here a week – stays another week, I suppose. She is very nice. We were over in my native place for a day or two – queer – I can accept it again – no longer have to fight it at all. We get a lot of the old people – people of my pre-London days – to see us. Arabella is the first from the South. – You said you were coming. But perhaps the hour isn't due yet. You'll come before the summer is over.

Are the Farbman's still at Eastbourne – and you alone with Fox?[3] You must have an abnormal *static* power – I should have gone mad long since. Aren't you afraid of becoming one day rooted and immovable, like a graven stone, or a wooden image? I think a bomb will have to fall *very* near to you, or

[1] Irene Whittley was, in 1919, at least, a teacher in Battersea. Her husband served in the Navy during the war and was employed in Barclay's Bank after it.
[2] 'The cheque for £10 is dated 19 June 1918. DHL never cashed it. It is preserved among the *Koteliansky Papers*' in BL (Zytaruk 141 n. 1).
[3] The name of the Farbmans' dog (Zytaruk 141 n. 3).

you'll metamorphose into a sort of rock. – But it needs a great effort to bear up against these days.

Write again soon. Frieda greets you.

DHL

1589. To Mark Gertler, 26 June 1918
Text: MS SIU; Huxley 448.

Mountain Cottage, Middleton by Wirksworth, Derby
26 June 1918

Dear Gertler

I suppose you are at Garsington now. Is it nice? Perhaps we should like to come to London for a while, next month, to see you all again. We will come if I get that money from that beastly fund.

How is Ottoline now? Do you think she would like to see us again? Do you think we might be happy if we saw her again – if we went to Garsington?[1] I feel, somehow, that perhaps we might. But tell me how it is – what you think.

We are alone again today for the first time for weeks – it is queer. I am very restless and at the end of *everything*. I don't work – don't try to – only just endure the days. There will either have to come a break outside or inside – in the world or in one's self.

Tell me about Garsington and Ottoline. Remember us both to her. – If you feel like it, you can come up here from Garsington. You come from Oxford to Birmingham – Birmingham to Derby – and then you are soon here. If it attracts you at all, do come.

Frieda sends her love.

DHL

1590. To Sallie Hopkin, 26 June 1918
Text: MS NCL; Huxley 446–7.

Mountain Cottage, Middleton-by-Wirksworth, Derby
26 June 1918

My dear Sallie

You will be feeling quite lost with all your folk gone off to Scarboro. Arabella also has left us today – in tears and grief. I hope she will come again soon – we became very fond of her.

---

[1] Commenting on this question, in a letter written from Garsington to Kot, Gertler remarked: 'It puts me in a very difficult position. Ottoline particularly objects to Frieda' (*Gertler: Selected Letters*, ed. Carrington, p. 160).

We had such a good time at the week-end. Did your people enjoy it as much as we did? I can't help wishing that Willie and Enid and Kitty[1] had stayed here for this week, and gone on to the sea with you. It was so jolly when we were all together. And it is the human contact which means so much to one, really. Do you know, I quite suffered when they had gone away on Monday – and usually I am so glad to be alone.

I do wish you could have had a few really peaceful days here, as you promised you would. Don't you think you might manage it when you come back from Scarborough? I find, for myself, nowadays, that change of scene is not enough – neither sea nor hills nor anything else; – only the human warmth, when one can get it, makes the heart rich. One no longer takes ones riches through the eye, I find – but in some subtler communication direct from being to being. And in a world where most of the human influence is now destructive and horribly humiliating, to be with people whose presence is an enrichment in the veins, is everything.

Tomorrow a friend is calling, on her way down to London from Edinburgh[2] – but staying only one night. I don't know what we shall do at the week-end. I wish we had a nice soft motor-car that could fetch you over here. But we haven't. – And you will be dreadfully tired with the business. – And of course Ada or somebody may be coming here. – But if Frieda and I ever do happen in on you will you *please* not make any bother of us. We are such simple people when we are by ourselves – and we really like that best.

I thought Willie and Enid both looked better on Monday – did you? They are both suffering the inevitable suffering of this crisis. It has to be got through.

Love from both of us   DHL

1591. To Catherine Carswell, 26 June 1918
Text: MS YU; Huxley 447–8.

Mountain Cottage, Middleton-by-Wirksworth, Derby
26 June 1918

My dear Catherine

Out of a sort of despair of the days, one lets the time slip by. How are you now, and what is your news? Are you better – and up – and going about? – and is Johannes a happy boy? – and is everything all right, in the immediate circle? I hope so.

---

[1] Kitty Allcock (b. 1897); see Nehls, i. 469–70.
[2] Unidentified.

We are alone again today for the first time for many weeks. The last fortnight Dorothy Yorke – Arabella, the American girl at Mecklenburgh Sq – has been with us. She was very nice. She has gone back today. I feel, at this time, it is better to have friends near one – and children – otherwise one thinks too much and is too much exposed. We had my little nephew of three, and my niece of seven, for a few weeks – and I was very glad of their presence.

I have no particular news. Perhaps I shall get a bit of money from the Royal Literary Fund, next month. If I do we might come to London for a little time, to see you all again. I should like to see you again, and to see the newcomer for the first time. One's heart gets very dry and weary with the day after day of this life – all suspense and tension and nullity and humiliation. There will come a break soon. I am very glad you have got the baby, you will be happy.

The flowers are nearly all gone – just wild roses, and meadow flowers. We have been for several long walks in this country. It is rather fine. I hope you will come and see it before long. I feel, somehow, as if we should be seeing you again soon.

Frieda sends her love – greet Don from me.

DHL

1592. To William Hopkin, [1 July 1918]
Text: MS NCL; Postmark, Ripley 1 JY 18; Unpublished.

Grosvenor Rd, Ripley, Derby
Monday 1 July

Dear Willie

I had a very nice Sunday with Sallie: who seems well and brisk. She read me some bits of your letters[1] – I can see you are enjoying yourself in the right old style.

This is to ask you do you know where the key of the water-well is – I haven't been able to find it last week. Do you remember where you put it when you so nobly filled up the water jar in the kitchen.

It is very hot and lovely – I am just setting off for Ambergate to go back to the cottage. Hope we shall see you when you are back. You might get over on Sunday – I'm not sure if Ada will be driving over with the Clarkes – or with the old man Clarke – damn him.[2]

Best greetings to the girls.[3]   D. H. Lawrence

[1] Hopkin was on holiday in Scarborough.
[2] Ada's father-in-law, William Clarke (1856?–1929); he had a tailor's shop in Ripley.
[3] Enid Hopkin and, probably, Kitty Allcock (see Letter 1590).

1593. To S. S. Koteliansky, 2 July 1918
Text: MS BL; Postmark, Wirks[worth] 2 JY 18; Moore 559–60.

Mountain Cottage, Middleton by Wirksworth, Derby
2 July 1918

My dear Kot

I wrote to Gertler thinking we might see the Ott. again – then we should have come to London for a bit. But I got such a stupid answer from him – vague and conditional like Mr Balfour discussing peace terms.[1] To Hell with Ott. – the whole Ottlerie – what am I doing temporising with them.

Now why don't you come here. Plainly and simply, why don't you come here for a time. You said you would – so just do it. If you don't want to report yourself to the police, well, *don't.* Arabella didn't – and she is American. She just came and stayed her two weeks and took no notice. You could do the same, if it is the reporting which irks you.

There isn't any news – everybody seems immersed in the most hopeless stupidity and vacuous misery – I have no patience, and no hope from such spiritless *Canaille.* But I don't care. I do verily believe the war is going to fizzle out – though what next, I don't know – nor how we are going to live. It is the end of the tether – and what when the tether breaks, God knows: it even may not break, and we shall strangle ourselves.

Never mind, I don't care. We'll just hang on while we can. Do really uproot yourself and come and stay here for a bit. It's a case of move or perish: so move.

I am still hanging on in the hope that I need not use your cheque. The meeting that decides the money from the Literary Fund is on the 10th. I hope the dogs and swine will have sufficient fear of God in their hearts: *fear,* that is the only thing that will do them any good: fear of the wrath of the Lord.

We are alone, save for my little nephew – who is only three years old, and therefore quite decent. Next week my sister may be here for two or three days – no more – but that need not prevent your coming.

Gertler's letter made me mad. What in the name of hell do I care about the Ott's queases and qualms.

Now then stir yourself to take a train.

DHL

Frieda greets you, and will be glad to see you.
I had another letter from Lewis – which I ignored.[2]

---

[1] A. J. Balfour in his capacity as Foreign Secretary (1916–19).

[2] DHL first met A. P. Lewis in June 1914 at Spezia where he was employed by Vickers Maxim (*Letters,* ii. 184); in August Lewis may have been one of the four-man group which undertook a walking tour in Westmorland (*Letters,* ii. 268 n. 2).

1594. To Cecil Gray, 3 July 1918
Text: MS StaU; Huxley 449.

Mountain Cottage, Middleton by Wirksworth, Derby
3 July 1918

What Zennor ructions – W[illiam] H[enry] married, Katie going away: what will be left of Zennor? W.H. is rather a fool, and bores me. I feel distressed for the old ewe – his mother. If he had any decency he would go and live with Mary Quick in my cottage, and leave his mother on the farm. When they write to me I'll tell them that. But he'll be too 'big', I know. – And then the Fish suddenly opening her mouth and barking.[1] No, it's too much, there should be a general extirpation of the race.

Our news is no news, as usual. Arabella is back in Mecklenburgh – She was very[2] nice here, we had some splendid walks in the country, and really enjoyed them. We get rather crowded with people. For the moment we are alone save for my little nephew, aged 3. Frieda is well, and about as happy and unhappy as you might expect.

I sent the American Essays to a friend in London, who was going to put them with a 'safe' friend to have them typed. The friend collapsed, and they are hung up.[3] I don't want them to go to the ordinary typist. So I don't know quite what will eventuate. I'll let you have a typed copy if ever I get one. – I am still waiting proofs from Beaumont.[4] He sent me *New Paths* – the anthology in which I figure, cum Richard cum Flint etc.[5] It is a very mediocre production, in all but paper and print. Of Maunsel and the philosophy nothing actually came.[6] It may, after the war. The Oxford Press said I might do a school-book, of European History.[7] If only I could get books of

---

[1] Mrs Fisher: see Letters 1509 and 1511.

[2] MS reads 'She very'.

[3] The reference to two friends is obscure, though presumably Kot was the one who 'collapsed'. In mid-February DHL had asked him to undertake the typing (Letter 1527) and sent him the 'first part' on 25 February (Letter 1532); Kot had sent some typescript by mid-March (Letter 1547) but apparently abandoned the task by the end of that month (Letter 1550).

[4] Proofs of *Bay*.

[5] See p. 202 n. 2. The volume included two poems by Richard Aldington ('The Blood of the Young Men' and 'Soliloquy') and two by F. S. Flint ('Oak' and 'Swan'); other poets represented included W. H. Davies, Walter de la Mare, W. W. Gibson, Harold Monro, Aldous Huxley and Edith, Osbert and Sacheverell Sitwell. Also reproduced in the volume were pictures by Augustus John and Walter Sickert, John and Paul Nash, Mark Gertler ('Study for "The Bathers"') and Ivan Meštrović on whom DHL's old friend Ernest Collings wrote an appreciation (see p. 137 n. 2). Sadleir himself contributed an article on 'The Young Novel' in which he spoke highly and at some length of DHL's achievement.

[6] See Letter 1507; the 'philosophy' referred to was 'At the Gates'.

[7] DHL's first reference to what became *Movements in European History*, published by Oxford University Press – using DHL's pseudonym Lawrence H. Davison – in February 1921. The initiative in proposing this venture to DHL came from Vere Collins (see p. 194 n. 1).

reference, I would. I feel in a historical mood, being very near the end of Gibbon. The chief feeling is, that men were always alike, and always will be, and one must view the species with contempt first and foremost, and find a few individuals, if possible – which seems at this juncture not to be possible – and ultimately, if the impossible were possible, to *rule* the species. It is proper ruling they need, and always have needed. But it is impossible, because they can only be ruled as they are willing to be ruled: and that is swinishly or hypocritically.

There is a great upset here about the munitions explosion near Nottingham – 86 people answered the roll-call, out of 2000. The paper says 60 killed. So much for the paper.[1]

There is raging influenza – but not just here.

God knows how we shall all end up. Frieda sends her love to both.

DHL

1595. To J. B. Pinker, 11 July 1918
Text: TMSC NWU; Keith Cushman, *DHL Review*, vi (1973), 23.

Mountain Cottage, Middleton by Wirksworth, Derby.
11 July 1918.

My dear Pinker,

I have a friend whose husband, Leigh Henry, is interned in Ruhleben.[2] He has sent over the MS. of a book of poems, which are good. It makes a little vol. of 42 poems, all short – called 'Poems of a Prisoner'. Some are written in Ruhleben – though they haven't much to do with it, that's a fact. I wondered if you would try to place these poems, for Mrs Henry. If you would, I will send the MS. along. But if it would not be worth your while, I will send them to Duckworth – or somebody – for her.

Don't you have any success with the 'Coming Awake' poems? Perhaps Secker would do them – I believe he is amiably disposed towards me just now.

Yrs.   D. H. Lawrence

---

[1] There was a serious explosion on 1 July at 'a national shell-filling factory in the Midlands' (*Times*, 3 July 1918). The *Times* reported the official death-toll on 10 August: 134 people had been killed.

[2] Leigh Vaughan Henry (1889–1958), who was interned in Ruhleben camp for most of the war, was a composer and music critic as well as poet. Before 1914 he was the musical director of Gordon Craig's School for the Art of the Theatre in Florence. Henry was the author of *The Story of Music* (1935), *Dr John Bull, 1562–1628* (1937), etc. (See Cushman, *DHL Review*, vi (1973), 21–32.) So far as is known, the volume of poems in which DHL interested himself was never published. His wife, Nancy Henry, was most likely a free-lance, part-time editor for Oxford University Press; she was actively involved in the production of DHL's *Movements in European History*.

1596. To Nancy Henry, 11 July 1918
Text: MS Lazarus; Cushman, *DHL Review*, vi. 24–5.

Mountain Cottage, Middleton by Wirksworth, Derby
11 July 1918

Dear Mrs Henry

The poems all came safely – and the letters. They were very interesting. I have made a book of the poems – called it 'Poems of a Prisoner'. I have left out the *Chinoiseries* and the poems from *Moon Robbers* – have kept practically all the rest – but have dropped the divisions and inscriptions etc and simplified the form as much as I can. – It makes a nice little book of 42 poems – I have written my agent about it – if he doesn't think it worth his while, I will send it round myself.

I don't think the 'Tufty poems' are so good – and the 'Moon Robbers' absolutely needs the music – with which it might be beautiful. Some of the poems in the MS. I am going to send out are very lovely, I think. I hope we'll have a success with it.

I have done the first essay of the *European History*.

Greetings from my wife.

Yrs   D. H. Lawrence

1597. To Cyril Beaumont, 11 July 1918
Text: MS UCin; Unpublished.

Mountain Cottage, Middleton by Wirksworth, Derby
11 July 1918

Dear Beaumont,

I got my copy of *New Paths* – very handsome it is to look at and touch and handle – something *really* clean and fresh in this world of frowsty books. It is very interesting as a venture – tentative as it ought to be. I hope it'll go.

How is your hand press and proofs of *Bay*?

Yrs.   D. H. Lawrence

1598. To S. S. Koteliansky, 12 July 1918
Text: MS BL; Postmark, [. . .] 12 JY 18; Zytaruk 144.

Mountain Cottage, Middleton by Wirksworth, Derby
12 July 1918

My dear Kot,

I got a miserable £50 from that dirty Royal Literary Fund – so I shall not need your £10 for the moment. I send you the cheque back.[1] You can't be

---

[1] See p. 256 n. 2.

offended, because I'm afraid that in a few months' time, I shall be asking you for it again.

I can't come to London. Really, I haven't the energy. But you should really stir yourself, and come here. The people at the police station at Wirksworth are the most aimiable on earth. We shall be quite alone for the next fortnight. Rouse yourself up – it will be so good for you.

I haven't any news – have you? Do take a trip up here, it is *necessary* for you.

DHL

1599. To Arthur Llewelyn Roberts, 12 July 1918
Text: RLFund; Unpublished.

Mountain Cottage, Middleton by Wirksworth, Derby
12 July 1918

Dear Sir,

Thank you for your letter and the enclosed cheque for £50, from the Royal Literary Fund. Please convey my thanks to the Committee of the Fund.

Yours faithfully   D. H. Lawrence

A. Llewelyn Roberts Esq.

1600. To Lady Cynthia Asquith, 13 July 1918
Text: MS UT; Unpublished.

Mountain Cottage, Middleton by Wirksworth, Derby.
Sat. 13 July 1918

Yes, you can get to Edinburgh from Derby in about 8 hours, on the Midland Railway, if that will do for you. *Derby 11.12 – Edinbro 7.34.* Derby is about 14 miles from here. So it is directly on your way to Scotland, if you come on the Midland Railway.

If you come, come from *St. Pancras 12.15*, arrive Derby 3.30, change there, wait a few minutes, leave Derby 3.43, arr. *Cromford* 4.30. It is better to come to Cromford, rather than Wirksworth. Or if you don't want to change, you can stay in your London train till *Matlock*: arr. 4.3. I can meet you there and we can come on by motor-bus to Cromford. *Can you walk about 3 miles, hilly?* – if not we must find some sort of conveyance. I hope this is clear – the express stops at Matlock, but not at Cromford. Please yourself which you come to. I'll meet you.

Of course you would have to take this Flu – you are always so abominably in the swim – vulgar. – Hope it's better. We are as yet uninfected.

I got £50 from that dirty Literary Fund – which is something, anyhow. Many thanks to you and to Whibley, who shall be unnamed, as he desires. I got the money yesterday – should have written to you anyhow.

I hope your husband will go on enjoying himself – rolling home, so to speak.[1]

When do you think you will be coming?

DHL

1601. To J. B. Pinker, 17 July 1918
Text: TMSC NWU; Unpublished.

Mountain Cottage, Middleton by Wirksworth, Derby.
17 July 1918.

My dear Pinker,

Thanks for your letter of this morning. I send Leigh Henry's poems. Why are Chattos so slow making up their minds?

Yrs. D. H. Lawrence

1602. To Cecil Gray, 22 July 1918
Text: MS StaU; Huxley 450.

Mountain Cottage, Middleton by Wirksworth, Derby
22 July 1918

Dear Grigio

Capt. Short has let me down again. I understood my bigger house was not occupied, and that he had put my furniture into it. So I let it to a Miss A.M. Taylor. The poor female arrives, finds the house stuffed with Miss Pilchard's land-workers, all my furniture monopolised – and so on – she is in a pretty pickle, I'm sure. If you feel like it, I should be glad if you would send her a line, and if you would see her, to help her if you can – perhaps find her a few necessities. And I should be glad if you could get my books over to Bosigran one day – I am afraid I shall lose *everything* in that treacherous hole of Tregerthen.

How are you now? I wish I could see you. Do you remember this time last year we talked of the Andes? – and you used to say, you were not *ready*. There won't be any Andes. And I don't suppose any of us were ready. But do you feel now as if the old world – or self – were about cleared out of you? – a sort of

---

[1] Herbert Asquith was on leave from the army, 6–19 July 1918.

– moi, après le Déluge? When you feel like leaving Bosigran for a bit, you will
come and stay here, will you, and we'll see where we are.

I don't get any proofs or any MS. typed to send you. I want you to read the
American Essays when they *are* typed.

Is the Fish with you? – and for how long?

I have a man and wife wanting a house in Cornwall.[1] Will you be letting
Bosigran for the winter?

I don't think I shall ever come back to Cornwall now.

DHL

We may go to London for a week or so in August.

1603. To Captain John Short, 22 July 1918
Text: MS UT; Unpublished.

Mountain Cottage, Middleton by Wirksworth, Derby
22 July 1918

Dear Capt. Short,

I have received the enclosed letter from Miss Taylor, and am most distressed on her account. I had *no idea* there were land-workers in the bigger
house – nor that you had taken the cooking utensils and so on. Again, you see,
you are *not* straight in your dealing with me.

If Miss Taylor stays, I hope you will do what you can to make her
comfortable. But I hope she will find another place. I am ashamed enough at
being responsible for her present situation.

Yours Sincerely   D. H. Lawrence

1604. To J. B. Pinker, 24 July 1918
Text: MS UT; Unpublished.

Mountain Cottage, Middleton by Wirksworth, Derby
24 July 1918

My dear Pinker

Will you give these three poems to Austin Harrison – I had meant to ask
you to take them out of the MS., for him.[2]

Have Chattos still not made up their minds about 'Coming Awake'? They
are over long. They should have given them back to you. And Secker? –
anything from him?

Yrs   D. H. Lawrence

[1] Probably Mr and Mrs Collard: see Letters 1608 and 1609.
[2] The poems have not been identified.

1605. To S. S. Koteliansky, [25 July 1918]
Text: MS BL; Moore 561.

Middleton –
Thursday.[1]

My dear Kot,

Are you still living, and can you still speak? I'm sure I feel about as bad as you do, altogether.

Will you still be in No 5. next month – and if we wanted to come for a few days, would it be feasible? Frieda will be seeing her children – I don't know exactly when. But we just *might* want to come in a week's time – might: probably it will not be for a month.

Oh my dear Kot, for these months and years of slow execution we suffer, I *should* like my revenge on the world. Are we *really quite* impotent, all of us? Quoi faire? – che fare?[2] – Can't you answer?

DHL

1606. To Sallie Hopkin, [25 July 1918]
Text: MS NCL; Unpublished.

Middleton –
Thursday

My dear Sallie

I wrote to you before, but we papered the walls, so the letter disappeared.

I hope your mother's death wasn't a shock to you.[3] I hope things are all right. What is Mrs Hicks going to do?[4]

My Aunt and Uncle are coming from Leicester for Bank Holiday. He is German – Fritz Krenkow – Arabic scholar.[5] I don't know how long they'll stay nor what day they'll come. I wish you could get over to see them one day. Frieda wants to go to London to see her children – probably on Aug 12th. – wants me to go. That would sadly interfere with your visit. But you would come as soon as we get back. – We should see Enid.

[1] The conjectural date presumes a fairly lengthy silence on Kot's part after DHL's previous letter on 12 July 1918, and a short span before his next (on 30 July, Letter 1610) which refers again to the possibility of a visit to London.
[2] 'What's to be done?'
[3] Sallie Hopkin's mother was Maria, née Hewson. m. James Pead Potter.
[4] Rosamond Hicks, née Potter, was Sallie Hopkin's elder sister. She was regarded as the invalid of the family (hence the tone of DHL's enquiry); she was cared for by her eight brothers and sisters; she outlived them all.
[5] Ada Rose Beardsall (1868–1944), DHL's maternal aunt, m. Fritz Johann Heinrich Krenkow (1872–1953). At this time Krenkow earned his living with a hosiery firm in Leicester; he later acquired a high reputation as an Arabic scholar (see *Letters*, i. 77 n).

I should like to see you and Willie before we go. Couldn't you really drive over one day. Who will be coming to you?

Let us hear how you are.

Love from both   DHL

1607. To Captain John Short, 26 July 1918
Text: MS UT; Unpublished.

Mountain Cottage, Middleton by Wirksworth, Derby
26 July 1918

Dear Captain Short

Your letter has just come. I understood, of course, from Miss Taylor's wail, that she had four or five land workers[1] in the house with her, and was destitute of the barest necessities. – Whereas, if she has the place to herself; and the things as you say, she is really impertinent to set up such a scream. What indeed does she want for 7/6 a week? Yes, leave her alone to come to her senses. I will do the same. Of course I don't *know* her – and don't want to.

I apologise for my remarks in my last letter. How wretched it is, that Westyr is so ill![2] What is really the matter with him? What a life of misery and worry altogether! No, I'm sure I don't want to add to your troubles. I only hope that there will be an end of this business, and that we can have some happy times, as before. When I am in my garden here, I think all the time of Tregerthen – your garden there – your beans on that lattice work.

Remember us very kindly to Mrs Short – and to Mrs Whitley, and to Whitley. Where are they now? I shall see them again one day.

Greetings to you from my wife and me –   D. H. Lawrence
P.S. I laughed at your 'Dear Sir', to me.

1608. To Nancy Henry, 26 July 1918
Text: TMSC NWU; Huxley 450–1.

Mountain Cottage, Middleton by Wirksworth, Derby
26 July 1918

Dear Mrs. Henry

I send you the first three chapters.[3] They are perhaps rather long. The others, some of them, will be much shorter. I wanted to make a serious reader that would convey the true historic impression to children who are beginning

---

[1] DHL wrote 'landowners' (cf. Letter 1602).
[2] Westyr was Captain Short's second son.
[3] Of *Movements in European History*.

to grasp realities. We should introduce the deep, philosophic note into education: deep, philosophic reverence.

I've no doubt your people won't like this style. I shan't mind if they don't want me to go on. But please tell me your own full opinion.

I wrote to Collard[1] that my cottage is let.

I wonder what Vere has decided.[2]

I haven't any news yet about poems. It is always so slow. Have you heard of your husband?

Greetings from us both.   D. H. Lawrence

1609. To Nancy Henry, [29 July 1918]
Text: MS ColU; Paul Delany, *DHL Review*, ii (1969), 196.

Middleton by Wirksworth
Monday.

Dear Mrs Henry

I got your letter just when I had sent off the chaps. of the *History*. Hope they'll come to you all right in London.

The news is interesting, about the press; will save it, anyhow.

I've just heard from a friend about his house near mine in Cornwall.[3] I mentioned it to Collard. Now, like a fool, I've lost Collard's address. Send it me by return, will you. – Or just drop him the enclosed note.

I want to see the story. We must arrange a meeting soon. Let us get next week over – people coming here.

What about your husband? I have no news of his poems yet from Pinker, my agent. – What has Vere decided? Oh God, what a *muddle* everything is. – To know how to interpret dream-hints is *not* to destroy dream knowledge – only to verify it.

D. H. Lawrence

1610. To S. S. Koteliansky, [30 July 1918]
Text: MS BL; Zytaruk 146.

Middleton –
Tuesday

My dear Kot

The coming to London depended on other people. – My aunt and uncle,

---

[1] Unidentified. (The letter is missing.)
[2] Vere Collins.
[3] Cecil Gray: see Letter 1602. (The note, or a letter, to Collard has disappeared.)

whom I have not seen for 6 years, are coming here next week for a day or two.
– But then Frieda wants to come immediately to London to see her children.
So we might come on Friday week – Aug 9th. is it? – or more probably the
Monday following – Aug. 12th. Would that do? – As for gas etc, they won't
matter.

Like you, I hate the reformers worst, and their nauseous Morrellity. But I
count them my worst enemies, and want my revenge on them first. Ça ira.

Frieda thanks you for your invitation, and is pleased to come to the cave.
Where is Gertler? – still Ottling?

DHL

1611. To J. B. Pinker, 3 August 1918
Text: TMSC NWU; Huxley 451–2.

Mountain Cottage, Middleton by Wirksworth, Derby.
3rd. August 1918.

My dear Pinker,

I am sending you the first of the *Studies in Classic American Literature*.
There are six or seven more – these I will send in about a week's time. Do read
this essay on the 'Spirit of Place'. You will find one MS. complete – the other
lacking the last eight pages. Would you let somebody type out these eight
pages, and then you will have two copies.

I think we may really sell these essays, both in America and in England –
and really make something with them. I have a feeling that they will make all
the difference. Will you send Harrison this first essay at once? He might do it
quickly.[1] Let me know what you think.

I may come to London in a week or ten day's time. If you are in London I
will come and see you, shall I.

Really, I place my hopes of the world on these essays, so you will help me
with them as much as possible. I know it has been a thankless job so far. But it
won't always be so.

Yrs.   D. H. Lawrence

1612. To Catherine Carswell, 3 August 1918
Text: MS YU; Huxley 451.

Mountain Cottage, Middleton-by-Wirksworth, Derby.
3 Aug. 1918

My dear Catherine

I had been thinking so often of you these last days – so glad to hear your

---

[1] The essay was published in *English Review*, xxvii (November 1918), 319–31.

news peaceful and nice. Everything is very quiet here, for the moment –
nothing to tell, *at all.*

But Frieda has promised to go to London on the 12th. to see her children –
and I may go with her. I think we shall stay with Koteliansky. Thanks very
much for offering the house. If it is not let, do you think Frieda might have it
for a meeting place for her children once or twice – spend a day or two there –
not sleep, just some hours per day?

I *do* wish we could come with you to the Forest of Dean for two or three
days. I don't know that Wye Country. Do you think it might be done – from
London to Ross – and from Ross to Derby? I should like it so much. – If it
were possible, it would be about the 19th or 20th. – And I do want you to
come here for a bit. Let us think.

Love from both to you three   DHL

1613. To S. S. Koteliansky, [6 August 1918]
Text: MS BL; Zytaruk 147.

Middleton by Wirksworth, Derby
Tuesday 6 Aug.

My dear Kot

I expect we shall come next Monday – 12th. I will let you know exactly. We
will bring our rations – don't get much in.

I am quite thankful that you have got to scrub etc. We might find you
inseparably glued to a chair.

à bientôt   DHL

1614. To Enid Hopkin, 8 August 1918
Text: MS UCLA; cited in Moore, *Poste Restante* 49.

Mountain Cottage, Middleton by Wirksworth, Derby
8 Aug 1918

My Dear Enid

We think of coming to London on Monday – 12th. – stay at 5 Acacia Rd,
St. Johns Wood, N.W. I expect we shall be in town about a week. Let me
know when you are free – what time in the evening. We must certainly meet.
Everybody is out of town – just everybody – but we'll see what we can do. –
Shall be glad to see you.

D. H. Lawrence

1615. To Lady Cynthia Asquith, 8 August 1918
Text: TMSC NWU; Unpublished.

Mountain Cottage, Middleton by Wirksworth, Derby.
8th. August 1918.

Right, I'll believe you when I see you – about coming here.

As for your secretariate, after beating my brains, . . . I want to know.[1]

Also, *when* you have done your first month's duty, and drawn your first month's donation, I shall believe this new little official report of yours. Till such time, I must turn up a sceptical nose. Nay, I demand sixpence a month, from your receipts, as a pledge and payment for my belief.

We are going to London on Monday for about a week – staying at 5 Acacia Road, St. Johns Wood, N.W. – with a disreputable Russian. Frieda is seeing her children.

I believe I'm going to have that Flu – my nose hurts. Are you all right? Tell me about your boss – divulge.

DHL

1616. To S. S. Koteliansky, [9 August 1918]
Text: MS BL; Zytaruk 147.

Middleton-by-Wirksworth, Derby.
Friday

My dear Kot

We shall come on Monday, Deo Volenti – arriving St. Pancras 3.37. It seems very strange to be coming to London – I can hardly believe it will happen. But I am glad to come.

My uncle and Aunt are here. He is interesting – my aunt bores me a bit.

Will you be alone in the house, or will the Farbmans be there? I should like to see Mrs Farbman – and Farbman. I hope they'll come.

If my uncle and Aunt should come to London on Wednesday night, just for a night – do you think we could put them up? Perhaps we might, if the Farbmans are not there.

I will bring what food I can. We shall be glad to see you, and talk out all things.

DHL

---

[1] Lady Cynthia became secretary to Sir James Barrie on 24 July 1918 and remained so until his death in 1937.

1617. To Catherine Carswell, 10 August 1918

Text: MS YU; Unpublished.

Middleton by Wirksworth, Derby.

Sat. 10 Aug. 1918

My dear Catherine

We got your letter this morning: we want *very much* to come to Ross. We can get back, a good train, Midland, Gloucester to Derby. But don't think about the tickets. The address is

5 Acacia Rd. St. Johns Wood. N.W.

Do let us know if we can come. I suppose we shall stay in London about a week.

Yes, in all faith, I shall sprinkle Johannes, if you wish it – with a potent and magical blessing.

We also are suffering badly from relatives – badly.

We do look forward to coming – Frieda as much as I.

Love from both to three   DHL

1618. To Enid Hopkin, [14 August 1918]

Text: MS UCLA; cited in Moore, *Intelligent Heart* 244.

5 Acacia Rd. – N.W.8.

Wed.

My dear Enid,

We have been here two days – came Monday. London is horribly boring and stultifying. It is like living in a sort of vacuum. – And we have to go out every evening – it is difficult to get things fitted in. I wish you were free in the daytime. Tell us how to get at your seed-testing place – the exact address – and I'll probably come in on Friday at lunch-time to find you. Couldn't you get an hour off then? Some people want us to go down to Colchester for the week-end[1] – which we may or may not do. If we don't, we'll arrange a meeting then.

Ring me up here tomorrow morning, won't you? We are in the book under 'Bourse Gazette' – 5 Acacia Rd.

London is detestable.

DHL

---

[1] Barbara Low and Edith Eder: see Letter 1621.

1619. To Catherine Carswell, 15 August 1918
Text: MS YU; Unpublished.

5 Acacia Rd. St. Johns Wood, N.W.8.
Thursday – 15 Aug. 1918

My dear Catherine

We are here till next Monday or Tuesday – then we *may* go for a day or two to Hermitage. Let me know about Herefordshire – *Don't* put yourself to any trouble about us. If you are not *quite* free, then we will go back to Derbyshire from Hermitage next week, and you must come up and see us there. Be sure not to let the thought of our coming west be any trouble to you. Only just send a line.

With love from both to three   D. H. Lawrence

1620. To J. B. Pinker, 16 August 1918
Text: MS UT; Unpublished.

Mountain Cottage, Middleton by Wirksworth, Derby[1]
16 August 1918

My dear Pinker

Thanks for your letter about Secker and the poems. Yes, give him the book[2] – I suppose his terms are better than nothing – a trifle better than nothing.

Yrs   D. H. Lawrence

1621. To Catherine Carswell, [20 August 1918]
Text: MS YU; cited in Carswell 102.

5 Acacia Rd. N.W.8.
Tuesday.

My dear Catherine

We have just got back from Mersea, where we have spent a week-end with Barbara and Mrs Eder – find your letter and post card here – we are very thrilled at the thought of coming. I am sad to take the cheque – but do so to save myself from any imputation of wastefulness.

We are going on Thursday to Hermitage –
Chapel Farm Cottage, Hermitage, nr. Newbury, Berks.
Margaret Radford is there alone – very seedy – we shall spend a day or two with her. They have had to put Mr. Radford into a home. Maitland's baby was born two days ago. Dollie is going to Lyme Regis.

---

[1] Though writing from London, DHL used his Derbyshire address.
[2] i.e. *New Poems.*

We will come next Monday, shall we? – catch that 10.45 at Didcot or Newbury or Gloucester. We are both most excited at the thought. I have got a feeling of peculiar anticipation. Hope everything will come off properly.

Love from both to you all   DHL

1622. To Dr Maitland Radford, 22 August 1918
Text: MS UN; Unpublished.

5 Acacia Rd. N.W.8.
22 Aug 1918.

Dear Maitland

I was very glad to hear of the coming of your daughter[1] – and that Muriel is safe and well. All blessings on the child – and what are you going to call her? – I wonder what she will be like – fair like you or brown like Muriel. She is the *real* younger generation.

We are going down to Hermitage today to see Margaret. I am sorry your mother is so knocked up.

All good wishes to the three of you.

D. H. Lawrence

1623. To S. S. Koteliansky, [23 August 1918]
Text: MS BL; Zytaruk 148.

Chapel Farm Cottage, Hermitage, nr Newbury, Berks.
Friday

My dear Kot,

We got our train and got here all right.

We were very happy in Acacia – stay on there, I think probably we shall come again later – then we will make a proper arrangement.

The plums are out of the garden – I picked them from the tree last evening. I hope they'll arrive nicely. They are not many, alas – but share them with Sophie Isaayevna and Ghita.

Frieda left tooth brushes and tooth-paste, and the little black nail-brush, in the bathroom. Send them to us, will you. – On Monday we go to

'The Vicarage, Upper Lydbrook, Ross-on-Wye, Herefordshire'.[2]

I feel we shall meet again soon.

DHL

Have asked Arabella to send the *Rainbow*. Let me know if she does.

---

[1] Anne Radford, b. 15 August 1918.
[2] Where the Carswells were staying: see Carswell 100.

1624. To Nancy Henry, [23 August 1918]
Text: MS ColU; Delany, *DHL Review*, ii. 197.

Chapel Farm Cottage, Hermitage, nr. Newbury, Berks
Friday

Dear Mrs Henry

I was not able to come again – had only one evening in town, and some old friends came in. But we will have a meeting before long.

We stay here till Monday – then are going on to

'The Vicarage – Upper Lydbrook, Ross-on-Wye, Herefordshire'.

We stay there till the 31st – or till 2nd. Sept. – then back to Middleton.

If Ely really decides to have the history I shall work hard at it when I get back.[1]

I have got more typed MS. of the Essays – am revising – will send you the little books if you like. One feels a curious nascent quality in the world – perhaps something is going to appear. There needs a crisis – a cataclysm of some sort. It would liberate us all into a free and good relationship. At present there is some intangible counteraction between us all – so I find it – between me and everybody.

DHL

1625. To Enid Hopkin, 24 August 1918
Text: MS UCLA; cited in Moore, *Poste Restante* 49.

Chapel Farm Cottage, Hermitage, nr. Newbury, Berks.
Sat. 24 Aug. 1918

My dear Enid

I hope you get to Richmond all right today. I had promised to ask you to go to Richmond straight, and meet Koteliansky there, at Mrs Farbman's. Like a fool, in the rush of going about, I forgot. I trust you either rang up Koteliansky, or found him at 5 Acacia Rd.

It is very pleasant here – corn in stook – very many blackberries – very peaceful, somnolent. On Monday we are going to

'The Vicarage, Upper Lydbrook, Ross-on-Wye, Herefordshire'.

I suppose we shall stay about a week, then back to Middleton, where I shall ask your mother to stay with us.

These last days I feel much too sleepy and vague to have any grip on anything. – I will write to Koteliansky, and if you have missed him this week, you must see him again.

au revoir   D. H. Lawrence

---

[1] Herbert Ely was an editor with Oxford University Press; he was responsible for the Juvenile and Elementary Schools Department. With a colleague he produced many books under the pseudonym, 'Herbert Strang'.

1626. To Edith Eder, [August? 1918]
Text: Hobman, ed., *David Eder*, p. 120.

[Chapel Farm Cottage, Hermitage, nr Newbury, Berks]
[August? 1918]

How weary one feels. What heaven to ride on an ass from Jerusalem to Jericho.[1]

1627. To J. B. Pinker, 25 August 1918
Text: MS UT; Unpublished.

Middleton-by-Wirksworth, Derby
25 Aug 1918

Dear Pinker

Let Secker label the goods with whatsoever he thinks best in the dignified straightforward line – that being his line.[2]

Will you ask him in the agreement to give me twelve copies, not six.

Yrs   D. H. Lawrence

1628. To S. S. Koteliansky, 27 August 1918
Text: MS BL; Zytaruk 149.

The Vicarage, Upper Lydbrook, Ross-on-Wye, Herefordshire
27 Aug 1918

My dear Kot,

We got here yesterday – rather lovely – in the Forest of Dean – a real forest. – The Carswells very nice but depressed. Margaret Radford was horrible. – Everywhere a nasty sense of sordid despair.

You, my dear Kot, are a tower of strength – a real tower of strength to us both – and a solitary tower in the land, at that. We must meet again soon. Thank you for the boots etc.

Frieda quite loves you since open enmity is avowed.

We go back to Middleton Saturday or Monday.

DHL

[1] This fragment (noted by Hobman, ed., *David Eder*, as written from Hermitage in the same year as Letter 1729) is hesitantly assigned to August 1918 to associate it with DHL's brief visit to Hermitage and with his reference to 'Eder in Jerusalem' in Letter 1637.

[2] See p. 291 n. 3.

1629. To Donald Carswell, 1 September 1918
Text: MS YU; cited in Carswell, *Adelphi* 392.

Mountain Cottage, Middleton-by-Wirksworth, Derby.
Sunday 1 Sept. 1918

Dear Don,

We got home quite nicely last evening – but a terrible crush in the train from Gloucester to Derby. It seems very quiet here – strangely quiet, though the wind blusters and the rain beats on this little house.

We were very happy with you, after the malaise of the first tumbling into that forest of Lydbrook – which for some reason is curiously upsetting. You were both awfully nice to us – it leaves a warm feeling. I hope you will be able to come here. – I loved the walk to Simmonds Yat[1] – particularly through that parky place: also the Monmouth day – particularly the Church by the Monrow bridge – the bright, sunny town, and the tears in one's inside because there isn't *real* peace; – and then, *very nice*, the meal in the green riding: also our evenings. – They are good memories – worth a lot, really. And it pleases me that we carried the child about. One has the future in one's arms, so to speak: and one *is* the present.

If you would care to, I wish you would read the essays I left with Catherine.[2] You will say I repeat myself – that I don't know the terms of real philosophy – and that my terms are empty – the empty Self – so don't *write* these things to me, I know them beforehand, and they make me cross. None the less, read the essays and see if you find anything in them.

I imagine you in that vicarage room this evening – no more 'What are the Wild Waves Saying' for a bit[3] – But I hope you'll come here in a fortnight.

Love, from us both, to Catherine and you, and little J.P.

D. H. Lawrence

1630. To J. B. Pinker, 7 September 1918
Text: MS UT; Unpublished.

Middleton-by-Wirksworth
7 Sept. 1918

My Dear Pinker

I don't care if Secker leaves out the poem[4] – but I don't want to hear his literary criticisms.

Yrs   D. H. Lawrence

---

[1] Symonds Yat is a well-known beauty-spot 8 miles s. of Ross-on-Wye.
[2] Presumably some of the essays on American literature. (See Letter 1642.)
[3] A song by Joseph Edwards Carpenter (1813–85). DHL and Donald Carswell used to sing it as a duet (Carswell 105). See also *Letters*, ii. 62 n. 2.
[4] 'Late in Life': see Letter 1636.

1631. To Nancy Henry, 10 September 1918
Text: MS NWU; Unpublished.

Mountain Cottage, Middleton-by-Wirksworth, Derby
10 Sept. 1918

Dear Mrs Henry

I got your letter in Lydbrook. – The only thing for us to do is to keep a real friendly feeling – I doubt if one can do more. I doubt if one person can help another, save by just *being*. – As for my struggles, they will have to resolve themselves somehow. One can neither help them nor force them. – But someone in the world whom one can really trust as a friend is a great blessing. We ought to be able to be friends as long as we live – have a sense of decent permanency. – My wife gets angry when she reads your letter. – Why can *three* people never be proper friends? Nothing will be any good till they can. Perhaps we shall manage it. – *I* feel that we might be friends, in the permanent sense, so long as we adjust ourselves properly. – I have a great desire for permanency – the feeling of the unalterable, for ever – in my relationships henceforward.

It rains and blows and is wild and autumnal already. – What about the history? – What news of your husband?

D. H. Lawrence

1632. To Donald Carswell, 11 September 1918
Text: MS YU; cited in Moore, *Intelligent Heart* 244.

Mountain Cottage, Middleton by Wirksworth, Derby
11 Sept. 1918.

Dear Don,

Glad you like 'Moby Dick'.[1] I send you four songs. The carol Bertie Farjeon sent me[2] – probably Catherine will like it. I will get you the *Oxford Song Book*.

Today being my 33rd birthday – sacred year[3] – comes the papers calling me up for medical re-examination. I am determined to do nothing more at the bidding of these swine.

I wonder when we shall see you again, actually.

DHL

---

[1] Most likely DHL was referring to his essay on Melville's novel. ('Herman Melville's "Moby Dick"' did not receive magazine publication; it was first printed in *Studies in Classic American Literature*.)

[2] Herbert Farjeon (1887–1945), dramatist and editor of the Nonesuch Shakespeare. DHL had known his sister, Eleanor Farjeon, for several years (see *Letters*, ii. 321 n. 4).

[3] 'Sacred' because Christ is thought to have been aged 33 at the time of the crucifixion.

1633. To Amy Lowell, 11 September 1918
Text: MS HU; cited in Damon 482.

Mountain Cottage, Middleton-by-Wirksworth, Derby.
11 Sept. 1918

My dear Amy,

I have today received your letter with the little cheque for the anthologies:[1] the other letter I had a few days ago. – About the anthologies, you certainly know best. – Thank you for saying the nice things about me, in your essay.[2]

Martin Secker is doing the poems which I inscribed to you: a small half-crown volume called *New Poems*. I am expecting proofs now: the book should be out in six weeks' time. Secker will send you copies. I hope you'll like the book – or some of the things in it, at least.

Today I heard from Robert Nichols – you will have read his *Ardours and Endurances*.[3] He is coming to America, lecturing on poets. You will see him – he is a friend of mine.

I haven't seen Hilda or Fletcher for a long time. Hilda has left Cornwall, and even had some idea of coming to America, I believe. But I don't expect she will. – Richard is still all right – in France, back of the firing lines.

I got the copy of *Poetry* with a notice on me by Fletcher – very nice of him to take the trouble.[4] When you are writing Harriett Monroe, thank her from me, will you, and please give her this address of mine.

Frieda and I are here trying to be patient. I am slowly working at another novel: though I feel it's not much use. No publisher will risk my last, and none will risk this, I expect. I can't do anything in the world today – am just choked. – I don't know how on earth we shall get through another winter – how we shall ever find a future. Humanity as it stands, and myself as I stand, we just seem mutually impossible to one another. The ground dwindles under one's feet – what next, heaven knows.

I wish we could see you.

Warm greetings   D. H. Lawrence

[1] i.e. DHL's share of the royalties on the three *Imagist* anthologies edited by Amy Lowell and to which he had contributed. (See *Letters*, ii. 209 n. 4, 610 n. 3; and p. 104 and n. 4.)
[2] It appears from Amy Lowell's answer to this letter (Damon 483) that DHL was here reiterating his thanks for her remarks made in the lecture she delivered in March 1918 (see p. 253 and n. 1).
[3] Nichols's volume of poems had appeared in June 1917.
[4] John Gould Fletcher had reviewed *Look! We Have Come Through!* in *Poetry*, xii (August 1918), 269–74; the editor, Harriet Monroe, had sent DHL a copy of this issue. Fletcher insisted that DHL's value to contemporary society – 'so rich in half-measures, and compromises' – was as 'a fine, intolerant fanatic' who challenged received opinions. He compared DHL with Whitman and emphasised 'the power with which [DHL's] imagination pierces its subject' as in his poem 'The Sea'. (See R. P. Draper, ed., *D. H. Lawrence: The Critical Heritage* (London and Boston, 1970), pp. 121–4.)

1634. To Robert Nichols, 11 September 1918
Text: MS UTul; Unpublished.

Mountain Cottage, Middleton-by-Wirksworth, Derby.
11 Sept. 1918

Dear Nichols

I got your letter today. I thought you had gone to America. – Will you see *Amy Lowell* there –? – *Heath St. Brookline. Mass.* – Do – she is a friend of mine.[1]

Yes, I am very nicely stranded – like a fish chucked up above high-water mark, and gasping. Humanity spits me out, and I spit humanity out. So there we are. As for Bennett, with his manly bluff, and his huge literary harvest, why hasn't he the decency to help a man whose work he professes to admire![2] Here am I, can't make a living to save my life, without caving in and accepting the filthy world at its own value. Which I won't do. – There remains the serious prospect of starving oneself out. – And manly Bennett, having got huge sums by literature, knowing quite well, through Pinker, my agent, what the circumstances are, contents himself with discreetly ignoring me, save in the safe company of another man who takes the initiative to speak well of me. – As for being a genius – the very word becomes an insult, at last.

Today is my 33rd. birthday – the sacred age. So today once more I receive a notice calling me up for medical reexamination. But having been badgered about as I have, kicked out of Cornwall, and pushed about by the police, I'm damned if I will move one step at the bidding of such filthers. – You know, that on our famous evening in Mecklenburgh Square, the police were listening under the door, and detectives came following me when I moved to Earl's Court?[3] – But I've *soupé*: I've had my bellyful.

Yes, I like the free soul, that an artist is and must be, in you. How much you'll sail with, and how much against, the wind: that is your affair. But the wind is dead against a free spirit and a *real* art: it requires 'The Bull'.[4]

For biographical details – I suppose you've got Ralph Hodgson's, and will treat of him as among the highest of genius: tant pour votre 'genius' – but I'll send you what you ask for.[5]

David Herbert Lawrence (it is like filling in another form).

born Eastwood, nr Nottingham
Sept. 11th. 1885.

---

[1] Whether Nichols took DHL's advice is not known, but he did substitute for Amy Lowell at a speaking engagement in Philadelphia on 10 February 1919 (Damon 487).
[2] See *Letters*, ii. 479 n. 3; see also p. 205 n. 1.   [3] See Letter 1495 and n. 3.
[4] A poem by Ralph Hodgson (1871–1962); it was privately printed in 1913 and included in *Poems* (1917). For DHL's opinion of Hodgson's poetry see *Letters*, ii. 92–3.
[5] It is presumed that Nichols had requested the information for use on his American lecture tour. (For details of DHL's family see the genealogical table, *Letters*, i. xxiv–xxv.)

Father – Arthur Lawrence, coal miner.

Mother – Lydia Lawrence.

Father's family – great Grandfather supposed to be French refugee,[1] from the Revolution: supposed to have fought against Napoleon in Waterloo: grandfather, at any rate, brought up as a tiny baby in some military hospital – or home: *barracks*, my father says, though that can hardly be: taught to be a military tailor: a tall, silent, strange man, whom I remember – he lived to be 86. He was famous in South Notts as the best dancer and the best boxer.

Mother's family – old, well-to-do, puritan family – fought with Cromwell – ruined in a smash in the lace industry.

My life – very poor but honest touch – *Sons and Lovers* contains a good deal of it – won scholarships – went to Nottingham High School and University – was a teacher for a time – went to Germany with Frieda – who is a Baronesse of a good,[2] old German family, cousin of that Richthofen flying-man[3] – went to Italy – always lived with no money – always shall – very sick of the world, like to die with the nausea of it.

assez. –   D. H. Lawrence

1635. To Lady Cynthia Asquith, 12 September 1918
Text: MS UT; Huxley 453–4.

Mountain Cottage, Middleton-by-Wirksworth, Derby.
12 Sept. 1918

Are you in Scotland still?[4] We were away for three weeks – in London, and in your Gloucestershire – on the Wye. We wished you were at your Stanway.

Are you being a secretary really? Do you think there is anything the *I* could do – that I *would* do. – I can type, rather badly – not shorthand. I feel the war is going to end. And I would dearly love to be active, in the afterwards. And surely I am a valuable person. I only wish I were in Lloyd George's position. I would love to have some of my own way. I've been shut up long enough. See if there is anything possible. – Of course I know you can't do more than just tell me what you think. – I want to burst this sort of coccoon that I'm in – it is

---

[1] refugee,] refugees,

[2] good,] big,

[3] Manfred von Richthofen (1892–1918), commonly known as 'The Red Baron', a famous German air ace; he had been shot down and killed on 21 April 1918.

[4] Lady Cynthia had returned from a visit to her father's Scottish seat, Gosford House, on 23 August 1918.

likely to prove a shroud, if I don't. It is time I had an issue. And one can do nothing from here. As for the people – Labour itself – it is hopeless, as hopeless as Lloyd George or Balfour – just the green half of the same poisonous apple. It's awfully hard to find an issue.

Yesterday I got papers to be medically re-examined – at Derby, on the 21st. I sent them back – and said, how could they expect me to do anything, if I am still a black-marked person. I feel like hitting them all across the mouth. – However, if it comes to, I suppose I shall submit to another medical examination. But beyond that, I submit to *nothing*. – However, they would reject me again, – it is not of any great importance.

The importance is the coming winter. I look at the months and *know* there must be a change. I can't merely go on hanging on to nothing but the skin of my own teeth. I think I'd rather get myself arrested. But I'm not going to be a martyr either – enough of those pitiful objects in the world.

We've kept some sort of a flag flying so far. Now I shall either have to begin to plant mine, or get off the face of the earth. But I go my own way, either way. Curse the sodden, abject *men* of today.

Hope things are well with you.

à toujours   D. H. Lawrence

1636. To Martin Secker, 13 September 1918
Text: MS UInd; Secker 11.

Mountain Cottage – Middleton-by-Wirksworth, Derby.
13 Sept. 1918

Dear Secker

I return the proofs. I took out 'Late in Life'[1] – also two last verses from 'Everlasting Flowers'[2] – which just makes it that the five sections of 'Two

---

[1] The poem has never been published. It survives in an autograph MS of *New Poems* and in a corrected proof copy (Roberts E269.5 and E193.7d respectively).
[2] In the UT MS of *New Poems* the stanzas omitted read as follows:

> How you've taken my breast to rest in,
> My eyes to look forth from, now.
> How you take what you want from my hand, and put
> Your power on my brow.
>
> Your ghost in me is identical
> Invested with life.
> I am lord in you of the kingdom of death,
> Master of Strife.

Wives' (Antiphony of Widows) can have each a page to itself.[1] I think that
counts just 64 pages. If you want to take out another page, let it be 'Letter
from Town: The Almond Tree'.[2]

I think it makes quite a nice little book. Hope it'll do alright.

                                                    Yours   D. H. Lawrence

1637. To S. S. Koteliansky, [18 September 1918]
Text: MS BL; Moore 562–3.

                                                          Middleton –
                                                          Wednesday
My dear Kot

I am thinking I shall never be able to sit at Middleton this winter. If I don't
do something I shall burst or go cracked. I *must* move.

Now would it be all right if we came to you – not as guests – but as
Campbell would have come – just to share expenses, all expenses? I will get
money somehow. We would probably come in two weeks time – and stay
some weeks, at least. – I want to know Robert Smillie and Snowden and Mary
Macarthers and Margaret Bondfield.[3] I must find somebody to bring me to
them. It is no good, one cannot wait for things to happen. One must actually
move.

I got notice to go and be medically examined once more. I sent it back.
They replied with their usual insolence. I must go on the 26th. It infuriates
me to such a degree, that I feel I will not go. – One must have one's own back –
oh, thoroughly.

Grisha was a wise man, to go. – Did Sonia get the *Rainbow*? I sent it to her.

As for Russia, it must go through as it is going. Nothing but a real smelting
down is any good for her: no matter how horrible it seems. You, who are an
ultra-conscious Jew, can't bear the chaos. But chaos is necessary for Russia.

---

[1] 'Two Wives' was duly published in *New Poems* in five sections; two further sections were
added when the poem was revised for *Collected Poems* (1928).
[2] This poem was printed (for the first time) in the volume.
[3] They were all well-known political figures of the day, associated with the Independent Labour
Party. Robert Smillie (1857–1940) was President of the Scottish Miners' Federation, a close
friend of Keir Hardie (d. 1915) whom DHL may have met at William Hopkin's house in
Eastwood, and a pacifist. Philip (Viscount) Snowden (1864–1937), another politician
associated with 'the old "progressive" clique' in Eastwood (*Letters*, i. 176), was chairman of
the I.L.P., and M.P. for Blackburn. Mary Reid Macarther (1880–1921), a trade-union leader,
had married William Anderson, chairman of the I.L.P. executive. She was a close friend of
Margaret Grace Bondfield (1873–1953); together, in 1906, they formed the National
Federation of Women Workers. Margaret Bondfield was later to become the first woman
cabinet minister as Minister of Labour in 1929.

Russia will be all right – righter, in the end, than these old stiff senile nations of the West.

I don't think chaos is any good for England. England is too old. She'll either have to be *wise*, and recover her decency – or we may as well all join Eder in Jerusalem.

Well, my dear Kot, I am at the end of my line. I had rather be hanged or put in prison than endure any more. So now I shall move actively, personally, do what I can. I am a desperado.

DHL

Is Campbell back? I was a bit disgusted with him last time. – But I must see him again, if only to abuse him. – How is Gertler? – Did Murry fetch his books? – Tell me about them.

1638. To Amy Lowell, 23 September 1918
Text: MS HU; cited in Damon 482.

Mountain Cottage, Middleton by Wirksworth. Derby.
23 Sept. 1918

My dear Amy

I send you the proofs of the poems.[1] I expect the book will be out in a month's time. You will get a copy.

Perhaps Harriett Monroe would care to publish some of these verses:[2] if she would it would mean a few dollars – or if anyone else would do them. I don't know if my agent has arranged for American publication. I'll ask him.

Let me know how you like these. Write to us.

D. H. Lawrence

1639. To Nancy Henry, 24 September 1918
Text: MS ColU; Huxley 454–5.

Mountain Cottage, Middleton-by-Wirksworth. Derby.
24 Sept. 1918

Dear Mrs Henry

I have got the story, and have read it through.[3] You have put all the stuff into it right enough. But I'm afraid you haven't created that subtle atmosphere of unbearable, nauseating or exalting terror, which you wanted. I doubt if it could be done, or conveyed from the mouth of a speaker, as you

---

[1] The proofs are unlocated.
[2] The verses were not published in *Poetry*.
[3] The story is unidentified.

have done it. I think it would have to be in the third person: so that you can get the pure horrific *abstraction* of it, as it were. It is a story which, in its inner significance, makes me a little sick with the same kind of fear. I'll see if I can gather myself together and write out a version: then I'll send it to you and let you compare, and you can have another go if you feel like it. I am afraid, to tell you the truth, of tackling the story, because of the shock it will mean, to do it. But probably I'll try.

I got your other letter. Yes, I thought it good, and as far as I know, on the right track, nearly all. But one needs to be able to *talk* about those things. Philosophic realisation means to me painful, bitter, and rather sickening experience, so I rather shrink from it – except of course from the purely intellectual attitude, when it is more like a game of chess, extraneous and not rooted in the bowels. As you feel about your story, so I feel about the reality of the moon, for example. I can hardly talk about it, it goes so deep into one's bowels and makes one a little sick.

I haven't heard from Vere – but it doesn't matter, as at the moment I am going over my American essays, which are coming back from the typist. The history can wait a bit.

Also on Thursday I've got to go up for medical re-examination. It infuriates me to be pawed about by the swine. If I felt it were any good at all, I would send them to hell. But there is no spirit of resistance or freedom in the country, and I have only a contempt for martyrs. If only men roused up and stiffened their backbones, and were men. I wouldn't mind how much I risked myself. But offer myself as a martyr of self-sacrifice I couldn't do, it is too shoddy, too late.

Probably in a while we shall go to London again: it may be very dreary here. We must see what happens. In London we may really meet and talk. And I will let you know again soon about the story, if I can do it. It is the 'over the edge' reality which makes one feel ill.

[   ]¹ wife sends her regards.

D. H. Lawrence

1640. To J. B. Pinker, 25 September 1918
Text: MS UT; Unpublished.

Middleton – Wirksworth, Derby
25 Sept. 1918

My dear Pinker
Harrison wants me to accept five guineas for the Study on American

¹ MS torn.

Literature.[1] Shall we do this? I suppose he is very hard up – but so am I. – However – he might do some more of the essays. They are coming back from the typist now – I am waiting for the last. They are good – and they would make a decent little book – about 70,000 words.

Will you let Harrison know about the essay he has got.[2]

Yrs   D. H. Lawrence

1641. To Lady Cynthia Asquith, 26 September 1918
Text: MS UT; Huxley 455–6.

Mountain Cottage, Middleton-by-Wirksworth. Derby

26 Sept. 1918

I don't mind if you use Sir J[ames Barrie][3] – so long as you *can* use him. The only thing that infuriates me is that he is in the position to use *you*.[4]

Your poems: that miserable little Beaumont is waiting for some opportunity or other: they *will* come, certainly: and I expect before Christmas. I'll make him be definite. – Meanwhile Secker is bringing out a little 2/6 vol., almost immediately – called *New Poems*. I'll give it you when it comes. – Your book *Bay* will be thin – about 20 pieces in it – but[5] [hand-printed and beautiful, 7/6 a copy. That is very nice.

Now as for me. These accursed people have put me in Grade 3. It kills me with speechless fury to be pawed by them. They shall *not* touch me again – such filth.

You know I have had all the training and spent three years as a schoolmaster. I really know something about education. I want a job under the Ministry of Education: not where I shall be kicked about like an old can: I've had enough of that. You must help me to something where I shall not be ashamed. Don't you know that man Fisher?[6] He sounds decent. Really try and get me introduced and started fairly. I need a start – and I'm not going to be an under-servant to anybody: no, I'm not. If these military *canaille* call me

---

[1] Harrison's offer apparently referred to a particular essay on American literature; it cannot be identified.

[2] See Letter 1611.

[3] See Letters 1615 and n. 1, and 1635.

[4] Someone tried to delete the whole of this paragraph on the MS. It is perhaps significant that the paragraph is omitted by Huxley.

[5] The remainder of the MS is missing; the text is taken from Huxley.

[6] Herbert Albert Laurens Fisher (1865–1940), President of the Board of Education, 1916–22; he introduced the Education Act of 1918. He was subsequently Warden of New College, Oxford (1925–40). Lady Cynthia records meeting him on only one occasion though the tone of her remarks suggests more than casual acquaintance (Asquith, *Diaries* 279).

up for any of their filthy jobs – I am graded for sedentary work – I shall just remove myself, and be a deserter.

I've had enough of the social passion. Labour and military can alike do their dirty businesses to the top of their bent. I'm not going to squat in a cottage feeling their fine feelings for them, and flying for them a flag that only makes a fool of *me*. I'm out on a new track – let humanity go its own way – I go mine. But I *won't* be pawed and bullied by them – no.

I don't care much what I do – so long as it is nothing degrading. I would like to do education.

I shall come to London next week. We can all spend a winter in town, and do some jolly things. I want to have a good time with the *individuals* I care for – very few, they are.

Now even if you take some trouble for me – do it. You won't regret it. Frieda sends her love.

DHL]

1642. To Catherine Carswell, [26 September 1918]
Text: MS YU; Carswell 102.

Middleton –
Thursday

My dear Catherine

I have been examined – am put in Grade III – and from this day I take a new line. I've done with society and humanity – Labour and Military can alike go to hell. Henceforth it is for myself, my own life, I live: a good jolly personal life, with a few people who are friends, and the rest can do what they like. – I am going to try to get a job: quick, before the military attempt to paw me again – for they shall *never* touch me again. I shall go to London next week. We shall meet again soon. Then we can talk.

About the essays, I crossed out the 'children' passages.[1] Who am I to dictate when hope does or doesn't lie? Let it lie when it likes.

Tell Don I shall see him again soon. No more of the social passion and social insistence from me. I can understand I've been a nuisance and a fool.

Love from both to you all   DHL

I sent on the shirt. Thanks for the other. – I think I shall come to London alone, Frieda will follow in a week or so.

---

[1] The reference may be to the 'Herman Melville I' essay: 'It is absurd to speak of savages as "children", young, rudimentary people. To look among them for the link between us and the ape is laughably absurd. Of all childish things, science is one of the most childish and amusing. The savages, we may say *all* savages, are remnants of the once civilised world-people, who had their splendour and their being for countless centuries . . . It is we from the north, starting new centres of life in ourselves, who have become young' (MS Smith, p. 6).

1643. To J. B. Pinker, 1 October 1918
Text: MS UT; Unpublished.

Mountain Cottage, Middleton-by-Wirksworth, Derby.
1st Oct. 1918

My dear Pinker,

Did you agree with Harrison about the American study? I hope so.

I am coming to town next week. I shall come and see you. I shall have to try and find some work, to solve my difficulties, financial and otherwise. I suppose you don't know of anything I could do. I am Grade III. I don't suppose the military would bother me – but I shall have to do something.

Would Arnold Bennett like to see me, do you think? If so, I would like to meet him.

Yrs   D. H. Lawrence

1644. To Mark Gertler, 2 October 1918
Text: MS SIU; Unpublished.

Mountain Cottage, Middleton by Wirksworth, Derby
2 Oct. 1918

Dear Gertler

We shall be coming to London next week – Monday or Tuesday. I was med. re-examined – Grade III. I shall have to get a bit of a job, to prevent them calling me up for some of their dirty work: also because it is hopeless to go on any longer, with no money and no hope. I don't know what I can get. I must try round. Tell me if you hear of anything for me.

We shall stay 32 Well Walk – alone there – the Radfords are away.

How are you? What news? We shall see you next week.

DHL

1645. To J. B. Pinker, 3 October 1918
Text: MS UNYB; cited in Moore, *Poste Restante* 50.

Mountain Cottage, Middleton by Wirksworth, Derby.
3 Oct. 1918

My dear Pinker

Thanks for your letter. I shall come to London on Monday – to 32 Well Walk, Hampstead, N.W. Shall I come to see you on Tuesday afternoon?

Yrs   D. H. Lawrence

1646. To Martin Secker, 5 October 1918
Text: MS UT; Unpublished.

                    Mountain Cottage, Middleton by Wirksworth, Derby
                                                              5 Oct. 1918
Dear Secker,

I am coming to town for a time – coming next Monday. I should like to call and see you one day. Will you tell if I shall come, and when – the address is
                        32 Well Walk, Hampstead. N.W.
When do you expect the *Poems* will appear?

                                                    Yrs   D. H. Lawrence

1647. To J. B. Pinker, [8 October 1918]
Text: MS UNYB; Unpublished.

                                          32 Well Walk. Hampstead, N.W.
                                                              Tuesday.
My dear Pinker,

Thanks for your letter. I shall come tomorrow at 3.0.

                                                    Yrs   D. H. Lawrence

1648. To Martin Secker, [10 October 1918]
Text: MS UInd; Secker 12.

                                          32 Well Walk, Hampstead, N.W.
                                                              Thursday
Dear Secker,

I was coming to see you this morning, then suddenly people turned up and prevented me. I am sorry. May I come some time later?

Thank you for the poems, which came this morning. The grey cover looks very nice.

Would you please send two copies for me, to
          Miss Amy Lowell, Heath St, Brookline – Mass. U.S.A.
I shall be much obliged.

                                                    Yrs.   D. H. Lawrence

1649. To Lettice Berry, 14 October 1918
Text: MS Clarke; Unpublished.

                                          32 Well Walk, Hampstead, N.W.
                                                              14 Oct. 1918
Dear Aunt Lettie[1]

I can't tell you how shocked and grieved I was to hear from Uncle Fritz of

---

[1] Lettice Ada Berry, née Beardsall (1857–1938), DHL's maternal aunt.

Hedley's death, and how very sorry I am that you should have to bear this unspeakable blow.[1] There is nothing one can say that will make it any better. Things have become unbearable. – But I feel curiously that the dead are with us now, that they stay with us and help us through. I feel that very much about my mother – and about a friend who was killed. They are not lost: they come back and live with one, in one's soul. It is only the faith in what is beyond, that saves us.

Remember me to Ivy and Douglas.[2] I hope one day to see them again. I do hope you will be able to find some support and relief for your sorrow. I feel how useless it is to say anything.

Your affec. nephew   D. H. Lawrence

1650. To Arthur McLeod, 16 October 1918
Text: MS UT; Postmark, Hampstead 16 OCT 18; Unpublished.

32 Well Walk. Hampstead, N.W.
Wed. 16 Oct 1918

My dear Mac,

I am glad you found the old poems in the *New Poems*. It was Secker who wanted that decidedly false title.[3]

I am, like you, Grade III, and so far quite free – intend to remain free, which is more. We have been living in Derbyshire – came to London last week. I have been to see Freeman – sub-editor of *The Times*[4] – he will give me some work for the *Supplement* – perhaps both *Literary* and *Educational* – because I am so hard up. So I must keep the accursed military at bay till the war ends – which I believe will be soon.

Don't be apologetic when you write to me – I don't like it, it isn't fair to our old friendship. Come and see us here: I want you to. We may be staying only a week or two – perhaps three weeks. So come soon. Come to Hampstead Tube Station – Well Walk is near. Come any time – just send me a line. *Don't* be scared of me because I have a beard – for the good of my throat –; apart[5] from the beard I am the same man.

---

[1] Hedley Berry, the son of John (b. 1852) and Lettice Berry, was killed in France.
[2] Douglas is known to have been the Berrys' son; Ivy is likely to have been their daughter.
[3] The title-page of the original MS of *New Poems* read: 'Coming Awake. Poems. by D. H. Lawrence.' This title was blue-pencilled and a new one – 'New Poems' – written in its stead. Many of the poems had been written and several published at a much earlier period (some as early as 1910); in this sense Secker's was a 'decidedly false title'.
[4] George Sydney Freeman (1879–1938) was editor of the *Times Educational Supplement* from 1910, and deputy editor of *The Times*, 1914–24.
[5] apart] and

I have just corrected proofs of such an amusing essay for the *English Review*.[1]

My wife wants to be remembered to you. Come and see us – yes.

DHL

1651. To William Hopkin, [18? October 1918]
Text: MS NCL; cited in Pinto, ed., *D. H. Lawrence after Thirty Years*, p. 28.

32 Well Walk, Hampstead, N.W.
Friday.[2]

Dear Willie,

I send you the poems. Frieda is in bed with a cold. No news from here. Wish something nice would turn up.

DHL

Please send the bill for the wine.

1652. To S. S. Koteliansky, [20? October 1918]
Text: MS BL; Zytaruk 152.

[32 Well Walk, Hampstead, N.W.]
[20? October 1918][3]

[   ][4] to be peace soon. So be damned to all jobs and jobbers.

Frieda has a bad cold and throat – Maitland Radford says she must stay in bed. She won't be able to go out for some days. So we can't go to Mrs Farbman on Wednesday. I have written to Richmond to say so.[5] When Frieda is well enough we shall move down to 66 Adelaide Rd. N.W.3.[6] – it is near Chalk Farm station. But if there is peace we shall go back to Middleton in about a fortnight's time.

I don't care about anything, if there is peace. – See you one evening.

DHL

---

[1] 'The Spirit of Place'; see p. 270 n. 1.

[2] The date of this letter is very uncertain. The MS was found in a copy of *Bay* but it is unlikely that those are 'the poems' referred to in DHL's letter: *Bay* was published on 20 November 1919 and DHL was not staying at Well Walk either shortly before or after that date. Frieda is known to have been ill in mid-October 1918 (see Letter 1653) when they were at Well Walk, and it is assumed that 'the poems' must have been *New Poems*.

[3] The reference to Dr Maitland Radford lends support to the supposition that this letter was written when the Lawrences were staying at Dollie Radford's house, 32 Well Walk; it was clearly written before the Armistice, though at a time when the possibility of peace was fairly substantial; and Letter 1654 – also alluding to Frieda's illness – suggests that they had left London on 22 October. Thus, 20? October is the date proposed.

[4] The beginning of the letter is missing.

[5] The letter is missing.

[6] Nancy Henry's address.

1653. To Arthur McLeod, 24 October 1918
Text: MS UT; Postmark, Hermitage 24 OC 18; Unpublished.

Chapel Farm Cottage, Hermitage, nr Newbury, Berks.

24 Oct 1918

Dear Mac

We have had to flee down here – Frieda was ill in London and wanted to come out at once. It is so pleasant here – we have been out all afternoon getting chestnuts. I think we shall stay two or three weeks – then come back to London. When we are coming I shall let you know, so that you can come up – for I want to see you.

Look in next month's *English Review* and tell me if you like my essay.

a rivederci   D. H. Lawrence

1654. To Lady Cynthia Asquith, [28 October 1918]
Text: MS UT; cited in Delany 382.

Chapel Farm Cottage, Hermitage, nr. Newbury, Berks.

Monday.

We came down here last Tuesday – country *very* nice and yellow – Frieda better, nearly – I had the same old cold – more or less better. How is John? How are you and young Mick, the slayer of Bel, the Great Dragon.[1] – I haven't been able to rouse myself to a *Times* effort. But I've written a play – very nice – which *might* be acted.[2] Shall I send it you, and you can ask Whibley about it, perhaps. I will remain anonymous – my name is like red pepper in people's noses. – Of course we are thrilled – one must be thrilled. I see myself a second Sir Jas,[3] with a secretary. – But no, truly, I am ashamed in daylight to confess it, I have written a play out of my deep and earnest self, fired up my last sparks of hope in the world, as it were, and cried out like a Balaams ass.[4] I believe the world yet might get a turn for the better, if it but had a little shove that way. And this is my attempt – I believe the last I am capable of – or the first, perhaps – at a shove. You must take it very seriously, of course – save our ironical grimaces till these sparks have fizzled out: if they must.

Let us know how you are, any way. F. sends love.

DHL

[1] The story of 'Bel and the Dragon' is to be found in the Apocrypha. The connection with Lady Cynthia's second son, Michael, is not known.
[2] *Touch and Go*; see p. 371 n. 4.
[3] Sir James Barrie.
[4] Numbers xxii. 28–30.

I meant to give you these poems. Secker called them *New Poems* – they are Old Poems – many of them juvenilia – a few new. I forgot to give you a copy – not very important anyhow.

1655. To Stanley Hocking, [30 October 1918]
Text: MS BucU; Postmark, Hermitage [. . .] OC 18; cited in Nehls, i. 367.

> Chapel Farm Cottage, Hermitage, nr Newbury, Berks.
> Wed. 29 Oct. 1918

My dear Stanley

I got your letter this morning with all its unfortunate news. Zennor is having a bad time. – We went to London about a month ago, intending to stay some little time. But Mrs Lawrence immediately became ill – the doctor said pleurisy – and she was so depressed that we fled away here again to the country as soon as she could travel. She is much better. – The flu. is really like a plague, everywhere – London absolutely stricken.

I was reexamined in Sept. – after a row with the Nat. Service people. They put me in Grade III. I don't expect to be bothered.

As a matter of fact I think peace will actually come before Christmas: if that old scoundrel Clemenceau doesn't put his spoke in. Lloyd George personally wants peace – quite emphatically now – so does Milner – so they should be able to manage Englands part.[1] I feel as if *this* war were [near?]ly over, anyhow: heaven knows what the peace at home will be like.

I don't quite know what we shall do – perhaps go back to London for a short time, if the flu. slacks off – then perhaps to Middleton. If the war ends we shall come to Tregerthen, at least for a while. But everything seems so shaky and indefinite. Nevertheless we shall probably be seeing you soon.

In town we saw the Murrys again. They have a house in Hampstead. Poor Mrs Murry has consumption of the lungs – cannot go outside the house. – But still, I think if the war ends, and she could go away to Italy or somewhere warm, she might get better. Mr Murry is quite flourishing – rather to my disgust, seeing she is so ill. – We also saw Mrs Tarry. She has her son home from France – after a whole year's absence. She was the one happy person we saw. – I heard Mr Gray was in town – but did not see him.

Don't bother about Grade I. They ought soon to stop recruiting altogether.

---

[1] The three statesmen named by DHL exerted major influence on the outcome of the war and the peace negotiations. Georges Clemenceau (1841–1929) was the French prime minister, 1917–20; Viscount Alfred Milner (1854–1925) was Lloyd George's Secretary of State for War. All three were shortly (4–5 November) to be in Versailles to discuss peace terms.

I am sorry about Katie. Your mother always worries most about her. But she will perhaps soon be all right. We must all drag ourselves out of this Slough of Despond. – For myself, I have been exceedingly well this year – so has Mrs Lawrence, till now. – It seems to me London is a veritable death-trap at present, with its flu and sickness.

Here the woods are all yellow – big, yellow woods. I never saw them more lovely. The other day we went getting chestnuts. There were quite a number, sweet and good. This is a pleasant place – not so rocky and sombre as Middleton – and not bare, like Tregerthen.

Well, Stanley, I suppose you've forgotten all your French.[1] – Never mind – better than going to France to learn it. – Tell Mary I owe her a letter and will write soon. – Remember us both very warmly to everybody.

Yrs   D. H. Lawrence

1656. To Amy Lowell, 5 November 1918
Text: MS HU; Damon 484–5.

Chapel Farm Cottage, Hermitage, nr. Newbury, Berks.

5 Nov. 1918

My dear Amy,

I have received *Can Grande's Castle*.[2] You are wrong when you say I only like subjective poetry – I love visions, and visionary panorama.[3] I love 'thunderheads marching along the sky-line' – and 'beautiful, faded city' – and 'fifty vessels blowing up the Bosphorus' – and English Coaches – all those things.[4] I love the pomp and richness of the past – the full, resplendent gesture. The sordidness of the present sends me mad – such meagre souls, all excusing themselves. – But why don't you write a *play*? I'm sure you could write a handsome drama. Pity we can't do it together. – I do wish we could have some rich,[5] laughing, sumptuous kind of days, insouciant, indifferent to everything but a little good laughter and splendeur de vivre which costs

---

[1] DHL taught Stanley Hocking sufficient French for them to hold 'a little conversation' in it: see Nehls, i. 367.

[2] The book was published in USA on 24 September 1918. It consisted of four 'poems' in what Amy Lowell described in her preface as 'polyphonic prose' (pp. ix–xiv). (The castle of Can Grande was Dante's refuge and thus the poet's refuge from the world and the vantage point from which he can view it.)

[3] Amy Lowell had written to DHL on 4 October: 'I am sending you my new book. I do not know whether you will like it or not. Sometimes I think you will not. You see, this poetry is entirely objective, and you rather like the subjective kind' (Damon 483).

[4] See *Can Grande's Castle*, pp. 3, 145 and 132; the poem 'Hedge Island' (pp. 87–102) is devoted to English coaches.

[5] MS reads 'have some have some rich,'.

nothing. – Why not, one day. – Meanwhile as it happens to be a very sunny day, and the war will soon end, I feel already like a holiday.

No, Amy, again you are not right when you say the india-rubber eraser would let me through into a paradise of popularity.[1] Without the india-rubber I am damned along with the evil, with the india-rubber I am damned among the disappointing. You see what it is to have a reputation. I give it up, and put my trust in heaven. One needn't trust a great deal in anything, and in humanity not at all.

I too have written a play: not wicked but too good is probably the sigil of its doom. Que n'importe! I go my own way, regardless. By good I mean 'sage': one of my unspotted 'sagesses'.

We went to London, Frieda and I – got the Flu. – fled here – have recovered – shall probably return soon to Middleton. I have one really passionate desire – to have wings, only wings, and to fly away – far away. I suppose one would be sniped by anti-aircraft guns. But one could fly by night. Then those indecent search-lights fingering the sky.

Frieda sends her love. Remember us warmly to Mrs Russell.

D. H. Lawrence

1657. To J. B. Pinker, 5 November 1918
Text: MS UT; Delany 383.

Chapel Farm Cottage, Hermitage, nr. Newbury, Berks
5 Nov. 1918

My dear Pinker

I have an idea that you would rather not be bothered any longer with my work: which certainly must be no joy, nor profit, to you. Will you let me know if this is so. I remember you said when we made the agreement that it might be broken if either was dissatisfied. If you have any desire to break it just let me know.

Do I still owe you money? Will you tell me how much.[2]

Yrs   D. H. Lawrence

---

[1] In the letter of 4 October Amy Lowell wrote: '. . . I regret sincerely that you cut yourself off from being published by an outspokenness which the English public does not understand, I regret it . . . because it keeps the world from knowing what a great novelist you are . . . You need not change your attitude a particle, you can simply use an India rubber in certain places, and then you can come into your own as it ought to be' (Damon 483).

[2] A note written on the MS, most likely by Pinker, reads: £15-4-3. See Letter 1662.

1658. To Catherine Carswell, [6 November 1918]
Text: MS YU; cited in Carswell 111.

Chapel Farm Cottage, Hermitage – nr Newbury, Berks
Wed¹

My dear Catherine

This is a mere line to say that I sent the play² to Katharine Mansfield, because she is so ill. I wish you would call for it – 2 Portland Villas, East Heath St. I told her you would. Then tell me if you like it, and if you would show it to that friend. *I* was rather thrilled by it. K.M. is in bed, so you needn't see her – can't get up.

I'm glad you are well and happy. Hope the book goes.³ Let me see it as soon as there is enough done.

I couldn't write the Educational stuff⁴ – I tried so hard – it wouldn't work in me – no go.

We shall perhaps go back to Middleton next week – shall be a night or two in town – so shall see you.

DHL

1659. To Catherine Carswell, [9 November 1918]
Text: MS YU; PC; Postmark, [. . .] 9 NO [. . .]; cited in Moore, *Poste Restante* 51.

Hermitage –
Sat

Just a line to say, did you get the play from Katharine Murry – and that that is the only MS., so I hope it won't get lost. – I want to know what you think of it – very much want to know. I remember you once did theatres.⁵ – 2 Portland Villas is on East Heath Rd., a little way above the end of Well Walk. I wonder if you will see Katharine. – We had a marvellous Peace report on Thursday night – great celebrations and hurrahing.⁶ We still feel a little crestfallen. – We are both better – hope you are still all right. You must be worried for J[ohn] P[atrick] – you never told me if Don had got any briefs. I *can't* do the

<hr>

¹ Dated with reference to the letter following.
² *Touch and Go.*
³ Catherine Carswell's novel most recently mentioned in Letter 1552.
⁴ See Letter 1650.
⁵ She was a reviewer and drama-critic for the *Glasgow Herald*, 1907–11.
⁶ Though hostilities had not yet ceased, the Armistice was awaited. 'All the world awaits with eager desire news that Germany has taken the next step towards peace' (*Times*, 8 November 1918).

Times work – I gnash my teeth. But I'm doing a short story about a blind man.[1] – The weather is lovely – wish you could all come down here.

Love from both   DHL

1660. To Catherine and Donald Carswell, [11 November 1918]
Text: MS YU; cited in Moore, *Poste Restante* 51.

Hermitage –
Monday.

Dear Catherine and Don,

We have not heard a word from you – do hope you are not ill. Kath. Murry told me you fetched the play.

I am coming to town tomorrow – staying 66 Adelaide Rd. – I shall call and see you, probably tomorrow evening. Hope I shan't be in the way. – Frieda will stay on here till the week-end, I think – and next Monday we shall go back to Middleton.

I do hope you are not down with flu, any of you.

au revoir   DHL

1661. To Nancy Henry, [13 November 1918]
Text: TMSC NWU; Huxley 476.

Chapel Farm Cottage, Hermitage – nr Newbury, Berks.
Wed.

Dear Mrs. Henry

Many thanks for your letter and the MS. of history[2] – and for your good efforts. I should have written before but am never sure where to write. We were coming to London this week-end – but Austin Harrison, of the *English Review*, is coming down. We shall come next week. Could we come to your rooms? Could you be in town *next* week-end? Could we have your rooms next Tuesday? I shall go back to Middleton soon, and do the history there. I can do it better there. We'll stay in London about a week. Wonderful that there is peace. The first of the American Essays is in this month's *English Review* – the next in next months. The rest of the MS. is out. Try and get hold of Mme. Blavatsky's books – they are big and expensive – the friends I used to borrow

---

[1] 'The Blind Man' was published in *English Review*, xxxi (July 1920), 22–41. (It is set in the Vicarage, Upper Lydbrook, where the Lawrences had stayed with the Carswells. See Bridget Pugh, 'Locations in Lawrence's Fiction and Travel Writings', in *A D. H. Lawrence Handbook*, ed. K. Sagar, Manchester, 1982, p. 250.) On its genesis see Carswell 105–6.

[2] i.e. *Movements in European History*.

them from are out of England now.[1] But get from some library or other *Isis Unveiled*, and better still the 2 vol work whose name I forget.[2] Rider,[3] the publisher of the *Occult Review* – try that – publishes all these books. I think he is in Paternoster Row. But look in the *Occult Review*. You see I never owned the books I had – and they are all big, 10/6 and £1„1„0. And they're not *very* much good. But try Riders: he has a good shop – Vere will tell you the right address.

The tiresome thing is to be so poor and to have to depend on precarious borrowing.

You will have your husband *very soon*. How strange peace is. Is it peace?

Kindest regards from both.   D. H. Lawrence

1662. To J. B. Pinker, 23 November 1918
Text: TMSC NWU; Unpublished.

5, Acacia Rd. – N.W.8.
23 Nov. 1918.

My dear Pinker,

Thank you for your letter, which I had at Hermitage.

I have sent Harrison two more of the American Essays, which are coming out in December and January.[4] I really think these should be published in America. Harrison says an American bought 20 copies of the first essay – this month's – to send over there. I suppose I ought to let you have the MS. Unfortunately that which is ready is not typed, and it costs so much to type. I really have no money at all. Would you defer the paying of the £15. I owe you for a short time, and send me what little comes in. For English purposes there is no need to type MS., is there?

I am going back to Middleton on Tuesday. I have written three short stories which ought to sell: two are very good. I shall send them to you next week, from Middleton.[5] I hope we shall sell them, for I can't live.

Here I send you a play. I know I ought to write something saleable – but

[1] Probably Dr David and Edith Eder, then in Jerusalem (see p. 150 and n. 1).
[2] *Isis Unveiled: a Master-Key to the Mysteries of Ancient and Modern Science and Theology* (1910); the two-volume work would be *The Secret Doctrine*.
[3] William Rider (of 8–11 Paternoster Road, London, E.C.).
[4] The two essays were entitled 'Benjamin Franklin' (*English Review*, xxvii, December 1918, 397–408) and 'Henry St. John de Crèvecoeur' (*English Review*, xxviii, January 1919, 5–18).
[5] The stories being written were: 'The Blind Man'; 'The Fox', published in *Hutchinson's Magazine*, iii (November 1920), 477–90; and 'John Thomas', published as 'Tickets, Please' in *Strand* (April 1919). (See Letter 1685.)

chis is rather a wonderful play, and I wanted to do it. You will see what you think of it. One day it will be acted.

Write to me at Mountain Cottage, Middleton-by-Wirksworth.

Yrs.   D. H. Lawrence

1663. To Katherine Mansfield, [29 November 1918]
Text: MS NYPL; [John Middleton Murry, ed.], 'Nine Letters (1918–1919) from D. H. Lawrence to Katherine Mansfield', *New Adelphi*, iii (June–August 1930), 276–7.

Mountain Cottage, Middleton-by-Wirksworth, Derby
Friday[1]

My dear Katharine,

I got home last evening: we got a motor car (Cath. Carswell was going to Kings Cross) – from Lansdowne in Heath St., just above Tube Station – 12/6 for the journey, doing the two stations – 10/- for one station: I come from St. Pancras. When you come, you come St. Pancras to Cromford, leave 12.15: but trains are very full, so arrive early. The change at Derby is easy – step out of one train into the other, two strides, and wait only four or five minutes: arrive Cromford 4.30, in the dark rain, to find Talbot waiting with the Vektawry, as he calls it.[2] The Vektawry has its hood up, one creeps inside to fill in the features, and so away into the night, through a rustle of waters. I found Mrs Doxey here[3] – a fire with a full ½cwt. of coal, a great red furnace – but no bread to be had for love or money – tea and sup on milk and potatoes, and look at the night – very dark, moving softly with misty rain – soft chink of water in the stable butts – wash myself before the fire – and so to bed, very snug. – This morning find the world rather Macbeth-looking – brownish little strokes of larch trees above, the bracken brown and curly, disappearing below the house into shadowy gloom.[4] But the fields to the well are grey green and luminous almost like stone. – On the lawn the moles have turned up a circle of strange black mounds, very magical. But I regret it. – Tomorrow I am going to Ripley and Eastwood, for the week-end. My sister is at Ripley.

The wind is getting up. This place is a wind-centre, I warn you.

If you come soon, you must sit tight on your courage, and not be daunted, then you'll be all right. – I should like Jack to come too.

[1] Dated with reference to the previous letter.
[2] i.e. a 'Victoria': a carriage for public hire.
[3] A neighbour at Middleton.
[4] gloom.] gloom, below the house.

The Railway people, when one travels, seem rather independent and Bolshy.

Quick – sharp – get better.

DHL

One feels here rather like a man looking out from a fortress.

Please thank Ida Baker for the trouble she took for me.[1]

Bless my soul, the sun is shining – and Mrs Doxey has just brought me a patriarchal cake of bread cooked in a frying-pan.

1664. To J. B. Pinker, 4 December 1918
Text: MS BosU; Unpublished.

Mountain Cottage, Middleton by Wirksworth. Derby.

4 Dec. 1918.

My dear Pinker

I send you a story[2] – hope it may go. I will send you more soon.

What about the play? Is anything doing with it? If not, will you send it back to me here, as I would like to show it to a friend.[3] What did you think of it yourself?

Hope we'll make a start soon.

Yrs   D. H. Lawrence

1665. To Katherine Mansfield, [5 December 1918]
Text: MS NYPL; Murry, *New Adelphi*, 'Mansfield', 277–9.

Middleton –

Thursday

My dear Katharine

I received your letter this morning. I want to write a few little things I have on my mind.

First, I send you the Jung book, borrowed from Kot. in the midst of his reading it. Ask Jack not to keep it long, will you, as I feel I ought to send it back. – Beware of it – this Mother-incest idea can become an obsession. But it seems to me there is this much truth in it: that at certain periods the man has a desire and a tendency to return unto the woman, make her his goal and end,

---

[1] Ida Constance Baker (b. 1888), a close friend of Katherine Mansfield and author of *Katherine Mansfield, The Memories of L. M.* (1971).

[2] 'The Blind Man'.

[3] Lady Cynthia Asquith (see Letter 1654).

find his justification in her. In this way he casts himself as it were into her womb, and she, the Magna Mater, receives him with gratification. This is a kind of incest. It seems to me it is what Jack does to you, and what repels and fascinates you. I have done it, and now struggle all my might to get out. In a way, Frieda is the devouring mother. – It is awfully hard, once the sex relation has gone this way, to recover. If we don't recover, we die. – But Frieda says I am antediluvian in my positive attitude. I do think a woman must yield some sort of precedence[1] to a man, and he must take this precedence.[2] I do think men must go ahead absolutely in front of their women, without turning round to ask for permission or approval from their women. Consequently the women must follow as it were unquestioning.[3] I can't help it, I believe this. Frieda doesn't. Hence our fight.

Secondly, I do believe in friendship. I believe tremendously in friendship between man and man, a pledging of men to each other inviolably. – But I have not ever met or formed such friendship. Also I believe the same way in friendship between men and women, and between women and women, sworn, pledged, eternal, as eternal as the marriage bond, and as deep. – But I have not met or formed such friendship.

Excuse this sudden burst into dogma. Please give the letter to Jack. I say it to him particularly.

The weather continues dark, warm, muggy and nasty. I find the Midlands full of the fear of death – truly. They are all queer and unnerved. This Flu. is very bad. There has only been one flicker of sunshine on the valley. It is very grim always. Last evening at dusk I sat by the rapid brook which runs by the high-road in the valley bed. The spell of hastening, secret water goes over one's mind. When I got to the top – a very hard climb – I felt as if I had climbed out of a womb.

The week-end I was at Ripley. Going, on Sat. night, the train runs just above the surface of Butterley reservoir, and the iron-works on the bank were flaming, a massive roar of flame and burnt smoke in the black sky, flaming and waving again on the black water round the train. On Butterfly platform – where I got out – everything was lit up red – there was a man with dark brows, odd, not a human being. I could write a story about him. He made me think of Ashaburnipal.[4] It seems to me, if one is to do fiction now, one must cross the threshold of the human psyche. – I've not done 'The Fox' yet – but I've done

---

[1] precedence] submission
[2] precedence.] submission.
[3] unquestioning.] submissively.
[4] Ashurbanipal was the last of the great Assyrian kings; he reigned 669–626 B.C.

'The Blind Man' – the end queer and ironical. – I realise *how* many people are just rotten at the quick.

I've written three little essays 'Education of the People'. I told you Freeman, on the *Times*, asked me to do something for his *Educational Supplement*. Will you ask Jack please to send me, by return if possible, Freeman's initials, and the *Times* address, that will find him, so that I can send him these essays and see if he will print them. It will be nice if I can earn a little weekly money.[1]

I begin to despair altogether about human relationships – feel one may just as well turn into a sort of lone wolf, and have done with it. Really, I need a little reassuring of some sort.

DHL

Do you know the poem – Heine I think –

> Aus alten Märchen winkt es
> Hervor mit weisser Hand
> Da singt es und da klingt es
> Von einem Zauberland
> Wo grossen Blumen schmachten
> Im Goldnen Abendlicht
> Und traurig sich betrachten
> Mit bräutlichem Gesicht.[2]

I only object to '*Traurig*' – it fascinates me – if I remember it right.

Don't you think you and Jack might come here for Christmas? – would you be well enough? I've been getting wood in the well-fields – it's rather beautiful, these dark, gleamy afternoons.

---

[1] These essays were not accepted by Freeman for the *Times Educational Supplement*: see Letter 1681. The three essays eventually became twelve but what survives and was finally published as 'Education of the People' (in *Phoenix*, ed. McDonald, pp. 587–665) was probably the result of continuous writing begun in June 1920 (Tedlock, *Lawrence MSS* 90, 131–2).

[2] DHL quotes ll. 1–8 from an untitled poem by Heinrich Heine (1799–1856); it comes from a group of poems *Lyrisches Intermezzo* (1823) which later appeared as a section of *Buch der Lieder* (1827) ['. . . grosse . . . Und zärtlich sich . . .']:

> A white hand beckons from old stories, there's a singing and a ringing of a magic land where great trees languish in the golden evening light and tenderly gaze at each other with bridal faces; –

(Translation from *Heine: Selected Verse*, ed. Peter Branscombe, 1967.)

The word DHL selects for comment, 'traurig' (mournful, gloomy) is the one he misremembered: Heine wrote 'zärtlich' (tenderly, fondly).

1666. To Herbert Farjeon, 6 December 1918
Text: MS SIU; Nehls, i. 480.

Mountain Cottage, Middleton-by-Wirksworth. Derby.

6 Dec. 1918.

Dear Bertie

Please lend me *Legends of Charlemagne*, which you have in Everyman, grey, in your dining-room.[1] I am struggling with a European History for Schools – and cursing myself black in the face. – The weather is vile, so dark – I am here by myself – Frieda has not come – and I'm doing work I don't want to do – and I suspect myself of having Flu, though it may only be temper.

How are you and Joan and Jocelyn – and the staff – and the pond?[2] The Midlands are *very* gloomy. Influenza is really very bad, and they are all genuinely frightened – the fear of death is on them – not, unfortunately, a wholesome fear of the Lord, however: quite selfish. They'll never do anything, these people – though Railways will cause trouble if they possibly can. – One can only wait on the heavens – humanity is a nasty affair. – I do hope you are well and prosperous. I expect we shall be back at Hermitage in Jan. or Feb.

Till then, au revoir.   D. H. Lawrence

1667. To Harriet Monroe, 6 December 1918
Text: MS UChi; Huxley 457.

Mountain Cottage, Middleton-by-Wirksworth, Derby. England.

6 Dec. 1918

Dear Harriett Monroe

I have received your letter and the November issue of *Poetry*. – If you see Iris Tree, remember me to her.[3]

I asked Amy to let you have a copy of my *New Poems* (so called by Secker, the publisher) – in order that you might re-print any you liked. Has she not done so? I sent her proofs, and asked Martin[4] Secker to send her two copies, but have heard nothing from her. – I think you might find some little things you would like, in it. – I inscribed the book to Amy.

---

[1] *Legends of Charlemagne*, ed. Thomas Bulfinch (Everyman's Library, 1911).
[2] Joan, née Thornycroft (b. 1889), wife of Herbert Farjeon, and their elder daughter Joscelyn (b. 1917). The 'pond' was probably the beautiful pool in the garden of the Farjeons' Spring Cottage at Bucklebury Common, near Hermitage; 'the staff' would be their cook.
[3] Iris Tree (b. 1897), daughter of Sir Beerbohm Tree, had been a student at the Slade (with Dora Carrington) and met DHL at a party given by Brett in early November 1915. She published *Poems* (New York, 1919) and *The Traveller and other Poems* (New York, 1927).
[4] asked Martin] asked the

I send you a number of elegiac poems[1] – some which I like best of any I have done. I feel a bit tender about them – don't print them unless you feel them. They may seem nothing in Chicago.

England is gloomy. I think I shall come to America.

Greetings to you   D. H. Lawrence

Please note the address.

Beaumont is doing these poems, in a little volume de luxe – these I enclose you – I suppose they'll be out in February.

1668. To Lady Cynthia Asquith, 6 December 1918
Text: MS UT; Unpublished.

Mountain Cottage, Middleton-by-Wirksworth, Derby
6 Dec. 1918

I am sending you the play today – Read it, and tell me what you think of it. And if you like, show it to Mrs Patrick Campbell[2] – but just as you think fit. I'm afraid no manager would look at it at the moment. Later, however, it is possible.

I am here by myself. Frieda stayed in Hermitage – I believe she has gone to London today, and will come on next week. It is very lonely here – far-off feeling. One wonders what is real, and what not. – so very few things, so very few. Sometimes you seem to me to be sleep-walking. – But why not I? – Of this I'm sure, that all the world, as represented by the newspapers, is just prancing about in a meaningless sort of nightmare. It hasn't the shadow of reality: probably never will have. – Quoi faire, in the midst of such a stinking sea of unreality? – Make an island, I suppose.

Ah well, I saw you having your portrait painted.[3] Then I knew you were asleep.

DHL

[1] i.e. poems which would appear in *Bay* (the volume mentioned in the postscript). See p. 325 n. 1.
[2] Beatrice Stella Tanner (1865–1940), m. (1) in 1884, Captain Patrick Campbell (d. 1900) (2) in 1914, Major George Cornwallis-West (1874–1951), playwright. As well as being a friend of Lady Cynthia, she was also a well-known actress: the part of Eliza Doolittle in Shaw's *Pygmalion* (1913) was specially written for her.
[3] See p. 176 n. 3.

1669. To Unidentified Recipient, [6 December 1918]
Text: MS UN; Unpublished.

[Mountain Cottage, Middleton by Wirksworth, Derby]
[6 December 1918][1]

[   ] another shot at essays on education, as well as settling down to the *History*: so find myself very busy: for which to be alone is good. But the weather is very nasty and damp, and the Midlands stricken with the fear of death: this Flu. They are horribly frightened, all of them: but it is not fear of the Lord: merely selfish fear of death, petty and selfish. – When *will* one get the spark of a new spirit out of these people?

Let me hear from you.

Yrs   D. H. Lawrence

1670. To Catherine Carswell, [7 December 1918]
Text: MS YU; cited in Carswell 107.

Mountain Cottage, Middleton by Wirksworth, Derby.
Sat.

My dear Catherine

I had a card from Lettie[2] to say Don had Flu. I'm very sorry. Can you send me a line, if he is getting better all right? – It is very bad in these parts also – think I've got a touch – but slight. Frieda isn't back yet – coming next week, I suppose. – I do hope you and J[ohn] P[atrick] will be safe from this accursed Flu. – At least, have no more than a mild touch, and be done with it. It is a little plague, I'm sure. And the weather is *vile*: mist again today, though it's colder.

I wrote 4 little essays for the *Times* – 'Education of the People' – good, but most revolutionary. Still, as it is Education, not politics, Freeman might print them. If so, I'd go on with them. Send me his initials and address, will you, so that I can post them.

This weather maddens me. I suppose Edinburgh is lugubrious, too. Let me have a line.

DHL

---

[1] This fragment is dated by the obvious similarity of contents and phrasing to Letter 1666.
[2] The Carswells' servant (see Carswell 105–6).

1671. To Katherine Mansfield, [10 December 1918]
Text: MS NYPL; Murry, *New Adelphi*, 'Mansfield', 279.

Middleton-by-Wirksworth.
Tuesday.

My dear Katharine

No, it's damn well no good bothering about people. I had an S.O.S. from Barbara Low today, and she wants her Jung.[1] Let her have it by the week-end will you – post it to her direct – *10 Brunswick Square, W.C.1* – and *print* the address, dear Katharine, so that the Jewish magpie shall not settle chattering on my roof. – You will understand I can't be chattered at.

I went to Ripley – found my poor sister rather sick and wretched. We must get her husband home, to do the work.[2] I am writing to Campbell – though he's no good – I mean, he will never lift a finger.[3] Does Jack know anybody Ministry of Labour, who might tell us the best way to go about to get my brother-in-law out of the Marines. There is a special clause for one-man businesses, you know.

I also saw the Eastwood friends: one just on the point of dying.[4] Katharine – on ne meurt pas: I almost want to let it be reflexive – on ne se meurt pas: *Point!*[5] Be damned and be blasted everything, and let the bloody world come to its end. But one does not die. Jamais. – I bolted home to Matlock in the train. The Derwent (the river at Matlock) rushes very fast. This for some reason gives me extreme pleasure. I believe it would you.

We must find some way, next year, of getting *out* of the world: and if Jack doesn't want to go, let him stay and write for the *Nation*. *If* we are self-sufficient, a few of us, *what* do we want with the world?

When do you think you will be strong enough to come up here? Don't be long.

I'm sending you the *Times* essays, in despair of ever getting the address. You will be cursing me, probably, for bothering you. But do read them and post them on at once if you can, for the sake of the publication.

I wrote the fox story – rather odd and amusing. What is your story? – Perhaps I'll send both the 'Fox'[6] and the Education essays to Frieda, and she'll bring them in to you. Let me see your story. – Somehow I hate doing

---

[1] See Letter 1665.
[2] William Edwin Clarke (1889–1964), m. Ada Lawrence, 4 August 1913. He was a tailor but, at this time, still in the armed forces.
[3] Gordon Campbell was working in the Ministry of Munitions (see p. 48 n. 3).
[4] Frances ('Frankie') Amelia Cooper (1884–1918), one of DHL's childhood friends, was dying of tuberculosis; she was buried on 22 December 1918. See *Letters*, i. 34 and Letter 1675.
[5] 'one does not die . . . one is not dying. *Certainly not!*'
[6] the 'Fox'] it

that *European History* for the Oxford Press. Curse it – why shouldn't one do as one likes.

We'll stand free and swear allegiance, anyhow, shall we?

DHL

1672. To Selina Yorke, [16 December 1918]
Text: MS Lazarus; Unpublished.

Middleton –
Monday

Dear Mrs Yorke[1]

In haste to answer yours. Miss Taylor gave me 30/- for the cottage, for 12 weeks. She said she thought 2/6 a week quite enough. I said in reply that if *she* thought so, then it was enough. She was not very polite – except in the last letter when she sent the thirty shillings. But leave her alone, for heavens sake.

Frieda came up here on[2] Saturday. We shall stay over Christmas. I suppose you and Arabella couldn't come up? We should like it if you could.

Poor Hilda.[3] Feeling sorry for her, one almost melts. But I *don't* trust her – other people's lives, indeed!

DHL

1673. To Katherine Mansfield, 20 December 1918
Text: MS NYPL; Murry, *New Adelphi*, 'Mansfield', 279–80.

Mountain Cottage – Middleton by Wirksworth. Derby
20 Dec 1918

My dear Katharine

So, it is practically Christmas, and the shortest day. I wish you were better, so that we could kick off with a bit of a spree.

It snowed yesterday, and the dark valley was white. But it melted. Today there is a powder of snow, and a slow sunshine. In the wild storm yesterday evening arrived my sister and her husband[4] – They[5] went again this morning at 7.0, and I watched them in the dark, slightly snowy greyness. We are going

---

[1] The mother of Arabella Yorke; she is understood to have done some journalistic work but little further is known of her.
[2] on] over
[3] Hilda Aldington; she knew that Arabella was her husband's mistress.
[4] In view of the remark about Ada Clarke and her husband in Letter 1671 (also to Katherine Mansfield), they would seem to be the people referred to here.
[5] They] She

to Ripley on Christmas day, after all – leaving here about 10.0. Think of us en voyage. They are having a turkey.

We went to Matlock yesterday, and got you this bit of the Derbyshire underworld. It is Fluor Spar – mined just near, and cut in Matlock.[1] It is very difficult to cut. There is a purple sort – the common name for this stone is Blue John – but it was too expensive to buy you a purple bowl. And I liked this yellow one. It is a golden underworld, with rivers and clearings – do you see it? For some reason, it is like Derbyshire.

I have a sort of feeling that you are not very well. But tomorrow is the *shortest* day, and then the tide turns. I do so want to do nice gay happy things, to start at once. I hate work, and I don't want to work – write, that is. I wish we'd had our Rananim – or got it. I should so love gaily and easily to mess about. I can't bear any feeling of any sort of *importance* in things any more. One wants to be nice and easy and insouciant.

The barber cut my hair and shaved me bald and made me look like a convict, clipping my beard: also gave me an ensuing cold. – Courage, mon ami, le diable vit encore.[2]

I'm supposed to be doing that little European history, and earning my living, but I hate it like poison, and have struck. Why work?

I hope you won't get this days and days before Christmas.

Oh, did you send Pinker the stories[3] – I've had no acknowledgement from him? – And 'Aunt Barbara' the Jung?

Greet Jack from me.

Many Christmas greetings – let's be born ourselves, Jesus is a back number – time our star riz.

DHL

Frieda is writing tomorrow.

1674. To J. D. Beresford, 20 December 1918
Text: MS UT; Unpublished.

Mountain Cottage, Middleton by Wirksworth – Derby.
20 Dec. 1918.

My dear Beresford

I have received your cheque this morning – and very many thanks to you

---

[1] in Matlock.] just near.
[2] 'Courage, my friend, the devil is still alive'; a play on a colloquial remark ('Courage . . . diable est mort'), perhaps remembered from Charles Reade's *The Cloister and the Hearth* (1861). See *Letters*, ii. 305.
[3] 'The Fox' and 'John Thomas' (see Letter 1685).

and the unknown. What a lot of trouble you are taking for me. I wish I were a more satisfactory person. – But now I have got £10. money ceases to trouble me, I go gaily on, since the morrow, at any rate, is all right. And I shall try and get some money from Austin Harrison. He can only give me £5. a time, from the *English Review* – and I owe Pinker. But I'll get Pinker to wait, and divert Harrison's £10. to me, so I shall manage. Don't[1] you bother any more: the skies may open.

                                                        Yrs   D. H. Lawrence

1675. To S. S. Koteliansky, 22 December 1918
Text: MS BL; Zytaruk, ed., *Malahat Review*, i. 34.

                        Mountain Cottage, Middleton by Wirksworth, Derby.
                                                            22 Dec. 1918

My dear Kot,

Frieda told me you had influenza. I hope it is better by now, and that you are prepared for laying waste to various Christmas preparations for feasting. I too have got a bad cold, and feel like crawling into a deep hole to hide there. The weather is very dark and bad. I have been going to Eastwood to a friend, who has now died. 'Christmas comes but once a year[2] – And that is once too often, dear.' We are going to my sister's on Christmas Day, if ever I get so far, which I probably shan't.

For news, there is none. I wrote four little essays for the *Times*, and sent them in, but have heard nothing at all of them. It is not likely they will come to anything. – I wish I need never write another line of any sort, for publication, in my life. I've had enough. If only I had a small income, I'd chuck writing altogether. I'm really sick of it. The necessity to earn something is all that drives me – and then I earn nothing, so I might as well keep still. – Well, there's a Carol for you.

Greet me very kindly to Sophie Issayevna and to Ghita, and I hope Ghita will have a good and festive time. Send me some news of you. It is four years since the Bucks cottage christmas[3] – my God, what wrecks we are!

                                        Nevertheless, all good wishes   DHL

---

[1] Don't] You
[2] Ascribed to Thomas Tusser, *Five Hundred Points of Good Husbandrie* (1580), chap. XII.
[3] See *Letters*, ii. 252 n. 2 for Frieda's description of the Christmas party in 1914.

1676. To Lady Cynthia Asquith, 22 December 1918
Text: MS UT; Huxley 462–3.

Mountain Cottage, Middleton by Wirksworth, Derby
22 Decem. 1918.

I don't know where you are spending Christmas – but hope you will have a high and festive time, and that Michael will suitably enjoy himself. We are going across to my sister's on Christmas Day, if ever I get so far – having got a bad cold, under which I crawl dismally for the time being. The weather is very dark and nasty, and Christmas is an institution that really should be abolished. I don't want to hear of it, it wearies me. – I suppose you will be in town, tripping round and refusing turkey. But one needs the spring to come, when the skies will lift a bit and one can wander forth. – Sorry the play irritated you. Keep it as long as you feel any use in keeping it. I wrote four nice little essays for the *Times*, nicely curried. *The Times* refrains even from acknowledging their receipt. I chuckle a little to myself, when my cold leaves me enough energy. – Ah, what a happy day it will be, when I need not write any more – except a letter occasionally. I am tired of writing. – We heard from F[rieda]'s mother in Baden-Baden – I believe her God-father – Frieda's – has left her a legacy – he should have done: he has just died.[1] I suppose the Allies will swallow it: just the thing that would happen to us. But then my brother-in-law is now Minister of Finance for Bavaria, so he might hook out the fish for us.[2] Oh my dear sweet Jesus, if I had even £100 a year I would never write another stroke for the public. Pray that I may get this provision.

I don't know that my wishes for a festive Christmas are worth much, but here they are. F. sends hers also.

DHL

1677. To Sallie Hopkin, 24 December 1918
Text: MS NCL; Unpublished.

Mountain Cottage, Middleton by Wirksworth.
24 Dec. 1918

My dear Sallie
We are going to Ripley tomorrow, which is Christmas Day, to stay

---

[1] DHL's remark about a legacy cannot be verified.
[2] Dr Edgar Jaffe (1866–1921), the estranged husband of Frieda's sister Else, had become Finance Minister of the short-lived revolutionary government of Bavaria. His appointment ceased in February 1919.

presumably till Friday. Frieda says she wants to see you – so might we perhaps come over on Thursday to tea, or is that a wrong time.

Frieda has made you the bag: she sends her love, and all good wishes for the Christmas.

I thought we might have seen Enid here: have been half expecting her all along.

Au revoir   DHL

1678. To Katherine Mansfield, 27 December 1918
Text: MS NYPL; Murry, *New Adelphi*, 'Mansfield', 280–2.

c/o Mrs Clarke. Grosvenor Rd., Ripley, nr Derby
Friday 27 Dec 1918.

My dear Katharine

We got your parcel on Christmas morning. We had started off, and were on the brow of the hill, when the postman loomed round the corner, over the snow. It was all white and snowy and sunny, with a wind like an axe. I floated out my hanky for a flag over the snow, and Frieda dropped the tangerines in her anxiety to get the wheat-sheaf unwrapped, and it was terribly cold and windy just on that edge. Frieda's wheat-sheaf looked so strange, such a queer indescribable darkish colour, somehow elephant, over the snow which is so candid in comparison. It was queer and like Africa, and a bit like a meteor. She has worn it on her yellow slip, with the red silk skirt and red coat, at our two parties here – but I can't get used to it now, it seems like a little torch or brand of elephant-grey, tropical, lush twilight. Funny how things disturb one. – But my hanky fluttered very nice and lively. – I wish you could have been there on the hill summit – the valley all white, and hairy with trees below us, and grey with rocks – and just round us on our side the grey stone fences drawn in a net-work over the snow, all very clear in the sun. – We ate the sweets, and slithered downhill, very steep and tottering. The children had the tangerines and the fan.

We read your letter in the wind, dropping down to Cromford. It made me feel weary, that we couldn't all be there, with rucksacks – I'd got mine on – setting off for somewhere good, over the snow. It *is* disappointing. And unless one decorates one's house for oneself alone, best leave it bare, for other people are all wall-eyed. I do so want to *get out* – out of England – really, out of Europe. And I *will* get out. We must do it.

There was hardly any snow in the valley – all green, with the yew-berries still sprinkling the causeway. At Ambergate my sister had sent a motor car for us – so we were at Ripley in time for turkey and Christmas pudding. – My God, what masses of food here, turkey, large tongues, long wall of roast loin of pork, pork-pies, sausages, mince pies, dark cakes covered with almonds, chiscakes,[1] lemon-tarts, jellies, endless masses of food, with whiskey, gin, port-wine, burgundy, muscatel. It seems incredible. We played charades – the old people of 67 playing away harder than the young ones – and lit the christmas tree, and drank healths, and sang, and roared – Lord above. If only one hadn't all the while a sense that next week would be the same dreariness as before. – What a good party we might have had, had we felt really free of the world.

We had a second turn-to yesterday – and at half past eleven went roaring off in the dark wind to Dr Feroze's[2] – he is a Parsee – and drank two more bottles of muscatel, and danced in his big empty room till we were staggered, and quite dazed. – Tonight we are going back to Middleton – and I feel infuriated to think of the months ahead, when one waits paralysed for some sort of release. I feel caged, somehow – and I *cannot* find out how to earn enough to keep us – and it maddens me.

Still, it might be very much worse. One might be tied tight to a job, or to a sickness. I do wish you were better. But you *sound* stronger. I long to make *plans* – new plans. But not Europe: Oh God!

I pledge you 'the days to come'.

DHL

1679. To Amy Lowell, 28 December 1918
Text: MS HU; Moore, *Intelligent Heart* 248–9.

Mountain Cottage, Middleton by Wirksworth, Derby.
28 Dec 1918.

My dear Amy

Why haven't we heard from you for so long? Did you ever get my *New Poems*? You have not written since October, I believe, not since you sent *Can Grande*.

Christmas is over now, and we must prepare for a New Year. I hope it will be a real new year, a new start altogether. The old has been bad enough. – I was in London in November – saw Richard, who was on leave. He is very fit,

[1] DHL was remembering the Nottingham version of 'cheesecakes'; 'chiskets'.
[2] Dr Dhunjabhai Furdunji Mullan–Feroze (1874–1959) was the Clarkes' family doctor and a close friend; he was also well known to and liked by DHL. (He qualified in Bombay in 1904 and Edinburgh in 1905.)

looking forward to peace and freedom. Hilda also is in town – not so very well. She is going to have another child, it appears. I hope she will be all right.[1] Perhaps she can get more settled, for her nerves are very shaken: and perhaps the child will soothe her and steady her. I hope it will.

England is wintry and uncongenial. Towards summer time, I want to come to America. I feel I want to be in a new country. I expect we shall go to Switzerland or Germany when Peace is signed. Frieda wants to see her people. Her brother-in-law is now Minister of Finance to the Bavarian republic, one of my friends is something else important, and F's cousin – Hartman von Richthofen, whom they turned out of the Reichstag six months ago, because he wanted peace – he is now a moving figure in Berlin. So Germany will be quite exciting for us. But I want to come to America, I don't know why. But the land itself draws me.

We shall see you then. What are you doing in the meantime? – are you coming over here? And why haven't you written a line.

Remember us to Mrs Russell. A good New Year to you.

                                                        Yrs   D. H. Lawrence

1680. To Captain John Short, 28 December 1918
Text: MS UT; Unpublished.

                              Mountain Cottage, Middleton by Wirksworth. Derby.
                                                                  28 Dec. 1918

Dear Captain Short

I find that we shall probably be able to go to Switzerland in February or March, so I think the best thing I can do is to sell my bit of furniture at Tregerthen, and give up the cottages. No doubt Benney would take the furniture. When I hear from you, I will write to him. I should like to keep only my books and desk, two mirrors, the two little clocks, all bedding, and the few ornaments, the two pictures, and two hair mattresses, one from the camp bed, one from the big bed, the primus stove, the brass lamp, the candlesticks and Primus lamp, and the remainder of the boots or clothes worth sending. These I would like to have sent to the cottage at Hermitage. The remainder – perhaps you or Mr Benney would make me a list of them, and give me an estimate of the value. Some things perhaps you would like to keep in the cottage. You must let me know. And then please let me know exactly what you wish as settlement for the rent.

Perhaps I may think of a few more things I should like to keep – small

[1] See Letter 1723 and n. 4.

things. I will make a list. I will write to the Hockings about the Persian rug and the piano.

I hope you had a pleasant Christmas, and that Westyr and Mrs Short are well. Remember us both very kindly to them, and to Mr and Mrs Whitley.

Yours Sincerely   D. H. Lawrence

1681. To S. S. Koteliansky, 1 January 1919
Text: MS BL; cited in Gransden 27.

Middleton-by-Wirksworth. Derby.

1 Jan. 1919

My dear Kot,

I got your letter this morning: a deep snowy morning, very still and isolated – the first day of the year. I do hope it will be a new start of a new time for us. I do want to get out, to get across into something freer and more active.

Yes, do give me a little New Year gift: but nothing extravagant and solemn. I should like a book – or perhaps two books, to read. One depends on reading here: and the more I live, the more I respect the good genuine books of mankind. I should like, from the Everyman Library

Bates' – *Naturalist on the Amazon.*   1/9
Scheffel – *Ekkehard: a Tale of the 10th. Century.*[1]   1/9

The first I want because I intend some day to go to South America – to Peru or Ecuador, not the Amazon. But I know Bates is good. The second I want because he will help me with my *European History*, and because I began him once and never had a chance to finish him. – I don't like the more expensive bindings of Everyman – only the ordinary pre-war 1/- sort, now 1/9, I believe.

About money, I got £10. from Harrison for two essays,[2] which I circumvented from Pinker's clutches, so please don't lend me anything yet. Later on, if I am cornered, I will ask you. I am doing the history – it will take about a month or six weeks, I suppose. – If Shearman likes to send me a little, well and good: but don't bother him.

Tell Gertler that Cynthia Asquith has the play and is seeing to it.[3] She has some part in some new theatrical concern – I suppose it is Bennetts. Tell Gertler also that Bibesco, the buffoon-prince, was approached last year on my behalf. He said he would rather help me to publish my work than give money

---

[1] Henry W. Bates, *The Naturalist on the River Amazon* (Everyman's, 1910); Joseph Victor von Scheffel, *Ekkehard* (Everyman's, 1911).
[2] See Letter 1662 and n. 4.
[3] *Touch and Go*: see Letter 1668.

direct. He had the MS. of the novel, returned it without a word, and did nothing.[1] So that, although these buffoon-princes have money and pretensions, they are just like the Bennetts and Wellses and Selfridges and Lyons of this world – or even the Howard de Waldens[2] – they will only pay for their own puffing-up. Tell Gertler that there is nothing doing in the Bennett–Bibesco quarter. Pah! So much the better.

We hear from Germany. My brother-in-law, Edgar Jaffé, a rich Jew and Professor, is Minister of Finance for Bavaria. From Frieda's mother also news that she has money for her. Between the Minister of Finance and the gute Schwiegermutter we may find a solution of this money difficulty – perhaps – and perhaps not.

I still have some sort of hope of our Rananim: the last hope.

My sister gave me a bottle of gin. I drink the New Year to you.

DHL

The *Times* sent me back my little essays on Education: 'Very interesting, but too deep, rather matter for a book than for a Supplement'.

1682. To Edith Eder, 2 January 1919
Text: Hobman, ed., *David Eder*, p. 121.

Mountain Cottage, Middleton by Wirksworth, Derby.
2 Jan., 1919.

Dear Edith,

I'm sorry you remain so seedy. But this winter is the devil. If one can get through it one will be on another shore.

Is Eder coming home? I very much want to see him. I feel now *I must get out*. I must get out of England, of Europe. There will never be anything here but increasing rottenness, generally slow, sometimes quick, but always rottenness. I want to know about Palestine, if there is any hope in it for us. I still keep to my old hope that we may go away, a few of us, and live really independently. I still think it possible. I like best to imagine my Andes. But if the Andes are impracticable, and if Palestine be practicable, then I'll go to Palestine. I want to see Eder. I *will* get out of Europe this year . . .[3]

---

[1] See Letter 1569 ; the novel was *Women in Love*.
[2] DHL here associates popular writers (Arnold Bennett and H. G. Wells) with equally popular stores (such as Lady Cynthia's favourite, Selfridges) and restaurants (Joseph Lyon's). Thomas Evelyn Scott-Ellis, 8th Baron Howard de Walden (1880–1946) was a man of wealth and diverse interests; he had written the libretti for an operatic trilogy; he was capable of great generosity; but DHL suspected that he wished his munificence (to artists, public institutions, etc.) to be publicly acclaimed.
[3] Hobman's text is incomplete.

1683. To William Henry Hocking, 2 January 1919
Text: Moore 574–5.

Mountain Cottage, Middleton
2 January 1919

Dear William Henry

I find that in all probability we shall be able to go abroad in February or March, and as I don't know when I shall be back, I have decided to give up the Tregerthen Cottages, and to sell the furniture. Mary knows most about the things, but as I am not sure whether she is at Tregerthen or not, I write to you about the things you have.

I wish you would please roll up the Persian rug, tie it up, and send it by *parcels*-rail to my sister: *Mrs Clarke, Grosvenor Rd, Ripley, nr Derby*. If this is a bother Capt. Short will get a man to do it.

If you would care to keep the piano, I hope you will take it as a gift. If not, let the man take it away.

Perhaps you will have the other things that may be at the farm carried up to my cottage, where Capt. Short will see to them. If there is anything out of the cottages that you would like, please let me know – or let Capt. Short know. You can decide before Benney comes to buy the things.

If you write to me, I will let you know from time to time what I am doing. Remember me very warmly to your Mother, and to all. I shall see them again one day. Kindest regards to your wife.

1684. To S. S. Koteliansky, 6 January 1919
Text: MS BL; Postmark, [Wirk]sworth 7 JA 19; cited in Gransden 27.

Mountain Cottage, Middleton by Wirksworth. Derby.
6 Jan. 1919.

My dear Kot

Ekkehard and the *Amazon* came today: what nice, happy kind of books they are to have: they mean such a lot more to one than Lloyd George or Ottoline Morrell or Middleton Murry. To me they mean real living mankind – not this squirming spawn which passes today for Man. I should never be a sad man, whilst it was possible for a real book to come along.

I knew that it was Desmond Mcarthy who had put a stopper on Prince B[ibesco], moaning on Ottoline's outraged behalf.[1] I knew that. And I knew

---

[1] Lady Cynthia Asquith recorded an occasion on 28 February 1918 when she, Prince Bibesco and the journalist and literary critic, (Sir) Desmond MacCarthy (1877–1952) discussed the possibility of publishing *Women in Love*: 'Unfortunately, Desmond MacCarthy, who might be

that Prince B. had not the courage to say a word either to me or to Cynthia Asquith, but returned the MS. wordless. And I knew that Desmond Macarthy was quite pleased with himself for having arse-licked Ottoline and the Prince both at once, both of them being pretty sound benefactors of Desmond, who rather enjoys his arse-licking turns. All these things, my dear Kot, I knew and know: in fact I know very many things which I prefer to leave, like manure, to rot down in my soul, unspoken, to form the humus of a new germination.

The Rainbow was printed by a Jewish publisher called Huebsch, in New York. Then the suppression came on, and he dared not bring it out. It still lies, no doubt, on Huebsch's hands. I had one copy – a paltry looking black book, rather like a text-book, with several pages of the English edition omitted in it. You have illusions, my dear Kot, about my being able to make money by my writing. Whilst President Wilson coos and preens in New York,[1] whilst Ottoline stinks in Garsington, whilst Clemenceau spouts in France, whilst Murry 'Dostys' and you 'Rimbaud',[2] I am not worth a penny: nay, even whilst Katharine attaches a purple Cashmere shawl in drapery behind her arms, and whilst Campbell says 'Ireland'. And the world will end before these things cease. So an end, my dear Kot, to those illusions of prosperity which I am to find through some *good* new journal here, or through some puff in the U.S.A.

I would like to hear Grisha, by now, on 'America'.

Here we are deep in snow, very white and strange, beautiful, not very cold, but the roads difficult. I am working away at the history: hope to get it done soon enough to save my situation: otherwise I shall come to you for £10. I will not ask the Prince for anything – not I.

I suppose we shall all be struggling for passports soon. The moment it becomes possible, I shall leave England. I don't care where I go, so long as I can turn my back on it for good. Nor do I care what I do in the future, so long as I can just walk away.

Remember me very nicely to Sonia and to Ghita: also to Gertler. When I

helpful, takes Lady Ottoline seriously as a friend and wishes her protected from the pain the (according to him) obvious lampoon of her would inflict . . . [He] spoke of Lawrence as indisputably a genius, but *no* artist' (Asquith, *Diaries* 415–16). Presumably DHL knew of the conversation from Lady Cynthia.

[1] Woodrow Wilson (1856–1924), American President, enjoyed unbounded popularity following the Armistice. (When DHL wrote this, Wilson was in Europe and had recently been in England.)

[2] Murry had a keen interest in Dostoievsky; he had published *Fyodor Dostoevsky: A Critical Study* (1916); see also p. 53 and n. 1. The reference to Rimbaud (1854–91) is obscure: no work on him or translation of him by Kot is known.

can get as far as Matlock I shall buy you a tiny thing as a memento of bad times – they have been pretty bad times, these four years, haven't they? Chi lo sa?[1] – we may come to reckon them as having been good.

Vale. DHL

1685. To J. B. Pinker, 9 January 1919
Text: MS UT; Unpublished.

Mountain Cottage, Middleton-by-Wirksworth, Derby.
9 Jan 1919

My dear Pinker

I suppose you received the two MS. of the little stories 'The Fox' and 'John Thomas', which a friend forwarded to you.[2] I will send you another story directly.[3] If you think these are not likely to be placed, don't bother to have them typed, will you. If you have them typed, will you send me back the scrubby MS.

I asked Harrison to give me some money for the American Essays, as I was completely landed. So he sent me £10,10,0, for the II and III. This is all right, isn't it.

Do you remember the MS. 'Poems of a Prisoner', by Leigh Henry, which I sent you? Would you please return this to *Mrs Leigh Henry, 66 Adelaide Rd, N.W. 3.*

I've got no news in the world. Hope things are all right.

Yrs D. H. Lawrence

1686. To Stanley Hocking, 10 January 1919
Text: MS BucU; Postmark, Derby [. . .]; cited in Nehls, i. 427–8.

Mountain Cottage, Middleton-by-Wirksworth, Derby.
10 Jan. 1919.

Dear Stanley

I had your letter yesterday. Capt. Short will have told you that we are giving up the cottages, and selling the furniture. I also wrote to William Henry and told him, but have had no reply. I said to him that if he wished he should keep the piano as a gift. Since he does not reply to my letter, to say whether he wishes it or not, I conclude he does *not* wish it. So I wish you

---

[1] 'Who knows?'
[2] The 'friend' was Katherine Mansfield; see Letter 1673.
[3] directly.] more. (The story in question was probably 'Wintry Peacock'.)

would let Mr. Benney have the piano, as he says he will give me six or seven pounds for it.

I also asked William Henry if he would roll up the big Persian rug, and fasten it well, and send it by *parcels* rail to my sister, Mrs Clarke, Grosvenor Rd, Ripley, nr Derby. Perhaps you would do this – or ask Capt. Short to do it. And perhaps you would put anything else you were taking care of for me back in the cottage, so that Capt. Short could pack it or dispose of it.

I should like to give you something. Would you like the big volumes of the Geography of the World, that you had[1] – or would you prefer something else? And tell Mabel to secure the little lantern we used to joke about, and ask her if she would like the rest of the tea-service. I don't think many pieces of it are broken. Tell her to take it if she likes it.

I don't know where Mary is. I have not heard from her since just before Christmas, when she said she was going to London. And you do not mention her. Let me know about her.

Write to me, and let me know about the piano, and the rug, and everything. If you send off the rug, tell me what it costs. Capt Short says your mother has the square mahogany table – she will keep that in remembrance of us both.

I expect we shall stay here till we can go abroad. That should be in March, unless the world gets still further upset: which is likely. One day I shall come to Tregerthen again, to see your mother and all. Mrs Lawrence, of course, is excited at the thought of going home. My brother-in-law is the new Minister of Finance for Bavaria. I expect we shall be in the midst of things. If you write to me from time to time I will let you know where we are.

Remember us both very warmly to your mother and all.

Yrs –   D. H. Lawrence

1687. To J. B. Pinker, 15 January 1919
Text: MS BosU; Unpublished.

Mountain Cottage, Middleton by Wirksworth, Derby.
15 Jan. 1919

My dear Pinker

I send you another story.[2] I've no idea what you will think of it. If you think it worth while to have it typed, send me the MS. again, – any time – will you. I received the others today – many thanks.

Yrs   D. H. Lawrence

[1] The set was actually entitled *The World of Today*; in several of the volumes Stanley Hocking wrote, 'From Mr. D. H. Lawrence, 1917'.
[2] See Letter 1685 and n. 3.

1688. To S. S. Koteliansky, [17 January 1919]
Text: MS BL; Zytaruk 158.

Mountain Cottage.
Friday.

My dear Kot.

Rather a blow to hear of you going into the War Office.[1] It *does* go against one's grain. If I had any capital you should share it. I am going to get about £10. from Cornwall, after selling up there, so I shall manage till the *History* is done: two more chapters now, and then revision. Barbara told you about the Stanley Unwin.[2] I loathe returning to my vomit: going back to old work.[3] And it won't mean more than £15. Still, I'll have a shot at it.

I am interested and a bit amused to know how the War Office works out in you. Tell me. And tell Campbell to come up here and see me for a day or two. Really, that man should shift. – I like Murry as the benevolent patron of us all:[4] tra-la-la!

I'm awfully mad and rampageous inside myself, but just hold my nose down and grind on at the history etc. Blast the world, blast it, it is soft-rotten, and if one takes a step one goes head over heels in soft-rottenness.

Very kind regards to Sonia. Grisha will find a way of some sort. Send me news.

DHL

1689. To Fritz Krenkow, 17 January 1919
Text: MS UN; Unpublished.

Mountain Cottage, Middleton by Wirksworth, Derby.
17 Jan. 1919.

My dear Uncle

Emily tells me you are going over to Ripley tomorrow in the car. If you care to come on here for the week-end, we shall be very pleased. There is a house for the car.

I didn't answer your letter. I've been struggling to get finished my little School history for the Oxford University Press. They want it, I am rather behind – and they will give me £50 when I give them the MS., so that will

---

[1] No information has survived of any service by Kot in the War Office.
[2] See Letter 1691.
[3] Proverbs xxvi. 11 ['As a dog returneth to his vomit, so a fool returneth to his folly', A.V.]
[4] Presumably a reference to the literary opportunities which Murry could offer when he took over the editorship of the *Athenæum* in March 1919. (See Letter 1705.)

solve my financial difficulties for the moment. I want to come to Quorn when this wretched piggling work is done.

The weather is stormy, we are alone, but busy, hardly notice the loneliness. Come over if you can.

Love from both to both   DHL

1690. To Nancy Henry, 23 January 1919
Text: MS ColU; Huxley 466.

Mountain Cottage, Middleton by Wirksworth, Derby.
23 Jan 1919

Dear Mrs Henry,

I'm sorry you have been so seedy. The very air has seemed a bit poisonous lately. I do hope you're feeling better. Are you fit to go on with your work?

We are very quiet here – my wife been in bed with a cold – rather better now – I going on with the history. I have only one more chapter. Every chapter, I suffer before I can begin, because I do loathe the broken pots of historical facts. But once I can get hold of the thread of the developing significance, then I am happy, and get ahead. I shall need to revise rather carefully. But you'll see, when you get these 4 last chapters, the book does expand nicely and naturally. I am rather pleased with it. There is a clue of developing meaning running through it: that makes it real to me. – I hope if you think of any other book I could do, you will propose me for it – if I am in England, that is.

I am tired of the state of things here, and want to clear out. As soon as one can travel I expect we shall go to Switzerland, then probably to Bavaria. Later I want to go on to America – south if possible – I am finished here in Europe.

Let me know how you are. Don't bother about the history till you feel free. Come and see us if you are in Derbyshire. We both send regards – Saluti a suo marito.[1]

DHL

1691. To Catherine Carswell, 23 January 1919
Text: MS YU; cited in Carswell 107.

Mountain Cottage, Middleton by Wirksworth, Derby
Thursday. 23 Jan 1919

My dear Catherine

I wondered whether you were back: your letter came yesterday: the MS.

---

[1] 'Greetings to your husband.'

D. H. Lawrence, 1920–1, from a portrait by Marie Hubrecht

Emily and Margaret King, 1918

Gilbert Cannan, c. 1910

Mary Cannan, c. 1910

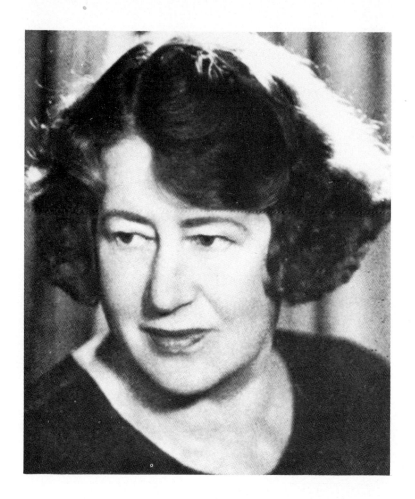

Beatrice Campbell, 1925

Godwin Baynes, 1913

Rosalind Baynes, c. 1911

Robert Mountsier

Hilda (Doolittle) Aldington, 1918

Michael Sadleir, 1921

Dorothy ('Arabella') Yorke, from a portrait by D. H. Lawrence

Ada Clarke, William Hopkin, Edwin Clarke, Frieda Lawrence, Sallie Hopkin,
Gertrude Cooper, D. H. Lawrence and Dr Mullan-Feroze,
near Mountain Cottage, Middleton-by-Wirksworth, 1918

Donald and John Patrick Carswell, 1921

Douglas Goldring, 1929

Thomas Seltzer

Max Plowman, 1917

Compton Mackenzie, c. 1918

Francis Brett Young, 1922, from a portrait by Cathleen Mann

Jessica Brett Young, 1914

Marie Hubrecht, c. 1914

Marie Hubrecht at Rocca Forte, Taormina

Albert Curtis Brown, c. 1921

Carlota Thrasher on her farm

today.[1] The MS. doesn't matter at all – I have duplicates. No news here. Freeman sent me back my little essays. 'I was deeply interested, but feel myself rather out of my depth. – I have consulted another opinion, and we feel that this is rather matter for a book than a supplement.' – So be it. They are just cowards, and there one must leave 'em, all the lot of 'em. Je m'en fiche of the whole show. – Barbara saw the essays – showed them to Stanley Unwin, who wants me to write as much again, and he will publish in a little book, and give me £15. down.[2] So it is not waste. – Meanwhile I am finishing my *European History*, for the Oxford Press: Have only one more chapter – I shall get £50 down for that. We have sold up in Cornwall and shall live on the proceeds in the interim. I feel I am shaking myself free to get out of this country, for good and ever.

Frieda has had a bad cold – is rather better. She sends love. I'm sorry you had a bad time in Scotland – I always feel bad when I turn north. I think one should set one's back to it, and to all the past, and strike out into a new line – if possible. – I hope the pots won't disappoint you: they'll match the other things in your room.

By now I am utterly bored with social and political England – Europe too – I don't believe in them in the least – none of 'em – don't even want to any more. I've really fallen out of the reckoning, so I ought to be able to walk off soon. It's all I want.

Glad J[ohn] P[atrick] is well again, in his native air. My God, teeth already! he'll be smoking a cigarette in our faces before we know where we are.

Love from both   DHL

1692. To Benjamin Huebsch, 27 January 1919
Text: MS UT; Postmark, [Wirk]sworth 27 JA 19; Moore 577.

Mountain Cottage, Middleton by Wirksworth, Derbyshire – England.

27 Jan. 1919.

Dear Mr Huebsch,

Thank you for the notice of your publications, which I received the other day. Will you please tell me how *Look We Have Come Through* is received in America. And will you tell me if there is any sale of the *Prussian Officer* and *Twilight in Italy*. I ask Pinker, my agent in London, but can get nothing out of him.

---

[1] Unidentified.
[2] Stanley Unwin (1884–1968) had founded the publishing firm of George Allen & Unwin Ltd in 1914.

Have you seen anything of my *Studies in Classic American Literature* –
essays that are appearing in the *English Review* here? I wrote them for
America, and think a lot of them myself. They've had a good deal of notice
here. I'll ask Harrison to send you those that are published – four, that will
be.[1] There are a dozen essays in all: I don't know if he'll go patiently on to the
end.

I want very much to come to America this summer, and expect to be able to
do so: though I don't know anybody in the whole USA., at present, save Amy
Lowell. I like your list of publications. I hope we shall meet before long.

                                    Yours Sincerely   D. H. Lawrence[2]

1693. To Katherine Mansfield, [29 January 1919]

Text: MS NYPL; PC v. The Green and Basin, Middleton; Postmark, [Matl]ock Bath 29 JA 19;
Murry, *New Adelphi*, 'Mansfield', 282.

                                              [29 January 1919]

I wonder if you are not so well again, that you have not written. Did you get
the white frock F[rieda] sent? – I doubt you wouldn't like it. – We have both
got bad colds, and curse the day. It is all snow on the ground, and a dark sky.
Oh Spring! Send us a word to say you are all right. Cath. Carswell is home –
depressed also. Wonder when we shall all get out? – everything seems so
shaky and nasty.

                                              DHL

1694. To Harriet Monroe, 1 February 1919

Text: MS UChi; cited in Harriet Monroe, *Poetry*, xxxvi (May 1930), 92.

                        Mountain Cottage, Middleton-by-Wirksworth, Derby
                                                      1 Feb. 1919

My dear Miss Monro,
    I have received your letter and the proof of the poems: I am glad you liked

---

[1] DHL is anticipating the publication of 'Fenimore Cooper's Anglo-American Novels' which
    appeared in the *English Review*, xxviii (February 1919), 88–99. The first three published were
    'The Spirit of Place', 'Benjamin Franklin' and 'Henry St. John de Crèvecoeur': see
    pp. 270 n. 1 and 299 n. 4.
[2] Huebsch replied on 22 April 1919 to this letter (TMSC LC). He warmly encouraged DHL to
    visit USA; offered help in arranging lectures by DHL to cover his expenses; and added his
    willingness to do 'anything else in which you think I may be of service'.
       The verso of DHL's envelope carries the official declaration: 'OPENED BY CENSOR'.

them.[1] – I have written to ask Martin Secker for a copy of the *New Poems*, for you. I will post it to you myself – am afraid he is not very trustworthy. If ever you want his address he is

Martin Secker, Publisher, 17 Buckingham St., Adelphi, London, W.C.

I have also asked Harrison to send you copies of the *English Review* with the essays on Classic American Literature which are appearing there. I wish you would tell me if you like them. I have worked at them for more than four years – hard work. They may not look it. – I want them to appear in America – there are twelve essays in all.

You will send me *Poetry*. I always like to see it. The American tone usually sets the English back up: and I suppose the English tone sets the American back up: in literature I mean. But I do believe America has a real will-to-live, and that attracts me most. It is not indecision which prevents my coming to America, but damnable circumstance. I do hope I shall see you and your Chicago this summer.

Excuse the crooked writing – I am laid up for the moment.

Yours Sincerely   D. H. Lawrence

1695. To Nancy Henry, 3 February 1919
Text: MS Lazarus; Huxley 466–7.

Middleton by Wirksworth, Derby
Monday 3 Feb 1919

Dear Mrs Henry

I am so sorry you have been laid up: do hope you'll get sound again soon. The weather is vicious, I think. I've been in bed a day or two also. – Here the snow lies: it is rather lovely, but very cold.

I don't know whether I ought to step in with advice. But I *do* think it would be unwise to give up your job, unless you have some other provision. Never has it been so difficult to make money by any form of art: never has the artist had such a bad chance: and never has the world been so coldly indifferent, never has it clutched its shillings more tightly. Everybody feels we are just marking time before a débâcle, and nobody is going to waste one *serious* moment on art at all, or on charity. Your husband doesn't know what the world is like now. It is not as it was five years ago. – If you are going to put yourself in a position to starve, starve you actually will: have no illusion about

---

[1] Harriet Monroe published six of DHL's poems in *Poetry*, xiii (February 1919), 258–64: 'Tommies in the Train', 'War-Baby', 'Obsequial Chant', 'Bread upon the Waters', 'Pentecostal' and 'Nostalgia'. (All the poems were published in *Bay*.)

it. The day has gone by when fairy godmothers stepped in. The tension of the struggle for possession of money grows so strong, that you must actually be on one side or the other, either earning or producing money, or you are less than nothing. – And he, if he is going to produce music, let him produce it out of the courage of his own soul. That other business is a form of prostitution. One should not prostitute oneself, even to art. The art can't be vital, anyway – must be spurious. If you are wise you will keep your job: there are days coming when art will not save us: neither you nor me nor anybody.

I am glad you like the history. I send you here the last four chapters. I thought of calling it *Movements in European History*. Do you think that is all right? – I suppose it will be anonymous – Ely won't want my name – and I don't want it on the book, either. If a pseudonym is useful to the publishers, we can apply one.[1] – Let me know about maps, will you. I hate bothering you when you are knocked up.

Kindest regards from us both   D. H. Lawrence

1696. To Amy Lowell, 5 February 1919
Text: MS HU; cited in Moore, *Intelligent Heart* 250.

Mountain Cottage, Middleton by Wirksworth, Derby
5 Feby. 1919

My dear Amy

I heard from Harriett Monroe that you did not receive the two copies of *New Poems* which Secker sent you. I am sorry. He is sending you now another copy.

You have not written at all since you sent *Can Grande* in the autumn – nor answered my letters. – By the way, is Can Grande's castle the Della Scala palazzo in Verona? – Can Grande was a Della Scala, I believe. – It is very cold here. We have both been ill. I want spring and summer, terribly.

Will you come to Europe? I shall probably manage to come to America in the summer. Let us have a word from you.

mila saluti buoni   D. H. Lawrence

1697. To S. S. Koteliansky, 8 February 1919
Text: MS BL; Zytaruk 159.

Mountain Cottage, Middleton by Wirksworth, Derby
8 Feb. 1919

My dear Kot,

I wrote you straight away, some time ago, and congratulated you on your

---

[1] This proposal coincided with the determination of Humphry Milford (1877–1952), Publisher to the University of Oxford since 1913, that *Movements in European History* should not appear under DHL's own name (see Nehls, i. 471). See p. 261 n. 7.

heroism, and asked you to come and stay with us a bit. Frieda enclosed a note also. Did you never receive that letter? I wondered why you did not answer.

I have at the present moment got £20; – £5. from Harrison and £15. from selling up in Cornwall. So I must send back your cheque, for I fear to imagine myself richer than I am. If I thought I had thirty pounds to lash out with, heaven knows what I might do. Sufficient unto the day is the good thereof.[1]

I read about London in the newspaper – and am not thrilled. What a great nation we are! If the tube stops running, the commonwealth collapses.[2] Basta! Here it is terribly frozen and snowy. I have been in bed for a week with a cold, but am much better. The sun shines, but the windows are covered with very magnificent ice flowers, so we are obscured as if in a frozen under-sea.

There isnt anything really to say. I hear the Derby railway men are anticipating a strike.

> 'Strike while the iron's hot, boys.'

I often wonder about Grisha, how he is getting on. Remember me very nicely to Sonia and Ghita. It is so cold, one could almost speak Russian.

Vale   DHL

1698. To Katherine Mansfield, 9 February 1919

Text: MS NYPL; Murry, *New Adelphi*, 'Mansfield', 282–3.

Middleton
Sunday 9 Feb 1919

My dear Katharine –

I send you *I Promessi Sposi*[3] and *Peru*.[4] I thought you would like the other two. I am very fond of George Sand – have read only *François le Champi* and *Maître Sonneurs* and *Villemer* – I liked *Maître Sonneurs* immensely.[5] Have

---

[1] Matthew vi. 34 ['. . . the evil thereof'].

[2] The London Underground was closed by a strike of motormen (over hours of work) on 4 February; the strike was settled on the 6th and train services were completely restored on the 10th. But this strike had been linked to a threat by the trade union to call out all its members and to bring the entire railway system to a halt (hence DHL's later reference to 'the Derby railway men'). The railway strike was only one among many in England, Scotland and Northern Ireland: DHL's remarks (here and later) reflect apprehension about the general state of the country.

[3] The Italian novel ('The Betrothed', 1827) by Alessandro Manzoni (1785–1873).

[4] William Hickling Prescott, *History of the Conquest of Peru* (1847).

[5] Novels by George Sand (Lucile-Aurore Dupin) (1804–76): *François le Champi* (Paris, 1856); *Les Maîtres Sonneurs* (Paris, 1852); *Le Marquis de Villemer* (Paris, 1860).

you any George Sand? and Mary Mann is quite good, I think.[1] – It is
marvellous weather – brilliant sunshine on the snow, clear as summer,
slightly golden sun, distance lit up. But it is immensely cold. – everything
frozen solid – milk, mustard everything. Yesterday I went out for a real walk –
I've had a cold and been in bed. I climbed with my niece to the bare top of the
hills. Wonderful is to see the footmarks on the snow – beautiful ropes of
rabbit prints, trailing away over the brows; heavy hare marks; a fox so sharp
and dainty, going over the wall; birds with two feet that hop; very splendid
straight advance of a pheasant; wood-pigeons that are clumsy and move in
flocks; splendid little leaping marks of weasels, coming along like a necklace
chain of berries; odd little filigree of the field-mice; the trail of a mole – it is
astounding what a world of wild creatures one feels round one, on the hills in
the snow. From the height it is very beautiful. The upland is naked, white like
silver, and moving far into the distance, strange and muscular, with gleams
like skin. Only the wind surprises one, invisibly cold; the sun lies bright on a
field, like the movement of a sleeper. It is strange how insignificant, in all this,
life seems. Two men, tiny as dots, move from a farm on a snow-slope,
carrying hay to the beast. Every moment, they seem to melt like insignificant
spots of dust. The sheer, living, muscular white of the uplands absorbs
everything. Only there is a tiny clump of trees bare on the hill-top – small
beeches – writhing like iron in the blue sky. – I wish one could cease to be a
human being, and be a demon. – Allzu Menschlich.[2]

My sister Emily is here, with her little girl – whose birthday it is today –
Emily is cooking treacle rolly and cakes, Frieda is making Peggy a pale grey
dress, I am advising and interfering – Pamela is lamenting because the eggs in
the pantry have all frozen and burst – I have spent half an hour hacking ice out
of the water tub – now I am going out. Peggy, with her marvellous red-gold
hair in dangling curl-rags, is darting about sorting the coloured wools and
cottons – scène de famille. – It is beautiful to cross the field to the well for
drinking water – such pure sun, and Slaley, the tiny village away across,
sunny as Italy in its snow. – I expect Willie Hopkin will come today.

Well – life itself is life – even the magnificent frost-foliage on the window.
While we live, let us live –

DHL

Emily's nickname was Pamela, or *Virtue Rewarded*.[3]

[1] The prolific and moralising writer, Mary E. Mann (d. 1929), whose works 'disappointed'
    DHL at an earlier stage. See *Letters*, i. 256, 525.
[2] 'But one is all too human.' (Probably carrying an allusion to Nietzsche's *Menschliches,
    Allzumenschliches*, 1876–8.)
[3] Cf. the title of Samuel Richardson's novel (1740).

1699. To S. S. Koteliansky, [26 February 1919]
Text: MS BL; Zytaruk 160.

[Grosvenor Road, Ripley, Derbyshire]
Wed[1]

My dear Kot

Thank you for all the things – dont send so much. Tea sweets and honey came today. Today for the first time I have food – not only accursed milk – also for the first time sit up in bed and write this – so shall soon be better – get out of bed for $\frac{1}{2}$ hour next Sunday. – Am very weary and a little downhearted however – the world seems so nasty ahead of one. Will write again. Hope to see you before long.

DHL

[Frieda Lawrence begins]

I will write to-morrow all about him – It is cheering to have you there,
F.

1700. To S. S. Koteliansky, [28 February 1919]
Text: MS BL; Zytaruk 161.

Ripley –
Friday

My dear Kot

Yesterday came the grapefruit – a godsend – they are so good – one doesn't want to eat, except these.

I am getting better – shall get out of bed on Sunday for $\frac{1}{2}$ hour – still have the cough and the heart-pains, but not so much.

I am going to the seaside – we want to find a cottage. My Uncle will drive me in his motor car, he says.[2] Do you know a place?

I think even my soul is recovering. I thought it was cracked for ever. But no, I shall shake off the world.

Perhaps you will come and stay with us at the seaside – will you?

I'll write again   DHL

My uncle has sent 2 champagne – what luxuries.

---

[1] Dated by DHL's remark that he will 'get out of bed . . . next Sunday'; the Sunday can be established as 2 March 1919 by reference to the postmarked letter to Catherine Carswell (Letter 1701).
[2] Most probably Fritz Krenkow.

1701. To Catherine Carswell, [28 February 1919]
Text: MS YU; Postmark, Ripley 28 F[. . .] 19; cited in Carswell, *Adelphi* 393.

Ripley –
Friday

My dear Catherine

I couldn't thank you before for the wine – it really started my inside into life. Thank goodness I am getting better – what a nasty disease – I have never felt so down in the mud in all my life – a putrid disease. – I shall get out of bed for ½ hr. on Sunday.

We want to find a cottage at the seaside. The Midlands will be the death of me. Do you know a place? We must meet in some nice place – life is too unbearably foul – we must meet and have a little happy time.

Thank D[onald] for his letter. I'll write again.

DHL

My uncle has now sent 2 champagne.

1702. To S. S. Koteliansky, [1 March 1919]
Text: MS BL; Zytaruk 162.

Ripley –
Saturday

My dear Kot

The brandy and port came on Wednesday – Frieda says she told you – I'm sorry you didn't know. The brandy is very good and soft. Spare Selfridges.

Tell Sophie Isaayevna I shall write to her. – Poor Beatrice, let me know if she lands safely. – Do you go and see Katharine? – I think she's been very ill too.

I shrink from putting my foot out of bed into the world again.

DHL

1703. To Harriet Monroe, 2 March 1919
Text: MS UChi; cited in Monroe, *Poetry*, xxxvi (May 1930), 92.

Mountain Cottage, Middleton-by-Wirksworth, Derby
2 March. 1919

Dear Miss Monroe

I have received your letter and the cheque for seven guineas[1] – which is very generous. I hope you got the *New Poems* I sent – also the *English Review*s.

[1] In payment for DHL's six poems in *Poetry*: see p. 325 n. 1. (The poems were re-published in *Bay*: hence the later reference to 'Beaumonts proofs').

I am not sure if I should have acknowledged *Poetry* in the *Poems*. Don't be angry with me if I have forgotten. I really will remember when I get Beaumonts proofs: heaven knows when he will send them, for I believe he is in difficulties – money. – Excuse the pencil – I have been struggling with the Flu for a month, and am still in bed, – am getting better: a very nasty disease. – As soon as I am well and Peace will be signed we are due to go to Germany, where my dear old Frau Baronin mother-in-law[1] sits in lament in Baden-Baden, my brother-in-law manages to weather the storms in Munich, and remain Minister of Finance to the new Bavarian republic, a cousin bobs up and down in Berlin, and so on. I want to come to America this summer, and I will, if the gods are not too spiteful. At present however a voyage autour de ma chambre[2] finishes me. – You have got a big lake at Chicago, haven't you? I should like that. – I should like to see you all in Chicago very much indeed – after all poetry is a great freemasonry.

I shall send you a copy of the Beaumont poems, when they appear. Anne Estelle Rice has done drawings for them – do you know her? – she is American.[3]

The sun shines – the snowdrops are out in the garden, under the bushes. I long to begin life afresh, in a new country.

mila saluti buoni   D. H. Lawrence

1704. To S. S. Koteliansky, [6 March 1919]
Text: MS BL; Zytaruk 163.

Ripley – Derbyshire
Thursday[4]

My dear Kot

The grape-fruit have come – just as the last were finished. I wonder if Katharine has them – they are such a good fruit.

I am getting better – today I shall try to go downstairs. It is the stairs I fear. But I want to go back to Middleton. Perhaps next Wednesday I can be driven up. I give up the seaside idea: too great a struggle to travel to a new place. Next month we might go to Hermitage – or we may stay at Middleton. Frieda

---

[1] mother-in-law] stepmother
[2] An allusion to the novel, *Voyage autour de ma Chambre* (Paris, 1794) by François Xavier de Maistre (1763–1852). Cf. *Letters*, i. 341.
[3] Painter, m. Raymond Drey. She was a close friend of Katherine Mansfield. See p. 238 n. 2, Letter 1742 and *Letters*, ii. 404 n. 7. (For an article on her Fauvist paintings, see the first issue of *Rhythm*, ed. Murry and Mansfield, 1911.)
[4] The contents of this letter make clear that it and the two following were written on the same day, Thursday 6 March 1919.

wants to go to Germany as soon as we can – I too want to leave England. – Eder will come this month to Middleton to see me – what if I went to Palestine! I feel I *must* get out or I shall die of soul-suffocation – out of this island. I wonder when one can go.

Murry has asked me to contribute to his *Athenæum*.[1] That is very nice, and I shall be pleased to have a try at it.

I will write to Pinker soon – it nauseates me, all that business of publishers and publication.

The day is sunny. I must lay fresh hold on life. – Thank you for the fruits. – How do you feel yourself? Are you very bored?

au revoir   DHL

1705. To John Middleton Murry, [6 March 1919]
Text: MS NYPL; cited in Murry, *New Adelphi*, 'Reminiscences', 324.

Ripley – Derbyshire
Thursday

My dear Jack

I am very pleased about the *Athenæum* – I do hope you'll enjoy it and that it will be successful. Thank you for asking me to contribute – that pleases me too. I should like to do it. But you must tell me exactly what you would like me to do, and I will try to be pleasant and a bit old-fashioned. I don't mind if I am anonymous – or a nom de plume.[2] When is it to begin? Tell me particulars as soon as you can – so that I can think about it while I am still not well, and make little ideas. That amuses me.

I've been awfully seedy and wretched with this Flu – but am getting better. Today I am going to make an effort, to creep downstairs. In a week's time I want to be taken back to Middleton – It is very shut in here. When it is possible, we want to go to Munich. When do you think it will be possible? If other things fail I might go to Palestine with Eder. I must leave England – no use for me here any more. I am quite at the end of everything here.

We may come to Hermitage in April – perhaps you would come and see us there. I want to get on my legs and feel I am moving again – moving into a new phase. A new phase starts now, for us all.

Write and tell me as soon as you can what you would like me to do, exactly, and when it is to begin.

Yrs   DHL

[1] See Letter 1688 and n. 4.
[2] DHL's only contribution to *Athenæum* – his essay 'Whistling of Birds' on 11 April 1919 – was printed under the pseudonym, 'Grantorto'. See p. 100 n. 2.

1706. To Lady Cynthia Asquith, 6 March 1919
Text: MS UT; Unpublished.

c/o Mrs Clarke, Grosvenor Rd, *Ripley* – Derbyshire
6 March 1919

I have received your letter and the play[1] here. About the latter, never mind. I am sorry about the infant, though I ought not to say so.[2] My mother never wanted me to be born, yet am I not a gem of life? – I have been miserably ill with the Flu and its complications – came here to my sister's house three weeks ago – suddenly collapsed – am still in bed, but get up for an hour at tea-time. – I dreamed of you two nights ago – that you came to see me and we went together to Heanor church, to some crowded service.

In a week's time I hope to be taken back to Middleton. We shall stay there some weeks, I suppose. Frieda's people want us to go to Germany as soon as possible. My brother-in-law manages to weather the storms and remain Minister of Finance to the Bavarian republic. Have you any idea when we can go to Germany? If you have, do tell me. – Later on I shall go to America – but perhaps first to Palestine. I think I shall leave this country for ever, now at last. It has no use for me nor I for it, and the world seems wide, outside.

Has your husband come home? What are you going to do? Let me know. – I have only one desire – to go out into the world, to wander. Perhaps it is a sick-room desire only.

The spring is coming, the sun shines. I do want to lay fresh hold on life, and start off in a new direction. A phase is finished now – a big phase. It remains to re-emerge.

Frieda is well. She wants to go to Germany – for a time only, of course. She sends her love.

Don't bother a bit about the play – the hour isn't ripe. I don't bother.

Well, I feel a bit sad – but things will probably turn out all right for you, quite soon. Write and let me know how you are.

DHL

1707. To Stanley Hocking, 8 March 1919
Text: MS BucU; cited in Nehls, i. 427.

Ripley – Derbyshire.
8 March 1919

Dear Stanley

I hope your sickness is better. – Your letter reached me here – where I have

---

[1] *Touch and Go.*
2 Lady Cynthia must have told DHL of her third pregnancy. See Letter 1794.

been in bed this last three weeks, with Flu and its complications – have been wretchedly ill, but am getting better – can get up for tea now. Next week I want to be taken back to Mountain Cottage – it is only twenty minutes in a motor car. I shan't be able to travel far for a couple of months. My uncle wants to drive me to the sea-side – Cromer or some such place – when I am well enough – but I dont want to be dragged about.

The rug arrived very nicely – thank you for packing it up. I heard from Capt Short in Cardiff some time back – I must answer him.

The spring is coming – I have all kinds of flowers in my room. I suppose at Tregerthen there are lambs, and the first primroses – far off it seems. I hate to be ill. – The idea of Jacky's marrying seems a little gruesome. What sort of woman would take him.[1]

We shall go abroad when I am well enough – to Germany or Switzerland, or perhaps even to Palestine for a little time. In Munich my brother-in-law manages to weather the storms, and remain Minister of Finance for Bavaria. But I don't quite know how things are going in Berlin. Europe is a stupid, wearisome place.

I do hope you are all well, and that your sickness did not amount to anything. Tell me how many lambs there are – and if they are flourishing – and if the blackthorn is in bud in the chapel hollow, and if celandines are out by the Zennor path.

Mrs Lawrence is well, and sends warm regards. Remember me very kindly to your mother, and all the others.

D. H. Lawrence

1708. To Beatrice Campbell, 10 March 1919
Text: MS UCin; Irvine and Kiley, *DHL Review*, vi (1973), 14–15.

c/o Mrs Clarke, Grosvenor Rd, Ripley, Derbyshire
10 March 1919

Dear Beatrice

Your letter came on Saturday, the sweets and butter today – glad you are better – understand that you feel like a bit of wreckage that will be swept off again next high tide. Gordon is like a strip of litmus paper, apparently. Dip him in a Dublin atmosphere, and he turns bright British red: dip him in a strong solution of St Johns Wood, and out he comes, the green, the green, the emerald green. – What are the chances that he'll be back in London

---

[1] Jacky was a tenant farmer and near neighbour of the Hockings. He was 'almost a dwarf and was regarded as something of a figure of fun' (see Richard Gilbertson, 'D. H. Lawrence in Cornwall', *Antiquarian Book Monthly Review*, February 1980, p. 75).

permanently, in a month or two?[1] Depends perhaps whether he feels London a safe investment for his services. – I am a wretched object like a drowned ghost creeping downstairs to tea – properly hate my condition, I can tell you.

I suppose I'll get strong enough again one day to slap Frieda in the eye, in the proper marital fashion. At present I am reduced to vituperation.

Shall we ever see the Emerald Isle, do you think? Somehow to me it is like a blank round O on the map – a sort of nowhere. Perhaps fate will fill it in.

I want to be taken back to Middleton this week – shut in here. I feel a bit as if I were sliding off the face of everything – heaven knows where the slide will land one. We've all sort of come unstuck – I see Kot rolling like black pebble to some Russian perdition, and Gordon swinging on a lamp-post, and Gertler casting himself into the Regents Park Canal, you floating a little luminous in the distance, like Dante's Beatrice down below, Murry with crape round his arm, for Katharine.

Do write and tell us the news. The butter is a great kindness, for I sicken at margarine. Frieda is well – has got her eye fixed on her Fatherland – sends her love. I wish we could bring off some nice happy scheme of a reunion.

Yrs DHL

1709. To S. S. Koteliansky, [11 March 1919]
Text: MS BL; Zytaruk 164.

Ripley –
Tuesday

My dear Kot

I am going to be motored up to Middleton next Sunday – it is so shut in here. I go downstairs to tea – but am so tiresomely feeble, I can't walk. – I suppose in a month we can go to Hermitage. My sister will go to Middleton with us, she is the responsible nurse. – Eder is coming – I don't exactly know when. – I feel as if we never should get out of this beetle-trap of an island – but June, you say – I'll look to June. – Murry vaguely asked me to contribute to the *Athenæum* – but he doesn't tell me what he wants, nor when he wants it. I feel fearfully mistrustful of him – feel sure we shall be let down. Poor Katharine – I'm afraid she is only just on the verge of existence. – Beatrice wrote to me very nicely from Ireland – told me about Gordon. Did you see him this week-end, and what was he like? Beatrice sent me a pound of butter – a great kindness, for margarine is uneatable. If ever you *can* get 4 ozs. of China tea, do – I hate the black taste of the other. – But $\frac{1}{4}$ lb will last me a long time,

---

[1] Gordon Campbell was Secretary to the Irish Department of the Ministry of Labour, 1919–22.

don't buy any more. – Of course if I went to Palestine it would only be for a little while, and as a *pis aller*. Don't become cynical. – Is there any newspaper news – I daren't read the papers, I become at once ill.

How reduced we all are – only a few fragments of us left! The world has walked over us and trodden us very small. I suppose one day we shall spring up like corn.

Remember me very nicely to Sonia and Ghita. I suppose we'll have a meeting before long.

DHL

1710. To Catherine Carswell, [11 March 1919]
Text: MS YU; cited in Carswell 107.

c/o Mrs Clarke, Grosvenor Rd, Ripley, Derbyshire
Tuesday

My dear Catherine

I got your little letter – did you receive mine, which must have crossed? I am getting well – but am so weak. I go downstairs to tea. On Sunday I am to be taken back to Mountain Cottage – only 20 minutes in a motor car. We have given up the seaside idea – shall stay at Middleton till I can travel, then go to Hermitage. I trust to see you there. I am glad you are all well, but imagine you feel a bit dreary. My God, how can it be otherwise. I long to get out of England. Eder is coming to Middleton to see us and talk about Palestine. Did you know that Murry is editor of the *Athenæum*, which is to be revived. I am to contribute. Good thing if I could earn a little weekly money. But I don't trust Murry.

I am glad J[ohn] P[atrick] is so flourishing – He is a satisfaction, at any rate. But life for us grown-ups is a dead rat, at present. I feel one must get out, by hook or crook – out into a new atmosphere. I suppose you have no plans.

When I can walk and feel a bit stronger, I shall be glad. I suppose in April we can go to Hermitage. Do come and see us there. Did you know the Campbells have gone to Ireland – he has taken a job there. Soon there will be nobody left. – Cynthia Asquith is going to have another baby – and feels doomed. Oh Lord! – Has Don got any briefs?

Don't you wish we could make real wild departure plans? Damn it, we've been buried long enough, like toads under a muck-heap. Time we crawled out.

Did I ever properly thank you for the muscatel? It was *so* good, and so reviving. I liked it better than the champagne.

Come, I feel we've been down long enough. Time we got up. Let us have a meeting soon, and defy the devil. Don't you feel you've been Hampstead-stifled, or England-stifled, long enough. Let us breathe.

Send me your news. Love from us both to you three. Write soon.

DHL

1711. To S. S. Koteliansky, [14 March 1919]
Text: MS BL; Moore 581.

Ripley – Derby
Friday

My dear Kot

The grape fruit came. They are at their best now – perfectly ripe. I am getting stronger. I am feeble now because the doctor says I was run down to start with, and have been very ill – for two days he said he feared I should not pull through. But doctors – bah! Anyhow I am nearly myself again, in my soul if not in my body. I have walked out a few yards. But it is *so* cold: as cold here as at Middleton. If the weather is fine we are going to Mountain Cottage on Sunday.

It would be fun to go to Ireland soon – perhaps we can do it. The expense deters me a little. We'll see.

My sister goes with us to Middleton. I am not going to be left to Frieda's tender mercies until I am well again. She really is a devil – and I feel as if I would part from her for ever – let her go alone to Germany, while I take another road. For it is true, I have been bullied by her long enough. I really could leave her now, without a pang, I believe. The time comes, to make an end, one way or another. If this illness hasn't been a lesson to her, it has to me.

Write next to Middleton – I will tell you how we get on. – My sister also broke her glasses last week – so she cannot laugh at you. But she borrows mine.

I have been trying to write for the *Athenæum*. Why is it such a cold effort to do these things? – Have you seen Barbara lately – she is suddenly very silent. – I *do* wish it would be warm.

DHL

1712. To J. B. Pinker, 15 March 1919
Text: MS BosU; Unpublished.

Mountain Cottage, Middleton by Wirksworth, Derby.[1]

15 March 1919.

My dear Pinker

I send you this play, which you saw before.[2] Some time it might be useful.

I have been ill for some weeks – am just getting better – nearly died with that damned Flu. and its complications. This winter is absolutely too much. It still snows fitfully here. I shall come south as soon as I can travel.

Would you send me that MS. of tiny poems – was it called 'All of Us'. You gave it to me, because C.W. Beaumont asked to see it.[3] He says he thinks he sent it back to you.[4] Did he? – or has he got it still? If he has, would you ask him for it.

And when will he publish that little volume *Bay*, I wonder.

I hope things are well with you.

Yrs   D. H. Lawrence

1713. To Katherine Mansfield, [20 March 1919]
Text: MS NYPL; Murry, *New Adelphi*, 'Mansfield', 284–5.

Middleton –
Thursday

My dear Katharine

Deledda is very interesting[5] – except the middle bit, in Rome: so is *Martyrdom of Man*.[6] The latter I really know – one has read so many fat books on Egypt and Africa and Gaul and what not. The *Martyrdom* would stand a good bit of correcting, really.

It is snow snow snow here – white white white. Yesterday was the endless silence of softly falling snow. I thought the world had come to an end – that I was like a last inhabitant of the moon, when the moon shed all its snow and went into a white dream for ever, slowly breathing its last in a soft, dim snowfall, silent beyond silence. Nobody comes, the snow is white on the shrubs, the tuft of larches above the road have each a white line up the trunk. Lord, Lord! Only the rabbit feet and bird feet are all over the paths and across

---

[1] By using this address DHL was anticipating his return to Middleton; the move occurred on 17 March (see Letter 1714).
[2] *Touch and Go.*
[3] See p. 219 and n. 1.
[4] Pinker, or someone in his office, wrote on the letter: '(we haven't it)'.
[5] See Letter 1322 and n. 2.
[6] William Winwood Reade, *The Martyrdom of Man* (1872).

the yard. – I am still very limp with my cold – but F[rieda] is better. – We got two newspapers today – occasionally the postman brings us one. – Pretty place London seems. It seems as if the dear old régime of happy industrial England is slowly and greasily melting like a dead thaw. I suppose it will take it ages and ages really to thaw itself out, yellow and slushy, without fire or swiftness, lapsing by the passive resistance of strikes. I hate it – but let it go.

Your last letter was cryptic. Do tell me what you mean by 'The bowl and the tureen have just come – but you will know by now'. That is how you began – utterly mysterious. Also what is Murry's fame? I half expected to see in the newspaper Lloyd George, like another John in the desert, asserting of your John 'Behold him, the latchet of whose shoes I am not worthy to unloose[1] – John Middleton Murry!' – But I didn't see it. Please explain these deep things.

My sister Ada has got her husband home, out of the navy. I suppose my elder sister, whose husband is in hospital at the moment, will soon get him discharged. Then I really think we shall come to Hermitage – next month – to see the wild snowdrops – there are wild snowdrops – and the white violets, and the wood anemones – and the trees coming in bud, the plum blossom in the garden. I feel Hermitage would be a pleasant meeting-ground – not so grim as here.

I think these two are the books that would amuse you most, for the moment. I think the others didn't attract you. I got these from my sister. – There is a pheasant comes and lies by the wall under the gooseberry bushes, for shelter. He is so cold, he hardly notices us. We plan to catch him, by throwing over him the netted hammock. But for the sake of his green head and his long, pointed feathers, I cannot. We thought we would catch him and send him to you to eat. But when I look at him, so clear as he is and formal on the snow, I am bound to respect a thing which attains to so much perfection of grace and bearing.

Love from both   DHL

I shall send your books back when Frieda has read them.

1714. To S. S. Koteliansky, 20 March 1919

Text: MS BL; Postmark, Wirksworth 20 MR 19; Zytaruk, ed., *Malahat Review*, i. 34–5.

Mountain Cottage, Middleton by Wirksworth, Derby.
20 March 1919.

My dear Kot

We came here on Monday – it was sunny then. Tuesday was a mild sweet

---

[1] Luke iii. 16 ['but one mightier than I cometh, the latchet . . .', A.V.].

morning. Tuesday afternoon it began to snow – it has snowed ever since – deep and white. My sister Ada is here, with her little boy Jackie. Ada and Frieda beat the trees, which are being smashed down by weight of snow, I stare stupidly out of the window like a sick and dazed monkey. – I shall have to stay here for another month, as the doctor – the Parsee[1] – is coming over from Ripley to give me certain injections for the lungs. At the end of the month I shall fairly flee to Hermitage.

I had a letter from Horne, who is back from 2½ yrs. in Salonika, and is in London on leave not discharged.[2] I wrote to him, and shall see him if it is easy. If I don't like him I shant see him twice.

No news, save snow and blank stupidity – except, oh yes, Eder came to Ripley last week-end – brought me a bottle of claret, cake, sweets, and was very nice indeed. He is sailing with Mrs Eder and the younger boy on April 3rd. I have promised to go out to Palestine in September, leaving Frieda in Germany. In Palestine I am to view the land and write a Zioniad. What do you think of it?

My sister has given me 10/- for books – I haven't a shred to read. Get me these four books out of the *Everyman* series, will you? – they cost 1/9 each, don't they? – that will allow you to buy one vol. for Ghita – buy her *Swiss Family Robinson* or Johanna Spyri's *Heidi* – or Ballantyne's *Ungava* – or Collodi's *Pinocchio*[3] – or better still, let her choose for herself from the Everyman list. Anyhow buy Ghita a volume. 5 books at 1/9 = 8/9. That just leaves enough for postage. If they cost more than 1/9, leave out *Charles Auchester*.[4] – I have to make a scrupulous account, or you will be further robbing yourself, or sending back 6d in stamps, or some such tiresomeness. – I have lent Bates' *Amazon*, that you gave me, to Katharine. It is such a good book – takes one into the sun and the waters.

Au revoir   DHL

See Letter 1678 and n. 2.
[2] William K. Horne was employed, with Kot, at the Russian Law Bureau, 212 High Holborn. See *Letters*, ii. 205 n. 5.
[3] Popular children's books: Johann David Wyss, *The Swiss Family Robinson* (1818; Everyman's Library, 1910); Johanna Spyri, *Heidi* (1880?; Everyman's Library, 1910); Robert Michael Ballantyne, *Ungava: A Tale of Esquimeaux-Land* (1858; Everyman's Library, 1908); C. Collodi (Carlo Lorenzini), *Pinocchio: The Story of a Puppet* (1891; Everyman's Library, 1911).
[4] DHL is here referring to the list of books appended to his letter: Thomas Belt, *The Naturalist in Nicaragua* (1873; Everyman's Library, 1911); Nathaniel Morton, *Chronicles of the Pilgrim Fathers* (Everyman's Library, 1910); Edward Gibbon, *Autobiography* (1896; Everyman's Library, 1911); Elizabeth Sara Sheppard, *Charles Auchester: A Memorial* (1853; Everyman's Library, 1911).

1715. To Mark Gertler, 20 March 1919
Text: MS SIU; Huxley 474–5.

Mountain Cottage, Middleton by Wirksworth, Derbyshire
20 March 1919.

Dear Gertler

Here we are, deep in snow again. I am an irritable sort of convalescent. It would make me happy to paint. What I would best like to do is Ucello[1] – those hunting and fighting scenes – I would like to copy them. But send me a book, or two books, of reproductions, will you – black and white is all right – Fra Angelico, Giotto, Mantegna, Van Gogh – anybody with 'Composition' and hard figures and topical interest. Don't mind being bothered. – I shall send the books back safely.

In a month we come to Hermitage – I am not doctor-free till then. And then you will come and see us. I feel we must have great meetings, because great partings are probably imminent.

If you send an Ucello print, tell me the colours if you can – scarlet trunk-hose, snow, tree-shafts – you know.

Lord, I am sick of this winter.

D. H. Lawrence

Tell us your news – I have none – nothing.

1716. To S. S. Koteliansky, [25 March 1919]
Text: MS BL; Postmark, Wir[ksworth] 26 MR 19; Zytaruk 168.

Middleton –
Tuesday.

My dear Kot

The books, the grape fruit and the tea came this morning, and I was very glad. Please don't buy[2] Karavan tea – the very name sounds beyond words costly, like camels and eastern merchandise. I am ashamed at receiving so much from you. If you were the banker of the portrait I wouldn't turn a hair: but since you are the widow with the widow's mite,[3] in *my* excellent portrait of the future, it worries me. – I am sorry too that those damned books have risen to 2/-. I rook you of the postage now.

You read Anatole France first,[4] as I have got my books now. They look *very*

---

[1] Paolo Uccello (1397–1475), Florentine painter. He was distinguished by his use of geometrical composition and a particular feeling for abstract pictorial design. (See J. W. Pope-Hennessy, *The Complete Works of Paolo Uccello*, 1950.)

[2] MS reads 'by'.   [3] Mark xii. 42.

[4] Letter 1724 makes it clear that *Le Petit Pierre* (1918) by Anatole France (François Anatole Thibault) (1844–1924) was the book referred to.

attractive. Often I would give you a book – but I feel you would never read it, and it would only be an encumbrance to you. Tell me if that is so. Tell me if you would like me to send a book now and then – one that I have read and found good. I should like to do it.

Tell Gertler I got his postcards and the book. Tomorrow I will start. I copied a Teniers in the meantime – very nice.¹ But painting is not *my* art – only an amusement to me.

It is terribly cold here – deep snow still – and impossible for me to set foot out of doors. But now I have books and paints I shall be quite busy.

It is awfully nice to have china tea. Substitutes like the ordinary tea and margarine and jam become just offensive when one has been seedy. But I am really a lot *stronger* – if only I could go out.

Hope you and Gertler are both happy again by now.

au revoir   DHL

Horne didn't write again.

1717. To Louis Golding, 26 March 1919
Text: MS UT; Unpublished.

Mountain Cottage, Middleton by Wirksworth, Derby
26 March 1919

Dear Mr Golding²

Thank you for your letter, the essay, and the copies of *Voices*.³ The essay praises me too much – but why shouldn't I be praised, I have been insulted enough. – I have only looked through *Voices* as yet. I like it, it isn't Café Royal.⁴ The touch of preciosity I like, the quality of reverence. How old is Branford? – *why* do you print him Flight-Lieutenant, it seems almost comic.⁵

I will write later and send some poetry.

Yrs   D. H. Lawrence

¹ David Teniers (1610–90), the Dutch painter some of whose work in the Dulwich Art Gallery delighted DHL in 1909. See *Letters*, i. 124.
² Louis Golding (1895–1958), novelist, poet and critic; his first book – *Sorrow of War: Poems* – had appeared in February 1919.
³ The first issue of *Voices* (edited by Thomas Moult and published in Manchester, in January 1919) contained poems and a prose introduction by Golding.
⁴ i.e. unpretentious, avoiding the merely fashionable.
⁵ Flight-Lieutenant F. J. Branford (as he was described in *Voices*) contributed eight poems to the first issue. He was also a regular contributor of poems to the *English Review*.

1718. To Katherine Mansfield, [27 March 1919]
Text: MS NYPL; Murry, *New Adelphi*, 'Mansfield', 285.

[Mountain Cottage, Middleton by Wirksworth, Derby]
Thursday.

Frieda said you were cross with me, that I *repulsed* you. I'm sure I didn't. The complication of getting Jack and you and F. and me into a square seems great – especially Jack. But you I am sure of – I was ever since Cornwall, save for Jack – and if you must go his way, and if he will *never* really come our way – well! – But things will resolve themselves.

I dreamed such a vivid little dream of you last night. I dreamed you came to Cromford, and stayed there. You were not coming on here, because you weren't well enough. You were quite clear from the consumption – quite, you told me. But there was still something that made you that you couldn't come up the hill here.

So you went out with me as I was going. It was night, and very starry. We looked at the stars, and they were different. All the constellations were different, and I, who was looking for Orion, to show you, because he is rising now; was very puzzled by these thick, close brilliant new constellations. Then suddenly we saw one planet, so beautiful, a large, fearful, strong star, that we were both pierced by it, possessed, for a second. Then I said 'That's Jupiter' – but I felt that it wasn't Jupiter – at least not the everyday Jupiter.

Ask Jung[1] or Freud about it? – Never! – It was a star that blazed for a second on one's soul.

I wish it was spring for us all.

DHL

1719. To Irene Whittley, 29 March 1919
Text: MS UT; Unpublished.

Mountain Cottage, Middleton by Wirksworth, Derby.
29 March 1919

Dear Mrs Whittley

I am slow answering your letter – My wife wrote to you a short time ago, but she is very careless about addresses, so heaven knows if you got it.

I have been ill – since six weeks ago – with Flu. and its complications – am convalescent now, taking little shaky walks. It has been hateful.

We are staying here till April 24th., then going down to the cottage at

---

[1] MS reads 'Yung'.

Hermitage. Perhaps you and Whittley will come and see us there – will you? My wife expects to go to Switzerland or Germany in June, but I think it is too soon; I would rather we went about August, when things will be quieter and travelling easier. I dread the effort of a long, struggling journey to Munich – or even to Baden-Baden or Bellinzona.[1] At present I don't want to bother with anything. I hope my uncle will motor us down to Hermitage, to avoid the hateful train.

Here round the house and in our fields the snow lies thick. But the roads are free, and the valley below quite clear. But it is very cold still. I am weary beyond thought of this winter.

What is Whittley doing? Is he staying on in the Navy, or whatever it is? If we stay the summer in England, I should like to go to Tregerthen again, and look at it again, for I loved it. But Cornwall is a malicious place.

Do you ever see Starr or Gray in town – though I believe Meredith has left now.[2] He was usually to be found in the Café Royal. I hear Lady Mary had a baby, but have not ascertained the precise tint. Gray is still wandering round like a lost infant. – The Murrys are still in Hampstead: she still a great invalid. I expect she will go to the South of France, or to Madeira, this summer, to stay the winter through. He will remain in London. He is out of the War Office – editing the *Athenaeum*, which re-appears on April 4th. She also writes – signing herself Elizabeth Stanley.[3] As for me, I choose to be anonymous in the *Athenaeum* – Your father,[4] no doubt, would enjoy reading Elizabeth Stanley's small masterpieces. I think you should give him that pleasure.

I should like to see you and Whittley again. Do you remember a misty day, down in the wet fields, and big mushrooms which you had found when we came upon you? Ah Lord, how it all passes!

Best of wishes to you both from F[rieda] and me.

D. H. Lawrence

1720. To Else Jaffe, 29 March 1919
Text: Frieda Lawrence, *Nur der Wind* . . . (Berlin, 1936), pp. 139–40.

Middleton, Derby.
29. März 1919

Liebe Else,

Schon lange wollte ich Dir schreiben, bin aber an Influenza und ihren

---

[1] In Switzerland, 10 miles e. of Locarno.
[2] i.e. Meredith Starr (see p. 130 n. 4).
[3] Katherine Mansfield appropriated the name of her paternal grandmother.
[4] i.e. Captain Short.

Folgen krank gewesen. Eigentlich soll Frühling sein, aber um dies Haus liegt
noch Schnee – wir wohnen ziemlich hoch – und der Wind ist bitter kalt. Am
24. April wollen wir nach Chapel Farm Cottage. Dort ist es milder. Wir
wollen dort bleiben, bis wir England verlassen. Frieda sitzt wie auf Nadeln,
bis wir weg können. Vielleicht im Juli. Ich möchte auch kommen – sehr gern.
Von den Dingen hier habe ich genug. – Glaubst Du, daß einem Engländer in
Deutschland mit viel Abneigung begegnet würde? Ich denke nicht. Hier
machen die Arbeiter und inneren Sorgen den Krieg schon zu einem
abgeblaßten und halb vergessenen Ereignis und in Deutschland muß das
noch mehr so sein. Die psychische und geistige Atmosphäre ist unerfreulich.
Die menschlichen Wesen befinden sich wie es scheint in ihrer denkbar
übelsten Verfassung. Weiß der Himmel wie sich das klären soll. Wie Du
hasse ich eine vulgäre Demokratie, die sich über allem Leben breit macht.
Alles wird dadurch so niedrig, so gemein, nur materiell. Zwar war die alte
Kaiser- und Aristokraten-Ordnung veraltet, sicherlich. – Der gegenwärtige
Zustand scheint wie ein häßlicher Gedankenstrich in der Geschichte – eine
Art verkrampftes Nichts. Es wird wohl so sein müssen. Aber ich hätte lieber
nichts damit zu schaffen. – Ich glaube an die Auserwählten: die Auserwählten
sollten eine Welt aufbauen: nicht die Massen. –

Frieda geht es gut. Wir leben hier sehr still. Ich freue mich riesig, Euch alle
wieder zu sehen, wieder in einer größeren Landschaft zu sein – England ist
eng, in jeder Beziehung, außer im äußeren Behagen, das gibt es so reichlich
wie immer. Ich hoffe, daß Ihr endlich Nahrungsmittel bekommt.

Liebevolle Grüße, auf baldiges Wiedersehen

DHL

[Dear Else,
I've long wanted to write to you, but have been ill with influenza and its
effects. Really it ought to be spring, but snow still lies round the house – we
live rather high up – and the wind is bitter cold. On 24th April we want to go
to Chapel Farm Cottage. There it's milder. We want to stay there till we leave
England. Frieda sits as if on needles, till we can get away. Perhaps in July. I
should also like to come – very much. I have had enough of things here. – Do
you believe an Englishman would meet with a great deal of antipathy in
Germany? I think not. Here the workers and internal worries make the war
already a faded and half forgotten event and in Germany that must be even
more so. The psychic and spiritual atmosphere is unpleasant. The human
creatures are, as it seems, in the nastiest frame of mind imaginable. Heaven
knows how that will be resolved. Like you, I hate a vulgar democracy, lording
it over all life. Through this everything becomes so low, so mean, only

material. To be sure the old imperial and aristocratic order was antiquated, certainly. – The present condition seems like an ugly dash in history – a sort of cramped nothing. It doubtless must be so. But I would rather have nothing to do with it. – I believe in the elect: the elect should build a world: not the masses. –

Frieda is well. We live here very quietly. I look forward immensely to seeing you all again, to being in a larger landscape – England is narrow, in every respect, except in external comfort, that's as plentiful as ever. I hope you are all at last getting food.

Loving regards, for an early get-together

DHL]

1721. To S. S. Koteliansky, 3 April 1919
Text: MS BL; Moore 584–5.

Mountain Cottage, Middleton by Wirksworth
3 April 1919.

My dear Kot.

I send you the *Scarlet Letter* – a very great book – no doubt you know it already. But read it again. My next month's *English Review* essay is about this.[1] – Keep the book if you like it.

I heard from Murry, very editorial – he sort of 'declines with thanks' the things I did for him. He will publish one essay next week[2] – too late to ask for it back – and that is the first and last word of mine that will ever appear in the *Athenæum.* Good-bye Jacky, I knew thee beforehand. – But don't say anything at 2 Portland Villas.[3]

I heard from Horne – foolish, I thought. He is living in Acton – is still in the army – and 'very busy' with demobilisation – wants to get an 'administrative' job – has applied for a post in Palestine or Damascus or somewhere else – thinks his barrister's qualification will help him to get an appointment. Let's hope they'll appoint him to the moon. – Maisie meanwhile is putting a 'sketch' on the boards, at her own expense, and starts her tour at Exeter next week. – 'If it is not a success she will lose money by it –' (Horne).

---

[1] 'Nathaniel Hawthorne', *English Review*, xxviii (May 1919), 404–17. (This was revised extensively and published as 'Nathaniel Hawthorne and "The Scarlet Letter"' in *Studies in Classic American Literature.*)

[2] See p. 332 n. 2.

[3] The Murrys had moved into 2 Portland Villas (known as 'The Elephant'), East Heath Road, Hampstead, in August 1918.

Who is it that has been telling small petty mean lies, now, to depress you? – instead of world-mighty Alexandrian lies. Ach Kot, who cares about the little fleas, or the big fleas either!

Don't bother about any book – in vulgar debt I owe you 2/- for postage for the others. And let me pay for Karavan, please.

I am very thrilled about Sonia. When she sees Grisha, she is to be sure and give him my blessings. Let me know what takes place.

It is true, one has to be in the mood to read books: no use trying if one is out of the mood.

I have set to, revising my history.[1] It will take about three weeks – pray God not longer – and then I hope speedily to receive the £50. There is a sum for you!

Tell Ghita I received her bob-curtsey little letter, and wish to know if I am the little-boy-blue of the illustration and exhortation: and if so, what tune shall I strike up.

Vale   DHL

1722. To Amy Lowell, 5 April 1919
Text: MS HU; Damon 492–4.

Mountain Cottage, Middleton-by-Wirksworth, Derby. England.

5 April 1919

My dear Amy

I am sorry you have been so seedy – one gets so pulled down.[2] I had Flu. also – nearly shuffled off the mortal coil – am well on in convalescence. It was a vile sick winter for us all. – Hilda also had pneumonia some weeks ago, and it left her weak. I hear her baby, a girl, was born last Sunday, and that both are doing well. We shall be going to London soon, and may see her.

I am sure you are wise to defer your lectures on poetry – but I wish you were coming over to Europe. One feels a great longing for a bit of a gathering of friends in some sunny, careless, genial place. But the world is all at cross purposes, and gets worse: everything seems tangled in everything by a million bits of string. I want to go to Switzerland or Germany, and then come on to America this summer. But I can see we shall never manage it. I want awfully to come to America – first to the north, then later to go south, perhaps to Central America. It is what I intend to do when the world becomes sane again, and oneself free.

---

[1] i.e. *Movements in European History*.

[2] .Amy Lowell had influenza and then was profoundly shocked and distressed by the sudden death of a nephew whom she had regarded almost as a son (Damon 491).

Here in England nobody cares about anything, literature least of all: all bent on scrambling uneasily from day to day, as if we were all perched on a land-slide, and the days were stones that might start sliding under one's feet. I don't know why it all seems so uncertain, so irritable, such a sequence of pinpricking moments, with no past to stay one, and no future to wonder over. But it is so. And it is hateful to have life chopped up into disagreeable moments, all gritty.

We hear from Frieda's people: terrible distress there seems to be. F. worries – we all worry. I suppose it will soon end. My brother-in-law is Minister of Finance to the new Bavarian republic. He seems to weather the storms. But it is a perpetual question of what next. – We want to go to Munich when we can. Frieda wants to see her mother and her sisters: I too want to see them all again.

When you write will you address me at – Chapel Farm Cottage, *Hermitage*, nr. *Newbury*, Berks. We are going down there at the end of the month, and I suppose we shall stay there till we leave England. I have not written anything these last few months – not since I have been ill. I feel I don't want to write – still less do I want to publish anything. It is like throwing one's treasures in a bog.

I agree with you, that the poetry of the future, and the poetry that *now* has the germs of futurity in it, is rhymeless, naked, spontaneous rhythm. But one has an old self as well as a new. – I hope you got the copy of *New Poems*. It was much better received than *Look we have Come Through*. The press only spat on that. – What is Huebsch publishing of mine in New York, do you know? I never hear anything.[1]

I do hope you are well and happy. I would love to see your garden, particularly to get the scents at evening. I would love the gorgeous, living lavishness that America is capable of, naturally – and Europe isn't.

Remember us to Mrs Russell. Frieda and I send warmest greetings.

                                                                        D. H. Lawrence

1723. To S. S. Koteliansky, [7 April 1919]
Text: MS BL; Moore 583–4.

                                                    Middleton by Wirksworth, Derby
                                                                            Monday
My dear Kot
    Thank you for grape fruit, Karavan, and Anatole France. Karavan I sip

---

[1] Huebsch was to write on 22 April 1919; see Letter 1734.

happily as I look out of the window at the motionless valley: by the way I owe you half a dollar for it: grape fruit I have eaten one and made a design for embroidery with it: Anatole I have read four pages, and such a mess of parturition, babies and puppies being spawned on the floor, that I go outside and wipe my feet on the mat.

> No stir on the land, no stir on the sea
> The Murrys are silent as silent can be.[1]

That is, he's done me in over one of my essays, which now becomes out of date, since he neglects to return it to me.[2] – I saw the notice of the *Athenæum*: what a rechauffé of dead men!

I have in preparation a very charming little present for you, so you may as well know it beforehand, in case it never comes off. Anyway it will be a week or two.

A letter from Margaret Radford; – how happy, dear Lawrence, she is that she can be at Hermitage to receive us and stay ten days with us. 'Love rules the camp, the court, the grove.'[3]

Another hair in Sonia's soup! Tell her to save it, she will have enough to weave a rope to hang somebody with, soon. – Tell me about her and Amsterdam. Say to Ghita I began the tune of 'Rule Britannia', because her father sings it so well. Hope this is quite according to programme.

Heard from Arabella: Hilda's baby born last week: a girl:[4] 'Gray behaving wretchedly, Richard very fine' (quots. Arabella). A. herself seems in low water. – Hilda and baby doing well.

Tell Ghita, for a second tune, we'll sing that inspiring hymn

> 'We're marching to Zion
> Beautiful beautiful Zion
> We're marching homeward to Zion etc –'[5]

I hope she'll join in.

Don't say anything about Hilda – except to Sonia.

DHL

My envelopes are awful, but they knock your long coupons into a cocked hat.

[1] Cf. Robert Southey, 'The Inchcape Rock' (1803), ll. 1–2 ['No stir in the air, no stir in the sea,/ The ship was as still as she could be'].

[2] Unidentified.

[3] Sir Walter Scott, *The Lay of the Last Minstrel* (1805), III. ii. 5 ['. . . rules the court, the camp, the grove'].

[4] Hilda Aldington's first child was stillborn (in 1915); her daughter Frances Perdita, b. 31 March 1919. (Aldington was not the father.)

[5] A refrain added to Isaac Watts's hymn, 'Come we that love the Lord,/ And let our joys be known'.

1724. To S. S. Koteliansky, 17 April 1919
Text: MS BL; Postmark, Wirksworth 17 AP 19; Zytaruk, ed., *Malahat Review*, i. 36–7.

Mountain Cottage, Middleton by Wirksworth, Derby.

17 April 1919.

My dear Kot,

We are still here – my sister with us, with her little boy – she rather ill. She too had Flu., and it left her with boils that keep on coming. They make her weak and depressed – I do wish they would stop.

We are coming to Hermitage next week – 24th., I think – I shall let you know when we arrive. Perhaps you will come and see us there. Margaret will be at the cottage till first week in May, alas! I hate the bother of hauling out all my things and shifting again.

Your present – evidently you did not deserve it, for it has gone wrong in the post – envelope arrived torn across, little box missing. I am filling up forms and hope still to recover it. If not I'll try and get another. – It is of no value, only it was really nice, and not to be replaced – one could only get something more or less the same. – It sounds cryptic, and even shady, like a present posted by the Murrys. But it was a real thing, and I have a faint hope it may turn up even yet.

I haven't heard from the M's – only received back the bit of my MS. I hadn't asked for, containing also my own letter to Jack – nasty bit of oversight; also last week's *Athenæum*. Of all the wet and be-snivelled rags, this *Athenæum* is the messiest: soulful, spiritual journalists moaning because they *can't*, and probably never *will*, make pots of money, poor darlings! The Athenæumites are snivellers, *piagnoni*[1] one and all – even K[atherine]'s sprightly wit has a wet-nosed sniff in it. Pah!

I see you are getting a little telegram-official fever. Keep cool. – But it is irritating. Poor Sonia, hopping between the frying-pan and the fire. I hope she'll get back all right. Are you meanwhile all alone?

I read ½ Anatole France: but Pierre was so Petite that I could hardly see him at all,[2] and began to suffer from eye-strain. But Anatole is a very graceful piffler, and so *easy* that to me he becomes impossibly difficult. I feel like a parrot born to crack nuts trying to feed itself on pap. – I'm glad you like *The Scarlet Letter*. I shall send you another Hawthorne. – Hope I don't sound conceited about A.F. and *P.P.*

I have got only two more chapters of the history before me. When these are done, I have nothing on hand at all, can turn tramp or bolshevist or government official, any of those occupations one takes up in one's leisure. It

[1] 'snivellers, weepers'.   [2] See p. 341 n. 4.

seems we are to be kept dormant and apathetic and anaesthetised for ever. I am afraid of becoming bored at last.

People are coming here for Easter. I nearly cut and run – bolted to you. Seriously I thought of descending on you for Easter. But I suppose I shall have to stick it out.

Thank you very much for the grape fruit. My sister shares them with me. She likes them extremely, and I believe they're good for her. – If I can get to Matlock I will send you an Easter egg. But it rains: and I have never walked so far since I was ill. I am better: can again chop wood and carry water and potter in the garden. I mean no more questions are to be asked about me, I am normal.

Poor Sonia: tell me how she gets on.

Au revoir   DHL

1725. To Catherine Carswell, [22 April 1919]
Text: MS YU; cited in Moore, *Poste Restante* 54.

Shirley House, Ripley, Derby.[1]
Tuesday

My dear Catherine

I had your letter – sorry you are so badly off. I am better, go about nearly as usual – just get tired rather easily, that's all. – We are going down to Hermitage on Thursday or Friday – this week anyhow – for good – giving up Mountain Cottage. Come and see us at Hermitage, wont you. I am just finishing the *History* – beyond that I know *nothing* – nor what I shall do nor anything. We hope to go to Germany.

au revoir   DHL

1726. To S. S. Koteliansky, [23 April 1919]
Text: MS BL; cited in Gransden 27.

Middleton by Wirksworth
Wednesday

My dear Kot

We are going away on Friday, leave here 8.0 o'clock – all the things packed up now. My sister with her boy leaves tomorrow evening. How many times have I packed our miserable boxes! – and when will they ever come to rest. – I feel as if we were setting off on a real new move now, as if we shouldn't

---

[1] Though DHL uses headed notepaper with this address, it is plain from the letter following that the Lawrences and Ada Clarke were still at Middleton.

be long in Hermitage, as if soon the bigger journey would begin, away from England. Perhaps they will make peace for the time being, and let us out.

If you won't come to Hermitage I will come to London and see you soon. The history is finished, I am a free man. The other day I got papers revoking the Cornwall order against us.[1] – I think Sonia will come back soon. Meanwhile it makes you cross.

The Murrys do not write to me – which is what I prefer. K[atherine] writes to F[rieda] – foolish would-be-witty letters. They bore me merely.

I send you now your *Petit Pierre* – for which many thanks. I will send you more books from Hermitage. Margaret will be there. You remember the address:

>   Chapel Farm Cottage, Hermitage, nr Newbury, *Berks*.

Let us have a meeting soon.

>   Au revoir   DHL

1727. To Mark Gertler, [23 April 1919]
Text: MS SIU; Unpublished.

>   Middleton by Wirksworth
>   Wednesday

Dear Gertler

Kot thanked you for this book, no doubt – but the reproductions are bad – and I daren't tackle the Uccello from these postcards. Still, we did two pictures. Many thanks for sending.

We have been packing our boxes once more today. On Friday we are coming to Hermitage – Chapel Farm Cottage, Hermitage, nr. Newbury, Berks. Come and see us there, with Kot, if you can persuade him to move. Margaret Radford will be there for the first week. – She wrote me how good she thought *Mendel* – so simple, so sympathetic, so direct.

I hope things are going all right with you – I would like to tramp off to the end of the world. – Write to Hermitage.

>   D. H. Lawrence

1728. To Ada Krenkow, [23 April 1919]
Text: MS SIU; Unpublished.

>   Mountain Cottage, Middleton by Wirksworth, Derby.
>   Wednesday

My dear Aunt,

I think that we will go direct to Hermitage on Thursday. It would be

---

[1] See Letter 1463.

painful for me to see Louie.[1] I was fond of her, and have always a good feeling for her in me. But it would be wrong to meet again, I think, and to start the old feelings again. Anyhow it would be a shock to all of us.

So we shall go via Birmingham tomorrow. I hope it won't annoy you, this changing about. We shall see you and uncle at Hermitage.

DHL

I think these are Mr Blaggs[2] cuffs and links.

1729. To Dr David Eder, [post 25 April 1919]
Text: Hobman, ed., *David Eder*, pp. 121–2.

[Chapel Farm Cottage, Hermitage, nr Newbury, Berks]
[post 25 April 1919][3]

My dear Eder,

Oh, do take me to Palestine, and I will love you for ever. Let me come and spy out the land with you – it would rejoice my heart into the heavens. And I will write you such a beautiful little book, 'The Entry of the Blessed into Palestine'. Can't I come and do the writing up? Because as a *possibility*, I have a hot little interest in Palestine. But I have a horror of the dreadful hosts of people, 'with noses', as your sister said. It needs kindling with a spark of magic, your Palestine – it will be a dead failure otherwise.

First Law: There shall be no laws: every man shall hold up his hand in token that he is self-responsible and answerable to his own soul.

Second Law: Every man shall have food, shelter, knowledge and the right to mate freely – every man and woman shall have this, irrespective of any other claim than that of life-necessity: and every man who enters, and every woman, shall hold up a hand to signify that in these two principles we are at one.

Then everything else can be done by arrangement, not by law. There are many deep and bitter and sweet things to know and learn, afterwards. But in

---

[1] Louisa ('Louie') Burrows (1888–1962), DHL's fiancée from December 1910 to February 1912 (see *Letters*, i. 29 n. 3). She maintained her friendship with the Krenkows for many years after DHL broke the engagement; indeed the friendship with Fritz Krenkow continued after the death of his wife, Ada.

[2] Unidentified.

[3] The letter is dated 'post 25 April 1919' to take account of the following facts: Hobman (*David Eder*, p. 121) says it was written 'from Hermitage at the beginning of 1919' whereas DHL did not arrive there until 25 April; Eder had visited DHL at Middleton in March and then returned to Palestine on 3 April; and Kot was told on 20 March (Letter 1714) that DHL had promised to go to Palestine. This letter is thus seen as a follow-up to the discussions about Palestine between DHL and Eder in March; it is likely to have been written from Hermitage soon after the Lawrences' arrival.

accepting the first two principles, we put ourselves, like beginners, into the state of pure attention, like acolytes. And so our State begins.

Now, isn't this feasible, and right? Whatever else is said, it must be said as well. And all the other wordly chuffings will be only a trick to spoil those European Egyptians.

I wish you would take me to Palestine. I don't believe you'll pull it off, as a vital reality, without me . . . I seriously want to go to Palestine.

DHL

1730. To S. S. Koteliansky, [30 April 1919]
Text: MS BL; Moore 585–6.

Chapel Farm Cottage, Hermitage, nr Newbury, Berks
Wednesday

My dear Kot

We came here last Friday – I am just recovering from the journey. The weather is not nice. Margaret Radford is here: under the circumstances I'd much rather be at Mountain Cottage.

What swine they are about Sonia. They make my blood go a little darker – if that be possible. Tell me if your efforts have availed you anything.

Are we going to have peace? – Do you hear the Herald Angels sing? Ah God!

I would come and see you at once, but have got a sort of obstinate sulky stupidity which prevents my doing anything. Partly it derives from the sweetly-loving Margaret. I wish one could exterminate all her sort under a heap of Keating's powder. I feel utterly 'off' the soulful or clever or witty type of female – in fact, the self-important female of any sort.

I should like to come to London, if my disagreeableness would let me. I should like to talk for about half an hour: I should like to go with you to the opera, en garçon, in the cheapest seats: I should like to go to the National Gallery. But I don't want to see anybody at all – don't want to let anybody know I am there – save perhaps Cath. Carswell and Gertler. When I get over my fit I will come.

Tell me about Sonia. Tell me if you know of any charm to cure my fit of enduring hatefulness.

DHL

1731. To J. B. Pinker, 30 April 1919
Text: MS BosU; Unpublished.

Chapel Farm Cottage, Hermitage, nr. Newbury, Berks.
30 April 1919

My dear Pinker

Thank you for your letter. I am living here for the present. The *Cosmopolitan* offer is very rosy, and I am quite ready to do what you think well in the matter.[1] But you know they will look at my stories and find they are not in their line. – However, I promise you that for the next six weeks I will write nothing but short stories, if the short stories will come. It's as good a promise as I can make.

Yrs   D. H. Lawrence

1732. To J. B. Pinker, 5 May 1919
Text: MS UNYB; Moore, *Intelligent Heart* 252.

Chapel Farm Cottage, Hermitage, nr Newbury, Berks.
5 May 1919

My dear Pinker

Thank you for the cheque for fifty-five pounds which came so nicely on Saturday.

Yrs   D. H. Lawrence

1733. To S. S. Koteliansky, 9 May 1919
Text: MS BL; Moore 587.

Chapel Farm Cottage, Hermitage, nr. Newbury
9 May 1919.

My dear Kot

So glad to hear of Sonia's safe arrival, and of your relapse into quiescence. From Sonia's letter I gather she has sent a bit of Dutch cake: I shall write to her tomorrow, when it has arrived.[2]

Now the weather is warm I am quite happy – dolce far'niente.[3] The world is very lovely, full of flowers and scents. One can be out most of the day Would you like to come down?

I haven't read Wm James *Religious Experiences*.[4] He is an interesting man.

---

[1] The details of the *Cosmopolitan* offer are not known; DHL never published in the magazine.
[2] DHL's letter has not been found.
[3] 'a happy life of leisure'.
[4] This statement appears to clash with Jessie Chambers's remark in her *D. H. Lawrence: A Personal Record* (1935), p. 113: DHL 'also liked *Some Varieties of Religious Experience* and recommended me to read it'. William James's book, *Varieties of Religious Experience: Study in Human Nature*, was published in 1902.

Lend it me if it is quite easy to do so. You really seem to be reading. I shall send you more books, in that case.

Katharine wrote to me, but somehow I couldn't answer her. When I can I will. Of him, nothing – and forever nothing.

I feel that soon we ought to be talking plans. I feel that soon we shall be scattering: God knows where to. We ought to have a meeting soon. Are you sure you wouldn't like to come down? I could get you rooms in the village, if you don't want to stay in the house here. Let me know.

DHL

1734. To Benjamin Huebsch, 9 May 1919
Text: MS UT; Postmark, Hermitage 9 MY 19; Moore 586–7.

Chapel Farm Cottage, Hermitage, nr. Newbury, Berkshire, England.

9th. May 1919

Dear Mr Huebsch,

Thank you for your letter and the cuttings.[1] I sent you yesterday a copy of the *New Poems* – the Secker book – and asked Duckworths to forward you a

---

[1] DHL's letter was in reply to Huebsch's of 22 April 1919 (TMS LC) which read as follows:

Dear Mr. Lawrence,

Please forgive me for not having replied sooner to your letter, which I was greatly pleased to receive. I have often wished to get in direct touch with you but hesitated because of the possible misinterpretation of such a course by your agent. You know how sensitive agents are! I cannot tell you how great a satisfaction it is to me to be in some way concerned in placing your work before American readers. The degree of my interest is not to be measured by the extent of the sales, but I think that my methods will probably be advantageous to you in the long run even though the immediate results may seem rather meager. The demand for your books, though not large, is persistent. I much prefer this to the more rocket-like success.

The episode of "The Rainbow" is one that perhaps requires a longer explanation than I can give in a letter, but I may say this much; upon the advice of friends who are quite as much interested in your work as in me, I withheld the book when the ghouls were lying in wait for me to publish it, and a few months ago I quietly distributed the edition that I had prepared in the autumn of 1915 without advertising or any other publicity, so that at least the book is not buried.

Having labored under numerous difficulties due first to the war and latterly to moving my office, I cannot yet give precise data of sales later than May 1918. Up to that date, as you can see by statements furnished to Mr. Pinker through George H. Doran Company (Our dealings have been roundabout!), the sales were approximately as follows: "Amores" 300, "The Prussian Officer" 600, and "Twilight in Italy", 250. As to royalties, some time ago I sent a check to G. H. Doran Company settling to May 1, 1918.

Making due allowance for the limited circle to which anything intelligent appeals, you have a great many admirers here and you would be warmly welcomed if you were to make your proposed visit. America expects every man to be a lecturer and, if it is not totally against your desires to appear on the platform, I am quite sure that enough engagements can be secured to cover the expense of a trip. If such a course is not disagreeable to you, I suggest that you advise me very soon of the time and possible duration of your visit and I will then, with your

copy of *The White Peacock*, from me. I will send directly a complete MS. of the *Studies in Classic American Literature*. Harrison has gone on publishing them in the *English Review*: the eighth comes in June.[1] I wish they could have appeared in an American review. Do you think that is in any way possible?

I hope the *Seven Arts* will be revived. – It is my intention to come to New York in August or September, and come I will, if it is any way possible. I have never lectured, and don't see myself on a platform. But if it needs must be done, I will do it: for I must make a living somehow. I might lecture on American Literature. Thank you for thinking of an agent for me. The worst of it is, I am not a public man – not a bit – always have a 'Strictly Private' notice in my hat. Also the thought of New York is much more awful than the thought of a savage jungle: not because it is savage, but because of the overweening mechanical civilisation. So when I come I shall have to beg you to receive me and set me down a little gently among the skv scrapers.

I hope you will come to England this summer. That would be much nicer, if we could meet here and arrange ourselves. Do let me know.

permission, arrange with a responsible lecture agent to secure engagements for you, and I will, of course, cooperate with him because lecture agents are, I think, somewhat worse than literary agents in achieving results for newcomers. I have already spoken to several persons here and in Chicago about the likelihood of your coming with a view to engaging their assistance in the lecture project. I mentioned it to Miss Lowell, too, thinking that she might be able to help in Boston, but she warned me not to expect anything from that rather conservative town. I think, however, that she underrates the possibilities because of her too close proximity.

Recently the editor of The Century expressed a desire to see some of your short stories. If I am not encroaching on your agent's rights, I shall be glad to handle such material as you may send over here, doing it, of course, strictly as a friendly and not a business matter.

You will be interested in knowing that there is a project to revive "The Seven Arts" if the necessary funds to guarantee its existence can be secured. If the magazine should be published it would be with James Oppenheim again as editor, Louis Untermeyer assisting and with me as publisher. If we realize our hopes, it would mean a more certain market for some of your work. Owing to long delays in transatlantic shipment, the sheets of "Look! We Have Come Through" arrived only late in the winter, so that few important reviews have as yet been printed. I am enclosing a sympathetic notice by Llewellyn Jones, literary editor of the Chicago Evening Post, together with an editorial paragraph also by him, and Miss Lowell's review that has just been printed in The New York Times. Doubtless, her intentions were of the best, but I cannot understand why she makes it seem as if you were only now being discovered. Very soon there will be a review in The New York Evening Post by Louis Untermeyer.

I shall have to ask you for more patience before I reply with regard to your articles in The English Review. In the meantime, if you have a manuscript of the complete work, will you not send it to me? Do not hesitate to consult me freely about the American trip and, in fact, about anything else in which you think I may be of service. I am hoping to get over to your side in the early summer but the chances are only slight.

Yours sincerely,

[1] 'The Two Principles', *English Review*, xxviii (June 1919), 477–89. This essay was not included in *Studies in Classic American Literature*; it had its first book publication in *The Symbolic Meaning*, ed. Armin Arnold (1962).

I daren't send you any stories, Pinker would be too furious. But when I come to America, then I shall please myself – I shall have an understanding with Pinker beforehand. – Let us hope we may meet in England this summer.

Yours Sincerely   D. H. Lawrence

I haven't any photographs at all. If it were best to have one, I will get one taken.

1735. To Edward Marsh, 10 May 1919
Text: MS NYPL; Huxley 477–8.

Chapel Farm Cottage, Hermitage, nr. Newbury, Berks.
10 May 1919

Dear Eddie

Your letter has come this morning, with the twenty pounds from Rupert.[1] Queer, to receive money from the dead: as it were out of the dark sky. I have a great belief in the dead – in Rupert dead. He fights with one, I know. – That is why I hate the Oliver Lodge spiritualism[2] – hotel bills and collar-studs. The passionate dead act within and with us, not like messenger boys and hotel porters. Of the dead who really live, whose presence we know, we hardly care to speak – we know their hush. Isn't it so?

Thank you for thinking of me. – Yes, I am happier now the war is fought with the soul, not with filthy guns.

I'll send an inscribed copy of the *New Poems*. Shall I send *Look!* – also?

Yrs   D. H. Lawrence

1736. To Lady Cynthia Asquith, 10 May 1919
Text: MS UT; Unpublished.

Chapel Farm Cottage, Hermitage, nr Newbury, Berks.
10 May 1919

We have come down here: not so far off, so perhaps we shall see you. – I had your letter prescribing childbirth – or rather childbearing – as a cure for all the ills: sorry it is denied me: must think of a substitute. You had a war-baby:

[1] The money was paid from a fund (consisting of royalties from Marsh's 'Memoir' of Rupert Brooke) which Marsh had decided to administer on behalf of needy writers. (Gordon Bottomley and W. H. Davies also benefited on this occasion.) See Christopher Hassall, *Edward Marsh* (1959), pp. 461–2.
[2] Sir Oliver Joseph Lodge (1851–1940), eminent scientist and well known for his writings on psychic phenomena. He was a former president of the Society for Psychical Research. See *Letters*, ii. 440.

now a peace-baby.[1] I tell you, you are a perfect chronicle of current events. Your deliver the times to a T. – I suppose the baby will be Gabriel: or Gabrielle: unless it has to be Bolshevina.

Eddie sent me £20. from Rupert. As a matter of fact, I expect you were the agent in the matter. So I must thank you, Rupert, and Eddie: merci Madame et Messieurs.

The country at present is very lovely. If you are in town – you wrote from Stanway – I will send you some cowslips. Send us a line.

We are thinking to go to Germany about August. Will it be possible? Chi lo sa? Anyhow my feet feel unfastened, I know we shall be departing soon, somewhere, somehow.

I shall probably be in town very shortly: then let us meet, if you are within reach.

F[rieda] sends her love   DHL

1737. To Catherine Carswell, 14 May 1919
Text: MS YU; Unpublished.

Chapel Farm Cottage, Hermitage, nr Newbury, Berks.
14 May 1919

My dear Catherine

Come next Tuesday. The best train leaves Paddington at 3.0, for Newbury: change Newbury and come on to Hermitage station, arrive 4.30. Come by that – only just look and see if there is any alteration in the 3.0 train: I know the 4.15 out of Newbury to Hermitage is all right.

The other train, the only one later, is 5.5 Paddington, Newbury 6.23 – wait an hour for the 7.25 out to Hermitage. Best come 3.0.

No, don't sue Beresford, they've got the golden angels on their side.[2]

The country is marvellous – I don't care about the world. – Let's make plans.

F[rieda] sends love – she has some scraps of child-clothing for Johannes.
DHL

P.S. – I can give you £1. for the journey: wish it were £1000.

---

[1] Michael Asquith was born in 1914, Simon in 1919 (see Letter 1794).
[2] The reference is obscure.

1738. To J. B. Pinker, 14 May 1919
Text: MS BosU; Unpublished.

Chapel Farm Cottage, Hermitage, nr Newbury, Berks.
14 May 1919

My dear Pinker

I send you 'Fanny and Annie'.[1] I hope it is the right sort. If you think it would be better with a different ending, I will write a different ending if you send the MS. back.

I will write six stories, and we'll see how they go.

Yrs   D. H. Lawrence

1739. To J. B. Pinker, 20 May 1919
Text: MS BosU; Unpublished.

Chapel Farm Cottage, Hermitage, nr Newbury, Berks
20 May 1919

My dear Pinker

Will you please send me the MS. of that play of mine *Touch and Go*. I should like to look at it again, and a friend wants to criticise it.

I sent you a second story yesterday.[2] Hope it is the sort.

Yrs   D. H. Lawrence

1740. To Cyril Beaumont, 23 May 1919
Text: MS UCin; cited in Beaumont, *First Score*, p. 35.

Chapel Farm Cottage, Hermitage, nr Newbury, Berks.
23 May 1919

Dear Beaumont,

Im sorry you are not well again – hope it'll get better.

The wood-cuts are very amusing – almost comic.[3] Only I do think the tail piece is a bit incongruous with the text.

I send back the MS. – Let me have the other poems when you can, will you, that I can copy them. When will the book be ready? – I am anxious to see it. I expect it to be *very* nice.

[1] The story was presumably written in response to Pinker's initiative over the *Cosmopolitan* (see Letter 1731). In fact it remained unpublished until 21 November 1921 when it appeared in *Hutchinson's Magazine*.
[2] Probably 'Monkey Nuts'; see Letter 1748. It was published in *Sovereign*, 22 August 1922.
[3] For a further, more forthright reaction to Anne Estelle Rice's illustrations for *Bay*, see Letter 1742.

Don't forget, will you, to put the acknowledgement somewhere: 'Some of these poems have appeared in *Poetry* and in *The English Review*.' I do wish this to be done, as I am always in trouble for [. . .] forgetfulness.

I'll come in to see you before long: as soon as I am in town.

Yrs   D. H. Lawrence

1741. To Catherine Carswell, [24 May 1919]
Text: MS YU; Unpublished.

Chapel Farm Cottage, Hermitage, nr Newbury
Sat.[1]

My dear Catherine

Mrs Lowe hasn't let her rooms for Whitsun, but if you want them write at once.[2] She charges 35/- a week, board and all included: 5/- a day, but if it is only week-end, a little extra. She is busy doing district nursing, but would be quite pleased to let you have her rooms if you would more or less look after yourself: that is, for a longer period. You would be much more comfortable there than at Mrs Brown's.[3] I think she would charge very moderately for the rooms alone – 15/- or £1. a week, probably.

Barbara has come – she seems pretty well. – We are busy making me a blue linen coat.

I do hope you feel stronger again. Greet John Patrick and Don from me.

au revoir   DHL

1742. To Amy Lowell, 26 May 1919
Text: MS HU; Moore, *Intelligent Heart* 251.

Chapel Farm Cottage, Hermitage, nr Newbury, Berks.
26 May 1919

Dear Amy,

I had a letter from Huebsch the other day, about the publishing of the poems etc.[4] He seems very nice. He said he would arrange for me to lecture in

---

[1] The letter is dated with reference to Whitsunday (8 June 1919) and the letters exchanged with Catherine Carswell and others before that date. Letter 1744 was written on 30 May in anticipation of Catherine Carswell's arrival on 5 June; this letter seems to have been written on the Saturday before 30 May.
[2] The Lawrences had themselves stayed at Mrs Bessie Lowe's in February 1918 (see Letter 1532). She kept the village shop in Hermitage; according to Catherine Carswell, she was also the local midwife (Carswell 110).
[3] Mrs Brown's cottage adjoined Chapel Farm Cottage.
[4] See p. 356 n. 1.

America. I am not bent on lecturing but don't mind if it *must* be done. I am making every arrangement possible to come to New York in August or September. I want very badly to come – to transfer myself. Huebsch said you told him you didn't think Boston would be the place for me to lecture in. Are you shy of me? – a little doubtful of the impression I shall, or should make? I hope not. I believe you are the only person I know, actually, in America, so I was hoping you'd help me a bit to find my feet when I come. Anyhow, tell me how you feel about it, won't you. – Probably I shall come alone, and Frieda will follow. If you don't want to be bothered – I admit it is a bother – just tell me. – I do hope your health is good now.

Have you any news? – any publications? I have nothing – except that I had some proofs of a little vol. of verse that C.W.Beaumont is hand-printing. It is illustrated by absurd and unsuitable wood-cuts, by Anne Estelle Rice. Do you know her? She is American – one of the Matisse crowd from Paris – married a man called Drey. Well, her wood-cuts are silly, to my poems.

Here it is hot and dry, summer has almost exploded into leaf this year; violence is really catching. We are waiting to be able to move. Frieda badly wants to go to see her people, but heaven alone knows when it will be possible.

I always hope to see you and have some happy times.

Remember us to Mrs Russell.

D. H. Lawrence

1743. To Catherine Carswell, [30 May 1919]
Text: MS YU; PC; Postmark, Hermitage 30 MY 19; Unpublished.

Hermitage.
Friday

Mrs Lowe says she wrote you Wednesday, so no doubt you have her letter by now. She seems quite pleased at the thought of your coming – and can give Ivy a bedroom also – share sitting-room with you. She thinks she can find you a pram. – If not we can take that old push-chair we went wooding with. Let Ivy write Mrs Lowe and say when she will be coming – I suppose you will all come together on Thursday. We'll meet you at the station.

Thanks for enquiring about type-writer. – Your parcel was so refreshing – I was just feeling sick. – So glad about the good luck. Till Thursday.

DHL

1744. To S. S. Koteliansky, [30 May 1919]
Text: MS BL; Zytaruk 180.

Chapel Farm Cottage, Hermitage, nr Newbury
Friday

My dear Kot

This is your present at last. The lost seal was chrysoprase – bright green – lovely: this is jade. I drew a little man: a thunder-evoker, from an African symbol – but they have no proper engravers in Cornwall now, so I had to have your initials. But I hope you'll like your seal, and keep it as a rather bomb-like peace-sigil.

It is hot, and I had a little colpo di sole,[1] so felt sick. Barbara is here – chatters. – Cath. Carswell et famille, and Mme Litvinov et fils are coming to this village for Whitsun. – not to this house. If you hear of my disappearance don't wonder.

This isn't a letter – a barren note. Greet Sonia Issayevna and Ghita Grishevna from me, tell them I am speechless, and am rapidly becoming stone deaf, through the sound of voices.

DHL

1745. To Siegfried Sassoon, 4 June 1919
Text: MS HL; Unpublished.

Chapel Farm Cottage, Hermitage, nr Newbury, Berks
4 June 1919

Dear Mr Sassoon

If you will send the sheet of paper I will write out a poem as you suggest.[2] I received your letter here only today.

Yours truly   D. H. Lawrence

---

[1] 'sunstroke'.

[2] DHL may have been answering a request in connection with what the poet Siegfried Sassoon (1886–1967) eventually published in *Vanity Fair*, xv (September 1920), 55, as: 'Fireflies. A Set of Parodies of the Work of Some Modern British Poets'. Sassoon included a parody of DHL beginning 'I say to you, my firefly: Flash around and fill me to the core with power.' Other poets parodied were W. H. Davies, John Drinkwater, Walter de la Mare, W. W. Gibson, Robert Graves and John Masefield.

1746. To J. B. Pinker, 4 June 1919
Text: MS UNYB; Unpublished.

Chapel Farm Cottage, Hermitage, nr Newbury, Berks
4 June 1919.

My dear Pinker

Thank you for the cheque for twenty-nine pounds, which has come this morning.

Yrs   D. H. Lawrence

1747. To Benjamin Huebsch, 8 June 1919
Text: MS UT; Postmark, Hermitage 9 JU[. . .]; Unpublished.

Chapel Farm Cottage, Hermitage, nr. Newbury. Berks. England.
8 June 1919

Dear Mr Huebsch,

I wonder if you got my last letter, in answer to yours.[1] I am waiting to hear from you.[2] I do hope you can fix up for me some lecturing, or something that may enable me to earn a little money, for I want to come to America at once. As soon as I hear definitely from you I will get a passport and book a berth – though that no doubt will take some little time. But write and let me know as soon as you can, will you? I hate having to bother you, but don't see how I am to manage without. And I do want to come right away to America, I weary myself here.

I am doing a quite 'proper' novel,[3] which I hope may be done by the time I start. If so, I will bring you the MS.

Anyhow let me hear from you, that I needn't wait vaguely.

Yours Sincerely   D. H. Lawrence[4]

1748. To J. B. Pinker, 18 June 1919
Text: MS StaU; Unpublished.

Chapel Farm Cottage, Hermitage, nr. Newbury, Berks
18 June 1919.

My dear Pinker

I'm glad you sold 'The Fox'.[5] I suppose they won't pay the £30. until they print – worse luck.

---

[1] See Letter 1734 and n. 1.
[2] Huebsch had written to DHL on 2 June 1919 (TMS LC), but the letter had not yet arrived. It acknowledged DHL's letter of 9 May and expressed the hope that the two men might meet early in July if Huebsch's plans to visit England materialised.
[3] Probably the early version of *Aaron's Rod*.
[4] Huebsch noted on the MS of DHL's letter: 'Answd July 4'. The envelope is stamped 'OPENED BY CENSOR'.
[5] See p. 299 n. 5.

I'll try and get more stories done. Thanks for the MS. of 'Monkey-Nuts', which I received.

Yours   D. H. Lawrence

1749. To Cyril Beaumont, 18 June 1919
Text: MS Lazarus; Beaumont, *First Score*, p. 35.

Chapel Farm Cottage, Hermitage, nr. Newbury, Berks.

18 June 1919.

Dear Beaumont

I return MS. – I altered the Hyde Park[1] – hope it is now plain. – Don't be very long setting up, will you, as I may be leaving England, and I should like to see the book before I go. But I suppose it won't be ready for some months.

Yrs   D. H. Lawrence

You might let me *see* proofs, anyhow.

1750. To Catherine Carswell, [19 June 1919]
Text: MS YU; Unpublished.

Hermitage.

Thursday.[2]

My dear Catherine

I had this letter from the type-writing people. Two pounds seem little – but perhaps one may as well let it go at that. What do you think?[3]

I'm glad you got home safely. My sister *loved* the beads: she liked them much better than the shawl. That was nice. It was good of you to give them. – The Cornish people said they would send an estimate for the jade: so I'll let you know when they do.

Nothing new in the world – except that Huebsch, my American publisher, is coming over to England early next month, and will arrange with me about going over there. Oh my God, everything seems so wrong, somehow.

Mrs Lowe continues to say 'sweet baoy, John!'

I'll probably be in town before you go to the New Forest.

DHL

---

[1] The poem (first published in *Bay*) was entitled: 'Guards, A Review in Hyde Park, 1913'. It is not known in what ways DHL altered the poem.

[2] The conjectural date is arrived at on the assumption that the Carswells (having come on 5 June) would stay over the Whit weekend; Catherine Carswell had also had time to write and announce their safe return home. Huebsch's letter of 2 June (see Letter 1747 n. 2 and letter following) had arrived in the meantime. Taken together these facts suggest that 12 June would be too early for this letter whereas 19 June would be possible and likely.

[3] Catherine Carswell recorded: 'He had asked us to sell his typewriter for him, and my brother bought it for £4, which seemed a lot to all of us' (Carswell 111). Cf. Letter 1743.

1751. To Lady Cynthia Asquith, 20 June 1919
Text: MS UT; Unpublished.

Chapel Farm Cottage, Hermitage, nr. Newbury. Berks
20 June 1919.

Silence has overtaken you – suppose it is only peace and summer-stillness and childbearing. We are here, a bit at a loose end.

I send you the wood-cuts which will 'adorn' your book of poems.[1] I had them from Beaumont. He is setting up the book by hand – has it half done – suppose he will live to finish. These wood-cuts are done by an American woman I know – Anne Estelle Rice. I think they're pretty bad: no good at all. Ah but Beaumont and his 'beautiful books' – he must run his little course.

Next month the man who publishes me in New York is coming over to England – wants to arrange for me to go over there, and lecture and become a stunt. See me 'Ladies and Gentlemen –' pah! But probably I shall go – here I'm spun out. One must live – and see the world.

I hope your new little 'Colombe' sleeps softly before her coming: I have decided it is a girl.

Send us a line. I wrote you a note before – to London – so I'll send this to Stanway.

F[rieda] sends love.

DHL

1752. To S. S. Koteliansky, 30 June 1919
Text: MS BL; Moore 588.

Hermitage, nr. Newbury, Berks.
30 June 1919

My dear Kot.

I haven't been able to write to anybody lately – simply stiff-fed with everything. However, the PEACE is signed[2] – sweet peace – Peace Perfect Peace – Pea – Pea – Pea – Pea – Peace: 'the very word is like a bell'[3] – pah!

Murry suddenly descended on us on Saturday – a bolt from the blue: not very startling. Truly, he was quite nice. But by now I am an old suspicious bird. He was looking for another house, *for Katharine*!!

---

[1] i.e. *Bay*.
[2] The Treaty of Versailles was signed on 28 June 1919.
[3] DHL may have had in mind Shakespeare's *Midsummer Night's Dream* V. i. 425 or *Richard II* IV. i. 103; the well-known hymn (1875) by Edward Henry Bickersteth (1825–1906); and Keats, 'Ode to a Nightingale', l. 71.

Huebsch, the American publisher – did you say to Murry that he was no good? – did Farbman suggest that? – but however, Huebsch is supposed to be coming to London 'early in July': that is, within the next fortnight. There I am to meet him. Then we are to discuss my going to America: particularly a lecturing tour wherein I lecture on poetry. Pah! Pfui-i! But if it must be done it must. I put my faith in no man – and in no bundle of men.

What about you and Sophie Issayevna? You must have plans. I must get out of this country as soon as possible. But having no money, and all, it is hell. How on earth are you fixed? Curse, damn, and blast!

I want to come and see you very soon. I would come tomorrow, but I feel I must wait a bit longer to hear from that Huebsch, who I am ready to call Hässlich.[1]

Frieda of course wants to go to Germany as soon as possible. When do you think that will be possible? It is my plan to go straight to New York. Though I hate it, I shall do it. But if it is quite impossible, I shall go to Germany with Frieda, for a bit.

The Radfords, with stinking impudence, having let us this cottage, want us to clear out by July 25th., so then we shall have nowhere to go. However, I hope and trust that we can leave England by August, or during that month. But what about you? However, I must come soon – very soon – and talk. Perhaps I'll come this week – shall I? Ask Sophie Issayevna.

Many mingled greetings   DHL

1753. To Lady Cynthia Asquith, 1 July 1919
Text: MS UT; Huxley 478–9.

Hermitage, nr Newbury. Berks.
1 July 1919.

Sorry you feel all wrong: you should never go to the East Coast except with genial other people. Why stay there? Why not go to London at once?

Yes, we'll see you in town – Deo Volente. I am going up immediately – this week-end probably – to see about our departing, and to apply for passports. It was a great mistake that we did not clear out in 1915, when we had those other passports. Still, there is nothing for it. One must keep one's flag flying, and sail off for new scenes. Over here it really isn't any good hanging on or trying afresh. I'm sure I can make enough to live on in America, fairly easily. One

---

[1] 'ugly' ('Huebsch' means 'pretty').

day you will most likely come over there to see us, in some log hut out west – or out somewhere. Life let us cherish.

What is your husband doing, and what are your prospects? Don't take them gruesomely – the world is big, once one gets out of one's own little hole. The great thing is not to give in – not to lose one's sense of adventure. Truly one is a dead failure at this life over here – I am – but there are lots of lives. I've not lived more than two, out of my nine. That's seven to the good: and life's the only thing that matters, not love, nor money, nor anything else – just the power to live and be one's own Self. Love is heavily overweighted. I'm going to ride another horse. I mean love in general – humanity and all. Life let us cherish. – See you in town.

DHL

1754. To Clifford Bax, 2 July 1919
Text: MS UT; Unpublished.

Chapel Farm Cottage, Hermitage, nr. Newbury.
2 July 1919

Dear Mr Bax[1]

I intend to come to town tomorrow – staying with Mrs Farbman, 5. Acacia Rd, St. Johns Wood. I believe it is near you – though I don't know Fellows Rd.

Would you care to meet quietly and have a talk – either at Mrs Farbmans or at your rooms.

Yrs   D. H. Lawrence

1755. To Amy Lowell, 3 July 1919
Text: MS HU; Damon 498–9.

Chapel Farm Cottage, Hermitage, nr. Newbury, Berks. England
3 July 1919

My dear Amy

This morning comes your long letter. I do understand and believe perfectly what you say: particularly about lecturing. As for an El Dorado, when I set out to look for one, I shall find one: for nothing is easier to find than money, if a man sets out straight for it. I don't want El Dorado: only life and

---

[1] Clifford Bax (1886–1962) had trained at the Slade but abandoned painting for literature (particularly drama and poetry). DHL met him in 1912 (*Letters*, i. 405 n. 8); Bax had subscribed to *Signature* (*Letters*, ii. 407).

freedom, a feeling of bigness, and a radical, even if pre-conscious sympathy. I don't want to lecture – never did.[1] I only want to be able to live. And I believe that, once in America, I could soon do that by writing. All I want is to feel that there is somewhere I could go, if necessary, and somebody I could appeal to for help if I needed it. That's why I am afraid of putting a burden on your friendship.

Huebsch said he was coming to England early this month. I am going to London today to see about things – a passport for Frieda, etc. She will go to Germany to her people quite soon: this month, I hope. I shall come to America, because I mean to come. Probably I shall sail in August. I shall come alone, Frieda will stay in Germany till I am a bit settled, then I shall send for her. – I am not afraid of prejudices: they are rarely in the very blood, only in the mind, on top.

I want to feel that I may come to you, to stay with you for a week or two, if I can't provide for myself just at the very first. Don't fear, I can soon get on my own feet. It is merely the start.

My articles in the *English Review* were on *Classic* American literature. I hope to do a series on the Moderns, next.[2]

Anyhow and anyway, I shall be seeing you soon – quite soon – The wind blows that way. Then we can have a laugh and many a talk.

D. H. Lawrence

1756. To Edward Marsh, [3 July 1919]
Text: MS NYPL; Unpublished.

13 Guilford St., W.C.1.
Thursday.

Dear Eddie

I am in town for about five days. Shall we see each other?

D. H. Lawrence

---

[1] DHL was responding to a letter from Amy Lowell (Damon 497–8) in which she warned that he would not find himself welcomed as a lecturer in New England. She warned, too, against false expectations of the USA in general: 'You must not look for El Dorado, because it is anything but that . . . I do not think it would be possible to get you any large quantity of lectures until you have made yourself known in other ways'.

[2] It was never written.

1757. To Edward Marsh, [4 July 1919]
Text: MS NYPL; Unpublished.

13 Guilford St. W.C.1.
Friday

Dear Eddie

London made me so sick, physically, not metaphorically that I couldn't go out today. I should have liked so much to hear some Scarlatti also.

This place is so noisy. I am going tomorrow to

5. Acacia Rd. St. Johns Wood. N.W.8.

You can always ring me up there Hampstead 6534. I shall probably stay till Thursday. I should really like to see you. But let us meet for an hour somewhere quiet, will you – not dine out.

Yrs   D. H. Lawrence

1758. To Edward Marsh, 7 July 1919
Text: MS NYPL; Huxley 479.

Chapel Farm Cottage, Hermitage, nr. Newbury. Berks.
7 July 1919.

Dear Eddie

Could you tell me if Robert Nicholls is back from America – and if so, what is his address. I want to ask him about America. I want to go there now – at last it will be possible. It is just hopeless, my trying to live here – I can't. My publisher said he would arrange a lecture tour for me – I mean the New York publisher. I guess I should loathe trying to lecture on English and American novels – yet I'd do it, if only for the sake of trying a new start in life, in another country.

Frieda wants to go to Baden-Baden to see her mother. She is applying now for a passport. I wonder if she'll get it. And then, as soon as she is off to Germany to her people, I shall struggle to New York. She can come over there when I've got a bit of a footing.

What a tiresome life, really. – I heard from Cynthia Asquith – in Suffolk – ill and depressed. Things have gone badly since the days when Michael was going to be born.

Tell me about Nicholls – he's a man I like, really, and he'll let me know perhaps how it feels in America. I dread it horribly, but must go. Advise me of anything you can, will you.

Yrs.   D. H. Lawrence

1759. To Edward Marsh, 7 July 1919
Text: MS NYPL; Unpublished.

Hermitage, nr Newbury
7 July 1919
Dear Eddie

I was away when your note came – wrote before I received it. Yes, do use the 'Seven Seals'.[1]

D. H. Lawrence

1760. To J. B. Pinker, 8 July 1919
Text: MS BosU; Unpublished.

Chapel Farm Cottage, Hermitage, nr. Newbury. Berks.
8 July 1919
Dear Pinker

Your letter dated July 2nd. arrives here this morning. I have never received from you any suggestion concerning the cutting of 'The Fox'. If the editor wants to cut it down, however, let him send me the MS. and I will do it.[2]

Yrs D. H. Lawrence

1761. To Douglas Goldring, 8 July 1919
Text: MS UT; Unpublished.

Chapel Farm Cottage, Hermitage, nr. Newbury. Berks.
8 July 1919
Dear Mr Goldring[3]

The idea of the 'People's Theatre' is very attractive.[4] I wish I had known

---

[1] The poem had been included in *New Poems*: Marsh reprinted it in *Georgian Poetry 1918–1919* (1919), pp. 93–4.

[2] send . . . it.] do it.

[3] Douglas Goldring (1887–1960), novelist, playwright and editor. He was sub-editor (1909) of *English Review* under Ford Madox Hueffer's editorship; editor of *The Tramp* (1910–11); literary adviser to Max Goschen Ltd (1912–14). He lived in Dublin 1916–19 and was a close friend of Joseph Hone. Author of *The Fight for Freedom* (1919), *The Black Curtain* (1920), *South Lodge* (1943), etc. m. (1) Beatrix ('Betty') Duncan, 1917, (2) Malin Nordström, 1927. Goldring met DHL through Kot; he also knew Barbara Low.

[4] In *Odd Man Out: The Autobiography of a 'Propaganda Novelist'* (1935), pp. 247–8, Goldring states that the 'People's Theatre Society' was an offshoot of the international socialist society, 'Clarté' (see Letter 1776); he adds that his principal aim in founding the Society was 'to secure the production of one of Lawrence's plays'. He intended that the Society should produce a series of 'Plays for a People's Theatre'; the plays were to be published by C. W. Daniel; and *Touch and Go* was to be the first in the series. In fact it was the second (Goldring's *Fight for Freedom* was the first), but Daniel did publish it in 1920. DHL's preface to his play was designed to propagate the idea of a People's Theatre.

before – I have just come back from town – I might have met you and talked about it. I should like you to do *Touch and Go*. But I am under Pinker – that is, he is my agent. I must settle with him. But if the People's Theatre is really going to come off, I should love to be in it.

I've not done anything with regard to publishing the play. I would much prefer you to do it, rather than an ordinary publisher. I feel we ought to talk about it. I think I shall be in town in about a fortnight's time – would that be all right?

Yours Sincerely   D. H. Lawrence

1762. To Helen Thomas, 9 July 1919
Text: MS StaU; Postmark, Hermitage 10 JY 19; cited in Moore, *Poste Restante* 54.

Chapel Farm Cottage, Hermitage, nr Newbury. Berks.
9 July 1919

Dear Mrs Thomas[1]

I got back here last evening – no nearer to America. Mrs Henry came over for the one night – seemed better, I thought. – I asked about my own English copy of the *Rainbow* – it should reach you in a few days' time. If not, send a line to S. Koteliansky, 5. Acacia Rd., St. Johns Wood, N.W.8. I have asked him to post it to you. He may mislay your address.

Probably we shall be hung up in England for some weeks. In that case you might meet my wife too – it would be nice.

Thank you for the week-end. You were quite as good a hostess as I was a guest, – I talk too much.

Tell Vere I'll write to him. Remember me to Mifanwy.[2]

D. H. Lawrence

1763. To Eleanor Farjeon, 9 July 1919
Text: MS UT; Huxley 479–80.

Hermitage, nr. Newbury.
9 July 1919

Dear Eleanor

I was in town a day or two – but so short, and rushed, or I should have told you.

[1] Helen Berenice Thomas (1877–1967), widow of the poet Edward Thomas (1878–1917). She was a friend of Leigh and Nancy Henry, and of Vere Collins; it was Collins who took DHL to her cottage, 'The Forge House', Otford, Kent. Her lively account of this visit first appeared in the *Times*, 13 February 1963; it is reprinted in her *Time and Again* (Manchester, 1978), pp. 100–4.

[2] Helen Elizabeth Myfanwy Thomas (b. 1910), Helen Thomas's younger daughter.

I am sending you an address which came this morning. You have to get from The Emergency Committee, 27 Chancery Lane, W.C.2.[1]

1. Forms of application for Vouchers: one voucher must accompany each parcel.

2. They return you a Voucher, and you proceed with it to a tradesman. I found Selfridges very slow. Perhaps being on the spot you could see it was done quicker. Above all things they want stockings, sewing cotton, and soap: then for food milk, cocoa, sugar, dripping, bacon – then beans or peas.

The parcels we ordered, June 14, were not sent till July 4. It is too bad. Tell me if you have any success.

I enclose all that my sister-in-law says about your poor woman – who must be a munition-worker or some such thing. München, full of artists, is a town of 'fallen' women – Roman Catholic in that respect.

Hope to see you soon   D. H. Lawrence
Helen Thomas expects you at Otford this week-end. I *liked her*.
The address is

Fräulein Creszenz Weingärtner, Erzgiesserei-strasse 4,
Rückgebäude II, Munich.

she has two small children, and one child she has adopted – all sehr verhungert.[2]

I enclose you an application form for Voucher. Address your letter 'Parcels', and enclose addressed envelope for yourself. – Best to be quick. – Ask for an information leaflet.

1764. To J. B. Pinker, 10 July 1919
Text: TMSC NWU; Huxley 480–1.

Chapel Farm Cottage, Hermitage, nr. Newbury, Berks.
10 July 1919.

Dear Pinker,
The letter about shortening the story,[3] with the enclosure from Vivian Carter, came yesterday.[4] Why it should be so many days behind I don't know. I would rather do the cutting myself.

---

[1] The Board of Trade had licensed the formation of the Emergency Committee for the Assistance of Germans, Austrians and Hungarians in Distress (*Times*, 29 May 1919). Parcels – strictly prescribed in size and content – could be sent only through the agency of the Committee.
[2] 'all of them very short of food'.
[3] 'The Fox'; see Letter 1760.
[4] Vivian Carter (1878–1956), journalist. He worked on *Pearsons Magazine*, the *Daily Express* and (according to *Who Was Who*) 'kindred publications'. In 1919 he was a publicity officer in the Ministry of Labour. (See *Times* obituary, 24 February 1956).

A man called Douglas Goldring wants to do my play *Touch and Go* in a 'People's Theatre Society' venture. It may not come to much, but the idea attracts me. Also he wants to publish the play in a series of *Plays for the People's Theatre*. I wish you would let me go ahead and do as I like with this play – on my own.

Probably in a few weeks time I shall go to America. But I will let you know.

Yrs.   D. H. Lawrence

1765. To Douglas Goldring, 10 July 1919
Text: MS UT; Unpublished.

Chapel Farm Cottage. Hermitage, nr. Newbury. Berks.

10 July 1919

Dear Mr Goldring

I have written to Pinker to tell him I want to do as I like with *Touch and Go*. I want you to do the play for the Peoples Theatre. I want it to be the first production, and I want it to be a success. It is so very, very rarely I feel in sympathy with a new attempt. Now I do – so I shall go ahead. – You may announce it in your series of plays, too – and before the month is out I will come up and talk it over with you.

Yours Sincerely   D. H. Lawrence

Did you ever see my play *The Widowing of Mrs Holroyd*? Shall I ask Duckworth to send you a copy?

1766. To J. B. Pinker, 10 July 1919
Text: MS UT; Huxley 481.

Chapel Farm Cottage, Hermitage, nr. Newbury. Berks.

10 July 1919

Dear Pinker

I send 'The Fox' by return. I wish I could have cut more – but I simply can't, without mutilating the story.[1]

I will tell Douglas Goldring to arrange with you in a little while. The thought of a People's Theatre pleases me – probably it will fail – but it is a vital *idea* anyhow. I want to talk with Goldring about it – He said he would ask Fagan to let them have the Court Theatre.[2] They two might have a little

---

[1] DHL reduced the story by only some 650 words (out of about 9,000) and modified a few sentences (see Brian Finney, 'The Hitherto Unknown Publication of Some D. H. Lawrence Stories', *Notes and Queries*, xix n.s., February 1972, 55.)

[2] James Bernard Fagan (1873–1933), actor and playwright; he became well known as a London producer after giving up his acting career; he took over the management of the Royal Court Theatre in September 1918. On 31 October 1919 (TMS NYPL) Fagan returned *Touch and Go* to Pinker and commented: 'It is well written but I am afraid in my opinion it would not succeed on the stage.'

understanding, even about the play itself. I should so like a People's Theatre to materialise. Goldring will see you in due course.

Yrs   D. H. Lawrence

1767. To S. S. Koteliansky, [12 July 1919]
Text: MS BL; PC; Postmark, Hermitage 13 JY 19; Zytaruk 182.

Hermitage
Sat.

Have written Goldring – he is 7. St. James Terrace, Regents Park. N.W.8. – and asked him to ring you up. I have agreed to give him the play *Touch and Go* – for publication and production both. He says he will see Fagan about the Court Theatre. – I'll enquire about Daniel.

DHL

1768. To Eleanor Farjeon, [15 July 1919]
Text: MS UT; Postmark, Hermitage 15 JY 19; Huxley 477.

Chapel Farm Cottage, Hermitage, nr. Newbury. Berks.
Tuesday.

Dear Eleanor

I suppose you are back by now from Otford. I'm glad the Weingärtner parcel went off. I am asking my sister-in-law about children's names. – I am asking the Emergency Committee to tell me if one may post letters and parcels now direct to Germany, and if one may send what one likes. Have you any information? – is there any notice in the post office? Tell me if so.

Yesterday we went to look at a place for you: a nice little bungalow, like a little house – about 20 years old – cosy, but small – also an old cottage, spoiled by having two big rooms, one up, one down, added to the end – and a good big orchard garden and paddock effect – all the lot £400 – would take less. The worst of it is it is right out of the world – Summerhurst Green, near *Headley*, nr. Kingsclere, Hants. – about 5 miles from Newbury, 5 from Thatcham: a far off end-of-the-world place, up a narrow forsaken trough of a lane: don't know if you'd like it – don't think you would.

A new venture in a small way – The People's Theatre Society – Douglas Goldring – will do my play (D.V.) *Touch and Go* – in the autumn. It might be nice. I may be in town soon – shall see you then.

Pop down and see us if you feel like it. Margaret expects you here the 1st. week in August.

DHL

1769. To S. S. Koteliansky, [17 July 1919]
Text: MS BL; Zytaruk 183.

Hermitage.
Thursday.[1]

My dear Kot

What do you think of Huebsch. Somehow it puts me off America: to lecture like a fool to fools.

I am glad you liked Douglas Goldring.

I think I shall come to town next week, for a week. Margaret is coming here – and I can't be in the house along with her. – I have written to Barbara, and shall stay in her rooms, probably. She is going to Cambridge for a week or so. Her rooms are in Guildford St. I shall be by myself and in peace. I won't come so soon again to the cave,[2] lest I wear out my welcome. But I'll be round to see Sophie Issayevna and all.

Huebsch makes me hang fire about America. If only one could go as an independent man. Pah, these lectures, these innumerable *suffisant*[3] swine.

I have a pleasant feeling about the Peoples Theatre – but take nothing to heart these days.

DHL

1770. To Thomas Moult, 21 July 1919
Text: MS Lazarus; Unpublished.

Chapel Farm Cottage, Hermitage, nr. Newbury, Berks
21 July 1919

Dear Mr Moult[4]

I expect to be in town on Thursday, and to stay about five days. When and where shall we meet?

Yrs   D. H. Lawrence

Send me a line
c/o Miss Barbara Low, 10 Brunswick Square, W.C.1.

---

[1] The date is selected with reference to DHL's proposal to visit London on 24 July 1919 (see Letter 1770). Also it appears that he has just heard again from Huebsch; Huebsch wrote on 4 July (as indicated on MS of Letter 1747) and, judging by Letter 1787 written on receiving Huebsch's letter of 11 August 1919, mail took approximately twelve days to reach England from New York.

[2] See p. 250 n. 1.

[3] 'self-satisfied'.

[4] Thomas Moult (1880?–1974), poet, critic and editor. He founded and edited *Voices*, a magazine in which he printed two of DHL's poems, 'Nostalgia' and 'Obsequial Chant', in July 1919. (See also Letter 1790 and n. 3). Moult was also reviewer (he reviewed *Touch and Go* in the *Athenaeum*, 11 June 1920); poet (Marsh included him in *Georgian Poetry 1918–1919*);

1771. To Unidentified Recipient, [22? July 1919]
Text: Bookseller's Catalogue (John Wilson, 1981).

5 Acacia Road, St John's [Wood]
Tuesday[1]

[Lawrence announces his presence in London till the following day; he asks whether his correspondent would care to see him; and he gives his address in Pangbourne for the next fortnight.] . . . lunched with Eddie – he says he dines with you on Thursday – so you may be already in town. In that case, and if you would like to see me, perhaps you will ring me up, Hampstead 6534, and I will come.

1772. To Thomas Moult, [25 July 1919]
Text: MS Lazarus; PC; Postmark, St. Johns Wood 25 JUL 19; Unpublished.

5. Acacia Rd. St. Johns Wood.
[25 July 1919]

Dear Mr Moult
    London has rather knocked me up – would you and Mrs Moult care to come to tea here tomorrow. You take any bus that goes up the Finchley Rd, get down at Acacia Rd (Ayre Arms) – but take care of the house numbers – No. 5 is on the right, quite near to the Ayre Arms. – You can ring me up Hampstead 6534. – I should like to see Golding.[2]

Yrs   D. H. Lawrence

1773. To Rosalind Baynes, [1 August 1919]
Text: MS BucU; Nehls, i. 498.

Myrtle Cottage.
Friday[3]

Dear Rosalind[4]
    I send on the letters.
    We are liking The Myrtles so much. I have been working, in the garden all morning, Frieda busy about the house.

anthologist (he produced annual volumes of *Best Poems*, 1922–45, and included DHL's 'Triumph of the Machine' in the 1930 volume); and critic (he wrote *Barrie* (1928), *Mary Webb* (1932), etc.). m. Bessie Boltanskye. (See *Times* obituary, 22 November 1974.)
[1]   The Lawrences moved to Pangbourne on Monday, 28 July (see Letter 1782); this letter – dated 'Tuesday' – could therefore not have been written the day before their departure from London. It is conjecturally placed on the Tuesday nearest their departure date.
[2]   See Letter 1717 and n. 2.
[3]   The letter following announces the arrival of DHL's relations on 3 August; this letter must have been written before that date and thus on the first Friday of his stay in Pangbourne.
[4]   Rosalind Baynes, née Thornycroft (1891–1973), wife of Helton Godwin Baynes (1882–1943) whom DHL had known since 1912 (see *Letters*, i. 475 n. 3). Rosalind was staying in the house

We are expecting my sister any time. We won't come to Spring Cottage on Sunday particularly if Margaret will be there. But we will come on Monday or Tuesday if we may. Perhaps my brother-in-law can get us over in the motor-bicycle.[1]

au revoir   D. H. Lawrence

1774. To Cecily Lambert, [2 August 1919]
Text: MS SIU; PC; Postmark, Pangbourne 2 AU 19; Unpublished.

Myrtle[2] Cottage. Pangbourne
Saturday

Had your pc. – half expected you to turn up today[3] – my sister and brother-in-law come tomorrow. – It is very quiet and nice here – but we hardly go outside the garden. A few apples are ripe, and pears – good for me. – Let us know if possible the day you are coming or else come pretty early – as our visitors may want us to go off picknicking (can't spell) or on that steamer. My brother in law will row you on the river. I blush to make an exhibition before all the nuts and their daisies, so numerous here.

Au revoir to both   D. H. Lawrence

[Frieda Lawrence begins]

Tell Mrs Low to come, we can put you all up easily –
We have *no* butter, Mrs Brown may have some for me from Mrs Allen –[4]

---

belonging to her brother-in-law and sister, Herbert and Joan Farjeon, Spring Cottage, Bucklebury Common, where she had first met DHL (see Nehls, i. 497). The Lawrences were staying in Rosalind's house, 'The Myrtles' in Pangbourne.
[1] Subsequent letters make clear that Edwin and Ada Clarke were the relatives in question.
[2] Myrtle] Spring
[3] Cecily Lambert, with her cousin Violet Monk, had taken over Grimsbury Farm, Long Lane, near Hermitage, on the death of her grandfather. She had first (accidentally) met the Lawrences when they temporarily moved out of Chapel Farm Cottage and were staying with Mrs Lowe in early 1918. Misses Lambert and Monk are, by tradition, associated with DHL's 'The Fox', though Cecily Lambert insisted that in all essentials the story 'was sheer fantasy' (Nehls, i. 465).
[4] Dolly Allan lived near Chapel Farm Cottage; she was the 'odd-job' woman of the village and probably did some house-cleaning and washing for the Lawrences.

1775. To Martin Secker, 6 August 1919
Text: MS UTul; Unpublished.

Myrtle Cottage, Pangbourne – Berks.
6 Aug 1919

Dear Secker

I am glad the *New Poems* are coming in another edition.[1] Let me see what it is like, as soon as possible.

Yes, I should like all my poems to be collected.[2] But if you settle it with Chattos and Duckworth, let me know, will you. I should like to discuss with you the arrangement, and to insert two or three poems.

Yrs   D. H. Lawrence

I am at above address for another fortnight.

1776. To Douglas Goldring, [8 August 1919]
Text: MS Lazarus; Unpublished.

Myrtle Cottage, Pangbourne – Berks.
Friday[3]

Dear Goldring

I couldn't get to a lunch – and couldn't stop on in London. – We are here for another fortnight.

Let me know what happens in Holland. I am always ready to do anything I can towards sanity and real *clarté* – but feel that perhaps one must wait a little longer for events.[4] – I have a feeling, though, that a Peoples Theatre would go all right.

Thank you for lending me the book. It was interesting to me – but Oh God, so dreary the life: such dreariness, weariness.

---

[1] Secker published a 'New Edition re-set' in August 1919.

[2] It was many years before this proposal came to fruition: Secker published DHL's *Collected Poems* in 1928.

[3] The letter following shows that DHL expected to leave Myrtle Cottage on 20 August: this letter was written on a Friday approximately a 'fortnight' earlier; hence the conjectural date of 8 August.

[4] Goldring described himself, in the post-war years, as 'an uncompromising anti-war propagandist, rapidly turning into a Socialist revolutionary' (*Odd Man Out*, p. 177). He became secretary of the English branch of 'Clarté', an international leftist movement for brotherhood and peace; Henri Barbusse, a prominent founder-member, and others, sought what they regarded as 'intellectual clarity'; but 'Clarté' was later exposed as a communist front-organisation. Goldring was about to visit The Hague at the invitation of the editor of a socialist weekly journal (see p. 391 and n. 4).

Remember me to Mrs Goldring.[1] I'd like to see her act. Be sure and write
to me if there is anything I can do, and tell me of your own doings.

D. H. Lawrence

1777. To Thomas Moult, 9 August 1919
Text: MS Lazarus; Unpublished.

Myrtle Cottage, Pangbourne, Berks
9 Aug 1919.

Dear Moult

Thanks for *Voices*. I don't forget I promised you some prose – but I have to
get it out of the Hermitage cottage, which is occupied by other people at
present. Next week I hope to send.[2] – I have written about a cottage. We are
here till the 20th.

Beyond this, no news. How nice it would be if one were pleasantly far off.

D. H. Lawrence

1778. To S. S. Koteliansky, [9? August 1919]
Text: MS BL; Zytaruk 184.

Myrtle Cottage, Pangbourne
Saturday

Dear Kot

I have done a certain amount of the translation – 'Apotheosis'. I began
'Russian Spirit', but either Shestov writes atrociously[3] – I believe he does –
or you translate loosely. One sentence has nothing to do with the next, so that
it seems like jargon. The 'Apotheosis' is more intelligible. His attitude
amuses me – also[4] his irony, which I think is difficult for English readers. But
he isn't anything wonderful, is he? 'Apotheosis of Groundlessness' will never
do. What can one find instead, for a title.

---

[1] DHL 'was anxious that she should play the part of "Mrs Holroyd" if I succeeded in getting
my "People's Theatre Society" to stage a production of that play' (Goldring, *Odd Man Out*,
p. 251). See also Letter 1941.
[2] See Letter 1790 and n. 3.
[3] Leo Shestov (Lev Isaakovich Svartsman) (1868–1938), Russian philosopher and critic. His
work (for which 'Apotheosis of Groundlessness' would have been an accurate title) was
translated by Kot; DHL then acted as editor for Kot's version; and the book finally appeared as
All Things Are Possible, Translated by S. S. Koteliansky with a Foreword by D. H. Lawrence
(Secker, 1920). (On the translation see G. M. Hyde, *D. H. Lawrence and the Art of Translation*,
1981, pp. 21–5, 33–4.)
[4] also] and

Monstrous hot here. – My younger sister and family have gone – my elder sister comes today. Beyond that no news.

Too hot to write an[1] intelligent letter.

DHL

1779. To S. S. Koteliansky, [10 August 1919]
Text: MS BL; Zytaruk 186.

Pangbourne.
Sunday.

Dear Kot.

Could you get a little hand-book of philosophies (or look at one in a public library) and find out the correct term for your 'consequentialness', your 'law of consequences', 'law of sequence' 'causality' – look at *Positivism*.[2] I know nothing about Positivism. *Encyclopædia Britannica* will tell you – in any public library.

Also will you send me Shestov's 'Introduction' if possible before – or with – Part II. Also will you send me a small Introduction of your own – the facts of Shestov's life and purpose.

Don't ask the Woolfs[3] – we will make Heinemann or somebody such print the stuff. Also why not print weekly in *The Nation* or *New Statesman*? We must do this.

Look up Moleschot and Vogt in a big biographical dictionary.[4]

I hope Part II is not so long as Part I. We shall have to cut down if it is. There is more chance of printing a smaller book.

I send you this part – Let me have it back, and we'll make some selections to offer to *The Nation* or to *New Statesman*.

I don't want my name printed as a translator. It won't do for me to appear to dabble in too many things. If you don't want to appear alone – but why shouldn't you? – put me a nom de plume like Richard Haw or Thomas Ball. –

[1] MS reads '&'.
[2] Positivism originated with Auguste Comte (1798–1857), French philosopher who set out his theory in *Cours de Philosophie Positive* (6 vols, 1830–42) and other works. It proved to be a highly influential philosophical system based on science and socialist theory; Comte attempted to provide a corrective to the evils of capitalism and to replace religion with science. (For its influence on the later DHL, see *Apocalypse*, ed. Kalnins, p. 237.)
[3] Presumably Kot had suggested that the Hogarth Press, founded by Leonard and Virginia Woolf in 1917, might undertake the publication of the Shestov translation.
[4] Jacob Moleschott (1822–93), Dutch–German medical writer; Nils Collett Vogt (1864–1937), Norwegian lyric–reflective poet.

Also, when it comes to payment, in mere justice my part is one-third. Don't argue this with me. If you are a Shestovian, accept the facts.

We might try the *English Review*.

Please go through my version and alter anything you think fit.

DHL

1780. To Cecily Lambert, [11 August 1919]
Text: MS SIU; Unpublished.

Pangbourne.
Monday.

Dear Miss Lambert,

You will wonder what we are doing. – My sister and Peggy – also Hilda B[rown][1] – are here, the former till Thursday. Mrs Baynes comes back on Friday. She wants us to stay with her: so we'll stay, I expect, till the Monday following: next Monday, that is. Then we shall have to be trotting off. Do you think you might come for us, with Tommy,[2] next Monday? – Tomorrow the women and children are going – steaming – to Reading. On Wednesday we propose to come to Hermitage. We should bus to Streatley, walk over the downs to Compton, and take train to Hermitage. It will be necessary to see Margaret, to settle up with her. She is going to London on the 21st. – but coming back to the cottage in September. – I shall have a plain understanding with her about the cottage.

We shall lunch at Chapel Farm C. – bring it with us. Shall we come over to you for tea in the afternoon? Tell us if you are busy. We shall come back here by train – 6.20 or 7.30.

At last it is cooler. I feel cooked to a turn – cooked right through. Pangbourne is – or has been – too much like a casserole for me.

Hope you are both safe and sound – particularly sound.

Greetings from everybody   D. H. Lawrence

1781. To S. S. Koteliansky, [12 August 1919]
Text: MS BL; Zytaruk 187.

Pangbourne.
Tuesday

My dear Kot

I have done also 'The Russian Spirit'. Send it at once to Austin Harrison –

---

[1] See Nehls, i. 498–500 for Hilda Brown's recollections of her visit to Pangbourne.
[2] Unidentified.

tell him I recommended you to do so – and tell him a few words about Shestov

The English Review, 19 Garrick St. W.C.

Harrison is mean. *Manage* him about money. He might like to print a series of Shestov-paragraphs.[1] If so, go and see him and have a definite arrangement with him.

DHL

1782. To Catherine Carswell, [15? August 1919]
Text: MS YU; Moore, *Intelligent Heart* 253.

Myrtle Cottage, Pangbourne. Berks.

Friday[2]

My dear Catherine

We are here – since July 28th – Rosalind Baynes lent us her house – pleasant house – hate Pangbourne itself.

Thos. Cook said pass-ports would not be granted till Peace was *ratified*: God knows when that will[3] be. Will Don please fill in the passport, and forward it to Thos. Cook. At any rate it will be ready.

We are here, I think, till the 25th. – then to Hermitage, either to stay in the Cottage or with those farm girls.[4] The wretched Margaret is at the cottage now – she turned us out. She leaves on the 23rd, but comes back again in Sept. for a week or fortnight – so we shall probably stay at the farm. We had my younger sister here last week – now my elder sister.

I don't quite know what is going to happen with us. I shan't go to Germany at present – nor even America, I think. When I come near to the thought of U.S.A. – New York, Prince of Wales etc – it sickens me.[5]

What is your place like? This hot weather I suppose you live out of doors. Are you leaving at end of August?

Nothing happens – except Martin Secker wants to bring out my Collected Poems – why, heaven knows.

Hope J[ohn] P[atrick] is well and happy, also his mother.

Au revoir   DHL

See that Don endorses a photograph.

---

[1] *All Things Are Possible* comprises a series of short paragraphs.
[2] Dated with reference to the arrival and departure of DHL's sisters.
[3] will] would
[4] i.e. Cecily Lambert and Violet Monk.
[5] The Prince of Wales left on 6 August for a tour of Canada and a visit to USA.

1783. To S. S. Koteliansky, [15? August 1919]
Text: MS BL; Zytaruk 185.

Myrtle Cottage, Pangbourne.
Friday[1]

My dear Kot,

I'm glad you went to the New Forest[2] – it's a first step out, anyhow.

I am sending in Frieda's application for a passport today.

I have done 71. of the Shestov paragraphs – more than half. No, I don't hate doing it – rather like it – only he often irritates me when he will keep on going on about philosophers, and what they do or don't do. One gets sick of the name of philosophers. – But sometimes he blossoms into a kind of pathetic beauty.

I'll send you the MS. when finished – Shall you have to get it typed? I might do a bit of typing at Hermitage. We go back there on the 25th. I expect.

I'll let you know as soon as I finish.

DHL

1784. To Catherine Carswell, [20 August 1919]
Text: MS YU; PC; Postmark, Pangbourne 20 AU 19; cited in Moore, *Poste Restante* 55.

Pangbourne.
Wed

Sounds so jolly with you – wish we could have come, but am afraid we can't manage. How long are you staying? We are here till Monday – then to Hermitage. – If you were staying two more weeks, we might dash down. It rains now – so grey, looks as if it would rain for weeks. – Autumn must be beautiful in the Forest.

love from both   DHL

1785. To Cecily Lambert, [22 August 1919]
Text: MS SIU; Unpublished.

Pangbourne.
Friday

Dear Miss Lambert

You'll think we are as vague as Margaret. – Mrs Baynes has come back –

---

[1] The evidence for dating this letter precisely is scarce; it is placed at this point to accord with the sequence of references to the Shestov translation.

[2] Probably to visit the Carswells at Decoy Pond Farm, Marchwood, Hants.

says she has asked Captain Baynes[1] to come down next week, specially to see us, and to talk about a fruit-farming bee which he's got in his bonnet – wants us to stay till he's been. – It's rather a bore upsetting the arrangement. Would you mind coming for us Wednesday or Friday, if these days are possible. I'll write the moment I know when Baynes will be here. – I feel horribly shut in here – think with such relief of the space round the farm.

Tell Miss Monk to have patience with us. I hate this changing business.

D. H. Lawrence

1786. To J. B. Pinker, 23 August 1919
Text: MS UT; Unpublished.

Myrtle Cottage, Pangbourne. Berks.
23 Aug. 1919.

Dear Pinker

Huebsch wrote and asked me if he might begin printing the *New Poems* which Secker published.[2] I said Yes. I suppose that is all right.

About *Touch and Go* – I'm sorry, Douglas Goldring and Walter Peacock were arranging it before I really knew.[3] Peacock arrange[d] with Daniels to publish the play as the first of a 'Plays for A Peoples Theatre' series. Do you mind if it goes through now with these other people?

Yours Sincerely   D. H. Lawrence

---

[1] i.e. Godwin Baynes; he had been a captain, RAMC, during the war; in 1919 he was on the resident staff of Maudesley Hospital.

[2] Huebsch wrote to DHL on 11 August 1919 (TMS LC):

Dear Mr. Lawrence,

I have had no word from you about 'New Poems' and though I presume that you wish me to bring that book out, I wish that you would drop me a line about it. Better still, if I am to go ahead, cable the one word, 'Proceed.' Use the cable address as printed above.

As the book is unprotected by copyright and may be reprinted by anyone who wishes to do so, I suggest that some slight change, substitution or addition be made; or you might include a short foreword if you can appropriately do so. This will make it possible to copyright the book because technically it becomes a different book than the one already published in England, though actually it will not interfere with anyone's right to reproduce the English volume. If you will act in accordance with my suggestion cable 'Proceed alteration' and I will understand that you are immediately posting me the information that will enable me to go ahead with the volume.

Yours sincerely,

[3] Walter Peacock, associated with the literary (principally drama) agency, Golding Bright Ltd, acted as agent for the People's Theatre (see Letters 1807, 1861).

1787. To Martin Secker, 23 August 1919
Text: MS UInd; Postmark, Reading 26 AU 19; Secker 12.

Myrtle Cottage. Pangbourne. Berks
23 Aug. 1919.

Dear Secker

I have heard from Huebsch in New York. He wants to begin printing the *New Poems*. He says they are not copyrighted in America. Is that so?

How is the new edition going?[1] – and the 'Collected Poems' – what of them? I have no photograph of myself – if you really need one I will come up and go to the man you suggest.

Yrs   D. H. Lawrence

1788. To Benjamin Huebsch, 26 August 1919
Text: MS UT; Unpublished.

Panbourne
Aug 26 1919[2]

Proceed alterations.[3]

Lawrence

940 AM

1789. To Cecily Lambert, [26 August 1919]
Text: MS SIU; Unpublished.

Pangbourne.
Tuesday

Dear Miss Lambert,

Do you still invite us to the farm, or are you tired of the continual variations? If we are to come, could you and Miss Monk come to fetch us on Friday or Saturday or even Sunday – whichever day is convenient to you and Tommy. But come to lunch on Friday, for choice. Capt. Baynes is here – we've just been sailing and rowing down to Mapledurham[4] – very windy. Ive agreed to go back into the cottage Sept 16. Can you endure us so long?

Frieda sends greetings.

au revoir.   D. H. Lawrence

Send me a line.

[1] See Letter 1775 and n. 1.
[2] Details of address and date are taken from the cablegram.
[3] See Letter 1786 and n. 2.   [4] Two miles s.e. of Pangbourne.

1790. To Thomas Moult, 29 August 1919
Text: MS Lazarus; Unpublished.

c/o Miss Lambert. Grimsbury Farm, Long Lane. nr. Newbury.

29 Aug 1919

Dear Moult,

I asked Murry *quick* for the MS. he has.[1] He kindly tells me he has *lost* them. tant pour lui!²

I send you a little Preface I wrote for an American publisher, who asked for it. If you like to print it, do so.³ – If you like to cross out the 'Written for the American etc' – cross it out.

We are at Pangbourne – I would have sent sooner, but only finished enclosed yesterday. This evening we go to above address.

D. H. Lawrence

1791. To S. S. Koteliansky, [29? August 1919]
Text: MS BL; Moore 591–2.

Grimsbury Farm, Long Lane, nr Newbury. Berks.

Friday

My dear Kot

I have finished Shestov – have compressed him a bit, but left nothing out – only 'so to speak' and 'as all know' and many such phrases and volatile sentences – no *substance* at all – Sometimes I have added a word or two, for the sake of the sense – as I did in 'Russian Spirit'. What I leave out I leave out deliberately. There is a many-wordedness often, which becomes cloying, wearying. I do get tired of his tilting with 'metaphysics', positivism, Kantian postulates, and so on – but I *like* his 'flying in the face of Reason', like a cross hen. I don't know what I have done with the 'Russian Spirit', which you returned to me. I have written to Pangbourne to see if it's there. If not, I shall have to copy it out from your MS. – Let me have the Preface as soon as possible: also everything you know about Shestov, and I'll write a tiny introduction, and we'll approach the publishers.

So you will be home Tuesday. – Greet Sophie Issayevna and Ghita.

DHL

---

¹ Some (unidentified) pieces offered by DHL to Murry for publication in *Athenæum*.
² 'so much for him!'
³ The preface, written for Huebsch's American edition of *New Poems*, was printed by Moult under the title, 'Verse Free and Unfree', in *Voices*, October 1919. (It also appeared in *Playboy* Nos. 4 and 5 (1919), as 'Poetry of the Present'.)

1792. To Benjamin Huebsch, 29 August 1919
Text: MS UT; Postmark, Pang[bourne] 29 AU 19; Moore 591.

Chapel Farm Cottage – Hermitage, nr. Newbury, Berks
29 Aug. 1919.

Dear Huebsch,

I sent the cable on the 26th. Here is the preface.[1] It is nice, I think. Will you please print on the fly-leaf of *New Poems*: 'Thanks are due to *Poetry*, for permission to re-print some of these poems.' And please send a copy of the book to Harriet Monroe. *Please don't forget this.* – I told Pinker you were printing, so he replied in haste that he would draft an agreement as for *Look* — — as he knew nothing of your intentions. This is what one has an agent for. – I wish you would tell me personally what the sales are, and what becomes due in royalties: the business part: also make the arrangements with me – and if Pinker has to come in, he can come in after.

I can't get to America now: various reasons. I *shall* come though – suddenly one day. – Soon I shall send you the complete MS. of the *American Literature* essays. I haven't done anything. I get angry with things and everybody, and stick. But I'll do them.

D. H. Lawrence

I wish you would send me six copies of *New Poems*, when the book is out: also one copy of *Look*—.

Can I also have a couple of copies of *The Rainbow*. Can English people write to you for a copy of *The Rainbow*? and if so, how much is the cost? Many people bother me about this.

If you feel in a benevolent mood, send Brother Cyprian what he asks for.[2]

1793. To Edward Marsh, 2 September 1919
Text: MS NYPL; Unpublished.

Grimsbury Farm, Long Lane, nr. Newbury. Berks
2 Sept. 1919

Dear Eddie

Thank you for the cheque.[3] – I am here for the moment – Frieda waiting for her passport to Germany – me busy chopping bushes and clearing the meadow. Are you going to Italy?

Chapel Farm Cottage will always find me.

D. H. Lawrence

[1] See Letter 1790 and n. 3.
[2] See p. 399 n. 1.
[3] Probably for the reprinting of 'Seven Seals': see Letter 1759 and n. 1.

1794. To Lady Cynthia Asquith, 2 September 1919
Text: MS UT; Huxley 482.

Grimsbury Farm, Long Lane, nr. Newbury. Berks.

2 Sept. 1919

We are here for the time – F[rieda] waiting for her passport home.

How are you? We saw in the newspaper of the arrival of the third boy.[1] Do you feel better, and happier? Do send a line.

D. H. Lawrence

1795. To Martin Secker, 2 September 1919
Text: MS UInd; Postmark, Hermitage 2 SP 19; Huxley 481–2.

Grimsbury Farm, Long Lane, near Newbury. Berks.

2 Sept. 1919.

Dear Secker

I have been editing, for a Russian friend of mind, a rather amusing, not very long translation of a book of philosophy by one of the last of the Russians, called Shestov. It is by no means a heavy work – nice and ironical and in snappy paragraphs. Would it be in your line?[2]

Yrs   D. H. Lawrence

1796. To Thomas Moult, [4 September 1919]
Text: MS Lazarus; Unpublished.

Grimsbury Farm, Long Lane, nr Newbury.

Thursday 5 Sept 1919

Dear Moult

Thank you for your letter and the cheque: very nice, I had forgotten you were going to pay me.[3] – Did you like that little essay? – you didn't say.

My wife like an unhappy hen flutters from roost to roost. But I like not to have a home.

Remember me to Mrs Moult.

D. H. Lawrence

---

[1] Simon Anthony Rowland Asquith, b. 20 August 1919.
[2] Secker agreed to publish *All Things Are Possible*; it appeared in April 1920.
[3] See Letter 1790 and n. 3.

1797. To Cyril Beaumont, 7 September 1919
Text: MS UCin; Unpublished.

Chapel Farm Cottage, Hermitage, nr. Newbury.
7 Sept 1919

Dear Beaumont,

I have arranged the indenting all right – it will cost you no space or trouble, and will look better. I want that slightly fantastic formation. Unfortunately you missed a line, so I don't know now quite what you will do. Can't you get another line on the first page? – the odd line wouldn't look so bad at the top of p.29. – 'Shades' will be all right as it stands – only insert a dash.[1]

It must be a bother fitting up these small pages.

Hope you are keeping better.

D. H. Lawrence

At the end, let me see a complete set of revised proofs, will you? – I won't alter anything of mine.

1798. To Thomas Seltzer, 7 September 1919
Text: MS UT; Ross, *DHL Review*, viii. 207.

Chapel Farm Cottage, Hermitage, nr. Newbury. Berks, England.
7 Sept 1919.

Dear Mr Seltzer[2]

I had your cablegram – at least as enclosed. I was away, so there is some delay. I wanted moreover to go through the MS. of the novel once more. – I consider this the best of my books.[3] – Please be careful with the MS., as it is the most complete one: – I am forwarding it to you by the next mail.

Meanwhile Martin Secker writes that he would like to publish the book

---

[1] The proofs of *Bay* sent by Beaumont (now at UT) show 'Obsequial Ode' (pp. 29–31) marked by DHL for indentation just as it is printed in *Complete Poems*, with the exception of stanza 1 which – because of the way it is printed in *Bay* – he did not mark for indentation. What is line 19 in the final poem ('Their fingers in sunset shine') had been omitted by the printer; DHL wrote it in. Nine lines of the 'Ode' were printed on p. 29 under the illustration. In 'Shades' DHL inserted a dash at the end of line 1; he added 'we' to line 18 ('One shadow, and we need not dissemble'); and made several minor changes in punctuation.

[2] Thomas Seltzer (1875–1943), journalist, translator and publisher. Born in Russia, he lived in America from the age of 12. He translated Gorky, Leon Trotsky, Andreas Latzko, *et al*. His publishing career began with Boni and Liveright in 1917; he and Temple Scott formed the partnership, Scott and Seltzer, in 1918; during the period 1920–5 he published more first editions by DHL than any other American publisher has ever done. m. 1906, Adele Szold (1876–1940). (See *D. H. Lawrence: Letters to Thomas and Adele Seltzer*, ed. Gerald M. Lacy, Santa Barbara, 1976.) His London representative was Douglas Goldring who presumably drew his attention to DHL.

[3] *Women in Love.*

next spring, under its old title 'The Sisters'. He has another copy. – I would like the book to come first in America. I shall never forgive England *The Rainbow*. – If you wished to publish this novel, would you like me to write a short Fore-word?[1] – And which title do you prefer, 'Women in Love', or 'The Sisters'.

Yours Sincerely   D. H. Lawrence

Hermitage, Newbury, England is sufficient address for me.

1799. To Martin Secker, 8 September 1919
Text: MS UInd; Postmark, Newbury 9 SP 19; Secker 13.

Grimsbury Farm, Long Lane, nr. Newbury. Berks.
8 Sept 1919

Dear Secker

Thanks for your letter – I will send the Shestov translation this week. – About *Women in Love* – I am just corresponding with America about it. If it actually comes off, and is published there this late autumn, would you like to have sheets?[2] I'll tell you in about 3 weeks time. – 'The Sisters' was one of the original titles – but somebody – some woman – has used it.[3] To me the title is a matter of indifference. I would like you to publish the book – I know it is my best – but don't speak yet to Pinker, wait a bit till I let you hear about America.

Yrs   D. H. Lawrence

1800. To Douglas Goldring, 9 September 1919
Text: MS UT; Unpublished.

Grimsbury Farm, Long Lane, nr. Newbury.
9 Sept 1919

Dear Goldring

I had your letter from Holland – glad you made a good thing of your visit. I am doing an essay on Democracy for *The Word*.[4]

---

[1] The first edition of *Women in Love*, privately printed, was published by Seltzer in New York in November 1920; Secker's first English edition appeared in June 1921. Seltzer published the 'Foreword' separately in an advertising leaflet in autumn 1920; see also p. 144 n. 2.
[2] After publishing the first English edition in 1921, Secker issued a limited autographed edition of 50 copies made up of sheets bought from Seltzer, in June 1922.
[3] Ada Cambridge (b. 1844) published her novel, *Sisters* in 1904. See also DHL's reference to May Sinclair's novel, *The Three Sisters* (1914), in *Letters*, ii. 639.
[4] Goldring stayed in The Hague at the invitation of the editor of 'a curious publication called *The Word in Three Languages . . .* run by a group of enigmatic and highly improbable Germans who pretended to be International Socialists . . . I fancy I got them to print one or two articles by Lawrence' (*Odd Man Out*, p. 243). See Letter 1818 and p. 404 n. 1.

Are you at home now? Let me know when you come to town. I may be coming up shortly also.

Did you get to Germany?[1] My wife is awfully anxious to go and see her mother – in Baden-Baden. But they don't issue passports here to Germany. How did you manage about getting in? Do tell me if there is anything we could do to get my wife a passport – or an entry into Germany. She has a permit from Baden, to enter there.

We are going back to Chapel Farm Cottage directly. It is quite near. – You might come and see us – both of you – this sunny lovely weather. Would you care to?

Yrs   D. H. Lawrence

1801. To S. S. Koteliansky, [9 September 1919]
Text: MS BL; Zytaruk 189.

Grimsbury Farm.
Tuesday[2]

My dear Kot

I got your letter this morning. I feel I can't come to London: feel the town would be more than I could stand at this minute: even the train journey would do for me. Here one can chop bushes and milk the goats.

I had a letter from Secker – he said he would like to see the Shestov, with a view to publishing it. Connie Garnett has the Tchekhov letters in print – is now correcting proofs for Heinemann.[3] – I hear that a book on Tchekhov, by Shestov, is published in England[4] – one of those black-covered translations. Could you find out about that, I wonder? Or shall I write and borrow it? – We must find out enough about Shestov.

Let me have the Introduction as soon as you can.

I'll write to Tidmarsh[5] about the Shestov *Tchekhov*.

DHL

---

[1] Despite the considerable difficulties put in the way of travellers, Goldring managed to visit several places in Germany. One person whom he met – who was subsequently important to DHL – was Dr Anton Kippenberg (1874–1950), the head of Insel-Verlag; Goldring claimed that he interested Kippenberg in DHL's writings (*Odd Man Out*, p. 245).

[2] The contents of the letter suggest that it was written on the Tuesday before Letter 1803; that in turn was written when the Lawrences returned to Chapel Farm Cottage on 12 September 1919.

[3] Constance Garnett (1861–1946), the eminent translator of Russian literature, was the wife of Edward Garnett (1868–1937), DHL's early mentor. Her translation, *Tchekhov, Letters to his Family and Friends* was published by Chatto & Windus in February 1920; Heinemann published her translation of Dostoievsky's *An Honest Thief and Other Stories* in October 1919.

[4] Letter 1803 lends weight to the idea that DHL had heard of a book which proved to be the translation by Kot and Murry of Shestov's *Anton Tchekhov and Other Essays* (1916).

[5] It is conceivable that DHL proposed to enquire of Lytton Strachey, or one of his friends, at Tidmarsh Mill, only one mile from Pangbourne.

1802. To Max Plowman, 11 September 1919
Text: MS Plowman; Unpublished.

Chapel Farm Cottage, Hermitage, nr. Newbury, Berks.[1]

11 Sept. 1919

Dear Mr Plowman[2]

I shall be very glad to have your inscription, and a word spoken for *The Rainbow*. One shouldn't look for consolations, but it's nice when they come. Shall we meet one day?

Yours Sincerely   D. H. Lawrence

1803. To S. S. Koteliansky, [12 September 1919]
Text: MS BL; Zytaruk 190.

Chapel Farm Cottage, Hermitage, nr. Newbury. Berks.

Friday

My dear Kot

I got the Shestov book, and preface: also heard from Rosalind Baynes about the Shestov *Tchekhov*. It was your essay – I thought she meant a whole vol. on Tchekhov.

I will send the Shestov in to Secker on Monday. If only we had a duplicate, we could send to America.

We came back here this evening – wonderful autumn weather.

When I hear from Secker, perhaps you will go and see him.

DHL

1804. To Gordon MacFarlane, 15 September 1919
Text: MS Carswell; Unpublished.

Chapel Farm Cottage, Hermitage, nr. Newbury. Berks

15 Sept 1919

Dear Macfarlane,[3]

Thank you for your letter and cheque. Are you sure the typewriter is worth so much to you?[4] For heaven's sake don't give me £5. unless it is fair dues. –

---

[1] DHL was anticipating his return to this address on 12 September (see the letter following).

[2] Mark ('Max') Plowman (1883–1941), journalist and poet. m. Dorothy Lloyd Sulman, 1914. He had served as an army officer from 1914 but, in 1918, had resigned his commission as a conscientious objector. He published several volumes of verse and *An Introduction to the Study of Blake* (1927); later he was editor of *Adelphi* (1938); but he had recently – in June 1919 – published *War and the Creative Impulse*. It may be that Plowman had offered to present an inscribed copy to DHL. *The Rainbow* is not mentioned in the book, and no explanation can be offered of DHL's remark about the novel.

[3] See p. 146 n. 4.

[4] See p. 365 n. 3.

Does the hateful old thing go all right now? She can't have an oil bath –
Cleopatra luxuries; she must be content with a smear. – Hope you won't curse
the day you met her.

Yrs   D. H. Lawrence

1805. To Martin Secker, 15 September 1919
Text: MS UInd; Secker 13.

Chapel Farm Cottage, Hermitage, nr. Newbury. Berks.
15 Sept. 1919.

Dear Secker.

I send you the Shestov: it's really worth doing, and will probably take well
with young people. – You can put 'Edited by D. H. Lawrence', or leave it
out, as you like.[1] – I find Shestov's 'Preface' long and tedious and
unnecessary. You could leave it out if you thought fit, and put in the little 4-
page Foreword I enclose. Shestov's Preface is too heavy, to my thinking.

Let me know fairly quickly, will you. I want to send the MS. to America.

When I hear from New York about the novel, I'll tell you. You see I want
you to print from the MS. that is now over there. Either they will return it and
I'll send it you, or they'll send proof-sheets which I'll send you.

What about the new edition of *New Poems*? – and the Collected Edition?

D. H. Lawrence

Would it be very expensive to have the Shestov typed?

1806. To Lady Cynthia Asquith, 16 September 1919
Text: TMSC NWU; Huxley 482–3.

Chapel Farm Cottage, Hermitage, Nr Newbury, Berks.
16th September 1919

Will Simon be called Peter, and super hanc Petram shall you found your
fortress?[2] I suppose we shall have to see you Madonnaing in the penny
pictorials for a while. But beware, you know what comes to over pictorialised
ladies. Didn't one fall through a sky-light?[3] Don't Madonna for the Sunday
press.

[1]   See p. 380 n. 3 and Letter 1779.
[2]   See Letter 1794 and n. 1. Cf. Matthew xvi. 18 ['thou art Peter and upon this rock I will build
      my church'].
[3]   Moore states that DHL is referring to an accident which befell Lady Diana Cooper (Moore
      593). She is reflected in Lady Artemis Hooper, the society lady who has managed to fall
      through the window of a taxi, in *Aaron's Rod*, chap. XII.

So I expect you are on your legs again, cast forth from the hallucinary Patmos of your bed.[1] Simon! Simon! It has a Judaic sound. Better make a dart for the foam again, Aphrodite is better than any Judith, or than any Mary. *Plus fière.* Loathsome Judaea.

What other news, save Simon? Are you richer? Are you glad to go back to Sussex Place? What is your husband doing? When I say richer, I merely mean 'Bradburys'.[2] Are you preparing to sally forth into the 'monde' as a sort of young matron? Pfui!! Ah bah! What is the new line? You'll have to have a new line. *Mère de trois.* It's a bit of a quandary. Capitoline Juno? Ox-eyed Hera?[3] [Many-breasted Artemis?] Ficherie! *Mais toujours mère de trois.* Super hanc Petram. That's how it always is, nowadays. *Fate attenzione al sasso.* Mind the stone. Cave petram.

No, I'm not angry with the world. I've got tired of being angry. I also want a new line. It's time the world began to amuse me. I insist on being amused.

I believe in a little while I shall be having a sort of success: in America. Better spend it in England. Time one had a bit of fun. [Perhaps soon you may even be enjoying again a governmental daughter-in-lawdom.][4]

Frieda, who still insists on 'feeling' her trials, gets very cross, or weeps, when the letters come from Germany. She has set her mind on going: and she can't go. Another quandary. Patience is justified of all her children.[5] [I suppose when you acquire again a governmental lustre,][6] Frieda will get her passport: *quand nous avons changé tout cela.*[7] But really I don't care a jot about changing it.

Beaumont [dear, foetid little Beaumont,] slowly filters through the poems. He must be nearing the end. Perhaps by Christmas he will actually spawn his production.

Martin Secker will bring out *Women in Love* in the Spring. Probably it will come out this autumn in America.

---

[1]   Patmos was the island of exile or retirement for St John (see Revelation i. 9).
[2]   i.e. banknotes (especially £1 notes) signed by Sir John (later 1st Baron) Bradbury (1872–1950), Secretary to the Treasury.
[3]   Juno, the 'ox-eyed' wife of Jupiter in Roman mythology was identified with the Greek Hera; she was the special protectress of marriage. (The typescript copy on which the text of this letter is based lacks the interrogative phrase, 'Many-breasted Artemis?', which appears in Moore 592. The authority for Moore's text is not known.)
[4]   The bracketed sentence is taken from Moore 593.
[5]   Cf. Luke vii. 35 ['wisdom is justified . . .'].
[6]   These bracketed words (as on two occasions later in the letter) are taken from Moore 593; they replace ellipses in the textual source. The remark at this point (which Huxley omits) glances at the 'lustre' enjoyed by the Asquith family when H. H. Asquith was Prime Minister (1908–16).
[7]   Molière, *Le Médecin malgré lui* (1666), II. iv ['mais nous . . .'].

When I lunched with [Eddie,] he says 'Isn't it remarkable, how the poets are returning to Beauty!' – he was afraid to walk with me up the Mall afterwards, and ran away like a respectable rabbit. What I want to know is, was it my appearance, or my reputation, or his? *Bel Dio!*

Pleasant mild Autumn, many mushrooms, smoke from cottage gardens, chilly evenings, etc. – *toujours perdrix*[1] – no, not even that – *tojours lapin en casserole.*

When I am in town again – before long – I will call at Sussex Place, if I am duly invited. Frieda sends her love: emotional goods not rationed.

DHL

1807. To J. B. Pinker, 17 September 1919
Text: MS BosU; Unpublished.

Chapel Farm Cottage, Hermitage, nr. Newbury. Berks
17 Sept 1919

Dear Pinker

Thank you for your letter. – I think I explained to you that owing to circumstances I had to settle[2] *Touch and Go* with the People's Theatre agent, Walter Peacock, – so that he'll have to go through with it. – You have copies of the play. You had *two*[3] type-written copies made. – Anyhow, I'll bet it won't suit these New Yorkers.[4]

Yours Sincerely   D. H. Lawrence

1808. To Martin Secker, 23 September 1919
Text: MS UInd; Postmark, Hermitage SP 23 19; Secker 14.

Chapel Farm Cottage, Hermitage, nr. Newbury.
23 Sept. 1919

Dear Secker

A week ago I sent you the MS. of the translation of Shestov's 'Apotheosis of Groundlessness' – to Iver. – I haven't heard if you received it. If not, I must enquire about it quickly.

Let me hear about it as soon as possible, will you.

Yrs   D. H. Lawrence

---

[1] A favourite but obscure phrase meaning literally 'always a partridge'. Cf. *Letters*, ii. 536 and 'The Novel and the Feelings' (*Phoenix*, ed. McDonald, p. 755).
[2] settle] settle with
[3] A marginal note (probably made in Pinker's office) on the MS reads: 'one'.
[4] See Letter 1812.

1809. To S. S. Koteliansky, [24 September 1919]
Text: MS BL; Postmark, Hermitage 24 [. . .] 19; Moore 593–4.

Hermitage.
Wednesday

My dear Kot

I have been a long time – waiting to hear from Secker. He always offers filthy terms. What do you say? Let me know, and then I'll write and tell him you'll see him and make the agreement direct.

What about an American publisher? Shall I write to one, direct, or will you see an agent?

I am troubled about your finances. At present I've got to see Frieda off to Germany – the policeman came Monday to verify her passport application, and said the passport would come all right – probably it will – so I must provide for that trip, otherwise I could have given you something. – Have you been to Harrison?[1] Go to him, make him publish 'Russian Spirit', and even other sections. Try and get an advance out of Secker – and really, out of common decency, do keep whatever money can be made. I owe you heaven knows how many pounds. – Soon I shall, I believe, begin to make money in America. Then you can have some freely. At present it's the same old hand to mouth.

I thought the Shestov Preface the worst part of the book – don't think Secker will do badly if he omits it. – I wrote a 4-page Foreword.

Another thing – if you aren't busy, do you think you might copy out for me three of the American essays?[2] Huebsch worries me for them – an American[3] came to see me last week. If you would copy out three for me – I'll send my MS. – it would save me weary work. – You would let me pay you, like a type-writer. Your handwriting is so nice and plain. – But be sure you don't do it if you don't want.

If Frieda gets her passport I shall be in London, and shall see you.

Is Sonia home – yes surely. Remember me very nicely to her and Ghita.

DHL

---

[1] See Letter 1781.
[2] Letter 1811 makes clear that DHL was not referring here to any of the essays published in *English Review*. Kot was therefore being asked to copy three of the following: 'Dana's "Two Years Before the Mast"'; 'Herman Melville's "Typee" and "Omoo"'; 'Herman Melville's "Moby Dick"'; 'Whitman' (this being the least likely).
[3] Presumably 'Schaff', mentioned in Letter 1812.

1810. To Martin Secker, 26 September 1919
Text: MS UInd; Postmark, Hermitage [. . .] 19; Secker 14–15.

Chapel Farm Cottage, Hermitage, nr. Newbury.
26 Sept. 1919

Dear Secker

I sent your letter to Koteliansky: of course it's his translation. He is badly off, and would wish to sell the copyright to you at once, for a lump sum. If you wish, he would sell both the American and the English rights. – You would make the agreement direct with him – or with me, it amounts to the same thing: no Pinker. – I have a man in America who, I think, would take the book all right. If you preferred only to buy just the English rights, I should be very glad if you really let me have sheets in a month's time, as you said. – Koteliansky wants Shestov's Preface published – but really, do you think it matters?

I am writing to Duckworth about the poems. I know he's obstinate. He faithfully expects me to sell one day: and is content with the steady sales he has. I think he sold about 150 *Love Poems and Others* last year – but I'm not good at remembering.

Let us settle quickly about Shestov. – 'Groundlessness' is a horror! – but what else?

I thought of offering a few selections from the 'Apotheosis' to Harrison, for the *English Review*. Do you agree? – or do you prefer not?

If you would care to see[1] Koteliansky, or write him, he is S. Koteliansky, 5 Acacia Rd., St. Johns Wood, N.W.8. – on the telephone under *Bourse Gazette* – I believe *Hampstead 6534*. – But if you prefer to settle with me about everything, do so.

Yrs   D. H. Lawrence

Could you give me Compton Mackenzie's address?[2] Is he in Italy? I want to go to Italy – and I want to write to him about it.

1811. To S. S. Koteliansky, [26 September 1919]
Text: MS BL; Zytaruk 192.

Hermitage.
Friday

My dear Kot

I have written to Secker just what you said. I'll let you know as soon as he

---

[1] see] go
[2] (Sir) Edward Montague Compton Mackenzie (1883–1972), novelist. He and DHL had first met at Chesham on 24 August 1914. See *Letters*, ii. 212. Secker was Mackenzie's publisher.

replies. – I have another publisher in America – Scott and Seltzer – I believe they'd be better than Huebsch.

Will there be peace with Russia?

I send you the three essays. Will you please do them on smallish sheets like this – so that they can make one MS. with the *English Review* pages. I wish I could have sent you a writing block – but none here – and it rains. I shall send you a few pears – for you and Sophie Issayevna – when it doesn't rain.

DHL

1812. To Benjamin Huebsch, 30 September 1919
Text: MS UT; Moore 595–6.

Hermitage, nr. Newbury. Berks.

30 Sept. 1919.

Dear Huebsch,

I had your letter yesterday, saying you would probably postpone the *New Poems* till after Christmas.[1] – I understand that the smut hunters want to raise

[1] Huebsch had written on 17 September 1919 (TMS LC):

My dear Lawrence,

The difficulty of producing books is increasing to such an extent that I may possibly postpone issuing "New Poems" until after Christmas. The labor situation is acute and we are facing the possibility of a strike which may interfere with the printing and binding of autumn books long since planned.

I have read through the preface once but after it is copied on the typewriter I will read it again with greater concentration than was possible when reading your wonderful microscopic orthography, but I got the sense of it and I think you have done a fine job. I don't like to let anyone use it before it goes in the book, yet I feel that if I can get some money for you by selling it to The New Republic or The Nation it will be worth while foregoing its exclusive use in the book. I will let you know if I should succeed.

I shall not forget your injunction with regard to "Poetry" and a copy to Miss Monroe. The contract from Pinker came promptly on top of your letter. Agents!

I posted you a copy of "Look! We Have Come Through" and two copies of "The Rainbow", the latter being from among the half dozen that I have saved. Don't refer any English inquirers to me as the book is out of print. I am confident that the friends who advise me not to restore it to print at present have at heart your best interests and mine. Our self-appointed censors (smut hounds as Henry L. Mencken calls them) would love to make a "case" out of this, and unfortunately under our postal laws and system of justice the book would be officially suppressed (which it is not now) I would be fined or sent to jail and your reputation would suffer.

As to Brother Cyprian, he is a grafter, to use our flexible American speech. Whenever he sees a review of a book that promises to interest him he becomes the mendicant friar of fiction.

There are reasons why you should not regret too much not being able to come over now. Personally, I am very sorry but in the long run I think that you lose nothing by postponing the visit. But I know how you feel at having your plans interfered with. Am I not in the same boat?

I will have the account with your books fixed up and let you know how matters stand.

Cordially yours,

a howl over you – canaille! – A week ago last Saturday Schaff[1] called to see me – told me about America. Today I have a parcel of books from Jane Burr – read the *Glorious Hope*[2] – Humanly, what a horror of a place your U.S. seems – sends ice to my heart. – Quoi faire! I swear people are no longer people, over there with you – sort of stalking emotional demons. You no doubt are a Jew – capable of the eternal detachment of judgment – connoisseurs of the universe, the Jews – even connoisseurs of human life – dealers in fine arts and treasures – dealers – you might just tell me what you *really* think of the U.S.

I have finished the *Classic American* essays – end up with an essay on Whitman. The essay on Whitman you may find it politic not to publish – if so leave it out altogether – don't alter it. The rest is unexceptionable. – These essays are the result of five years of persistent work. They contain a whole Weltanschauung[3] – new, if old – even a new science of psychology – pure science. I don't want to give them to a publisher here – not yet. – I don't really want people to read them – till they are in cold print. I don't mind if you don't publish them – or if you keep them back. – I only know the psychoanalysts here – one of them – has gone to Vienna, partly to graft some of the ideas on to Freud and the Freudian theory of the unconscious – is at this moment busy doing it.[4] I *know* they are trying to get the theory of primal consciousness out of these essays, to solidify their windy theory of the unconscious. Then they'll pop out with it, as a discovery of their own. – You see Ive told Ernest Jones and the Eders the ideas. – But they don't know how to use them. And no one has seen the essay on Whitman – no one in the world. – Look after the MS. for me, won't you. – Schaff says you're the only 'white' publisher in America. – Superlative. – I arranged with a man here – Daniels – to publish a play *Touch and Go* – he arranged the American rights with somebody – Tobey or somebody[5] – I don't know. – Also I sent the novel *Women in Love* – sort of sequel to *The Rainbow*, to some other New York people who asked to see it[6] – presumed you were not keen on it – you must have seen the MS – Pinker has had it for two years. – I edited a translation of a Russian philosopher – Shestov – for a Russian friend of mine – Secker will publish it in the spring – a short, amusing book, about 50,000 or 60,000 words. Would you like sheets of that? – let me know at once. – It's called 'Apotheosis of Groundlessness' – written in short, ironical, amusing paragraphs.

---

[1] Unidentified.
[2] Jane Burr had been responsible for publishing her own book, in 1918; in 1921 both Seltzer and Duckworth published it.
[3] i.e. philosophy of life, creed.
[4] The psychoanalyst was Dr Ernest Jones. He was an associate and close friend of Freud; he later published *Sigmund Freud: Life and Work* (1953–7).
[5] Unidentified.   [6] Scott and Seltzer.

I shall send you the MS. of the American essays as soon as this railway strike ends[1] – I expect this week.

I might possibly go to Italy for the winter – for health.

Schaff said the *Atlantic Monthly* might publish the Dana and Herman Melville essays: but if you don't want them to appear in periodicals, don't bother.

Good luck to you   D. H. Lawrence

I think I shan't let Pinker make any more agreements – anyway I'll tell you first.

1813. To S. S. Koteliansky, [1 October 1919]
Text: MS BL; Zytaruk 193.

Hermitage.
Wed.

My dear Kot.

Yes, the paper is quite all right. I feel you'll hate doing it.

Secker says he has written to you, making offers. – He wants a new title.

Let us hope the insects will bite K[atherine] to death.[2]

Things will never be *lively* – they may be deadly. It is a process of attrition, not violence.

Good for Grisha.

I *may* – just possible – go to Italy for the winter – but *not* San Remo – which is really France still.

DHL

Tell me what Secker says.

Railway will compromise with Govt – encore!

1814. To Martin Secker, [1 October 1919]
Text: MS UInd; Postmark, [Hermit]age 1[. . .] 19; Secker 14.

Hermitage.
Wednesday

Dear Secker

Thanks for Mackenzie's address – I have written to him[3] – I do hope I can get off soon – how nice if we had a time all together on Capri! I wonder if there will be any passport difficulties. Do you know?

---

[1] The strike dragged on until 5 October 1919.
[2] In mid-September 1919 Katherine Mansfield went to live at the Casetta Deerholm, Ospedaletti, San Remo, on the Italian Riviera.
[3] The letter has not been found.

I agree about 'Apotheosis' – give it a nice English title 'Why Believe?' – 'Away with Dogma.' – 'The Bounds of Possibility' – 'Illimitable Possibility' – the last is a fair translation of 'Apotheosis of Groundlessness'. – or 'Boundless Possibility' – or *All Things Are Possible* – I like the last best. But you'll probably think of something you prefer.

D. H. Lawrence

1815. To Martin Secker, 2 October 1919
Text: MS UInd; Postmark, Hermitage 2 OC 19; Secker 15.

Chapel Farm Cottage, Hermitage, near Newbury.
2 Oct. 1919.

Dear Secker,

Koteliansky is furious at your offer of £20. for all rights, and asks me to write to you. Truly, if for all the work we have both done, £20. is the beginning and the end, best have sat still.

Let me know if you really want to have the book. If you aren't keen on it, send me the MS. back here, and I'll go elsewhere with it.

Koteliansky says, if you do the book at all, we will revert to your first offer. These are his terms.

1. That the book be published before April 1st. 1920: that you pay 10% royalty, with a settlement for the copies subscribed on publication day.
2. That you supply me with proofs within one month's time after signing agreement.
3. That we have the right to publish paragraphs from the book in periodicals, in the meantime, before you are ready for publication.

Koteliansky is also rather keen that Shestov's Preface be included. I can't see that that matters, and leave it to you.

You can make the whole agreement with me, if you like – or with Koteliansky. – Or you can just return me the MS. and make an end of it.

Hope this will be all right.

Yrs   D. H. Lawrence

1816. To S. S. Koteliansky, [4 October 1919]
Text: MS BL; Zytaruk 194.

Hermitage.
Saturday

My dear Kot

The MS. has come this morning – thank you very much indeed. Did it bore you very much to do it? I shall send it to America now.

I laughed at your fury with Secker. Didn't you know he was a scurvy little swine? They are all like it. Pah! – I wrote to him your terms – told him he could make the agreement with me – was quite plain to him: showed him what I thought of him.

Poor Fox:[1] after all, if he doesn't come back, he'll be *your* tragedy more than anybody's. But in my secret heart, je voudrai qu'il soit perdu.[2]

I will send you whatever Secker writes. – I told him to send me Shestov back again, if he wasn't keen on him – and I'd try elsewhere.

DHL

1817. To S. S. Koteliansky, [6 October 1919]
Text: MS BL; Zytaruk 195.

Hermitage –
Monday

My dear Kot

I send you Secker's letter and agreement.[3] The world of business is *never* decent – it lies and lies and lies again – by now I am callous to it. – You will see the agreement is made with me – I suppose you don't care – I don't. Oh Lord, it is hard to imagine the pitch to which I don't care. I'm always having to kick myself into making an effort for my own rights. – I don't care for Seckers 'America' clause – why should he have $\frac{1}{3}$ if we arrange rights? – and 10% of sheets sold won't do – no. What do you think of this? – Anyhow, I so insisted that Secker should return me the MS. if he wasn't keen on publishing it, that he must go ahead now.

DHL

1818. To Douglas Goldring, 6 October 1919
Text: MS UT; Unpublished.

Chapel Farm Cottage, Hermitage, nr. Newbury. Berks.
6 Oct. 1919

Dear Goldring

I wondered what had become of you: was glad to hear from you. My wife is still waiting for her passport – but will get it soon, I believe. We shall see you

---

[1] See Letter 1588 and n. 3.
[2] 'I hope he'll stay lost.'
[3] The agreement signed by DHL is dated 4 October 1919; the provisional title of the volume was 'Apotheosis of Groundlessness'; the royalty payment was to be 10%; and DHL was to receive six complimentary copies. The 'America' clause to which DHL refers guarantees a 10% royalty if Secker sold sheets to an American publisher; two-thirds of the profits would be paid to DHL on any separate copyright edition in USA.

before she leaves for Germany. I think I shall have a shot at going to Italy for the winter.

Today I have sent off four essays on 'Democracy' to *The Word*.[1] I *do* think it should be a monthly, not a weekly. I want to see you about it.

Any news whatsoever about A People's Theatre, and the play?

I suppose you wouldn't have time to come down here for a week-end with your wife? feel there is so much to talk about.[2]

Yrs   D. H. Lawrence

1819. To Martin Secker, 8 October 1919
Text: MS UInd; Postmark, Reading 8 OC 19; Secker 16.

Chapel Farm Cottage, Hermitage, nr. Newbury.
8 October 1919.

Dear Secker

I enclose the signed agreement. I sent it to Koteliansky and he agreed. But do let us have the proofs in the month, if possible.

How long do letters take to Italy? I am wondering about Mackenzie. My wife has got her passport for Germany, so will be off almost at once.

Yrs   D. H. Lawrence

1820. To S. S. Koteliansky, 10 October 1919
Text: MS BL; Zytaruk 196.

Chapel Farm Cottage, Hermitage, near Newbury.
10 Oct 1919

My dear Kot

I send you the agreement, and Secker's last letter.

Frieda has got her passport: waits for the Dutch visa – may set off next week. If so, we shall be in town and shall see you.

I really think I may go to Italy – if conditions are possible there.

---

[1] The first essay, carrying the sub-heading 'The Average', appeared in *The Word*, xii (18 October 1919), 11–12; the second, 'Identity', in xiii (25 October 1919), 2, 11; and the third, 'Personality', in xiv (6 December 1919), 7. The fourth has not been traced. The text of the first three sections follows very closely that of 'Democracy' in *Phoenix*, ed. McDonald, pp. 699–713. (Though Goldring gives the title of the publication as *The Word in Three Languages* – see p. 391 n. 4 – and though the contents of the periodical are in German and French as well as in English, its title is simply *The Word*.) Cf. *Kangaroo* (Secker, 1923), chap. vi: a 'series of articles on Democracy . . . in that absurd international paper published at The Hague, that they said was run absolutely by spies and shady people'.

[2] See Goldring, *Odd Man Out*, pp. 251–2, for his account of the weekend.

I enclose 10/-. to pay for paper and postage etc. of the MS. – for which I again thank you.

au revoir to all, including Fox.

DHL

I offered Secker a set of possible titles.

You keep the Agreement – I am so careless.

1821. To Benjamin Huebsch, 10 October 1919
Text: MS UT; Unpublished.

Chapel Farm Cottage, Hermitage, nr. Newbury.
10th. Oct. 1919.

Dear Huebsch,

I am sending you today the *Studies in Classic American Literature*. As I said before, if you find it better not to publish 'Whitman', leave it out altogether. I include four little essays on 'Democracy', which I expect will come out in that little weekly International paper *The Word* – published at The Hague. – You could, if you liked, include these instead of 'Whitman', or as well as 'Whitman' – as you like.

I gather that you feel me a risky venture just now. Why not get some monthly, like the *Atlantic*, to publish the Dana and Melville essays? Mr Schaff said he had personal acquaintance with the editor, and would put the thing before him. If you could get some of the essays in respectable sound periodicals, I'm sure it would help my reputation immensely, and simplify your job. Somebody might do the 'Democracy' essays: I am not sending them out in England just yet.

Well, good luck to you. Remember what I say about these *American* essays: don't publish them, don't bother with them, just send them me back, if you feel doubtful.

My wife has got passport etc for Germany – her people are German – and is just about to set off. I think I shall go to Italy – perhaps spend the winter with Compton Mackenzie on Capri. Anyhow I'll let you know.

D. H. Lawrence

I'm sorry I can't send you typed MS. You must excuse me.

1822. To Beatrix Goldring, [14 October 1919]
Text: MS StaU; PC; Postmark, Hampstead 14 OCT [. . .]; Unpublished.

c/o Mrs Carswell, Holly Bush House, Holly Mount, Hampstead, NW3
[14 October 1919]

Came here today – brought your gloves and wax[1] – shall probably see you
Thursday – tomorrow rushing for visa and F[rieda] departing if possible.

D. H. Lawrence

1823. To Douglas Goldring, [15 October 1919]
Text: MS StaU; PC; Postmark, Hampstead 15 OCT 19; Unpublished.

Hampstead.
Wed night.

Frieda goes off tonight. I shall come and see you in the morning – or afternoon
– think I shall go to Hermitage tomorrow night. Ring me up in the morning,
about 10.0 at Mrs *Carswells* – Holly Bush House – Hampstead 4059 I believe
– verify it – and tell me when you'll be in.

DHL

1824. To Cecily Lambert, [15 October 1919]
Text: MS SIU; PC; Postmark, Hampstead 15 OCT 19; Unpublished.

Hampstead –
Wednesday

Frieda sets off for Harwich tonight – I shall probably be home on Friday –
shall have to go to the Midlands, my sister is ill – but I shall call round. Is
Miss Monk home again? – Im sorry for that trouble.
    Kind regards to your Mother and father.

D. H. Lawrence

1825. To Martin Secker, [16 October 1919]
Text: MS UInd; Postmark, Hampstead 16 OCT 19; Secker 16.

Chapel Farm Cottage, Hermitage, nr. Newbury.
17 Oct 1919

Dear Secker
    I have just sent off to America the completed MS. of my *Studies in Classic*

---

[1] Presumably left after the Goldrings' weekend with the Lawrences.

American Literature. It makes a book about 80,000 words, I believe. – I don't want to send it to Pinker – feel tender about having it displayed before promiscuous publishers – Do you think you might do it?

I haven't heard from Capri.

D. H. Lawrence

Koteliansky wants to put part of Shestov in the *Athenæum* – that is all right, of course?[1]

The *English Review* has printed about ⅔ of the Essays[2] – not quite so much.

1826. To Catherine Carswell, [30 October 1919]
Text: MS YU; cited in Carswell, *Adelphi* 395.

Hermitage.
Thursday[3]

My dear Catherine

I am preparing to go to Italy – selling my books in Reading. I thought you and Don would like the De Quincey.[4] When you are well off you can have him re-bound, and he will look nice. He is a *very* nice man – I can go on reading and reading him. I laughed over 'Goethe' yesterday. I like him De Quincey because he also dislikes such people as Plato and Goethe, whom I dislike.

I went to the Midlands last week: my sister frail and seedy, but getting better.[5] I've been stuck indoors with a cold this week.

I wonder if you would hate writing to your cousin in Rome to ask if she could find me a very simple room in Rome for a few days.[6] I am going to Caserta, near Naples – hear of a farm there. I don't seem to be able to get a ship, so shall go by land.

I shall come to London on Monday, most probably: stay with Koteliansky: shall ring you up and come and see you. Do hope you are all well: such awful weather – Frieda arrived in Baden.

DHL

---

[1] No portion of the book appeared in the *Athenæum*.
[2] i.e. the essays on American Literature.
[3] Dated with reference to DHL's move to London which had taken place by 5 November: see Letter 1832.
[4] DHL 'gave us his tattered but complete set of De Quincey's works' (Carswell 113). For the essay on Goethe see *Works*, ed. David Mason (Edinburgh, 1890), iv. 395–421; on Plato's *Republic*, viii. 42–83.
[5] Ada Clarke.
[6] Ellesina, the daughter of the painter Francesco Santoro, was, strictly, not Catherine Carswell's cousin: Catherine Carswell's aunt, Ina, had married Santoro but was not Ellesina's mother.

1827. To Martin Secker, [31 October 1919]
Text: MS UInd; Postmark, Reading 31 OC 19; Secker 16.

Hermitage.
Friday

Dear Secker

I haven't any word yet from Scott and Seltzer: and I want you to print from the MS. they have.[1] They haven't had much time, it is true. But would you care to write them, or cable them? – or shall I do it? The man is Thomas Seltzer, of Scott and Seltzer, 5 West 50th. St. New York City. Let me know. – They haven't had very much time – the post office delayed the MS – expect I shall hear next week. – Dont mention *them* to Pinker.

I shall be in town on Monday, preparatory to going off for Italy – have everything ready – my address 5 Acacia Rd. St Johns Wood, N.W. 8. – telephone under *Bourse Gazette*.

Yrs   D. H. Lawrence

1828. To S. S. Koteliansky, [2 November 1919]
Text: MS BL; PC; Postmark, Newbury 2 NO 19; Zytaruk 197.

Hermitage.
Sunday

I shan't get away till Tuesday. But I will come for certain on Tuesday, arrive about 1.30. Shall bring all the luggage.

Hope this is all right for S[onia] and you.

DHL

1829. To Thomas Seltzer, 2 November 1919
Text: MS UT; Postmark, Hermitage 2 NO 19; Lacy, *Seltzer* 3–4.

Hermitage – Newbury
2nd Novem. 1919

Dear Mr Seltzer

I have no news from you of *Women in Love* – presume you have MS. – Unless you are already printing, will you return the MS. *at once*, as Secker urgently wants it to print from. He is including the novel in his Spring list – title The Sisters. If you are printing, send sheets, proofs, as soon as you get them from the printer, to *Martin Secker, 17 Buckingham St., Adelphi,*

---

[1] *Women in Love.* See Letter 1798.

London, W.C. Please do this. And if you are not printing, do please send the MS to *Secker*, not to me, as soon as you get this.

If you have to write to me, will you address me at *5. Acacia Rd., St. Johns Wood, London, N.W. 8.* I am going to Italy next week.

Yours Sincerely   D. H. Lawrence

1830. To Benjamin Huebsch, 2 November 1919
Text: MS UT; Unpublished.

Hermitage, nr Newbury
2 Novem. 1919

Dear Huebsch

I have cable[1] – *have written asking for novel back*, unless they have started printing. I am going to Italy next week – don't know where – address me here at *5. Acacia Rd. St. Johns Wood, London, N.W. 8.* That always finds me.

D. H. Lawrence

1831. To Norman Douglas, [November 1919]
Text: [Maurice Magnus], *Memoirs of the Foreign Legion* (1924), p. 11.

[5 Acacia Road, St Johns Wood, N.W.8]
[November 1919][2]

[Lawrence recalled: 'I had written to N[orman] D[ouglas] to get me a cheap room somewhere in Florence, and to leave a note at Cook's.'][3]

---

[1] Probably the undated cable (TMSC LC) which reads: 'Certainly I want novel. Pinker never submitted. Cant you cable withdrawing manuscript and transfer to me. Huebsch.'

[2] In his introduction to the posthumous publication of Maurice Magnus's *Memoirs of the Foreign Legion* (over which DHL quarrelled with Norman Douglas), DHL says that he had written to Douglas before he set out for Italy on 14 November 1919. It is not possible to assign a more precise date to the letter.

[3] George Norman Douglas (1868–1952), novelist and essayist. b. Scotland; educated at Uppingham and Karlsruhe. He entered the Diplomatic Service in 1893; served in St Petersburg, 1894–6; and later in Italy where he eventually settled in Capri. Douglas was assistant editor to Harrison on the *English Review* c. 1911 and first met DHL then. See *Letters*, ii. 31. He established his literary reputation with the novel *South Wind* (Secker, 1917). He was a restless, unconventional, witty and uninhibited hedonist. DHL portrayed Douglas as James Argyle in *Aaron's Rod*. DHL was introduced to Maurice Magnus by Douglas who defended Magnus in *D. H. Lawrence and Maurice Magnus: A Plea for Better Manners* (1924). m. Elsa FitzGibbon, 1898. (See *Times* obituary, 11 February 1952.)

1831a. To Richard Aldington, [4? November 1919]
Text: Nehls, i. 507

[5 Acacia Road, St Johns Wood, N.W.8.]
[4? November 1919]

['It was no great surprise . . . in 1919 when I [Aldington] had a note from
Lawrence to say that he was on his way through London to the Continent.']

1832. To Douglas Goldring, [5 November 1919]
Text: MS StaU; PC; Postmark, St. Johns Wood 5 NOV 19; Unpublished.

5. Acacia Rd. N.W.8
Hampstead 6534
Wed

Dear Goldring
    Am here for a day or two – going to Italy – like to see you and Mrs Goldring
– busy today – Could you ring me up in the morning.
    Hope all is well with you both.

D. H. Lawrence

1833. To Max Plowman, [5 November 1919]
Text: MS Plowman; PC; Postmark, St. Johns Wood 5 NOV 19; Unpublished.

5. Acacia Rd. St. Johns Wood. N.W.8.
Wed.

I am here for a few days en route for Italy. Will you be in to tea tomorrow? Are
you on the telephone? You will find this house under Bourse Gazette –
Hampstead 6534, and I am in in the morning. But you can always leave a
message.

Yours Sincerely   D. H. Lawrence

1834. To Martin Secker, 6 November 1919
Text: MS UInd; Postmark, St. Johns Wood 6 NOV 19; Secker 17.

5. Acacia Rd. St. Johns Wood. N.W.8.
6 November 1919

Dear Secker
    I wrote to America, asking that the MS. of *Women in Love* should be sent
by return post, direct to you at 17 Buckingham St, unless it is in the printers

hands: and if it is being printed, it should be sent in proofs as the proofs come. Hope that will do.

When are you going to Italy? I am expecting a ship – hope it will turn out all right.

Yrs   D. H. Lawrence

1835. To Max Plowman, [6 November 1919]
Text: MS Plowman; PC; Postmark, St. Johns Wood 7 NOV 19; Unpublished.

5 Acacia Rd. NW8
Thursday

Dear Plowman

I have been thinking, if you could let me have the MS of your plays at once, I would like to read them and then if I thought they'd suit Daniel's series, introduce him to them quickly, while there is still time.[1]

Yrs   D. H. Lawrence

1836. To Cecily Lambert, [8? November 1919]
Text: MS SIU; Unpublished.

[5 Acacia Road, St Johns Wood, N.W.8.]
[8? November 1919][2]

Dear Miss Lambert

I saw my Consul yesterday – he wired to Leghorn about a ship.[3] The overland travelling is *such* a sweat now, I am told, I will wait a bit for my ship – but do wish it would come soon.

I have been seeing various people – went to a Tolstoy play yesterday – Henry Ainley – awful rubbish it seemed to me.[4] – Don't like London.

Are you coming to London? Probably not, or you would have written. If you go to Joan's tomorrow, ask her about the apples, the sending off – and tell her I haven't heard from her. If you are in Hermitage, ask Mr Boshier if he has forwarded my letters.[5]

[1] The plays in question may have been 'Andy's Adolescence' (later retitled 'The Tyranny of Years') and 'Love's Martyr'; neither was ever published. (MSS at University College, London).
[2] The top of the MS has been torn off, removing DHL's address and date, and a small portion of text on p. 2. The conjectural date is based on evidence from adjacent letters.
[3] The consul was Thomas Dunlop; see Letter 1302 and n. 1.
[4] *Reparation*, based on Tolstoy's *The Live Corpse* (and translated by Aylmer Maude), was produced at St James's Theatre, with Henry Ainley and Marion Terry in the leading rôles. On DHL's hostile reaction see Carswell 136.
[5] Walter Edward Boshier (1865–1940) ran the village store which was also the post office. The 'Louie' mentioned later was Louie Flitter who worked for Boshier.

I don't feel at all *gone* yet – feel anyhow as if we should all meet again, before so very long – let's hope it will be in a nice new place with a good climate. Let us [sail?] to Africa. The thing to do is to get on the move – or to get ready to move. Don't forget. – Had a letter from Rosalind – she seems to fear she may not get off.[1] See her soon, won't you? – I'm sure she'd be glad. – Heard from Frieda – luggage still lost. She says food *very* scarce there – am afraid she is none too happy.

Is Miss Monk back?

Kindest regards to Mrs and Mr Lambert.

Au revoir   D. H. Lawrence

Doubt if Louie is to be trusted to send on my letters. Just ask her, will you, if she's done it.

1837. To Martin Secker, [8 November 1919]
Text: MS UInd; Postmark, St. Johns Wood 8 NOV 19; Secker 17.

5. Acacia Rd. St. Johns Wood, N.W.8.
Saturday

Dear Secker

I should be glad if you would send a copy of the Shestov proofs here to Koteliansky: then my Italian address I will give you in Italy, and I will do the *real* proof correcting.

I am waiting till Monday[2] to see if I can have a passage to Naples on a cargo boat. If that is arranged I shall sail about the 16th. If it is *not* arranged, I shall go overland – and in that case, shall we go together on Friday? I shall be 2nd. Class – Paris – Turin – Rome direct.

Yrs   D. H. Lawrence

1838. To Cecily Lambert, [10 November 1919]
Text: MS SIU; Unpublished.

5. Acacia Rd. N.W.8.
Monday.

Dear Miss Lambert

I have your letter this morning. My ship won't take me, so I have decided to go on Friday morning, leave Charing Cross at eight o'clock: so early! travelling with a friend through France. If you come up, let me know. I will

---

[1] The marriage between Godwin and Rosalind Baynes had broken down; divorce was contemplated (see Letter 1933); and Rosalind wanted to leave England with her children to avoid adverse publicity.

[2] Monday] tomorrow

keep Thursday open, anyhow. London is very nasty – Grimsbury is quite heaven in comparison. But this November is a bitter pill to swallow.

I haven't heard from Frieda again – not since last Tuesday: nor have I heard from Joan. Hope you had a pleasant lunch last Thursday.

Well – I shall see you if you come to town this week – otherwise next spring, en route for Zululand.

My regards to Miss Monk – also your mother and father – also Miss Furlong.[1] – Margaret said – a post card – she was going to the cottage for the week-end: wonder if she appeared.

The days are really hideous just now. Mind you, we must sail right off next year: it isn't good enough here.

Au revoir DHL

How much did you get for the pears?

1839. To Benjamin Huebsch, 12 November 1919
Text: MS UT; Unpublished.

5 Acacia Rd. St. Johns Wood. N.W.8.
12 November 1919.

Dear Huebsch

Thank you for your letter of the 1st. November, and for the cheque for £20. Tomorrow – God Willing – I am leaving for Florence and Rome – spend the winter in Italy – health – My wife, who is in Baden-Baden seeing her people, will join me. I'll send you an address.

When you have time, send me accounts of the transactions between us up till the present, will you. I understand you had not made up your accounts for my books since last year. Surely then this £20 does not derive out of the unborn future, surely it comes from the past.

I hope to have the MS. of the novel to send you shortly.

By managing the rate of exchange, I expect I shall be able to live in Italy.

Yours Sincerely D. H. Lawrence

1840. To Rosalind Baynes, [12 November 1919]
Text: MS BucU; cited in Moore, *Poste Restante* 56.

5. Acacia Rd. St. Johns Wood, N.W.8.
Wednesday

I am going by train on Friday morning. That actual ship didn't come off – but

---

[1] The dancing and physical education teacher at Hermitage; she occasionally stayed at Grimsbury Farm with Cecily Lambert and Violet Monk.

I could definitely have another in ten more days – However, I hear there is a big strike in Genoa harbour, ships can't leave, passengers cant find hotels – best get on by land. My luggage I am sending to Rome by Gondrand Frères: I shall only have what I can carry. I shall take a ticket to Turin – Cooks swindle one on the exchange – which is today 50–52 Lira for £1. – enormous. Tomorrow I shall try to buy Italian money at the Banca Italiana. I think I shall stay in Turin – perhaps with some people,[1] until I hear from Frieda. Charing Cross to Turin is about 22 hours only, all being well. – I have no letters from Frieda – hear that the passenger train service is completely suspended in Germany. It must start again. – From Turin I may go to Florence, and wait for F. there – then to Rome – then to Picinesco. What did you put for Grazio's address?[2] I shall write him from Italy. If you think of starting very soon, wire me tomorrow and I could look after you at Turin or Rome: otherwise I shall write you immediately I have an address. – Your luggage you can send direct from Pangbourne to Gondrand – 46 Gt. Tower St. E.C.3. But write him first. – Will you take Ivy? – Nasty about that cheque and Nellie[3] – Can one trust *anybody*? – Did you send the books? If you didn't, have you still got that big Children's book – the Dulac?[4] If you have, post it for me to Mrs Dunlop, 63 Worple Rd, Wimbledon, S.W.19. Dunlop is the consul, and he has done a lot of inquiring for me – I feel I owe his children something – they love fairy tales. – You can have those books of mine – or the proceeds – to pay for Dulac. I can't afford to buy anything. Watch the Italian exchange, and buy before it goes down. It can't be much higher. A good bank should give you 51 Lira – but ask them first. Your father or Godwin might do that for you. – It is perfectly easy getting the visas at the Italian and French Consulates – but go pretty early in the morning – Italian at 10.0 – French next – 8/- each. You can get them both in one morning – Push forward in the Italian, ask the clerk if you can go inside the barrier to fill up the inquiry form. Ivy would have to go personally. You want an extra photograph for each visa.

au revoir DHL

I leave Charing Cross 8·0 a.m Friday.

[1] See Letter 1844 and n. 1.
[2] DHL's reference should have been to Orazio Cervi who had acted as an artist's model for Rosalind Baynes's father, the sculptor, Sir Hamo Thornycroft (1850–1925), R.A. Cervi (who provided the model for Pancrazio in *The Lost Girl*) lived at Picinisco Serre, 45 miles n. from Naples. (For his letters to Rosalind Baynes and Sir Hamo, October–November 1919, see Nehls, ii. 6–8.)
[3] Ivy was Rosalind Baynes's children's nurse, Nellie her maid.
[4] Edmund Dulac (1882–1953), renowned for his illustrated editions of well-known works, e.g. *Arabian Nights* (1907). Recently published were: *Edward Dulac's Fairy-Book* (1916) and *Stories from Hans Andersen* (October 1919); both were large and expensive.

1841. To Douglas Goldring, [13 November 1919]
Text: MS StaU; PC; Postmark, St. Johns Wood 13 NOV 19; Unpublished.

5. Acacia
Thursday

Sorry couldn't come today – leaving tomorrow morning – will write you from
Italy.

DHL

1842. To Rosalind Baynes, 17 November 1919
Text: MS BucU; cited in Moore, *Poste Restante* 56.

train.
Monday 17 Nov. 1919

I must say, trains in France and Italy are the dead limit – I got to Paris about
6.30 p.m Friday evening – taxi to Gare de Lyon – left Gare de Lyon 9.30 p m
– arrive Modane (frontier) about 1.30 p.m. next day – Turin 8.0 p.m
(Saturday). The trains simply sit still half the time. I left Turin this morning
at 8.30 – am now still sitting in a motionless train, beside a lovely sunset sea,
and it is 5.30. From Genoa for 50 miles it is all sea, the sea almost touching the
rails, and most beautiful, blazing sun and blue sky and Italy quite herself.
Only you do as you like here – if you don't want the train to go, you just stand
with the door open, and they graciously wait for you. – I shall stop the night in
Spezia, go to Florence in the morning.

If you come by train, get a *sleeper* from Paris to Rome – wagon-lit – never
mind the expense. I believe then the *night* boat is best, and the 2.0 train out of
Paris (Gare de Lyon). Make Cooks tell you. But have a sleeper, and you'll be
perfectly all right.

If you come day boat, they tell me the 10.0 train Victoria Newhaven
Dieppe is best – longer on sea, shorter on land. I had a lovely crossing. This
the Dieppe train gets to Paris about 6.0 p.m, but usually is an hour late; so it is
7.0 or more. Then a taxi quick to Gare de Lyon. You can come second class
perfectly happily from London to Paris – but after that, have a sleeping car.
Make Cooks tell you very definitely if the 2.0 p.m train out of Paris is better
than the 9.35 p.m. – if so, about the right boat.

It is all perfectly easy – only *slow slow – slow*. No bother at frontiers – only
rather a crush – Change a little French money on boat in 1st Class saloon – get
ready to disembark as boat draws near, and move to the passport gangway on
the boat – near the Lower deck 1st class cabins, in front. – Seize the first

porter, give him *all* your luggage, let him take it to the Douane, and let him get you 3 seats. Always seize a porter the moment you get anywhere, and make him do everything for you. They are very trustworthy and sensible. – The Customs is a very slight business – so is passports – only the crowd – which is not so bad on the trains, however.

At Modane, every confusion. But an English Tommy will tell you everything. Leave the children in their carriage[1] – don't open your bags for Italian customs – they'll just chalk them. Take three or four bags in the train with you – porters will cope with them. Also take some nice food – my train had no restaurant car from Paris to Turin.

– As I say, at Modane seize a porter – tell him 1st Class or 2nd Class to Rome or wherever it is – he does the rest, you merely go in front of the bench and see them chalked. There are plenty of nice porters – In Italy shout 'facchino'.

Italy is nice – very nice indeed – lovely lovely sun and sea.

I'll tell you when I have an address –

The sea is going dark – the sky is still a brilliant red line.

DHL

1843. To Cecily Lambert, [18 November 1919]
Text: MS SIU; PC; Postmark, Lerici 19. 11. 19; Moore 597.

Hotel des Palmes, Lerici, Golfo di Spezia
Tuesday.

Well, I have got so far – reached Turin Saturday night – came on here Monday – it is the place where we used to live.[2] I have seen all the people – tomorrow I go on to Florence, where I shall wait for Frieda. Dont write until I send an address. – Yesterday Italy was at her best, such brilliant sun and sky – today rather grey, and the sea under the window falls with a half-angry, half-sad noise. But it is considerably warmer than England – no overcoat. It is evening, and the lights twinkle across the harbour, and the lighthouse beats time with the same measure as six years ago: yet everything seems different – not so gay any more. Everything is expensive, but counting the exchange, about the same as in England. – I shall go further south – feel I want to go further and further south – don't know why. Did you write to Nip[3] about

---

[1] Her children were Bridget (b. 1914), Chloë (b. 1916) and Jennifer Nan (b. 1918).

[2] The Lawrences lived at Lerici and Fiascherino, 28 September 1913–8 June 1914.

[3] DHL is referring to Cecily Lambert's brother whom he had met at Grimsbury Farm; 'Nip' was on 'sick leave from the East Africa War Zone' (Nehls, i. 466). Cf. Letter 1899.

Zululand? I'll send an address tomorrow or Thursday – am going on tomorrow to Florence to wait for Frieda.

Best greetings to Miss Monk and Miss Furlong.

DHL

1844. To Lady Cynthia Asquith, 18 November 1919
Text: MS UT; Huxley 484–5.

Albergo delle Palme. Lerici. Golfo della Spezia
18 Nov. 1919

Well, I've got so far – travelling now is the devil, if you can't afford a sleeper. The train sits still half her time to hatch out her ideas for the next Kilometre – Paris is a nasty city, and the French are not sympathetic to me. – I stayed two nights in Turin with rich English people[1] – Knight, K.C.B. OBM or OB something – parvenu etc – great luxury – rather nice people really – but my stomach, my stomach, it has a bad habit of turning a complete somersault when it finds itself in the wrong element, like a dolphin in the air. The old knight and I had a sincere half-mocking argument, he for security and bank-balance and power, I for naked liberty. In the end, he rested safe on his bank balance, I in my nakedness. We hated each other – but with respect. But c'est lui qui mourra. He is going to die – moi non. He knows that, the impotent old wolf, so he is ready in one half to murder me. I don't want to murder him – merely leave him to his death.

I couldn't get further than this yesterday. O trains! The sea is marvellous – Yesterday a blazing blazing sun, a lapping Mediterranean – bellezza! The South! The South, The South! Let me go south – I must go south. – Why don't we go to the Pacific? – why don't we? Is it only snipe and pop-guns detain us, or something more?

Italy is still gay – does all her weeping in her press – takes her politics with her wine, and enjoys them. Great excitement over the elections[2] – but lively and amused excitement, nothing tragic or serious.

---

[1] DHL's hosts were Sir Walter Frederick Becker (1855–1927) and Lady Delphine Therese Becker, who lived at Val Salice, near Turin. Becker had been a shipowner in Sicily and Italy from 1880; he had established and directed a hospital in Turin for the British forces, and undertaken local propaganda work, during the war. He was made KBE in 1918 but had been invested by the King only on 31 October 1919, less than three weeks before DHL's visit. The Beckers were the originals of the wealthy Sir William and Lady Franks in *Aaron's Rod*, chaps. XII and XIII. For Becker's reactions to the discovery of his fictional counterpart, see Nehls, ii. 12–13.

[2] Italian general election.

I am going to Florence tomorrow. You can write me
        c/o Thomas Cook and Son, Via Tornabuoni. Florence
– or you can wait for another letter with an address. – For your sleeplessness,
move – there is nothing like it – but move away from the old trimmings – move
away.

The sea is under the window – the sea! My God, what wouldn't I give to
sail far off on it – South. What wouldn't I give to be off to Nukuheva or
Numea.[1] Bello, bello il mare! The sea! Let us go.

                                                                            DHL

1845. To Stanley Hocking, [20 November 1919]

Text: MS Sagar; PC v. Firenze – Piazza della Signoria – Fontana del Nettuno; Postmark,
[. . .] 20.XI.19; Unpublished.

                            [Pension Balestra, 5 Piazza Mentana, Florence]
                                                        [20 November 1919]
Dear Stanley

Here I am for the moment in Florence, waiting for Mrs Lawrence to come
down through Switzerland – I suppose we shall winter near Naples. – I
wonder how you all are – if you are all at home still. I will send you an address
later, and you must tell me your news. Italy is a good bit spoilt by the war. My
kindest regards to everybody.

                                                                    D. H. Lawrence

1846. To Margaret King, [20 November 1919]

Text: MS Needham; PC v. Firenze – Panorama dal Piazzale Michelangiolo; Postmark,
[. . .] 20.XI.19; Unpublished.

                            Pension Balestra. 5. Piazza Mentana, Florence.
                                                                Thursday.
My dear Peg.

Here am I waiting for your Auntie Frieda to come down through
Switzerland – then we shall go on to Rome. I expect we shall be here for a
week or so – so tell your mother to send me a line, to say if there is any news. –
I've got two friends here, so am not quite alone – but alas, it rains.

                                                        With love. DHL

[1] For Nukuheva see Letter 1343 and n. 4; Numea (Noumea) is the capital of New Caledonia in
the South Pacific.

1847. To Catherine Carswell, [20 November 1919]
Text: MS YU; PC v. Firenze – Palazzo Vecchio; Postmark, Torino 21.11.19.; cited in
Carswell 117–18.

Pension Balestra. 5. Piazza Mentana, *Florence.*
Thursday

Am here in the rain, waiting for Frieda, of whom I hear nothing yet. – Italy is
rather spoiled by the war – a different *temper* – not so nice a humour by far. – I
wrote again to Ellesina[1] – hope for an answer. I expect we shall be here a week
– then to Rome. The coat-lining was a treasure, I tell you – cold trains here.

DHL

1848. To Gertrude Cooper, [20 November 1919]
Text: MS Clarke; PC v. Firenze – Ponte Vecchio; Postmark, Firenze 20.11.19;
Lawrence–Gelder 115.

Pensione Balestra – 5. Piazza Mentana, Florence
Thursday.

My dear G[ertrude]

Here am I on my lonely-o, waiting for Frieda. My room looks on the river –
quite near this bridge – but alas, it rains today. It is an awful business
travelling – if you come you'll have to come *train de luxe,* and have a sleeping
car. I suppose I shall be here about a week – so send a line –

Love. DHL

1849. To Catherine Carswell, [24 November 1919]
Text: MS YU; PC v. Firenze. Galleria Uffizi. Adamo; Luca Kranack; Postmark, Firenze
24.XI 191[. . .]; cited in Carswell 118.

5. Piazza Mentana. Florence.
Monday

I had a letter from Ellesina – very nice – she will find us a room. I hear from
Frieda – she is worrying to get her passport fixed up, so I am waiting on here.
I like it. I've got a really sunny room over the Arno, there is good wine, and
there is a nice carelessness – and the people in the house are very nice and easy
going. Keep this address. Send me a line to say how everything is. I feel I shall
loaf away all my substance – *but I do* enjoy it.

DHL

---

[1] See Letter 1826 and n. 6.

1850. To Emily King, [24 November 1919]
Text: MS Needham; PC v. Firenze – Angelo del Tabernacolo – Beato Fra Angelico – Gall. Uffizi; Postmark, Firenze 24.XI [. . .]919; Unpublished.

5. Piazza Mentana. Florence.
Monday.

Am waiting for Frieda – had a wire from her – she has not yet fixed up her passport. It is very nice here – sunny – a charming room over the Arno – and good friends, where I can dine out. Truly, Italy is pleasant to live in. If you write here, I shall have it forwarded even if we go on – and I should like to know how you are – so send a line. I believe F. has got her lost luggage. The days pass quickly – soon I have been here a week. One loafs ones life away in Italy.

Love.   DHL

1851. To Hilda Brown, [24 November 1919]
Text: MS Cotterell; PC v. Firenze – Panorama da S. Miniato al Monte; Postmark, Firenze 24.XI 1919; Nehls, ii. 16.

5. Piazza Mentana. Florence.
Monday.

Dear Hilda,
    Here I sit in my room over the river Arno, and wait for Mrs Lawrence. I had a wire from her – she is arranging her passport, and will come down through Switzerland. – Italy is very nice, sunny and gay still, with good red wine. I have friends here in Florence, so amuse myself. When Mrs Lawrence comes, we shall stay a few days more here, then go down to Rome. – I wonder how you all are.

Kindest Greetings.   D. H. Lawrence

1852. To Martin Secker, 24 November 1919
Text: MS UInd; Postmark, Firenze 24.XI 1919; Secker 17.

Pension Balestra, 5. Piazza Mentana, Firenze
24 Nov. 1919

Dear Secker
    I am here – in the same house with Norman Douglas – waiting for my wife to come down from Baden-Baden. I hope she will be here quickly – then by the end of the week we may leave for Rome, where we shall stay a day or two, after which proceed towards Naples to look for a house or flat. Perhaps we may see you somewhere before you go back to England.
    Tell Mackenzie I shall come one day to Capri, to see him.

Yrs   D. H. Lawrence

1853. To Ada Clarke, [24 November 1919]

Text: MS Clarke; PC v. Firenze – La nascita di Venere – Botticelli – Gall. Uffizi; Postmark, Firenze 24.XI [. . .]919; Lawrence-Gelder 114–15.

5. Piazza Mentana – Florence.
Monday

I had a wire from Frieda – she has not yet fixed up her passport – hope she won't be long. But I am quite happy here, in my room over the river – have English friends in the house, and dine with people in town. Florence is beautiful, and full of life and plenty. – I wonder how things are going with you – shall be glad to have a line. – Keep this reproduction of this *very* famous picture – *Birth of Venus*. –

With love. DHL

1854. To Katherine Mansfield, [24? November 1919]

Text: The Letters of Katherine Mansfield, ed. Murry, i. 315.

[Pension Balestra, 5 Piazza Mentana, Florence]
[24? November 1919]

['Lawrence wrote from Florence. He said Florence was lovely and full of'] extremely nice people.

1855. To S. S. Koteliansky, [26 November 1919]

Text: MS BL; PC v. Firenze, Galleria degli Uffizi. Sacra Conversazione. Bellini; Postmark, Firenze 26.1[...]19; Zytaruk 197.

5. Piazza Mentana. Florence.
Wed

I have your letter with enclosures this evening: think I shall see Secker in Rome, and will mention *Green Ring*:[1] but he does not care for plays: doesn't *Constable* do a modern play series? – and I'm sure Daniel would do it. – Let us arrange English publishers first. I will be thinking, and will write tomorrow. Turin, *les riches*, dried me up – and it was Sunday, I arrived late Sat. evening – Travelling is truly horrible – it *feels* like accidents, the permanent way all dilapidated.

Have you any idea who sent the telegram about the ship.

DHL

My pen is stolen.

---

[1] Kot's 'authorised translation' of *The Green Ring*, a play by Zinaida Hippius (Merizkowsky), was published by Daniel in his 'Plays for a People's Theatre' series, in February 1921.

1856. To Cecily Lambert, [26 November 1919]
Text: MS SIU; PC v. Alberto Dürer, L'Adorazione dei Re Magi, Firenze – Uffizi; Postmark, Firenze 26.11.19; Moore 599.

5. Piazza Mentana, Florence
Wednesday

Here I still sit in my room over the river, which is swollen with heavy rain, and yellow. The horses and mules, as they cross the bridge, have nice grey bonnets on their heads, and the carters are hidden under big green umbrellas. On they trot in the rain, busy as ever. Here they always cover the horse's *head*, to keep him warm. – I had a wire from Frieda – she is coming this day week – so we shall be here till December 6th, I suppose: then to Rome. – Rosalind wrote she wanted that picture – tell her she can have it, will you. And do you know of any little furnished cottage that would do for the Yorkes – whom Margaret let down so nastily –

Miss Dorothy Yorke, 19 Kingsway Mansions,
Red Lion Square, W.C.1.

– I have not had a word from England yet. Let me know the news.

DHL

1857. To Amy Lowell, [26 November 1919]
Text: MS HU; PC v. Firenze. Galleria Uffizi – Ritratto di Gentildonna – Piero della Francesca; Postmark, [. . .] 27.XI.19; Unpublished.

5. Piazza Mentana. Florence.
26 Novem.

My dear Amy –
I have not thanked you for your letters, which were really kind, and which I understood. I have come to Italy for the winter – Frieda is coming down from Baden-Baden next week, to join me here, then we are going further south. – I have a room here over the Arno, which is noisy and swollen with rain. The war has left its mark on people here too – but not so much. There is still some blessed *insouciance* in the Italians. I wonder how you are. Send me a line.

D. H. Lawrence

1858. To Benjamin Huebsch, [26 November 1919]
Text: MS UT; PC v. Firenze. Galleria Uffizi. La Madonna che adora il Bambino. Cettaglio. Filippo Lippi; Postmark, Firenze 26. 1[. . .]. 19; Unpublished.

5. Piazza Mentana. Florence.
26 November

So I have come to Italy for the winter. Will you write to me either here, or: presso il Signor Grazio Cervi, *Picinisco*. Prov. di Caserta.

I think I shall be there about Dec. 16th. – am leaving here when my wife comes down from Baden-Baden, next week. I want to know about the *Classic American Literature* essays. We shall probably stay in Picinisco for a few months. – I will write about the novel as soon as I have the MS.

Yrs.   D. H. Lawrence

1859. To Max Plowman, [26 November 1919]
Text: MS Plowman; PC v. Firenze. Galleria Uffizi. Madonna del Capellino. Van der Werff; Postmark, Firenze 27.XI 1919; Unpublished.

5. Piazza Mentana. Florence.
Wed

Here I am in a nice room over the Arno – which is rushing with much rain. Italy is still magnificently sunny, in spells, and still has her own insouciance. But the war has spoiled a good deal. – My wife arrives on Dec 2nd – on the 8th. we go to Rome. Let me know about Daniel, and if need be I'll write him about the plays – wish I could have read them. I'll introduce them to Norman Macdermott, if you like, when I have seen them.[1] Hope you are all three happy.[2]

D. H. Lawrence

1860. To Rosalind Baynes, [28 November 1919]
Text: MS BucU; cited in Moore, *Poste Restante* 56.

5. Piazza Mentana, Florence.
Friday 28 Nov.

Dear Rosalind

I have your little note – see that you will come early in January.

Frieda will come next Wednesday – Dec. 3rd. We stay here till about Dec. 9th. – then to Rome for 5 or 6 days: and then to Picinisco, at least to see what it is like. I want ultimately to have a house in Sicily for a more or less permanent place. But Picinisco can be a base.

You will probably go to a pension in Naples for the winter, you say. Most

---

[1] Norman Macdermott (1889–1977), theatrical producer. Became particularly well known in 1920 when he founded the Hampstead repertory theatre, 'Everyman', and bridged the gap (made by the war) with the work of Granville Barker at the 'Court'. Produced Sean O'Casey and Eugene O'Neill's plays, revived Shaw, etc. He had an option to produce *Touch and Go* but irritated DHL by his inactivity (see Letters 1891 and 1941). For Plowman's plays see Letter 1835 and n. 1.

[2] Plowman; his wife, Dorothy; and their first son (b. 1916).

places are expensive: Rome is enormous. Cooks will book you an hotel for a night: but you *must* have a room booked, or you'll be on the street, in Rome.

This is a very good and cheap pension. It comes to about 85 francs a week, including *everything*, save wine. 10 francs a day pension, about 10 francs a week heat and light – then washing. The food is good and plenty. It is as cheap a place as any in Italy. If you feel like trying this, let me know about your rooms and requirements. I got 50[1] Lira for £1. So that 100 francs is just £2. You might perhaps have your meals in your room, with the children, for about 300 francs a week, *all included*: probably for 250 francs. The rooms are large, overlook the Arno, – and central heating. Everything is a bit haphazard and untidy, but pleasant, kind, easy going. Signorina Pia speaks English well. Of course you would have 2 rooms, with a connecting door. But you'd have to wire to me, because we're going away. I think you might like Florence for a couple of months – there is an English Institute, everything English you need for a start.

I feel one must coast round before settling on any *permanent* place.

You could no doubt have a day nurse here.

DHL

You might possibly arrive here before we leave – fun it would be. I feel one *must* go south – but carefully, because of money. Florence is a good town, the cheapest in Italy probably. I would really advise you to try it.

If you wire: say rooms, date of arrival, length of stay, nurse etc.

You[2] change at Pisa: which is not quite 3 hours from here. The through train leaves Paris on Tuesdays,[3] Thursdays, and Saturdays, at 2.0 p.m. arr. Modane (frontier) at 2.0 a.m. – leave Modane 4.10 a.m, arr. Pisa *3.15 p.m.* In Pisa you must wait, unfortunately, till *8.30 p.m.* arrive Florence *11.5 p.m.* If you like, I will meet you in Pisa, if we are still in Florence. We could have a meal, look at the Cathedral, and so to Florence.

I don't see why you should stay in Paris – what's wrong with the night crossing? The children can sleep in the train.

Trains may alter for Dec. 1st – Cooks will know. – You would have to say on your wire 'Meet me Pisa'.

Of course, if you come here, you can see Italy stage by stage, on your way down. Venice isn't very far. – If you wire, say if you will bring nurse – and for how long here. – No doubt you could come at once.

---

[1] 50] £5   [2] You] I expect you   [3] Tuesdays,] Mondays,

1861. To S. S. Koteliansky, [29 November 1919]
Text: MS BL; Postmark, Firenze 29.XI 1919; cited in Gransden 27.

5. Piazza Mentana. Florence
Sat.

My dear Kot,

I have your letter this evening, enclosing one from Herbert Trench, (*Napoleon*) who is in London:[1] a bus ran in to his taxi on *Napoleon* night and cracked his skull a little – he invites me to go to Settingnano to stay with his *wife and daughter* – moi non!

It is warm here, but a good deal of rain. Yes, it is *much* better than England – not that pressure. One moves lightly – and then there is wine. It is 3 francs a litre: but with the exchange at 50, still possible.

Frieda comes on Dec. 2nd. We shall stay for 5 or 6 days: then to Rome: and then, nothing preventing, to that model I told you of. That will be:

presso il Signor Orazio Cervi, Picinisco, Prov. di Caserta.

We shall be there, I think, by Dec. 20. The Rome address I don't yet know. We leave Florence, I think, on Dec. 9th. or 10th. – Letters apparently take 5 days. – The moment the Huebsch parcel comes I shall write to him about the *Green Ring*. But alas, oh Lord, I fear you may get no money out of him. Would you like to see or write to Walter Peacock, 20 Green St., Leicester Square, W.C.2. He is a really decent dramatic agent, chiefly for America. Tell him I said you would find him useful. I will write to him also – I am waiting to hear from Secker. If he sees me in Rome, I will press the *Ring* on him. But he is a slippery worm. – I have changed altogether £40 of my money – and got Lira 2000 for it. They will take English cheques here. – I wrote to Radford – perhaps she wants more rent. – I can live here *well* for 100 francs a week – £2. – How are you to get money?

– au revoir   DHL

I am being dentisted here.
I have written to Peacock – he is the man – go to him at once.[2]

---

[1] Frederic Herbert Trench (1865–1923), Irish poet and playwright, who lived at Settignano, near Florence. m. Lilian Isabel Fox, 1891. DHL had known and liked him when they met in Italy in 1914 (see *Letters*, ii. 167, 173). Trench's play, *Napoleon*, was first produced on 19 October 1919 ('*Napoleon* night') by the Stage Society, with Sybil Thorndike, Leon Quartermaine, Basil Rathbone *et al.*; it was well reviewed in the *Times*, 21 October 1919.

[2] The letters to Peacock and to Radford have not been found.

1862. To Ada Clarke, [29 November 1919]
Text: MS Clarke; PC v. Firenze. Galleria Uffizi. La Calunnia (part.) Sandro Botticelli dip.;
Postmark, Firenze 30.XI [. . .]919; Lawrence–Gelder 116.

5. Piazza Mentana. Florence.
Sat. evening. 29 Nov

I have just heard from Emily, so the post is beginning to go through. Frieda is coming, arrives from Switzerland on Wednesday morning at 4.0 a.m. – hope she'll have a decent journey. She has got her trunk back – though the Dutch thieves kept all the *new* stuff. I had a p.c. from Aunt Ada, sent from Schönberg to London, and forwarded to me here, to say that Uncle Fritz arrived at his native place to find his mother had died just three hours before his arrival: died of joy. Did ever you know such people. – We shall stay here till Dec. 9th. – then to Rome. I will send you an address later – but letters will come on from here. – Florence is very pleasant, very nice to live in – lots of English friends here. Let me know how you all are.

With love. DHL

1863. To Benjamin Huebsch, 3 December 1919
Text: MS UT; Moore 599–600.

presso il Signor Orazio Cervi, *Picinisco*, Prov. di Caserta. Italy
3 Dec. 1919.

Dear Huebsch

I have just received *Winesburg*[1] – lay in bed and read it – gruesome it is – everybody dotty, *non compos* all the lot – good, I think, but somehow hard to take in: like a nightmare one can hardly recall distinctly. Thank you for sending it.

The post is *very* slow. I am waiting to hear of the MS. of *Women in Love*, which I ordered back to me.[2] Secker wants to print it at once – would you like sheets from him? – When *Women in Love* is really published, I shall have another novel ready – not before – a more possibly popular one.[3]

A friend of mine – S.Koteliansky, 5 Acacia Rd., N.W.8. has done a translation of a play *The Green Ring*, by Merizkowsky's wife. It made a stir in Russia. He wants to know if you would like to consider it.

I am going to do various small things – on Italy and on Psycoanalysis[4] – for

---

[1] Huebsch had very recently published *Winesburg, Ohio; A Group of Tales of Ohio small town life* (New York, 1919), by Sherwood Anderson (1876–1941).
[2] See Letter 1829.
[3] See Letter 1747 and n. 3.
[4] DHL was working on *Psychoanalysis and the Unconscious* in January 1920: see Letter 1916.

the periodicals. I wish I knew the American magazines – weeklies and monthlies. Would you hate to advise me about the placing of these things? It is time we made a sort of systematic attack on the American public. I'll do the writing if you'll help with the placing.

You asked about that play of mine *Touch and Go*. Did I tell you that Daniel, the English publisher, arranged the American rights without telling me. But in future, before publishing anything in England, I will let you know, and we can have some sort of understanding in time.

You will issue *The Rainbow* later, won't you? And then I wish you would send some to England – about 500 really. I'll arrange it. I do wish England could have even *sheets*. Couldn't you send some over? Do contrive that – let me know, and I'll arrange it in England.

D. H. Lawrence

1864. To Emily King, [4 December 1919]

Text: MS Needham; PC v. Firenze. Il David di Michelangiolo all'ingresso di Palazzo Vecchio; Postmark, Firenze -5.12.19; Unpublished.

Firenze.
Thursday 4 Decem.

Frieda arrived last night quite safely – a good bit thinner for her stay in Germany, but very well in health – brought pretty things from her mother. I expect we shall leave here on the 10th. – will let you know. Florence has had a strike – over now – some rows. Firenze of course is the Italian for Florence.

This statue of David, outside the Old Palace, is very famous.

Love from both.   DHL

1865. To Ada Clarke, [4 December 1919]

Text: MS Clarke; PC v. Firenze – Ponte Vecchio; Postmark, Firenze -5.12.19; Unpublished.

[Pension Balestra, 5 Piazza Mentana, Florence]
Thursday.

Frieda arrived quite safely last night – thinner, but very well – and quite rich owing to your £10. – which was very good of you. She brought some such nice things from Germany! I shall send yours directly. – We propose to stay here till the 10th. – then to Rome – then to Picinisco – where the address is:

presso il Signor Orazio Cervi, Picinisco, Prov. di Caserta.

– But you'll hear again. – The house by the lamp-post is the one we're staying in – in the picture. I'll write again directly.

Love from both.   DHL

1866. To S. S. Koteliansky, [6 December 1919]
Text: MS BL; PC; Postmark, Firenze -6.12.19; Zytaruk 200.

5. Piazza Mentana. Florence.
Saturday

Have registered letter today – it enclosed £50. from Scott and Seltzer, who will not send me back *Women in Love*, yet can't see their way to publishing – fear! – I wrote to Huebsch and everybody about the *Green Ring*. – I sent Murry an essay from here.[1] – I beg you, please *do not* send me ½ of the 'Russian Spirit' money: if you have any regard for me, don't bother me about this: please do keep it: I so much wish you to make some money. – I am not Katherine.[2] – I have a letter from the Altrincham stage society – they are acting *The Widowing of Mrs Holroyd* on March 10th. to 13th. inclusive. I wish somebody saw it.[3] – Frieda is here. We leave on Wed. for Rome. On the 17th we are at Picinisco:

presso il Signor Orazio Cervi, *Picinisco*, Prov. di Caserta.
Write there. The skunk Secker has not answered my letter to Capri: that MS. must be printed by now.[4] I'll write again. – The address of the Altrincham stage society is

Garrick Rooms, 8 Post Office Hill, Kingsway, *Altrincham*, Cheshire.
– The place is near Manchester. Write to me at Picinisco – I don't know our address in Rome. – I have been to a dentist here – everything finished, 125 francs. – Did Sophie Issayevna get my letters?[5] Secker is

C/o Compton Mackenzie, Casa Solitaria, Isola Capri, Naples.
– Or perhaps he is in London. Wring that MS. out of him.

DHL

[1] Probably 'David', an essay on Michaelangelo's statue of David (see *Phoenix*, ed. McDonald, pp. 60–4; Tedlock, *Lawrence MSS* 180). Cf. the illustration on Letter 1864.
[2] i.e. Katherine Mansfield.
[3] Catherine Carswell did see it: see Letters 1947 and 1956, and Carswell 134–6.
[4] i.e. *All Things Are Possible*.
[5] None has survived.

1867. To Cyril Beaumont, 6 December 1919
Text: MS UCin; PC v. Michelangiolo Buonarroti. La Notte (dal monumento a Lorenzo de'
Medici); Postmark, [. . .]; Unpublished.

Picinisco. Prov. di Caserta, Italy
6 Dec. 1919.

Dear Beaumont
     This is my address. What about *Bay?* – When will it open its leaves? Do
send a line and tell me. I shall ask you to post a few copies for me to people in
England – will you do that? – Send me only a couple to Picinisco. Italy is nice
– Florence charming at the moment.

D. H. Lawrence

1868. To Lady Cynthia Asquith, 6 December 1919
Text: MS UT; Unpublished.

Florence.
6 Dec. 1919

You have not answered my letter and card – hope you aren't more seedy. If
you are – *move*.
     We leave here on Wednesday 10th. for Rome:
          presso la Signorina Santoro, Via Sistina 126. Rome.
     But we shall stay in Rome only a week. After the 17th. we shall be
          presso il Signor Orazio Cervi. *Picinisco*. Prov. di Caserta.
That is in the mountains about 40 miles south of Rome. I want to stay there
and do a bit of work.
     Frieda is a bit thinner for her reduced diet — but *very* well.
     Send a line to say if you are better: you seemed so shivery-nerved.

D. H. Lawrence

1869. To Benjamin Huebsch, 6 December 1919
Text: MS UT; Unpublished.

Picinisco, Prov. di Caserta, Italy
6 Dec. 1919.

Dear Huebsch,
     I hear from Scott and Seltzer today. They will not send me back MS. of
Women in Love – but pledge to print it, and send me money in advance of
royalties. This I cannot refuse, as I sent them the MS. – I really thought
Pinker had shown it to you long ago. – So there you are. It's not my fault.

I shall wait to hear from you. If you do not want the *Studies in Classic American Literature*, please return them to me at once, to this address.
Have a letter from Jane Burr today.[1]

D. H. Lawrence

1870. To Max Plowman, 6 December 1919
Text: MS Plowman; Unpublished.

presso il Signor Orazio Cervi, *Picinisco*. Prov. di Caserta. Italy
6 Dec. 1919

Dear Plowman

We are going to above address on the 17th. – On the 10th. leave Florence for Rome. Send a line to Picinisco. – I hear from the Altrincham Stage Society that they are producing *The Widowing of Mrs Holroyd* next Spring – March 10th. to 13th. inclusive. I dearly wish somebody saw it. – The address is

The Hon Secretary, Garrick Rooms,
8 Post Office St., Altrincham, Cheshire.

You might even go. –
My wife is here, from Germany. Italy is lovely. Send a line.

D. H. Lawrence

1871. To Cecily Lambert, [13 December 1919]
Text: MS SIU; PC v. Roma – Foro Romano; Postmark, [Ro]ma 13.XII [. . .]; Unpublished.

Rome –
Saturday

This town impossible and crowded – we are going straight on – the permanent address is

Picinisco, Prov. di Caserta. Italy.

It is about 50 miles south of Rome. I haven't had a line from you – hope all is well. F[rieda] greets you.

DHL

[1] See Letter 1812.

1872. To Emily King, [13 December 1919]
Text: MS Needham; PC v. Roma. Veduta dall'Accademia di Francia; Postmark, [Rom]a
13.XII [. . .]; Unpublished.

Rome –
Saturday

Beautiful weather here – but the town so crowded, you never saw anything
like it. We are going straight to Picinisco – I gave you the address, didn't I.
Picinisco, Prov. di Caserta.
Shall write a letter from there.

Love.   DHL

1873. To Hilda Brown, [13 December 1919]
Text: MS Cotterell; PC v. Roma. Basilica di S. Pietro in Vaticano; Postmark, [Ro]ma
13.XII 19[. . .]; Nehls, ii. 18.

Rome –
Saturday.

This is the great St Peter's Cathedral – Mrs Lawrence and I don't care for
Rome very much – we are going on – the permanent address
Picinisco, Prov. di Caserta – Italy.
Mrs Lawrence will send you a little thing from Picinisco – hope it will come
for Christmas.

Best wishes.   D. H. Lawrence

1874. To Ada Clarke, [13 December 1919]
Text: MS Clarke; PC v. Roma – Pincio; Postmark, Roma 13.XII [. . .]; Unpublished.

Rome
Saturday

Rome so crowded and impossible, we are going on to Picinisco at once –
Beautiful weather, such a blue sky.

Love   DHL

1875. To Rosalind Baynes, 16 December 1919
Text: MS UN; Huxley 485–7.

presso Orazio Cervi, *Picinisco*, Prov. di Caserta.
16 Dec. 1919

Dear Rosalind
    Rome being vile, we came on here. It is a bit staggeringly primitive. You
cross a great stony river bed, then an icy river on a plank, then climb

unfootable paths, while the ass struggles behind with your luggage. The house contains a rather cave-like kitchen downstairs – the other rooms are a wine-press and a wine-storing place and corn bin: upstairs are three bedrooms, and a semi-barn for maize cobs: beds and bare floor. There is one tea-spoon – one saucer – two cups – one plate – two glasses – the whole supply of crockery. Everything must be cooked gipsy-fashion in the chimney over a wood fire: The chickens wander in, the ass is tied to the doorpost and makes his droppings on the doorstep, and brays his head off. The natives are 'in costume' – brigands with skin sandals.

[sketch]¹

and white-swathed strapped legs, women in sort of swiss bodices and white shirts with full, full sleeves – very handsome – speaking a perfectly unintelligible dialect and no Italian. The brigand men are by no means fierce: the women are the fierce half of the breed. – The village 2 miles away, a sheer scramble – no road whatever – The Market at Atina, 5 miles away – perfectly wonderful to look at, costume and colour – there you buy your weeks provisions. We went yesterday. There is milk – also bread when you get it – also meat – no wine hardly – and no woman in the house, we must cook over the gipsy fire and eat our food on our knees in the black kitchen on the settle before the fire.

Withal, the sun shines hot and lovely, but the nights freeze: the mountains round are snowy, and very beautiful.

Orazio is a queer creature – so nice, but *slow* and tentative. I shall have to dart round. We are having a little fireplace in an upstairs room – shall buy grass mats and plates and cups etc – and settle in for a bit. But if the weather turns bad, I think we *must* move on. At the moment a terrible commotion, bagpipes under the window,² and a wild howling kind of ballad, utterly unintelligible – Christmas serenade. It happens every day now, till Christmas.

I believe you would enjoy it here – but what about the children? They are impossible. There isn't anything approaching a bath: you'd have to wash them in a big copper boiling-pan, in which they cook the pigs' food.

If the weather turns bad, I really think we must go on, to Naples or Capri. Poor Orazio!

Be careful, when you travel, of *thieves*. Be careful even in a sleeping car, of your small luggage. They have opened my bag, and stolen pen, 400 francs and things – also picked my pocket.³

Frieda sends love –   DHL

¹ DHL gives a rough sketch of a 'skin sandal' and leg straps.
² window,] river
³ Cf. Carswell 118–19.

1876. To Irene Whittley, [17 December 1919]

Text: MS UT; PC v. Picinisco – Panorama; Postmark, Picinisco 17.12.19; Unpublished.

presso Orazio Cervi, *Picinisco*, Prov di Caserta, Italy

17 Dec

Received your letter this minute – will write tomorrow. Best of regards from us both.

DHL

We are staying at above address for a time.

1877. To S. S. Koteliansky, [17 December 1919]

Text: MS BL; Zytaruk 201.

Picinisco.

17 Dec.

My dear Kot

I got your letters, both, today, when I struggled up the long hour's goat-climb to Picinisco post-office.

About the Foreword – I will write to Secker, and tell him you strongly wish it omitted – I will send him your letter.[1] As far as I am concerned he can leave it clean out. But I mean what I say in it: and as it would be my signed opinion, I don't see that it matters: not a bit. Secker will no doubt inform you.

When I get proofs I will go through them. But if he sends me one set only, how can I post them to America. I have spoken of them to Huebsch. But I will post them as soon as I have them. Very many thanks for the notes of misprints.

This place is the devil of inaccessibility – I curse the post here. I shall probably carry this, with Secker's letter, a long five miles to Atina tomorrow.

Has Sophie Issayevna had any letters from me? My best Christmas greetings to her and Ghita – wish distances weren't so absolute.

I should be so glad if you would ignore that dividing of Murry's miserable cheque.[2] Are you afraid of me? Don't I owe you fifty times 35/- – – per Dio!

DHL

---

[1] See the letter following.
[2] See Letter 1866.

1878. To Martin Secker, [17 December 1919]
Text: MS UInd; Postmark, Villa Latina 18.12.19; Huxley 487.

presso Orazio Cervi, *Picinisco*, Prov. di Caserta. Italy.
17 Dec.

Dear Secker,

The post comes once in a blue moon here. – I enclose a letter from Koteliansky. I am perfectly willing to have the 'Foreword' omitted altogether – my foreword, that is. Let Koteliansky know, will you, what you decide.[1] And please arrange a title page to suit him, will you. Ach, Ach! these little businesses! Every hen is occupied with her own tail-feathers.

I suppose I am to return to you the corrected proofs of the Shestov. If so, be so good as to let me have a duplicate set for America.

Be *sure* and tell me when you have the MS. of *Women in Love* – The Sisters if you like – and tell me what you are doing with it.

This place is off the map entirely – I tell you, the post comes when a peasant happens to be coming down to the river – unless I scramble up an accursed goats climb of about 80 minutes, to the God-lost village of Picinisco. However, à la guerre comme à la guerre.

Inform me of things. Send me a book to read, if you've got an interesting one nowadays.

Yrs   D. H. Lawrence

Possibly Koteliansky returns corrected proofs to you. If so, tant mieux. For me, my foreword is what I think: though it is immaterial to me whether you print or not. It is between you and Koteliansky, I suppose.

1879. To Margaret King, [18 December 1919]
Text: MS Needham; PC v. Picinisco – Costume; Postmark, Villa Latina 18.12.19; Unpublished.

[presso Orazio Cervi, *Picinisco*, Prov. di Caserta, Italy]
Thursday –

I have sent off the little parcel to your Auntie Ada, but could not post your parcel, with the Crèche,[2] at Picinisco – they could not take it. I am sending it straight to you, to Carlton,[3] today if possible – do hope it will come all right.

With love from us both for Christmas   DHL

---

[1] Secker decided to include the 'Foreword'.
[2] i.e. a doll's cradle.
[3] The King family were now living at 480 Main Street, Carlton, Nottingham.

1880. To Irene Whittley, 18 December 1919
Text: MS UT; Unpublished.

presso Orazio Cervi, *Picinisco*, Prov. di Caserta. Italy
18 Dec. 1919

Dear Mrs Whittley

I got your letter when I had sweated up the mountain to that damned Picinisco today. The post is utterly irrelevant – if a peasant happens to be coming down this way, well and good – or so-so – and if not – it's all the same in the end. – Frieda went to Germany early in October – stayed with her mother in Baden-Baden for about two months – is a bit thinner after living on carrots – came down and joined me in Florence – ate so much and drank so much wine that her pancia – her paunch, as they say here – went on strike for a bit: was soon on its legs again, however. We came to Rome – couldn't stand the crush and the swindle – and now are here, some 100 miles south of Rome, 15 miles from the railway, lost among wild mountains. When the sun shines, it is gorgeous – so brilliant and marvellous. When it is cloudy, we look at the snow-topped mountains and curse the day.

I suppose we shall stay here for a time – don't know how long – don't know whither or whence. I am turned into a wandering Jew, my feet itch, and a seat burns my posterior if I sit too long. What ails me I don't know – but it's on and on – Frieda is not quite sure where she is – and her Italian is so hopeless after two months in Germany and five years in England – that I am going to pose next as a deaf-mute, for the delectation of these damned peasants. – It's very picturesque here, and all that – brigands and costume – women and donkeys and gibberish of a dialect which is no language of men – but – immer fragt der Seufzer wo[1] – if you'll excuse the bit of hackneyed German. – And so you sit in Battersea – and you teach! Do you box their ears? And Whittley sits in a bank – bel Dio! Has he grown a moustache again? Must I forever remember him in a dark blue uniform and brass buttons and a clean mouth?[2] – I prefer to remember you both crouched over a fire in the empty house before the Murry's came[3] – airing mattresses – and the dark hour when he used to come home late from St. Ives, with the motor-bicycle – and was so tired too. – Is there any news from Cornwall? – your father and mother both well? – your father still enjoying himself tarring and making fences and contrivances up at Tregerthen? – your mother still wrapping a shawl round herself and feeling

[1] Literally the remark means 'always the sigh asks where'.
[2] Cf. p. 256 n. 1.
[3] i.e. before Murry and Katherine Mansfield joined the Lawrences at Higher Tregerthen, in April 1916.

rather cold, and laughing at me secretly? Ah well, but I was mostly happy at
Tregerthen, and shall always remember gratefully.

I don't know a bit what we shall do next – we might come before long to
England – then we could have a little wine, or beer, or gin or whatever
belongs, and lay to.

It is nearly christmas – men come with prehistoric bagpipes and serenade
us every day, with a wild howling ballad about that eternal Maria. What our
actual Christmas here will be, God knows – we are miles from everywhere.
But best of wishes from us both to you two.

D. H. Lawrence

1881. To Compton Mackenzie, [c. 19 December 1919]
Text: Mackenzie 164.

[presso Orazio Cervi, *Picinisco*, Prov. di Caserta, Italy]
[c. 19 December 1919]

['a letter arrived from D. H. Lawrence, who was finding the climate of
Picinisco, a beautiful mountain village in Southern Italy, too cold in
December. In this letter, which is lost, he wrote that he had been driven from
England by the melancholy of elms; he had never forgotten a remark I
[Mackenzie] had made about them when I visited him in 1914 at that cottage
in Buckinghamshire. I had told him then I had a cottage in Capri which I
should always be glad to lend him if he ever decided to return to Italy. Was
that cottage vacant now? If it was, might he and his wife take advantage of my
offer to lend it to them?']

1882. To Emily King, [20 December 1919]
Text: MS Needham; PC v. Picinisco – Il Castello; Postmark, Villa Latina 20.12.19;
Unpublished.

– Picinisco
Saturday

Snowing here – on Monday we are going on to Naples, then across to the
island of Capri, to a friend – the address

    c/o Compton Mackenzie Esq, Casa Solitaria, *Isola Capri*, Naples.

Much love for Christmas   DHL

    Can't post Peg's parcel here.

1883. To Martin Secker, 20 December 1919
Text: MS UInd; Postmark, Villa Latina 20.12.19; Secker 18–19.

Picinisco.
Sat. 20 Dec. 1919

Dear Secker

I have done the Shestov proofs: please correct from *my* corrections, Koteliansky will miss a thousand things, particularly German misprints. Let me know if you decide to keep the foreword as it is. – The book is quite long enough.

About a title-page – you will put 'Authorised translation by S. Koteliansky', won't you? No need to figure me, unless you wish – I am quite indifferent. I wish you would print in one place, under the present title, the original Russian title in brackets – 'An Apotheosis of Groundlessness'. It should appear.

I have only corrected misprints, and changed about $\frac{1}{2}$ doz. words – except one little paragraph, which was wrong.

Here it is snowing all day. If we can get out, we shall leave on Monday and go to Capri, find rooms or something there. Address me c/o Mackenzie, will you, as I don't know what my address will be.

Yrs   D. H. Lawrence

Please send me another set of Shestov proofs, for America.

1884. To Ada Clarke, [20 December 1919]
Text: MS Needham; PC v. Picinisco – Il Castello; Postmark, Villa Latina 20.12.19; Lawrence–Gelder 117.

[presso Orazio Cervi, *Picinisco*, Prov. di Caserta, Italy]
[20 December 1919]

Picinisco is too cold – on Monday we are going on to Naples and the Island of Capri: the address

c/o Compton Mackenzie Esq, Casa Solitaria, *Isola Capri*, Naples.
Mackenzie is a novelist – Capri will be warm.

Merry Christmas   DHL

1885. To Francis and Jessica Brett Young, [24 December 1919]
Text: MS UB; Unpublished.

[Rosaio]
Wednesday[1]

We called today, wondering if you were going down to the Piccola Marina, or staying here – and if we could have one or other of the houses. Leave word for me at Morgano's will you.[2]

D. H. Lawrence

1886. To Cecily Lambert, [25 December 1919]
Text: MS SIU; PC; Postmark, Capri 26.12.19; Unpublished.

Palazzo Ferraro, *Capri*, Italy.
Christmas Day

After many buffetings we are here on this small island, in a little apartment of our own. I really think we shall stay here a while. – I see the ships come sailing from England into the bay of Naples – and setting out from Naples for Africa – and wonder what the future brings. There hasn't been a single line from you all the time I've been in Italy. Why not? I wonder what you're all doing this Christmas Day – if you're having a good time. Frieda sends best of wishes, with mine, to you both.

DHL

1887. To Martin Secker, 27 December 1919
Text: MS UInd; Postmark, Capri 28.12.19.; Huxley 488.

Palazzo Ferraro, *Capri*. Italy.
27 Dec. 1919

Dear Secker
    Picinisco was too icy – mountainous – we escaped here: and like you, we

---

[1] Jessica Brett Young (*Francis Brett Young*, 1962, p. 95) claims that she and her husband found DHL's note on a visiting-card in 'January' 1920; other evidence points to his having written it on 24 December 1919. It was written when DHL was investigating the possibility of living in one or other of the houses owned by Compton Mackenzie – 'Rosaio' or 'Piccola Marina' – and before he moved into the flat over Morgano's café. (The Brett Youngs were living in 'Piccola Marina' and had formerly lived in 'Rosaio'.) DHL's move into the flat was completed by Christmas Day (see the letter following).

[2] Francis Brett Young (1884–1954), novelist, had trained as a doctor and served (with the rank of major) in the RAMC in the East African campaign. m. Jessica ('Jessie') Hankinson, 1908. His health was endangered in East Africa; this led to their settling in Anacapri where they remained, for the most part, till 1929. Published *Robert Bridges* (1913), *Deep Sea* (1914), *The Young Physician* (1919), *Poems 1916–1918* (1919), etc.

were rejected by the Sirens: the sea threw us back, we spent a night on board
that rolling saucepan of a boat, off Sorrento. Now we have a little apartment
here, right over Morgano's, on the neck of Capri, looking to the sea and
Naples on the right, the sea and space on the left: the duomo[1] the apple of our
eye – gall-apple.

Mackenzie seems well. – This place is sympathetic, for a time. But it seems
to me like a stepping-stone from which one steps off, towards elsewhere: not
an abiding place.

I hope you got the proofs of Shestov which I returned. Please send me a
nice little vol. of corrected proofs, will you, for America.

Mackenzie said you thought of printing the *Rainbow*. Do that, and you
have my eternal allegiance. He suggests it be called 'Women in Love Vol I.',
with a foreword by himself. I think 'Women in Love, Vol I and Vol II' is a
very good idea. I am anxious to hear from you. If you do this, *The Rainbow* as
a Vol I of *Women in Love*, then I must make a sort of permanent agreement
with you. I am waiting for MS. of a novel three parts done, 'Mixed
Marriage', which I left in Germany before the war. This would make a
perfect selling novel when I've finished it.[2]

About Pinker. I should like to break with him altogether: shall I simply
write to him to that effect, before I go any further? Can you give me any hint?
Gilbert[3] had a row with him and broke. I must do it.

D. H. Lawrence

1888. To J. B. Pinker, 27 December 1919
Text: TMSC NWU; Huxley 489.

Palazzo Ferraro, *Capri*, Italy.
27th Dec. 1919.

Dear Pinker,

We are here for a time – moving out of Europe before long, I hope.

I think, there is not much point in our remaining bound to one another.
You told me when we made our agreement, that we might break it when
either of us wished. I wish it should be broken now. What bit of work I have to
place, I like to place myself. I am sure it isn't much worth to you.

Let me know, will you.

D. H. Lawrence

---

[1] i.e. the cathedral.
[2] The MS was that of 'The Insurrection of Miss Houghton' left behind in Bavaria when the
Lawrences stayed there May–June 1913. DHL had stopped work on it in March 1913 because
it had proved 'improper' (*Letters*, i. 549). The MS arrived in February 1920 but was soon
abandoned; DHL began afresh on the novel which became *The Lost Girl* (1920). (For the
history of the MSS see *The Lost Girl*, ed. Worthen, pp. xix–xl.)
[3] Gilbert Cannan.

1889. To Emily King, 31 December 1919
Text: MS Needham; PC v. Pompei – Casa dei Vettii; Postmark, Capri 31.12.19.;
Unpublished.

Palazzo Ferraro, *Capri*, (Naples)
31 Dec. 1919

I was able to send off Peg's toys from here. Would you wrap three or four ounces of tea in a bit of paper, and put it in a long envelope, and send it to me by registered *letter* post: put in a letter as well. We shall be out of tea in a few days.[1] – I sent you a letter – believe I put the wrong number. – I heard yesterday from Ada, with news of you. If it is so, perhaps it will be a good thing and will make you happy. Let me know.

Love. DHL

The cost of postage may be rather dear – but can't be helped.
The p.c. is a copy from the wall of a house in Pompei.

1890. To Francis Brett Young, [1 January 1920]
Text: MS UB; PC; Postmark, Anacapri -3.1.20; Unpublished.

Palazzo Ferraro, Capri
Thursday

Mackenzie said you had sent a note – it hasn't come, so I send a postcard to you. Will you come in and see us, you and your wife, when you are in Capri.

1891. To Douglas Goldring, 3 January 1920
Text: MS UCin; Postmark, Capri -5.1.20.; Goldring, *Odd Man Out*, pp. 257–8.

Palazzo Ferraro, *Capri*. (Naples)
3 Jan 1920

Dear Goldring
We have struggled our way down Italy, perpetually on the move, and no sort of rest. That's why I haven't written before. I suppose we shall sit here for a time.

There, if I'd known, I wouldn't have let Macdermott have that option – but it doesn't much matter, and if necessary, could no doubt be bought back from him for his £15.[2]

---

[1] A postcard (postmarked Taormina 27 3 20) from Frieda to Margaret King showed that the King family were a reliable and presumably frequent source of supply: 'Tell your mother we got the tea and were very glad . . . My people are as thankful for your mother's parcels.'
[2] See p. 423 n. 1.

I heard from Scott and Seltzer – they sent me £50 for the novel[1] – but I doubt if they'll publish it. Probably Secker will do it in England.

Italy is frightfully expensive, particularly travelling. I daren't shift again – and Berne is far off. One lives on the financial verge as ever – but so be it. – I expect *Touch and Go* will soon be out. Could you give Daniel my address here, and let me know when he is sending out publishers copies. I might write to one or two people, and make the reviewers act, anyhow.

I am glad Chapman and Hall are going to do you. Yes, I am pleased if you inscribe to me.[2] Why the devil did the reviewers ignore your play.[3] Could you send me a copy? I might get the *Times* to come in, at this late hour.

My wife loved Baden – really better than Italy. The Italians have a grudge against us now. Perhaps in May we shall go to Germany. Let us all meet there and have a good time. We often speak of you. – I don't want to come back to England, anyhow.

I do hope Mrs Goldring gets out of that pamphlet shop: it's horrible.[4]

a thousand greetings from us both   D. H. Lawrence

1892. To S. S. Koteliansky, 4 January 1920
Text: MS BL; Postmark, Capri -5.1.20; Moore 604.

Palazzo Ferraro, *Capri*, (Naples)
4 Jan 1920

My dear Kot

I have got all the letters today – no post for four days – sea too rough for the ship.

Now look here, I think all this about the preface is perfect nonsense. What I say can't hurt Russian Literature – nor even Shestov: much more likely to *provoke interest.* You are being unnecessarily fussy. I haven't had a reply from Secker, so don't know what line he is taking. I am waiting for revised proofs, to send to America.

The letter from Huebsch contained an unexpected £25, so I feel I really can

---

[1] *Women in Love* (Goldring was Seltzer's London representative.)
[2] Goldring dedicated his novel, *The Black Curtain* (Chapman & Hall, March 1920), to DHL. (He inserted a dozen lines from DHL's poem, 'Craving for Spring', as part of the epigraph to the novel – along with a quotation from Henri Barbusse.) In Goldring's view it was 'the most violently anti-war and revolutionary work of fiction to appear in England in 1920 and for some years afterwards' (*Odd Man Out*, p. 277).
[3] *Fight for Freedom* was published (by Daniel) in November 1919. (The *Times* did not review it.)
[4] The Goldrings were both passionately devoted to humanitarian causes; he campaigned for the 'Fight the Famine Council', she for the 'Save the Children Fund'. DHL's term 'pamphlet shop' was dismissive of their feverish enthusiasm for such 'good causes'.

give you back £10. of the sums I owe you. It's the first time I've had a real *extra* £25, so it's very good. If Italy weren't so blasted expensive, I should feel momentarily rich. If any trifle accrues from Shestov, you will merely keep it till your ship comes home.

I found Mary Cannan here, large as life. But she's very nice, and brought us some butter.

I feel Capri isn't big enough to stay long in: and *so* cosmopolitan, in a small way. But I must get some work of some sort done, before I can move.

I have written to Pinker that I want to be rid of him.

Francis Brett Young – a Secker novelist, is here – with wife: humble waiters on Compton Mackenzie.

The weather is stormy, blowy, rainy – but not cold.

Don't be tiresome   DHL

The Green Ring will be published, anyway.

1893. To Catherine Carswell, 4 January 1920
Text: MS YU; cited in Carswell 121, 122, 124, 125.

Palazzo Ferraro, Capri, (Naples)
4 Jan. 1920

My dear Catherine

I had your letter today – we have moved and moved in such a state of restlessness. I could not write letters. Picinisco was beautiful beyond words, but *so* primitive, and *so* cold, that I thought we should die. The mountains stood round in a ring, glittering white like devils. On the Saturday before Christmas it snowed all day long: so on Monday we did extricate ourselves: got up at 5.30, walked 5 miles to Atina, caught the post omnibus 10 miles drive to the only station, Cassino. We got to Naples, caught the Capri boat at 3.0 p.m. The sea rose as we left the bay – by 7.30 we came in to the shallow port of Capri, but the seas were running so high, the boats couldn't come out to take us off. Back we had to go, to lie all night rolling on board, in the semi-shelter of Sorrento. The Italians *were* sick: oh dear: luckily we managed to keep all right.

We have got an apartment – two beautiful rooms and a kitchen we share – 150 francs a month – at the top of this old palazzo, which has a staircase like a prison, not a palace. It is extremely beautiful – just on the very neck of the little town, on the very neck of the island: we can touch the queer bubbly Duomo, almost, from our balcony: all the island life goes beneath us: and then away on the right, the sea, Ischia in the distance, and the bay of Naples: on the left the wide open mediterranean. In each case it is a short mile down to the sea – but steep down. The narcissus flowers still are many in the rocks, but passing: sweet they are, Greece. A few pink cistus-flowers too. It is warm, but rather stormy. We have had one fire one evening – for the rest, we aren't cold. Your plaid, however, is a valuable thing: and your little jersey a treasure for Frieda. They are just the things for Italy: to wrap oneself up indoors a bit. The apartment is part of the top flat, owned by a signorina Palenzia, a Bourbon relic from Naples – nice. There is a young and amusing Rumanian who fans his fornello[1] so hard and seizes me to pour Socialism into me. It is pleasant and bohemian. I wish you were both here: this is the life we could enjoy together.

We lunch or dine sometimes with Compton Mackenzie, and he is nice. But one feels the generations of actors behind him, and can't be quite serious. What a queer thing the theatre is, in its influence. He seems quite rich, and does himself well, and makes a sort of aesthetic figure – 'head of the realistic school of England, isn't he?', asks my Roumanian, – walking in a pale blue suit to match his eyes, and a large woman's brown velour hat to match his hair. It was a sight on New Years Eve, when we were down in Morgano's café – the centre of Capri, downstairs. F. and I sat with an old old Dutchman and a nice man called Brooks,[2] drinking a modest punch, and listening to the amazing bands which come in, with the Tree, on New Years Eve: a weird, barbaric affair. The Anacapri lot intoned a ballad, utterly unintelligible, of about 38 verses, with the most amazing accompaniments. – At about 11.0 came in Mackenzie with *rich* Americans – rather drunk. The Tiberio band came – Monty (Mackenzie) took the tree and bobbed it in the faces of the Americans, and looked like Christ before Pilate in the act. The Tiberio boys, two of them, danced the Tarantella to the same grunting music – a funny indecent pederastic sight it was (Don will chase my spelling – I mean paederastic). At midnight the Monty crowd ordered champagne, and tried to look wine and womenish. But my God, it was an excruciating selfconscious effort, a veritable Via Dolorosa for Monty, who felt his stomach going. Oh God, the wild rakishness of these young heroes! How conscious they are of the Italian crowd in the background. They never see the faint smile of the same crowd – such a smile. – A glass of champagne is sent out to the old road-

---

[1] 'stove'.

[2] John Ellingham Brooks (1863–1929), read Law at Cambridge and German at Heidelberg; a homosexual, he went to Capri after the Wilde trial and lived there for the rest of his life. m. Romaine Goddard, 1903; she was a painter and a lesbian; they parted a year later. Two books were dedicated to Brooks: Norman Douglas's *Birds and Beasts of the Greek Anthology* (Florence, 1927) and Compton Mackenzie's *Vestal Fire* (1927); Somerset Maugham presented him as 'Brown' in *The Summing Up* (1938).

sweeper – de rigeuur (can't spell). Meanwhile we sip our last drop of punch, and are the Poor Relations at the other end of the table – ignored – to our amusement. – Mackenzie is going to begin tomorrow, at 10.30 precisely, 'Rich Relatives'. He thinks *Relatives*, as an offset to *Relations, so* good.[1]

Well, I find I am nearly as spiteful as the rest of Capri. This island is covered with a small brand of cosmopolitans – English, American, Russian, German – everything. The English-speaking crowd are the uttermost uttermost limit for spiteful scandal. My dear Catherine, London is a prayer-meeting in comparison. We get it from Mary Cannan! Here we found her! Ana she is one of the decentest people here on this island – brings us butter and figs: butter costs 20 francs a kilo. But she is staying with an arch-scandalmonger – wife of a local judge of some sort – she's English. The stories Mary is told are *incredible*. We've got a long way to go, such mere people as us. It would be an interesting document, to set down this scandal verbatim. Suetonius would blush to his heels, or Tiberius would feel he'd been a flea-bite.[2]

There are here also the Brett-Youngs –. Francis Brett-Young, novelist and poet, and his wife. We hardly know them. They come when Mackenzie says come, and go when he says go.

Now for your news: *good.* Of one thing I'm certain, and that is, your novel is the best that Melrose or any of the rest of them has had the chance of seeing.[3] I wonder if I could review it anywhere? But there, I should do it no good. But it's coming out, and that'll hearten you to another shot, especially as J[ohn] P[atrick] will be growing up. We'll carry the field yet, you see if we dont.

But about the £50 – don't give it us, you really need it more.

Though in the next breath, I must lament the dearness of Italy: butter 20 francs, wine 3 francs a litre the cheapest, – sugar 8 francs a kilo, oil 7 or 8 francs a litre, carbone a franc for two kilos – a porter expects ten francs for bringing one's luggage from the sea – and so on. With the exchange at 50, it is just possible, and only just.

[1] Mackenzie's novel, *Poor Relations* (October 1919) was followed in 1921 by *Rich Relatives*. Jessica Brett Young applied the term 'Poor Relations' to the Lawrences, Mary Cannan, herself and her husband: indeed to the group who spent Sunday afternoons at Mackenzie's house, 'Solitaria' (*Francis Brett Young*, p. 96). (For Mackenzie's comment on the incident described by DHL, see Mackenzie 166.)

[2] Suetonius (c. 69–c. 122), Roman biographer and antiquarian. DHL probably had in mind *De Vita Caesarum* in which Suetonius seasons his biographies with gossip and scandal. Tiberius (42 B.C.–37A.D.), Roman emperor who ruled from Capri for the last ten years of his reign and indulged his love of cruelty and perverted vice.

[3] Andrew Melrose Ltd, publisher; see p. 525 n. 1.

Still, you might come for Easter. How jolly it would be. You could have a
room with us here, independent and splendid. Nourish the idea.

I liked Ellesina very much: glad Fanny is all right again, *hate* these shocks:
hope Don is feeling happy.

a million good wishes.   DHL

1894. To Benjamin Huebsch, [4 January 1920]
Text: The Collector (Walter R. Benjamin, 1978), p. 16.

[Palazzo Ferraro, Capri, (Naples)]
[4 January 1920]

[Lawrence thanks Huebsch for a cheque for £25.7.7] which you tell me is a
gift from Louis Untermeyer and Jean Untermeyer and Emile Tas.[1] That is
very good of them – though I feel a bit ashamed, receiving the money. But
anyhow, it is a nice human thing of them. If I have luck with the exchange, I
shall get Lira 1,250 for it: which means a good five weeks' living for the two of
us . . . We have buffeted our way down Italy, and landed here in Capri. It is a

---

[1] Huebsch had written to DHL on 5 December 1919 (TMS LC) as follows:

Dear Lawrence:

I have been wanting to write to you about a number of things and in answer to several of your
letters but I always make the mistake of putting off such correspondence until leisure offers. I
will write you some short notes instead of one long one.

I am terribly sorry about the misunderstanding with regard to your novel and I hope that
you have been trying to get the manuscript back as you said in yours of November 2d you
were doing. Who on earth has it and how did you come to let them have it?

Among my friends here who are great admirers of yours are Louis Untermeyer, a poet, Jean
Starr Untermeyer, his wife and also a poet and Emile Tas, a fine type of Dutch-American who
cuts diamonds for a living but really enjoys playing the cello, reading good books – in a word, a
cultivated European connoisseur. Finding no other way of expressing their admiration for you,
they ask me to send you the enclosed check which is the equal of one hundred American
dollars.

I hope there will be no difficulty in utilizing it in Italy if this letter should be forwarded to
you from London. If your letters are being opened by someone on your behalf, I trust that the
most practicable means of conveying the money to you will be employed. That is all for the
present as I want this to catch tomorrow's steamer.

All good wishes to you.

Sincerely yours,

For Untermeyer see p. 141 n. 1. Jeanette ('Jean') Starr (1886–1970), m. Louis Untermeyer,
1907. She had published her poems, *Growing Pains* (1918), and was to follow it with *Dreams out
of Darkness* (1921): Huebsch was the publisher of both volumes. Emile Tas is unidentified.
Writing to Richard Aldington over thirty years later, on 1 June 1950 (TMS LC), Huebsch
referred to the gift of money and added that this was the money DHL 'turned over to
M[aurice] M[agnus]'.

beautiful little island by itself; but it's had so many civilizations rather violently poured over it, that "e don't know where 'e are'. [Lawrence mentions various people who are on Capri including Compton Mackenzie and Brett Young.] We are at the top of this old palace, which is the very key of Capri: Morgano's Cafe is downstairs. We have a roof and Naples and Vesuvius to the right, the Gulf of Salerno behind, and the open sea to the left, shining. I get a strange nostalgia for I know not what. I stand on my roof and evoke so many gods, and look at the four corners of the winds, and begin to feel even a bit frightened, as if I'd got to the middle and did not quite know how to get out. The past is simply immense here, and not yet dead. I feel like bursting into tears, and begging Parthenope and Leucothea please to let me go.[1] Aber wohin?[2]

1895. To Sallie Hopkin, 5 January 1920
Text: MS NCL; PC v. Capri – Marina Grande; Postmark, Capri -6.1.20.; cited in Keith Sagar, *Review of English Literature*, vi (July 1965), 94.

Palazzo Ferraro, *Capri*, (Naples).
5 Jan 1920

Dear Sallie

Here we are on this little island, with Naples 20 miles off, and Vesuvius mildly smoking. It is very beautiful, but stormy, the winds blowing round the high rocks: not cold, however, we don't have fires. It is a nice apartment high in this old palace – big rooms, rather a cold splendour. The life of the tiny world – the town – all goes on below us. – We have friends here – Compton Mackenzie, the novelist – and Mary Cannan – and others. It is all lively and jolly. But when the boat can't come, no post, no anything.

Love from both   DHL

1896. To Cyril Beaumont, 5 January 1920
Text: MS UCin; Unpublished.

Palazzo Ferraro, *Capri*, (Naples)
5 Jan. 1920.

Dear Beaumont

I got your letter in Picinisco, in the midst of a snowstorm: Picinisco being deeply buried among the snow-mountains. However, we extricated our-

---

[1] Parthenope was the siren who threw herself into the sea out of love for Ulysses and was cast up on the bay of Naples; as a result Naples was known by her name. Leucothea threw herself into the sea after the murder of one of her sons; she was deified and known as the 'White Goddess'.
[2] 'But where?'

selves, and are here for a time, at least. If you are sending me [those?] sheets
to sign; or anything else, send them direct will you, here.

Compton Mackenzie is here – and Brett Young – and a few other English:
as the Roumanian next door remarks: toute une Parnasse anglaise, Capri. We
all come to it sooner or later, Parnasse, as to a cemetery. But I have to answer
my Roumanian: poco Parnassiano, io.[1]

All good wishes for the New Year.

D. H. Lawrence

1897. To Lady Cynthia Asquith, 5 January 1920
Text: MS UT; PC v. Pompei – Casa dei Vettii; Postmark, Capri -6.1.20.; Unpublished.

Palazzo Ferraro, *Capri*, (Naples)
5 Jan. 1920.

Much buffetted and bedraggled, we have landed at last here in an apartment
high in this old palace, on the very neck of Capri, centre of the tiny town –
rather charming: the weather stormy and blowy, but not cold. We don't need
fires. The wild narcissus are out, very perfumy, and the blue anemones just[2]
coming. – Find Compton Mackenzie nice and amusing. Also whom do we
find here but Mary Cannan (Mrs Sir J[ames] B[arrie]) – a good friend of ours.
All the world's a stage etc.[3] I hope you are better – will write in a day or two.
Buon' anno from us both.

DHL

1898. To Baroness Anna von Richthofen, 7 January 1920
Text: MS UCB; PC v. Capri – Panorama; Unpublished.

Palazzo Ferraro, *Capri*, (Napoli).
7. Jan. 1920.

Liebe Schwiegermutter,

Gestern kam dein Brief vom 23 Dezember: deine Weihnachtfeste waren
gewiss schön: hier in Italien sieht man wenig oder Seele oder Geschenk. Aber
wir haben auch ein bissel getrunken und gelacht, hier auch. – Hoffentlich
kommt das Manuskript gleich. – Wir haben wieder viel Wind und Sturm

[1] 'Capri is all one English Parnassus . . . I am not much of a Parnassian'.
[2] just] very
[3] *As You Like It* II. vii. 140.

gehabt, bis gestern Abend kein Schiff, für drei Tage. – Siehst du den Turm in diesem Bild? wir wohnen ganz in der Nähe, von unserm Balcon können wir beinah die grosse Uhr mit der Hand erreichen. Es ist der Mittelpunkt von Capri. Unten liegt das Meer. Brauchst du noch etwas aus England.

Love. DHL

[Dear Schwiegermutter,

Yesterday came your letter of 23 December: your Christmas celebrations were no doubt lovely: here in Italy one sees little or soul or gift.[1] But we too drank and laughed a bit, here too. – I hope the manuscript will come directly.[2] – We've had again a lot of wind and storm, till yesterday evening no ship, for three days. See the tower in this picture? we live quite near it, from our balcony we can almost reach the big clock with our hand. It is the very centre of Capri. Below lies the sea. Do you need anything else from England.

Love. DHL]

1899. To Cecily Lambert, 9 January 1920
Text: MS SIU; Moore 607–8.

Palazzo Ferraro, *Capri*, (Naples).
9 Jan 1920

Dear Lambert,

We had your letter the other day – when at last the ship managed to come. For some days we had storms of wind, and the poor little iron tub of a steamer could neither get here nor to Naples, but had to hide at Castellamare. Now however she arrives again, and toots as if she bossed the Mediterranean.

Capri is a funny place – a real mountainous island, like this as you approach –

[sketch]

– You are dropped out of the steamer into a little boat, where I mark x, then you are hauled up in the funicular to Capri town, which lies in the neck of the island. This old palace – palazzo means palace – is right in the very middle of it all, and looks over to the sea north, to Naples, and South, to Africa. We've got a big big sitting room, with two window-doors and balconies high over the narrow street by the so-called cathedral – a whitewashed oddity. All the life of the island passes beneath. – We've got friends here – Compton Mackenzie, the novelist – and Brett-Young, another – then Mary Cannan, who was

---

[1] Here DHL's German is incomprehensible. Presumably his reference is to the spirit of Christmas and Christmas presents.
[2] See Letter 1887 and n. 2.

Barrie's wife. There are all kinds of people – English, German, Russian, American, Dutch, Danes – all sorts – many rich: too many for this island, which is only 4 m. by 2. – quite small though bigger, because so mountainy.

The days pass rather lazily. I ought really to work. But one loses the desire. Now the weather is sunny again, we think of starting bathing. – Italy is a lazy country. One meets people, and lounges till the next meal; and so life passes. But why not!

I still think of Africa. I hope it isn't true that Nip is losing on horses. If he seriously says he would like us to go out to Zululand, I shall certainly go: the money can be scraped from somewhere, and I can make £300 a year there as easily as at Hermitage, by my spasmodic pen.

I heard from the Browns that Aldington and the Yorkes were at the cottage. They are not very easy people to get on with so I won't send you to them on spec. You'd only find it uphill work. They have their own special brand of conversation, and it's no good if you can't do it. I can't do with so much specialising. – Margaret and her mother wrote so *sweetly*: but too late.

I don't expect Rosalind will ever get out to Italy. Really, all things considered, it's *too* difficult with three children. If she could *deposit* them somewhere, and come out alone, well and good. But no, with three Bridgets! – one doesn't attempt it. – As for the embroidered picture, unless Rosalind *demands* it of you – I said she could have it, before I left – why, just keep it where it is, if it pleases you. – We have postcards from Bucklebury – all seems spick and span as ever there.[1] – What are you doing to your farm? – making the walls white? What about *goats* and ducks?

One of the best things about Italy is that there is still wine, even if it's dearer, to make glad the heart of man.[2]

I wonder if it's very dark and muddy at Grimsbury.

Tell the Monk to write to me, with all *her* side of the information. I hope she's girding her loins for the Veldt, or whatever it is in Zululand. – I hear my big luggage is still in Customs at Turin. One ceases to bother about these trifles.

I wish we could just pop over for one cosy evening: or that you could both come here for many days. – Remember me to Æ.[3] I did send her a postcard. I get so tired of writing letters – one's laziness here is shameful. Do send all the news.

F[rieda] joins in love to both.   DHL

[1] i.e. Spring Cottage, Bucklebury Common, the home of Herbert and Joan Farjeon.
[2] Psalms civ. 15 ['wine that maketh glad . . .'].
[3] Unidentified.

1900. To Sallie and William Hopkin, 9 January 1920
Text: MS NCL; Huxley 492–4.

Palazzo Ferraro, Capri, (Naples)
9 January 1920

My dear Sallie and Willie

Today came the hanky and letters from Florence, after so long a time. But we have been straggling about – to Rome, to the wilds among the Apennines south of Rome – then here. The hanky is very lovely with its green sheen through the red: reminds me a good deal of grass going dark under a heavy crimson sunset. The socialist Roumanian from next door, who would please Willie, save that his Italian is of a Roumanian and difficult brand, brought in the post, and with true socialistic communism must at once carefully fold the hanky and try it round his neck, looking very much pleased with himself, and cocking his black eyebrows. But I didn't let him appropriate it.

Frieda came down to Florence about a month ago: a bit thinner for her vegetarianism, but very well: had enjoyed Baden-Baden. Everything is very short there – no fat, no milk, practically no meat, no coal. I must have some things sent from England. The French seem really *foul*, and some of these *trials* by the Allies of condemned German war-officials hideously unjust and Inquisitorial.[1] Ah Lord, the *filthy* world.

Florence was so nice: its genuine culture still creating a certain perfection in the town: Rome was tawdry and so *crowded*, I hated it. In Picinisco we got right into the wilds, where the ass lived on the doorstep and strolled through the hall, and the cock came to crow on the bent-iron wash-stand: quite a big, fine looking house, but lo and behold, one great room was a wine-press, another a corn and oil chamber, and as you went upstairs, half the upstairs was open, a beautiful barn full of maize cobs, very yellow and warm-looking. The kitchen, a vaulted cave, had never been cleaned since the house was built. One ate ones meals on a settle in front of the great chimney, where the pots swung on the hooks and the green wood sputtered. No one dreamed of a table, let alone[2] a table cloth. One blew up the fire with a long, long ancient iron tube, with a winged foot to stand in the ashes: and this tuba was handed from person to person in the process of blowing up a blaze. Hygienics not yet imagined. – Add to this, that all round circled the most brilliant snowy mountain-peaks, glittering like hell: that away below, on our oak-scrub hills, the air had a tang of ice, while the wild river with its[3] great white bed of

---

[1] The Allies claimed the right to try German war criminals by military tribunals of the accusing country. The *Times* reported (22 December 1919) that the list included 1500 names; subsequently (10 January 1920) it was reduced to 800.

[2] let alone] with

[3] MS reads 'is'.

boulders rushed pale and fizzy from the ice: that there was no road to the house, but everything had to be piled on the ass and forded over the river: that the nearest shop was $1\frac{1}{2}$ hours away, the nearest railway 15 miles of terrific mountain road: and that on the Saturday before Christmas it snowed all day long, and you have it.

We fled here. We got on the ship – a little iron tub of a steamer – takes 4 hours to Capri. Of course the sea rose – we got to Capri, where there is no landing stage, in the darkness about 8.0 at night, after 5 hours wallowing: the sea so high, that when a boat came to take us off it almost hopped onto our deck, and then fell back into an abysmal gulf of darkness; amid yells unparalleled almost, even in Italy. In terror, half swamped, it turned for shore, leaving us rolling with a lot of spewing Italians. We had to put back to mainland, and roll at anchor in the shelter of Sorrento till morning, when once more we pushed across to Capri, as the magnificent red dawn came up over the Mediterranean – and like sacks we were hurled into the curvetting boats.

However, here we are, high in this old palace, with two great rooms, three balconies, and a kitchen above, and an enormous flat roof, one of the most wonderful places in the world: Ischia, Naples, Vesuvius slowing smoking to the North – the wide sea to the west, the great rock of our Monte Solaro in front – rocks and the Gulf of Salerno – South. Below us, all the tiny jungle of Capri town – it is about as big as Eastwood, just from the Church to Princes Street – oh, less than that, very tight and tiny. Below is the piazza, the little square, where all the island life throbs – across the little gulf of the street by the end balcony is the comical whitewashed cathedral.

The island here is about $1\frac{1}{2}$ miles wide, we're on the very neck – steep round ridge of the hill. Altogether Capri is about 4 miles by 2 miles: but really almost mountainous, sheer precipices above us even here. – There are heaps of cosmopolitan dwellers – English, American, Russian by the dozen, Dutch, German, Dane – everybody on this tiny spot. Compton Mackenzie has a nice villa here and does the semi-romantic – but I like him, he's a good sort: also we found Mary Cannan, who was Barries wife: also Brett Young, a novelist with wife: and lots of other people if we cared to know them. But I prefer the Italians.

Italy is expensive, but works out with the high exchange about equal to England. – It is warm – we have had two fires only, just two evenings. We are thinking of starting to bathe now in the sea, which is very beautiful.

There is a real Italian shop behind Mecklenburg Square, where you can get good, or at least, *real* oil. But I forget the street. If I can get a sound vessel to send it in, I'll send you some from here. I'll see about it.

My dear Willie, I thought Ada had sent those library books back *long ago*. I'll write her.

I *do* wish you could come out here to see us. Couldn't you manage it? It would cost only the *fare*. Thomas Cook and Son, Ludgate Circus, E.C.4. will do all your passport business, and tell you everything, if you write them. Why not plunge?

Frieda sends her love, with mine   DHL

1901. To Thomas Moult, 10 January 1920
Text: MS Lazarus; Unpublished.

Palazzo Ferraro, *Capri*, (Naples)
10 Jan. 1920

Dear Moult,

Today I have received your telegram, forwarded from Grimsbury Farm. You will see where we are. Miss Monk writes from the farm that she forwarded your letter to Florence – I haven't had it, neither that nor the cheque. But it may arrive later – sent on from Florence.

We fled from England. My wife went to Baden-Baden early in October – I stayed in England another month – was too much for me, went to Florence. My wife joined me there in December – we went on to Rome – then into the mountains – and at last here, seeking a warm and inexpensive place. Thank goodness this is pretty warm – one rarely needs a fire – and not outrageously expensive. But Italy is no longer the delightfully cheap place it was before the war.

Capri is pleasant. Compton Mackenzie is here – the 'rich young novelist': but nice. Francis Brett Young also here – and other friends. The island is lovely enough, when the wet scirocco wind isn't stickily raving: but it is overcosmopolitanised, in its small way. I expect however we shall be here for a few months.

I hope I shall get the letter from Florence. But anyhow write and tell me about *Voices*: I guess it isn't drowned even by all these hooting Owls and babbling Mercuries.[1] Tell me also how are you and your wife.

Yrs   D. H. Lawrence

---

[1] *The Owl*, Nos. 1 and 2, had appeared in May and October 1919; it was edited by Robert Graves and published by Secker. The *London Mercury* began its twenty-year independent life in November 1919, edited by J. C. Squire.

1902. To J. B. Pinker, 10 January 1920
Text: TMSC NWU; cited in Carswell 123.

Palazzo Ferraro, *Capri*, (Naples).

10 January 1920.

Dear Pinker,

Thank you for your letter. Yes, I am grateful to you for all you have done for me in the past. But I am an unsatisfactory person, I know. And therefore it would be best for me to act just on my own responsibility. So do please let us conclude our agreement.

What things you have to return to me, please tell me. But don't send any MS. to me here. I will arrange with my sister, or a friend, to keep the things for me.

I feel I have been an unpleasant handful for you, and am sorry.

Yrs.   D. H. Lawrence

1903. To Violet Monk, 12 January 1920
Text: MS SIU; Moore 611–12.

Palazzo Ferraro, *Capri*, (Naples).

12 Jan 1920

Dear Monk,

Many thanks for the letter, with the Moult telegram. Neither of the letters you forwarded has come on: heaven knows why. The post is very erratic. One has to register anything that matters at all. – But the mighty cheque wouldn't be for more than £4., I'll bet my boots, so we won't alarm ourselves.

How nice that the Silence ladies prove so congenial.[1] Life opens itself in little new circles. Here we struggle along in Italian and German and French and English, on this island which is a little Babel. My neighbour is a Roumanian, and we spend fierce evenings in a discussion of idealistic philosophy, I in my bad English-Italian, larded with French, he in his furious Roumanian-Italian, peppered with both French and German. You may guess what it's like: a sheer farce.

The weather keeps very uncertain – but never cold. Sudden storms rise up, and blow their heads off, and ours. The little steamer which wallows its way from the mainland once a day can't come. We stand on the dark terrace and peer into the gulf of the sea: nothing. Then the bread gives out in Capri. Everybody runs to buy biscuits – biscuits give out: a run on potatoes. – But

---

[1] Members of the 'Order of Silence' had their convent in what is now Downe House School at Cold Ash, 2 miles *s*. of Hermitage.

today is a great day. All the boats got across yesterday, so there is to be a supply of flour, rice, cheese, macaroni, coffee, and sugar, sudden abundance after scarcity. Frieda got a christmas present from Germany yesterday also – a beautiful scarf: which at the moment she is showing to the servant, who sings out Come è bello! – come è be-e-e-e-ello! – Isn't it lovely. I expect the dear Liberata will be donning the scarf when we are out. – She's not our own servant – belongs to the whole flat: is handsome, and eats the jam.

We get most marvellous days. On Saturday I went with the Roumanian to the top peak of the island, Monte Solaro. It is a high climb, more than two hours steady going. But from the top it is beautiful beyond words: this island at one's feet, the dark sea all round: the mainland at Massa coming close, pale grey rock, very steep, and slopes of white-specked villages – then snow-mountains above, behind. Naples clings close to the exquisite long curve of her bay, far off, and Vesuvius rolls a white glittery smoke level on the wind. And the other islands stand pale and delicate in the sea – and the coast veers far away into the south and east – and away inland runs the snow-ridge, high up – and on the sea a white steamer loses herself southward. – In Italy the tones are all delicate and pearly, really, tending to blue. The olive trees themselves are misty coloured and frail. Only orange clumps are dark, with round yellow oranges.

It is a pity we can't all go and picnic on Monte Salaro. There are two lovely rooms here, with a terrace, that you and Lambert might have.

So you know Richard Aldington! Do you like him? And Arabella?

I'm glad Mr and Mrs Lambert have[1] a house. Ventnor is very pleasant indeed – though a bit far.[2] When are they turning in?

If only I did some work! We are doomed, like butterflies, to flutter our little day, I suppose. – 'Consider the ant!'[3] I hate ants.

Remember me to Mrs Lowe: also to Mr Boshier: also to Ernie.[4] One thinks a lot of Hermitage. Who helps you saw wood? How is Becky? Betty?[5]

I really think I *couldn't* bear the mud. Here it is so steep and rocky, the island is always dry – Makes such a difference not to have to bother where one steps. The sound of England in mud simply is too much.

My kindest regards to Mr and Mrs Lambert. Frieda sends greetings.

D. H. Lawrence

---

[1] MS reads 'has'.
[2] On the Isle of Wight.
[3] Proverbs vi. 6 ['Go to the ant, thou sluggard; consider her ways, and be wise'].
[4] Ernie Prior was a cripple who owned a cycle shop; DHL befriended him and knew him particularly well when Ernie had rooms with Mrs Lowe at the same time as the Lawrences.
[5] Unidentified.

1904. To Max Plowman, 12 January 1920

Text: MS Plowman; PC v. Capri – I faraglioni dalla Marina piccola; Postmark, Capri
12.1.20.; Unpublished.

Palazzo Ferraro, *Capri*, (Naples)

12 Jan. 1920

I sent you a letter from Florence, but didn't get any answer.[1] I wonder if you
are back in Hampstead. Send me a line, and tell me: tell me also what is
happening, and if you feel like making a dash to Italy. Here also it is stormy,
but not cold, thank goodness. We've got an apartment high in this old palace –
airy and light and the sea beyond on both sides. My wife likes it immensely.

Greetings   D. H. Lawrence

1905. To Benjamin Huebsch, 15 January 1920

Text: MS UT; Postmark, Capri 17.1.20; Moore 613.

Palazzo Ferraro, *Capri*, (Naples), Italy

15 Jan 1920

Dear Huebsch

I am sending you the Martin Secker first proofs of the translation of the
Russian philosopher Shestov. My friend Koteliansky did the translating, I
Englished it. I think you'll find it rather amusing. Koteliansky is the
authorised translator of this work. He wants to sell the translation outright –
not bother with copyrights. I wonder if you would care to do the book – if so,
will you tell me how much you'll give for it? – If you don't care for it, would
you give it to Hermann Schaff, for him to consider – I have lost his address.
Also my compliments to him. Please do hand the proof on, if you don't
intend to publish it.

There are many errors in this proof. I will send a perfect proof shortly.
Koteliansky is like the rest, hard up – wants some bit of ready money.
Answer me direct about this; quickly, will you. – Secker publishes in March
or April. You could have sheets, of course.[2]

D. H. Lawrence

Revised proof will contain a short notice of Shestov himself.

---

[1] See Letter 1870.

[2] Huebsch does not appear to have responded until 27 February 1920; he then wrote (TMS LC):

Dear Lawrence,
   Since writing to you yesterday, I noticed that you wish me to deal with you direct in the
matter of Koteliansky and the Shestov book.
   I am ready to give him £50. outright for the American rights, assuming that no translation of

1906. To Benjamin Huebsch, 16 January 1920
Text: MS UT; Postmark, Capri 17.1.20; Moore 613–14.

Palazzo Ferraro. *Capri*, (Naples), Italy.
16 Jan. 1920

Dear Huebsch,

I am writing again to Scott and Seltzer about *Women in Love*. Your cablegrams came on from Picinisco today.[1] About a month ago Seltzer sent me £50. on account of royalties for the novel. This I accepted conditionally. I write to him today, asking him if he will release the MS. to me again, and telling him I wish to return his £50. We must wait for his answer. I can't act without his acquiescence.

Anyhow, I want to get everything on a straightforward basis now. I am breaking my agreement with Pinker – he is willing. I want to act now for myself. And I must be clear and sure about everything. I don't like this vague, half-friendly, in-the-air sort of business. It leaves me irritated and dependent. I don't want charity or kindness or anything of that sort: at least I don't want it mixed up with business. Let us make a start now, at precise dealing with one another.

I want you first to send me an account of sales of all my books up to date.

I want you, further, to agree to send me accounts every six months, and to settle the accounts within three months of their falling due.

Presumably, Pinker will return to me his agreements with you on my behalf. If not, I want you to send me copies of our agreements.

I want to know precisely what you are doing about *New Poems*: also, to know if you have received the MS. of *Studies in Classic American Literature*. Tell me please if you are going to publish these *Studies*, and give me the approximate date. If you are not inclined to publish, will you please return the MS. to me *at once*.

Before we go any further, let us get on to a clear, sure footing. I can't bear to fumble my way any further through a half-sentimental mist of business. If

the book has appeared in America and that K was authorized to dispose of the American rights. Please get in touch with him immediately and ask that he cable (using the above cable address) promptly, if he accepts, the single word 'Koteliansky' will signify an affirmative reply. If he declines let him cable the word 'no' Koteliansky.

I have just written Secker on another subject and have added that I am accepting the book and asked that he send me some proofs immediately and also that he withhold his publication, if possible, so as to enable us to copyright over here.

Yours as ever,

[1] The first (sent on 30 December 1919) read: 'Lawrence Avoid serious mistake. Cable Scott [& Seltzer] withdrawing novel. Writing. Heubsch.' The second (31 December 1919): 'Lawrence Cannan opposes Scott strongly advocates my publishing. Huebsch.'

according to account rendered I am in your debt, so be it. If twopence is due to me, let it be twopence. Only I will be sure, before I go a step further.

Yrs   D. H. Lawrence

Also, please tell me the precise fate of *The Rainbow*: if it is really out of print, or only nominally: if you are re-issuing, and when. I understand the difficulties. But I want *to know*.[1]

1907. To Thomas Seltzer, 16 January 1920
Text: MS UT; Postmark, Capri 17.1.20.; Lacy, *Seltzer* 4.

Palazzo Ferraro, *Capri*, (Naples), Italy
16 January 1920.

Dear Mr Seltzer,

I hear from Huebsch that he is anxious to secure the publishing of *Women in Love*. I understood that my agent Pinker had sent him the MS. long ago. Apparently it was not so. Since Huebsch has done *The Rainbow* it is most fair that he should have the offer of *Women in Love*. If you can see your way to do so, I wish you would relinquish to me again the MS of the novel, and I will at once return the £50 advance. If you have gone to the expense of type-written copies, I will pay that bill also. Please let me know *by return*.

If you cannot see your way to relinquishing the MS., then first and foremost will you let Martin Secker have the copy you promised. He writes insistently about it, and I am concerned that he has not received it.

Then will you please draw up a short agreement according to the terms of my last letter:[2] stating definitely the royalty per-centage, the sale-price of the

---

[1] Though Huebsch's response to DHL's enquiry does not seem to have survived, reference can be made to his later report to Richard Aldington, 1 June 1950 (TMS LC). In it Huebsch explains that, in order to avoid the attention of the American censor, he told his travellers 'to let the book dribble out to the trade with a caution against talking too much about it, and thus the edition (I do not remember the quantity) was eventually sold out without, I think, any advertising or copies for review. Perhaps there were some reviews at that stage but if so the editors must have asked for copies; I know that I did not offer any because that would have balked my plan. The book having gone out of stock there were demands for more, of course, but I was still timid and decided to take refuge in the old trick of a limited edition, a little larger in dimensions and a little more expensively produced than the first. I have a copy dated 1920, but as I several times reprinted this "limited" edition (at $5, which was pretty high for a novel in those days) I am not sure of the date of the first limited edition. In justice to myself let me add that I did not try to deceive anybody by the term "limited" edition, but made it clear through the travellers that I was feeling my way, printing a lot at a time during a ticklish period. I wanted to fulfill my obligation to Lawrence by keeping the book available but I was in no position then, working almost single-handed, to defend a suit which, following on the London suppression, might have had serious consequences for me.'

[2] This seems to have disappeared.

book, and the date before the expiration of which the book shall be published; also will you agree to send me an account of sales every six months, and to settle the account within three months of the date of rendering.

My agreement with my agent Pinker lapses now, and I wish to act as my own agent henceforth. If this is to be in any way satisfactory, I must have every point of agreement between myself and my publisher precise and explicit. I don't want tedious formality. But a short, concise, explicit agreement, signed by both of us, I must have.

Yours Sincerely   D. H. Lawrence

1908. To Martin Secker, 16 January 1920
Text: MS UInd; Postmark, Capri 17.1.20.; Huxley 495–7.

Palazzo Ferraro, Capri, (Naples)
16 January 1920

Dear Secker,

I had your letter with the offer for *The Rainbow* and *Women in Love* – and I talked it over also with Mackenzie. I had written to Duckworth asking him if he would sell back my copyrights:[1] he replied he could not see his way to sell them back, but was ready to make me an offer for the re-publication of *The Rainbow*. I wrote and asked him what offer he could make. There it stands.

With regard to your letter – I should never sell the *Rainbow* for £200. I'd rather go back to my old arrangement with Duckworth, of royalty and £50. advance: or even no advance. The fact that I have no money would never make me jump at a lump sum. I have lived so long without money, that I know I can go on living without money, and £200 is really nothing to a man who has nothing. Moreover I believe in my books and in their future, and don't really bother. Vogue la galère – she won't sink, anyhow, of that I'm sure.

But apart from this: I should like to join with you: I should like to be a part-publisher of my own work: I should like to be one in a real guild. Mackenzie and I get on with one another: also Brett Young.

I should like to be with you, because you really care about books. The thought of our being partners all in Secker and Co. pleases me, so long as we are really in sympathy, and so long as we are all free souls.

Mackenzie suggested £200 for *The Rainbow*, £300 for *Women in Love*, and £500 for the book which I am expecting – it is in the post now – and which I will call provisionally A Mixed Marriage:[2] this total of £800 is to represent the sale of all copyrights until your books prove a return of £1000, after which I

---

[1] The letter has been lost.   [2] See Letter 1887 and n. 2.

am to resume my royalty of 20%, the proceeds of which are to pass into the firm of Secker and Co until such time as I shall have, say £2000 invested in the firm – after which they are to be my own separate property. This, with minor provisions, is Mackenzies scheme. And this seems to me pretty sound.

But I dont want you to imagine for an instant that I am trying to force an issue, with Mackenzies help. I don't want anything that doesn't seem to you just and fair. But I want you also to treat me justly and fairly. I hate tentative methods. I do like plain outspokenness. I don't want to cadge anything. Tell me exactly and flatly what you think. In an affair like this, we have either to be a genuine *alliance*, a certain real accord between us: or else we must keep entirely to the old, purely commercial relationships such as I had with Duckworth, and which I found always, with Duckworth, decent: – or else we merely part.

Then, honestly, I think you are wrong about the title *Women in Love*. Everybody jumps at it, as an excellent title. *The Rainbow* and *Women in Love* are really an organic artistic whole, I cannot but think it would be well to issue them as *Women in Love* Vol I and Vol II. *The Rainbow* must appear as a new book. Best give it a new title and make some few alterations. I should like to know what alterations you would suggest. As far as the legal proceedings of the suppression are concerned, Pinker could supply you with all information: so could that man – Thring, is it? – secretary to the Authors Society.[1] I was given distinctly to understand that the magistrates order destroyed only the existing edition: that any further edition would have to be proceeded against all over again, it could not be automatically suppressed. Best re-issue as a new book, with a new title, anyhow. – The magistrates proceeded on the reviews by James Douglas, in the *Star*, and one by Clement Shorter, I think in *Pall Mall*.[2] The scene to which exception was *particularly* taken was the one where Anna dances naked, when she is with child. I don't think it's very important, anyhow. Sufficiently past.

The MS. which is now in the post, coming from Germany, has lain in Bavaria since early 1914. It is a novel, two-thirds finished – quite unlike my usual style – more eventual[3] – I am very keen to see it. I thought if I finished it, it would be quite *unexceptional*, as far as the censor is concerned, and you might publish it soon after *The Rainbow*, if you liked – or leave it till *Women in Love* is also done.

[1] George Herbert Thring (1859–1941) was Secretary to the Society, 1892–1930. See *Letters*, ii. 433n.

[2] James Douglas (1867–1940) and Clement King Shorter (1857–1926) wrote hostile reviews of *The Rainbow* in the *Star* and *Sphere* respectively. See *Letters*, ii. 462 nn. 1 and 2.

[3] i.e. focussing on events.

These are just suggestions. Tell me just what you think. Let us either agree sincerely, or remain merely commercial, or break off. – I wish we could meet, pity you are so far.

Yrs   D. H. Lawrence

Pinker replied that, if I really wished, he would let me go. I have written to say I want to go. So I am as good as free in this respect. I want to act for myself.[1]

1909. To Cecily Lambert, [22 January 1920]
Text: MS SIU; PC v. Capri – Marina piccola; Postmark, Capri 23.1.20; Unpublished.

[Palazzo Ferraro, Capri, (Naples)]
22 Jan.

We've had a postal strike for the last ten days – no letters – but it's ended now, and so there's a railway strike – probably it will end. O Italy! – O Europe! It makes me want to go to a new continent. I am quite serious about Africa. Could you send me Nip's address? – also Wally's?[2] I should like to write to both of them direct. Do send the addresses. – I wrote a letter to you, also one to the Monk: hope they'll arrive. It's all a gamble. – It's a bit colder here – but we're eating new potatoes, and in the tiny fields the broad beans are in flower, and the butterflies flutter on the warm side of the island. Hope all is well at Grimsbury.

DHL

[1] Secker's response to DHL's proposals can be clearly gauged from his letter to Mackenzie:

I have thought over your suggested arrangement, but the affair is becoming too complicated. To be quite candid I am not at all convinced that he is a commercial proposition anyway and I am lukewarm about reprinting *The Rainbow*. I would only do so after I had got clear away with *Women in Love*. I do not want the advertisement of a cause celèbre which can be purchased at too great a cost, and I am advised that as matters stand its publication would automatically constitute a contempt of court. I do not think the authorities would move of their own volition, but some purist busybody would compel them to take notice. I can only repeat my original offer, £300 for all rights of *Women in Love* with the option of following up with *Rainbow* at £200. This I should probably exercise if *W. in Love* did not involve me in any kind of lawsuit and did something to rehabilitate the author. It must not be forgotten that at the moment no bookseller would buy a single copy of the *Rainbow* even with my imprint unless he dealt in 'curiosa'.

If he does not like this proposition I can revert to the original plan of trying *W. in Love* on an ordinary contract, royalties starting at 10%. But I am a little tired of the whole thing and, now Duckworth is in competition, am quite ready to retire in his favour. Lawrence's books are not worth competing for from a money making point of view (Mackenzie 168–9).

[2] Unidentified.

1910. To Lady Cynthia Asquith, 25 January 1920
Text: MS UT; Huxley 497–9.

Palazzo Ferraro, *Isola di Capri*, Italy.
25 Jan 1920.

I've been intending to write – but what with a postelegrafonico strike, and now
the railway strike, we have been cut off from the communicating world. I sit
dearly waiting for an MS. which is in the post, and which will lie in the post
till Doomsday, along with my Christmas parcels, my sweet cake and my nice
mincepies from my sister, my pound of tea and my pound of coffee and my
chocolates: all inestimable treasures in Italy: all, no doubt, gone down the
throats of the postelegrafonico strikers. There is always a fly in the ointment,
be it even spikenard, always a hair in the soup. – So – dolce far niente. Here I
sit at the top of my palace, and do nothing, sweet nothing – except go out to
lunch, or walk from one end of the island to the other. As for walking across it,
needless: one bestrides the narrow world without being a Colossus.[1] My
palace-roof, where F[rieda] and I hang the washing, is the very saddle of
Capri, on which we ride the island. It is Hiddigeigei's roof:[2] and this Palazzo
Farraro is the hub of island Capri.

Well – as it happens, the weather is wondrous fine – brilliant, hot sun,
brilliant, beautiful. I watched him go down red into the sea. How quickly he
hurries round the edge of the horizon, as if he had an appointment away
below. A lovely red evening. We went with our Signorina, from whom we
rent this apartment, to look at the Villa Lo Smeraldo, of which she has the
keys: it is to be let furnished. It is very beautiful, and we collected wood in the
grounds, and made a fire in the drawing-room, and had a joyous tea, and
danced on the marble floor while another Italian played the piano – altogether
what one should not do – till the sun went. It is a beautiful villa above the clear
sea and the Faraglioni,[3] all sun. I wish you came and took it. It costs 1000
francs a month – which is £20. at the present rate – Then you could let us
have an apartment, and we'd rejoice in the land. There is a sort of little
dependence – a world of ones own. – Compton Mackenzie lives away below.

---

[1] Cf. *Julius Caesar* I. ii. 135–6.
[2] Hiddigeigei is a cat created by Joseph Viktor von Scheffel (1826–86) in his long epic poem, *Der
Trompeter von Säckingen* (1853) which was popular well into the twentieth century. In one
adventure the cat finds itself on the roof of a garden house besieged by peasants.
[3] A group of rocky stacks off the s.e. corner of Capri.

He is amusing and nice. He talks also of the South Seas: and of my going: but alas, a sort of réclame-trip,[1] written up and voiced abroad and even filmed. Alas, I could not be filmed. I should feel, like a savage, that they had stolen my 'medicine'.

You ought to come to Capri – it isn't very cold, ever – particularly on the South side. You only need a fire some evenings – really: and you can get milk and butter in plenty, and with the exchange at 50 it costs perhaps a bit less than England. I believe I've got about £100. at the moment, so am rolling.

There are a few people – Mackenzie – and the Brett Youngs – Francis Brett Young, protegé of Eddies – pas grande chose – also Mary Cannan, whom you call Lady B[arrie] – also others – even too many.

I am going to the Mainland, to look round for a little house. There doesn't happen to be one empty here – only big ones. Do you know Capri? To look down the Salernian Gulf, South-east, on a blue day, and see the dim, sheer rocky coast, the clean rock mountains, is so beautiful, so like Ulysses, that one sheds ones avatars, and recovers a lost self, Mediteranean, anterior to us.

But Capri itself is a gossipy, villa-stricken, two-humped chunk of limestone, a microcosmos that does heaven much credit, but mankind none at all. Truly, humanly it is a bit impossible – for long.

Of news – it is possible *The Rainbow* will be re-published shortly in London – then *Women in Love*. Beaumont has actually finished the poems: but his edition on Japanese vellum-rubbish will still wait, for the leaves that have to be signed by me still lie here.[2] I shall try again to post them tomorrow. If you see Eddie tell him I'll send him a copy, also that history, of which I've finished the proofs.

Italy is a ridiculous kingdom, politically, governs itself so badly that one becomes indifferent to all political fates – Fiumes, JugoSlovakias and such like my-eye,[3] and merely curses because there's no coffee and no post. Meanwhile the sun shines brilliantly, and the sea ruffles its shoulders and doesn't care, so why should I or anybody care. So many worlds have passed – but there's only one Me.

Frieda greets you. We think, of course, of South Seas or of Africa. Do you know anybody in Africa, in a nice climate, who'd let me live on his land and help him – no wages or anything – but I should like to help a man make some

---

[1] i.e. advertising trip.
[2] See Letter 1564 and n. 2.
[3] Fiume (or Rijeka, the second city of Croatia) became a major issue in the peace settlement after 1918: it was first yielded to Yugoslavia; in 1924 it was returned to Italy (and then reverted to Yugoslavia in 1945).

sort of a farm in Africa – and I can always keep us two by writing. I feel like advertising in the *Nairobi Herald*. – More anon.

D. H. Lawrence

1911. To Lilian Trench, 26 January 1920
Text: MS UT; Postmark, Capri 27.1.20.; Unpublished.

Palazzo Ferraro, *Capri*, (Napoli).
26 Jan. 1920

Dear Mrs Trench[1]

We have buffetted our way here – at least it is warm and sunny. We find friends here too – Compton Mackenzie among them.

Please do a kindness for me. Let Miss Trench call on a friend of ours, at 5 Piazza Mentana (our old pension), will you. The friend is Mrs Rosalind Baynes, daughter of the old sculptor R.A., Sir Hamo Thorneycroft. She has just come out with her three tiny children, and nurse, and I'm afraid she feels a bit forlorn. I am a bit worried for her too. Douglas is in the same pension, and I've half a feeling he's making new scandals for himself, and I don't want her in any way to be touched or frightened. If you could just give a look in, I should be so glad.

Where is Herbert Trench – is he home, and better?[2] How is Miss Trench? – is her friend still with her? How glad Rosalind will be to know you all – she was unhappy with her husband, Dr Baynes, and they are just separated.

Let me thank you now for your kindness to us in Florence. My wife sends greetings. My best remembrances to Trench and the girls – I beg your pardon for the familiarity – their pardon too.

au revoir.   D. H. Lawrence

Where is Stein?[3] no word from him.

1912. To Margaret King, [27 January 1920]
Text: MS Needham; PC v. Amalfi. Valle dei Muliar, Portatrici di Vino; Postmark, [. . .]; Unpublished.

Hotel Capuccini – Amalfi.
27 Jan.

We got in such despair, never receiving any letters, because of the post strike

---

[1] See p. 425 n. 1.   [2] See Letter 1861 for details of his injury.
[3] Leo Stein (1872–1947), brother to Gertrude Stein (1874–1946), was one of the Trenches' neighbours in Settignano.

and the railway strike, that we have come a trip to the mainland. Amalfi is very lovely – this hotel was an old monastery, high over the sea. – The women in the picture are carrying wine down from the mountains. – There are wild crocuses all on the slopes, and narcissi, and magenta anemones, and violets – and almond and peach trees in full bloom – and so hot, we are sunburned. – Today the strike is over – letters will come.

Love. DHL

1913. To Ada Clarke, [27 January 1920]
Text: MS Clarke; PC v. Amalfi – Hôtel dei Cappuccini – Il Chiostro del 1200; Postmark, Amalfi 28.1.[. . .]; Lawrence–Gelder 188–9.

Amalfi –
27 Jan.

We have come a trip to the mainland, tired of the post strike and the railway strike and no letters and no work possible. Amalfi is marvellous – the picture shows the cloisters of this hôtel where we are – it was an old monastery. It is blazing sun, so hot we are sunburned. – We came 8 miles by steamer, 8 miles on foot, 12 miles in carriage. The coast is full of flowers – crocuses, violets, narcissi, and purple anemones, wild everywhere – and peach and almond in full flower – and beans and peas in flower, and potatoes being dug – I do wish you were here. – The strike has ended today.

Love DHL

We've had no post for nearly three weeks – these strikes. – We are going back to Capri in two days – a 3 day trip.

1914. To William Hopkin, [28 January 1920]
Text: MS NCL; PC v. Amalfi. Panorama dei Cappuccini; Postmark, Amalfi 28.1.20; Unpublished.

Amalfi
28 Jan.

We are making a small trip on the mainland – staying in this hotel on whose terrace sits the old monk. It is lovely – hot as our midsummer – on the slopes the wild crocuses are spread wide, like great lavender stars – and there are violets and narcissi and purple anemones – most beautiful. The oranges on the trees are quite hot with sun – and peach and almond trees are clouds. Its an adorable coast. We're returning Sat. to Capri. Hope everything is well with you.

DHL

1915. To Cyril Beaumont, 29 January 1920
Text: MS UT; Postmark, Capri 31.1.20. (MS UCin); Beaumont, *First Score*, pp. 36, 38–9.

Palazzo Ferraro, *Capri*, (Naples).

29 Jan. 1920

Dear Beaumont,

Today I have received the first copy of *Bay*. Yes, I think it's charming. – But now *why* did you forget to inscribe it to Cynthia Asquith? I promised it her, and I *know* she's looking forward to it. Can't you do anything about it?[1] please print it in, if you can. Just put 'To Cynthia Asquith.' I reminded you so often. – Then the picture on p. 14, over 'Last Hours,' is, I think, upside down. – Then, on p. 42, last line of 2nd. stanza down – 'till the roots of my vision seems torn.'[2] The last 's' should go out of 'seems' – not that it matters much. – Your binding is awfully pretty – but isn't it rather like spring? – and doesn't the inside open rather black? Don't you think it might be more sombre: purple, grey and black, or something like that. – If ever you want patterns of those binding papers, I think I could get some from a place I know in Florence.

The essential format is, I think, quite beautiful. The points I mention are details which can soon be altered. But I am really put out about the inscription. Let me know if you can do anything. I think I shall inscribe the vellum sheets myself. They still lie here. I have tried and tried to send them off – the postal strike and the railway strike have prevented me – the post office refuses responsibility. – I am surprised you haven't included the two poems you had in your anthology, which you stipulated you should include: 'Labour Battalion' and the other.[3]

Please send out for me several copies of the book: I shall put the addresses on a separate sheet.

Tell me about the new kind of book you have in your mind – I should like to hear.

Yrs   D. H. Lawrence

---

[1] Beaumont provided his own explanation in *First Score*, pp. 38–9: 'Lawrence had inscribed the poems: "To Cynthia Asquith." But I did not receive this until after the MS. and, putting it away in a drawer until I was ready to start on the book, I forgot all about it when the time came ... The omission of the dedication was rectified by printing the requisite number of single leaves on the three pages of the edition and pasting them in.'

[2] 'Nostalgia', l. 12.

[3] See Letter 1564; the 'other' poem was 'No News'.

1916. To Benjamin Huebsch, 29 January 1920
Text: MS UT; Postmark, Capri 31.1.20.; Moore 618–19.

Palazzo Ferraro, *Capri*, (Naples).
29 Jan. 1920

Dear Huebsch

It is just as well you are angry – I have been so angry, something has happened to me. Pinker, publishers, everybody – even you, previously – treated me with such vagueness and evasiveness, as if I were an aimiable imbecile, and left me to contrive to live on sixpence – no, basta! Abbastanza.[1] One could eat ones old shoes, while Pinkers and publishers were complaisant and vague. That's why I've done with Pinker: whatever mess I make in the future, I'll make myself, not through an agent.

Simply, it never occurred to me that Pinker could have had that MS. for almost two years, all the while assuring me that he was doing everything possible, without ever even mentioning it to you. It just didn't occur to me. I thought you'd seen it and turned it down months and months before. Then Seltzer, having heard of it from a friend, wrote and cabled, and I sent him the only final MS: he was decent, and I more or less agreed with him. – If I'd thought Pinker hadn't shown you the MS. – he had *3* copies – wouldn't I have sent it you a year ago? – Of course I would. There's nothing I believe in more than in sticking to one publisher. – But you seemed to leave me in the same vague and airy cart as all the rest: very friendly, but never telling me *anything*.

There you are. I'll write once more to Seltzer, and absolutely demand the MS. back, and refund anything he's spent. But still, I can't *legally* do anything – and what good is law, anyhow – and I entered with him in good faith. – But I'll get it back.

I'm going to send you six little essays on Freudian Unconscious.

This cursed strike still prevents the Shestov being posted: but perhaps it can come letter post – I'll have another shot tomorrow. Italy is damnable, as far as management goes. – When you get Shestov, if you can see your way to do so, just buy the American rights for a certain sum – no royalties – for Koteliansky's sake.

I don't want to write more tonight.

D. H. Lawrence

I got your Jan. 2nd. letter tonight.[2]

If you see Cannan you might tell him I got another cable from him, with half of it completely incomprehensible.

---

[1] 'No, that's enough.'   [2] Missing.

1917. To Thomas Seltzer, 29 January 1920
Text: MS UT; Postmark, Capri 31.1.20; Lacy, *Seltzer* 6.

Palazzo Ferraro, *Capri*, (Naples)
29 Jan 1920.

Dear Mr Seltzer

Huebsch writes that I have put him in the cart with *Women in Love*. It is my agent's fault. I thought Huebsch had turned the book down a year ago: it seems he never saw it. Now since he did *The Rainbow* when no-one would touch it in America: and since he has stuck to my work, I *very much* want you to give me back the MS. Any expense incurred, over and above the £50 advance I had and of course including the £50, I will refund at once, but I do wish that you would cable to me that you are willing to return the MS. Anyhow, if you are going strong on Goldrings work, I'm sure you will never bring mine in with any success: not that I depreciate Goldring, far from it: but he appeals to a public which would reject me.[1] – Moreover I don't want a semi-private publication. – I don't believe it is good for a new publisher to handle *Women in Love*. Do please cable me – 'Will release Manuscript' – and send (unless that is disagreeable to you) a line to B.W. Huebsch to that effect.

I am so sorry to be tiresome – but I honestly think it would be best all round if you left such a book alone. Huebsch has lost his reputation, in that line, already.

Yours Sincerely   D. H. Lawrence

1918. To John Middleton Murry, 30 January 1920
Text: TMSC UT; Unpublished.

Palazzo Ferraro, *Capri*, (Naples)
30 Jan. 1920

Dear Jack

I received your letter and also the returned articles, forwarded from Ospedaletti.[2] I have no doubt you 'didn't like them' – just as you didn't like the things you had from Derbyshire. But as a matter of fact, what it amounts to is that you are a dirty little worm, and you take the ways of a dirty little worm. But now let me tell you at last that I know it – not that it's anything new: and let it be plainly understood between you and me, that I

[1] Seltzer published Goldring's *Margot's Progress* and *Fight for Freedom* (with a preface by Henri Barbusse) in 1920; he had already published *The Fortune* (1919).
[2] See p. 401 n. 2. (Katherine Mansfield left Ospedaletti on 21 January 1920). For one of the essays see p. 428 n. 1.

consider you a dirty little worm: and so, deposit your dirty bit of venom where you like; at any rate we know what to expect.

D. H. Lawrence[1]

1919. To Benjamin Huebsch, [30 January 1920]
Text: Bookseller's Catalogue (Parke–Bernet, 1963), pp. 31–2.

[Palazzo Ferraro, *Capri*, (Naples)]
[30 Jan. 1920]

[Lawrence 'comments on the number of errors in the proof' of Shestov, *All Things Are Possible* 'and mentions the difficulty he has had in sending it to Huebsch because of a strike . . . Lawrence claims in his note not to have corrected the proof.']

1920. To Catherine Carswell, 5 February 1920
Text: MS YU; Postmark, Capri -6.2.20.; cited in Carswell 127, 128, 130, 131, 134.

Palazzo Ferraro, *Capri*, (Naples).
5 Feb 1920.

My dear Catherine

I had your letter at last – after all these strikes. Good news that the novel still goes well. *Don't* have a foreword if you can avoid it. But I believe at the bottom you quite like Melrose: he sounds a character. I shall be so interested to see the novel again: want to read it again.

I hope Don's case really goes well and leads up to something. It is absolutely killing, I know, to keep wrestling with the void. I can feel that he gets depressed. But one should not take the world too seriously. I wish you could both come out here to Italy and vegetate – why should one always strive and struggle.

Secker wrote and said he would publish *The Rainbow* if I would sell him *all rights* for £200. Well, I won't, so he is furious. Now I am in communication with Duckworth, who will probably (touch wood) publish it and give me the just royalty, which is all I want. Then he would do *Women in Love* also. Of course Duckworth is a bit timid. I wish he could be reassured some way or

---

[1] Added beneath DHL's letter, on the TMSC from which this text is printed, is Murry's reply dated 8 February 1920:

Dear Lawrence,
    This is to tell you that it is my fixed intention, when ever or wherever I meet you again, to hit you in the face. There is no other way of treating you.

other. – I feel that this is the time to make our grand-slam. I feel that we have stuck together through so much disappointment – now we ought to unite and make a success all together. Why shouldn't you get away from London – why shouldn't you write another novel, and make enough to live on. And why shouldn't Don help us through *The Times*?[1] I feel times have been hatefully hard for you. Now they ought to come easier. I'm sure once I start I can make money – then we'll share mine. It won't be long, you see if it is.

I received from Beaumont, after all these months, the little book of poems he has been handprinting – 17 months he's been at it. But he's *non compos*. You should see his letters. He hasn't done a thing I want him. He's left out poems, he left out the inscriptions, he left out everything. To my violent expostulations he writes inane imbecilities – the man is hopeless. Have you ever seen him? Such a silly-looking little book, I think it – *Bay*, except it's beautiful paper and print. But oh dear, the silly little wood cuts, so out of keeping with the poems, some of which I think really beautiful and rare. I wonder if you'd care about a copy.

Daniel is supposed to have issued that play *Touch and Go* by now, though I've heard nothing. That will be another fiasco. Yesterday I got Douglas Goldrings play – *The Fight for Freedom*.[2] It is the first of the series – and is a pamphlet play with a detestable and inartistic motive. Goldring got *Touch and Go* out of me, saying it *Touch and Go* would be the first of the 'Plays for a Peoples Theatre'. Then the sly journalist went and put this offensive *Fight for Freedom* as the first play – and for sure has damned and doubly damned the lot. I don't *want* to be associated with the *Fight for Freedom* and it's knavish preface. And there is *Touch and Go*, with a preface written specially. Curse the sly mongrel world. Fortunately the *Fight for Freedom* has been utterly ignored – so that, publicly at least, *Touch and Go* escapes much connection. – I know you don't like the play – but anyhow it's not *base*.

Well, there we are. We went a little excursion on the mainland last week, down the Amalfi coast. I tell you it is lovely there – much lovelier than Capri. I am very sick of Capri: it is a stewpot of semi-literary cats – I like Compton Mackenzie as a man – but not as an influence. I can't stand his island. I shall have to risk expense and everything, and clear out: to Sicily, I think. One gets to Palermo in twelve hours by steamer from Naples. So I think we shall go. – My luggage hasn't come yet – I heard of it from Turin. You know we've had three weeks railway strike. – And I *can't* get that MS. of a novel from Germany out of the post. – But come what may, I must clear out of this Cat-Cranford of Capri: too much for my nerves. At present I'm in bed with a

---

[1] See p. 57 n. 1.   [2] See p. 371 n. 4.

bronchial cold: not serious though. – No, I don't want to do a satire. It all just dries up one's bowels – and that I don't like. – I shall go and find a place in Sicily, and you will come for a few months, won't you. J[ohn] P[atrick] runs about now – we can find him an Italian nurse. You could come by sea.

It is brilliant sunny weather. Do hope all goes well.

DHL

1921. To Katherine Mansfield, [6 February 1920]

Text: MS NZNL; *Katherine Mansfield's Letters to John Middleton Murry 1913–1922*, ed. John Middleton Murry (1951), p. 470.

[Palazzo Ferraro, *Capri*, (Naples)]
[6 February 1920]

[Katherine Mansfield, writing to Murry on 9 February 1920, reported: 'Lawrence sent me a letter today, he spat in my face and threw filth at me and said'] I loathe you, you revolt me stewing in your consumption . . . The Italians were quite right to have nothing to do with you ['and a great deal more. Now I do beseech you if you are my man to stop defending him after that and never to back him up in the paper. *Be proud.* In the same letter he said his final opinion of you was that you were a'] dirty little worm. ['Well, *be proud.* Dont forgive him for that, please'.]

1922. To Martin Secker, 6 February 1920

Text: MS UInd; Postmark, Capri -7.2.20.; Huxley 501.

Palazzo Ferraro, *Capri*, (Naples).
6 Feb. 1920

Dear Secker

Thank you for your letter. No, I don't see in the least why I should raise any ill-feeling: I don't dream of it.

I am going on with Duckworth – hope it works out all right.

I suppose you never received the promised MS. from Scott and Seltzer? – Liars they are. – If it does come, let me know at once, will you, and I will tell you if I should like it sent direct to Duckworth – I speak of *Women in Love.*

Let me have a copy of Shestov – or revised proofs – as soon as you can, will you – for America.

Will you send Brooks a copy of *New Poems*: I should like him to have them: J.Ellingham Brooks, Villa Ferraro, *Capri.*

Tell me one day what you are doing with *New Poems.*

Yrs   D. H. Lawrence

1923. To S. S. Koteliansky, 8 February 1920
Text: MS BL; Postmark, Capri -9.2.20.; cited in Gransden 27.

Palazzo Ferraro, *Capri*, Prov. di Napoli.
8 Feb 1920

My dear Kot

Your letter today. The three weeks strike, and practically no post all the time, made it seem useless to write. And now I've had flu again – it is very bad in Italy – and am only just going to get up. – Sonia's parcel has not come – parcels never come. – I sent the Shestov to Huebsch – he asked for it – with urgent instructions to pay a lump sum. We will await the result – from him as from your Knopf – of whom I believe I have heard, but know nothing.[1] Post is very slow here, to America. – Secker of course is going on with Shestov – but you know how *slow* Secker is – impossible. He will send you a copy as soon as he has one ready. – He wanted to buy the *Rainbow* out and out for £200. Of course I wouldn't, so we broke off, and Duckworth is considering. – I have never heard from Gilbert again – not since that letter you sent on. – Mary is still here – but goes to Sicily soon – afraid of flu and death. Very much afraid of death. – Gilbert is saying disgusting things about 'us writers' in American papers – Mendelling.[2] Mackenzie showed me cuttings. Curse Gilbert, if he's worth it. – Douglas Goldring sent me his *Fight for Freedom*. A nice thing for my play to be following on the heels of such a shit: especially as, since I was purported to open the series, *I* have got a little preface on 'A Peoples Theatre'. O crotte mondaine![3] – I have broken with Pinker. Te deum laudamus.[4] – It's fine and sunny here. – But I'm sick of this island: a nice cats cradle of semi-literary and pleni-literary pussies. Oh my dear English countrymen, how I detest you wherever I find you! Notwithstanding Mackenzie is nice. – But as soon as I've got my legs I'm going over to the mainland to find a cottage where, if possible, are none but Italians. – The exchange, I hear, rose to 66: but they won't give it. Meanwhile prices soar up. – I haven't heard anything from Daniel about the play.

a riverderci, e sia bene.[5]   DHL

Katharine gone to Mentone – 'L'Hermitage', Mentone – as I suppose you know.[6] I wrote my final opinion of Jack to Jack. Basta.

---

[1] Alfred A. Knopf (1892–   ) had founded the publishing firm which bears his name, in 1915; president, 1918–57. m. Blanche Wolf, 1916. Knopf later published several of DHL's books, including *St. Mawr* (1925), *The Plumed Serpent* (1926), *David* (1926) and *Mornings in Mexico* (1927).
[2] See Letter 1314 and n. 3.
[3] 'O shit of the world!'
[4] 'We praise thee, O Lord.'
[5] 'and I hope things go well'.
[6] 'L'Hermitage' was a private nursing-home in Menton. She stayed there until 15 February.

1924. To J. B. Pinker, 8 February 1920
Text: MS Forster; cited in Carswell 123.

Palazzo Ferraro, *Capri*, Prov. di Napoli
8. Feb. 1920

Dear Pinker

I have your letter of 27th. January, with cheque for £105, settling Huebsch's account. What is the £25 refunded to E.A.Bennett?[1] I don't know anything about it, do I? And who is E.A.Bennett?

I wish you would send to me here the manuscripts named in your list (except of course *Women in Love*) – by registered manuscript post.[2] I think there is nothing very heavy. Please don't send by parcel post, anyhow, as it never arrives. And will you please include my agreements, so that I can keep them by me.

Yours Sincerely   D. H. Lawrence
J. B. Pinker Esq.

1925. To Benjamin Huebsch, 10 February 1920
Text: MS UT; Postmark, Capri 12.2.20.; Moore 621–2.

Palazzo Ferraro, *Capri*, Prov. di Napoli
10 febbraio 1920

Dear Huebsch

I had this Cable today from Seltzer, of Scott and Seltzer, in reply to my cable.[3] It is no use my cabling again, as he will have my letters by now, telling him I want you to have *Women in Love*. I expect he will communicate with you – at any rate, I will let you know what he says. Apparently he will let the book go. He said he was having it re-typed, as the MS. was written over. I have told him I will pay all expenses, if he has incurred them. If you get the MS., I should be glad if you would have it re-typed, in case he has not done so. – I am going on with Duckworth rather than Secker, about the re-publishing of *The Rainbow*, and then of *Women in Love* – will let you know what Duckworth decides: but I want D. to have a copy of *Women in Love*, which I want you to send him, if Seltzer has not done so. Seltzer was supposed to have a typed copy of the MS. sent to Secker, but he hadn't done so, the last I heard.

---

[1] Arnold Bennett anonymously contributed £25 to help relieve the impoverished DHL in February 1918 (*Letters of Arnold Bennett*, ed. Hepburn, i. 261n.). See Letter 1515 and n. 1.

[2] DHL recorded the MSS on Pinker's list, in his diary (Tedlock, *Lawrence MSS* 89): 'Mortal Coil, Samson & Delilah, Miracle, At the Gates, Thimble, Bay, John Thomas, Fox, Wintry Peacock, Fanny & Annie, Monkey Nuts, You Touched Me. (*Ask for Witch à la Mode, Once, Primrose Path, Love Among Haystacks*)'.

[3] The cable, dispatched from New York on 8 February 1920, read as follows when transcribed in Picinisco: 'Relnquies for atother publisher entirely cable our ekpense. Selizer.'

I am more keen on *Women in Love* than on any of my books.

Will you tell me *what agent* you will go to, for the placing of my work. Pinker is returning to me all my MSS.. I have got several stories, which I want to place in America, so need a good New York agent. I am sending you directly some things you might put in the *Freeman*.

Tell me plainly and openly about everything. No more agents: and no more vagueness.

I feel it is my business now to secure an American public. I have been fooled long enough.

D. H. Lawrence

I told Seltzer plainly I wanted you to have *Women in Love*, and why: and that I would refund his £50. and pay his typing expenses, if any.

1926. To J. B. Pinker, 10 February 1920
Text: TMSC NWU; Unpublished.

Palazzo Ferraro, *Capri*, Prov. di Napoli.
10 Feb. 1920.

Dear Pinker,

Thank you for the cheque for £8-12-9, received this morning, on account of Huebsch's edition of *Look We Have Come Through*.[1]

Thinking over the list of MS. which was in your last letter, it seems to me there are several stories missing. Have you any track of 'The Primrose Path', 'Once', 'Witch à la Mode', 'Love Among the Haystacks'.[2] I have these on an old list.

Yrs.   D. H. Lawrence

1927. To Michael Sadleir, 10 February 1920
Text: MS UNCCH; Unpublished.

Palazzo Ferraro, *Capri*, Prov. di Napoli.
10th Feb. 1920

Dear Mr Sadler

I have your letter of the 3rd. – like the sound of the new review – seems sound. I shall send you a story as soon as I get my MSS. from Pinker – He is

---

[1] Huebsch had sent a cheque for $37.05 to Pinker, on 23 December 1919.

[2] All these stories had been written or drafted several years earlier: 'The Primrose Path' in June/July 1913 (*Letters*, ii. 52); 'Once–!' in June 1912 (ibid., i. 420 and n. 1); 'The Witch à la Mode', April 1911, under its original title 'Intimacy' (ibid., i. 258 and n. 3); and 'Love Among the Haystacks' in October/November 1911 and revised in July 1913 (ibid., i. 323 and n. 2; ii. 44 n. 5). None had so far been published.

returning all to me, as I am going to act without an agent for the future. – So that I should think I can let you have a story within a month's time.[1] Your pay isn't much – but I expect you haven't much capital.

I wish, however, you would tell me a little more about the projected review – I don't like to feel so vague and in the air – should like to know whom you think to include in your first numbers – and who are the actual editors. – I truly believe in avoiding another appearance of coterie and clique – let's hope we can avoid the reality as well as the appearance – but should like to know who are my associates. I have a bit of connection with the Oxford Press – and am not likely to render you liable to a prosecution in a short story.

I will say nothing at all about your letter, and your name shall not be mentioned by me.

Yours Sincerely   D. H. Lawrence

Hope I read your address correctly.

1928. To Compton Mackenzie, [11? February 1920]
Text: MS UT; Mackenzie 170.

[Palazzo Ferraro, Capri, (Naples)]
Wednesday[2]

I enclose Secker's letter.[3] – As you please, dear Martin. – I'll send *The Rainbow* to Duckworth, and get on with him. If he would really like a little foreword by you, would you still do it?

I'm staying indoors with a cold for the moment.

D. H. Lawrence

1929. To Amy Lowell, 13 February 1920
Text: MS HU; Damon 526–7.

Palazzo Ferraro, Capri, Prov. di Napoli. Italy.
13 February 1920

My dear Amy

Today I have your letter, and cheque for thirteen-hundred Lire.[4] How

---

[1] DHL, as good as his word, revised the story 'Wintry Peacock' (written as 'The Lance-Corporal Comes Home from the War' in January/February 1919) and sent it to Sadleir on 10 March (Tedlock, *Lawrence MSS* 89). However, the 'new review' (to be published by OUP) for which Sadleir requested the story, never appeared. Later, as editor of *The New Decameron* for Blackwell, he published 'Wintry Peacock' in June 1922.
[2] The conjectural date of this letter takes account of DHL's rejection of Secker's terms; Duckworth's receiving, reading and remonstrating on *The Rainbow* by 22 March (see Letter 1951); and DHL's suffering from 'flu' (cf. Letter 1923).
[3] The letter is missing.
[4] Amy Lowell had sent the equivalent in lire of $100 in January 1920 (Damon 523); but the

very nice of you to think of us this New Year. But I wish I needn't take the money: it irks me a bit. Why can't I earn enough, I've done the work. After all, you know, it makes one angry to have to accept a sort of charity. Not from you, really, because you are an artist, and that is always a sort of partnership. But when Cannan writes and tells me he has collected a few dollars – which, of course, I have not received – he wrote me to tell me he was collecting a few, but never wrote again.[1] Cannan annoys me, with his sort of penny-a-time attempt at benevolence, and the ridiculous things he says about me – and everybody else – in the American press.[2] I am a sort of charity-boy of literature, apparently. One is denied one's just rights, and then insulted with charity. Pfui! to them all. – – But I feel you and I have a sort of odd congenital understanding, so that it hardly irks me to take these Liras from you, only a little it ties me up. However, one must keep ones trust in a few people, and rest in the Lord.[3]

I am extremely sorry you are not well, and must have an operation. Such a thought is most shattering. Pray to heaven it won't hurt much and will make you right. – Blackwell is a good publisher for getting at the young life in England. He's much more in touch with the future, than old Macmillan.[4]

Secker has done another[5] edition of my *New Poems*, properly bound now. I shall have him send you a copy. I asked Beaumont to send you a copy of a tiny book of mine *Bay*, which he has hand-printed. He is not very responsible – tell me if you have received it.

No, don't go to England now, it is so depressing and uneasy and unpleasant in its temper. Even Italy isn't what it was, a cheerful insouciant land. The insouciance has gone. But still, I like the Italians deeply: and the sun shines, the rocks glimmer, the sea is unfolded like fresh petals. I am better here than in England. – Things are expensive, and not too abundant. But one lives for the same amount, about, as in England: and freer to move in the air and over the water one is, all the while. Southwards the old coast glimmers its rocks, far beyond the Siren Isles. It is very Greek – Ulysses ship left the last track in the

transaction ran into difficulties (see Letter 1940 and n. 1); and DHL finally received the cheque in dollars on 23 June 1920 (see Letter 2025).

[1] See Letter 1953.

[2] Cannan had published a short article, 'A Defense of Lawrence', in the *New York Tribune*, 10 January 1920; it was a rejoinder to an interview, published by the *Tribune*, with the publisher Sir Ernest Hodder. Cannan sponsored DHL as 'a man of genius and a person of vital importance to the intellectual and imaginative life of our time'.

[3] Cf. Psalms xxxvii. 7 and cxviii. 8.

[4] Macmillan had published Amy Lowell's *Six French Poets* in 1916; Blackwell was to publish the English edition of *Can Grande's Castle* in October 1920.

[5] another] another of

waves. Impossible for Dreadnoughts to tread this unchangeable morning-delicate sea.

Frieda came down to Florence from Germany: a bit thinner and wiser for her visit. Things are wretchedly bad there. I must have food sent all the time to F's mother from England, and for the children – there absolutely isn't enough to eat.

We have got two beautiful rooms here at the top of this old palace, in the very centre of Capri, with the sea on both hands. Compton Mackenzie is here – a man one can trust and like, which – as far as the first goes – is more than one can say of Cannan. – But Capri is a bit small, to live on. Perhaps I shall go to the mainland – perhaps not. Anyway this address will always find me. – I have just begun a new novel.[1]

I feel we shall see you in Italy. I do hope you will be better. Is Mrs Russell with you always?

A thousand greetings from both   D. H. Lawrence

1930. To Robert Mountsier, 16 February 1920
Text: MS Smith; Postmark, Capri 19.2.20.; Unpublished.

Palazzo Ferraro, *Capri*, (Naples), Italy.

16 Feb. 1920

Dear Mountsier

I got your letter of long ago, reached me yesterday. I am very sorry you have been knocked up – hope it isn't serious: that it is better now.

Frieda and I are here in an apartment at the top of this old palace. Capri is warm and sunny: one great improvement on England. I feel as if I should never go back to England anymore. A good many English people here – Compton Mackenzie among 'em.

Am glad I am not in America performing before the public. No – really. – But you will be glad to hear I have broken my contract entirely with Pinker. Am just awaiting the return of the last MSS. from him. No more Pinkers for me. – Yet I shall have to have some sort of Agent in New York – never again in England. I suppose it wouldn't be worth your while to act for me, in an unofficial sort of way – and take the percentage? When I get my short stories I shall have a number to ship over: also a few Psychoanalysis essays. – The sequel to the *Rainbow* lies in the hands of Scott & Seltzer at the moment – But

---

[1] In March 1916 (*Letters*, ii. 580) DHL referred to the MS of a novel – begun three years earlier as 'The Insurrection of Miss Houghton' – which he wanted from Germany. It had arrived on 12 February 1920 (Tedlock, *Lawrence MSS* 89). He began work on it at once; on 22 March he told Mackenzie that he had 'scrapped all the novel [he] did in Capri' (Letter 1952); and he then began afresh on the book which became *The Lost Girl*.

I am trying to recover it for Huebsch. I believe *The Rainbow* has gone quite well. I am busy with a novel now – rather nice – goes quite well. – Duckworth is considering a re-publication of *The Rainbow* in England.

But I want to plant my stuff *first* in America, and let England take second chance every time. And I want somebody to help me. I am sure I am going to have my day.

What do you think of Huebsch. – And do you know Scott & Seltzer – new people?

Write and tell us you are better. And tell me if you'd perhaps like to try planting my stuff in New York. Or suggest to me some decent agent who won't swindle me, and whom the publishers won't hate. – I believe the *Metropolitan* looks on me with a very favorable eye.

Yrs   D. H. Lawrence

Frieda greets you.

1931. To Catherine Carswell, 22 February 1920
Text: MS YU; Postmark, Capri 22.2.20; cited in Carswell 121.

Palazzo Ferraro, Capri, (Naples).
22 Feb. 1920.

My dear Catherine

You see enclosed. I should *so* like you to go and see the play, if you possibly can manage it.[1] It's a long way – but do go if you can: and write a notice of it for some paper. I do so much want to know what it looks like on the stage. I send £5. for the journey, for fear you're stumped. I know it's not enough – but it will pay the railway – Altrincham is Cheshire – near Manchester. I have told the Sec. you may come.

How are you? I've started a novel.

DHL

1932. To Gertrude Cooper, [25 February 1920]
Text: MS Clarke; PC v. Capri – Panorama dalla funicolare; Postmark, Capri 25.2.20; Lawrence–Gelder 117–18.

Capri
25. Feb.

I had your letter, inside Ada's tea, this evening. It is as hot as June here – all

---

[1] See Letters 1866 and 1956. Catherine Carswell had a commission from the *Times* to review the Altrincham production of *The Widowing of Mrs Holroyd*; thus she did not need the £5 DHL sent for her train fare (see Carswell 130, 134–6).

the butterflies fluttering among the flowers – wish indeed you could all be here. – Lovely green tea! – Tomorrow I am going by sea to Sicily – from Naples. If I find a house we shall go over. – Tell Ada I sent £2. to Emily for father. Do hope you're better.

DHL

1933. To Godwin Baynes, [March? 1920]
Text: MSC UN; Nehls, i. 500–1.

[Fontana Vecchia, *Taormina*, (Messina), Sicily]
[March? 1920][1]

[   ] Why bother about divorce?[2] The publicity is hateful and there isn't much to gain. One has to learn that love is a secondary thing in life. The first thing is to be a free, proud, single being by oneself: to be oneself free; to let the other be free: to force nothing and not to be forced oneself into anything. Liberty, ones own proud liberty, is worth everything else on earth: something proud within oneself. I believe if you would both come off the personal, emotional, insistent plane, and would be each of you self sufficient and to a degree indifferent or reckless, you and Rosalind would keep a lasting relationship. Its an ignominious thing, either exacting or chasing after love. Love isn't all that important: one's own free soul is first.

Excuse this impertinence. A second thing – you are a great admirer of Whitman, R. said. So am I. But I find in his Calamus, and Comrades one of the clues to a real solution – the new adjustment. I believe in what he calls 'manly love',[3] the real implicit reliance of one man on another: as sacred a unison as marriage: only it must be deeper, more ultimate than emotion and personality, cool separateness and yet the ultimate reliance.

For the rest of morality, je m'en fiche. One should keep one's own soul proud and integral, that's all.

Excuse the tirade. I felt you were running your nose against the wall, as I am. I speak on account of the stars I have seen, bumping myself against the eternal obstacles.

D. H. Lawrence

[1] This fragment of a letter – copied in an unknown hand – cannot be confidently dated. It is hesitantly placed in March 1920 because in this month (see Letter 1948) DHL raised with Rosalind Baynes the question of Godwin Baynes's divorce.
[2] Baynes rejected DHL's advice and instituted divorce proceedings; his wife did not contest the suit, and he was granted a decree *nisi* (see *Times*, 27 April 1921).
[3] 'Calamus. A Song' (3rd edn, 1860), l. 10: 'the manly love of comrades'.

1934. To Ada Clarke, [3 March 1920]
Text: MS Clarke; PC v. Vista dell'Etna da Taormina; Postmark, Taormina 4 3 20;
Lawrence–Gelder 118.

Fontana Vecchia, Taormina, Sicily
3 March.

I have found such a charming house here, in a big garden – Frieda arrives
Saturday, I hope. I'll write later.

love. DHL

Fontana Vecchia means old fountain – the name of the house.

1935. To Catherine Carswell, [7 March 1920]
Text: MS YU; PC v. [view of Mount Etna]; Postmark, Taormina 8 3 20; Carswell 131.

Fontana Vecchia, Taormina, (Messina), Sicily.
7 March

We have got such a lovely house and garden here – taken it for a year. Come
and see us.

Love DHL

1936. To Compton Mackenzie, [8 March 1920]
Text: MS UT; Mackenzie 169–70.

Fontana Vecchia, Taormina, (Messina)
Monday.

We've come in to our house this evening – I write by lamplight. Already
rather cosy. Returned to Giardini Sat. evening, and waited there till 9.30,
when F[rieda] and Mary arrived by the accelerato – ach! – and their trunks
not with them. We all stayed at Bristol – today I skipped to Catania for the
trunks – got them all right. Mary has turned in to Timeo[1] – seems a nasty
impudent place, like Etrangers, only more of it. – The woman upstairs here
leaves on Thursday morning – meanwhile, frigid gulf between two regions.
To hell with her. – I looked again at the Hindoo muslin stuff – but as the
woman was cheeky, with her English, and as the ragged rubbish has a dirtyish
look, to hell with it. Mary, of course, darted into the rag-shops like a sparrow
into a scullery, and emerged with a waistcoat. – I shall send your 50 francs
when there is ink for a cheque. – It is Scirrocco today[2] – grey like unshed

---

[1] The 'Bristol' and 'Timeo' were well-known hotels in Taormina.
[2] The sirocco, a hot, dry and dusty wind from North Africa.

tears, ages old and still unshed. That wall of mist met me as I left Messina,
rolling up the Straits[1] in a wall. There are many devils, little people, Tuatha
De Danaan,[2] dark influences, in Sicily. This is the Celtic land of Italy – with
the old fear in it. – I suppose tonight you are back at Piccola[3] – seems across a
space. – Frieda loves the house, so does Mary. – Do you imagine the balcony
at night? – the Plough pitching headlong into the sea on the left, terribly
falling, and Taormina in a rift on the right fuming tremulously between the
jaws of the darkness. – I wonder if I shall work – Heaven save us all! Did you
hear that one of F's diamond rings was stolen from the room in Capri. One
shouldn't have diamonds voilà tout! – Most bookless here. If you ever have
anything I might read and you don't want, remember me. Send me name and
address of *Land and Water* man, *please*, for Magnus.[4] Tell me the news. Hope
all is well.

                                                                        DHL

1937. To Compton Mackenzie, [8 March 1920]
Text: MS UT; Mackenzie 170.

                        Fontana Vecchia, *Taormina*, Prov. di Messina, Sicilia
                                                                      Monday.

We've turned in to our house tonight – strange lost soul I feel, with a bit of
heimweh[5] for Capri. But I am very grand here, in the house of the cook.[6]
Mary has gone in to Timeo tonight also: hateful place, Timeo, our Bristol
much nicer, smaller: she stayed with us till today, down there. – Well, I feel
I've reached my limit for the moment – like a spent bird straggling down the
Straits. We saw a great V of wild fowl wavering north up the straits –
Heimweh, or nostalgia then, for the north: yet I am wavering South. – But I
am at my limit for a year. Consider my exchequer with repulsion based on fear.

[1] Straits] Straights
[2] The gods of ancient Ireland (*Complete Poems*, ed. Pinto and Roberts, p. 1008). See DHL's
     poem, 'Mutilation', l. 37, in *Look! We Have Come Through!* (ibid., p. 213).
[3] See Letter 1885 and n. 1.
[4] Hubert James Foss (1899–1953), assistant editor of *Land and Water*, 1919–20. He joined the
     educational books department of Oxford University Press, 1921; he founded and became
     manager of the Press's music department, 1924–41.
       Maurice Magnus (1876–1920), an American who had enlisted in the French Foreign Legion
     during World War I; he later deserted and made his way to Italy; DHL met him, in Florence,
     in the company of Norman Douglas, in 1919. Magnus committed suicide in Malta in
     November 1920. DHL wrote an introduction to his *Memoirs of the Foreign Legion* (Secker,
     1924).
[5] i.e. home-sickness.
[6] See p. 506 n. 3.

But best not consider. – I hope you won't scorn us too much for moving to Taormina. It was chiefly, I think, the arid sort of dryness of the Capri rock: a dry, dry bone. But I don't know. – I feel a bit of a stranger here – feel the *darkness* again. There is no darkness in Capri. – Frieda said you had pains – do hope they're better. I get a sort of Wehmut.[1] Quoi faire! – Later I'll come to the South Seas – drift and drift. Don't let us lose sight of one another. We are opposite poles, in most things. But opposite poles are most inevitably mutually related. Don't let the world matter – it doesn't matter. I think we met well in Capri. – I'll see you again before very long. Let us weave fate somehow together – Hope your book goes – perhaps I shall write here – if only I could care again – or if only the ravens would walk up with the Capretto and macaroni.[2] Send us a line. – No ink here yet – I hope you got your typewriter safely – – many thanks.

DHL

1938. To John Ellingham Brooks, [8 March 1920]
Text: TMSC YU; Unpublished.

Fontana Vecchia, Taormina.
Monday.

Dear Brooks,

I haven't come back, have I? But I feel a bit of Heimweh for Capri. This evening we have come up to our house. It is very grand – once belonged to some Dutch people – Ybrecht, or Übrecht[3] – but now to the chief cook of the Timeo: peasants beneath. But the B[rett]-Y[oung]'s will tell you. – Oh, how *he* did weary me – like a fretful and pragmatical and dictatorial infant: always uttering final and ex cathedra judgments in the tone of a petulant little boy. – I am a little bit beyond myself here – not at home as in Capri. But there is more space, more air, more green and succulent herbage. – Mary has turned in to her Timeo – an uncharming place. I liked our Bristol Hotel much better – and only 22 francs a day if you have pension – and *so* good. Come and see Taormina again – come with your wife – you wont need a vestige of a passport, in hotels: only when you register as a *resident*. – I am going to send back your Baedeker: but your little brown pocketbook has, I am afraid, said its last farewell to you. It has become attached to me. – I wish you would call in the post-office and give them my change of address, so they can send my letters direct. I dont want them to go to Palazzo Ferraro. Excuse pencil – no ink bought. Frieda sends many greetings. Come and see us.

D. H. Lawrence

---

[1] 'melancholy'.   [2] Cf. 1 Kings xvii. 6.   [3] See p. 489 n. 2.

1939. To S. S. Koteliansky, [9 March 1920]
Text: MS BL; Postmark, Taormina 10 3 20; Zytaruk 205.

Fontana Vecchia, *Taormina*, (Messina), Sicily
9 March.

I scooted round Sicily looking for a house – Capri was too dry and small –
Now I have taken this, a nice, biggish place, with great garden, for a year –
2000 francs. The exchange will need to stay at 62. – Mary is staying here, at
the expensive Timeo hotel. – Sicily is a queer place – a touch of Saracen and
the East in it – sort of explosive gunpowder quality. But I like it. Wonder how
I shall stand it for a year.

I watch the Russian news, as well as I can: and watch the post. If only I can
get a £10. I am expecting, I shall send it you. But I had a blow – 1000 Lire
from America, which the Credito Italiano wouldn't cash. I hope I shall get it
back. Oh these American cheques.

Women in Love has gone to print in America. Has Daniel sent you *Touch
and Go?*

I imagine you setting off for the Ukraina. God, what a grand excitement,
after so long! Do let me know. Tell me about Sonia, what she will do. – That
parcel never came –

I want to work – I mean I ought to. Perhaps I shall, here, it is so still, and
festooned with flowers, beautiful.

DHL

1940. To Amy Lowell, 9 March 1920
Text: MS HU; Damon 527.

Fontana Vecchia, *Taormina*, Prov. di Messina. Sicily.
9 March. 1920

Dear Amy

My bank, Haskard and Co. of Florence, where I have a little account, sent
me the enclosed letter about the 1315 Lire which you gave me.[1] I don't know

---

[1] The letter (TMS HU) reads as follows:

Piazza Degli Antinori, Florence
March 1st 1920

David Herbert Lawrence Esq
Palazzo Ferraro, Capri (Naples)

Dear Sir,

Referring to our letter of February 18th ult. beg to say that the Credito Italiano, on which
your draft for *Lit.1315.70* was issued, have refused to pay us said amount, as they wish us to
send them a declaration with which we relieve them of all responsibility in respect to the

why the Credito Italiano is fussing. But stop the cheque at your bank, will you, lest they swindle us. – It is always easiest to have a cheque made out in dollars – they give much more for it here. For $100 I can sometimes get Lire 1800, which pays my rent for nearly[1] the whole year: a vast consideration. – Only don't let us *both* be done out of the money.

We have come here, and taken such a lovely house in a garden, for a year. It costs 2000L. It is really lovely. Only travelling is so trying and so expensive.

There are real good hotels here. If you are well enough, perhaps you will come during the course of our year.

I do wish you felt well and strong. Tell me if you get the various books I have ordered to be sent to you.

Italy feels shaky – Europe altogether feels most insecure. There'll be another collapse soon. Mais à la guerre comme à la guerre.

Send me a line to say how you are.

D. H. Lawrence

1941. To Douglas Goldring, 9 March 1920
Text: MS UT; Goldring, *Odd Man Out*, p. 258.

Fontana Vecchia, *Taormina*, (Messina), Sicily.
9 March 1920

Dear Goldring

I have just got yours of Feb. 28. We have taken a house here for a year. Note address.

About the *Fight*, Barbusse will put his party-umbrella over it all right. If you'd had a Barbusse preface at first, it would have been luck.[2] But best not be too political.

Yes, do squeeze *Touch and Go* out of McDermott – tell him he can have his £15 back. I *am* so curious to know what they do with *Mrs Holroyd* at Altrincham: should like to see B[etty], with her big nose, as Mrs H.[3] She's got the silent quality.

Istituto Nazionale dei Cambi, because said draft has been issued in America in Italian Lire, instead than in Dollars.

As we are unable to adhere to their request, we have today debited to you said amount, plus *Lit.2.75* interest from February 18th up to date, and plus *Lit.2.50* collecting charges.

We beg to remain, Dear Sir,

Yours faithfully   Haskard & Co. Ltd

[1] nearly] six
[2] See p. 467 n. 1. Henri Barbusse (1873–1935), French novelist and poet; his novel, *Le Feu*, was awarded the Goncourt prize in 1916. He became a zealous international socialist after his experiences during 1914–18.
[3] See p. 380 n. 1.

I like Irene Rook so much – or did when I met her – also Rosmer.[1]
I doubt if England will ever be Clarté'd.[2]
Everything feels unsure here – but at last, after 7 months drought, it rains a little. That will soothe the social nerves.
Send me word.

D. H. Lawrence

1942. To Benjamin Huebsch, 9 March 1920
Text: MS UT; Unpublished.

Fontana Vecchia, Taormina, (Messina). Sicily
9 March 1920

Dear Huebsch,

I've been coasting round looking for a house – found one at last. The above is my address for a year.

Would you please post a copy of *The Rainbow* to:

Signora Galata, Villa Farnesino, *Capri*, (Naples).[3]

Will write when my post comes on, and I know what is happening.

Yrs   D. H. Lawrence

1943. To Thomas Seltzer, 9 March 1920
Text: MS UT; Postmark, Taormina 10 3 20; Lacy, *Seltzer* 6–7.

Fontana Vecchia, Taormina, (Messina), Sicily
9 March 1920

Dear Seltzer

I have your letters of Feb. 9th. and Feb. 11th. and contracts. Duckworth must have Canadian rights: and I thought we could agree about terms for the next novel, when it is ready. Otherwise well and good.

I am sorry about Huebsch. But Pinker let me in for this: and Huebsch was always *so* vague and friendly: now it is as it is. Let us see how *we* get on together. Huebsch should have been more to the point with me, and not have acted behind the publisher's veil. Then I should have known how much Pinker and he had to do with one another. As it was, I was a third and mystified party. Let us go ahead. Huebsch will feel I've let him down – I hate

---

[1] Irene Rooke (1878–1958), well-known actress, and her husband, the actor and producer, Milton Rosmer (b. 1881), lived near Tring, Buckinghamshire from autumn 1914 to January 1915; they met the Lawrences and Cannans during that period.
[2] See Letter 1776 and n. 4.
[3] Unidentified.

that. But I would never have done so intentionally. There, people shouldn't have veils – except in season.

Twenty five dollars seems much for a price.[1] But I suppose I must depend on a succés d'estime at the best, and at the worst, a succés de scandale. If so, let them pay for their scandal. Pah! – and for their esteem. How it wearies me.

I'm glad you like *Touch and Go* – and your wife likes the *Rainbow* – son' contento.[2] *Women in Love* is best, next to *The Rainbow*. I am doing Mixed Marriage – it should be more popular – one withdraws awhile from battle.

Yes, put at the back of *Touch and Go* that the dramatic agent is Walter Peacock, 20 Green St., Leicester Square. London. He is a nice man.

Now is the beginning of my day.

We've taken this house for a year – guess you know Taormina. Italy feels shaky – but Sicily won't change much till Etna erupts again – and Etna is snowy silent.

When you have anything to pay me, please pay in American dollars, it is easiest, and the exchange so favorable for me.

Send a copy of *Touch and Go* to Amy Lowell, Heath St., Brookline, Mass, will you – and a copy to Robert Mountsier, 417 West 118 Street, New York.

I really ought to find somebody to place small work – short stories and articles – in America.

I shall *love* to have a copy of *Women in Love*, nicely printed. Send me a proof as it comes, will you.

D. H. Lawrence

1944. To J. B. Pinker, 9 March 1920
Text: MS Davis; Unpublished.

Fontana Vecchia, *Taormina*, (Messina), Sicily.
9 March 1920

Dear Pinker

Thank you for the bundle of agreements, also the two packets of manuscripts, which you sent.

The above is my address for the next year, if ever you should require it.

Yrs   D. H. Lawrence

---

[1] The first American edition of *Women in Love* cost $15.
[2] 'I'm pleased'.

1945. To S. S. Koteliansky, 11 March 1920
Text: MS BL; cited in Gransden 28.

Fontana Vecchia, *Taormina*, (Messina), Sicily.
11 March 1920

My dear Kot

I had your letter last night. I am waiting to hear from Huebsch. I sent him the Shestov, and asked him for a lump sum, some time ago. Let us see what he says.

I have been thinking about the other scheme. But I don't think I can come back to England. I don't much want to be associated with Mond and Gilbert on a paper.[1] What remaining belief I had in Socialism dies out of me more and more as the time goes by. I feel I don't care. I feel it wouldn't be worth while to give oneself to work on a rival show to little Murry. I am not interested in the public – it all seems so far off, here in Sicily – like another world. The windows look east over the Ionian sea: somehow I don't care what happens behind me, in the north west. – Lasciami stare.[2]

I am more or less busy on a new novel.

But if I can do anything from here, of course I will.

Tell Sonia *please* not to bother about that parcel – I feel she will curse the day. – Is Grisha happy in Russia? – you will have had letters by now from him.

Has Gilbert come back to England?

Whatever I undertook with the public of today would merely fail. One has to be a Murry or a Squire[3] or a Sassoon. Better stay still.

Best greetings to Sonia and Ghita   DHL

1946. To Edward Marsh, [11 March 1920]
Text: MS NYPL; Unpublished.

Fontana Vecchia, *Taormina*, (Messina), Sicily.
11 March

Dear Eddie

I had your cheque for £6„12„0 here yesterday – many thanks.

We have taken this house for a year – wonder if you know it? The owner –

---

[1] Henry Ludwig Mond (1898–1949), cr. 2nd Baron Melchett in 1930; at this time an artist and writer, later a politician and industrialist. m. Amy Gwen Wilson, 28 January 1920. (Mond's marriage to Cannan's former mistress occurred during Cannan's absence in USA.) It is not known what 'paper' the two men had in mind.
[2] 'Leave me alone'.   [3] See p. 555 n. 1.

who is cook at Timeo, says that Bob Trevelyan once had the house for some time.[1]

Capri is small – Sicily is better. Queer it is to look over the open sea eastwards – and to see the high coast of Calabria north-east. One's whole orientation is changed. I'm not used to it yet. The compass seems reversed. This is brink of Europe.

I wonder if Beaumont has sent you my little book of poems called *Bay*. I know it's ready. But he is terribly wessel-brained.[2]

That history shouldn't be long[3] – I've done proofs – will send you a copy, though it is only a school-book, since you said you'd like to see it.

DHL

1947. To Catherine Carswell, [14 March 1920]

Text: MS YU; PC v. [Taormina. Teatro Greco]; Postmark, Taormina 15 3 20; cited in Carswell 135.

Fontana Vecchia, *Taormina*. Sicily
14 March.

I have just got your card to say you will go to Altrincham[4] – and it will be this very week-end. I have a dreadful feeling it may be a fiasco, and you may hate the whole business. But let us hope not. Anyhow you've been awfully good about it, you and Don. – No news here – except after so much heat, it is raining and cool – very glad, I tell you, to see the rain. Hope you'll get my address in time, not to write to Capri.

DHL

1948. To Rosalind Baynes, [15 March 1920]

Text: MS UN; Huxley 501–2.

Fontana Vecchia, *Taormina*, Sicilia.
15 March.

Dear Rosalind

I feel at last we are settled down and can breathe – Capri was all the time

---

[1] Robert Calverley Trevelyan (1872–1951), poet, playwright and translator – whom DHL would vividly recall from Fiascherino in December 1913 (see *Letters*, ii. 116 n. 1) – had a long association with Taormina. When he went there about 1895, he met a Dutch girl, Elizabeth des Amorie van der Hoeven (1873–1956), (whom he married in 1900); and at the time she was staying with a member of the Hubrecht family in Fontana Vecchia.

[2] Dialect for 'weasel-brained'; i.e. unreliable, evasive.

[3] i.e. *Movements in European History*.

[4] See Letter 1931 and n. 1.

like a ship which is going to arrive somewhere, and doesn't. Here we are, in Sicily. We've got a nice big house, with fine rooms and a handy kitchen – set in a big garden, mostly vegetables, green with almond trees, on a steep slope at some distance above the sea – looking East. To the left, the coast of Calabria, and the straits of Messina. It is beautiful, and green, green, and full of flowers. Capri was a dry rock.

I must say I like this place. There are a good many English people, but fewer than Capri, and not so all-overish – and one needn't know them. It seems so peaceful and still – and the earth is sappy – and I like the strong saracen element in the people here. They are thin and dark and queer. It isn't quite like Europe. It is where Europe ends: finally. Beyond is Asia and Africa. One realises, somehow, how non-European, how Asiatic Greece was – tinged with phenœcian.

Frieda loves this place. We don't look at Etna – but Etna is a beautiful mountain, far lovelier than Vesuvius, which is a heap. We've got the house for a year – I think perhaps we might really sit still – more or less – for a year. But I believe the summer is very hot. Will you be still in S. Gervasio. Shall we plan to come and see you in the hot summer weather? – We *must* meet in Italy, now we are here. Do you think you could manage to get to Taormina? There is a room if ever you could. I expect the babies will hold you faster here even than in England. We are always wondering how they are getting on in the new conditions.

I've begun to try to work – begun a novel – don't know if it will ever end. How is Godwin's divorce proceeding?[1] It all seems far away and unreal, doesn't it – a weariness of the flesh. Things behind get more unreal every day. I feel one comes unstuck from England – from all the past – as if one would never go back. But there – who knows. – Frieda sends her love – I do hope all goes very well.

DHL

1949. To Lucy Short, [19 March 1920]
Text: MS UT; PC v. Panorama con l'Etna, Taormina; Postmark, Taormina 19 3 20; Unpublished.

Fontana Vecchia, *Taormina*, Sicily
19 March.

Dear Mrs Short,
    I have just received your letter, and have written to my mother-in-law,

[1] See Letter 1933 and n. 2.

Baroness von Richthofen, Ludwig-Wilhelmstift, Baden-Baden, for the medicine. Do hope you'll have it safely. Let me know. We have taken this villa for a year. – I'll write again.

D. H. Lawrence

1950. To Fritz Krenkow, 20 March 1920
Text: MS Clarke; Moore 623–4.

Fontana Vecchia, *Taormina*, (Messina). Sicily.
20 March 1920

My dear Uncle

I had your letter of 7th March yesterday – am so sorry you had so much trouble with the velvet, and then to no purpose. What a bother these things are! Will you let me know what luck you have with the Hague permission.[1] Because if it is not forthcoming, I shall ask Miss Hubrecht to see to the matter.[2] She is a Dutch woman who has a beautiful villa here, and who goes to Holland and Norway for the summer. She will be leaving in about two weeks time, I believe, for Holland.

I'm sorry you have so much trouble, – business and health. Why is Auntie so seedy? – She ought not to be. Why doesn't she come to Italy.

Monte Cassino is wonderful – and the monks are charming to one. But it seems pathetic, now, in its survival: so frail and hardly vital any more. Of course it should be *feudal*: like a great fortress hanging over the plain, what is it now it is divested of power and turned into a sort of museum where the forty monks linger on? – They have wonderful archives. We will go there one day.

I like Sicily – oh, so much better than Capri. It is so green and living, with the young wheat soft under the almond trees and the olives. The almond blossom of Sicily is over now – there are groves and groves of almond trees – but the peach is in blossom. – We have quite a lovely villa on the green slope high above the sea, looking east over the blueness, with the hills and the snowy, shallow crest of Calabria on the left across the sea, where the straits begin to close in. – The ancient fountain still runs, in a sort of little cave-place down the garden – the Fontana Vecchia – and still supplies us.

There are people here – many English. I know a few of them – don't want

---

[1] See Letter 2120.
[2] Marie ('Tuttie') Hubrecht (1865–1950) had inherited Fontana Vecchia, Rocca Bella and Rocca Forte in Taormina, but her home was the Witte Huis, Doorn, 20 km. s.e. of Utrecht. (Her brother, A. A. W. Hubrecht, a friend of Charles Darwin, was Professor of Biology at Utrecht.) Marie Hubrecht was a painter; her portrait-drawing of DHL (reproduced in this volume) is in the National Portrait Gallery.

to know too many, it is too distracting. Fortunately I have begun to work again. Most foreigners leave, end of May.

Etna is a lovely mountain – deep-hooded with snow – such a beautiful long slope right from the sea. He puffs flame at night, and smoke by day.

We have got this house for a year. I wonder if we shall find it too hot for the summer. If so, we'll go north a bit.

It is warm, wonderful weather again, after the rain. – You should bring Auntie to Sicily for a few months.

With love from both   DHL

1951. To Martin Secker, 22 March 1920
Text: MS UInd; Postmark, Taormina 22 3 20; Secker 22.

Fontana Vecchia, Taormina, Sicily.
22 March 1920

Dear Secker,

Duckworth wants me to leave out a chapter of *The Rainbow*. This annoys me.

Have you got the MS. of *Women in Love* yet? Seltzer says he sent it you. He is printing for a private edition.

You snapped off our last negotiations. Don't know if you feel like returning to them. – I wish you didn't ask me to sell my books outright. I don't like their going clean away from me.

Nevertheless, because you dont ask me to make alterations in the books, if you still offer me the same terms I'll take them, and thank you, and be damned to the rest.

Yrs   D. H. Lawrence

1952. To Compton Mackenzie, [22 March 1920]
Text: MS UT; Mackenzie 170–1.

Fontana Vecchia, Taormina
22 March.

So sorry you are seedy – hope it's better. Brooks wrote, and says you are working again – Do hope it goes. I have dreamed twice I was going to the South Seas. – I scrapped all the novel I did in Capri – have begun again – got about 30,000 words, I believe, done since I'm here.[1] Rather amusing. But as

[1] See p. 476 n. 1.

for me, I may come to a full stop any minute – you never know.

I had a letter from Duckworth, and he wants me to cut pieces from *The Rainbow*. It annoys me, so I break off with Duckworth. I wrote to Secker to say I'll take him at his old terms, if he is still willing. That too annoys me, to lose all my rights over the books. But I'd be glad to get them off my hands and be rid of the bother of them. – Enough of Europe and its ways. – If Secker doesn't want any more, then to hell with the lot, and there's an end of it.

This place is really awfully nice, for greenness and sappy growth and a little stream falling and tinkling, and water-cress, and the sunrise golden, and the shimmery pallid wide sea over which one walks, ach, treads far off, with one's back on Europe forever.

For people – I know a few already – the permanent evergreens are awful, while the deciduous are even awfuller. But the permanents, the evergreens like Miss Mabel Hill[1] are too sanctified to sniff at me, and the deciduous, like the Duca, are getting ready to shed themselves from Taormina.[2] So, as for people – peu ou rien:[3] save for a slit-eyed Dutch woman and two young men from South Africa, rather nice.[4] – I don't like people – truly I don't. And Taormina is a place where I can amuse myself by myself, in the garden and up the hills among the goats, for a long long time. I wish Taormina village weren't there, that's all – with Timeo, Domenico, and Villaolatry.

Is Secker coming out? If so, tell him what I say. – I should really like to be rid forever of the bother of those two novels. Damn the world, why is one such a fool as to offer it anything serious *di cuore*. I've finished forever – wish I'd never begun. Henceforth my fingers to my nose – and my heart far off.

When you are well, you might come to Taormina for a little bit: although you scorn it.

I wish you had a ship. Such a lovely steam yacht has been cruising off here – now she has gone eastwards, over the pale level floor of the sea. If only I had

---

[1] Mabel Hill had already lived in Taormina for nearly 20 years (and was to remain there until 1939). A profoundly religious and actively philanthropic woman, she founded two workshops to enable poor girls to learn embroidery and boys to learn joinery. A plaque – erected in Taormina in 1908 – records her generosity towards the children of a local orphanage.

[2] Hon. Alexander Nelson Hood (1854–1937), KCVO, brother of Viscount Bridport. He had been Private Secretary to Queen Mary when she was Princess of Wales, 1901–10, and Treasurer to the Queen, 1910–19. He was Grand Officer of the Order of the Crown of Italy and Duke of Bronte, Sicily. Hood lived at Castello di Maniace, Bronte, and at La Falconara, Taormina. He was generally known as the 'Duca'.

[3] 'little or nothing'.

[4] The woman was presumably Marie Hubrecht; one of the men would be the young South African painter Jan Juta (1897–), who was later to illustrate DHL's *Sea and Sardinia*. He had studied at the Slade (1919) and in 1920 was at the British School in Rome.

her! I invoke the ultimate heavens. Ah God, if one had the feet of the sea, and far spaces, and sails that kiss the wind. To sail outwards – outwards. That's the best of our Fontana Vecchia – she's a watch-tower of the sea. The young men say Africa.

How is Eric?[1] Remembrances to him. – I believe Douglas is in Naples just now, *en route* for Greece. Wonder if he'll appear.

Ethel Smythe is here[2] – haven't met her – but see her in the street. Niente bella.[3]

Frieda is going to write to you: so is Mary. You are the enfant gâté[4] of Capri – save for the Gods, who screw you with too much pain. I hate pain. To me the elements are lovely – the wind, and shadows, and the up and down of hills. One should not have any more pain. Assez de cela – it is of the sick world. So rise up.

DHL

– Oh, how is the Solaro house.

1953. To Benjamin Huebsch, 24 March 1920
Text: MS UT; Postmark, Taormina 24 3 20; Moore 624–5.

Fontana Vecchia, *Taormina*, Sicily
24 March 1920

Dear Huebsch

Yesterday came *Peter Middleton*. Please send this note to Dr Marks, for me.[5]

Last week I had Seltzer's letter – he says they have sent *Women in Love* to print, and that he won't think of relinquishing it – so there we are. I've signed his little agreement. – You'll think I did it all on purpose: but I didn't. Now I can't help it. – Cannan writes that Scott and Seltzer are bound to go

---

[1] Francis Brett Young's brother, Eric, had come to Sicily in January 1920 as Mackenzie's secretary.

[2] Ethel Mary Smyth (1858–1944), composer and author. She was well known as a suffragette (she served two months in jail in 1911), but more particularly as a writer of operas (*The Boatswain's Mate*, 1916, etc.) and other choral as well as orchestral works. She was made DBE in 1922. (See her autobiographical works: *Impressions that Remained*, 1919; *Streaks of Life*, 1921, etc.)

[3] 'Not much to look at.'

[4] 'spoilt child'.

[5] The note to Henry Kingdon Marks (1883–1942) has not survived. His novel, *Peter Middleton*, was published in Boston, 1919, and in London, June 1920. Marks's connection with DHL is not known; at this time he was an assistant physician at the Neurological Institute, New York. (Marks's novel presents the career of a young artist who, after the failure of his first marriage, contracts venereal disease and transmits it to his mistress and to his second wife. Finally he commits suicide. The story is told with skill and poignancy.)

bankrupt. Well, that's another issue. Let us see what happens. Seltzer says he would like the *Studies in Classic American Literature*. Do you feel inclined to let him have them?¹ If so, send him the MS., will you. If not, tell me what you propose. I shall have to give him the refusal of one other book, anyway.

It is some time since I heard from you. I have just got the set of short essays from the typist: *Psychoanalysis and the Unconscious*. I did them for your *Freeman*. But now feel doubtful whether to send them. Posting to America always seems like dropping an MS down the bottomless pit, and depending on the winds of hell to blow it back again. I have also got various stories from Pinker, but don't know what to do with them.

Cannan wrote me a departure letter from New York. Said he was handing to you four hundred dollars to send to me.² Don't suppose he ever did it. If he had an egg in his hand, he'd have to suck it. – I hear now, indirectly, that he is in Paris.³

If ever you should have money to send, please send it in American dollars. One negotiates such a lot better exchange over here.

D. H. Lawrence

1954. To Michael Sadleir, [24 March 1920]
Text: MS UNCCH; Unpublished.

Fontana Vecchia, *Taormina*, Sicily.
24 March

Dear Sadler,

Glad you like the story. I wonder if you'd do rather a boring thing for me. I heard from Huffey, editor of *The Metropolitan Magazine*, New York, that he'd like a story from me (at least Gilbert Cannan wrote that Huffey sent that message). I can't find my duplicate of 'Wintry Peacock'. It would be noble if you could let Huffey have a typed copy, and ask him if he can't print simultaneously.⁴ – You could take the costs out of my cheque for the story. – But perhaps it is too late. Do as you think best.

What is the *name* of your magazine? Does it come 1st May.

I forgot to say that Compton Mackenzie said to me you could have those sonnets, but he doubted if they were suitable. They were written about his

¹ Seltzer published the book in August 1923.
² See Letters 1962, 1963 and 1968.
³ When Cannan returned from USA, the newly-married Henry and Gwen Mond (see p. 486 n. 1) took him with them on a car-holiday via Paris to Italy.
⁴ Sadleir obviously did as DHL asked (see Letter 2027) and sent a typed copy of 'Wintry Peacock' to Carl Hovey (not 'Huffey'). The story appeared in the *Metropolitan Magazine* in August 1921.

staff in Greece.[1] – I'll ask him to send them on, anyhow. Or write to him, Casa Solitaria, *Capri.*, (Naples).

D. H. Lawrence

1955. To Lady Cynthia Asquith, [25 March 1920]
Text: MS UT; Huxley 502–3.

Fontana Vecchia, *Taormina*, (Messina), Sicily.
25 March.

I did get your letter, forwarded from Capri. I have been in Sicily this last three weeks. We've taken this house for a year – very beautiful, quite big (for us) – out of Taormina on the green height over the sea, looking east – like it very much – like Sicily extremely – a good on-the-brink feeling – one hop, and you're out of Europe: nice that. Frieda loves her house and her little blue kitchen – rich Dutch people built it – it is a bit Dutch as well – cousins of Robert Trevelyans wife – Hubrecht.

I should think Beaumont has sent you *Bay* – I hear from my sisters they have received copies – and that the inscription is in. I had a copy in Capri, and that bewildered chicken Beaumont had forgotten the inscription – among other of his forgettings. I abused him, and he said he would put it in.[2] I hope you'll like the poems: they are delicate, I think – in their own way the rarest things I've done.

I am so glad you are feeling gay. Quite right – one should. Mind you don't slip again. Courage goes a long way. Stay gay, and don't slip into that depression.

I am doing a novel – amuses me – perhaps I shall even finish it.

The worst of Taormina is that it is a parterre of English weeds all cultivating their egos hard, one against the other. Imagine nettle overtopping dandelion, the languors and lilies of virtue here very stiff and prickly, the roses and raptures of vice a little weedy and ill-developed. Save me from my countrymen.

Will you actually come to Italy. Twill be hot here by May, I expect. F. sends love.

DHL

[1] The poems are not known. [2] See Letter 1915 and n. 1.

1956. To Catherine Carswell, [31 March 1920]
Text: MS YU; cited in Carswell 138, 139–40.

Fontana Vecchia, *Taormina*, Sicily
31 March

My dear Cath.

I had your letter and the copy of *The Times*.[1] Am afraid *Mrs Holroyd* was altogether a bit of a bore, and that you were miserable. Am sorry. Hope you'll have a good time in Sussex anyway. – You seem to have been working very hard. London must be so *wearing*: everything that comes out of it seems so worn on the nerves. Sicily indeed is cross and swindles one because of the exchange: 82 when I last heard. But somehow it doesn't affect one: annoys and amuses one: which is different. But they *do* swindle us on account of our exchange, and get so cross with us all, all foreigners. But it isn't my fault, is it? – The days are lovely – the orange blossom is passing, northern trees, apple and pear and may-blossom, are out: the wheat is tall and green, the mornings are heaven. I feel I dont care a bit about the trials and troubles of the world – suppose they'll be coming down on my head just now to make me care: but even so, I can't trouble beforehand. They seem very much perturbed over here about the internal condition of Italy. Will one have to clear out?

But what stinking papers English newspapers seem to one, here: false and putrid from end to end. No wonder the Italians get irritated till they are beyond themselves.

I have done about $\frac{1}{2}$ of a novel which I find quite amusing, myself – don't know if it will amuse anybody else. It is meant to be comic – but not satire.

It's a pity you can't be here and right away. But probably you don't want to be right away. At the moment I feel I never want to see England again – if I move, then further off, further off – But one never knows.

Again, when you get your novel money, keep it for a while, *don't send any* till I see if I get the money down for the *Rainbow*, which I may, and then I shan't need the £50. If I don't get any money, I shall tell you. But wait for that, won't you. Hope things are nice for you.

DHL

The post comes ages late here. – Thank you so much for that sweat you had over *Mrs Holroyd*.

---

[1] Catherine Carswell's discriminating review of *The Widowing of Mrs Holroyd* appeared with all her 'warmest commendations' omitted (Carswell 137), in the *Times*, 12 March 1920. The review ends: 'It is a pity that the author (abroad just now for his health) could not for himself have seen a performance showing so clearly here and elsewhere what alterations are demanded by the action of his fine and stimulating play.'

1957. To Jessica Brett Young, [31 March 1920]
Text: MS UB; Sagar, *Review of English Literature*, vi. 95–7.

Fontana Vecchia
Wednesday 31 March

I had Francis' letter – see you are gone to Fraita[1] – hope it's nice and summery. We are already old inhabitants here – and terribly be-visited. Mary still sits, or rather struts, in Timeo, and wears one hat after another. We had lunch with her there on Sunday, and coffee on the terrace. – My hat, the people: the poor ricketty Baroness (American married to a Dane) with buttercup hair: the gaga Duca di Brontë, alias Mr Hood,[2] but always called (by the English, not by natives) The Duca – like The Lord: then the runaway French couple whom the police arrested (what for? is the motto): then Dr Rogers from Cambridge hypnotising Danish damsels with fox-skins over their shoulders and glaucous eyes across the lunch table, over poached eggs, and making the table heave when the oranges are skinned: then the actress from the Opéra, very chic de la chic: then – but why enumerate.[3]

Miss Hubrecht – Dutch – about 45 – in the big villa just below Bristol – being of the Minerva category, disapproved of Mary's Aphrodite, and took her (and us) to the Home For The Old (remember the affiche in the Bristol porch, with a little drawing at the top, like this

[sketch][4]

Well, Mary and the Hubrecht have declared a vendetta, and it's most funny. We had a HighTea and evening here – oh Lord – also an evening at Miss H's with Doctor Rogers, who sprang the scientific latest on us and to whom I was rude, telling him it was childish piffle. He didn't think at all well of me. Tonight a dinner at the Bristol with 2 South Africans[5] – Dutch English – and Miss Hubrecht and a young man – you see how it is.

The Sicilians are the greatest swindlers and extortioners. But one cuts them close. – We couldn't get honey except a vast greek amphora-full, for 84 Francs – 17 kilos: also butter in fat tins – 5 kilos for 80 francs. That wasn't a swindle but the rest is. – I never see a newspaper – but Atenasio was giving 80, exchange, on Monday. Now he's shut shop altogether. Suppose the Maffia made him – he's conscienceless. But the

---

[1] Villa Fraita was the house at Anacapri which the Brett Youngs first rented and then bought.
[2] MS reads 'Wood'.
[3] Except for Mary Cannan and the 'Duca', the dramatis personae here cannot be identified.
[4] DHL's pen-and-ink sketch is of a house with, on the drive, an aged woman leaning on a stick; it carries the caption: 'HOME FOR THE OLD subscriptions welcomed.'
[5] Jan Juta and his sister Réné Hansard (see p. 506 and n. 4).

Taorminese have got the exchange badly on their chest. I say Merde to them, politely. But they're feeling *very* perky about it. Merde to them again. Mary has got 47000 Lire in the Roman Sconto bank: feels in a funk about it. See what it is to have money. – Etna is very red at night lately. Sounds like Titus Livius and auguries.[1]

I've done about, I should think, about 50,000 words of a rather comic novel, which runs out of my control and jumps through the port-hole into the unknown ocean, and leaves me on deck painfully imploring it to come home. – I got my bit of typewriting home from the Albert Steinman typist in Naples. It's title appearing as *Psycoanalisis and the Unconsious*. After that of course I rushed it into a drawer lest it should bite me or convict me of perjury. – I wrote to Secker and said he could have *The Rainbow* and *Women in Love* at his old terms, because Duckworth wanted to cut a chapter (swine) and because I'm fed stiff and because I *know* we shall have to skedaddle from Italy before *very* long. Best have the ship fare. – Hope you're well. Send a line. Frieda greets you.

DHL

1958. To John Ellingham Brooks, [31 March 1920]
Text: TMSC YU; Norman Douglas, *Looking Back* (1933), ii. 354–6.

Fontana Vecchia, Taormina.
Wednesday, 31 March.

Dear Brooks,

I had your letter and glad to know your news. Which is your next home? And has your wife come to Cercola?[2] What is Capri doing? And how are your toes?

Here one feels as if one had lived for a hundred thousand years. What it is that is so familiar I dont know. You remember Stopford said Sicily had been waiting for me for about 2000 years:[3] must be the sense of that long wait. Not that Sicily waited for me alone

> She waits for each and other
> She waits for all men born[4]

[1] Titus Livius, the full name of the great Roman historian Livy (59 B.C.–17 A.D.).
[2] Compton Mackenzie relates that Romaine Brooks arrived in Capri at the beginning of August 1919; whereupon Brooks himself 'hastily evacuated the Villa Cercola for a *villino* and she moved into that large studio for the summer' (Mackenzie 158).
[3] Jessica Brett Young's version of this story is that Magnus had told DHL that 'Sicily . . . had been waiting for him since the days of Theocritus' (*Francis Brett Young*, p. 102). Albert Stopford (b. 1860) was an art dealer, related to the family of the Earl of Courtown.
[4] Swinburne, 'The Garden of Proserpine' (*Poems and Ballads*, 1866), ll. 57–8.

– What for? To rook them, to overcharge them, to diddle them and do them down. Capri is an unhatched egg compared to this serpent of a Trinacria.[1]

The moneychangers, thieves incomparable, have shut up shop, and if you want to buy anything the natives say 'il cambio'[2] and take you metaphorically by the nose.

I have done 50,000 words of a novel which amuses me but perhaps wont amuse anybody else. I am going to give it to Mary to criticise. I feel that as she sits in her room in Timeo she will represent the public as near as I want it. So like an 'aristo' before Robespierre, I shake in my superior shoes.[3]

Here is very beautiful. Yes, we are north of the village, outside. We dont see Etna. Beautiful flowers are out. There is a tiny blue iris as high as your finger which blooms in the grass and lasts a day. It is one of the most morgen-schön flowers I have ever seen. The world's morning – that and the wild cyclamen thrill me with this sense. Then there are the pink gladioli, and pink snapdragons, and orchids – old man and bee and bird's nest. Sicily seems so fascinating in the interior. If I can only get some money and finish this novel I shall walk into the middle of it. Perhaps away from the coast the exchange wont be stuck so tight in the native throat. Anyhow the exchange doesn't make *me* any less a human being, and it ought not to make them. But it does.

I look up at Monte Venere and think I will set off. Why dont I. But dawn is so lovely from this house. I open my eye at 5.0, and say Coming; at 5.30, and say yellow; at 6.0, and say pink and smoke blue; at 6.15 and see a lovely orange flare and then the liquid sunlight winking straight in my eye. Then I know its time to get up. So I dodge the sunlight with a corner of the blanket, and consider the problem of the universe: this I count my sweetest luxury, to consider the problem of the universe while I dodge the dawned sun behind a corner of the sheet: so warm, so first-kiss warm.

We do all our own work – which is fun. High on the top floor we live, and it feels rather like a fortress. You know we have two terraces, one above the other. There we pace the decks.

I wonder when we shall see you. If the heat makes us flee north later, I shall flee via Capri. Has the Roumanian gone?[4] If you see Palestra, be nice to her.[5] Tell me what flowers now below Tragara, and what in the gardens. Are cistus out? Frieda greets you.

D. H. Lawrence

[1] i.e. Sicily.
[2] 'the rate of exchange'.
[3] Maximilien François Marie Isidore de Robespierre (1758–94), one of the French revolutionary leaders; he was the virtual dictator during the Terror.
[4] See Letters 1900 and 1903.
[5] Unidentified.

Keeping your Baedeker a bit longer, for the map.

> Green
> The dawn was apple-green
> The sky was green wine held up in the sun
> The moon was a golden petal between.
>
> She opened her eyes, and green
> Her eyes shone, clear like flowers undone
> For the first time, now for the first time seen.[1]

10. 2. 1920   D. H. Lawrence

1959. To Ada Clarke, [2 April 1920]
Text: MS Clarke; PC v. Capri – Palazzo a Mare – Bagni di Tiberio; Postmark, Taormina
3 4 20; Unpublished.

[Fontana Vecchia, *Taormina*, (Messina), Sicily]
Good Friday

You will be glad to hear that *one* of the Xmas parcels arrived this morning – a
tin, containing sugar, cherries, mincemeat and a plum pudding – all perfectly
good – but only ½ the cherries and mincemeat remaining. – Alas for the other
– they have eaten it, for sure.

DHL

1960. To Martin Secker, [5 April 1920]
Text: MS UInd; Postmark, Taormina 6 4 20; cited in Huxley 503.

Fontana Vecchia, *Taormina*, Sicily.
Easter Monday 1920.

Dear Secker
    Yours of March 28th. arrived this morning, and I reply by return. I agree
to your proposal to publish *Women in Love* and *The Rainbow* on a royalty basis
of 1/- per copy on the first 2,000, 1/6 to 5,000, and 2/- after that. Start
with *Women in Love* if you wish: but only on condition that you publish *The
Rainbow* within a reasonable time after the publishing of *Women in Love*.
    Will you give me £100 on each book – advance? That covers the 2,000 at
1/-.

---

[1] This poem had first been published in *Poetry*, January 1914 and collected in *Look! We Have
Come Through!*

You *should* have heard from Seltzer and received that MS. Is he a hopeless liar like the most of them? – I enclose his letter. Return it to me. – You might cable him.

I love Sicily, and the Fontana Vecchia. Come when you are in Italy. Mackenzie says you are going to Capri soon: come on here, it is so nice.

I am waiting to hear from Huebsch about Shestov. I know he's a terrible payer, – to my sorrow I know it. What about Koteliansky's *Knopf*?[1] – or Scott and Seltzer? – But let us see what Huebsch says, as I asked him to buy outright.

Well, this is our Easter Egg. Hope it hatches immortally.

D. H. Lawrence

1961. To S. S. Koteliansky, [5 April 1920]
Text: MS BL; Zytaruk 207.

Fontana Vecchia, *Taormina*, Sicily
Easter Monday

My dear Kot

I wrote to you, and the letter got destroyed with old ones. – Today is Easter Monday – sunny – and still a festa. All the world goes to the sea today. – Today I have agreed with Secker to publish *Women in Love* and *The Rainbow*, on a fair royalty basis: beginning with *Women in Love*: good so far. I trust to nothing these days. – I haven't heard from Gilbert again, nor a single word of the 400 dollars etc: – only saw the announcement of the marriage.[2] Alas, the dollars. If my name has been abused surely I should see the pence. – Here is sunny and spring-like, and I like it. I have done half of my new novel – quite amusing. But I shan't say anything to Secker yet, I shall probably sell it to the highest bidder when it is finished. It is as proper as proper need be. – What are your news in the world? I see Lloyd George is coming to Italy – maybe he is Collyfogling something.[3] The exchange is over 80. In the village they offer 79.50, for cheques at sight. I feel I ought to cash out my remainder – but don't know how much I have: and there come such rumors of Italian financial collaps. But it will not be yet. – Mary is still here – seems to get old, but will never admit it: trips upstairs if she dies of fatigue. Poor Mary – a burden also. – Shall we offer Secker to sell Shestov for £20, or leave it on royalty basis as it is. I owe you money – you would get £20. – My dollars from

---

[1] See Letter 1923 and n. 1.
[2] See p. 486 n. 1.
[3] DHL uses a Westmorland dialecticism to convey his distrust for Lloyd George once again: 'collyfogle' means to deceive, cheat or scheme.

America are still absent – even those 100 which the Cambio Nazional disputed.[1] What do you think of Italian affairs? I feel quite reckless. – What news of Grisha? I wish this cursed Europe *did* explode.

Many greetings to you all   DHL

1962. To Benjamin Huebsch, 9 April 1920
Text: MS UT; Postmark, Taormina 10 4 20; Unpublished.

Fontana Vecchia, *Taormina*, Sicily.
9 April 1920

Dear Huebsch

I hear from Secker today that he has fixed up the American publication of the Shestov *All Things are Possible* – a bound proof of which I sent you about ten weeks ago. He waited so long, but I have heard nothing from you at all. Please don't bother any further with Shestov.

Cannan came here yesterday, and said he gave you a hundred and fifty dollars for me, before he left New York. Perhaps you have sent them. If not, please send in dollars, not in Lire, as I can effect a better exchange here.

You will have had my letter about Seltzer – and it is all irritating, but I can't help it. Hope otherwise things go well with you.

Yours   D. H. Lawrence

Please let me hear about the *Studies in Classic American Literature*.

1963. To Compton Mackenzie, 9 April 1920
Text: MS UT; Mackenzie 177–8.

Fontana Vecchia, *Taormina*, (Messina).
9 April 1920

I got Secker's letter on Good Friday. It says he will publish *Women in Love* and *The Rainbow* – 1/- a copy up to 2000, 1/6 to 5,000, 2/- after that: *Women in Love* first; *Rainbow* later. I wrote and accepted. If he publishes at a normal price, it is quite fair and I am satisfied. So far so good.

We received the Scarlet's two days ago, and Frieda is reading fast.[2] She

---

[1] See p. 482 n. 1.

[2] 'At the beginning of April [Mackenzie] had sent the Lawrences some books, including the two volumes of *Sylvia Scarlett* to Frieda' (Mackenzie 176). The 'two volumes' in question were his novels: *The Early Life and Adventures of Sylvia Scarlett* (1918) and *Sylvia and Michael: The Later Adventures of Sylvia Scarlett* (1919). For Frieda's response see Mackenzie 176–7.

likes *Sylvia Scarlet* immensely – says it is a break away into a new world. I am going to read it as soon as she's done. 'Mortality, Behold and Fear!'[1]

Your letter to F. today – also a note from F[rancis] B[rett] Y[oung]. I am really wretched to think of you so much sick. You will have to leave Capri for a bit – yes truly. Leave it for a while – come to Sicily, go to England, but leave Capri for a bit. Nip over here for a short while! Fun!

Yesterday I heard a fumbling on the terrace – and there Gilbert at the foot of the stairs, in a brown hat rather like yours: gave me quite a turn: thought it was somehow you-not-you. He came express from Rome in one of his tantrums because of the nasty letter I'd written him[2] – fume! – But – nay, I'll say nothing. The main upshot is that in his indignation he disgorged a cheque for £75 – SEVENTY-FIVE POUNDS STERLING – as the equivalent of $300 which he had collected from Americans for me. Benone![3] Fortune so had it that *for once* Mary wasn't here to tea: and that he had taken a room at Domenico, as being a *little grander* than Timeo. He is tout américain – L'Americanisato![4] – pocket book thick, fat, bulging with 1000 Lire notes – 'these beastly hotels' – 'Oh yes, picked up quite a lot of money over there' – 'Oh yes, they seemed to take to me quite a lot' – 'Yes, have promised a quantity of people I'll go back this Fall.'

Oh what a Fall was there!![5]

However, we parted as friends who will *never* speak to each other again.

> And Life is thorny, and Youth is vain
> And to be wroth with one we love
> Doth work like madness in the brain –[6]

Poor Gilbert – a soap pill.[7] However, I've sent my 'check' like lightning to the bank, to see if it'll be cashed safe and sound. Aspettiamo![8] – And today the filbert[9] returns to Rome, to his deux Monds. – 'Gwen is a wonderful and beautiful character –' – this to my nose – Do you wonder I made a nose at it? 'Gwen's isn't a forgiving nature,' says he. 'Neither is mine,' reply I. Assez de ça. He's returned to his revue des deux Monds[10] – and shortly the Mond, the

---

[1] Francis Beaumont (1584?–1616), 'On the Tombs in Westminster Abbey', l. 1.
[2] The letter has not been found.   [3] 'Excellent!'
[4] 'quite the American – Americanised!'   [5] *Julius Caesar* III. ii. 197.
[6] Coleridge, *Christabel*, ll. 411–13.   [7] i.e. a suppository. (Mackenzie prints 'soup frill'.)
[8] 'Let's wait and see!'
[9] DHL alludes to a well-known musical hall song (from which he quotes in 'Monkey Nuts'): 'Gilbert the filbert, colonel of the Nuts'. (A 'filbert' was a very fashionable man about town; a 'nut' was a dandy.)
[10] DHL is punning on the Monds (Henry and Gwen) and the Parisian journal, *Revue des Deux Mondes*, with which he was very familiar (cf. p. 533).

Demi-Mond, and the Immonde, (to parody one of Mary's 'sayings') – return en trois to London. ' It has made no difference to *me* –' This from the filbert, regarding the marriage of Gwen. Ça parait, mon cher.

I had a letter from FBY –, But not a word of his landed proprietorship.[1] It's no good, my dear fellow, you may wrestle with him for the tight little island, but he's got his teeth in, so you may as well let go. Now, early, with a good grace and a *bonne mine*, carissimo – Tulips, daffodils, Nec Tecum nec Sine Te, all the lot, relinquish, let go. A la bonne heure, mon cher,[2] if you *will* invite young writers to Capri. – My novel is page 245, and I like it so much, it does so amuse me. I want to wind it up about page 400 MS.

rivederci   DHL

1964. To Martin Secker, 9 April 1920
Text: MS UInd; Postmark, Taormina 10 4 20; Secker 23.

Fontana Vecchia, Taormina, Sicily
9 April 1920

Dear Secker

I have your letter of March 24, from Mackenzie, and have written to Huebsch to say that you have fixed up the American publisher of Shestov, and therefore he is to go no further. As I haven't heard from him for about six weeks, it's as well to be clear of him.

Have you got the *Women in Love* MS. from Seltzer. If not, do cable him about it before you ask Pinker for the previous MS. I want you to print from Seltzers MS. Wouldn't it be well to buy sheets from Seltzer – he is sure to print well and use good paper. No offence – I know you do both – but hear such moans about costs – Anyhow, communicate with him.

Cannan came here yesterday, from Rome – he returns there, to the jeunes Monds, today. They are coming shortly to London, he says. – He says Seltzer will go bankrupt.

I have done more than half of my new novel – think it is amusing, and might be quite popular. Hope to have it done before end of May. – What about it? Do you want to saddle yourself with it, having already the other two books, or shall I go to a commercial firm?[3] Can you tell me of a typist who won't charge me the eyes out of my head to type it for me. – I am a bit scared of putting the sole MS. into this Italian post.

---

[1] See p. 496 and n. 1.
[2] 'and putting a good face on it, my dear fellow – Tulips, daffodils, neither with you nor without you, . . . In good time, my dear chap,'.
[3] Secker published *The Lost Girl* in November 1920.

> We are not sure of sorrow
> And joy was never sure –[1]

Will you tell me about *New Poems* – how many you sold of the paper-backs, and how much you are selling the cardboards at, and if they're going to make me another £6-5-0.

I am most anxious about that Seltzer MS. Damn him, why doesn't he keep his word.

Are you coming to Italy.

You hear F[rancis] B[rett] Y[oung] has bought a house at the other extremity of the Isle of Capri. I see him and Mackenzie, with the beloved Isola like a bone between their teeth, pulling like mad against one another at opposite ends: and mark my word, that sly dog F. has now got his teeth in, he'll pull our dashing M. into the Mediterranean.

Yrs   DHL

Send Koteliansky the cheque for subscription royalties, will you?

At what price do you think you will publish *Women in Love*?

1965. To Robert Mountsier, 11 April 1920
Text: MS Smith; Postmark, Taormina 12 4 20; Unpublished.

Fontana Vecchia, *Taormina*, (Messina), Sicilia
11 April 1920

Dear Mountsier,

I got your letter of March 26th. only yesterday – was so pleased to hear from you. Glad you sound better – I believe you are happier in Europe.

I will do everything you tell me: draw you up a full account of my stuff and its publication. It will be so jolly if you are for me in America.

Compton Mackenzie is being continually ill – and writing a novel.[2] I still think yearningly of the South Seas. Mackenzie offered to enrol me in his company: he is planned to go to the Pacific and do a serial account of it and a film record and a film novel all at once.[3] But though I like Mackenzie, I couldn't bear to be ravelled up in a film.

Here is much nicer than Capri. Come and see us before you leave Europe. We have got this quite lovely villa for a year.

---

[1] Swinburne, 'The Garden of Proserpine', ll. 73–4.
[2] Mackenzie was 'writing' *Rich Relatives* February–June 1920.
[3] Mackenzie records that, during the winter of 1919–20, he and DHL frequently discussed a project for taking 'a selected group of people to re-colonize the Kermadec islands' (Mackenzie 185).

What is *Noa-Noa* and *The Moon and 6d.*?[1] I should love to talk South Seas with you again. From here we see sometimes the coast of Greece – the long shore of Greece.

Wait a minute for the stodgy business account. Tell us where you are. Frieda's sister is in Berlin, her mother in Baden-Baden, and her other sister in Munich. Frieda was in Baden-Baden for six weeks last autumn: got considerably thinner, but has lost it all again.

I am three quarters through a quite amusing novel.

au revoir   D. H. Lawrence

Have drunk a bottle of wine lunching out, so am not to be trusted.

1966. To Lucy Short, [18 April 1920]
Text: MS UT; PC v. Taormina. Teatro Greco; Postmark, Taormina 19 4 20; Unpublished.

Taormina.
18 April.

Had your letter yesterday – so glad you received the powders – hope you got the directions safely – if not, write direct to my mother-in-law, in English, and ask to have directions sent in English.

Fraū Baronin von Richthofen, Ludwig-Wilhelmstift. *Baden-Baden.*
Don't bother about the money – I paid it. Only hope the powders will be of use. – Shall be glad to see Whittleys here.

DHL

1967. To Marie Hubrecht, 18 April 1920
Text: MS UN; Unpublished.

Fontana Vecchia, *Taormina*, Sicily.
18 April 1920.

Dear Miss Hubrecht,

I suppose by now you are sitting safely in your thatched house in Holland:[2] wonder if you are glad to be home. Here is hot and lovely.

Many thanks to the Etna Wind for 250 francs she blew my way. It wasn't at all correct behaviour for the Etna wind, which is a breeze of separation and a gale of matrimonial disruption, according to description. Whereas F[rieda]

---

[1] *Noa Noa* (Paris, 1900) was the account by the French painter, Paul Gauguin (1848–1903), of his life in Tahiti. *The Moon and Sixpence* (April 1919), by Somerset Maugham (1874–1965), though not a strictly biographical account of Gauguin's Tahitian existence, was influenced by it.

[2] See Letter 1950 and n. 2.

and I trotted off to Catania next day and I bought shirts and sandals and she was dentisted and altogether we were restored to permanency. So, like any Greek god, I am now shod by the winds and vestured from the clouds.

Also for the flash-light, many thanks.

We have painted the shelves in our 'Salotta'[1] bright green, and Shakespeare reclines gracefully in the alcove, and the clock ticks discreetly. Fancy having to listen to it as he does.[2]

Perhaps you have heard from Juta that Mary is to have the studio from Cicio when the boys leave.[3] Juta says you will be 'oh so angry!', I say you will laugh. Poor Mary now hates Timeo, and longs to get down to the Studio.

A great scene when Gilbert Cannan, Mary's husband, suddenly arrived here at Fontana Vecchia. But he only stayed one night, then disappeared off to Rome, and Mary fortunately did not see him.

Today Juta and Insole and Mrs Hansard have gone off to Randazzo.[4] We were at the Bristol to lunch with them. Juta was in such a bad temper. He hates being chased about – wants to stay here and work: and the other two chivvy him out every day. You would hardly know him, he is so cross and wordless. The silent, moth-catching, grinning Insole secretly triumphs, setting poor Juta on thorns, and Mrs H. gets bored with both of them. They are an unjoyful trio, I tell you. We have promised to go to Randazzo tomorrow, returning Monday, but I don't know if we shall keep our promise, it is *so* hot. They are not staying here any longer. They return on Tuesday – then go to Palermo, Girgenti, Siracuse – then back to Rome. I suppose they will be in Rome in about 10 days time.

Meanwhile Taormina is much the same. Today F. and I sat in your big room at Rocca Bella, and looked at books. It was cool inside, the sun blazing in the garden. Gardeners are working, clearing all up for Mr Baldwin, who thinks (according to Wood) he will arrive here about May 10th.[5] It seems a

---

[1] 'reception room'.

[2] DHL made use of this detail in *The Lost Girl* when Alvina 'even admired Shakespeare on the clock' (ed. Worthen, p. 260).

[3] Francesco ('Cicio' or 'Ciccio') Cacópardo (d. 1965) had worked as a kitchen help in the Utrecht home of Marie Hubrecht's sister-in-law. From about 1910 he was with members of the family in Cambridge for several years; when DHL first rented Fontana Vecchia he was working temporarily as a chef in Manchester (Nehls, ii. 31); and, as DHL makes clear later, Ciccio became a cook-valet in Boston, Massachusetts. He owned Fontana Vecchia, having acquired it from the Hubrecht family. The other 'boy' mentioned here was Ciccio's brother, Carmelo (d. 1957).

[4] Juta's companions were his sister and the Welsh painter and writer, Alan Insole. Réné Hansard (wife of Luke Hansard) collaborated with her brother in producing three books: *The Cape Peninsula* (1919), *Cannes and the Hills* (1924) and *Concerning Corsica* (1926).

[5] As DHL would later discover, the man who subsequently owned Rocca Bella was Bowdwin (not 'Baldwin'). A wealthy American (d. 1943?), he had studied in Italy. DHL's informant,

little deserted and strange down there at Rocca Bella. The boys also haven't
been half so nice since the arrival of Mrs H. Altogether, since the Etna Wind
blew itself away to the north, Taormina seems to languish, and Rocca Bella is
dead.

We had another high tea, and another 'pollo',[1] and *no* Mary – Mary
sprained her ankle with high-heeled white shoes, and had to sit indoors in
Timeo. – It was jolly also, our second *thé alto*. But one feels a strange
restlessness and uncertainty, as if Etna might produce some wind much less
benevolent to us, and blow us all away.

I suppose you heard from Cicio that he and Emma[2] are going to Boston
U.S.A. with some rich Americans, for two years. Cicio is to be a sort of cook-
valet, and is to brush monsieur's trousers when he is not making omelettes.
For these and other services, our two Cacopardi are to receive 65 dollars a
month, all travelling expenses paid. I think they are pledged to go in June. I
am sorry they are going, it is pleasant to feel they are here.

Mary went to look at the house of a man Cuscona[3] – Miss White's old
house, under the Hôtel Pancrazio. Mr Cuscona suddenly came down on us,
said Mary had given her word that she would take the house, and threatened a
law-suit. Then he sent an avvocato to Timeo, and the young Floresta went
down to tell poor M. that unless she paid the money for the house, gendarmes
would arrive to seize her luggage. Great consternation on every hand – Mary
rushing to consult Wood. However, it seems to be blowing over.

The latest Timeo tit-bit. The baroness expostulated with Pancrazio the
waiter, said he brought them the poorest bits of food. 'Well,' said Pancrazio,
'you don't pay as much as the others, and so you get less.' This because the
poor Baroness, who arrived in December, has her *pension* at 30 francs. –
Imagine the storm raised by the Baroness. She summoned the whole
management, and raised hell.

The nespoli are ripe in the garden, and are very good. Pink gladiolus
flowers are lovely among the wheat under the olive trees. It is an exquisite
evening, with a white gold sea and Calabria all glimmering.

What is the world going to do?

I have ordered two books for you, from England.

Frieda sends warm greetings, with mine.

D. H. Lawrence

Wood, was another American, a water-colourist, who is remembered as an amusing
companion but impecunious.
[1] 'chicken'.
[2] Emma (sometimes Gemma) Cacópardo, née Motta, Ciccio's wife.
[3] Unidentified (along with Miss White, and the Baroness in the next paragraph).

1968. To Benjamin Huebsch, 21 April 1920
Text: MS UT; Unpublished.

Fontana Vecchia, *Taormina*, (Messina), Sicily
21 April 1920

Dear Huebsch

I got your letter of Feb. 26th. last night. Thank you for the cheque for 2700 Lire – representing Cannans $150. I wish you had sent me dollars, I might have exchanged at 21 instead of 18. But thank you none the less.

About all the rest of things, so many unanswered letters have intervened, I will wait now till you get them. But Secker seems definitely to have fixed up the Shestov with the Robert MacBride Company in America.[1] I should think you can use it for your *Freeman*. Write direct to Secker or the MacBride.

As for Seltzer and *Women in Love*, I say no more at the moment, but let you two settle it. I'm glad if you do recover the MS. – But do *please* see that Secker gets a type-copy of the MS. of *Women in Love* I sent Seltzer. Seltzer has promised it for months now – and Secker is waiting to print the book. Do, I beg you, make sure about this.

So I shall wait for further news.

D. H. Lawrence

1969. To Emily King, [25 April 1920]
Text: MS Needham; PC v. Siracusa (dintorni) – Latomia del Paradiso o dei Cordari; Unpublished.

Syracuse
25 April

Wondering how you are – The post is so bad, we get no letters – shall be glad to hear from you and Ada both. – We are here for a few days – friends invited us down.[2] – This is one of the Greek quarries. – Terribly hot sun.

Love   DHL

1970. To Ada Clarke, [25 April 1920]
Text: MS Clarke; PC v. Siracusa – Latomie dai Cappuccini; Postmark, Sira[cusa . . .]; Lawrence–Gelder 118–19.

Syracuse.
25 April

Friends invited us down to Syracuse for a few days – staying in this hôtel. The

---

[1] McBride & Nast were New York publishers. *All Things Are Possible* was not published in the USA.

[2] The Lawrences travelled with Jan Juta, Réné Hansard and Alan Insole (Frieda Lawrence, "*Not I, But the Wind . . .*", p. 130).

Latomia is one of the great quarries out of which the Greeks got the stone for the town, and in which the Athenian youths died so horribly.[1] – Its a wonderful place – quite near to Malta – which makes one feel near to England. Post all upset here.

DHL

1971. To Ada Clarke, [27? April 1920]
Text: MS Clarke; PC v. Piazza del Duomo e Fontana, Taormina; Postmark, Ta[ormina . . .]; Lawrence–Gelder 120.

[Fontana Vecchia, *Taormina*, (Messina), Sicily]
24 April[2]

Ages since we heard from you – have you written? I wrote you. – The post is very bad. We've both got colds, sneezing our heads off, after going rather high up Etna, to see the Duca di Bronte, who is Nelson's descendant, and who has a castle up there[3] – wonderful place. – Hope we shall hear soon.

Love. DHL

Going to Maniace F[rieda] wore that blue silk dress you gave her, and the people turned out to receive us as if we were royalty – such a joke.

1972. To Compton Mackenzie, [28 April 1920]
Text: MS UT; Mackenzie 183.

Fontana Vecchia
Wednesday[4]

Got your letter last night. We were away at Randazzo for 3 days. – About the theatre – thrilling but terrifying![5] You know my horror of the public! – Well, it's a phobia of phobias in Nottingham. Nottingham! Cursed, cursed

---

[1] The experience of visiting the Latomia quarry – where over 7,000 Athenian youths were left to starve in 413 A.D. – coloured DHL's presentation of Mrs Tuke in *The Lost Girl* (ed. Worthen, p. 274). It created 'a sinister dread impression' in Frieda too: see Frieda Lawrence, "*Not I, But the Wind . . .*", p. 130.

[2] The card was misdated by DHL. It was written in Taormina after he had returned from the visit to Etna which took place on 25 April.

[3] Castello di Maniace.

[4] Dated with reference to DHL's hope that he would complete *The Lost Girl* 'in 1 week': he finished it on 5 May.

[5] Mackenzie recorded that his mother, Mrs Virginia Mackenzie, was determined to give his sisters an opportunity to shine as actresses and 'was proposing to turn the Grand Theatre, Nottingham, into a repertory theatre . . . I had suggested to my mother that her Repertory Theatre in Nottingham should produce Lawrence's two plays' (Mackenzie 182–3).

Nottingham, gutsless, spineless, brainless Nottingham, how I hate thee! But if my two plays could be thrown so hard into thy teeth as to knock thy teeth out, why then, good enough.

There are only two plays – *The Widowing of Mrs Holroyd* – which Duckworth published years ago – and *Touch and Go* – which Daniel is publishing this minute. – They played *The Widowing* at Altrincham Stage Society the other day – believe it wasn't so very good. *Touch and Go*, I sold the dramatic rights to that Norman Macdermott man, for 1 year: that is, till next December. But I'm sure he wouldn't mind if you played it in Nottingham. You could do a good *Gerald*, in *Touch and Go* – and even the engineer in *Holroyd*. But as for me, I can't act one little bit. I confess that the very thought of the plays coming in Nottingham gives me such a fright I almost feel like deserting my own identity. But where the public is concerned I am a veritable coward.

I've written Duckworth to send you *The Widowing*, and I'm posting you now the MS of *Touch and Go*. – Then tell me what you think of them. – My idea of a play is that any decent actor should have the liberty to alter as much as he likes – the author only gives the leading suggestion. Verbatim reproduction seems to me nonsense. – I should like to see the things done, and done properly. Oh, if there were *actors*! I'd like to be there to *beat* the actors into acting. What terrifying thrills ahead! – But I *must* see you soon. Hang it all, you must be better, not so seedy. I hope to finish the novel in 1 week. – If we have to talk plays, I shall have to pop over to Capri. But read the plays first.

We went to Maniace to the Duca's. God, what a Duca! Shall write a farcical comedy.

Trust you're better   DHL

Shall write again immediately.

1973. To S. S. Koteliansky, 29 April 1920
Text: MS BL; Moore 626.

Fontana Vecchia, *Taormina*, (Messina)
29 April. 1920

We've been away in Syracuse for a few days – I find your letter and this from Huebsch, on my return.[1] I am cabling to Secker to let Huebsch have Shestov if possible. Go to Secker and explain about the *Freeman* also – if you don't hate to.

You see how long letters take to get here – sickening. It's a great bore that

---

[1] Huebsch's letter dated 27 February 1920 (see letter following) has not survived.

one gets ones business so criss-cross. And Secker is a little nuisance.

The draft Huebsch sends is 150 dollars that Gilbert collected for me. But damn Huebsch, why does he translate it into Lire. I get 2,700, whereas I myself here could easily make 3,400. So I lose *at least* 700 Lire. And I *tell* them not to transfer.

I wish you could have this £50 from Huebsch. Compare even £50 with Secker's dirty £10.[1]

It is very lovely here. I feel I shall never come north again. So hot at Syracuse.

What news of Grisha? I heard the Eders were arriving home from Palestine.

Gilbert drops into oblivion.

Many greetings to Sonia and Ghita.

DHL

1974. To Benjamin Huebsch, 29 April 1920
Text: MS UT; Unpublished.

Fontana Vecchia, *Taormina*, (Messina)
29 April 1920

Dear Huebsch,

I got your letter of 27th February[2] *today*. It is too maddening. I am wiring Secker at once to let you have Shestov if it is possible. – One must cable these days. You will hear from *him*. – Secure your things for *The Freeman* anyhow – say you have prior right from Koteliansky and me.

I send you a few – six – essays for *The Freeman*.[3] Use them as you like. They are good. No one else has seen them.

I can't make out about you and Seltzer – must leave it to you.

Maddening, this delay and criss-cross. Secker is a fussy little devil.

D. H. Lawrence

1975. To Martin Secker, 29 April 1920
Text: MS UInd; Postmark, Taormina 29 4 20; Secker 24.

Fontana Vecchia, *Taormina*, Sicily
29 April 1920

Dear Secker

I hear from Huebsch today that he wants to buy American rights of the

---

[1] Cf. £20 in Letter 1980.   [2] February] April
[3] See Letter 1916. None was published in Huebsch's periodical.

Shestov outright for £50. I am wiring you to let him have the book if possible. And don't fear his paying – he'll pay the flat sum alright. – Whether you are pledged to the Macbrides or not, however, please secure for Huebsch the right to publish selections from Shestov in his paper *The Freeman*.[1] It is due to him. – The delay is postal – his letter left New York on February 27th. – and reached me last evening.

Have you heard from Seltzer?

Are you making me the agreements for *Women in Love* and *The Rainbow*? I would really rather stick to the *Women in Love* title.[2]

I hope to finish my novel next week. It is called *The Lost Girl* – or maybe 'The Bitter Cherry'. Probably I will send it to you to be typed. But the post here is a howling insecurity. I may get it typed in Rome. – The American rights belong to Seltzer, when he has done *Women in Love*. – It is I think an amusing book, and I don't think it is at all improper: quite fit for Mudies.[3] I wish it could be serialised. Do you think there is any possibility? But you must see the MS.

I should like to have the agreement of the other two books.

Yrs   D. H. Lawrence

1976. To S. S. Koteliansky, [4 May 1920]
Text: MS BL; PC v. Taormina – Via Timoleone; Postmark, Taormina [. . .] 5 20; Zytaruk 209.

[Fontana Vecchia, *Taormina*, (Messina), Sicily]
4 May.

Had your letter with cheque today – wish you hadn't sent me the latter. Hope you have my letter and enclosed from Huebsch about Shestov. Chivvy Secker. – Wonderful news that Grisha has arrived – tell me about him. I suppose Sophie Issayevna hasn't time for a letter. Very hot here.

DHL

---

[1] See Letter 1980 and n. 1.
[2] An undated letter from Secker to Compton Mackenzie reveals the nature of the publisher's anxiety over DHL's title (Mackenzie 172): 'Why I want D.H.L. to change the provocative title of *Women in Love* to the quiet, even dull one of *The Sisters* is just for the very reason that it is important from D.H.L.'s point of view to be as unprovocative as possible in order to get the book taken anywhere. To give it that title is to tie a red rag on to it . . . I feel instinctively that anything to do with D.H.L. is rather dangerous, but I am prepared to take risks justified by what I know to be your wishes that I should give him another chance. I agree that he may go mad if he does not have something in print soon.'
[3] Mudie's Lending Library in London; it was founded in 1842 by Charles Edward Mudie (1818–90) and survived till 1937. Mudie's did not accept DHL's view of his novel: see Letter 2118.

1977. To Thomas Moult, [6? May 1920]

Text: MS Lazarus; Unpublished.

Villa Fontana Vecchia, *Taormina*, (Messina), Sicily
[6? May 1920]¹

Dear Moult

Had your letter today.

No, I never received the cheque.² Your bank must know that. If you feel like sending it again, well and good.

Surely 'Terra Nuova' was published in *Look We Have Come Through*.³ But I remember, in the anthology you speak of, there *is* one poem which has never been re-published – it has never appeared in England – a long poem.⁴ It was to go with 'Craving for Spring' and 'Frost Flowers', at the end of *Look*. Also there were two poems which Chattos refused to print in *Look*.⁵ I'll see if I can find them. They are *most* innocent. Let me know if you want them.

I'll do you a little rip of an essay – 500 words – soon.⁶ Rather fun.

I have taken this house for a year. – Did you get a copy of the play *Touch and Go*, from Daniel?⁷

I have finished a new novel. Secker is going to publish *Women in Love* and also *The Rainbow*: if he's not too frightened. There should be a committee for his moral encouragement.

Glad all goes well   D. H. Lawrence

1978. To Francis Brett Young, 6 May 1920

Text: MS UB; cited in Jessica Brett Young, *Francis Brett Young*, p. 106.

Fontana Vecchia, *Taormina*
6 May 1920

Had your letter yesterday. Alas, why didn't I know your wife was sailing for England.⁸ I'd have got her to take my novel. I've finished it, and sent the first

---

¹ The letter appears to have been written soon after 5 May 1920 when DHL finished *The Lost Girl*.

² Presumably for 'Verse Free and Unfree' (see p. 387 n. 3).

³ This poem had first appeared in *Some Imagist Poets* (1917) and was reprinted in *Look! We Have Come Through!*

⁴ The only poem which meets these criteria is 'Erinnyes': a poem of 55 lines, it had been included in *Some Imagist Poets* (1916) but had never been published in England.

⁵ 'Meeting Among the Mountains' and 'Song of a Man Who is Loved'. See Letter 1437 and n. 1. (Despite DHL's co-operative attitude, Moult printed no more of his poems in *Voices*.)

⁶ The essay (if it was ever written) cannot be identified.

⁷ Moult reviewed the play in June 1920. See p. 376 n. 4.

⁸ The Brett Youngs, having decided to stay in Anacapri, took steps to give up their house in England and sell some furniture; Jessica Brett Young had gone to make these arrangements (*Francis Brett Young*, p. 106).

half to Rome to be typed.[1] I'm terrified of the post. I never get my letters nowadays. I would have sent the thing in MS. so nicely to England by Mrs Brett Young, and felt so safe. Moreover the woman in Rome charges me 1/- per 100 words – which will come to £11. or £12. Imagine my despair at the figure. However, can't be helped. I shall venture to post the 2nd. half when I hear she's got the first. Burn a farthing candle for me to the saint of the post office: or much better, singe his posterior well, if you can lay hold of him, for being such an irresponsible thievish clown. – Secker seems to be haffling and caffling with me, now I'm promised to him. I get so irritated.

Well, as a sort of landed proprietor, you will take to wearing a velvet smoking cap with a tassel and you will cultivate the earth and a Neapolitan paunch. If that isn't a blessing it's a threat.

My luggage hasn't come *yet*: no sign of it. I got the Customs Clearance notice, and the keys from Turin. But the goods – niente, signore, niente. I tear my hair.

Meanwhile new troubles come upon us, à la Macbeth:[2] in the shape of that cherub Magnus this time.[3] But I can't write about it, it wearies me.

We had a concert in the Gk Theatre on Sunday evening – a long-haired individual called Barjansky on the cello, and the town band twinkling on guitars and mandolins, rather faintly, like grasshoppers and kindred insects. I preferred the insect noises to the all-too-human groans of the cello, maestro though Barjansky be. But I can't stand this twisting, squirming, whining modern music. I hated Bach and Schubert and Wagner and Brahms and all the lot of them, in the evening golden light – Imagine sitting there and looking through the broken windows at this coast swerving and swerving south, silvery in the gold of evening, swerving away into God knows what dawn of our world. That coast rouses a nostalgia that is half ecstasy and half torture in me, swooping in the great dim lines to Syracuse and beyond. – And then the snore of that sententious cello, and the Italian crowd in its ever-so-Sunday clothes! Is it to be borne? Will Etna not erupt, out of very shame of its modern fleas. Suppose I'm one of 'em.

The foreigners have all gone – all gone. Timeo shuts shortly. Taormina is strange and deserted, the natives are quite lost, with no one to jeer at and to swindle. Mary has deposited herself in Rocca Bella Studio – do you

---

[1] DHL's diary entry for 5 May 1920 reads: 'Sent first part MS. *Lost Girl* to Miss Wallace, 11 Via Vittoria Colonna, Rome' (Tedlock, *Lawrence MSS* 90).

[2] *Macbeth* I. iii. 144 ['new honours come upon him'].

[3] 'Magnus appeared at our Fontana Vecchia at Taormina, having fled from Montecassino. He came almost taking for granted that we would be responsible for him, that it was our duty to keep him. This disturbed Lawrence' (Frieda Lawrence, "*Not I, But the Wind . . .*", p. 117).

remember, that sort of chapelly building just behind the Bristol, with a naked bit of doorway terrace. There she sits, poor darling, like the old woman in the shoe.

I'm sorry for Mackenzie, being so ill. Can he do *nothing* to escape himself. Ach Gott!

I don't know what I shall do, my novel finished, myself out of work. Suppose I shall run hopelessly to seed one way or another. It has been ferociously hot, but now blows and rains a bit, thank goodness.

My novel is called *The Lost Girl*. How's that? – Cicio, the cook, my landlord, is a darling, but he sails for America – Boston, U.S.A. on June 12.

– I'd give you 2 pots for Fraita flowers, if you were near enough.

DHL

1979. To Martin Secker, [6 May 1920]
Text: MS UInd; Postmark, Taormina 7 5 20; Secker 24.

Fontana Vecchia, *Taormina*, (Messina)
6 May

Dear Secker

I've finished my novel – called it *The Lost Girl* – it's quite proper – I've sent the first part to Rome to be typed – hope to have it all typed and ready for England and America by June 1st.

Do you want me to send it to you? If so, what terms? Have you written me definitely about *Women in Love* and *The Rainbow*? The post is *awful* now – nothing comes. Anything important, register it.

Are you coming to Capri?

Best Wishes   D. H. Lawrence

1980. To S. S. Koteliansky, 7 May 1920
Text: MS BL; Moore 627–8.

Fontana Vecchia, *Taormina*, (Messina)
7 May 1920

Your letter of 13th. April, registered, came today. I had your letter with cheque for £5-, and news of Grisha in London, and the Caucasians, two days ago – and wrote you by return, as I always do when it is a matter of any moment.

Re – Shestov. I repeat what I have written before.

1. I had a letter from Huebsch a week ago, offering fifty pounds outright for Shestov. I telegraphed to Secker, and sent the letter to you. I thought if you were in need of ready money it would be a help to accept this £50. That is all.

2. Meanwhile – and I have written this long ago – I heard from Secker that the Robert MacBride Company had offered to set up a copyright American edition of Shestov on a 10% royalty basis, and that Secker had accepted this offer: on his own initiative, apparently. I don't know how final this is. See Secker and make it definite.

3. Huebsch makes no mention, as you will see, of separate payment for the articles from Shestov, in his paper *The Freeman*. This paper I received – one copy – a few days ago. I send it you. It contains a batch of extracts from Shestov, not mentioning translator or anybody. If Secker has agreed with the Robert Macbride, write yourself to Huebsch and demand payment at once for the articles. I will write also. – *The Freeman* is the issue of April 7th. – Why it should arrive, and no letter from America is a mystery of the Italian post.

4. I only mentioned the £20 English rights from Secker because I thought you might want money. As apparently there is no pressing need, let him go forward on his damned royalty basis.

5. I *do* wish you would make my share in Shestov one-fourth. A half is too much. – And Secker is going to give me £100 down, advance of royalties for *Women in Love*, and another £100 for *The Lost Girl* – my new novel, which is finished – and another £100 3 months after publication of *Rainbow*, *if nothing has happened*. So behold, riches in anticipation.

Your letter, this letter, is perfectly dreadful – the flue, and Annie,[1] and all. Hope by now you are happier with Grisha and the Caucasians. – Nothing will happen to the world: Bloomsbury will go on enjoying itself in Paris and elsewhere, no bombs will fall, no plagues, Etna will not erupt and Taormina will not fall down in earthquakes. One may as well accept the dribbling inevitable of this pettifogging fate. I am planning next Spring to go to the ends of the earth. Sicily is not far enough.

I hope you've had all letters by now: even about that imbecile Gilbert, whom please bury.

Many greetings to Grisha.   DHL

---

[1] Unidentified.

1981. To Lady Cynthia Asquith, 7 May 1920
Text: MS UT; Huxley 504–5.

Fontana Vecchia, *Taormina*, (Messina)
7 May 1920

Had your letter the other day – glad you are well and gay. Fun if you came to Taormina this summer: but August and September are *supposed* to be monstrous hot. But perhaps you like heat. Anyhow two hotels will be open, Bristol and San Domenico, and they'll give you pension at San Domenico, the swellest place, for 40 francs a day – which is 10/-. The Bristol is only about 26 or 28 francs. – We in our Fontana Vecchia are about ten minutes out of town, lovely and cool. We've had some sweltering days already – but our house with its terraces doesn't get too hot: so many green leaves. – Most of the foreigners have gone already – The Taorminese are lapsing into a languor and a sloth. I believe Sicily has *always*, since Adam, been run by a foreign incoming aristocracy: Phœnecian, Greek, Arab, Norman, Spanish, Italian. Now it is people in hotels, and such stray fish as me. They, the natives, verily droop and fade out without us, though they hate us when the exchange is too high.

It is very dry here – all the roses out, and drying up, all the grass cut, the earth brown. There is a lot of land, peasant land, to this house. I have just been down in the valley by the cisterns, in a lemon grove that smells very sweet, getting summer nespoli. Nespoli look like apricots, and taste a bit like them – but they're pear-shaped. They're a sort of medlar. Wish you had some, they are delicious, and we've got treefuls. The sea is pale and shimmery today, the prickly pears are in yellow blossom.

I've actually finished my new novel. *The Lost Girl*: not morally lost, I assure you. That bee in my bonnet which you mention, and which I presume means sex, buzzes not over loud. I think the *Lost Girl* is quite passable, from Mudies point of view. – She is being typed in Rome at the moment, which is going to cost me the monstrous figure of 1000 francs. If the exchange goes right down, I'm done.

Meanwhile Secker is actually doing *Women in Love* and *The Rainbow*. That is, he is sending *Women in Love* to press at once, so he says – and *The Rainbow* to follow almost immediately, if all goes well. Of course he is rather in a funk, fearing the censor. I wish someone could hold his hand while he gets the thing through. If there's any legal proceeding *I* shall have to pay for it. Lord, the world is a paltry place. The Great War has made cowards of us all: if it was possible.

However, we'll hope for the best, and devil take the hindmost. Let's hope my *Lost Girl* will be Treasure Trove to me.

Meanwhile life at Fontana Vecchia is very easy, indolent, and devil-may-care. Did you ever hear of a Duca di Bronte – Mr Nelson-Hood – descendant of Lord Nelson (Horatio) whom the Neapolitans made Duca Di Bronte because he hanged a few of them.[1] – Well, Bronte is just under Etna and this Mr Nelson-Hood has a place there – his Ducal estate. We went to see him – rather wonderful place – mais mon Dieu, M. le Duc – Mr Hood I should say. But perhaps you know him.

> Tell me where do dukedoms lie
> Or in the head or in the eye

– that's wrong.

> Tell me where are dukedoms bred
> Or in the eye or in the head.[2]

If I was Duca Di Bronte I'd be tyrant of Sicily. High time there was another Hiero.[3] – But of course, money maketh a man: even if he was a monkey to start with. – How are you, how well off? – beyond the exorbitant 20 guineas for the house? The tables were a good egg after all – better than editing poems, no doubt.

Frieda greets you. Salute your husband from me.

D. H. Lawrence

1982. To Thomas Seltzer, 7 May 1920
Text: MS UT; Postmark, Taormina 8 5 20; Lacy, *Seltzer* 9.

Fontana Vecchia, *Taormina*, (Messina)
7 May 1920

Dear Seltzer

I had your cable saying you were sending a hundred dollars – so am awaiting a letter to know why: presumably for *Women in Love*, I don't know anything else. Meanwhile I heard from Huebsch saying you were turning over the MS. to him. – I must wait for letters to enlighten me.

---

[1] Horatio, Viscount Nelson (1758–1805) received the Royal Licence (in 1801) to accept for himself and his heirs the title of Duke of Brontë from Ferdinand I, King of the Two Sicilies, for services rendered to Ferdinand.

[2] *The Merchant of Venice* III. ii. 63 ['Tell me where is fancy bred/ Or in the heart or in the head?'].

[3] Hieron I (d. 467? B.C.), the tyrant of Syracuse (who was also a patron of literature as Aeschylus and Pindar testified).

Secker says *you haven't sent him the typescript*. But you promised so plainly. I have done my new novel *The Lost Girl*. It is quite proper, to my idea, and might easily be popular. It is being typed in Rome. I hope to let you have a copy, by a friend who is sailing from Naples on June 10th., going to Boston.[1] Trust I shan't be frustrated in this despatch.

Meanwhile see if you can get a definite answer from Huebsch, as to whether he is doing the *Studies in Classic American Literature*. If not, ask him for the MS.

Meanwhile I wait for news from you in your letter with the dollars.

D. H. Lawrence

1983. To Martin Secker, 7 May 1920
Text: MS UInd; Secker 25.

Fontana Vecchia, *Taormina*, (Messina)
7 May 1920.

Dear Secker,

I have your letter of April 13th., with contracts, only today. Post is very bad.

1. I want to keep all my American rights quite separate, and to handle them myself. Therefore I cross out Clause 3.

2. I think *five* more books is many: three ought to be enough: because suppose we become disagreeable with one another, and are married for five succeeding children –

3. If you really do pay me the £100. on *Women in Love* on receipt of the agreement, I wish you would put £50 to my credit with the London County Westminster Bank, Law Courts Branch, 263 Strand, where I have an account:[2] and the other £50, if you were an angel, you would exchange for me at a good rate (alas, they are giving only 83 today in Taormina, as against your quoted 105 Lire –) and you would place it to my credit with *Haskard and Co., Bankers, Piazza degli Antinori, Florence*, where I have a couple of thousand Lire in a current account. They are good safe people, I think.

I have sent MS. of *The Lost Girl* to Rome to be typed. Horror of horrors, it will cost me about 1,000 Lire – which would keep the house going for five weeks. – But the post is abominable, I simple dared not send the only script to London. – I shall let you have a copy as soon as it is done. Hope you will like it – think you will. I think it's amusing. But I still think *Women in Love* my best – always shall, I believe – and *The Rainbow* second.

---

[1] Ciccio Cacópardo: see Letter 1967 and n. 3.   [2] See *Letters*, ii. 189 n. 3.

You might do *The Lost Girl* after *Women in Love*, if you preferred.

I agree to your provision about *The Rainbow* and the deduction if there should be legal expenses.[1] But there must not be legal expenses.

I had a cable from Seltzer to say he was sending 100 dollars, but no letter. I think all Americans are dotty. – The post from New York takes *at least* 4 weeks.

Huebsch is already publishing Shestov selections in his paper *The Freeman*. I don't know how this will suit the Macbride. You must settle that business now. And see Koteliansky about it, will you – he bothers me. And send Huebsch a *final* line, will you.

I will see you if you come to Italy, even if I must come to Capri.

D. H. Lawrence

Gamble my £50 for me in the Italian exchange.

1984. To Rosalind Baynes, 7 May 1920
Text: MS UN; Unpublished.

Fontana Vecchia, Taormina, (Messina)
7 May 1920

My dear Rosalind

My novel is done – primo.

I'm a free man, from work – secondo.

Was your flue bad?

Is it better?

Are Joan and Bertie gone back? I had one p.c. from Siena from Joan – wrote p.c's by return, hoping you might all pop down here. But no word further.

Now what are you going to do this summer? It won't be so very hot here – this house is so shady. But I do think we ought to effect a meeting somewhere. How long are you staying in La Canovaia?[2] What are you doing next winter? I think I could fairly easily find you a house here, for about 30/- a week, English money. – But what about the summer? Was it sea-baths you were wanting? – Of course we are a good $\frac{1}{2}$ hour above the sea – steep up. – Frieda would like to make a trip to Germany – don't know if it would be feasible. But almost for certain we shall be here this winter. It's quite lovely, and once

---

[1] Secker was fearful lest he should commit a contempt of court by re-issuing a book suppressed by a magistrate (see Mackenzie 172).

[2] Rosalind Baynes moved into the Villa Canovaia, San Gervasio, Florence, in January 1920 (see Nehls, ii. 44).

we're settled, not very expensive. – Shall we meet in July? – at La Canovaia, or where? Send plans.

Do hope you're better.

I got a copy of the Shestov – it is published – do you remember, in the Pangbourne garden.[1]

My novel *The Lost Girl* is being typed in Rome – going to cost me 1000 Lire for typing – horror! But it is pretty proper, and *might* have a success. – Secker says he is sending *Women in Love* to print now, and *The Rainbow* in early autumn, all being well.

How are Clive[2] and Earl Godwin? Oh you poor Lady Godiva, you'll have to use your wits to cover yourself, your hair isn't enormous enough.

But plans are the point.

How are the obstreperous cherubs?

F. sends love.   DHL

1985. To Compton Mackenzie, [10 May 1920]
Text: MS UT; Mackenzie 178–9.

Fontana Vecchia, *Taormina*, (Messina)
Monday May 10 or 11

Had your letter today. I've finished my novel – *The Lost Girl* – sent first part to Rome to be typed, and wait to hear if the woman's got it. Devil, it will cost me 1000 francs. I think it's good – amusing. Secker sent me finicky agreements – however I signed, except I reserve for myself *All* American rights and properties. He sounds funky. – You'll be able to hold his hand when you go to London. – I've read *Sylvia Scarlett* and *S[ylvia] and Michael* – amusing and witty – and alas, only too like life. This rolling stone business gets a little heart-rending in the end. One is rather busy at it oneself. Poor Sylvia – qu'est-il donc qu'elle cherche?[3] – It isn't *merely* adventure. She's all the while looking for something *permanent*. Don't like the Christ hankering – sign of defeat: alas, *S. and Michael* are a wistful pair. I'm terrified of my Alvina, who marries a Cicio. I believe neither of us has found a way out of the labyrinth. How we hang on to the marriage clue! Doubt if its really a way out. – But my Alvina, in whom the questing soul is lodged, moves towards reunion with the dark half of humanity. Whither your Sylvia? The ideal? I loathe the ideal with an increasing volume of detestation – *all* ideal.

[1] DHL's reference is presumably to some occasion(s) in the garden of 'The Myrtles', Rosalind Baynes's cottage, where she and the Lawrences were 15–29 August 1919.
[2] Unidentified.   [3] 'what is she looking for, then?'

Yes, I should like to see you before you go to England. Yet I feel I ought to sit tight on the Liras. I'm determined myself to hop off the known map by next spring: shall hoard Martins dear advances, and shan't buy a Fraita, not even a Pauline.¹ But I should like to talk once more *South Seas*. That interests me finally – I have to poke myself to be interested in novels and plays. *Are you really going?* – I had by the same post a letter from an American friend – in Paris at the moment – also South Seas.² He also plans to go. He has a friend in the US navy who knows the South Seas well, knows the natives of the Islands, who love him. He's looking for a ship to get out. He also will look for a place for us. And I am going to have enough money *by next year* to start off. Voilà! Free bird too. Meanwhile I shall cogitate a day or two, and may suddenly appear in Capri one morning.

At the moment Mary is madly keen to go to Malta, because at the hotel they give you Soles and ham and eggs for breakfast, raspberry jam and cream puffs for tea. And she's scared of going any more alone – begs us to go with her, she buy tickets. I don't know. – But if we went we should go next Monday, for about 4 days.

But if I come to Capri it will be because I want to talk South Seas for the last time before you start. I *can't* be *very* interested in plays, even my own. I somehow have no belief in the public: only in that other world which is dusky, I have a desire. – Don't imagine – since I mention tickets – that it is money which prevents my coming to Capri. I am quite well off as a matter of fact. The Malta affair is a mere excursion, a *niente* on which I would *not* spend.

But after my novel I am holidaying for one month. Then I should like to start again, with another I have in mind.³ I feel as if I was victualling my ship, with these damned books. But also, somewhere they are the crumpled wings of my soul. They get me free before I get myself free. I mean in my novel I get some sort of wings loose, before I get my feet out of Europe.

I am sending you a copy of *Touch and Go*. Perhaps the preface may amuse you.

Will you believe my *luggage* hasn't come yet. And do you imagine my weary despair.

Frieda greets you herzlich.

auf Wiedersehn – even if it's in Honolulu.

D. H. Lawrence

---

¹ Martin Secker; the house bought by Brett Young; and Mackenzie's 'dearly loved cat' (Mackenzie 145).
² See the letter following.
³ DHL had recorded in his diary for 7 May 1920, 'Began Mr Noon' (Tedlock, *Lawrence MSS* 90). He may be referring to this novel.

My gracious respects to your mother, and many thanks for her 'of course'.
I am just making marmalade with 1 chilo of sugar. Vlà!

After which I and Frieda and Mary are going down to the sea to bathe, like
Adam and Eve and Pinchme. I leave you broach the salvation of Pinchme.[1]

1986. To Robert Mountsier, [11 May 1920]
Text: MS Smith; Postmark, Taormina 11 5 20; Unpublished.

Fontana Vecchia, *Taormina*, (Messina)

12 May 1920

Dear Mountsier

I had yours of 21 April yesterday. Damn the Italian post.

I wrote to Compton Mackenzie and suggested you for the South Seas. But
he's a close and timid bird, and you and I, we'll have to take wing on our own.
However, I shall try and get him to bring you the MS. to Paris, in early June.
That do? Unless you come here. Come if you can. I put you a time-table on
the back.

Basel.	5.15 a.m.
Chiasso	12.40
Milan	13.50 dep. 20.25
Rome	8.50 –
Naples	14.0

Naples to Taormina – about 12 hours

But there is a lovely train leaves Modane (Mont Cenis – French frontier)
Tuesdays, Fridays, Sundays – Paris 9.35 p.m. – at 4.10 a.m.

Turin.	6.40
Genoa	10.16
Pisa	14.10
Rome	20.10

Which is Paris to Rome in 24 hrs. However – the only really good train from
Rome to Taormina leaves at 7.40 p.m. and arrives here next afternoon 2.40
p.m. So you can get the times. – It's a long way, alas. I wish we could even see
you in Rome. – But couldn't you sail back to America from Naples? There is a
boat on June 10th. only you'd never be ready for that.

Let me hear quickly where you are, and if I am to send MS. – I have done a

[1] DHL refers to the jingle:

> Adam and Eve and Pinchme tight
> Went down to the river to bathe.
> Adam and Eve were drowned,
> Who do you think was saved?

novel *The Lost Girl* – which you might take to Seltzer for me, and talk with him. It is being typed. I should love you to take it to America. Let me know.

If I cant get Barbara[1] dolce spumante you must have Asti, which I like better.

Live in hopes of seeing you – But you are so evanescent. I cant even write a letter, you don't seem at the other end.

If you travel in Italy, best buy your ticket at the frontier – or at Turin or Milan – people like Cooks rob on the exchange. The further the distance in Italy the cheaper the rate becomes. Our station is Giardini–Taormina. *Watch your luggage.*

Au revoir   D. H. Lawrence

1987. To Catherine Carswell, 12 May 1920
Text: MS YU; cited in Carswell 131, 133–4.

Fontana Vecchia, Taormina, (Messina).
12 May 20.

My dear Catherine

I had your letter yesterday – also, the day before, your photograph – a very good photograph indeed, I think, and very charming of you both, J[ohn] P[atrick] just smiling his nice smile.

Glad things are going fairly smooth. Of course the Rouen villa sounds awfully attractive: but you'd have to *see* it first, and see if it's in repair – look hard at it to see if it's in repair: that's the first thing. Then find out how heavy rates and taxes are: they're very stiff in Italy. – I wonder how the anti-British feeling is, in France? – nothing serious, I should think. Heaven knows which way we shall be moving next. Depends which way the wind blows us. But one's instinct is to go south, south – and away, away from Europe. Here we are almost on the last tip – and my face still looks south, as if one must step off into space somewhere. – I don't know, however, what we shall *actually* do. I've taken this place for a year – 2000 francs for the year. It's not enormous, anyway – only £25 with the exchange at 80. – We might go away a bit in July and August, but come back some time in September. They say it is still very hot in September – could you make it towards the end? – or don't you mind heat? It's lovely and cool in this house.

If you really think of coming, then you can, if you like pay the £50 into my account at the Law Courts Branch of the London County Westminster Bank – 263 Strand – and I'll just keep it for you for the holiday. But in any case, I

---

[1] Barbara Low.

wont do more than just keep it for you till you want it.

I have signed agreements with Secker. He is to publish first *Women in Love*, and is to give me £100 down, and usual royalties. After *Women in Love* he is to do *The Rainbow*, and give me £100 down 3 months after publication, but to deduct from my £100 all charges of any legal proceedings, if such should occur. He seems in a bit of a funk. If Don has spare time he might find out exactly the law. But perhaps he's busy – and I hope he is. – Anyhow I seem fairly sure of the £100 for *Women in Love*, pretty soon.

Then I've done my new novel *The Lost Girl*. I think it's quite amusing: and quite moral. She's not morally lost, poor darling. It's being typed in Rome – so *dear*, 1000 francs – alas for me! But post here is horribly slow. I had yours 21 April on 11 May – which is 20 days. Heaven knows what happens in the interim.

The weather is hot. Do you know what it is to be in a *dry* Southern country – dry, like Africa? I never knew before. But I like it. The sun is a bit overwhelming. Nearly all foreigners have left here already. Today we are going down to the sea to bathe. But it is a good ½ hour down, and 1 hour up. – Mary Cannan has a studio here – nice – for 3 more months. She is dying to go to Malta – the boat runs from Syracuse. But she can't go alone. So she wants us to go, if she pays our ship fare – it's only 8 hours crossing. It might be amusing, for 4 or 5 days. But Malta isn't wildly attractive, and I am doubtful if I want to spend the money.

Oh, your Melrose![1] But all these roses smell the same, no matter what their name. I believe publishing is a disease in itself – like many other professions. – But your book should be out now. I look forward immensely to reading it again. – My Lost Girl marries an Italian –

I haven't heard lately of my Hist of *Europe* (no, not The World! – not yet). I did all proofs – but await revised proofs, for indexing. God knows what they're doing. – I see *Touch and Go* is out. Have you got a copy? I ordered you one. If they haven't sent it, I'll send one.

Mila saluti to you both, and J.P. DHL

---

[1] Catherine Carswell's novel, *Open the Door!*, was published by Andrew Melrose Ltd in May 1920. It was selected (by Andrew Melrose himself) as 'Melrose's £250 Prize Novel, 1920' from the hundred MSS submitted. (Catherine Carswell, believing that DHL's 'funds were low enough', wanted him to 'have a slice' of her prize; hence the offer of £50 mentioned earlier in the letter. See Carswell 132.) Melrose's report on the novel – printed on the verso of the title-page – records the 'profound impression' the work had made on him: 'As a story of tumultuous emotion and the passionate efforts of a young girl for freedom and self-fulfilment, it is one of the biggest things that the Adjudicator has met with in a longish period, and a fairly wide acquaintance with the best fiction.'

1988. To Marie Hubrecht, 13 May 1920
Text: MS UN; Unpublished.

Fontana Vecchia, *Taormina*
13 May 1920

Dear Miss Hübrecht,

I had your letter yesterday. Cicio also received one from you.[1] He came to me very distressed about Mary. I am sorry it was so against your wishes to let the studio again. I thought you wouldn't mind, as you wouldn't be there – and Juta was quite glad to get his 150 Lire for this month. Mary went into the Studio on May 1st., when the Juta's went to Rome. She paid Juta the 150 francs for the month: so I suppose she can't very well be turned out till 1st. June. Cicio will ask her then to find another place – and will offer her *his* rooms downstairs here. I don't really want her in the Fontana Vecchia while we are here, it is *too* near. But if you are quite sure she must leave the Studio, I suppose we shall have to arrange it. She talks of going north in August, and of spending next winter with a friend in Cannes. Mr Bowdwin has not come yet.

I have not yet heard from Juta, from Rome – only a line from Palermo on May 31st.[2] But I know he wrote to you.

Taormina is already very quiet, most of the foreigners gone. The weather is hot. Sometimes we go to the sea to bathe.

We went to Randazzo with the Jutas. Knowing Mrs Hansard better, I liked her much more. She became simple again, dropped her social tiresomenesses, and I liked her. We had a jolly time at Randazzo, drove to Maniace and had tea with the Duca – Later on Insole invited us to Syracuse, and it *was* jolly. We miss them now they have gone. We talked of meeting once more, all of us, in Africa. But who knows.

I am glad you liked *Sons and Lovers*. Yes, it is more or less auto-biographical. Secker is doing *The Rainbow* again, also a new novel. I shall send you a copy of each, as soon as they appear. – I agree, Freud might be dangerous for weak-minded people – and I too detest him. But as we aren't weak minded, we can get something from his suggestions – But I'm sure you like the *Golden Bough*. – Get Blavatskys book one day.[3]

So will you be gone from the Witte Huis,[4] and this letter will probably follow you north. Ach, strange it must be to be in northern seas. Here it is very

---

[1] While Cacópardo was the owner of Fontana Vecchia, he appears also to have acted as Marie Hubrecht's agent in the management of her properties, Rocca Bella and 'the studio', Rocca Forte.

[2] The date is clearly an error (in a letter written on 13 May).

[3] DHL had read Sir James Frazer's *Golden Bough* in December 1915 (see *Letters*, ii. 470) and Blavatsky's *Secret Doctrine* by August 1917 (see Letter 1442).

[4] See p. 489 n. 2.

dry. Jutas larkspurs are out in Rocca Bella garden, and carnations and red lilies. But the earth is terribly dry.

My wife greets you. I am sorry about the studio.

Yours Sincerely   D. H. Lawrence

1989. To J. B. Pinker, [14 May 1920]
Text: MS UNYB; Unpublished.

Fontana Vecchia, *Taormina*, (Messina)
14 May.

Dear Pinker

Thank you for yours of May 3rd. I have written to Thomas Seltzer, of Scott and Seltzer, 5 West 50th. St. New York, to ask him to buy the plates etc of *The Widowing of Mrs Holroyd*, from the Little Brown Company.[1] Will they – Messrs Little Brown – please await his answer.

Yours Sincerely   D. H. Lawrence

1990. To Thomas Seltzer, 14 May 1920
Text: MS UT; Postmark, Taormina 14 5 20; Lacy, *Seltzer* 9–10.

Fontana Vecchia, *Taormina*, (Messina)
14 May /20

Dear Seltzer

I enclose letter from Pinker about my play *The Widowing of Mrs Holroyd* which was bought by Little Brown and Co, of Boston, some time back. I said to Pinker that if you want the plates etc you will write direct to Little Brown. – The play is just going to be produced in Hammersmith.[2]

No letters at all from America. – Hope to get the MS. of the *Lost Girl* off to you, by hand, by boat leaving Naples June 10th. It is being typed in Rome.

Yrs   D. H. Lawrence

1991. To Compton Mackenzie, [16 May 1920]
Text: MS UT; cited in Mackenzie 179.

Fontana Vecchia
Sunday. 16 May.

We're going to Malta tomorrow. Don't know why it sounds so thrilling – seems so thrilling. Perhaps it'll be a fiasco.

---

[1] Kennerley had published the first American edition of the play in 1914 and had disposed of the plates to Little, Brown & Co., publishers in Boston. Seltzer re-issued the work in 1921.
[2] No such production is known.

Secker says he may be able to serialise the new novel in *The Century*. Good
if he could! – Will you really take the MS. to London for me, as you pass?
Otherwise I don't believe it will ever arrive. You'll have E[ric] B[rett]-
Y[oung], won't you? The woman is
   Miss Wallace, Pension White, 11 Via Vittoria Colonna, Roma. 26.
I should think she'll have it done by first week in June.
   Secker prefers the title The Bitter Cherry – not *The Lost Girl*. My *Lost Girl*
amused me so – such a film title. But we shall have to let Secker have this, as
he yields me *Women in Love*.
   – I expect we shall be back here Friday. But if we miss the boat, it will be
Friday week, 28th. – because only one boat a week. Oh dear!
   Wonder if I shall see you.
   Cicio – my landlord – sails from Naples June 10th. for New York – leaves
here June 2nd. I was going to ask him to take one copy to Seltzer in N. York.
In that case, wouldn't Secker need two copies – one for self, one for *Century*?
– If so, he'd have to have my written MS. for himself. But it is quite plain.
   Don't curse me for bothering you.
   Hope you're better. – Post wouldn't accept *Stampa* – couldn't send play.[1]
   Wish I had heard from you before this Malta trip. – We stay there in Hotel
Great Britain.

                                                                   DHL
   Don't you think I might possibly have the novel serialised in England? I'm
dying to make enough money to trip off.

1992. To Martin Secker, 16 May 1920
Text: MS UInd; Postmark, Taormina 17 5 20; Secker 26.

                                              Fontana Vecchia, *Taormina*
                                                            16 May 1920
Dear Secker
   Yours of May 8th. today. I sent agreements. –
   I sent MS. of new novel to Rome to be typed. Hope Mackenzie will bring it
with him to London. If you prefer Bitter Cherry, well and good. – Seltzer has
only a claim on this one book – no claim on serial rights. Good if you could
serialise with *The Century*. – I was going to send one copy of the MS. direct to
Seltzer, by a man who sails from Naples for New York on June 10th. Shall I
do this? And in that case, shall Mackenzie bring you a type-script and the

---

[1] *Touch and Go*; see Letter 1972 and n. 5.

original MS., hand-written, for you and the *Century*? Let me know sharp, as Francesco leaves Taormina on June 2nd. and I must arrange with Rome. Anyway the MS will be typed by June 10th.

D. H. Lawrence

I had only two copies typed, of Bitter Cherry.

Wouldn't the Macbrides buy[1] Shestov for £50? Koteliansky does need money. – Have you sent a line to Huebsch?

I don't believe letters ever go from here to America – If you arrange with the *Century* to serialise the Cherry, be so good as to let Seltzer know – I'm sure my letters never reach him.

Thomas Seltzer, 5 West 50th. St. New York.

1993. To J. B. Pinker, 17 May 1920
Text: MS UNYB; PC; Postmark, Siracusa 17. 5. 20; Unpublished.

Taormina.
17 May 20

Thank you for your letter and enclosure for the story 'Foxed', which I received yesterday.[2]

1994. To Cecily Lambert, [20 May 1920]
Text: MS SIU; PC v. Malta – Grand Harbour; Postmark, Valletta 21 MY 20; Unpublished.

[Great Britain Hotel, Valletta, Malta]
20 May

We came over to Malta for a few days – but there's an Italian steamer-strike, so don't know when we shall get back. – Why have you and Miss Monk never sent a *line* since we've been in Taormina? That is too bad. You know the address – Fontana Vecchia, *Taormina*, Sicily. – I hope we shall get back to Sicily next week – meanwhile we are feeding ourselves stiff here, there is such a lot of food. Italy is rather Old Mother Hubbard just now. What's happening at Grimsbury? – So hot and dry here.

Mila saluti   DHL

---

[1] buy] sell
[2] It is presumed that DHL should have written 'Fox': be believed Pinker had the MS of that story in February 1920 (see Letter 1924 and n. 2.).

1995. To Emily King, [20 May 1920]
Text: MS Needham; PC v. Malta – Country Ciris; Postmark, Vallett[a] 2[. . .];
Unpublished.

Great Britain Hotel – Malta.

20 May –

It is wonderfully nice here in Valletta: most astonishing of all the abundance of food and of all things to buy, and it seems so cheap after Italy, where the shops are all so bare. – The Maltese women all wear this black silk arrangement in the street – gives them a dark, eastern look. – I expect we shall go back on Wednesday – arrive Fontana Vecchia Thursday evening. Think of you and hope you're keeping well.

Love. DHL

The land is *not* green,[1] but parched.

1996. To Jessica Brett Young, [22 May 1920]
Text: MS UB; PC v. Maltese – Lady; Postmark, Valletta 22 MY 20; Unpublished.

Gt. Britain Hotel. Malta.

22 May

Behold us on the razzle again – stuck in Malta till the Sicily boats stop striking. Did you enjoy England? British territory here is very easy and pleasant, and flowing with milk and honey, ham and eggs, marmalade and legs of mutton and Bass. It is hot as can be, and very dry. Valletta beautiful and gay. – I think we shall be back at Fontana Vecchia by the end of next week. I'm having a silk suit! Knock-out!

DHL

1997. To Margaret King, [22 May 1920]
Text: MS Needham; PC v. Maltese – Lady; Postmark, Valletta [. . .]; Unpublished.

Gt. Britain Hotel. Valletta

22 May

I sent you today a little embroidery thing – an exact copy of an Egyptian Wall-painting. It represents the river Goddess giving the new born god of the spring to the big god of the Sun and Creation: they all have their mysterious symbols. Ill tell you them one day. – It is so hot here, we gasp in the sun. I think we shall get a ship back next Wednesday. – Hang your goddess on the wall, – don't lie it flat.

Love. DHL

---

[1] The tinting on the picture is lurid.

1998. To Martin Secker, 24 May 1920
Text: MS UInd; Postmark, Valletta 24 MY 20; Huxley 507–8.

Great Britain Hotel, Valletta, Malta
24 May 1920

Dear Secker

We came here for two days – kept here for eight by the Sicilian steamer strike.

Land of plenty, land of comfort – Britain, wheresoever found.

Bacon and eggs for breakfast.

But a horrible island – to me: stone, and bath-brick dust. All the world might come here to sharpen its knives.

What I really have to say. Thinking about the title *Women in Love* – If you care to change it to *Day of Wrath*, I am willing.

> Dies irae, dies illa
> Solvet saeclum in favilla.[1]

That for the motto.

DHL

Taormina Thursday next.

1999. To Douglas Goldring, 26 May 1920
Text: TMSC NWU; Goldring, *Odd Man Out*, p. 259.

Osborne Hotel, 50 Strada Mezzodi, Valletta, Malta
26 May 1920

Dear Goldring

Ages since I heard from you – the post is simply abominable, I think they just *burn* the conglomerated mail when the strikes have done with it. But I got *The Black Curtain*, which we read and which is interesting.[2] But ugh, how I hate the war – even a suggestion of it.

We came to Malta for a few days – a strike held us up – no steamers. Thank God we go back to Taormina tomorrow. It's a *hideous* island, though Valletta is beautiful. But oh Lord, I'm glad to return to Sicily.

I got copies of *Touch and Go* just before we came here. It has a nice appearance – book. How *is* your Peoples Theatre? Hope it goes. Is there any news of it? A man here showed me MS. of various plays – good ones, really – translations.

---

[1] From the hymn by Thomas of Celano (fl. 1214–55); 'On that day, that wrathful day/Heaven and earth shall melt away'.

[2] See p. 441 and n. 2.

Love's Tragedy – by Knut Hamsun, 4 act – a famous thing, unknown in England.[1]

To the Stars – Leonid Andreyeff, 4 act – weird.[2]

The Snake Charmer – Very comic – 3 act – German, Julius Bierbaum.

Lady Sofia – George von Omptede – 4 act – comedy.

The White Fan – Hugo von Hofmannstal – 1 act – poetic.[3]

Do you think anything could be done with these? Magnus – the man who has the MSS. – wants to publish the things if possible – sell them outright to a publisher. But he retains the acting rights.

Let me know how everything is. You *may* of course be gone to Germany or the ends of the earth – or you may be producing plays like billy-o. I'm going back to Taormina to work. How is Mrs. Goldring? – feeding herself, for a change?

Yrs   D. H. Lawrence

2000. To Marie Hubrecht, 28 May 1920
Text: MS UN; Unpublished.

Fontana Vecchia, Taormina
28 May 1920

Dear Miss Hübrecht

I have your letter of 18th. May today – am glad you don't mind if Mary stays on in the Studio till August. We were waiting to hear from you. – All the things from Miss Hill were safely returned: also the Duca's candlesticks. There is nothing in the studio[4] but your things, and a few of Ciccios. The place looks very nice – it has been thoroughly scrubbed and carefully arranged, and really looks charming. Mary flutters round in her bits of ninon and fringe, and is quite happy. Sometimes we go to tea, and sit in the garden afterwards, and watch the moonlight mixed with sunset. It is always lovely, that coast.

---

[1] The play by the Norwegian novelist, Knut Hamsun (1859–1952), was translated by Maurice Magnus and sent to Goldring in June 1920 (see Nehls, ii. 40–1). There does not appear to have been any English printing or production.

[2] Though Magnus feared that it was 'too literary and subtle for the Anglo-Saxon theatre-going public' (Nehls, ii. 41), the play by the Russian, Leonid Andreyeff (1871–1919), in Magnus's translation, was published by Daniel in May 1921 as No. 10 in the 'Plays for a People's Theatre'.

[3] Otto Julius Bierbaum (1865–1910), German poet, novelist and playwright; Georg Baron von Ompteda (1863–1931), best known as a German novelist; Hugo von Hofmannsthal (1874–1929), Austrian poet, novelist and playwright who wrote several of Richard Strauss's operas. None of the three plays mentioned appears to have been published or produced in England.

[4] studio] flat

But it has been very hot. The corn is nearly all cut, the ground is dry and yellow, your garden is almost bare. Only the geraniums still flower red in the sun, above the dry withered grass, and that shrub hedge below your terrace is all in flower with pale-blue bunches. For the rest, yellow witheredness and sundried earth, and Etna dim in the glare.

Bowdwin has not come yet, because his mother has died. I haven't been able to get any books lately, because the gardener now has the key of the salon, and I can't catch him. We have nearly read all our *Revues des Deux Mondes*, so are nearly dried up.

Did I tell you we were going to Malta? We went, and I hated it. The island is a glaring gritty dry yellow lump with hideous villages. Only Valletta harbour is beautiful, particularly at night. – I hated also the British régime. There is something so beneficent and sterile, a kind of barrenness about it. English people seem so *good*, and so barren of life.

Today came the two blocks of writing paper: treasures they are. I want to begin to work again, and there they are, a clean field before me. – I sent you my play. Shortly I shall send you a small History of Europe which I did for the Oxford University Press. It may please you. I suppose the Doorn address will always find you.

Cicio leaves on Wednesday – 2nd. June, – for Venice. On June 11th. he sails from Naples. Strange it is to be going to America.

Frieda wants to go to Germany. If I get my new novel serialised in America, then we may both go to the Black Forest for a couple of months. Sometimes one sighs for a breath of the north, pine trees and wet, green grass and flowers full of sap, heavy, water-cool.

I will see that your things are safely put away, when Mary goes. – At present all your books are in their exact places.

Tell me where your new address will be. I'll send you all the news from here. Frieda greets you also.

D. H. Lawrence

2001. To Catherine Carswell, [28 May 1920]
Text: MS YU; cited in Carswell 134.

Fontana Vecchia
28 May.

My dear Catherine

Mary Cannan lured us away to Malta – we were to stay only 2 days – then a steam-boat strike, and we only got back tonight, after some 11 days. Oh, and it was *so* expensive, and I feel so displeased. Malta is a strange place – a dry, bath-brick island that glares and sets your teeth on edge and is *so* dry that one expects oneself to begin to crackle. Valletta harbour is wonderful: beautiful. But I get set on edge by the British régime. It is very decent, I believe, but it sort of stops life, it prevents the human reactions from taking full swing, there is always a kind of half-measure, half-length, 'not-quite' feeling about, which simply arrests my digestion.

I found your two letters and your cheque.[1] The last, you understand, I shall not use, I shall merely keep it for you for when you want it. – I find the book also, and shall start to read it tomorrow. Print makes a difference. – I hope it *will* have a success. It's evident *you* will have to make money, so the thing to do is to find the easiest way. One *has* to have enough money. It's time now we found it easily. – I'm sorry about Don. Damn them all, *Times* and Time-keepers and all. Damn them heartily. I find one fault with Don. He has too much respect for them. Shit to them all: that's my last word, even if it offends you.

France without the French sounded perfect. I would have loved it – without the French. Italy is *very expensive*: try as you may: the railway-fares are preposterous, carriages just an extortion, *everything* is extortion here. And the Italians are really rather low-bred swine nowadays: so different from what they were. None the less, I can bear Sicily better than anywhere else: better than Malta, which has its fascination, and which is very aboriginal still: the natives speak a strange ancient language – Arabic-Hebrew sort of thing – and they really *don't* understand English: – better also than England, better I feel than France. But even Sicily, *humanly*, one puts up with rather than enjoys. It's so everywhere.

As for Gilbert Cannan – he turned up suddenly to pull my nose for slandering his Gwen[2] – I saw him for 2 hours, and never again. The only tea-party we have is with Mary Cannan, a disappointed creature.

Send all news – nothing here.

DHL

It's terribly hot here.

I want to try to serialise my novel. Secker wants it to be called The Bitter Cherry, not the *Lost Girl*.

What do you think of the chances of serialising?

[1] See p. 525 and n. 1.
[2] See Letter 1963.

2002. To Jan Juta, [29 May 1920]
Text: MS UT; Unpublished.

Fontana Vecchia. Taormina
29 May.

Dear J[uta]

We got back last night, thank God, off that dry bone of Malta. Valletta harbour is beautiful – but I feel as if I'd been in a biscuit oven for a month.

I have your 2nd letter this morning. I could shed tears over that typing. I sent it 3 weeks ago to that Miss Wallace, 11 Via Vittoria Colonna. She is going to charge me *at least* 1000 Lire. I can't bear to talk of it. – But tell me the address of your woman. I shall want more done for me, quite soon. Shall you be gone by June 10th.? Cicio is going through, from Venice to Naples, and he is going to take an MS. to America for me. If you are in Rome you might perhaps take the MS. to the station to him – but probably you'll be gone.

Curse about your box. I'll go to the Bristol this afternoon, and to Giardini tomorrow. Have you got the *scontrino*?[1] I hate them at Giardini, so will make a row.

A woman pesters me to death for a photograph of myself. If you get the box, could you let me have a photograph of the Sketch?[2] Should be so glad. She wants it for *Vanity Fair*, New York particularly. 'Sketch by Jan Juta.' Put your name nice and plain on the paint.

Heard from Hübrecht – 'My bark is worse than my bite' – Quot. – Mary may stay on.

Magnus is a jewel. He was in Malta, in a white suit, floating in whiskies and soda and 'come to lunch tomorrow –' at the Osborne Hotel (vide envelope and Duca). He has taken a small house at Città Vecchia, and is going to sit elegantly on Malta till he bursts again. – No, I don't like him – shall not bother with him any more.

Glad you liked the books. Did Insole get his? I ordered ½ for you, ½ for him. *Bay* will come – but you'll find it slight. Beaumont, the publisher, is the most undependable insect on earth.

Glad of Réné's notices[3] – hope it means money. I got L2,400 (Italian) today from America. I had an official letter from Luke. But I *can't* go and have another full-fledged agent – – It is very hot. We *might* later go to Germany, if a bit more money comes. The Italians begin to sicken me a little. What is one

---

[1] 'the ticket' (i.e. luggage-check).
[2] Juta had 'managed only a charcoal sketch for the oil portrait [he] had in mind' (Nehls, ii. 85). The sketch is reproduced in Nehls, ii. 106 and is now located at UT.
[3] Réné Hansard had, under her maiden name, published *The Tavern* (April 1920). See also Letter 2020.

to do? – Don't like to think of you mixed up in child-birth. – Send the Anticoli address.

Frieda greets you di cuore.

DHL

Malta was bitterly expensive, and I rued it.

So *many* thanks for the typist – she is good for the future – But send name and address.

2003. To Richard Aldington, [30 May 1920]
Text: MS YU; Nicholas Joost and Alvin Sullivan, *D. H. Lawrence and 'The Dial'* (Carbondale, 1970), p. 37.

Fontana Vecchia
30 May.

Dear Richard

Here is the other sketch for *The Dial*, if it'll suit them. The money is very attractive.[1]

At last we're back from Malta – a dry chip of a place – didn't like it – frightfully hot. Hot also here – the corn cut, the earth autumn-pale. Alas! I can't bear to think of cowslips – There are no flowers like English flowers, say what you will.

Here it *never* rains.

If we get some money, we *might* go to Germany for a bit – to the Black Forest. –

Knees of the Gods.

Thank you very much for doing this for me. Send me the type bill.

Wiedersehn to A[rabella]   DHL

2004. To Catherine Carswell, 31 May 1920
Text: MS YU; cited in Carswell 134.

Fontana Vecchia, *Taormina*, Sicily
31 May 1920

My dear Catherine

I read *Open the Door* again – How well one remembers it! I find it a little altered and all improved – but essentially it is exactly as I remember it. Did

---

[1] The *Dial* had already accepted DHL's short story 'Adolf' and published it in the issue for September 1920 (pp. 269–76); the editor had apparently invited him to submit the companion piece 'Rex'. That story appeared in the *Dial*, lxx (February 1921), 169–76. DHL's diary for 20 June 1920 records: 'Sent Richard Rex, to go with Adolf, for the Dial' (Tedlock, *Lawrence MSS* 90). This letter, therefore, though written on 30 May, may not have been mailed until 20 June; it is written on the MS of 'Rex'. The 'attractive' money to which DHL refers was, according to *Dial* records, $40 for 'Adolf' and $50 for 'Rex' (Joost and Sullivan, *D. H. Lawrence and 'The Dial'*, p. 37).

Don chase the corners of some of your sentences? I believe I can feel his presence. – But I do think the book is good, and will stand. There's a satisfaction in that.

As for the cheque, I suddenly decided to burn it. I got 2000 Lire from America. I have enough money. And why should I hold any of yours in fee. So I accept the gift all the same: and have burned the cheque.[1]

Mary Cannan also is dying to write *her* novel. But she is so jealous because she says you have said all *she* was going to say, and so much better than she could do it. However, I'll bet she'll have her shot – Heaven knows how she'll find expression.

I hear you have jolly good notices. I saw the *Observer*. Am very glad. You get royalties still, don't you? My hat, I hope you're not sold outright to that Melrose. What you do want is money, so you must get it. Every congratulation and good wish still.

DHL

2005. To Martin Secker, 31 May 1920

Text: MS UInd; Postmark, Taormina 1 6 20; Secker 27.

Fontana Vecchia, Taormina, Sicily
31 May 1920

Dear Secker

I haven't heard from you lately. Have you got that MS. from Seltzer?

I had a letter from him. He says Alec Waugh wants to buy 500 sheets of the *de luxe Women in Love*.[2] Have you any objection to that? I suppose it wouldn't affect your public edition.

Can't I get the *Lost Girl* serialised in England? It would also be a safeguard against prosecutions, and it would bring me some money. I think I shall try.

I have got ready the MS. of my *Studies in Classic American Literature*. Do you want it, or have you enough on hand? I think you have. Shall I not try with it elsewhere?

I have begun another novel.[3]

DHL

Everybody cries out that *The Lost Girl* is so much better title than Bitter Cherry. More selling, I'm sure.

[1] DHL wrote in his diary on 31 May 1920: 'Cashed 1290 Lire (Seltzer) at Orlandi: sent Duckworths £10 to bank – burned Cath. Carswells £50' (Tedlock, *Lawrence MSS* 90).

[2] Seltzer was proposing a 'sort of private edition' of *Women in Love*, in 2 vols. at $15 (see Letter 2012).

Alec Waugh (1898–), himself a novelist, was reader for the publishers Chapman & Hall (of which his father, Arthur Waugh, was managing director); he was also an acquaintance of Douglas Goldring (see Nehls, ii. 42) who may have drawn his attention to DHL's difficulties in publishing the novel.

[3] *Mr Noon.*

2006. To Amy Lowell, 1 June 1920
Text: HU; Damon 538–9.

Fontana Vecchia, *Taormina*, Sicily
1st. June 1920.

My dear Amy

My landlord, a young Sicilian, is coming to Boston to be a cook, so he is bringing you this letter and this little ricordo.[1] He is Francesco Cacòpardo, called Cicio, and his address c/o Mr William B. Rogers, Potter and Rogers, 3 Doane St., Boston, Mass. His young wife Emma is coming with him. I like them very much. He speaks good English.

I wonder if you are well – fear you aren't. I wrote you three months ago about the cheque for 100 dollars which you sent me for New Year, but I have no answer.[2] The bank wouldn't cash the cheque – I haven't had it at all. I hope you stopped it at your bank, so that it is not just swindled away.

I have been very busy here at Taormina, and have finished a novel which I hope may get serialised, and then I shall be quite well off. Secker is to do it in England. He will also do *The Rainbow* again, and *Women in Love*, the sequel to *The Rainbow*. In New York Thomas Seltzer, of 5 West 50th. Street, is doing a limited edition of *Women in Love*, 2 vols., 15 dollars – he says. I shall tell him to send you a copy, and I hope you'll like it, because I consider it my best novel. – Seltzer will also, I suppose, do the new novel *The Lost Girl*; but I want to get this serialised first, perhaps in *The Century*, which Secker suggests.

We went to Malta, and it was so hot I feel quite stunned. I shouldn't wonder if my skin went black and my eyes went yellow, like a negro's. The south is so different from the north. I believe morality is a purely climatic thing.

The bougainvillia creeper is bright magenta, on the terrace here, and through the magenta the sea is dim blue and magical, summer-white. Nearly all the strangers have gone from Taormina, we are alone with the natives, who lie about the streets with a sort of hopeless indifference. Here the past is so much stronger than the present, that one seems remote like the immortals, looking back at the world from their otherworld. A great indifference comes over me – I feel the present isn't real.

The corn is already cut, under the olive orchards on the steep, sloping terraces, and the ground is all pale yellow beneath the almonds and the vines. It is strange how it is September among the earth's little plants, the last poppy falling, the last chicory flower withered, stubble and yellow grass and pale, autumn-dry earth: while the vines are green and powerful with spring sap,

[1] 'souvenir'.   [2] See Letter 1940.

and the almond trees, with ripe almonds, are summer, and the olives are timeless. Where are we then?

We love our Fontana Vecchia, where we sit on our ledge and look far out, through the green, to the coast of Greece. Why should one travel – why should one fret? Why not enjoy the beautiful indifference. Earnestness seems such bad taste, with this coast in view.

But Frieda is a bit scared of the almighty sun. She hankers after Germany, after the Schwarzwald – fir-trees, and dewy grass. She makes plans that we shall go north to Baden in August, for a couple of months. But I don't know. It costs so much, to travel, and is such a horrible experience nowadays, particularly in Italy.

We send you two bits of Taormina work. The women sit in the streets all day long, and do it. It is what the loom was to the pagan women, Penelope or Phaedra. Only the pagan women were indoors in some upper room, while these women sit together in the street, week after week, year after year. In the south there is no housework: no one knows what a Hausfrau is. Soup is boiled at evening, when the light fades. While the long day lasts the women sit with their frames in the street, dark, palish, intent, rather like industrious conspirators, working and talking: a wee bit sinister, as pagan women always seem to me sinister.

The brown strip, Frieda says, is for a dress or coat or something: the cushion is amusing. I wonder how many hours of Taormina life they represent. The women are Greek here – not Italian: lean and intense. The coast is all Greek – Naxos buried just below us, Polyphemos' rocks in the sea way down.

Well, I hope your health is good, that's the chief thing. Your garden will be gorgeous now. We both send many good wishes: [. . .] Remember me to Mrs Russell.

D. H. Lawrence

I send you a copy of my play. Seltzer will send you another copy, which you can give away.

2007. To Thomas Seltzer, 1 June 1920
Text: MS UT; Postmark, Coolidge Corner Jul 12 1920; Lacy, *Seltzer* 10–11.

Fontana Vecchia, Taormina, Sicily
1st. June 1920

Dear Seltzer

I received your letter yesterday, with the two drafts in Lire on the Credito

Italiano, Messina, representing twice $50. For the same, many thanks, they come very nicely.

I wrote to Secker about the sheets of the limited edition of *Women in Love* for Alec Waugh. If he objects, then we can't go forward with it. I will send a cable when I hear from him. – I hope by now he has really got the typed MS. from you. – I should very much like to have *proofs* of *Women in Love*, to correct them: but realise the horrible delays of the post. If you could post them on a ship coming direct here, I would get them back as soon as it is possible. – But if you think the delay would be too great, send me the proofs all the same, so that I can see them.

Secker said he thought he could get the new novel serialised in *The Century* in America. That would be a great protection for the other books. Secker prefers the title The Bitter Cherry, but I think my original *The Lost Girl* is better. *The Century* would have the option of the two.

I am sending this letter by hand, by the young Sicilian who owns this villa, which I rent.[1] He is a cook, and is coming to be *chef* to some Americans in Boston. He sails with his young wife from Naples on June 11th. I shall try to send a copy of the MS. of *The Lost Girl* by him; if only the typist has finished it.

We have just come back from Malta, where I went to see a friend. It is glaring hot. My health is quite all right. People like to exaggerate my delicacy. I am perfectly well, only too sensitive to shocks and influences.

I hear from Robert Mountsier in Paris, that he is returning soon to New York. He may get down to Taormina: hope he will. You will see him in New York.

Am looking forward to *Women in Love*.

D. H. Lawrence

Cicio's address in America (my landlord's, that is) is:

Francesco Cacòpardo, c/o Mr William B. Rogers, Potter and Rogers,
                    3 Doane Street, *Boston*, Mass.

I have just heard from Secker that he has not yet received the typescript of *Women in Love*. This is really annoying. You have said so often you were sending it.

Does nobody speak the truth? – I shan't send any MS. of *The Lost Girl* to America till that is settled about *Women in Love*.

DHL

---

[1] Ciccio Cacópardo posted this letter on 12 July 1920 (evidence from the postmark).

2008. To Irene Whittley, 2 June 1920
Text: MS UT; Postmark, Taormina, 3 6 20; Unpublished.

Fontana Vecchia, *Taormina*, Sicily
2 June 1920

Dear Mrs Whittley

I had your letter yesterday – so you are still in Battersea. We had been away to Malta for 10 days – it's not so very far from here: and it was so hot, so tremendous the sun, that we are still quite dazed.

Railway fares are an abominable swindle. I always travel second in Italy. – except for the 2 or 3-day journeys, when really, unless one has a sleeper, it is misery. But that is owing to the *length of time*. If you *did* come out, if I were you I should go London to Paris Third class – Paris to Rome *train-de-luxe* with sleeping berths. Then from Rome on, 2nd. class. – From Rome here is about 22 hours. If you come here, you can stay in this house with us – plenty of room. – But when will Whittley have his holiday? It will be *so* hot in August and September, and dry as a desert. We may go north then. If we do, we might meet somewhere in North Italy – much nearer for you. – It would be fun if you came and stayed here. But you'd be able to do *nothing* but laze the whole day away, and go to the sea in the evening to bathe. The sun is a monster even now. One dodges into the shadow as if one had been bitten. If only you had had time, your father might have got you berths on a tramp steamer, to Naples or Palermo or Malta.

Frieda wants to go to Germany again in the autumn. But we shall see. I don't think I shall come to England this year – though you never know.

The train de luxe leaves Paris on Mondays, Thursdays and Saturdays at 2.0 p.m., and arrives Rome at 8.10 p.m. on the following day – via Modane, Turin, Genoa, Pisa. – Stay a day in Rome. – Then Rome 7.40 p.m. – Taormina 2.37 next day – p.m. You can come 2nd. all the way if you break your journey in Turin and Rome, and sleep the night there.

We'll think about it all. We might meet on the Swiss-Italian Lakes – on Maggiore for instance. Why not? – so much nearer you.

Frieda sends many greetings.

DHL

We really might meet on the Lago Maggiore, and F's mother might come down there too. Good idea! It will be so hot here.

DHL

Has Whittley no hope of escape from that bank? Do you still sing? Who is in the Tregerthen cottages? – Mrs Murry is still in her consumption – back again from the Riviera, but not better.

I've quarrelled with Murry finally – told him he was a dirty little worm.

2009. To Rosalind Baynes, [2 June 1920]
Text: MS UN; Nehls, ii. 45.

Fontana Vecchia, *Taormina*, Sicily.
2 June.

My dear Ros.,

We went away to Malta, and were away nearly a fortnight: it isn't very far from here – sail from Syracuse. It was rather wonderful: but so *hot*, that we were quite stunned and dazed, and haven't quite got over it yet. – And therefore I think we shall sit still for some time now: not move this month. Where are you going, in the mountains? – near Florence? – Vallombrosa way? Where do you want to go, for the sea for Bridget for winter? Why not come here? I can find you a house, and Taormina is simply perfect in the winter.

We too love our house – it is so cool and high and beautiful. I was thankful to get back from Malta. Frieda wants to go to Germany in the early autumn. But why go so far. We might meet her mother on the Lago Maggiore, which is nearer – and then see you. We will make sure of a meeting in autumn – and you decide on your coming here for winter, and I'll find you a house now – not to fix you, that is, but just have it in one's eye.

If we come up north, I'd like to go to Venice for a little time. It's the one town I've not seen, that I'd like to see.

There'll be nothing to do here now but to aestivate – sort of summer sleep. But I want to get some work done, earn some money.

I was terrified Clifford Bax might turn up here – feel I couldn't bear to see him.[1]

How are your 2 heroes in England?[2] What news of them?

You've been quite at home, all your family with you. – Wish we were having a tea-party together.

How much does it cost you to live in San Gervasio?[3] I find we spend *more* than in Hermitage.

When Frieda has recovered a bit, she will write: at present she is sun-dazed.

Are the three young graces all well?[4]

DHL

---

[1] The feeling may have been shared by Bax himself: at least, in a retrospective view of DHL (in *Some I Knew Well*, 1951, p. 122), Bax regarded him as an arrogant 'pseudo-Messiah'.
[2] Perhaps Rosalind Baynes's estranged husband Godwin Baynes, and 'Clive' (see p. 521).
[3] See p. 520 n. 2.
[4] Rosalind Baynes's three daughters Bridget, Chloë and Nan.

2010. To Thomas Seltzer, 5 June 1920
Text: MS UT; Postmark, Coolidge Corner Jul 12 1920; Lacy, *Seltzer* 11.

Fontana Vecchia, *Taormina*, Sicily.

5 June. 1920

Dear Seltzer

I have just been going through the complete MS. of my *Studies in Classic American Literature*. Huebsch has had the duplicate MS. for six months, and I have no definite word even now of his intentions. No doubt he is a little scared.

Therefore I shall offer the book to you, if I don't hear from him within the course of a month from now. Let me know if you want it. I should like these essays to follow *Women in Love*. Secker will buy sheets.

You can speak to Huebsch, and tell him what I say. I will write him also. You might cable to me. *Lawrence, Taormina, Sicily* is enough address.

Yours   D. H. Lawrence

2011. To Benjamin Huebsch, 5 June 1920
Text: MS UT; Unpublished.

Fontana Vecchia, *Taormina*, Sicily

5 June 1920

Dear Huebsch,

Useless to talk any more about Seltzer and *Women in Love*.

I have no word from you about Secker and Shestov – but that is also evidently a finished thing. He has sold sheets to the Robert Macbride people, without consulting either Koteliansky or me. I cabled him, and he said he refuses to deal with you. I told Koteliansky to act, and Koteliansky wouldn't. Out of this Shestov, for which I get nothing, am I to have all the annoyance?

Will you please send to S. Koteliansky, 5. Acacia Rd., St. Johns Wood, London, N.W.8. the cheque for the articles which have appeared in *The Freeman as soon as possible* – because he wants to go to Russia, and has no money.[1]

I want to settle about the *Studies in Classic American Literature*. Hearing nothing from you, I conclude you don't intend to print them. If I don't hear from you before the end of this month, I shall go elsewhere with the MS.

[1] See Letter 1980.

How long do you intend to allow *The Rainbow* to remain out of print? I
wish to know, as it interferes with my rights too.

Yrs   D. H. Lawrence[1]

2012. To Robert Mountsier, 7 June 1920
Text: MS Smith; Postmark, [. . .] 7 – JU. 20; Unpublished.

Fontana Vecchia, *Taormina*, Sicily.

7 June 1920

Dear Mountsier

Yours from London today. I was hoping to see you, and scouring round for
the vino spumante. – Now I shall have to write business.

   1.   I am sending MS. of the *Lost Girl* by my landlord, Francesco
Cacopardo, who is sailing from Naples on the 11th. inst. – White Star – to
Boston. I have told him to keep the MS. till he hears from me. But I gave him
your New York address, as I might cable him: *Send Mountsier.* You might

---

[1] Huebsch replied on 8th July 1920 (TMS LC) as follows:

Dear Lawrence,
    There are a number of things to be covered in this letter. First of all with regard to "Studies
in Classic American Literature" I am handing this to Mr. Seltzer, to whom you say you are
obliged to give the refusal of another book. I don't blame you for your course concerning your
American publishing arrangements, I simply think that your judgment is bad.
    As to "The Rainbow" your remark that its remaining out of print interferes with your rights
suggests that you are ill advised in this matter. Every one of your friends here approves my
course and they are bound to know better than you, who can only judge from a distance. In one
of your letters you say that you are going on with Duckworth rather than Secker about
republishing "The Rainbow" in England but after that Secker wrote as if you were ready to go
ahead with him, he to pay you royalty on such copies as I supply to him in sheets. I made a
satisfactory price and he is now examining the copy of the American edition. If Secker should
order a supply I may print enough additional copies to supply the American demand if it
proves practicable to continue the distribution here.
    I don't understand the relations between Secker and Koteliansky and you and as the Shestov
transaction is closed so far as I am concerned, I am not going to try to understand them. While
I was negotiating with Koteliansky through you, Secker sells the American rights to someone
else. Meantime I use some of the material in The Freeman and naturally enough, offer
payment to the person who seems to have the right to sell it, namely Secker. If Koteliansky now
wants to collect, let him try to get the money from Secker. In view of this transaction and of
others that I am constantly having with Secker, it seems strange that he should say to you that
he refuses to deal with me.
    I am not sure that I acknowledged receipt of your articles on psychoanalysis. The articles
came and I am afraid that they are not available Freeman material. I suggest that you instruct
me what to do with the manuscript if I should not be able to use it in the paper or in a book.
    I expect to be in Europe, mostly in England, during late August and September and if you
should want to get in touch with me write c/o Curtis Brown Ltd. 6 Henrietta Street, Covent
Garden, London W.C.2. but with regard to the psychoanalysis manuscript any instructions
that you may send to this office will be observed. I expect to remain here until August 12.

write him for it. I want particularly to *serialise W[omen] in Love* in America. Secker said he thought he could arrange it with *The Century*. This is very important. See to it also.

Francesco Cacopardo, c/o Mr William B. Rogers, (Potter and Rogers), 3 Doane Street. *Boston*, Mass.

2.   My agreement with Seltzer is for *Women in Love* and the next book. Daniel made the agreement for *Touch and Go*: sold sheets, I suppose. For *Women in Love* I only get 10%, because Seltzer is doing it in a sort of private edition at 15 dollars (2 vol.). If he does it, I have promised him *The Lost Girl*, but at no fixed terms: that is to be decided. Beyond that nothing.

Seltzer writes that Alec Waugh has asked him for 1000 sheets of the private edn. of *W-in-L*. I have written Secker about this, and wait reply.

3.   My agreement with Secker is that he publish *Women in Love* and *The Rainbow*. He is waiting for a perfect copy of the former from Seltzer, who hangs on and won't part, curse him. For *W-L* and *The R*. I get £100 advance on royalties, each book: royalties 1/- per copy on the first 2000, 1/6 on the next 2000, 2/- after that – sale price 7/6 or 8/- net. I have also promised Secker the[1] option of 4 succeeding books, on the same terms. I do this because I want *The R*. and *W-in-L* published, and no one else will do them. – But for *everything* I keep all my American rights from Secker.

4.[2]   With Huebsch I have no agreement. He is very angry that Seltzer got *Women in Love*: but that was *Pinker's* fault. And once I had given my word to Seltzer, I had to keep it. – Huebsch has got the MS. of my *Studies in Classic American Literature*: has had it 6 months – and I can get nothing out of him about it. That is Huebsch all over. He may be 'the only white publisher in New York,' as his friends are continually writing me. But he is an unsatisfactory person, in that he doesn't reply to one's questions, is dilatory, and puts off paying till one really feels he never will pay. I have written to Seltzer telling him I shall offer him these essays if I can get the MS. from Huebsch – or if I get a definite word that Huebsch relinquishes. The only perfect MS. of these *Studies in C.A. Lit.* is the one I am finishing here. I want the print to be set up from this MS., not from Huebsch's. – I shall send this MS. to you direct to America – via England, I think.

Huebsch writes the *Rainbow* is out of print. He has had it out of print now for 6 months. If this is unnecessary on his part, and he persists, I can re-assume my rights over the book.

5.   The MS. of stories etc. I shall really have to collect and tabulate. Some

---

[1] the] four
[2] DHL misnumbered this paragraph '3.' and made corresponding errors in the two following.

are out wandering from Pinker still. Some suddenly appear in print and I know nothing of them. I will send all to you carefully indexed. Little Brown Co. of Boston did *The Widowing of Mrs Holroyd* (a play.). They wrote me they wanted to sell out, dispose of plates and sheets, as sale had more or less ended. I wrote to Seltzer to see if he wanted to buy these plates and sheets.

6. I had a letter from *Maurice S. Revnes, 10 East 43rd. Street, New York*, today, asking me to allow him to represent me in America for *film* rights.[1] This does not touch Literary rights at all. He asks for copies of all my works. – I shall write and tell him you will call on him and make an agreement with him, if you think well.

That's all the definite information, I think. For cables, *Lawrence, Taormina, Sicily* will always get me.

Now for opinions. *The Rainbow*, *Women in Love* and *Studies in C.A. Lit.* are all more or less 'dangerous.' I don't think a 'standard' publisher would handle them. Yet they are the works I set my heart on most – myself privately. My chief interest lies in them. I have to go softly and gently to get them properly published and established. If littler men like Huebsch and Seltzer

---

[1] Revnes wrote on 21 May 1920 (TMS UT) as follows:

My dear Mr. Lawrence:

Numerous English friends of mine have from time to time suggested to me your novels as having splendid material for the use in the making of motion picture plays.

It is for that reason that I take this opportunity to write you on the subject. As you perhaps already know American Film Producers are paying excellent prices for the film rights of novels and plays.

I personally not only represent a great many American Authors, Playwrights and Publishers in the sale of their work, but buy many stories for the films myself. And in spite of the fact that many English novels are not protected in this country by copyright I have numerous clients who are willing to purchase the film rights of English novels whether they are protected by copyright or not.

I should very much like to secure the film representation here in this country of your work, and I feel quite certain that I could obtain fairly good prices for the film rights to some of your material.

I devote all my time to the film business and do not in any way partake in any literary agency.

Should you desire references you are privileged to communicate with the Chief Editors of any of the big film companies here.

Should you agree to allow me to represent you in this country I would suggest that you mail me at once one copy each of your novels, short stories or dramatic compositions.

In looking after your film interests here I will agree to advise you by cable of any offer that I may receive for the film rights to any material you may send me.

I trust that it will be convenient for you to reply to my letter at any early date, I am,

Faithfully yours, Maurice S Revnes

Revnes wrote again, to Mountsier, on 13 November 1920 urging him to send 'the available Lawrence material' so that he could 'do something real soon'.

do them, I owe gratitude, up to a point. If Seltzer deals decently with me – as he has so far, save in withholding that typescript from Secker – then I don't mind if he is a Jew and a little nobody, I will stick to him. *I* don't really like Jews. But then I like still less the semi-gentleman, successful, commercial publisher, who is always on the safe side: Duckworth, Methuen, Chatto, all that crowd. They, *bourgeois*, are my real enemy. Don't be too sniffy of the risky little Jew. He adventures – these other all-right swine, no. Seltzer *may* do all well with me, and through me. Remember I am a *typo speciale*: you can't handle me like any other simple commercial proposition – J.M. Barrie or Hugh Walpole. I am different, and must approach the public rather differently.

I am going to order Duckworth to send you all my books. You can let this Maurice S. Revnes, the film agent, have them, if you agree with him.

Huebsch has published *The Prussian Officer*, *The Trespasser*, *The Rainbow*, *Look We Have Come Through*. – He wrote for *The White Peacock*, my first novel, but has said nothing about publishing it. It has not appeared in America.[1] Mitchell Kennerly did *Sons and Lovers*, but I don't know who has it now. – I put a list of my works on the back, in the order in which they have appeared (more or less).

Duckworth

The White Peacock (novel)[x]
The Trespasser (novel) – Huebsch, I think, now.
Sons and Lovers (,,) Kennerley
The Prussian Officer (Short Stories) Huebsch.
Twilight in Italy (Essays)[x]
The Widowing of Mrs Holroyd (Drama) Little Brown & Co, Boston.
Love Poems and Others (Poems)
Amores (Poems) – Huebsch, *I think*.

Look We Have Come Through (poems) – Huebsch. *Chatto & Windus*
New Poems – Martin Secker[x]
Bay (Poems – just out). C W. Beaumont, 75 Charing Cross Rd. W.C.[x]
Touch and Go (*Daniel*). – Seltzer.

The Rainbow (Methuen – suppressed) Huebsch.
Women in Love – sequel to *Rainbow* –. Seltzer doing it.
I take it you can get for yourself all the books of mine published in New

---

[1] DHL's memory was defective: *The White Peacock* was first published by Duffield in New York and by Heinemann, not Duckworth, in England.

York. I will order for you only *The White Peacock* and *Twilight in Italy* and *Love Poems and Others*. You must ask Huebsch what he is doing about those he has in consideration. Seltzer will have sent you *Touch and Go*, and I'll ask him to send you *Women in Love*. Or get proofs even from him. Meanwhile I'll try to rake together loose short stories.

I do hope I've remembered everything. I'll post this at once. Wish we'd seen you.

Yrs   D. H. Lawrence

2013. To Michael Sadleir, [7 June 1920]
Text: MS UT; PC; Postmark, Taormina 8 6 20; Unpublished.

Fontana Vecchia, Taormina
7 June.

Dear Sadler

Will you let me know about the story 'Wintry Peacock' – and if you had the MS. copied and sent to America, as you promised[1] – and how your magazine is going.[2]

Best wishes   D. H. Lawrence

2014. To Hilda Brown, [11 June 1920]
Text: MS Cotterell; PC v. Taormina – Fontana del Duomo; Postmark, Taormina 11 6 20; Nehls, ii. 45–6.

[Fontana Vecchia, Taormina, (Messina), Sicily]
11 June.

Very pleased to have your letter – We went to Malta, and found it when we came back. Malta isn't very far – about eight hours crossing over the sea from Syracuse, a smooth passage, but so hot, we gasped. It is cooler here now. All the corn is cut, practically, and they are making threshing floors to tread it out with the asses. We watch them from our terraces. The garden is drying up – but there are marrows and beans still – and little tomatoes. It is good to have such long sunny days. Sometimes we bathe in the sea. – But we often think of Hermitage, with all its flowers and woods. We shall come back one day. Mrs Lawrence sends her love.

DHL

---

[1] See p. 493 and n. 4.
[2] i.e. *The New Decameron* (see Letter 1927 and p. 474 n. 1.).

2015. To Compton Mackenzie, [11 June 1920]
Text: MS UT; Mackenzie 183–4.

Fontana Vecchia, *Taormina*
11 June.

Dear Mackenzie

I didn't write you because I didn't know if you'd gone – and no English address. This c/o Secker.

I hear this minute from Miss Wallace you are in Rome: so you are *en route*. How thrilling. With my mind's eye I see Nukuheva.[1] Ah God! Such a lovely sea here today, and a great white ship on the wind, making towards the South East. I'd give my fingers to be off. I read some of Stevenson. Idiot to go to Samoa just to dream and get thrilled about Scotch bogs and mosses. No wonder he died. If I go to Samoa, it will be to forget, not to remember.

I read $\frac{1}{2}$ of *The Lost Girl* in type – wonder how she'll seem to other people. It's different from all my other work: not immediate, not intimate – except the last bit: all set across a distance. It just came like that. May seem dull to some people – I can't judge.

Vanity Girl came yesterday[2] – have only just glanced at it. Mary is Hotel Bristol, Taormina.

Send thrilling news – *all news*.

DHL

Read Herman Melville's *Moby Dick*.

2016. To Martin Secker, 12 June 1920
Text: MS UInd; Postmark, Taormina 12 6 20; Huxley 508.

Fontana Vecchia, *Taormina*
12 June 1920

Dear Secker

Had your letter this morning. Damn and blast Seltzer for a liar. I sent him a letter by hand, by my landlord, who sailed yesterday to Boston to be a *chef* there. I told Seltzer I would not send him any MS. of *The Lost Girl* at all if he didn't keep this agreement about *Women in Love*. Every time he's written he's said he's sending the typescript at once – last time he said he had sent the book to press. – But he shan't have *The Lost Girl*, at this rate.

I will let him know about Waugh and sheets.

Presumably Mackenzie will be bringing you the original MS of *The Lost*

---

[1] See Letter 1343 and n. 4.
[2] Mackenzie's new novel, published in May 1920.

Girl. I had a wire from Rome yesterday about it. – I have the carbon copy, and am correcting it. There is not much to alter. Queer book it is. Being out here, I find it good – a bit wonderful, really. But when I get a sort of 'other people' mood on me, I don't know at all. I feel I don't know at all what it will be like to other people. Somehow it depends what centre of oneself one reads it from. – I wish I could get it serialised – in England too. One *must* make some money these days; or perish. To my horror it cost 1,348 Lire, typing – which I think preposterous.[1] – I sent a copy to USA with my landlord, but he is to hold it till I send him instructions. I will send you this carbon copy when you need it. Let me know.

DHL

If ever you want to wire, Lawrence, Taormina, Sicily is enough.

2017. To Ada Clarke, 12 June 1920
Text: MS Clarke; PC v. Carro Siciliano; Postmark, Taormina 12 6 20; Unpublished.

Sicily
12 June 1920

Had your p.c. this morning. So very thankful Pamela is all right – and a little girl![2] – wonder if she'd have liked a boy. – Mercy all has gone well. – Do wish you could both come out here for a time. Why don't you plan it for October – too hot till then – but why not then? I sent Jack a little 'Carro'[3] like this. – How are you yourself?

Love from us   DHL

2018. To Jan Juta, 13 June 1920
Text: MS UT; Unpublished.

Fontana Vecchia, *Taormina*, Sicilia
13 June 1920

Dear Juta

The photographs of the Wild Man of Borneo came this morning: very good they are: but my word, where will my reputation be, in the tender States, when he has reflected himself from the mirror of *Vanity Fair*?[4] Be that as it

---

[1] DHL wrote in his diary for 15 June 1920: 'Paid Miss Wallace 1360 Lire for typing Lost Girl: *too much*' (Tedlock, *Lawrence MSS* 90).

[2] DHL's sister Emily King had given birth to her second daughter, Joan Frieda.

[3] 'Cart' (as depicted on the postcard).

[4] See Letter 2002 and n. 2.

may, the woman shall have a copy at once: and can I get more from the man in Rome, case I need them?

Your Anticoli sounds *very* lovely, and I envy you the fountain and the flowers afresh.[1] Here the corn is cut, the almond trees below dangle their greenness featherily over a pallid stubble. All is dry and summer-still, suspended. The birds sing, however, strong, strange singing, in the early afternoon.

Yes, Cicio took the MS. – and Compton Mackenzie called for the other for England. Benissimo! Thank you for going to Wallace. That bitch charged me exactly 1348 Lire: which is exorbitant, even for a London expert, which she isn't.

My thoughts? – eh, carino, they'd make black writing, most times. – I've got two great big bottiglioni of good wine, down from the mountains, brought by Carmelo on his ass: 34 litres, 100 francs. We had a young *turkey* for dinner yesterday: Grazia[2] kindled the big oven, which is more like a cowshed than an oven: she puts blazing trees inside it, and hovers before the furnace like Beelzebub himself: and afterwards our young turkey, with potatoes in a pan, and it looked like a tiny boat under the dome of a hot black firmament, sizzling. But it was *very* good: 22 francs!!! Blame Frieda. – The almonds are ripe now, and we've had the first fat green figs. – All this in answer to your 'buon mangiare.'

Mary has gone with some cinematograph-filming people from the Bristol to climb Etna and peer down the crater. If she'll hop after Empedocles I'll write her an elegy.[3] At this moment she'll be among the lava on a mule – Deo volente. Whether she's already given her Twelve Pound Look down the throttle of Sicily, I don't know. – She's cut her hair. One day it thundered and lightened and was very Etnaish, and it got on her nerves all alone in the Studio, so she went and bobbed herself. Frieda says it suits her, but ever since, I can't bear the sights of her. It brings out all the pseudo-mannish street-arab aggressive selfish insolence, which affects me nowadays, as a male, like somebody throwing black pepper in my eyes. I plainly hate her. She began a novel on the strength of it: opened in studio, where lovely strange lady cuts her long black locks and is spied upon through one of the port-holes by a thrilled and enthralled young gentleman: 'nice young thing, quite young and *full* of enthusiasm, *full* of enthusiasm, and clean, hardly seen a woman before:

---

[1] Juta was living at 'San Filippo', Anticoli Corrado, Provincia di Roma where DHL visited him in mid-August 1920 (see Nehls, ii. 86).

[2] Ciccio Cacópardo's mother.

[3] Empedocles (493–433 B.C.), Greek philosopher, poet and statesman, is reputed to have thrown himself into the crater of Etna.

that kind of thing' (Quot.). – You see which way the minds of these elderly hankering bitches turns. – But I set my foot on that nasty worm of a novel, and killed it. – Conceit, hideous, elderly, megalomaniac sexual conceit, that's what ails these elderly scavenging bitches. If Etna had any sense of fitness he'd spit a fat mouthful of lava at her.

No news here: Taormina very quiet: the natives go dead without their foreigners, torpid, as if they were waiting to be wound up. Very little food procurable: insolent prices. – I stay most of my time in Fontana Vecchia, perched aloft. It is four oclock – Sunday – festa – a pale sea, summer white and soft, Calabria glimmering exquisite like a chalcedony – hens cackling – the landscape silent and asleep – fireworks threatened for the evening.

I hope, before you leave Anticoli, we may pay you a little visit. Who knows. Frieda gets a Heimweh for Germany – wants to go in early autumn. Chi saprei.[1] I feel, there are many things to say, which somehow we always avoided when you were here. Perhaps one day we'll say them – perhaps never – God knows whether it matters, anyhow. – Now Cicio is gone, it is very quiet down below here. – Bowdwin hasn't come yet. The Bristol porter has left – a little fool anyhow. Kitson leaves about 25th.[2] Did I tell you I had a tussore silk suit in Malta: £6.: very elegant. Magnus called it pongee, which sounds much less elegant. –

                                                                            DHL

Insole had my word about his tea-cloths: the woman says they will be done end of *this* month. – No sign of purple silk.

2019. To Martin Secker, 17 June 1920
Text: MS UInd; PC; Postmark, Taormina 17 6 20; Secker 28.

                                                                     Taormina.
                                                                    17 June. 1920
Dear Secker.

Thanks for your letter: Seltzer must wait for an answer about those sheets: am very much annoyed with him for not letting you have the MS.

You will have seen *The Lost Girl* by now. Let me know what you think of it, and if you think it will serialise. I have a copy by me: will send it if necessary. It is fully corrected, and with the few alterations in the actual text: only in one

---

[1] DHL's phrase is meaningless. He may have intended to write 'Chi saprebbe' : 'Who would know?'

[2] Robert Hawthorn Kitson (1873–1947), amateur water-colourist and expert photographer. Educated at Shrewsbury and Trinity College, Cambridge where he was offered a Fellowship but refused it. He lived in Taormina from 1900 until his death, except for absences during the Abyssinian and Second World Wars. (See *Times* obituary, 25 September 1947.)

place I have made a serious change – about two pages.[1] But that is serious.

I am just finishing a little book 'Education of the People', which Stanley Unwin asked me for last year: about 30,000 words.[2] Have you any objection to my offering it to him now? Let me know at once, about this.

Who was paid for those Shestov articles in *The Freeman*? Koteliansky *must* have that money. I feel already he has been done out of the £50. which Huebsch offered, and he needs it badly. Huebsch wrote him (Kot.) about having settled about those articles with *you*. But Koteliansky must[3] have that money. – Can't you buy out that Shestov at a decent figure, and have done with it. I find it very irritating. If Huebsch offered £50., why can't you?

DHL

2020. To Marie Hubrecht, 21 June 1920
Text: MS Young; Unpublished.

Fontana Vecchia, *Taormina*, Sicily
21 June 1920

Dear Miss Hubrecht

I have both your letters: the one of the 14th. this morning. Now I expect you are in England – and soon you will be in Norway. I suppose one carries one's own self wherever one goes. But one undergoes a metamorphosis also.

We waited for further news of your nephew; – now I understand we are not likely to see him. Mary sits quietly on in the studio. She has already paid the three months rent to Ciccio, so that is settled. Thank you all[4] the same, for a variable Etna wind that you are. I will see to it the blankets are put away with naphthaline. Mary's plan is to leave at the end of July, for Florence: and to spend the next winter on the French Riviera. Mrs Hansard plans to open an English library at Cannes. I suppose that will be quite a little centre. English people tend to move out of Italy into France, it seems.

Bowdwin has not turned up. Kitson is the last of the migrants: and he leaves on Wednesday. We have been to see him, and he seems quite nice, but no more than that. Wood of course remains: but him I don't know.

We have had beautiful days here. Once it rained quite heavily, and made the almond trees and vines bright green. Generally it is sunny, with a cool wind. The corn is all reaped and piled in bundles ready to be trodden out. The grapes are growing big. The first figs are ripe, and abundance of apricots and

---

[1] See Letter 2022. This is rather misleading; the corrections were far more extensive than DHL suggests: see *The Lost Girl*, ed. Worthen, pp. xxxiii–xxxiv, xxxviii.
[2] See Letter 1691 and p. 323 n. 2.
[3] must] would
[4] MS reads 'all all'.

cherries and yellow peaches. I am so glad the fruit has come: and cheap now, comparatively: apricots 80 c. al Chilo, cherries the same, figs 1.25.

The gardens are very dry – particularly that steep slope at Rocca Bella. The gardeners water the plants, without much effect. Only the blue plumbago is beautiful. – They have been blasting away some of the rock in the garden, near the road.

I wonder what to say of your vision. The bull has always been the symbol of generative power, since the world began: and the rose the symbol of fulfilment and the soul's expansion.

What will you think of the north? Blond, blond people, with the fair hair coming keen from the tanned skin, like ice splinters, and the physique sudden and sharp like foam, and eyes blue like water, and like sky, they have a great fascination for me. Sometimes one gets a desire, like a *thirst*, to go north. But not yet. I want to stay here yet.

Frieda talks of going to Germany in August. It all depends on circumstances. In any case we should come back here in October. Perhaps we shall stay on, right through. We are nearly always alone. Now Ciccio has gone Fontana Vecchia is deserted, we have it to ourselves. But there is the constant come-and-go of the peasants on the little road behind, the many goats stepping down the hill, the asses coming slowly, and processions of girls with great bundles of bright corn on their heads. So the peasant life threads almost through our fingers, perhaps the best of it. This frail streaming contact is what I like best: not to know people closely.

We had Mrs Hansard's book *The Tavern* – not very good, I think – I wish I did think it good.

We had dinner last night at the Bristol (it was Sunday). Then we sat on the tower, and looked down the coast – a small moon inland – Etna almost clear – lights on the shore, and continual fireworks splashing and cracking. I find that coast always wonderful, always magical. Your Rocca Bella is dark and sombre, waiting for an inhabitant. The pillars stand attentive in the night.

Frieda sends her greetings. I hope you'll love Norway.

Yrs.   D. H. Lawrence

2021. To J. C. Squire, 24 June 1920
Text: MS YU; Unpublished.

Fontana Vecchia, *Taormina*, Sicily
24 June 1920

Dear Squire

I've just done a little book 'Education of the People', about 30,000 words, for Stanley Unwin. It is 12 chapters, some 2,500 words each: quite amusing.

Think you might publish 2 or 3 chapters in your *London Mercury*?[1] If so, send
me a line quick and I'll let you have the MS. Plenty of kick in it, and *Mercury*
might profitably stub his toe: or try to: he flits so easily so far. – If not, send me
a post card will you.

Yours   D. H. Lawrence

2022. To Martin Secker, [24 June 1920]

Text: MS UInd; Postmark, Taormina 24 6 20; Secker 28–9.

Fontana Vecchia, Taormina
24 June

Dear Secker

I cant send you carbon copy, because I've sent it to Hubert Foss, asst.
editor of *Land and Water*, who said *The Queen* would like to see it for
serialising.[2] If you urgently need this carbon copy, *for serialising purposes*,
Foss will yield it up to you: I'll cable him. But it would be very good fun if *The
Queen* would serialise me. The American copy of the MS. I'm keeping low, in
Boston: Seltzer the swine shan't have it: I could cable it to be sent to *Century*
people any moment.

I enclose copy of the only long serious alteration in *The Lost Girl*. It comes
in the chapter where Alvina meets *Cicio and Mr Tuke* at Leeds, and Alvina
talks to Cicio – Chapter XI – in the hotel at night. The opening words are as in
original.

If the *Queen* is having the book, get this MS. from Foss and make all the
changes in your MS – It'll save proofs. – *Land and Water*, Windsor House,
Breams' Buildings, EC4. – But the *Queen* is only a chance.

DHL

Cicio is usually spelt Ciccio – short for Francesco. Think it matters?[3]

Let me know about those Education Essays quick.

2023. To Maurice Magnus, [ante 25 June 1920]

Text: Douglas Goldring, *The Nineteen Twenties* (1945), p. 205.

[Fontana Vecchia, Taormina, (Messina), Sicily]
[ante 25 June 1920]

[Lawrence told Magnus by letter that Goldring liked Magnus's *Memoirs of
the Foreign Legion*.][4]

[1] (Sir) John Collings Squire (1884–1958), editor of *London Mercury* (see p. 452 n. 1), did not
     accept DHL's offer.
[2] DHL's diary for 23 June 1920 reads: 'Sent carbon copy of Lost Girl to Foss, Land & Water, for
     the Queen' (Tedlock, *Lawrence MSS* 91). The novel was not serialised in the *Queen*.
[3] See Letter 2088 and n. 2.
[4] See p. 480 n. 4.

2024. To Cecil Palmer, 26 June 1920
Text: MS SIU; cited in Moore, *Intelligent Heart* 267.

Fontana Vecchia, *Taormina*, Sicily.

26 June. 1920

Dear Palmer,

I got your letter, dated December 31st, this morning. All things come to him who waits.

The *Studies in Classic American Literature* I finished revising ten days ago. They make a book about 70–80 thousand words. Secker wants me to sell the book[1] to America and he will buy sheets for England. I had rather it were set up in England: but am negotiating with America.

I warn you that publishers are a bit shy of the book. But if you *seriously* think you might print it, I will send the MS. Because I have fixed nothing yet.

What is Collings doing nowadays? I've seen nothing of him for ages.

Hope you flourish.

Yrs   D. H. Lawrence

2025. To Amy Lowell, 26 June 1920
Text: MS HU; cited in Damon 540.

Fontana Vecchia, *Taormina*, Sicily

26 June 1920

My Dear Amy

I had your letter with 100 dollar cheque three days ago: am very sorry about the cheque: wish you hadn't sent it again, but just cancelled the old one.[2] – They robbed you: plainly robbed you. But the banks always do it. The Lira is up again, so I only got 1550 for the 100 dollars: but still *I* make, while you lose. Too bad. A while back I should have got 2500 Lire for 100 dollars. – I hope my affairs are going to come right before long: time they did: then I shall be able to help others, instead of being helped. Meanwhile, – touch wood! – I think I'm all solvent for the next year – according to my prospects.

So you are a Doctor by now: of Divinity I nearly said![3] And Shall one address you as Doctor Amy Lowell? – and 'My dear Doctor –'? Well well – all titles seem to me comical: even Mr. and Miss and Mrs. I like my stark name best.

---

[1] the book] them
[2] See Letter 1940. DHL recorded in his diary, 20 June 1920: 'Recd. cheque 100 dollars from Amy – cashed for Lit. 1525. at Orlandi' (Tedlock, *Lawrence MSS* 90).
[3] By a jocular allusion to a well-known song in Gilbert and Sullivan's *Pirates of Penzance*, Act I, DHL refers to the conferment of the honorary degree of Litt.D. on Amy Lowell, at Baylor University, Waco, Texas, on 16 June 1920.

I wonder if Ciccio has arrived in Boston, and sent you the bits of Taormina work and my letter. You might even see him one day: he is a dear, so is Gemma. I'll tell you the romance of them. – Gemma and her family, with 1000 other refugees, were shipped down here from the Venetian province when the Austrians broke in. She was with her mother and nine brothers and sisters, barefoot, with nothing but a blouse and skirt, penniless. Ciccio fell in love with her: female half of Taormina enraged, for Ciccio's rich and speaks 3 languages. One irate woman attacked Gemma and tore the blouse off her back. The Mottas – Gemmas family – viewed Ciccio with wild suspicion and said he was going to make poor Gemma his concubine. Still they refused to believe he was married. So this time, before he left for Boston, he went up to the Veneto with his wife, and my heart, she was rigged up: silk stockings, suède shoes, georgette frock: she who had never worn a hat in her life till Ciccio bought her one: propria contadina.[1] I wish I could hear how the visit to San Michele went off. I hope you are well and happy, mon cher Docteur.

D. H. Lawrence

2026. To Jessica Brett Young, 26 June 1920
Text: MS UT; Unpublished.

Fontana Vecchia, *Taormina*
26 June 1920

Dear Mrs Brett-Young

We had your card yesterday: had wondered what was become of you. Sorry F[rancis] was ill: hope he's better. Of course it would be just like him to go and be ill[2] if you were tripping off a bit. Heard also of Mackenzie's departure[3] – but nothing in particular.

We sit here in the hot and cool. You heard of our exploit to Malta. My God, it was hot: that island like a bare and white-hot bone. Valletta harbour is wonderful: wonderful at night: call sometime and look at it, it is worth seeing: but never maroon yourself on that island of British beneficence and snobbishness.

Mary is in her studio. She went up Etna a fortnight ago, on mule-back, with a cinema-filming man and wife who were at the Bristol. They travelled for about 36 hours on end including departure from here: Mary's mule fell down with her: she sat in a gorse-bush: was so cold she fainted: and so on, and so on. She was like a dropped tea-cup, all in bits, when she got back. Now she

---

[1] 'a real peasant girl'.
[2] ill] if
[3] Mackenzie had gone to England in early June.

is stuck together again. – She leaves at the end of July, for Florence: Vallombrosa for a week or two – and then to find a little house with a friend on the French Riviera: Nice, Cannes. – Her programme. – Next year she's going Round the World

> 'Round the world if maybe
> And round the world again
> With a lame duck, a la-ame duck –'[1]

Taormina is very quiet, all the vim gone out of it with the departure of the foreigners. We slop about half dressed on our terraces. It is never too hot in the house and on this verandah: but walking is the devil. The corn is all cut and gathered in on the slopes below: and on the left, near that little barny place, they are treading it out with oxen. I suppose you are seeing just the same, living just the same, at Anacapri. We hardly ever get down to the sea to bathe.

Fruit is in, thank goodness: apricots (in Sicilian *crapoppi*) 70 and 80 al chilo: marvellous cherries, 80; figs 80 and L1.; peaches, not very many; tomatoes and cucumbers: thank goodness there is fruit, for there[2] isn't a great deal other stuff. New almonds in the garden, and grapes big. With abundance of fruit, and tomatoes and cucumbers and marrows and spinach, with a bit of meat twice a week, we get on very well. I've got two huge bottiglione of dark and powerful wine, down from the mountains: 100 francs worth. See me bibbing away.

Frieda wants you to do something. If ever you are in Capri, will you buy for an aunt of mine a tortoise-shell comb to stick in her hair at the back, dark tortoiseshell, nice, fairly simple. Mary says she got nice ones for about 25 or 28 francs, in that shop opposite our house. But you can see. Price doesn't matter, to a few francs. You might ask the shop to pack it for post, and you address it to Mrs F. Krenkow, The Hawthorns, *Quorn*, Leicestershire. F. promised the comb – never kept the promise – and impossible to get one here. – Then send me the bill. – Don't do it except when it is convenient and pleasant. – Post the thing 'registered letter.'

Do you get mosquito-bitten? We do: tigers they are, winged rattlesnakes.

Imagine that that woman Wallace charged me L1,360 for typing my novel: With the exchange at 60! Bitch.

You might come some time and have Mary's studio for a month: *such* a nice studio and garden: 125 a month. Perhaps we'll be moving north some time

---

[1] (Sir) Henry Newbolt (1862–1938), 'The Old Superb' (*Songs of the Sea*, 1904), chorus ['. . . if need be . . . lame duck lagging all the way'] (set to music by (Sir) Charles Stanford).
[2] for there] but so

before long. F. talks of Germany. If we come north at all we shall halt in
Capri: nice to see your Fraita. – Expect to be here for the winter.
 Do you see Mrs Di Chiara?[1] I owe her a line. What gossip afoot?

DHL

 You wont mind if I don't send the money now. It will be simpler when I
know what it is. – Do you want any 'roba Taorminese – ? –'

2027. To Michael Sadleir, [27 June 1920]
Text: MS UNCCH; PC; Postmark, Taormina 28 6 20; Unpublished.

Taormina
27 June.

Dear Sadler

 I had your card and a letter from Hovey both this morning[2] – my letter also
June 10th., which is real quick, for once. – I asked him to send the money
here, changed in New York if the exchange is good. I may as well have it
Italian. – I have an account at the Law Courts Branch of the London County
Westminster Bank, 263 Strand – when you pay me for the story, *minus the
typing and post*, you might pay it in there, for quickness and safety.

 Thanks for doing this for me: 250 dollars, nearly 4000 Lire today: a
windfall!

 Am curious to see your new magazine.

Yrs   D. H. Lawrence

2028. To Martin Secker, [28 June 1920]
Text: MS UInd; Postmark, Taormina 30 6 20; Secker 29.

Fontana Vecchia, *Taormina*
28 June.

Dear Secker

 Have your letter – sorry about Shestov. He may start later.

 Glad you have *some* MS. of *Women in L.*

 You can get the carbon copy of the new novel from Hubert Foss, *Land and
Water* – as I said in my last letter – and make corrections. They aren't many.
But I dreamed I had a very friendly interview with Queen Victoria; – so
there's hope in *The Queen* yet.

---

[1] Anna di Chiara, an American whom DHL had met in Capri.
[2] Hovey bought 'Wintry Peacock' for the *Metropolitan Magazine* for $250 (Tedlock, *Lawrence
  MSS* 91).

Round the world in the *Lavengro*.[1] Of course I see myself off!

If you think *The Century* might serialise the novel, they could have the copy which is in America:

> Sig. Francesco Cacopardo. c/o Mr. William B. Rogers,
> Potter and Rogers, 3 Doane St. Boston, Mass.

I'll cable Francesco if you let me know.

Send me more news. Don't bother, my star is rising all right.

DHL

I've got a rather amusing photograph of a portrait-sketch of myself, which Jan Juta made of me two months ago. Do you want one?

2029. To S. S. Koteliansky, 29 June 1920
Text: MS BL; Zytaruk 212.

Fontana Vecchia, Taormina
29 June 1920

My dear Kot

Your letter, with Secker's £5., today. Bad luck about Shestov: but he will start to sell later. – I have burnt your cheque: consider you owe me £5, if you like, but refrain from paying me till later on. I have sold a story for dollars 250: and have plenty of money. I should like to lend you £10. now: would you mind if I sent a cheque? you *must* be badly off. But you are so beastly high-handed. Say if you will let me lend you the £10. Don't be tiresome about money.

Ach Gilbert! Murry! all the wet little Schweinerei. Can't be bothered.

No news: it is extremely hot here: we lounge about half clad, but feel limp. Sea-bathing seems to make one hotter afterwards.

Frieda wants to go to Germany in August or Sept. – we must see if it can be managed – doesn't matter much anyhow. I have a horror of trains this hot weather, particularly Italian ones.

Do tell me if you are hard up. You have too much respect for money. What does it matter, so long as one gets along. I can't take anything seriously any more.

DHL

---

[1] The ketch in which Mackenzie and DHL were proposing to make a voyage to the South Seas; see Letter 2031. Mackenzie was staying with Secker and clearly the matter had been a topic of conversation; Secker was opposed to 'the South Sea plan' (Mackenzie 185).

2030. To Marie Meloney, 30 June 1920
Text: MS ColU; Delany, *DHL Review*, ii. 198.

Villa Fontana Vecchia, *Taormina*, Sicily.

30 June 1920

Dear Mrs Maloney[1]

I have your letter of 22nd June forwarded from Duckworths today: am sorry I can't meet you to talk about publishing. Is there anything one could write in a letter? – or are you coming to Italy?

Yours Sincerely   D. H. Lawrence

2031. To Compton Mackenzie, [30 June 1920]
Text: MS UT; Mackenzie 184–5.

Fontana Vecchia, *Taormina*

30 June

Dear Mackenzie

The *Lavengro* of course thrills me to my marrow. Yes, I'd sail the Spanish Main in her. How big was Drake's ship? Is she steam as well as sails? How many men do you consider you'd want to run her? I pace out her length on the terrace below. – Is she a pure pleasure yacht? – She sounds narrow in the beam – though I know nothing at all about it.[2] I suppose she's pretty. Why, one could soon learn to be an A.B. oneself, or at least $\frac{AB}{2}$.[3] And one could be one's own steward, and a good bit of one's own cook. If ever I have any money I'll go whacks in her – running her.[4]

For it's westward-ho, to Trinidad.

Don't believe Duckworth: he's an old woman.[5] One only needs guts: and his are nothing but lard. We've only one life: best live it.

London sounds sickening as ever. Curse their strikes.[6] I hate Labour and Capitalism and all that frowsty duality in nothingness. What a pity I haven't got a bit of money. I shall have some, you'll see, before long.

---

[1] Marie Mattingly Melony (1883–1943), editor of *Woman's Magazine*, 1914–20; of the *Delineator*, 1920–26; and of the *Sunday Magazine of the New York Herald Tribune*, 1926–43. m. William Brown Meloney.

[2] Mackenzie gives full details about the boat he considered 'the perfect craft for the South Seas': see Mackenzie 184.

[3] i.e. able-bodied seaman, second class; or, perhaps, half an able-bodied seaman.

[4] i.e. I'll share the cost of running her.

[5] Gerald Duckworth, the publisher (a fellow-member with Mackenzie of the Savile Club).

[6] There were several strikes in London (bus, train, printers, etc.) during May and June 1920; they culminated in a motion (which was defeated) for a general strike, at the Labour Party Conference on 23 June.

You can sell Capri. Anybody can have Capri.

I'm glad she's not called the Bible in Spain.[1]

> 'Round the world, if need be
> And round the world again –'

If you *do* buy her, then I beg you, send me a book where I can learn all about sloops, yachts, clippers and frigates, clewlines and bowlines and topsle gallants, ensigns and mizzen fore-peaks and so on, for I feel it's a question of becoming sea-born.

I shan't pray, because I believe Jesus is no good at sea. But I'll invoke Aphrodite and Poseidon and Dionysos, and keep my eye on the Mediterranean.

DHL

2032. To Martin Secker, 5 July 1920
Text: MS UInd; Postmark, Taormina 6 7 20; Secker 29–30.

Fontana Vecchia, Taormina, Sicily.

5 July 1920

Dear Secker

I had your wire this afternoon – so glad you like the novel. It was nice to have your wire.

I am dying to hear about the *Lavengro*. If M[ackenzie] asks me to go, I shall go. My wife will probably stay in Germany. – But perhaps it is no purchase.

If you haven't changed the second £50 into Liras, don't do it. The *Metropolitan Magazine* are sending me dollars 250 for a story, perhaps in Lire. And if we should go away –.

I do want *The Lost Girl* serialised in America, if not England. Carl Hovey of *The Metropolitan* is *very* sweet to me. And Schofield Thayer, of *The Dial*, 152 West 13th. Street, New York having heard a novel was finished, has written asking me to let him serialise it.[2] But they the *Dial* pay smaller. – American post here is hopelessly slow: English bad enough. I am anxious to know if[3] *The Century* is still a possibility. If not, these other two are possible.

---

[1] DHL plays on the fact that George Borrow (1803–81) wrote *The Bible in Spain* (1843) as well as the work of picaresque adventure, *Lavengro: The Scholar, the Gypsy, the Priest* (1851). MS reads 'call'.

[2] Scofield Thayer, editor of the *Dial*, had already accepted 'Adolf' and 'Rex' (see p. 536 and n. 1); he did not serialise *The Lost Girl*.

[3] MS reads 'of'.

Do let me know. And *you* write to Francesco and tell him where to send the MS., and I need only cable him one word (when it is decided, that is). – You have the address of the american MS.

        Sig. Francesco Cacopardo, c/o Mr William B. Rogers,
           Potter and Rogers, 3 Doane St., Boston, Mass.

Damn this slow post.

                                      D. H. Lawrence

Hope the carbon copy has arrived by now. – Have you got *all Women in Love?*

2033. To Compton Mackenzie, [8 July 1920]
Text: MS UT; PC; Postmark, Taormina 9 7 20; Mackenzie 185.

                    [Fontana Vecchia, *Taormina*, (Messina), Sicily]
                                            8 July.

Am dying to hear about the *Lavengro*. Hope it's a go.

I've got a *very good* book from America about the Marquesas Islands – *White Shadows in the South Seas*, by Frederic O'Brien – published by the Century Co. It gives a real impression of the Marquesas as they are now: I'll send it you if you like: also Gauguin's *Noa-Noa* which is Marquesas too.[1] O'Brien's book published last year, but written presumably 1913–14. Best thing I've read of late year travels. Say if you'd like it.

It is hot here, but I don't mind – I wish we could sail away, away from Europe. F[rieda] talks of going to Germany in August: but I shan't.

                                            DHL

Expect a letter every day from you.

2034. To Martin Secker, 10 July 1920
Text: MS UInd; Postmark, Taormina 10 7 20; Secker 30.

                                 Fontana Vecchia, *Taormina*
                                         10 July 1920

Dear Secker

Cecil Palmer wants me to send him the MS. of the *Studies in Classic American Literature* – says he wants to publish them. Seltzer wants to do them in America. – shall I send Palmer the MS.? – Is he any good? Or would you rather have sheets from Seltzer. – Tell me at once.

Also Seltzer asks for the MS. of *The Lost Girl* at once, as he wants to

---

[1] See p. 505 and n. 1.

publish in *Early Autumn*. What about that? The MS is in Boston, as you know.

I wish I heard from you – no letter – neither from Mackenzie. Has he bought the *Lavengro*? What is doing? – Post is bad again.

Yrs   D. H. Lawrence

Magnus is going to send you his *Legion* MS. I thought it awfully *good*.

2035. To Thomas Seltzer, 10 July 1920
Text: MS UT; Postmark, Taormina 10 7 20; Lacy, *Seltzer* 12–14.

Fontana Vecchia, Taormina, Sicily
10 July 1920

Dear Seltzer

Your letter of June 21st. today, with cheque for Lit.240. on account of the article in the *Evening News*: and many thanks.[1]

I heard from Secker he has received the first half of *Women in Love*: for which thank goodness. Hope by now he has got the second half.

I just had a cable from him also – '*Lost Girl* excellent, greatly pleased', it says. He has just got the MS. and read it. – I am trying to get it serialised in England, perhaps in *The Queen*.

Secker said he thought he could get *The Century* to serialise *The Lost Girl* in America. If that were possible, it would be a shield against all possible prosecutions, I should think. I am waiting to hear from Secker. English post here is now *abominable*. Italy is the devil of a country for business. – I expect the MS. of *The Lost Girl* will be in Boston by now: Ciccio took it some three weeks ago. I gave him your address with *The Century*s also, and said I'd cable him. You would like *The Century* to serialise, wouldnt you? Anyhow Ciccio's address is:

Sig. Francesco Cacopardo, c/o Mr. William B. Rogers,
Potter and Rogers, 3 Doane St. Boston. Mass.

When I hear from Secker – curse the post – I will wire Ciccio: either to send to you or *The Century*: with request to the latter (if they enter) to communicate with you. – I had a letter from Schofield Thayer asking me[2] to let him see *The Lost Girl* for *The Dial*, for a serial. I had a *very* nice and friendly letter from Carl Hovey, of *The Metropolitan*, accepting a story of mine which had been sent to him from London, through a friend – and asking

---

[1] The article in the *Evening Post Book Review* was 'The Poetry of the Present' already published in *Voices* and in *Playboy* (see p. 387 n. 3).
[2] me] him

me for more. – He might just possibly serialise. We ought to be able to do something.

I had funny letters from Huebsch about *Women in Love*: couldn't understand quite what you and he had been agreeing. I think he must be angry.

About *Studies in Classic American Literature*: I've just had a letter from Cecil Palmer asking me to let him publish them in England. I can't quite make up my mind. Secker wants to wait for American Sheets. – I don't *think*, myself, that Huebsch will do them. I wrote to him saying that unless I heard definitely from him *this month*, I should offer them to you. They have none of them been printed in America: The first eight essays were printed in *The English Review*, November 1918–June 1919 – long enough ago for them to be fresh for America. – The essays on Dana, Melville, and Whitman have never been published. But 'Whitman' would not do for a periodical. The earlier essays are the best for magazines. If you print the book, wait for a *revised* 'Whitman'.

I am glad you bought *The Widowing* –[1]

Hope this letter reaches you in decent time.

Compton Mackenzie was bargaining for a yacht to go to the South Seas: and was going to ask me. I very much doubt if it will come off. But if it should, I suppose we should call at New York, I think he would cross the Atlantic direct. Then I should see you. – Meanwhile it's very hot here.

I shan't do anything about publishing in America – save periodical stuff – without writing to you first and having your answer. I shall trust to you to tell me what you are doing with my work, exactly. Then we can get on. But I don't want you to feel at all hampered by me. If there is anything of mine you don't care for, say so without bothering.

Stanley Unwin asked me to finish a little book 30–40,000 words – 'Education of the People' – of which I showed him a sketch 2 years ago. I will let you see this also.

I got the six copies of *Touch and Go* this morning: many thanks.[2] Amusing it looks.

Have you sent me proofs of *Women in Love*?

Yrs   D. H. Lawrence

I have begun another novel – amusing it is.[3] But oh, the days are so hot just now – one lounges them away.

---

[1] See Letter 1990 and n. 1.
[2] Seltzer had published the first American edition on 5 June 1920.
[3] *Aaron's Rod* (begun in 1917).

A friend of mine, Robert Mountsier, is returning to New York just now from Paris, and I am asking him to look after my business a bit. He is not a literary agent – no agent of any sort – journalist. Perhaps you know him. – Curtis Brown bothers me to join him.[1] I see he acts for you. But I don't want professional agents any more.

2036. To Robert Mountsier, 12 July 1920
Text: MS Smith; Unpublished.

Fontana Vecchia, *Taormina*, Sicily.

12 July 1920

Dear Mountsier

I have been waiting for ages for an answer to my last letter to you, which I sent registered.

Two or three days ago I received *Noa-Noa*, *The Moon and Sixpence*, and *White Shadows in the South Seas*, from America. I guess you ordered them for me: and very many thanks for them. Gauguin seems to me a bit snivelling, and his mythology is pathetic: *Moon and Sixpence* not bad, but forcé: the third book very good, excellent, I am so glad to have read it, though it nearly broke my heart. To think what has become of Melvilles beautiful Typee! A million curses on European civilisation. It is collapsing, and it deserves to collapse. I spit on it.

Compton Mackenzie wrote me that he was negotiating to *buy* a yacht – 154 tons – *The Lavengro* – in which to sail the high seas. He was afraid of costs. But if he purchases he may ask me to go with him. And if he does, I shall go and F[rieda] will probably stay a few months in Germany.

Anyway I shall keep you informed. I wish I heard from you. A thousand thanks for the books – particularly for *White Shadows*. Do you know anything of Frederic O Brien? – a bit of a liar but an interesting person.

DHL

2037. To Jessica Brett Young, 13 July 1920
Text: MS UB; Sagar, *Review of English Literature*, vi. 98–9.

Fontana Vecchia, *Taormina*

13 July 1920

Dear Mrs Brett Young

A thousand thanks for sending the comb. I hope you didn't curse us for

---

[1] Albert Curtis Brown (1866–1945) began his career as a journalist with the *Buffalo Express* and the New York Press; he owned the Curtis Brown Newspaper Syndicate in London, 1898–1915. He became managing director of Curtis Brown Ltd in 1916 and built it up into one of the largest literary agencies in the world. m. Caroline Louise Lord, 1890. See his memoir, *Contacts* (1935). (See *Times* obituary, 25 and 27 September 1945.)

bothering you. It sounds very nice, the one you sent, and not at all costly.

The photographs of the Fraitani are very nice: F[rancis] just striding over into fame and immortality, so to speak. As for your 'Leaves from my past', the screen question is under consideration; 'Madame Jessie Brett Young'. You're nothing but Signora now – which is a comedown.

I had a letter from Mackenzie, and he was 'buying' (indef. participle) a yacht called *The Lavengro*. But that's three weeks ago, so the yacht may have been bought, sunk, salvaged and sold again by now. I've heard no more. I wish he'd buy her, and invite me to sail the Spanish and other Mains with him. In a little yacht, minus the cinematographing concomitants, I'd just love it. And Frieda¹ wants to go to Germany: and they advise my *not* going. And we had a wonderful book an American sent me, about the Marquesas. If we come up to Capri I'll bring it you.

For the rest, poco. Secker says he likes *The Lost Girl*. I am trying my head off to get it serialised, for the sake of the 'oof' – but no answer yet. I'm working with ever-diminishing spasms of fitfulness at a novel which I know won't go forward many more steps. It's like when you feel your motor-car breaking down – you poke its vitals and proceed 100 yards – then all u.p.

Mary leaves on the 22nd., going direct to Florence for Vallombrosa. Our plans are still indefinite, feel I can't come to any decision. In this climate one's very psyche is like a jelly that won't set: flux, flux, invariable flux: mind you don't spill it. – I feel a bit myself as if I'd been spilled out of my old jug, and can't quite pick myself up. – E don' know where 'e are. –. Many greetings, Fraitani, from the old fountaineers.

DHL

I hope 30 francs covers it.
Did you pick the capers, or let them flower?

2038. To Jan Juta, [16 July 1920]
Text: MS UT; Unpublished.

Fontana Vecchia, Taormina
16 July

Dear Janino

Poor darling! But the scirocco distresses me, on your account, more than the love affair.² I hope the throat etc is better. As for the American ladyette, all is vanity, on your part. If you weren't a beau garçon, and if you didn't know it, and if you didn't so *enjoy* being sweet and complaisant like anything, why,

---

¹ Frieda] Francis
² The lady in question may have been Elizabeth Humes; see Letter 2187 and n. 1.

they'd never love you. But just wire her 'Enough of this slop-doodle.'

Again many thanks for the photographs. They haven't come yet.

I am ordering you *The Peacock*. That damned Beaumont shows no signs of life – *Bay*. I'll give you the MS. – Did you have *New Poems* from Secker? If not I'll order them for you. – I'll give you the new novels when they appear. Secker wired '*Lost Girl* excellent – greatly pleased.'

Mackenzie hasn't written lately. Still I *might* go with him. – Failing that, F[rieda] wants to go to Germany in early August. Should we meet at Montecassino about 2nd or 3rd.? – and stay a day or two˙with you at San F[ilippo]? Fun. Then we'd go on. If I go north at all, I want to meet two friends, man and wife,[1] at Milan, about Aug. 18th.: make a little walking tour behind Como and Iseo and Garda: Get to Venice about Sept. 1st, and wait there for Friedas return. Sounds wildly extravagant: but when I'm alone I'm a gnat of economy. Do you know any *rooms* in Venice – where one needn't feed on the premises. I want a room only. Do tell me quick quick if I can find out. – We'd all be at Venice: too lovely. I must be cheap.

Write *at once*, post so bad.

Tell Insole cloths here, paid for, 480 francs. I have sent lace to Réné, which she asked for, in big linen envelopes, registered letter-post: cost about 5 francs a time: quite safe.

Send your letter espresso – last took 8 days.

Hope you're well.

Great fun meeting again.

Mary leaves on 22nd. for Vallombrosa: and if we're in Venice, she'll appear.

Tell Insole what fun!

                                                                    DHL

That's right, paint heaven and earth. My heart, the elbow grease! Slap at it – bull at a gate, and devil take the hindmost.

I'll post the cloths if Insole sends the addresses.

2039. To Irene Whittley, 16 July 1920
Text: MS UT; Unpublished.

                                        Fontana Vecchia, *Taormina*, Sicily
                                        16. July 1920

Dear Mrs Whittley

I reply at once to your letter.

There is just a possibility that I might be going to America in the early

---

[1] The friends were Percy and Irene Whittley (see the letter following).

autumn, and that would quash all other movement. But it is only a bare possibility, and not a probability. – Let us keep it in reserve.

Frieda wants to go in August to Germany: political weather permitting. In that case I should come north with her, and would meet you in Milan on the 18th. or so: and we would make a little walking tour from Lake Como to Lake Iseo and Garda, keeping within the Italian frontier: and then on to Venice from Verona. Would that do? Are you strong enough to walk with a little knapsack, and camp by the way? I heard from your mother you had pains in your back. I hope they're better.

We should have to be economical. We'd travel 3rd. Class for short journeys: that's cheap. We'd carry a spirit kettle and little saucepan, and a raincoat: fun it would be. – Bring *only* hand luggage, that you can keep in the carriage with you, and which will *lock*. Watch it like blazes. Bring as little as you can make convenient – one nice dress for town, one knock about. In Venice I'll try and get rooms, not an hotel or pension so that we can make our own breakfasts and lunch – and only get dinner out.

It will be awfully jolly – but don't count on me definitely until August 1st. or 2nd., when I will have settled my movement and Frieda's. She may be in Milan to see you: or she might be gone to Germany, and join us all in Venice. I will let you know finally by August 1st., even if I telegraph. A telegram here needs only: Lawrence, Taormina, Sicily.

I believe the Newhaven–Dieppe route to Paris is as quick as the other, and cheap. *Don't* change Italian money at Cook's: not more than £1.'s worth. – Bring 1 lb tea:½ lb each is allowed; and butter in a tin, if possible: nothing else. – Cook isn't very good nowadays. Be *firm* with him. – I came Charing X. 8.0 a.m. – Folkestone–Boulogne dep. 1.40 (thereabouts): arrive Paris 5.30 p.m. or so: take a taxi or any cab to Gare de Lyon (fare about 3/6: they'll take English silver gladly: 4/- or 5/- at most) – eat at the Gare de Lyon – (upstairs they give dinner, downstairs cold meat and beer etc) – leave 9.30 p.m.: arrive Modane about midday next day – frontier – luggage inspection and passport – they won't bother you at all. You can eat in Modane station restaurant – leave Modane about 3.0 – arrive Turin (Torino) about 7.0 – change, and arrive Milan (Milano) at about midnight – where I hope I'd be at that crowded station.

More anon.   DHL

The Italian for porter is facchino – pronounced as you know, fakēeno. At Turin you just say to any porter 'Milano' – and he'll take you to your train at once – say prima classa or seconda classa – and there you are. They are perfectly sensible.

At Folkestone and at Modane, let the porter take your luggage *at once*, you

take notice of his number: then you follow him when you can get through the
passport squeeze, to the customs – mere formality both at Modane and the
French port – but such a squeeze: tell the porter your class – deuxième or
première, whichever it is, so that he can get your seat: or at the port, one of
you get the seat.

If by any chance Germany and everything is off, we might meet you in
Rome, and come on here by stages: *Naples*: by sea to *Palermo*: then to *Taormina*.
Travelling second, it wouldn't be so dear: and here in Taormina I think we
can give you a lovely large studio with a big garden, all to yourselves. It would
cost no more than the northern trip because here would cost you *nothing at all*.
– Would that do?

DHL

One tips a porter about 1 franc for each bag: not more: one Lira in Italy.
I suppose you'll get your passports quickly: with French and Italian visés.

2040. To S. S. Koteliansky, 17 July 1920
Text: MS BL; Postmark, Taormina 18 7 20; Moore 633.

Fontana Vecchia, *Taormina*, Sicily
17 July 1920

My dear Kot

I had your letter two days ago, with the renewed cheque for £5. I am very
glad you are a rich man, and sorry I gave you the trouble of re-writing the
cheque. I cashed it in the village at 65.

I hope your Gorky book will have a success.[1] As for the Shestov, wait, he
will start later. It is not all over.

Here it is hot, too hot to do anything, save at morning and evening. Frieda
has promised to go to Germany in August: and I shall go north, to some
friends near Rome, then on with them perhaps to Venice – return here in
October. All this is yet indefinite. But I think we shall move in about a
fortnight's time. Summer is so long and dry, and already the leaves are falling.
– Though I am reluctant to move even so short a step nearer to the 'world'. –
I thought there *was* some sort of peace with the Bolshevists. – Think of a
Garsington-tea-party Bertie[2] pronouncing on Lenin! Pfui! – What *kind* of
realism is real nowadays – particularly on Gertler's part? – But I am limp and
misanthropic with a belly-ache today.

Vale.   D. H. Lawrence

[1] Gorky's *Reminiscences of Leo Nicolayevitch Tolstoi*, translated by Kot and Leonard Woolf, was
published by the Hogarth Press in July 1920.
[2] Bertrand Russell.

2041. To Thomas Seltzer, [18 July 1920]
Text: MS UT; Postmark, Taormina 19 7 20; Lacy, *Seltzer* 14.

Fontana Vecchia, *Taormina*, Sicily
18 July

Dear Seltzer

I hear from Secker he has written to Boston to have MS. of *The Lost Girl* sent to *The Century*. I have written to the *Century* asking them to communicate with you. If they don't accept for serialising, I wish you would let Hovey, of *The Metropolitan*, see the MS. – and then Schofield Thayer, of *The Dial*, if the *Metropolitan* turns it down. I'm sure the best thing is to be serialised in an important periodical.

I have begun another novel: such a queer mad affair. – Secker says he is *enthusiastic* about *The Lost Girl*.

Yrs   D. H. Lawrence

2042. To Robert Mountsier, [18 July 1920]
Text: MS Smith; Postmark, Taormina 19 7 20; Unpublished.

[Frieda Lawrence begins]

Fontana Vecchia

Dear Mountsier,

So we shant see you – it would have been fun seeing you here in Taormina – You ask about Germany? It was a great shock, finding it all so dilapidated, so *down* in the mouth – Germany that I had known with its bands and brass and spurs, it is strange to have known a thing like German militarism from your childhood and then find it gone *utterly* gone – It's gone for ever of that I am sure even if it still kicks a little now and then – The thing is gone. It's been an *experience* to the Germans a terrible one, let's hope they profit, to England it's not been a *vital* experience – Of course I only stayed at Baden-Baden with my mother – We went to see the old Grandduchess of Baden a remarkable old unbroken woman, the emperor's aunt she is[1] – I could tell you a lot I heard and saw – The French seem really fiendish in their victory, I suppose they had suffered and revenge is sweet – But they are very petty and stupid – I heard many stories from refugees – To our great joy we got your books, – The book on the South seas broke one's heart – how those people are dying out, the war seems not much in comparison – Tell us something of what you saw. Perhaps we shall meet, but where? On the island Rananim I hope –

[1] Louise, wife of Frederick (1826–1907), Grand Duke of Baden, and aunt to Emperor William II (1859–1941).

I am sorry it was not a 'Wiedersehen' this time –

Frieda Lawrence

[Lawrence begins]

18 July.

Wonder where this will find you. – No news of South Seas.

The MS. of *The Lost Girl* has been sent to *The Century*, on appro[val] for serialising. If *Century* turns it down I tell them to hand MS. to Seltzer, and I have asked *him* to hand it on first to Carl Hovey of *The Metropolitan*, who is very friendly to me, and after that to Schofield Thayer of *The Dial*, if the *Met.* is no go.[1] See to it for me if you arrive in time.

Hoping to hear from you.

DHL

2043. To Martin Secker, 18 July 1920
Text: MS UInd; Postmark, Taormina 19 7 20; Secker 31.

Fontana Vecchia, *Taormina*, Sicily.
18 July 1920

Dear Secker

I have your letter of 12th. I don't mind if you publish *Lost Girl* before *W[omen] in L[ove]*. But if there is a chance of the *Lost Girl's* being serialised, I must take it. I haven't heard yet if Foss has received the MS. I sent him. I want *The Queen* to see it.

I take it you have already written to Cacopardo and to the *Century* about the MS. that is in America. – Assure me of this. I am writing to him at once. Did you send him the *Century* address?

Yes, I have another novel in hand. I began it two years ago. I have got it $\frac{1}{3}$ done, and it is very amusing. But it stands still just now, awaiting events. Once it starts again it will steam ahead.

Let me know about Cecil Palmer and the *Studies in Classic American Lit.* at once, please.

I got very excited about Mackenzie and the yacht and the South Seas. But now it all seems in abeyance.

Frieda has promised to go to Germany in August. I shall probably wander about – Rome, Florence, Venice, for some 2 months – returning here in October. I will let you know. Probably we leave here Aug 1st.

---

[1] Mountsier faithfully carried out DHL's commission but each editor rejected the proposal in turn (see Letter 2092 and *The Lost Girl*, ed. Worthen, pp. xxxiv–xxxv and n. 96).

Seltzer wired me that he had sent complete MS. He also is very keen to publish the *Lost Girl* in 'the Fall'.

Yrs DHL

2044. To Douglas Goldring, 20 July 1920
Text: MS UNM; Huxley 508–9.

Fontana Vecchia, Taormina, Sicily
20 July 1920

Dear Goldring

I had your *Reputations* this morning: find it very witty and amusing.[1] God, it is time those stuffed geese were carved: the old stagers, and semi old-stagers. In the end, I suppose I shall have you hacking at me, for an old bird.

So glad to hear of you out of town, eating raspberries and spitting forth venom and other profitable matter. We are still here: I live in pyjamas, barefoot, all day: lovely hot days of bright sun and sea, but a cool wind through the straits. We do our own work – I prefer it, cant stand people about: so when the floors must be washed (gently washed merely) or when I must put my suit of pyjamas in the tub, behold me *in puris naturalibus*, performing the menial labours of the day. It is very nice to shed so much. It is wonderful to be able to pass the days anyhow, without having to resist the weather and the elements. I find that in England one spends so much of ones time merely holding out against the inclemency of the days: not to speak of the soul-stiffening one must perform, against a legion of windy-watery fools.

So you are getting quite rich. Good! I do hope you are taking it out of the mouth of the Murrys and Walpoles[2] of this world. I am creeping on in my own measured way, cook and the captain bold, etc.[3] But even we have a little bit more than usual.

Hence it is going to be busted. Frieda wants to go to Germany. It is still inhospitable to foreigners (so they say). Therefore she goes alone. And I shall

---

[1] Goldring's *Reputations: Essays in Criticism* was published in June 1920. *TLS* (10 June 1920) found it 'not so much about books as about men who write books . . . Generally, he is better at finding fault than bringing out merit . . . he is more at home with the personal than with the creative side of the literary life.' H. G. Wells, Mackenzie, Bennett are discussed, among others; Goldring reviews DHL's 'Later Work' on pp. 67–78 (see Draper, ed., *Critical Heritage*, pp. 136–40.)

[2] (Sir) Hugh Seymour Walpole (1884–1941), novelist and critic. His most recent novel was *The Secret City* (1919); it dealt with the 1917 revolution and was awarded the James Tait Black Memorial Prize.

[3] DHL's allusion is to Sir W. S. Gilbert's 'Yarn of the Nancy Bell' in *The Bab Ballads* (1869). Cf. *Letters*, i. 293 and n. 3.

move about Italy, seeing one person and another – Suppose we shall be back here in early October or Sept: leave in about two weeks time.

I finished a novel *The Lost Girl*. Secker's got it, and is enthusiastic about it. 'I am quite sure of your future.' What Jehovah is this squeaking. I am trying my head off to get it serialised – trying *The Queen* first. Secker rather put out. – He's going to hold *Women in Love* and *The Rainbow* till this book is out: spring, I suppose. Oh God, the dribblers!

I shall send you a *poste restante* address. So glad you are flourishing like a green bay tree[1] – and making wreaths for other people.[2]

2045. To Percy Whittley, [21 July 1920]
Text: MS UT; PC; Postmark, Taormina 22 7 20; Unpublished.

Taormina.
21. July.

I think it will be all right for the north Italy trip. My wife is preparing to go to her mother. We shall probably leave here about August 2nd., stay with friends near Rome for ten days or so, and meet you in Milan on the 18th. – or whichever day you arrive. Then we will be all four together in Milan for a day or two, after which F[rieda] will go north, and we will go to Como – or wherever we decide. Bring a few bits of toilet soap, and bring me two tubes of Kolynos tooth-paste – and perhaps better have with you a yard or two of mosquito netting: especially if mosquitoes trouble you.

If you arrive in Milan on the 18th., that would be a month today. I have asked my sisters to send a few trifling things for you to bring to me: quite quite tiny. You'll have to open the parcels, because of customs.

My next address is
          presso il Sig. Jan Juta, San Filippo, *Anticoli-Corrada*,
                    Prov. di Roma. Italy.
Write me there: expect we shall be there Aug. 4th. to 14th.

Au revoir.   DHL

2046. To Rosalind Baynes, [22 July 1920]
Text: MS BucU; Nehls, ii. 46–7.

Fontana Vecchia, *Taormina*
22 July

Dear R[osalind]
    Your letter this morning – sorry you won't come here – could have found you a house, very nice.

---

[1] Cf. Psalms xxxvii. 35 (A.V.).   [2] The MS is incomplete.

Mary Cannan (Mrs Gilbert Cannan, once Mrs J M Barrie) – is coming to Florence today – she's been here 5 months – came from Capri with us. She is staying at the Pension Lucchesi, on the Lung Arno della Zecca. You might see her, if you feel like it, and hear all news of Taormina. On 1st. Aug. she is going to Vallombrosa – Hotel Panorama. – I give her this letter to post in Florence.

F[rieda] thinks of going to Germany second week in August. Where will you be, in the mts.? I might come and see you – I shall come north, I think, but shan't go out of Italy. Give me your address at once – and I might meet you about end August.

Give me also address of those rooms in Venice,[1] and tell me how much they cost. I might wait in Venice for F.'s return, in Sept. – both come on here again end of Sept.

It isn't at all unbearably hot here, in the house.

Perceval is here for 1 month.[2]

Write at once, post is so slow.

DHL

2047. To Robert Mountsier, 23 July 1920
Text: MS Smith; Postmark, Taormina 23 [. . .] 20; Unpublished.

Fontana Vecchia, *Taormina*, Sicily.
23 July 1920

Dear Mountsier,

I have your letter of July 19., from Paris, this morning. This I post to New York.

I think Mackenzie is a swindle. Doubt if he will leave England, much less buy a yacht.[3]

Why did Germany make you so disgusted? Of course Frieda is angry. But anyhow, I am not going there. I don't suppose I shall leave Italy this year – but may spend August and Sept. in the north.

For business: I have already written Seltzer and Huebsch about you.

1.   The Cacopardo MS. of the *Lost Girl should* have been posted to *The Century*, in New York, for their approval for serialising. They have orders to refer to Seltzer. I will tell them by this post that you are entrusted. I want *The Lost Girl* serialised if possible. *The Metropolitan*,

---

[1] Venice] Florence
[2] Deane Perceval was the first Secretary of the British Institute of Florence, 1919–22.
[3] Though eventually DHL proved right, Mackenzie recalled that during July he 'made great efforts to raise the money for [*Lavengro*]' (Mackenzie 185).

Carl Hovey, very friendly: also Schofield Thayer of *The Dial* – also
Benet, of the *Evening News*, is it?[1] Secker is enthusiastic about *The
Lost Girl*. He has sent his MS. to the printer: wants to publish[2] in
Autumn. But I have sent a copy to *The Queen*, London, and want them
to serialise. There is no answer from them, whether they have received
MS. or not. Post here, for MS. particularly, seems abominable. I shall
post letter-post to you. Had a wire from Seltzer that he also wants to
print *Lost Girl* in early autumn. But I want it serialised, if possible.
Presumably *Women in Love* is about ready. I want to see *proofs* of this
book, even if Seltzer does not wait to have them corrected.

2. I think we can definitely ask Huebsch for the *Studies in C. A. Lit.* I
    promised Seltzer that MS. It is good as it stands, but I want to send a
    revised version of the last essay, the essay on *Whitman*. Tell me what
    you think of Seltzer. After *The Lost Girl*, I am under no contract with
    him. No contract at all with Huebsch.

3. Seltzer has bought *Widowing of Mrs Holroyd*.

4. I want you to enquire rigorously after *Sons and Lovers* in America. I
    can get no news of it. You know Kennerley had it, and I had nothing
    from him.

5. I am doing another novel.

6. This Story 'Fanny and Annie', will you have it typed, and if possible
    get it published simultaneously in England and America. In England
    The Strand, *Nash's*, *The English Review* print me – but there are
    others.

    The *Metropolitan* will no doubt take the story – and you can take
    expenses of typing from their cheque.[3]

7. I have done a History of Europe, for Secondary Schools, which the
    Oxford University Press is issuing. I await revised proofs, which I
    shall send you. The Oxford Press does not, I think, touch USA, but
    takes Canada and Colonies: my agreement says nothing of USA: have
    written enquiring.[4]

8. I want you one day to see Huebsch's books – his account books.

9. Cecil Palmer, London, asked me for MS. of *Studies in Classic Am. Lit.*
    Am deliberating whether to send or not. If I send, you will hear from
    him.

---

[1] William Rose Benet (1886–1950), American journalist and poet, was associate editor of the
     Literary Review of the *New York Evening Post*, 1920–4.
[2] publish] print
[3] If Mountsier followed DHL's instructions, they led to nothing. See Letter 1738 and n. 1.
[4] No American edition of *Movements in European History* was ever published.

About ourselves.
1. An agent, as you perhaps know, takes ten per-cent. Shall we agree to the same?
2. Shall I order all publishers to make payments to you, in your name?
3. Or shall I have an account in a bank in New York, and have drafts paid direct into it, and send you a cheque?

If you ever have to cable, Lawrence, Taormina, Sicily is enough.
Here's to you, in red Etna, since there is no Asti.

D. H. Lawrence

I send you a photograph: use it if you think good, but if it is printed anywhere, see that Juta's name is printed underneath '(from a portrait sketch by Jan Juta)'.

Fontana Vecchia, *Taormina*, Sicily
23rd. July. 1920.

I wish Robert Mountsier to act for me in all matters literary, dramatic, and cinematograph, in the United States of America, and hereby empower him to do the same, subject to my approval of his acts.

This agreement is to be null from the moment when either Robert Mountsier or I, D. H. Lawrence, hands in a written declaration that he wishes to withdraw from the agreement.

D. H. Lawrence
David Herbert Lawrence[1]

2048. To Cecil Palmer, 23 July 1920
Text: MS Smith; Unpublished.

Villa Fontana Vecchia, *Taormina*, Sicily
23 July 1920

Dear Palmer

I am sending you, then, the MS. of *Studies in Classic American Literature* – Because of irregularities of the post, I send the later essays here as registered Letter. That which was printed in the *English Review* I send as printed matter, separate. I send you a list of chapters. See they are in order.

First and foremost, I want you to do something for me. Have the essay on

---

[1] This formal letter of authority was written on a separate sheet.

Whitman typed out – it is the last essay – and post it at once to
          Robert Mountsier, 417 West 118 Street, New York.
Then send me the bill, and I will post a cheque by return. Please do this for
me.

     Then as to publishing. I am under contract with Secker. I have written to
tell him I am offering the book to you. But if he insists on my withdrawing, I
must withdraw from you. I don't suppose he'll insist.

     If you publish, I want you to give me 15% on the first thousand, 20% after,
and no advance on royalties. If the book sells a thousand, it will sell several
thousands. Let us see.

     I have practically settled the publication in America already.

                                                           Yrs   D. H. Lawrence
Change my mind, and send you the complete MS. as registered letter.
Anything else is too uncertain.

2049. To Percy Whittley, [30 July 1920]
Text: MS UT; Unpublished.

                                        Fontana Vecchia, *Taormina*, Sicily
                                                              Friday 30 July.
Dear Whittley

     As far as one can be certain of anything, we shall be leaving here on
Monday Aug 2nd. for Anticoli, where we intend to stay till about Aug. 12th. I
suppose you have had my letter and post card: I have no letter from you.

     Write me at once to Anticoli, and tell me if you are coming. I will meet you
in Milan, or wherever you decide: give the date and hour when you will arrive,
and I'll be at the station to meet you. If at the last minute there is any change,
you can wire Post Restante, Milan – or wherever it is.

     If this letter is very late, you might send a wire to Anticoli to say if you are
coming or not. The post address is
          presso Signor Juta, San Filippo, *Anticoli-Corrada*, Prov. Roma.
for a telegram, just
          Lawrence, San Filippo, *Anticoli-Corrada*, Rome.
See that the post office understands that the destination is Anticoli-Corrada,
not the town of Rome.[1]

     If you come to Milan, Frieda and I will both be there to meet you. Then
she will go on to Germany.

---

[1] What appears to be the text of a telegram is written cross the top of DHL's MS: 'Lawrence,
     San Filippo, Anticoli–Corrada, Prov. di Roma Arrive Milan Sunday [15 August] mid-night.
     Await your hotel. Whittley'.

I wonder what the exchange is! Being a banker, you will know: and you might buy cheaply in London. The last they gave me was 66.

Bring a pound of sugar, in case there is an absence of it. And bring 2 lbs tea – 1 lb each is allowed – in $\frac{1}{2}$ lb packets (don't put it all in one bag).

Also bring me 2 pairs cream woollen socks.

Also if you happen to bring a bottle of Carlsbad or Kruschen salts, just as well.

It has been *very* hot: cooler now, thank heaven. If you have got white duck suits, bring them: but anyhow, bring some sort of flimsy jacket, and thin trousers.

Would you mind sending a post card to my sisters to say if you're coming. Mrs Clarke, Grosvenor Rd, Ripley, nr Derby. and Mrs. King, 480 Main St., Carlton, Nottingham.

There are big clouds in the sky, and I can't tell you how thankful we are to see them.

I hope there won't be strikes and revolutions.[1] Anyhow we can dodge through them.

Shall be glad to hear definitely from you.

DHL

2050. To Jessica Brett Young, [30 July 1920]

Text: MS UB; PC v. Siracusa – Anfiteatro; Postmark, Taormina 30 7 20; Unpublished.

[Fontana Vecchia, *Taormina*, (Messina), Sicily]
30 July

Hope you had letter, cheque, and book – all sent some time since. We are going north on Monday – Aug 2nd. – for a fortnight to friends: presso Sig. Juta, San Filippo, *Anticoli-Corrada*, Prov Roma – afterwards F[rieda] to Baden, I to wander – May stray to Anacapri. It's been awfully hot: clouds today, thank Goodness. Heard from Mackenzie: no Pacific: but theatre Nottingham and C[ompton] M[ackenzie] dramatised right through.[2]

DHL

---

[1] Italy was currently suffering from a wave of strikes: a threat of a general strike was issued on 1 July; on 14 July there was a national tramway strike; gas and electricity supply workers were on strike in Rome, 16–27 July. The red flag was displayed in Rome and Milan: DHL was perhaps responding to its implications.

[2] Presumably Mackenzie had told DHL of his plans to stage the play *Columbine* (a version of his *Carnival*, 1912) in Nottingham's Grand Theatre; he directed rehearsals in the autumn (Mackenzie 182, 192). See Letter 2114.

2051. To Marie Hubrecht, 30 July 1920
Text: MS UN; Unpublished.

Fontana Vecchia, *Taormina*, Sicily
30 July 1920

Dear Miss Hubrecht

I had your letter from the north – full of the sound of leaves and water running, and stream dabbling birds. I suppose there are bilberries and cranberries. – Here it has been very hot, but now thank Goodness there are clouds. Still no rain. They are beating down the almonds everywhere, and leaves are falling, leaving the trees almost bare.

Bowdwin has come: he came to tea: very pleasant, and not exciting, I found him. Rocca Bella is having its windows painted and floors mended, and the beam that showed in the dining room, under the paint, removed. Mary has gone, the studio is empty – quite safe and tidy.

We are leaving next Monday – Aug 2nd. First we are staying with Juta and Insole at Anticoli, nr Rome, for 10 days. Then Frieda goes to Baden-Baden, and I meet some friends in north Italy. I don't know quite what I shall do. But we shall be back here almost certainly by early October. Do you think of coming to Taormina for the winter?

I am glad to be going away for a time – the heat has been oppressive, and Taormina feels humanly rather barren just now.

I heard from my publisher, they are all delighted with the novel I did here, *The Lost Girl*. Probably it will be out in the autumn – when I'll send you a copy. Hope for once that it will sell.

There are many strikes and disturbances, and a feeling of unrest. I suppose in the end Europe will break into eruption. But I feel I can't bother. Only it is like a thunderstorm hanging over and never breaking.

At this minute, I wish I was in Norway, to see the birch-trees moving and to hear the water among the stones. The dryness here seems to parch one's soul. Perhaps I shall go to Switzerland.

Write here and say what you will be doing in the coming winter.

Frieda joins in best greetings   D. H. Lawrence
the Anticoli address is
'San Filippo', *Anticoli Corrada*, Prov. Roma.

2052. To Hilda Brown, 30 July 1920
Text: MS Cotterell; Nehls, ii. 47–8.

Fontana Vecchia, *Taormina*, Sicily.
30 July 1920

Dear Hilda

The holiday is come, and we think of last year and Pangbourne, and hope that this year you'll have a good time. We are just going away also: first to some friends in the mountains near Rome – then Mrs Lawrence is going to Germany again to see her mother. I shall go with her as far as Milan – and from Milan to Baden is only about twenty hours. We rather dread the journey – from here to Milan about 36 hours direct. But thank heaven the weather is cooler. It has been hot blazing sun for week after week, day after day, and so hot lately it was too much. I have lived for weeks in a pair of pyjamas and nothing else – barefoot: and even then too hot. Now thank heaven clouds have come from the north, welcome and lovely. It has rained a tiny spattering today. Everywhere is burnt dry, the trees have shed nearly all their leaves, it is autumn. Only the vines are green. The grapes are just about ripe, hanging purple under the broad leaves.

Vegetables are all gone – except melanciani – egg-plant, purple things. But there are tomatoes in abundance – twopence a pound, fresh from the gardens. And the second lot of figs and peaches just coming. We had a nice lot of apricots – quite cheap, for once. Potatoes are twice as dear as apricots, and about the same price as peaches. But Italy is very expensive nowadays, for ordinary things, worse than England.

We often wonder about you, and the cottage, and the garden. Are there many greengages? – will there be apples? – how are the potatoes and marrows, and the good beans? Is there a black pig in the sty? What news of Hermitage? Does your Dad still trudge across to Oare, and your mother ride on Polly Wernham's bicycle?[1] And is Mrs Allan better? – remember us to her.

I send you a pound for your holiday. Put your name on the back, and anybody will cash the cheque for you: Mr Boshier or Mrs Lowe. It is for you to spend exactly as you please, on as much nonsense as you like.

Have we told you that Peggy has a baby sister? – born about a month ago. *There's* an addition to the family.

Send a line and tell us how you are, and address it to me:

presso Signor Juta, San Filippo,
Anticoli-Corrado, Prov. di Roma, Italy.

Mind you write decently, or heaven knows what the Italian postman will say to me. Mrs Lawrence sends love.

D. H. Lawrence

I'll bet you've never got that scholarship, you careless young baggage. Peg of course has got one – sharp-shins that she is. They say no news is good news: but not about scholarships. – Kindly say what the flower garden looked like

---

[1] Polly Wernham (Malthouse Farm, Hermitage) delivered bread, butter and milk around the village.

this year, if any of my efforts came to anything, and if your Dad was any less scornful than usual.

DHL

a lovely moonlight night, tonight, with a moon bright on the sea, and a few moving dark cloud-shadows. So nice to see clouds and their darknesses. Are the phlox out?

2053. To Robert Mountsier, 1 August 1920
Text: MS Smith; Postmark, Taormina 2 8 20 (MS ColU); Unpublished.

Fontana Vecchia, *Taormina*, Sicily
1 August 1920

Dear Mountsier
Your letter of 27th today. Accuse the post of the tallow. – I wrote to you already to New York, and sent you MS. of a story 'Fanny and Annie'. You might send a copy of it to England, to J C Squire, *The London Mercury*, Windsor House, Breams Buildings, London, E.C.4. I promised him something. I sent the 'document' empowering you to act for me. Hope you won't curse the bother of me.

I shall send you tomorrow morning my complete copy of *Studies in Classic American Literature*.[1] I have decided after all not to give it, just yet, to Cecil Palmer. I would rather it came in America first. I mistrust England horribly. Give it to Seltzer. I have a letter from Huebsch saying that he is giving his MS. of these essays to Seltzer. – Huebsch has more or less quarrelled with me.[2] He will be in England in August. – I prefer Seltzer, as far as I can judge from letters. – Huebsch has also some little essays on Psychoanalysis which he says he doesn't want. Get them from him.

I have written to *The Century* to hand the MS. of the *Lost Girl* to you in case it rejects the book. If the *Met[ropolitan]* doesn't want it, then let Seltzer go ahead with it. Cross out *Dial*. – The MS. I sent to England for the *Queen* has not arrived there after five weeks. Curse! –

Secker wants to print and publish *Lost Girl* before he does *Women in Love*. Funker. Curse England.

I wish I was going with you, to some new land. But we'll make money before long, and then we'll go.

We are leaving here for a bit. F[rieda] going to Germany, I to wander in north Italy, to be cooler. We shall be back here, God Willing, in October. We

---

[1] DHL recorded in his diary for the next day, 2 August 1920: 'Post Studies in Classic American Lit. to Mountsier in Paris for America' (Tedlock, *Lawrence MSS* 91).
[2] See p. 544 and n. 1.

leave tomorrow. – If you get the registered MS. of the *Studies*, send me a wire
        Lawrence, 'San Filippo', *Anticoli-Corrado*, (Rome).
San Filippo is the house of some friends – Anticoli-Corrado is the village,
Rome the province. We are there till Aug 14th.

If Seltzer prints the *Studies*, he can arrange the English publication, either
with Cecil Palmer, Oakley House, 14 Bloomsbury St. London, W.C. – or with
whom he likes: but he must supply the English publisher with the MS.

Best of voyages, best of luck to you. We'll make things move, before we've
done.

D. H. Lawrence

I had made up the MS. and sealed it for Palmer. I will not undo it, but just
paste on a new address.

2054. To Emily King, [6 August 1920]
Text: MS Needham; PC v. Roma. Colosseo con Pino visto dal Palatino; Postmark, Roma
10. VIII 1920; Unpublished.

Palazzo Moroni – Rome.
6 Aug

We are in Rome for a day or two – I posted you the cap for the nameless niece
from Montecassino – hope it arrives – we are motoring out to Anticoli
tomorrow with Juta. Do you like this view of the Coliseum?

Love   DHL

2055. To Ada Clarke, [6 August 1920]
Text: MS Clarke; PC v. Roma. Foro Romano. Casa delle Vestall; Postmark, Roma 10.
VIII 1920; Unpublished.

Palazzo Moroni. Rome
6 Aug

Staying a couple of days here – motoring out with Juta to Anticoli tomorrow –
expect to find a letter from you there – Rome is hot but pleasant. This is all
that is left of the house of the Vestal Virgins, in the Forum.

Love.   DHL

2056. To Robert Mountsier, [6 August 1920]

Text: MS Smith; PC v. Roma – Foro Romano. Basilica Giulia e Templo di Castore e Polluce; Postmark, Roma 10. VIII 1920; Unpublished.

Palazzo Moroni. Rome.
6 Aug

We are on our wanderings – Till mid-September 'San Filippo', *Anticoli-Corrado*, Prov Roma, will always find me. I'll send you an address if I have one before I return to Taormina. I am anxious to hear about the *Century*. If I can rake money I shall come to America early next year. Rome is hot but rather nice – travelling in Italy is hell – the railway.

Hope all goes well with you.   DHL

2057. To Percy Whittley, [7 August 1920]

Text: MS UT; Postmark, Anticoli [. . .]; Unpublished.

San Filippo, *Anticoli-Corrado*, Prov Roma
7. Aug.

Got your wire tonight. I will meet you in Milan on 17th. – don't know your train – I am wiring to the Hôtel du Nord, Milan. If I miss you, enquire there. I'll call at the poste restante. But I expect to hear from you before I leave here. We shall be in Milan on the 15th. and probably at Hotel du Nord.

au revoir   D. H. Lawrence

2058. To Cyril Beaumont, 10 August 1920

Text: MS SIU; Unpublished.

San Filippo, *Anticoli-Corrado*, Prov. Roma.
10 Aug 1920

Dear Beaumont

I still haven't received the vellum copy of *Bay*:[1] is it not done? – And you didn't send the copy of the simpler edition to Signor Juta, to this address, as I asked you.

I want to arrange an American edition – ought to have done so before. Will you please send a copy of the book to

---

[1] See p. 238 n. 2.

Mr Robert Mountsier, 417 West 118 Street, New York City.
Please don't fail to do this. I'll pay your bill the moment you send it.

I am moving about just now. Write to me to this address, until mid-September.

Hope all goes well.

D. H. Lawrence

2059. To Rosalind Baynes, [10 August 1920]
Text: MS BucU; cited in Moore, *Poste Restante* 60.

San Filippo, *Anticoli-Corrado*
10 Aug.

My dear Ros.

Had your letter yesterday – glad to hear: We move north on Thursday – get to Milan about 17th. I'm meeting two friends, man and wife, from London. They will be in Italy about 3 weeks. I think we shall walk round Como – perhaps go to Venice – many thanks for address. We *might* come to Florence. Is Canovaia empty? Might we stay a week there?

I'm not sure about coming to Rifredo. But certainly we'll be with you in Canovaia in October. We can linger with you before going down to Sicily. I look forward to that.

Here is very nice – the Abruzzi – hills and trees, cool after Sicily.

Send me a line c/o Thomas Cook and Son, *Milano*. If we went to Florence, the Whittleys and I, it would be about Sept 1st. When are you coming back?

I feel all unstuck, as if I might drift off anywhere.

rivederci   DHL

2060. To Robert Mountsier, 10 August 1920
Text: MS Smith; Postmark, Anticoli Corrado 12. AGO. 20; Unpublished.

'San Filippo', *Anticoli-Corrado*, Prov. Roma.
10 Aug 1920

Dear M[ountsier]

Here by the fountain under the trees – nice and cool – but a fierce sun in heaven.

I have written to C.W.Beaumont, of 75 Charing X Rd. W.C. to send you a copy of my little book of poems *Bay*. He is a sort of precious publisher for young bloods down from Oxford. He gave me £10. for the book – he has the English rights for 2 years. The two years must be almost expired. *Bay* has not been offered to America. Seltzer could make a *chic* little book of it, if he liked:

print in front that portrait photograph I sent you: I'll send you another one, *signed*: print the signed photograph in front, and sell *de luxe*. In case I forget, in the American edition I want 'Some of these poems have appeared in *Poetry*[1] – Chicago.' I told Beaumont, but he is a slip-shod imbecile.

The *Queen* funks *The Lost Girl*. If the *Century* follows suit, try the *Metropolitan*, and then let Seltzer go ahead.

Best write to me

c/o Martin Secker, 5 John St. Adelphi, London, W.C.

I'll let you know when I have an address. – You sail tomorrow.

DHL

2061. To Martin Secker, 10 August 1920
Text: MS UInd; Secker 31–2.

San Filippo, *Anticoli-Corrado*, Prov. Roma
10 Aug 1920

Dear Secker

I hear from Foss he has sent you the MS from the unsatisfactory *Queen*. You can do the proof corrections from it, can't you – and go right ahead without sending me proofs: because I suppose, if the *Century* behaves like the *Queen*, you will go ahead at once with the book, and publish this autumn.

As soon as you've got a set of proofs, send one to Seltzer, please. In spite of his *Women in Love* procrasts – please do this at once.

I have first batch of *W. in L.* proofs. Will let you have them corrected and exact, and you can print from them.

Send me a line

c/o Thomas Cook and Son, Milan.

Don't know where I shall find my next address.

Please send to Signor Jan Juta, at this address, a copy of *New Poems*, registered Book.

I enclose a photograph of his Sketch – too Bolsheviki for you, no doubt.

This is edge of Abruzzi – hills and trees – cooler than Sicily, but hot. Travelling is *hell*.

DHL

You know that Beaumont of Charing X Rd. has done a little book of my poems *Bay*. He had the rights for a year – expect that has well expired, he is such a procrastinator. You might do *Bay* if you like and stick this photograph in front.

If you were printing this in front of a book of poems, I would sign it – makes it sell better.

[1] in *Poetry*] in the *Poetry*

2062. To Francis Brett Young, 11 August 1920
Text: MS UB; cited in Jessica Brett Young, *Francis Brett Young*, p. 109.

San Filippo, *Anticoli-Corrado*, (Roma).

11 Aug 1920

Dear F[rancis] B[rett] Y[oung]

Had your letter and card here: many thanks for being willing to courier me: but I'm a cold egg: nothing at all to send to England, except you can spit on it for me if you feel like it.

We leave here for Florence tomorrow – Milan Monday – I'm meeting a couple of friends there, and F[rieda] is going on to her Fatherland, unless the gods, Lloyd-Georgelike, prevent. My address Cooks, Milan. – I intend to walk among the hills behind Como with the Whittleys, sleep out, etc. Travelling by rail is H^n – which means, not heaven, but Hell to the nth. power. It is truly agony. I feel I wouldn't care if I left Italy tomorrow, and for ever: but not to go north.

It is pleasant here – a courtyard with a fountain, and painters dropping in – yes, also in the fountain: nudes bathing: brutte nude. Country pleasant and hilly, Abruzzi: many trees, very nice: stinking villages: biggest hill burning, burning, a ring of flame round a black desert.

How long will you be in England. Will Mrs Brett Young be alone in Fraita?

The South Seas have receded into Infinite space. Nottingham Theatre looms large in the foreground.[1] Pah! – I agree with you, the theatre today is a vomit-pot, and no better.

It's a far cry to Lochaber.

Saluti buoni   DHL

2063. To Lucy Short, [18 August 1920]
Text: MS UT; PC v. Como. Piazza Cavour; Postmark, Como 18. 8. 20.; Unpublished.

Como.

18 August.

Dear Mrs Short

Here we sit in the Piazza Cavour drinking orange ice – a little table just at the corner of that bit of green grass in the bottom corner of this card. My wife has gone on into Switzerland, en route for Germany – so now we are three. We are going up the lake into the mountains for a few days, then round to Venice. Jolly it is to see Mrs Whittley and Percy – and to stroll round with them. Seems far from Cornwall.

Best wishes   D. H. Lawrence

If you write to Frieda, at her mothers address, she will see about the strength of that medicine: – in Baden Baden.

[1] See Letter 2050 and n. 2.

2064. To Margaret King, [19 August 1920]
Text: MS Needham; PC v. Como. Imbarcadero; Postmark, Como 19. 8. 20.; Unpublished.

Como.
19 Aug.

Had the letter-case and 'Housewife' from the Whittleys in Milan: the former much too grand and costly: every pick-pocket in Italy will be trying to steal it from me: the housewife a very satisfactory wife indeed: I have already darned a sock with her help. – Frieda has gone on to Germany. I am going up the lake with the Whittleys – about end of month we shall be at Venice –
c/o Thomas Cook and Son. Venice.
Shall write a letter when we reach a settling place.

Love. DHL

2065. To Gertrude Cooper, [19 August 1920]
Text: MS Clarke; PC v. Lago di Como. Primo bacino e Como; Postmark, Como 19. 8. 20.; Unpublished.

Como.
19 Aug.

Had your letter and parcels from the Whittleys in Milan – very nice everything – Frieda loves the cuff-studs – a thousand thanks. – After burning dryness, here among the mountains it pours with rain – and I must say I love to see it. – Arent you having a holiday?

Love. DHL

2066. To Robert Mountsier, [26 August 1920]
Text: MS Smith; PC v. Venezia – Stazione Ferroviaria; Postmark, Venezia 26. 8. 20; Unpublished.

c/o Thomas Cook. Venice.
27 Aug

Had your note from Anticoli – glad you got the MS. – F[rieda] in Baden – I am waiting round – feel I've about done Italy – will come to America soon. Am correcting proofs of *Lost Girl* for Secker – but he doesn't think he can publish till next spring – Write me Taormina – Hope America rejoices you.

DHL

2067. To Emily King, [26 August 1920]
Text: MS Needham; PC v. Venezia – Canal Grande e Palazzo Franchetti; Postmark,
Venezia 26. 8. 20; Unpublished.

c/o Thomas Cook. Venice
27 Aug

Came here yesterday – like Venice very much – many thanks for my pocketbook. – Haven't heard yet from F[rieda].

Love. DHL

2068. To Ada Clarke, [26 August 1920]
Text: MS Clarke; PC v. Venezia – Piazzetta S. Marco; Postmark, Venezia 26. 8. 20;
Unpublished.

c/o Thomas Cook. Venice
27 Aug.

Got here last night – Venice lovely. I may stay here a month – or only a week –
not heard yet from F[rieda] – shall wait here or in Florence.

Love. DHL

2069. To Gertrude Cooper, [28 August 1920]
Text: MS Needham; PC v. Venezia – Canal Grande – Palazzo Franchetti; Postmark,
Venezia 28. VIII 1920; Unpublished.

c/o Thomas Cook. Venice
30 Aug

Venice is quite lovely – not too hot, but the bathing still going strong. The
Whittleys return to England next week – I shall probably go to Florence,
where I have plenty of friends – will let you know.

Love to all DHL

2070. To Violet Monk, [28 August 1920]
Text: MS SIU; PC v. Venezia – Chiesa di S. Maria della Salute; Postmark, Venezia 28.
VIII 1920; Unpublished.

Venice.
30 Aug.

Here for a time – Frieda gone to Baden-Baden – Venice very lovely just now.

I ought to be getting on with that work, but don't. I think I shall go to Florence – plenty of friends there – send a line c/o Thomas Cook, Florence.

Greet the L[ambert].   DHL

2071. To Thomas Seltzer, 30 August 1920
Text: MS UT; Lacy, *Seltzer* 14.

Accademia, Ponte delle Meravegie, 1061, *Venice*
30 Aug. 1920
Dear Seltzer

I send you corrected proofs of *Lost Girl* – will let you have the rest as soon as I get them from Secker. Have been moving round this last month – think I shall leave Venice end of this week, and go to Florence. Best write to me at Taormina, where I expect I shall be by end of October.

D. H. Lawrence

2072. To Martin Secker, 31 August 1920
Text: MS UInd; Postmark, Battersea 6 SEP 20; Secker 32.

Venice –
31 August 1920
Dear Secker

I send you off the proofs I had received (2 lots) the other day.

I am leaving Venice tomorrow for Florence.

c/o Thomas Cook and Son, Via Tornabuoni, Florence.

Love Venice to look at, but not to smell, and not to live in – melancholic with its dreary bygone lagoons.

Whittley will post this in London on Sunday.

I expect really to be in Florence a month – waiting for my wife – plenty of friends there. Send proofs there.

DHL

2073. To Carl Hovey, 1 September 1920
Text: MS HL; Unpublished.

Venice.
1 Sept. 1920
Dear Mr Hovey

Thank you for the cheque for 250 dollars which I received from Taormina – for 'Wintry Peacock'. I cashed it for Lire 5,300/- – which is good. I expect

by now my friend Robert Mountsier will have sent you in another story. – I
expect to be back in Taormina in October.

                    Yours Sincerely   D. H. Lawrence

2074. To Percy Whittley, 2 September 1920
Text: MS UT; Unpublished.

                    c/o Thomas Cook, Via Tornabuoni, Florence.
                    2 Sept. 1920

I got here this morning after a night in the corridor – not so bad: am *so sorry*
our picnic à trois is all over: wish you were here in Florence. – Have got a
room in Miss Godkins pension[1] – which by the way is 1. Lungarno
Guicciardini, not Serristori, as Orioli told me.[2] It is quite nice, but I don't like
the little people here. No cant do with them. Shall leave again tomorrow – go
more into the country. But write to Cooks.

I do so wonder how you are getting on with your travelling today: feel quite
lost, by myself, quite outside everything. What a curse you aren't free to do as
you like.

Send me word how you are as soon as you are back. Oh for Argegno!

                    DHL

2075. To Robert Mountsier, 7 September 1920
Text: MS Smith; Postmark, Settignano -7. 9. 20; Unpublished.

                    c/o Thomas Cook, Via Tornabuoni, *Florence*
                    7 Sept 1920

Dear M[ountsier]

Send you this introduction.[3] Perhaps it might appear in a periodical.
Write a line to me *here*: quick.
Any news?

                    Many greetings   DHL

---

[1] The pension was run by Georgina Godkins (d. 1923) and her sister. It was located only a few
doors from the British Institute of Florence (at 9 Lungarno Guicciardini).
[2] Giuseppe ('Pino') Orioli (1884–1942), Italian antiquarian bookseller and publisher. First met
DHL in Cornwall (1916–17). He owned a famous bookshop on Lungarno Corsini in Florence;
he arranged for the printing and distribution of *Lady Chatterley's Lover* (1928); and he
published DHL's *The Story of Doctor Manente* (1929), *The Virgin and the Gipsy* (1930) and
Apocalypse (1931).
[3] 'America, Listen to Your Own', published in *New Republic*, xxv (December 1920), 68–70; the
magazine paid Mountsier $40 for it on 15 December 1920 (TMS UT). Mountsier later referred
to this piece as 'the "Knights of Columbus" introduction to *Studies in Classic American
Literature*' (see p. 626 n. 2).

2076. To Cyril Beaumont, 8 September 1920
Text: MS NYPL; Postmark, Firenze 9. IX 1920 (MS UCin); Unpublished.

c/o Thomas Cook and Son, Via Tornabuoni, *Florence*
8 Sept. 1920

Dear Beaumont

Thanks for copy of *Bay*, which has wandered after me round Italy. I enclose your bill, and cheque. Did not know you were selling for 12/6.

Yrs   D. H. Lawrence

Shall expect Vellum copy.

2077. To Irene Whittley, [8 September 1920]
Text: MS UT; PC; Postmark, Firenze 9. IX 1920; Unpublished.

Florence.
8 Sept.

Thought about you Sunday evening and Monday – your bitter Monday.[1] I stayed one night in Miss Godkins' pension – then fled – too intimate – old ladies etc. Have come to a villa out on the hill – a great rambling old place, with windows shattered by the explosion.[2] The gardener and family are at the back, but I have about eleven rooms all to myself. I cook for myself and do my room. Think how we might all three be camping here in this space. – It is great fun, even alone. I give luncheon and tea parties to elegant people, mostly American. We picnicked out behind Settignano today[3] – my word, such a gorgeous rich tea. But it wasn't fun like our Como days. – F[rieda] is enjoying Germany. Insole wants us to join them in Venice. I am not keen. F. might go alone, from Verona. – I am anxious to hear how you got on, on your journey. – Vine harvest begins today – also a sharp earthquake shock at 8.30 this morning.[4] Hope London is nice for you.

DHL

---

[1] Irene Whittley would probably re-start teaching on 6 September.
[2] 'All the windows of the Villa Canovaia [which DHL had borrowed from Rosalind Baynes] had been blown out by an explosion at a nearby ammunition dump in the Campo di Marte' (Nehls, ii. 48).
[3] Herbert Trench and his family lived at Settignano (see Letter 1861 and n. 1).
[4] The earthquake – most severe n.w. of Florence and Pisa – killed 174 people (*Times*, 9 and 17 September 1920).

2078. To J. B. Pinker, 10 September 1920
Text: MS UNYB; PC; Postmark, Firenze 10. IX 1920; cited in Moore, *Poste Restante* 60.

Florence
10 Sept 1920

Dear Pinker

Thank you for the cheque for £14-10-2 which I received yesterday, and the account accompanying it.

Yrs   D. H. Lawrence

2079. To Amy Lowell, 12 September 1920
Text: MS HU; cited in Moore, *Intelligent Heart* 273.

Florence.
12 Sept 1920

My dear Amy

I had your nice long letter a few days ago, in Venice. Glad you got the bits of embroidery, shall be amused to see your tilting against the *New Poems* preface.[1] Agree with you about *Bay*. – You'll send me your review on *Touch and Go?*[2]

Frieda wanted to go to Germany: has gone: so I have been wandering round Lake Como and Venice, and now am here for a while in an explosion-shattered, rambling old villa which a friend has lent me. It is hot, wine harvest has begun, the Italians cry out that they are persecuted like Job: what with earthquakes and manquakes.

F. talks of coming south again in early October when, I presume, we shall wander our way south to Taormina. We left in early August. It was *very* hot. I like warm countries, but it was too much for me, month after month. I sympathise with Mrs Russell.

Do you like Venice? I think it is so lovely to look at. I thought you were coming to Italy. Myriad Americans are here. With the exchange, it is cheap. All feels very fizzy and bubbly: but don't suppose anything big will happen – though it just might. – Why don't you trip over? Greet Mrs Russell.

D. H. Lawrence

I got the 9 dollars for *Imagist* – many thanks. I ought to dart and change them at 22/50.

---

[1] The preface had appeared in the first American edition of *New Poems* dedicated to Amy Lowell.
[2] She reviewed the play in the *New York Times Book Review*, 22 August 1920.

2080. To Compton Mackenzie, 12 September 1920
Text: MS UT; Mackenzie 190.

c/o Thomas Cook, Via Tornabuoni, Florence
12 Sept. 1920

Dear M[ackenzie]

What is this I hear about Channel Isles?[1]

The Lord of the Isles. I shall write a skit on you one day.[2] There will be a Lady of the Lake in it, and a rare to-do between the pair.

I am sitting in a rambling old explosion-shattered villa out under Fiesole: like it. Douglas away with his amico:[3] Reggie back from Capri, rather shaky.[4] Mrs Di Chiara here, and blooming, and a little ironical about homes and husbands. Various picnics.

My novel jerks one chapter forward now and then.[5] It is half done. But where the other $\frac{1}{2}$ is coming from, ask the Divine Providence.

Frieda gone to Munich: enjoying Germany: peasant drama and marionettes and return to innocent bare-footed dance under heaven: one of the reactions into sentimental naïveté, I presume. At same time, she says there is a very bad feeling between French and German – row brewing. – She proposes to come south early October – suppose we shall dribble our way to Taormina.

I bought a very nice old travel book *An Account of the Pelew Islands* – by Capt. Wilson,[6] wrecked in the 'Antelope' on those shores 1783.[7] – It is a quiet, very pleasing narrative, and a book something like your Mariners *Tonga*[8] – bound in calf and with maps and illustrations, published in Dublin 1785. If only it were about the Channel Isles, I'd send it you.

Tell Secker I sent what proofs came – from Venice, about a fortnight since. Nothing has come to me later.

---

[1] Applications had been invited for a sixty-year lease of the islands of Herm (at £900 per annum) and of Jethou (£100 p.a.); Mackenzie, encouraged by Secker, had applied; and on 20 August he was informed by the Treasury that he had been accepted (Mackenzie 185, 187).

[2] Six years later DHL wrote 'The Man Who Loved Islands', and Mackenzie threatened legal action as a result.

[3] Maurice Magnus.

[4] Reginald Turner (d. 1938), journalist, novelist and well-established member of the expatriate colony in Florence. Among his novels were *Uncle Peaceable* (1906), *Samson Unshorn* (1909) and *King Phillip the Gay* (1911). The *Times* obituary (8 December 1938) describes him as 'a friend of Oscar Wilde in his adversity' and as a man who was 'conversationally generous'. He was probably the prototype for Algy Constable in *Aaron's Rod*.

[5] *Aaron's Rod*.   [6] by Capt. Wilson] from Capt. Wilson's

[7] George Keate, *An Account of the Pelew Islands . . . composed from the Journals and Communications of Captain Henry Wilson . . . who in August 1783 was there shipwrecked in the Antelope* (London and Dublin, 1788).

[8] *An Account of the natives of the Tonga Islands . . . from the Communications of William Mariner . . . by J. Martin* (1817).

Very hot still here – and no rain to speak of. Am alone in this villa at San Gervasio – save for gardener's family at the back.

tanti saluti   DHL

2081. To Louis Untermeyer, 13 September 1920
Text: MS UInd; Unpublished.

Florence

13 Sept 1920

Dear Mr Untermeyer

I got your letter and cutting from *New Republic* just now[1] – go into post office and write an acknowledgement at once, or it will never be written.

I suppose all you say is true. All seems very far off too – Naples–Maine – and the English language in the United States – so far off, everything.

Bay was done in a sort of de luxe little way by

C W Beaumont, 75 Charing Cross Rd, London, W.C.

He bought the rights for 2 years for £10. – sells I think at 12s/6d a copy: is a scatterbrained chap. I would send a copy to you but it wearies me to write to him.

But always remember I prefer my strife, infinitely, to other people's peace, havens, and heavens. God deliver me from the peace of this world. As for the peace beyond understanding,[2] I find it in conflict.

Yrs   D. H. Lawrence

2082. To Margaret King, [13 September 1920]
Text: MS Needham; PC v. La Vergine col Figlio. Firenze – Galleria Uffizi (Filippo Lippi); Postmark, Firenze 13. 9. 20.; Unpublished.

Florence

13 Sept.

I had your mothers letter today – how excited you will be feeling in your first days at Mundella.[3] I hope it all is jolly for you. Yes, you'll have to stay to your dinners at school in the winter. – Glad baby is fat and bonny, but Ada says

---

[1] Louis Untermeyer had published an impassioned, critical piece entitled 'D. H. Lawrence' in *New Republic*, xxiii (11 August 1920), 314–15 (see Draper, ed., *Critical Heritage*, pp. 132–5).

[2] Philippians iv. 7 ['the peace of God which passeth all understanding'].

[3] Margaret King (aged 11) had just become a pupil at Mundella Grammar School in Nottingham.

she's a bit of a tartar. Hope she'll mend her ways. The earthquake killed 2 people in Florence – but quite mild here really. Shall write a letter tomorrow.

love.   DHL

2083. To Robert Mountsier, 15 September 1920
Text: MS Smith; Unpublished.

c/o Thomas Cook and Son. Florence.
15 Sept. 1920

Dear M[ountsier]

I send you these poems 'Fruit Studies'[1] – send them to the *New Republic* at your discretion (see note requesting poetry).[2] Probably plenty of other people would publish them, even if *N. R.* didn't.

If there is any money to collect, do collect it, and if possible open me a banking account (current) in New York.

Am writing to this man.

Hope to hear from you soon.

D. H. Lawrence

Think these 'Fruits' quite good, so don't be scared by them.

If there is money, take it for your expenses of typists, etc.

Don't abuse me for the vile MS. I can't write it out any more.

2084. To Robert Mountsier, [16 September 1920]
Text: MS Smith; Unpublished.

Florence.
16 Sept.

Dear M[ountsier]

Always something turning up. Today proofs of this story 'The Fox',

---

[1] When staying at the Villa Canovaia DHL wrote a number of the poems which were later collected under the sub-title 'Fruits' in *Birds, Beasts and Flowers* (Seltzer, 1923). *New Republic* published 'Medlars and Sorb-Apples' on 5 January 1921 and 'The Revolutionary' on 19 January; it paid $20 for each poem, on 6 and 19 January 1921 respectively (TMS UT).

[2] The note (TMS Smith), dated 24 August 1920, reads as follows:

Dear Sir:

Will you not give this American weekly, The New Republic, the pleasure of publishing some of your poetry in its pages? We shall be glad to receive as much as possible from you, and we remit payment promptly upon acceptance.

Very sincerely yours,   Ridgely Torrence
For The New Republic.

Frederick Ridgely Torrence (d. 1950), American poet, was associate editor of *New Republic*, 1920–34.

which *Nash's* Story *Magazine* is going to publish, presumably in November.[1]
Think you might get it in by then in an American magazine? It is rather long.
The Dial would probably do it.

Damn *Nash's*. They have been hanging fire with this story ever so long. I
thought they'd printed it – have had proofs before. I shall ask Pinker to
inform you, by return.

Enclose another poem.[2]

DHL

Keep me posted of what you do with me.
Chicago *Poetry* likes my verse.

2085. To J. B. Pinker, 16 September 1920

Text: MS UNYB; cited in Moore, *Poste Restante* 60.

c/o Thomas Cook and Son, Via Tornabuoni, *Florence*.
16 Sept. 1920

Dear Pinker

Thank you for letters and proofs forwarded.

I should be very much obliged if you could send a line to
Mr. Robert Mountsier, 417 West 118 Street, *New York City*,
telling him when *Nashs* intend to publish this story 'The Fox': if you could do
so at once. – I thought the thing must have been printed, they hang fire so long.

I am in Florence till the beginning of October – then Taormina.

Yours Sincerely[3]

2086. To Dr Anton Kippenberg, 16 September 1920

Text: MS SVerlag; Unpublished.

presso Thomas Cook and Son, Via Tornabuoni, *Florence*. Italy.
16 September 1920

Herr. O. Kippenberg
Insel-Verlag. Leipzig

Dear Sir

Mr James B. Pinker sent on to me your letter of Aug. 31st., as he is no
longer acting as my literary agent.

---

[1] DHL makes a mistake here: 'The Fox' was to be published in *Hutchinson's Story Magazine* iii
(November 1920), 477–90. (DHL reiterated his error in December 1921 to Curtis Brown and
told Mountsier in the same month that the story had appeared in *Strand*.)

[2] The poem cannot be confidently identified but it may well have been another of the 'Fruits'
poems which were noted in *Birds, Beasts and Flowers* as having been written at San Gervasio:
'Pomegranate', 'Peach', 'Figs' or 'Grapes'.

[3] DHL's signature has been removed from the MS.

I understand that you offer forty pounds sterling for the rights of German translation and publication of each book of mine which you care to undertake. This I am prepared to accept, for any volumes of mine which you bring out in German within the next twelve months.

I enclose a list of my books. If you have not already got a copy of the *English* edition of *The Rainbow*, I think my mother-in-law

Fraü Baronin von Richthofen, Ludwig-Wilhelmstift, *Baden-Baden* would be able to lend you one. The American edition is not quite complete.

My wife is German: at the moment staying in Baden-Baden with her mother. She will be glad, and so shall I, if you produce my books in Germany.

Yours Sincerely   D. H. Lawrence

Works of D. H. Lawrence.

Novels	*The White Peacock.*	1910.	Duckworth and Co
	The Trespasser.	1912.	3. Henrietta St.
	Sons and Lovers.	1913.	London, W.C.2.
	The Rainbow.	1915.	

Drama   *The Widowing of Mrs Holroyd.*   1911.   (Duckworth)
         Touch and Go.   1920.   (C.W.Daniel, 3 Tudor St. E.C.)

Poems   *Love Poems and Others.*   1912. } Duckworth
         Amores.   1915. }
         Look, We Have come through.   1917.   (Chatto and Windus
                                              111. St. Martins Lane
                                                 London, W.C.)
         New Poems   1918.   (Martin Secker, 5 John St.
                                           Adelphi, London. W.C.)
         Bay   1920   (C.W.Beaumont, 75 Charing Cross Rd, W.C.2.)

Stories   *The Prussian Officer*   1914.   (Duckworth.)

Travel Sketches   *Twilight in Italy*   1916.   (Duckworth)

In my opinion, most suitable for Germany are the novels – particularly *Sons and Lovers* and *The Rainbow*[1] – the short stories: *The Prussian Officer* – the drama: *Touch and Go* – and the *vers libre: Look We Have Come Through.*

---

[1] Kippenberg accepted his advice. Insel-Verlag published a translation of *The Rainbow* in 1922 and of *Sons and Lovers* in 1925; Franz Franzius was the translator.

2087. To John Ellingham Brooks, 17 September 1920
Text: TMSC YU; Unpublished.

c/o Thomas Cook and Son, Florence.

17 Sept 1920

Dear Brooks

I have wandered Como, Venice and here: Frieda is in Germany and I'm not quite sure when [she][1] thinks of leaving. But if she stays much longer I dont want to wait for her here in Florence. Should like to come to Capri to see you again: even to share Casa Solitaria and housekeeping with you for a fortnight, if that was feasible and agreeable. Will you send me a line? I should come about 23rd. or 25th. of this month – in a week's time. I suppose di Chiara will have come here by then.

I see Mrs. di Chiara and Reggie, and so have news.

Au revoir   D. H. Lawrence

2088. To Martin Secker, 18 September 1920
Text: MS UInd; Postmark, Firenze Centro 18 9. 20; Secker 32–3.

c/o Thomas Cook, Florence

18 Sept. 1920

Dear Secker

Had your wire today. Yes, please do correct the proofs in the office: but do them from the typed MS which *The Queen* had.[2] You will *at once* see my handwritten corrections over the type. Don't fail – as there are a few rather

---

[1] It is presumed that the typist omitted the word.
[2] Secker replied on 22 September 1920 (Secker Letter-Book, UIll):

Dear Lawrence,
    Many thanks for your letter from Florence of the 18th which reached me this morning, also for your telegram giving the title of the last chapter of the book [see DHL's next letter]. I am comparing the proofs carefully with the typed manuscript from the Queen and giving effect to all your alterations. The only thing it will not be possible to alter is the spelling of the name Cicio. Directly I received your postcard sometime ago I communicated with the printer but found it was too late to make the alteration. I wrote to you to this effect but evidently my letter never reached you. It would have been a very costly proceeding, indeed, to alter the name throughout and after consulting Mackenzie, who thought that comparatively few of your readers here would notice it I wrote as I have said to ask your permission to allow it to remain.
    The book is now being machined as quickly as possible and I shall do my very best to publish on November 1st which will be the latest it can appear this autumn.

Yours sincerely

DHL had tentatively drawn Secker's attention to the spelling of 'Ciccio' as early as 24 June 1920 (see Letter 2022): this was *before* the *Lost Girl* MS went to the Edinburgh printer.

important alterations later on. And remember the proper way to spell Cĩcio is with three c's – Ciccio.

My wife wants me to meet her, and other friends, in Venice, on the 28th.: so there I go in a week's time. Send me a line there –

c/o Thomas Cook and Son, Piazza dei Leoncini, Venice.

Hope all is well.

D. H. Lawrence

Suppose we shall be in Taormina end of October.

2089. To Martin Secker, 21 September 1920
Text: MS UInd; Postmark, Firenze Centro 21 9. 20; Secker 33.

Florence
21st. Sept 1920

Dear Secker

Got your wire this minute – you hadn't mentioned the chapter title – However call it 'Suspense'.[1]

This should reach you in three days – I'll wire also.

Think I shall be going to Venice on 27th to meet my wife and friends – stay about 10 days – then southward.

Tell Mackenzie to write me about the Channel Isles.

D. H. Lawrence

2090. To Reginald Turner, [24 September 1920]
Text: MS UCLA; Moore 635.

[Villa Canovaia, San Gervasio, Florence]
Friday evening[2]

Dear Turner,

Would it bore you to come into Piazza V. Emmanuele on Sunday and have tea with me and a certain American Mrs Thrasher at 4.0 on Sunday. I shall be there anyhow, so come if you are free. I think of going to Venice on Monday. Mrs Thrasher is charming – husband was a sculptor killed in the war.[3]

---

[1] Chap. XVI in *The Lost Girl* lacked a title in MS.

[2] Dated by DHL's proposal to go to Venice on Monday 27 September (he actually went on the 28th).

[3] Carlota Davis Thrasher (1883–1975) reappears a number of times in subsequent letters as the lady who offered the Lawrences a lease on her farm in the village of Westminster, Connecticut (see Letter 2165). Her husband, Harry Dickinson Thrasher (1883–1918), was killed in action in France, September 1918. As a sculptor he was considered of exceptional promise; a memorial to him exists in the American Academy, Rome, where he spent the years 1911–14. (See Rilla E. Jackman, *American Arts*, New York, 1928, pp. 454–5.)

Mackenzie sent his love to you in a letter about Channel Isles etc.

D. H. Lawrence

Is it Paskowskis café? – where we sat with Mrs Cannan – same place.

2091. To Baroness Anna von Richthofen, 26 September 1920
Text: MS UCB; Unpublished.

Florence.

26 Sept. 1920

Meine Liebe Schwiegermutter

I thought a great deal of coming to Baden-Baden. But I feel, it is so late in the year, and the autumn with the leaves falling would be sad. I would much rather come in spring. I should love to come next April, when we leave Taormina, and perhaps we could spend a whole summer together, you and F[rieda] and me. After the war, and with this bad exchange, one shrinks from coming. Next year it will be better.

I intend to go to Venice on Tuesday – Sept 28th. – and wait for Frieda. Then we can stay about eight days, and start to wander back to Taormina. The winter will soon go by, next year will soon come. And then perhaps we shall have more money and can spend it freely.

I enclose a letter from 'Insel-Verlag'.[1] Stupid of me to misread him. However, I write and say I will make an arrangement to receive the money in Marks. And these Marks he can pay to you. They would be no good out of Germany. If he writes to you for books which you haven't got, let me know, and I will order them for him from England. It might amuse Else to translate something: but probably it wouldn't.

Mila saluti, Liebe Schwiegermutter   D. H. Lawrence

The Venice address is

Casa Petrarca, Canal Grande, *Venice*, San Silvestro 1095.

2092. To Thomas Smith, 26 September 1920
Text: MS SIU; Unpublished.

Florence.

26 Sept 1920

Dear Mr Smith[2]

I have your letter of 3 Sept. here: am sorry you can't see *The Lost Girl* as a serial, but I quite understand why.

---

[1] The letter from Kippenberg is missing.

[2] Thomas R. Smith (1880–1942) had been literary adviser to several publishing houses; 1914–20 he was the managing editor of the *Century* magazine. He had written to Mountsier (the letter to which DHL refers) rejecting the proposed serialisation of *The Lost Girl* in the *Century* (see *The Lost Girl*, ed. Worthen, p. xxxiv).

I shall ask my friend Robert Mountsier to give you a short story to read, for *The Century.* Hope we shall be able to[1] work together.

Yours Sincerely   D. H. Lawrence

Am returning shortly to Taormina.

2093. To Jessica Brett Young, 26 September 1920
Text: MS UB; Sagar, *Review of English Literature,* vi. 100–2.

Florence.
26 Sept 1920

Dear Mrs Brett Young

I had your letter in Venice – there you sit lonely on that dry rock. Too bad! Why didn't you do a little gira[2] while F[rancis] was away. That's what I'm doing. My F[rieda] wanted to go to Germany: so I wandered with her as far as Milan, and saw her off. Then I went with friends to Lake of Como for 8 days: lovely: Venice for 8 days: lovely to look at, but couldn't stand it long: now I've been at Florence for 3 weeks. We left Taormina Aug 2nd. – stayed in Montecassino and Rome and with Juta in Abruzzi. Sounds all very expensive, but isn't. Here in Florence I camp in a big rambling old villa which a friend had and from which she was driven when the powder factory exploded just below, in August. I've got no glass in the windows – but a garden and a lovely view and air and peace and the gardeners family behind. But I cook and clean for myself: my old style.

I think of going to Venice on Tuesday: friends there want us to join them for a bit. Frieda writes for me to go to Germany. But too late this year. I expect she will be in Venice about Oct 2nd.: and by Oct 14th. I hope to be back in Taormina. My word, it *was* hot there in July. I should like to call at Capri as we go down: very much like to: perhaps we shall. Mrs Di Chiara was here – and him – left for Perugia Friday. We picknicked.

I have been thankful to get a bit of northerliness, greenness and comparative cool, and sound of brooks running and falling among stones: even sound of the Arno swishing green. I hear Capri no rain yet. Taormina quite got on my nerves, no sound of water anywhere, no green hollows. One needs one's proportion of the waters over the earth and under the earth. The sun at last seems malevolent, don't you think, if he wont let it rain. It has poured torrents in Taormina, Carmelo writes. The sea isn't water.

I suppose we shall stay our year out. My novel – the new one[3] – has stuck half way, but I don't care. I may get a go on him at Taormina. If not, I think I can sort of jump him picaresque.

---

[1] MS reads 'able work'.   [2] 'tour'.   [3] *Aaron's Rod.*

Hope *Lost Girl* will make some money, or I shall be whistling.

Hear from Mackenzie about Channel Isles, but indefinite. – Have a little farm offered me in Connecticut – New York 4 hours. I'd do it if I had another man: grow currants – not dried ones.

Is your F. returned?

Send a line

      presso Thomas Cook, Piazza Leoncini, Venezia.

                    Yrs   D. H. Lawrence

2094. To Gertrude Cooper, 26 September 1920
Text: MS Clarke; Unpublished.

                                          Florence.

                                 26 Sept 1920

My dear G[ertrude]

I send you a little purse of stamped leather, which is a Florentine speciality. Hope you'll think it pretty.

I am still here, alone in a big rambling old villa which Rosalind had, but which she left because the powder factory exploded and blew out the windows. Powder factories always explode in Italy. It's a nice old house, about three miles out of Florence. The gardeners family looks after me. – I think I shall go to Venice again on Tuesday. Frieda very much wants me now to go to Baden Baden. But it is so late in the year. I'd rather leave it till spring. – Juta and Insole are in Venice at the moment. I expect F. will come down next week. Write me

      c/o Thomas Cook, Piazza Leoncini, Venice.

We shall stay eight days or so – then to Rome for two days – then Taormina. That's the programme.

Autumn setting in here, but still *very* hot. I thought of you at Hove. Did you have a good time? Do you still collect for Feroze?[1]

I wonder how Ada is! What a curse that illness! Why can't she come to Italy for the winter. Tell her to let me know if she got the picture I sent from Alinaris.[2]

                        Love to you all   DHL

---

[1] See Letter 1678 and n. 2.
[2] Since 1852 the firm of Fratelli Alinari (Istitute di Edizione Artistiche) has been photographing works of art and architecture throughout Italy; the collection is now unrivalled. It is not known to which reproduction DHL refers.

2095. To Irene Whittley, [27 September 1920]
Text: MS UT; PC v. Nascita di Venere. Firenze – Galleria Uffizi (Botticelli); Postmark,
Firenze 27. 9. 20; Unpublished.

Florence.
27 Sept.

Tomorrow I am going to Venice again – expect F[rieda] about Oct 2nd. Write
me a line c/o Cooks, Piazza Leoncini. Lovely autumn days, sunny and hot at
midday. Have you forgotten all your Italian – could Whittley still buy honey.
Shall miss you there.

DHL

2096. To Percy Whittley, [29 September 1920]
Text: MS UT; PC v. Venezia; Postmark, Venezia 29. IX 1920; Unpublished.

Venice
29 Sept

I tried to buy you Noah, but could only find *Adam*![1] Am with the Scolari – she
inquires affectionately after you both. I miss you *frightfully* there. Juta and
Insole have a gondola and gondolier hired by the month, so we lounge on the
water. But I liked our picknicky days. Hope all goes well.

DHL

2097. To Rosalind Baynes, [29 September 1920]
Text: MS BucU; PC v. Venezia; Postmark, Venezia 29. IX 1920; Unpublished.

[Ponte delle Maravegie 1061, *Venice*]
Wed

Poured with a cloud-burst when I got here. Venice autumnal. Juta has hired a
gondola for a month – so we lounge on the water. Expect F[rieda] in a few
days – she writes tiresomely from Germany. Wonder what you are doing for a
house. I ate all my pan'forte[2] in the train – loved it – with *mediocre* white wine.
Send a line Cooks, Piazza Leoncini.

DHL

[1] The picture on DHL's postcard shows a corner of the loggia of the Ducal Palace; among the
decorations of the capitals of the colonnade those at the corners are particularly impressive; and
at the corner of the Piazzetta are found Adam and Eve, while facing the Ponte della Paglia is
Noah inebriated. DHL had obviously hoped to find a postcard showing the latter; he had to be
content with the former.
[2] Panforte is a kind of Sienese cake flavoured with almonds.

2098. To Robert Mountsier, 30 September 1920
Text: MS Smith; Unpublished.

Venice.

30 Sept. 1920

Dear R[obert]

I am sending you another photograph – also enclosing Smith's letter.[1] Am expecting to be hearing from you. You will have got a copy of *Bay*. Will you arrange about the American publication? And I should like to have this photograph put in front, with the words

'From a portrait sketch May 1920 by Jan Juta.'

I expect Frieda will be here in a few days time – then we shall stay another week or so – then really back to Taormina. I am anxious to hear from you.

I have done a little book of those *vers libre* like the fruit studies.[2] I'll send them and perhaps they can go in magazines.

A woman offers me a little farm in New England – near Norfolk – 4 hrs from New York, if I'll go and live there. It's a gone-wild farm. What do you say – 70 acres.

It seems years since I had a line from you: do hope you are safe and sound.

Saluti. DHL

2099. To Martin Secker, 2 October 1920
Text: MS UInd; Postmark, Venezia 2. X 1920; Secker 33.

Ponte delle Maravegie 1061, *Venice*

2 Oct 1920

Dear Secker

Thank you for your letter – Hope you'll manage *Lost Girl* by Nov 1. – don't think the 'Cicio' matters anyhow. What I hope is that you are sending, or have already sent, a set of corrected proofs to Seltzer.

I wish you would put another fifty pounds to my account in the London County Westminster Bank, Law Courts branch: or else send me cheque. I fear I am getting low. So far, I understand, you have paid me £50. That is correct? Pay me *English* money, don't transfer to Italian. I mistrust Italy.

---

[1] See Letter 2092.
[2] According to Catherine Carswell (Carswell 138), these poems – also referred to in Letters 2101 and 2102 – were the sequence of six later published by Seltzer as *Tortoises* (December 1921): 'Baby Tortoise', 'Tortoise-Shell', 'Tortoise Family Connections', 'Lui et Elle', 'Tortoise Gallantry' and 'Tortoise Shout'.

Expect my wife any day – after she[1] arrives, about a week more here, then south for Taormina, where I hope to arrive about mid October.

                                      Best wishes   D. H. Lawrence[2]

2100. To Marie Hubrecht, 2 October 1920
Text: MS UN; Unpublished.

                                                            Venice.
                                                        2 Oct 1920

Dear Miss Hubrecht.

Your letter reached me here, from Florence. I am waiting for my wife, who is coming down from Germany next week. By Oct 16th. I hope to be in Taormina once more. I am a little tired of wandering about, feel like settling to work.

Juta and Insole are here – but Juta is writing to you.

I am glad you enjoy the north. Frieda loved Germany, also. Here the autumn is fine, with sudden downpours: Venice lovely to look at, but rather shallow, I find her. I wouldn't want to stay here long.

We shall be in Taormina till March, I expect: and after that, I don't know where. Everything feels vague. Perhaps I shall go to America. But at any rate, if you come after Christmas to the Studio, we shall see you. Don't make too much of Carmelo's communication. Can one *entirely* trust Ciccia? Besides, the man Pasquale is now married.[3] I spoke to Bowdwin about the affair, and he seemed inclined to disbelieve it.

I'll go to the Studio as soon as I get back and see if everything is all right.

---

[1] MS reads 'after that she', DHL having inserted 'she arrives' as an afterthought.
[2] Secker replied on 14 October 1920 (Secker Letter-Book, UIll):

Dear Lawrence,
    Your letter of the 2nd only reached me a few days ago. Posts seem to be getting bad again. The corrections in the latter half of the book were rather heavy for you had made considerable alterations in the typescript from your original written copy from which I had set up. However, all this was carried through and I hastened to send a set of finally corrected proofs to Seltzer. I shall be publishing the book on November 1st.
    I am placing another £50 to your account in London which makes in all £100 that I have paid so far. I am now enclosing proofs up to page 128 of 'Women in Love' which I hope to issue some time in February. I hope you will not mind adding chapter titles, for especially in such a long book (it will make 512 pages) I think these tend to lighten the general appearance of the book. I am posting these to Taormina to await your arrival there. How is the new novel getting on?
                                                          Yours sincerely
[3] Pasquale has not been identified. 'Ciccia' (Francesca Cacópardo), whose first husband Guiseppe Testa had recently died, later married Vincenzo Falanga.

Thank you for bothering about the translation. All that is to be done, is that someone should translate a book, and get a Dutch publisher to accept the translation. Then the publisher will arrange with my publisher, or with me, the sum to be paid for the *Dutch* rights. Or a translator, if he or she likes, can write to me for authorisation, and thus be quite sure that no one else can interfere or rush in before. But don't trouble about it.[1]

My new book, the one I wrote in Taormina, is *due* for November 1st. I shall send you a copy to Doorn: – *The Lost Girl*. Hope it will remind you, if indirectly, of our jolly times.

Best of greetings   D. H. Lawrence

Tell me if you like Jutas portrait of me.

2101. To Amy Lowell, [3 October 1920]

Text: MS HU; PC v. Venezia. Piccioni a S. Marco; Postmark, Venezia [. . .] 10 [. . .]; cited in Moore, *Poste Restante* 60.

Venice –
3 Oct.

Am back here waiting for Frieda, who comes in a day or two. Venice looking very charming – but a bit hollow, I feel her, poor old thing. Robert Mountsier is back in New York, and is looking after my affairs. Do you know him?[2] 417 West 118 Street. He's a friend. I've done a new little volume of *Vers Libre* – so queer. Shall send Mountsier an MS. Should like to know what you think of it.

Yrs   D. H. Lawrence

2102. To Catherine Carswell, 7 October 1920

Text: MS YU; cited in Carswell 138.

Ponte delle Maravegie 1061. *Venice*
7 Oct. 1920

My dear Catherine

I just had your letter from St. Agnes, forwarded from Florence: had wondered so much why I never heard. I have come back here to be with friends – expect Frieda this evening, and hope to be back in Taormina by the 16th. Am sick of mouching about.

---

[1] No Dutch translation is known of any work by DHL in his lifetime.
[2] So far as is known, Amy Lowell did not meet Mountsier until 1921.

Cornwall sounds queer and far away: am glad old Ma. Dixon is flourishing.[1] You didn't go and see the Hockings at the farm?

Secker hopes to get *The Lost Girl* out by Nov 1st. I'll send you a copy. Will you make anything out of American rights of your book?[2] – Trust to the Lord you can write short stories. Sell them to America, never mind London. 250 dollars a story.

I am still stuck in the middle of *Aaron's Rod*, my novel. But at Taormina I'll spit on my hands and lay fresh hold. I wrote in Florence a little book of vers libre which I like.

Venice is lovely to look at, but very stagnant as regards life. A holiday place, the only one left in Italy – but even here écœuré.[3] Italy feels very unsure, and for the first time I feel a tiny bit frightened of what they might do, the Italians, in a sudden ugly 'red' mood. However, Sicily will be moderately safe.

America seems to you looney? Well, I don't care, perhaps there's more sense in lunacy than in our rational mechanism. God knows what one will do. I am thinking of next spring. I shan't stay in Taormina, I think – perhaps go to Germany for the summer, perhaps to Sardinia. Taormina blazes too hard, after June. You always London?

I was only on the edge of the earthquake. They're horrid frightening.

So glad J[ohn] P[atrick] is a triumph and a comfort in his youngness. How is Don?

DHL

2103. To Compton Mackenzie, 7 October 1920
Text: MS UT; Mackenzie 191–2.

Ponte delle Maravegie 1061. *Venezia*
7 Oct 1920

Dear M[ackenzie]

I have been hearing about the islands, Herm and the one ending in 'hou.[4] They sound rather fascinating. Are you going to farm Herm? – and who is going to be your farmer? I've half a mind to come and help, in the stormy Channel. Tell me about them, anyway. Are you going to make a cinema studio on Herm really, or is that just gossip?[5] They sound expensive, but probably you can make them pay.

I expect Frieda here today – then we shall go almost at once to Taormina. I expect to be there by the 16th.: want to get back, and work: have done nothing

[1] Unidentified.   [2] *Open the Door!*   [3] 'nauseating'.
[4] i.e. Jethou (see Letter 2080 and n. 1).
[5] On his dealings with film companies see Mackenzie 186–7.

but a little book of vers libre, which please me. I cant do anything in Venice.

Italy feels awfully shaky and nasty, and for the first time my unconscious is uneasy of the Italians.

I wonder how you find Nottingham.[1] I dread it for you, because I loathe the town. But I hope all goes merrily. Tell me about it.

I'll write to my sister. You might have tea with her in some café. She lives out of town.

Yrs. DHL

My sister is Mrs Clarke, Grosvenor Rd. *Ripley*, nr Derby. She comes to Nottm. every Wednesday. |

2104. To Rosalind Baynes, [7 October 1920]

Text: MS UN; Nehls, ii. 50.

Ponte delle Maravegie 1061. Venezia
Thursday.

Had your letter yesterday: so you didn't go to Canovaia after all. I can't imagine the Villa Ada, but it sounds all right.

I expect Frieda this evening 'if her passport is ready'. – And I'm sick of mouching about in Venice, and a gondola merely makes me bilious. I hope we can leave by the 14th., and be back in Taormina by the 16th.

I do no work, am out all day, either alone or with Juta and the others. The Lido is deserted, and, in the open part, quite lovely now, with tall clouds advancing over the sea, and many burnt sails. I take my lunch and sit and watch from the sand hills, and bathe. Sometimes we all go in gondola a long way over the lagoons, past Malamocca.

I hear from Mary. She *loves* Monaco, and says it is heaven after Italy. There seems more and more bolshy scare here – not in Venice, but in the Romagna. I suppose we shall just have to be wise and wary, that's all.

Insole and Mrs Hansard and her husband are coming to Florence. I'll give them your address, you *might* like Mrs H. She is a Juta, from South Africa, wrote a novel called *The Tavern*. I believe Insole would like to see Canovaia, to have it in spring if possible.

We had our first touch of autumn chill yesterday: but brilliant sun.

Wonder where we'll meet next.

DHL

---

[1] See p. 579 n. 2.

2105. To Hilda Brown, [12 October 1920]
Text: MS Cotterell; PC v. Venezia – Canal Grande in festa; Postmark, Venezia 12. X 1920;
cited in Moore, *Poste Restante* 61.

                                                                                    Venice.
                                                                                    12 Oct.
Dear Hilda
    Mrs Lawrence is back from Germany – we are leaving on Sunday for Rome
– then to Taormina. Write us a line there, and tell all the news.
                                        Love to you from us both   D. H. Lawrence

2106. To Margaret King, [12 October 1920]
Text: MS Needham; PC v. Venezia – Gondola Veneziana; Postmark, Venezia 13. X 1920;
Unpublished.

                                                                                    Venice
                                                                                    Oct 12.

Your Auntie Frieda is back here – quite flourishing after her trip. We leave on
Thursday for Rome, on our way to Taormina. Hope to be home by the 18th.
Haven't had any word from you here. Am tired of moving – want to be back
and quiet. Let me know how you are.
                                                                            Love. DHL

2107. To Percy Whittley, [12 October 1920]
Text: MS UT; PC v. [Map of Venice and estuary]; Postmark, Venezia 13. X 1920;
Unpublished.

                                                                                    Venice –
                                                                                    Oct. 12.

We are leaving for Florence and Rome on Thursday – hope to be in Taormina
by the 18th. Venice chilly – Lido deserted and beautiful. Frieda and I
picknicked there today and talked of you. Why have you never sent a line
since you left? Frieda quite well after Germany: sends remembrances.
                                                        Hope you're all right DHL

2108. To Edward Marsh, 13 October 1920
Text: MS NYPL; Marsh, *A Number of People*, p. 233.

Ponte delle Meravegie 1061, *Venice*
13 Oct 1920

Dear Eddie

I found your letter at Cooks this morning: also cheque, which is inspiring:[1] had a bottle of Lacrimi Cristi Spumanti on the strength of it, and in the clear, pure, pale-blue autumn sunshine felt the world magical. Many thanks. – Frieda is just back from Germany, which land seems to be looking considerably up. Tant mieux. Meanwhile Italy is going socialist, not to be avoided. But I believe, with a bit of sanity outside as well as in, Italy might take to a socialist government fairly naturally – more naturally than anybody. We are going to Florence tomorrow – shall be in Taormina next week. – Secker hopes to publish *Lost Girl* beginning of November. I'll send you a copy.

Hope you're feeling nice   DHL

2109. To Gertrude Cooper, [13 October 1920]
Text: MS Clarke; PC v. Venezia – Ponte dei Sospiri; Postmark, Venezia 13. X 1920; Unpublished.

Venice.
13 October

We leave Venice tomorrow for Florence and Rome. Hope to be in Taormina by the 18th. Frieda flourishing after her trip to Germany. I had your letter here – wish we could all be in Italy this winter. Am thinking about the coal strike.[2]

Love.   DHL[3]

2110. To Robert Mountsier, 18 October 1920
Text: MS Smith; Unpublished.

Fontana Vecchia, *Taormina*, Sicily.
18 October 1920

Dear Mountsier

I got back here this afternoon, find your letters of September 24th. and

---

[1] DHL was being paid his share of the royalties on volumes of *Georgian Poetry*. (See Letter 2113.)

[2] There had been serious discontent in the coal industry for several months; a strike had twice been threatened by the Miners' Federation but postponed at the request of the Prime Minister (Lloyd George); it was eventually called on 17 October 1920.

[3] DHL also translated the caption on the verso of the postcard: 'Bridge of Sighs'.

25th. – no others, after a struggle of a journey down from Venice, where I met Frieda. I think Italy will inevitably revolute, but what will be the final effect I don't know. I know there is fear here that Italian exchange will drop as low as German, or even Austrian. And you have Lire 5,000 and I have about 6,000 in the bank. If all goes to pot, you must let me buy yours at a better than market-price, *for you*. It will always have value inside the country.

Do have any payments of mine from publishers made out to you, and open some[1] sort of New York Banking account for me.

Secker is publishing, or *trying* to, *The Lost Girl* on 1st. November. He is supposed to have sent Seltzer complete corrected proofs. But Secker is a shifty dog, as they all are. – Let Seltzer go ahead with *Lost Girl*, as soon as possible.

I had a letter from Duckworth saying that the parcel containing *White Peacock*, *Love Poems and Others*, and *Twilight in Italy*, was returned unclaimed from your present New York Address. Some mistake: I will make them send again.

Very well, let Seltzer do *Studies in Classic American Literature* in a limited edition, if he sees fit.

The Oxford Press is sending me now final proofs of the Hist. of Europe. By the way they *won't* assure me that I have full rights (American) at my disposal, I'm sure I have. But I await their next letter, and will send you a copy of corrected proofs and final information, next week. – This book might sell for schools.

Get *Sons and Lovers* from Kennerley. I have never had a penny from him for it, only a *bad* cheque for £20, which I sent him back (the date was altered) and he never answered or wrote another word.[2] Get *Sons and Lovers* from him, with a club [sketch].[3] I certainly approve of our buying plates from Kennerley if we can afford. I would be only too glad to have all the American rights of my books in our own names.

The Huebsch agreements were made via Doran, through Pinker.[4] I never saw them (tyranny!) But I can demand copies. The Kennerley agreement was made through Duckworth. Again, I can demand to be informed regarding it. I will do so.

---

[1] some] me
[2] DHL told Edward Garnett on 22 April 1914: 'I have had £35 from Kennerley' (see *Letters*, ii. 165 and n. 1.). On the '*bad*' cheque' (for £10), see *Letters*, ii. 174, 210, 217, etc. (Garnett (1868–1937) was DHL's close friend and mentor in his early years as an author; see *Letters*, i. 297.)
[3] DHL added a small drawing of a wooden club.
[4] See *Letters*, ii. 419 n. 2 and 420 n. 2.

'Fannie and Annie' is not offered to the English publishers. *You have the only copy.*

I will begin to collect short stories for a book, as you suggest.

(end of answers to yours of Sept. 24th.)

I am half way through a novel called *Aaron's Rod*, – hope to finish before Christmas.

I find here full proofs of *Women in Love*, from Seltzer.

If there is time, tell Seltzer the usual spelling of the abbreviation of Francesco is Ciccio, with three c's, and not Cicio, as I write it.

I sent you some *vers libre* called 'Fruits'.[1] I shall send you a complete MS., *Birds, Beasts and Flowers*, of these and such-like poems. They will perhaps suit periodicals in the meantime before book publication.

Secker proposes to issue[2] *Lost Girl* in November, *Women in Love* in February, and *Rainbow* in April. I don't want *Rainbow* to lie dead in America, owing to Huebsch.

end of business

Frieda is very well – comes back enthusiastic for Germany, and wants me to go there in spring. Probably I shall. Italy is going bust. But Sicily, I believe, will be quiet enough.

As for what you say of Germany, let every man speak exactly as he feels.

Yes, I liked my spin round Italy – now I am glad to be back, in the thunderstorm and silence of here, and all the strangeness of the eastern sea, and the lifted-upness of Fontana Vecchia. I feel most things coming to an end.

Not having received one word from you, having received various other American letters forwarded on, I was afraid you were ill. So glad you are well. – But your father was old, wasn't he? The old must be glad to die.

au revoir.   D. H. Lawrence

Nonsense, the Juta portrait is very good. Do use it, or have it used.

DHL

You say I must modify the parts about Indians in *The Lost Girl*. I don't understand. Do you mean in *Studies in Classic A. Lit?*

---

[1] See Letter 2083 and n. 1.   [2] issue] do

2111. To Reginald Turner, 19 October 1920

Text: MS UT; Postmark, Taormina 21 10 20; Unpublished.

Fontana Vecchia, Taormina, Sicilia

19 October 1920

Dear Turner

Here we are, back; – glad to be back, in the quiet: horrible journey down.

I never saw you again – am sorry. Hope you are well, and happy. You didn't seem happy this time.

Would it trouble you to ask Ancoras to send a little pattern-book of those coloured papers for decoration covers of books to

C.W. Beaumont, 75 Charing Cross Rd, W.C.2

I remember that last year you called at Ancora's shop for the same patterns –[1] in one of those streets near the Piazza Signoria, parallel with the Corso, coming out into the road where is the Bargello. I don't know names of streets in Florence, or I would write myself. Don't do it if it is out of your way.

Mrs Cannan is in Monaco. My wife came back quite flourishing from Germany. Sicily feels so extraordinary *quiet*, after the north, almost like a lost land.

Greetings   D. H. Lawrence

2112. To Cyril Beaumont, 19 October 1920

Text: MS UCin; Postmark, Taormina 21 10 20; Unpublished.

Fontana Vecchia, *Taormina*, Sicily

19 Oct 1920

Dear Beaumont

Thank you for the vellum copy of *Bay*. Your letter was too late to get me at Florence – I went to Venice, arrived here yesterday. I have written to Florence to Ancoras to ask them to send the pattern papers. Let me know if they come.

I've got a little book of vers libres, rather more than in *Bay*. Am wondering whether to send it you.

Yrs   D. H. Lawrence

---

[1] patterns –] patterns last year –

2113. To Irene and Percy Whittley, [23 October 1920]
Text: MS UT; Unpublished.

[Frieda Lawrence begins]

Fontana Vecchia
Saturday

Dear Mrs Whittley!

They actually stole your address out of my little black purse – they evidently hoped for 'gold', but I would have rather lost that than your address in Germany – That's why I haven't written – Lawrence is telling me how jolly it was with you both – I hope that next time I will be there too – Why not the Black Forest next time?[1] I *loved* it – We are back here again, it is a long long way, but it's worth it, we both thought it beautiful after the rain and like spring the flowers are out, roses and creepers and the grass so green after the brown desert of summer – We are glad to be together again – – I wonder what your English winter will be like, not without its excitements I think – No chance of England for me, so I must wait!

With my love to you both and hoping for another good time with you.

Frieda Lawrence

[Lawrence begins]

22 Oct.

Dear Whittley

Your letter today – after many days. We sit and see the rain come straight down, silent, isolated, strange, after so much knocking about: clean, and far off it feels here – so far off.

The Signorina's cat, the big one, died in Venice, and she cried her eyes out, poor thing. It stole a large piece of liver, and ate it, and never ate again. The little sandy kitten was very lively.

John Lane offered me £150 to write a little book on Venice.[2] Why wasn't he three months sooner.

I got Eddie Marshes letter and cheque, for poetry, in Venice – benissimo!

Now I'm settling down to work: correcting proofs like an angel, and washing my clothes betweenwhiles. Wonder how Mrs Whittley is getting on with her singing.

You've got a strike.[3] Perhaps your bank will break and you'll become a

---

[1] At this point in the MS Frieda had to avoid what appears to be a brief shopping-list in DHL's hand.
[2] See Letter 2120.
[3] The miners' strike was still continuing; it was not settled until 4 November 1920.

workless gentleman. Italy will go pop this winter, I believe. When the flood comes, we shall rock when the boughs rock, and watch waters rise.

I ordered you my coming novel.[1] No need for you to read it – still less need for you to like it.

Hope something nice will happen.

Saluti   D. H. Lawrence

2114. To Compton Mackenzie, 25 October 1920
Text: MS UT; Mackenzie 192–3.

Fontana Vecchia, Taormina, Sicily
25 Oct. 1920

Dear M[ackenzie]

Your letter today. We got back here last week: peace and stillness and *cleanness*, flowers, rain, streams, birds singing, sea dim and hoarse: valley full of cyclamens: poem to these, among other *vers libre*.[2]

Today *Lost Girl*, brown and demure and anything but lost-looking. Glad you were amused. She looks testamental.

Heard from my sister, who saw *Columbine*, and loved it. Heard from my elder sister, that Nottingham thought it a *great* success.

Heard all about Herm from a man called Hansard:[3] sounds very lovely. I must come and see it next year. Meanwhile write me more about it. Who is going to farm it? How many houses? Are you *letting*, or having a farm bailiff? News – !

We are quite alone at Taormina – I haven't been out to see who, English, is here. Feel I don't want. Prefer to be quite alone this winter, rather than that sort of well-to-do riff-raff, Ducas etc. – Don't feel *at all* drawn to Capri – do you?

Douglas has gone to Mentone with his Réné.[4]

Frieda back very chirpy from Germany: me pledged to go there in spring. Who knows what spring will bring.

You seem all business now.

D. H. Lawrence

---

[1] *The Lost Girl.*
[2] 'Sicilian Cyclamens', later printed in *Birds, Beasts and Flowers.*
[3] See p. 506 n. 4.
[4] René Mari (1905?–33) whom Douglas had met in 1919 and who was to be a particularly close friend for many years.

2115. To Martin Secker, 25 October 1920
Text: MS UInd; Secker 34.

Fontana Vecchia, *Taormina*, Sicily.

25 Oct. 1920

Dear Secker

Lost Girl came today: nice sober lady she looks, weighty and to be taken seriously, poor darling.

When you broke up my loaves and fishes into a thousand little chapters, why didn't you break up Chapter XIV on p. 178, at the word 'lake', line 17: and call the next bit *Under Water*.[1]

I've got to ask you to send two more copies of *Lost Girl*.

Capt. Herbert Asquith, 8 Sussex Place, Regents Park. N.W.1.

and

Richard Aldington, Chapel Farm Cottage,
Hermitage, nr Newbury, Berks.

Bear with me. You can send me a bill for them all.

DHL

2116. To Dr Anton Kippenberg, 4 November 1920
Text: MS SVerlag; Unpublished.

Villa Fontana Vecchia, *Taormina*, Sicilia, Italy

4 November 1920

Dear Sir

I have your letter of October 26th., forwarded from Baden Baden. I wrote you a second letter from Florence, in answer to yours, but apparently it did not reach you.

I said in it, that if you would prefer to pay in German Marks, would you quote me a figure. But perhaps it is simpler to leave it in English money.

You say *übertragen*, not *übersetzen*. I trust it is a faithful translation which you intend, and not a German *adaptation*.

If you promise a faithful translation of whatever books you undertake, and if you will let me see proofs of the German text before you finally print, then I am pleased to agree to the terms you state: viz, that I shall cede to you the sole authority to translate into German any or all books of mine which shall have

---

[1] Through a reference to Christ's miraculous feeding of the five thousand (Matthew xiv. 14–21), DHL alludes to the proofs of *Women in Love* which he was correcting. His page and line numbers refer very accurately to the first English edition: the word 'lake' occurs just before the section of 'Water Party' where Gerald dives 'under water'.

appeared before January 1st., 1924, the agreement to terminate on that date: and that you shall pay me £35-sterling for every book you undertake.

Sons and Lovers and *The Rainbow* seem to me the best suited for translation.[1] Martin Secker is bringing out another novel of mine this month: *The Lost Girl*. I will order a copy to be sent to you. At the end the scene is laid in Italy. – Also I am just correcting proofs of *Women in Love*, which forms a sequel to *The Rainbow*. Secker intends to publish it in February. It has been held up for two years, for fear of suppression.

I am posting you a copy of my play *Touch and Go*. It may interest you.

Will you be so good as to have sent to me a copy of the Insel-Verlag catalogue.

It gives me a good deal of pleasure to think of appearing in German. I have known your little yellow 'Almanach' for a long time, and like to think of being connected myself with the Insel-Verlag.

Yours Sincerely   D. H. Lawrence

2117. To Ada Clarke, [4 November 1920]

Text: MS Clarke; PC v. Giardini, Panorama; Postmark, Taormina 6 11 20; Unpublished.

[Fontana Vecchia, Taormina, (Messina), Sicily]
4 Nov.

Had your letter and photograph of Jackie with Peter:[2] a rackapelt[3] couple they look. Glad your new rooms are so nice: but you sound quite rakish, what with dances etc. No, don't for heavens sake think of a hamper: unless you come and bring it. Post is impossible for parcels. I wish I could send you almonds and figs – the only things Sicily produces fit to send.

Love   DHL

2118. To Thomas Seltzer, [6 November 1920]

Text: MS CorU; Postmark, Taormina 6 11 20; Moore 635.

Villa Fontana Vecchia, Taormina, Sicily.
7 November 1920

Dear Seltzer

Thank you for all the proofs of *Women in Love*. I went through them. There are only very slight incorrections. I am looking forward to your volume: it comes out immediately, Mountsier says.

---

[1] See p. 598 and n. 1.
[2] Ada's son and a Pekinese dog owned by her sister Emily King.
[3] Nottinghamshire dialect word meaning 'rascally' and 'boisterous'.

You will have received from Secker final corrected proofs of *The Lost Girl*.[1] Please print from these. Secker was due to publish on 1st. Novem., but Smith's and Mudies objected to page 256, so I re-wrote it for him, and I hope it will delay so that he can publish simultaneously with you. I asked him to send you *at once* the revised page, so that you can please yourself.[2] Of course the original is best. – Via England is quicker post than direct to America.

Secker intends *Women in Love* for February. I still think it the best of my books. Will you please send a copy to:

Miss Amy Lowell, Heath Street, *Brookline*, Mass.

And will you please send me *two* copies for myself. Of course you will give one copy to Mountsier.

I have various bits of work to do: haven't settled to anything serious yet. Do hope all goes well and happily.

D. H. Lawrence

2119. To J. B. Pinker, 7 November 1920
Text: MS UNYB; Unpublished.

Fontana Vecchia, *Taormina*, Sicily.

7 Novem. 1920

Dear Pinker

Would you please tell me whether *Hutchinson's Story Magazine* has retained *all* magazine rights on 'The Fox' story, or whether the American rights are mine.

Yours   D. H. Lawrence

2120. To Marie Hubrecht, 8 November 1920
Text: MS UN; Unpublished.

Fontana Vecchia, *Taormina*, Sicily.

8 November 1920

Dear Miss Hubrecht

Since we are back here it has done nothing but pour in masses of rain, so that the sea is yellow and the streams are impassable: of all of which I am tired. But I like Fontana Vecchia: so still and remote and sweet scented. The roses are out, if they weren't knocked to bits by the rain: and the wild

---

[1] Seltzer did not receive the proofs from Secker until early December; the American edition of *The Lost Girl* was thereby delayed until 28 January 1921.

[2] On the lending libraries' objections and DHL's revised text see Letter 2121 and n. 1. Seltzer did please himself: he printed the unaltered original text of p. 256.

cyclamens, if they weren't gone under Noah's flood. Still I suppose one mustn't grumble, after ten months of sun.

Taormina seems disconsolate and forsaken. There are few English people, but a moderate number of Scandinavians. If you come you will imagine yourself still in Norway. – The Duca was here, but has left again for Maniace. Kitson came to tea yesterday – our only visitor. Bowdwin is in Rome, fussing over some furniture. The Major is so shaky on his thread of life, it is a marvel. But still he hangs on. Very few people in Timeo: and in the new and should-be startling Diodoro, only 3 visitors. – Carmelo wants to go to America to join Ciccio. Vicenzo, the youth whom Ciccia is going to marry, is dismissed from Mrs Dashwood's – she said he wasnt honest – and hangs round here. He seems quite nice. – There isn't much food to be bought in the village: but thank heaven, one goat has her kid, so a thin trickle of milk has begun: we had the first drop today. A barren land.

Juta and Insole are in Rome, Palazzo Moroni – not very happy together: Juta having tender interludes with young females, and Insole's nose out of joint. He talks of going to Tunis for the winter. – We shall stay on here till spring. John Lane asked me to write a book on Venice, to have Brangwen pictures.[1] I might go to Venice in March: have promised to go to Germany in May. The Insel-Verlag have decided to translate *Sons and Lovers*, and *The Rainbow* into German, and to pay for the translation rights. We will see how this goes. I ordered for you from London *The Lost Girl*, which I wrote here: though I believe novels bore you.

Now I am going to bother you about a little thing. Last year, last October, when Frieda went from England to Germany via Holland, one of her trunks went astray in Holland. It was found after two weeks, and sent on to Baden-Baden: but the Dutch authorities confiscated a piece of velvet, a piece of blue cloth, and two woollen vests, which she was taking to her mother. After much wrangling, the Dutch authorities released the goods, but would not allow them to pass into Germany, as there was a law against the export of cloth and clothing. So the things *still* lie in the hands of an old friend of my uncle's: more than a year they are there, and there seems to be no getting them out of Holland, in any direction. My mother-in-law would be more than glad of the stuff: she is threadbare, like most of Germany. If you could do anything in the matter, and if it wouldn't be a nuisance to you, I should be so glad. The cloth lies with *Mr. F. Buckesfeld. Bloemgracht 142*[1], *Amsterdam*. He is a friend of my uncle, *F. Krenkow, Quorn*. My mother-in-law is *Frau Baronin von*

---

[1] Frank Brangwyn (1867–1956) was a painter whom DHL particularly admired in his youth: 'to copy a Frank Brangwyn is a joy, so refreshing' (*Letters*, i. 491; see also i. 196).

Richthofen, Ludwig-Wilhelmstift, Baden-Baden. I would gladly pay all expenses if the material could be sent. Parcels going into Germany may go duty-free if inscribed *Liebesgabe.* – If the things can't go to Germany, they might even come here.

You won't mind my asking you, will you. Don't trouble if it is a nuisance – Are you coming to Taormina? Frieda greets you.

D. H. Lawrence

2121. To Martin Secker, 10 November 1920
Text: MS UInd; Secker 34–5.

Fontana Vecchia, Taormina, Sicily
10 Novem. 1920

Dear Secker

Enclosed proofs of *W. in Love* up to page 320.

Had your telegram saying revised page received, yesterday.[1] Post bad. Put not your trust in the British public.[2] Seltzer wants you to publish simultaneously with him – in January, that is. I believe his *W. in L.* is out – am waiting to see the vol.

Could you please get for me a copy of *Hutchinson's Story Magazine*, published *October 8th.*, and containing a story of mine 'The Fox'. I know nothing of the magazine. Please try and send me the copy.

Did I ask you to send a copy of *The Lost Girl* to Miss Marie Hubrecht, Witte Huis, *Doorn*, bei Utrecht. Holland. I believe I did: but if not, please take the address now. Also please send one copy to

Don Mauro Inguanez, Badia di *Montecassino*, Prov. Caserta.
There is no end to me and my sendings.

I am interested to know if you cajoled those MudieBootie people.

---

[1] Page 256 of *The Lost Girl* was re-written by DHL in response to a letter from Secker, 22 October 1920 (see *The Lost Girl*, ed. Worthen, p. xxxix) in which he warned DHL that three lending libraries – Smith's, Mudie's and Boots' – had voiced serious objections.

As a matter of fact they now decline to circulate it and the passage to which they specifically object is on page 256 . . . you should seriously consider whether it would not be possible for you to rewrite the passage in question in such a way as to remove their objections. After all these three libraries should account between them for some 2,000 copies, possibly more if the book should have the success I anticipate, and as well as this direct result there is the even greater indirect benefit of your work gaining the widest publicity which only the libraries can afford.

For the text of DHL's revised page see Worthen edn, pp. 386–7. The libraries were satisfied with the changes and duly bought copies of the novel.

[2] Cf. Psalms cxlvi. 3 ['Put not your trust in princes'].

The Insel-Verlag, Leipsic – the best publishing firm in Germany – write me that they want to translate and publish *Sons and Lovers* and *The Rainbow*: others later: give me £35 a time: or 10,000 Mark. I write I am willing. We'll see if it comes off.

Hope soon to have some news from you: hope for your sake even more than mine that this *Lost Girl* will bring her eggs safe to market.

Am not working – too unsettled yet: and this autumn-winter is my uneasy time. Let the year turn.

                                                                          DHL

Wail from Francis B[rett]-Y[oung].

2122. To Rosalind Baynes, 16 November 1920
Text: MS UN; Huxley 509–10.

                                        Villa Fontana Vecchia, *Taormina*, Sicily
                                                                    16 Nov. 1920

Dear Rosalind

It rains with such persistency and stupidity here that one loses all one's initiative and remains cut off. Had your letter this morning: hope you'll like the *Lost Girl* – or be a bit amused, anyhow. The libraries objected to page 256 (I think it's that) so it had to be altered, for Secker's sake, and delay in issuing. You've probably got the unaltered.

No news: it only rains. I've been swotting Ital. history: having finished proofs of the hist. for the Oxford Press, they ask for another chap. on Italian unification. Have read all up, now proceed to write.[1] Nothing else doing.

I'm copying a *very* amusing picture – Lorenzettis – *Anacoreti nelle Tebaidi*[2] – thousands of amusing little monks doing things in the *Thebaid*: like it very much: success so far.

Everywhere seems very far off. Sicily at the moment feels like a land inside an aquarium – all water – and people like crabs and black-grey shrimps

---

[1] This produced chapter XVIII of *Movements*. The reading to which DHL refers included Bolton King, *A History of Italian Unity* (1899); G. M. Trevelyan, *Garibaldi's Defence of the Roman Republic* (1907), *Garibaldi and the Thousand* (1909), *Garibaldi and the Making of Italy* (1911); and E. M. Jamison, *Italy Mediæval and Modern* (Oxford, 1917).

[2] The picture (in the Uffizi, Florence), known as *La Tebaide*, was attributed in DHL's day to Pietro Lorenzetti (1280?–1348?); it is now associated with the Florentine School of the early fifteenth century. (See *Gli Uffizi: Catologo Generale*, Florence, 1980, p. 487: P. 1479.) In citing the name of Lorenzetti DHL was probably quoting the caption on his photograph (perhaps by Alinari), or Baedeker or one of several art historians who attributed the picture to that artist. (The misattribution may have sprung from the likeness between the picture and the fresco of the *Thebaid* in the Campo Santo at Pisa. Vasari linked the name of Lorenzetti with the fresco; others, following his lead, associated the same painter with the picture.)

creeping on the bottom. Don't like it. Don't think Christmas would be any good here either. We shall be coming north in the spring – have promised to go to Germany – perhaps do a book on Venice as John Lane asked me – perhaps Sardinia – who knows. Will let you know.

It is becoming almost impossible to live with other people in the house, I agree. That's why, though I curse this rain, I really prefer the isolation. There is no contact, except one which makes one almost squeal with impatience.

Remember me to Eleanor: she's just getting the worst of Italy. How are the children? – and Godwin and Analysis![1]

DHL

2123. To Baroness Anna von Richthofen, 19 November 1920
Text: MS UCB; Unpublished.

[Fontana Vecchia, Taormina, (Messina), Sicily]
19 Novem 1920

Liebe Schwiegermutter

I made you such a nice parcel of figs and almonds, but try in vain to send it to you. The Italians are fools, they make so many difficulties.

The paper and envelopes came yesterday, and are appropriated by your daughter – who, since you ask how I find her, is, I am sad to say, no better behaved than she should be. But – speriamo – .

I wrote to the Insel-Verlag, and trust that business will go off all right – and we shall all be millionaires – in Marks, alas. – Don't bother to send them *The Lost Girl* yet.

We are wondering if Else is with you, and how she found Friedel Schloffer.[2]

Here it rains heavens hard, and I am tired of seeing and hearing so much water. If it continues all the soft part of Sicily will tumble into the sea, which is yellow already with the land washed into it.

Frieda is always talking about Germany and the spring. Let us hope all goes well and we can have a good time.

Many greetings to Else.

Love   DHL

---

[1] Probably a reference to Godwin Baynes's having been appointed Jung's assistant in Zurich; he went on to specialise in Jungian analytical psychology.
[2] The estranged wife of Otto Gross (see *Letters*, i. 395 n. 1. and 409 n. 2); she had been a friend of Frieda's sister, Else Jaffe, for many years.

2124. To Mary Cannan, 22 November 1920
Text: MS Lazarus; Moore 636–7.

Fontana Vecchia
22 November 1920

Dear Mary

Yes, I was a bit cross with you 'and your money', as you say. But – tout passe.

Here we are, like marooned sailors. Kitson has been once to tea – and once a Frenchwoman – otherwise, dead silence. But I don't want people – feel a dead blank in their direction.

We've had the awfulest weather – these last two days great guns of wind, slashing masses of rain, impossible to open the doors almost. But we've sat in the big room with a good fire and felt like Noah in the ark.

The Taorminesi natives are as mean and creeping as ever – really begin to feel like you, that one must have done with Italy. Exchange was 96.50 last week – doubt if it'll get better. If I were you I should change into French if there is a momentary improvement – at least part of your sum. Doubt if ever you'll want to come to Italy again, things being as they are, prices much higher, stuff scarcer, people more and more tiresome.

Glad you like Monte Carlo. Réné Hansard said France was *much* better to live in, materially, than here.

The Brett Youngs *may* be coming here – to Taormina that is – for Christmas.

Juta and Insole not agreeing very well, like a married couple, Insole has dashed to Tunis and writes from the Sahara.

No, I'm not going to Capri. I said we *might* only – one of my mites.

Very few English here – many Scandinavians poking about.

Am doing nothing serious.

Libraries objected to p. 256 (I think) of *Lost Girl* – so I re-wrote it for Secker's sake: delayed in England, therefore, not out yet, I think.

Am doing no serious work, but painting a picture.

tanti saluti   DHL

2125. To Thomas Seltzer, 22 November 1920
Text: MS UT; Postmark, Taormina 24 11 20; Lacy, *Seltzer* 15–16.

Fontana Vecchia, *Taormina*, Sicilia
22 Novem 1920

Dear Seltzer

Thank you for the cuttings – I send them back at once – don't bother to send me any more.

I had your letter – look forward very much to my copies of *Women in Love*.[1]
As for Italy – she'll get through the winter all right, I suppose. The South is a dead letter. Things are so shaky that nobody will give the last push.

Saluti   D. H. Lawrence

2126. To Martin Secker, 22 November 1920
Text: MS UInd; Secker 35.

Fontana Vecchia, Taormina, Sicily.
22 Novem. 1920

Dear Secker

Herewith the last, final, and concluding proofs of *Women in Love*: 508 pages, as you say. But it is the book I have most at heart. Don't you think it will be best *not* to send it out – not to send out review copies *at all*, but just to publish and leave it at that. I do so hate the critics, they are such poisonous worms, especially for a book like this.

Here there are great storms of·wind and rain and violent weather, the soft part of Sicily is all washing down into the sea. Goodbye to it.

When will *Lost Girl* come out? Tell me about it.

Did you get all the other proofs of *Women in Love*, and letters enclosed.

Will you send out still one more copy of *Lost Girl* – to:

Douglas Goldring Esq, 7. St. James' Terrace, Regents Park, N.W.8.

Vale   DHL

2127. To Douglas Goldring, [22 November 1920]
Text: MS SIU; PC; Postmark, Taormina 24 11 20; Goldring, *Odd Man Out*, p. 252.

Taormina
22 Nov

Dear Goldring

I ask Secker to send you a copy of the *Lost Girl* to this address: hope you will get it all right.

We are back here, after various wanderings – nothing doing – weather masses of rain and wind incredible. Promised to go to Germany in Spring – Insel-Verlag supposed to be publishing *Sons and Lovers* and *Rainbow* in translation. No news besides – hope you're[2] doing well, both.

Yrs   D. H. Lawrence

---

[1] Seltzer had published the novel on 9 November 1920.
[2] MS reads 'your'.

2128. To Ada Clarke, [25 November 1920]
Text: MS Clarke; PC v. Taormina. Vicolo con Venditrice di frutta; Postmark, Taormina 2[. . .] 11 20; Unpublished.

[Fontana Vecchia, *Taormina*, (Messina), Sicily]
25 November.

Haven't heard yet if you had my letter with cheque for father.[1] – If you get me a blazer, get it not too pale, as it will get dirty. Is there anything you would like that we could get for Christmas for you.

Love. DHL

2129. To Francis Brett Young, [29? November 1920]
Text: MS UB; Sagar, *Review of English Literature*, vi. 102.

[Fontana Vecchia, *Taormina*, (Messina), Sicily]
Monday

Dear B[rett] Y[oung]

Pity you cant see Sicily, or set foot on her again before Africa. Not that she's worth seeing at present, damn her, for she she's like a land in an aquarium, it rains so.

But it's left off today and we're going to a fair of cattle on the beach of Letojanni: it is still only 8.0 o clock.

No news here – we are quite alone, see nobody here – by choice – except a couple of people who bore me. I did more than half of *Aaron's Rod*, but can't end it: the flowering end missing, I suppose – so I began a comedy, which I hope will end. Who knows.

No news at all at all. Shan't afford Africa as soon as you, but shall say Ta-Ta! to Europe when I can: Ciau!

DHL

2130. To Robert Mountsier, 30 November–1 December 1920
Text: MS Smith; Unpublished.

Fontana Vecchia, *Taormina*, Sicily.
30 Novem 1920

Dear Mount.

Received yours of 10th Nov. today.[2] Right about the 10% up to 5,000

---

[1] DHL noted in his diary on 1 November 1920: 'Sent £5 to Ada for father' (Tedlock, *Lawrence MSS* 91).

[2] Mountsier's letter (TMSC Smith) read as follows:

Dear Lawrence: –

In view of the high cost of materials and labor for the publication of books, it is desirable to change your royalty percentage for "The Lost Girl," as you will see by the attached letters.

copies on *Lost Girl*. If Seltzer does at all well with *L.G.*, we'll give him the next: we must stay by him if possible, since he has been, I feel, very decent so far.

I had enclosed from Duckworth[1] – expected something further: but nothing so far.

I got from Pinker that the *English rights only* were sold to the *Hutchinson Story Mag.* of 'The Fox.' The end – yes, have all the opinions you can – is clipped as short as possible because editors complain so bitterly that the stories are too *long* for magazine work. I'd alter it for a book.

The Huebsch contracts were made, I believe, via Doran. I'll write Pinker about them – have written once.

I will write now to Secker forbidding him to send any *Lost Girl*s or *W. in Love*s to America.

Two months of torrential rain here – no work in me. – The *Dial* paid £14. sterling for 'Rex'.

I kept quiet when Seltzer first broached the subject to me, but two friends, one the manager of the American John Lane Company and the other the head of the book section of Marshall Field's department store strongly advised me to agree to 10% on a $2 price basis. Seltzer could go on with the publication at 15%, but he would have to fix the price at $2.50 or more, and publishers feel that that price will kill a novel. I got Seltzer to agree to 12½% on the second 5,000 and 15% on any copies over 10,000.

He wants to publish in January, so he is anxious to start the composition work. And he wanted the written permission of the attached letter. I am convinced that the new contract is the best way out of it.

Seltzer also wants to put a clause into the contract tying up your next novel or two. I consider this highly undesirable. He is a new publisher, and he has not yet shown us what he can do with the two novels he has, in the line of sales. Besides, he has "Studies in Classic American Literature" yet to publish. I understand his viewpoint, but that doesn't make me forget ours.

Please write Duckworth and ask him, if he has not already done so, to send me immediately a copy of the contract with Kennerley for the American publication of "Sons and Lovers."

Also add your word to mine to Secker to refrain absolutely from sending any copies of your books that he publishes to the States.

Torrence, of "The New Republic," is now considering "The Revolutionary" and "Sorb-apples and Medlars." "The New Republic" also is considering what I call the "Knights of Columbus" introduction to "Studies in Classic American Literature."

By the way, did you get a letter from me when you were in northern Italy? I wrote you as requested – c/o Thomas Cook, Via Tornabuoni, Florence.

Yesterday Huebsch could not see me because he is too busy! Day before yesterday Kennerley was not in, and his secretary said an appointment would be made for me, but as yet no word. There'll be some doing with these two birds before long, believe me.

Can't you get some sort of a detailed statement from Pinker that would show you where you stand with the various publishers? It would be useful in checking up over here, and incidentally we might check up Pinker on this side.

With best wishes,

Yours,   R. Mountsier

[1] Missing.

The Connecticut farm was to be a loan. The woman is a Mrs Thrasher, widow of a sculptor killed in war: a nice woman.

Mackenzie felt he must *make sure of money* before he took his boat. So he is staging his novels as plays for all he is worth: and succeeding, I believe. Meanwhile he has leased two *Channel Isles* – next Guernsey – Herm and a little one – for £3,000 a year from British govt., and is inviting me there. I am not enticed. What he'll do with 'em I don't know: a cinema studio is rumoured.

Lost Girl is out in England: Secker had orders for 1,300 – I've seen no crits. yet. Don't care.

My wine is Etna. Asti has gone up to 19 a bottle.

Best of wishes from us both. But *whatever* are you going to do without a job?

DHL

The parcel of books was re-sent from Duckworth.

1 Dec.   Enclose various agreements, come now. Tell me what more you want.

2131. To Martin Secker, 30 November 1920
Text: MS UInd; Secker 35–6.

Fontana Vecchia, *Taormina*, Sicily.
30 Nov. 1920

Dear Secker

Have your letter[1] – glad *Lost Girl* is out – hope she goes well.

I return proof of Chap VII.[2] Have altered it a bit: enough, I think. If enemies want to fasten, they'll fasten anywhere. As I say, I think it would be much best not to send out review copies. But we'll see how *Lost Girl* goes.

How is Mackenzie?

D. H. Lawrence

---

[1] Secker had written on 25 November 1920 (*Letters from a Publisher*, p. 7) as follows:

Dear Lawrence,
   I should have written to you some time ago to acknowledge one or two letters but I have been hoping every day to be able to let you know the total subscription to your book. After a great deal of delay with the printers and binders in fixing up the cancel pages it is only today that the book is actually out and the sales up to the present amount to roughly 1300. I think this is very good and if we can get the reviews which I expect I have great hopes of doubling this figure by the end of the year. . .

[2] This chapter in *Women in Love*, 'Totem', was later the cause of threatened legal action by Philip Heseltine who claimed to be libellously portrayed as 'Halliday'. Further alterations were eventually required. (See Eldon S. Branda, 'Textual Changes in *Women in Love*', *Texas Studies in Literature and Language*, vi (1964), 306–21.)

Please send a copy of *Lost Girl* to
    Miss Amy Lowell, Heath Street, *Brookline*, Mass. U.S.A.
If you like to send me a bill for the excess copies, I'll pay it.
Don't send any copies of *The Lost Girl* or *Women in Love* to America, *please*, except the one copy to Amy Lowell.

2132. To Amy Lowell, 30 November 1920
Text: MS HU; Damon 550–1.

Fontana Vecchia, *Taormina*, Sicily.
30 November 1920.

My dear Amy

I wonder how you are. Here we sit in Sicily and it has done nothing but rain masses of rain since we are back. But today a rainbow and tramontana wind and blue sea, and Calabria such a blue morning-jewel I could weep. The colour of Italy is blue, after all. Strange how rare red is. But orange underglow in the soil and rock here.

The little rose cyclamens are almost over: the little white and yellow narcissus are out among the rocks, scenting the air, and smelling like the world's morning, so far back. Oranges are nearly ripe, yellow and many – and we've already roasted the autumn kids: soon it will be Christmas.

I had your review notice of *Touch and Go*.[1] Did I thank you? I hope you've got *Women in Love* from Seltzer: I asked him to send it you. Of all my novels, I like it far best. But other people don't and won't. Tell me *please* what you think. – I've ordered Secker to send you also *The Lost Girl*, which is just out in London. Perhaps this will sell, and make me some money. I don't think *Women in Love* will sell.

I did a little book of vers libre – *Birds, Beasts, and Flowers*: am awaiting it from the typist.[2] Frieda hates it: I like it. 'Songs without Sound' I'd like to call them. When I get the MS. I think I shall send it to you for your opinion, am so curious to know.

Haven't you got a new book?[3]

We keep making plans for the Spring – I think I shall go to Germany for a time. Where are you going.

Greetings from both of us to you for Christmas.

D. H. Lawrence

---

[1] See Letter 2079 and n. 2.
[2] DHL recorded in his diary for 4 November 1920: 'Sent poem. MS Birds, Beasts, and Flowers to Miss Wheelock to type' (Tedlock, *Lawrence MSS* 91). Though he had devised a title which he later used for his volume of poems, DHL had not yet written all the poems themselves. Ruth Wheelock (1891–1958) worked at the American Consulate, Palermo (see Letter 2152).
[3] Her next book was *Legends* (May 1921).

1 December 1920

Even if you don't like *Women in Love* very much, have a certain gentle feeling towards it, because I ask you.

2133. To Professor John Metcalf, 1 December 1920
Text: MS UV; Postmark, Taormina 3 12 20; Unpublished.

Villa Fontana Vecchia, *Taormina*, Sicily.
1 December 1920

Dear Sir[1]

I have your letter forwarded from Duckworth today.

I enclose two poems, which are for the restless ghost of Poe.[2] Use them or not, as you like, but kindly let me know. And I should like to have a copy of the book when it comes.

Yours Sincerely   D. H. Lawrence

to Professor Metcalf and Professor Wilson
University, Virginia. U.S.A.

But I shall publish the poems later in a book.

Two Poems
for the unappeased spirit of Poe
by D. H. Lawrence

Tropic

Sun, dark Sun
Sun of black, void heat
Sun of the torrid midday's horrific darkness

Behold my hair twisting and turning black
Behold my eyes turn tawny yellow.

The milk of northern spume
Coagulating and going black in my veins
Aromatic as frankincense.

[1] The recipient was Professor John Calvin Metcalf (1865–1949), Linden Kent Memorial Professor of English Literature, University of Virginia, 1917–40. His name is associated at the foot of the letter with that of Professor James Southall Wilson (1880–1963), Edgar Allan Poe Professor of English Literature. The two men collaborated in publishing *The Enchanted Years: A Book of Contemporary Verse* to celebrate the University's centenary; it appeared in June 1921 (New York).

[2] 'Tropic' and 'Slopes of Etna' were printed in *The Enchanted Years*; later they were both collected (the former as 'Peace') in *Birds, Beasts and Flowers*. (It is presumed that Metcalf had made some reference to Poe's connection with the University of Virginia: he was there for ten months in 1826.)

Columns dark and soft
Sunblack men
Valved nostrils, sunbreathing mouths
Eyes of yellow, golden sand
As frictional, as perilous, explosive brimstone.

Rock, waves of dark heat
Waves of dark heat, rock, sway upwards
Waver perpendicular.

What is the horizontal rolling of water
Compared to the flood of black heat that rolls upward past our eyes.

Slopes of Etna

Peace is written on the doorstep
In lava.

Peace, black peace.
My heart will know no peace
Till the mountain bursts again.

Brilliant, intolerable lava
Brilliant as a powerful burning-glass
Walking like a royal snake down the mountain towards the sea.

Forests, cities, bridges
Gone under again in the bright trail of the snake
That has slept so long inside the mountain;
Since Naxos, thousands of feet below the olive-roots;
To wake again, and walk over the olive leaves
And lay black roads above the aloe-spikes.

Peace in lava on the door-step.
White-hot serpent in my heart, trying to lift its head
Never at peace.
Till lava breaks.
Till it burst forth white-hot, withering
To set in black rock.

Call it Peace?[3]

---

[3] l. 10 the bright . . . snake] the trail of the brilliant snake of the sun
l. 11 inside the mountain] in the mountain dormant in earth's bosom
ll. 13–14 To wake . . . walk . . . lay] And now wakes . . . walks . . . lays

2134. To S. S. Koteliansky, 3 December 1920
Text: MS BL; Postmark, Taormina 4 12 20; Zytaruk 214.

Fontana Vecchia, *Taormina*, Sicily.
3 December 1920

My dear Kot

Your letter today – I feel I simply can't write letters –

F[rieda] went to Germany – I was in Florence and Venice – we are back here for six weeks, and it has rained all the time. I will go to that 'far country' when I can afford – as soon as I can afford.

All your news is entirely new to me. Poor Gertler, what a curse and a misery.[1] And what a pretty thought, of your mother. Hm!

I've got no news – merely wrestle with publishers. I'll send you *The Lost Girl*, don't buy it – I am not wildly interested in it.

I never received Gorky's *Reminiscences*.[2] Did you send it? When? By registered Book Post? Curse this Italian post. But let me know, and I'll enquire here, and warm their ears. Not that it has the slightest effect on the swine.

Mary is in Monte Carlo, wearing her glad-rags with gusto. Haven't heard more of Gilbert – Mond.

Suppose we shall sit here till March – might leave before. I promised to go to Germany for a while in spring, but am not sure.

Remember me to Grisha and Sonia.

DHL

2135. To Robert Mountsier, 5 December 1920
Text: MS Smith; Unpublished.

Taorminad
Dec 5 1920

Mounthier
417 West 118 St New York
Very angry cabled Secker[3]

Lanretece[4]

---

[1] Gertler was in a sanatorium at Nordrach-on-Dee, Banchory, suspected of having tuberculosis. He was to remain there till early May 1921. Kot had probably conveyed to DHL the depression evident in a letter (28 November 1920) he had received from Gertler (see *Gertler: Selected Letters*, ed. Carrington, pp. 188–9).

[2] See Letter 2040 and n. 1.

[3] DHL noted in his diary for 3 December 1920: 'cabled Secker strongly' (Tedlock, *Lawrence MSS* 91). The cable has not been located. See p. 637 and n. 4.

[4] The spelling of the Western Union cablegram is retained.

2136. To Eleanor Farjeon, 6 December 1920
Text: MS UT; Huxley 510–11.

Fontana Vecchia, *Taormina*, Sicily.
6 Decem 1920

Dear Eleanor

Yours arrived yesterday. I stayed at Hotel Cappuccini in Amalfi – terms 35–40 a day: very nice, charming old monastery and orange garden – I liked it. Hotel della Luna also good, and I believe a bit cheaper. Write for rooms. Don't know how you intend getting there – there is a bus from Vietri station: 2 hours.

It has poured masses of water and still isn't clear here – vile – no sign of cotton except in umbrellas. I shall find you a room here in an hotel or pension – housekeeping is *so* irritating and tiresome. Tell R[osalind] *never* to think of living in Sicily, though it's a pity she can't see it. Tell me if you'd rather have a *pension* for about 22–25 a day, or a really rather nice hotel for 35?

Get your courage up for the railways – or pray for luck. They are normally vile south of Rome. You can go to Amalfi via Naples – Naples to Sorrento by steamer – Sorrento to Amalfi by carriage, fee about 35 francs. Don't get stranded, particularly in Rome, without having engaged a room – though Amalfi season is the early spring – swanky then. It is beautiful. – It's no good thinking of rooms – one must go to hotels, and fairly good ones.

Hope it's nice.

DHL

2137. To Robert Mountsier, 9 December 1920
Text: MS Smith; Postmark, Taormina 10 12 20; Unpublished.

Fontana Vecchia, *Taormina*, Sicily.
9 Dec. 1920

Dear M[ountsier]

Yours dateless telling me about 'The Blind Man' story in *The Living Age:*[1] Pinker's doing: and no word to me, and no cheque: sharp letter to him.

Had your cable on 3rd, about *Lost Girl* selling New York. Cabled Secker and wrote him pepper. He'll be offended for life. *Tant mieux pour lui.* Forbade him to issue *W. in Love* till May 1st – and altogether went it – I was, and am, furious with the little mongrel: he is no better. But his *W. in Love* won't be ready till May, I'm sure.

---

[1] After publication in *English Review*, July 1920, the story re-appeared in *The Living Age*, 7 August 1920.

No further news of *Lost Girl* in London. Post very bad here.

Had your proofs of 'Rex' from *Dial*. Do capture a copy of *The Dial* containing 'Rex' and 'Adolf' – which appeared earlier.[1] I should be glad if you kept a copy, in print, of everything of mine that appears in America.

I am sending you *Birds Beasts and Flowers* – poems – under registered manuscript cover. Sell as much as possible to periodicals first: also Harriett Monroe – she likes me – or did. I've neglected her. – I promised to let Amy Lowell see the MS. You might mail it to her and ask her for it back quick – Miss Amy Lowell, Heath Street, Brookline, Mass: and say who you are. – But don't bother if you don't want. Out of this MS. I sent to *Professor Metcalf, University, Virginia* – he wrote and asked me – two poems, 'Peace', which I called ' Slopes of Etna' and 'Tropic' – which I find I have omitted. I'll write it out and you will type it in – 'Tropic'. – The Virginia University has a centenary and a Poe memorial book. You could ask Prof. Metcalf if he is using the two poems, or avoiding them.

The *Movements in European History* is being published under nom de plume – Lawrence H. Davison – and the Oxford Press settling with me for America. They are slow.

I left off *Aarons Rod* – more than half done – but the end won't blossom. I began *Mr. Noon* – $\frac{1}{3}$ done – sudden stop – may go on soon.

Let me know if you have got all agreements etc. you want.

– End of business.

Taormina is a pretty place with hotels and English artists – well-to-do – used to be really swank – now nowhere is swank. A man Bonner, American, is sailing from here in early January for New York, with an *Opera* which he wants the Metropolitan to put on.[2] I shall get him to meet you and you can talk Taormina.

We live very quietly – nice house, quite swank compared to Cornwall – see a very few people.

Of Wm. Henry – he is married, with two little girls, prosperous in money – but household not happy – Mrs Hocking ill and miserable. I don't hear from them direct. I think Wm H. was scared when we were kicked out of Zennor and you were a 'Spy'.[3]

Whatever are you doing if you have no job?

If this finds you anywhere near Christmas, here's to your health and happiness from both.

Yrs   DHL

When you come to Europe, sail to Naples and so come here.

---

[1] See p. 536 n. 1.   [2] Unidentified.   [3] See Letter 1343 and n. 1.

2138. To J. B. Pinker, 9 December 1920
Text: MS UNYB; Unpublished.

Fontana Vecchia, *Taormina*, Sicily

9 Dec. 1920

Dear Pinker

I heard from America that 'The Blind Man' story had appeared in a periodical there some time ago. Would you mind telling me when and where – and if they have paid – and if Harrison has ever paid for the *English Review* rights of the same story.

Yours Sincerely   D. H. Lawrence

2139. To Thomas Seltzer, 11 December 1920
Text: MS UT; Postmark, Taormina 14 12 20; Lacy, *Seltzer* 16.

Villa Fontana Vecchia, *Taormina*, Sicily.

11 Decem 1920

Dear Seltzer

Today have come ten copies of *Women in Love*. I am very pleased indeed with it: feel it has made us friends for life: and sincerely hope so. It's a real book. Now I pray it will bring you your money quickly, and be a success in that way. It is my best book. I was glad you said you began to like it. It needs a bit of getting used to.

I was furious with Secker for letting his *Lost Girl* appear in New York – had Mountsier's cable – and wrote and cabled him, Secker, such a smack in the eye that he'll probably never forgive me. So much the better for me.

Be sure and tell me[1] how this book goes: I am *most* anxious about it: the others I don't fret myself about so much.

I hope we can go on all the way together, you as publisher and me as writer. I haven't Mountsier's respect for big publishers like Doran and Co: – they are excellent sellers of old hat, but fatal for new: witness Methuen and *The Rainbow*.

Many Christmas Greetings, and New Year. This was my best Christmas present.[2]

Yrs   D. H. Lawrence

---

[1] MS reads 'he'.
[2] Seltzer, replying to this letter, wrote on 5 February 1921 (TMS Smith) as follows:

Dear Lawrence,
    It was good to get your letter. It was *my* best Christmas present. It cheered me, and I needed to be cheered. The sudden business depression hit us all very hard. The dealers would not stock up with books, the people would not buy books and the banks would not give any money, and in publishing you need bushels of money every hour. But conditions are beginning to

2140. To Mary Cannan, 12 December 1920
Text: MS Lazarus; Moore 637–8.

Fontana Vecchia, *Taormina*, Sicilia.
Sunday. 12 Dec 1920

My dear Mary

Your letter today – also the 1000 Lire to Frieda – which makes me laugh at you up my sleeve – which you won't mind.

Sorry Montecarlo proved tiresome: Douglas, at Mentone, *loathes* the French. Here things have brightened up: sun again, blue sea, long mornings, and quite warm. We have suddenly dashed into society – or been popped in by Kitson. But don't take it seriously. Teaparty at Bowdwins little house with B. and young American who is just off for New York with an opera under his arm – also various others – bit boring. – Tea with Miss Rosalie Bull, who has that house with a sort of a bit of tower you see from us – near Cipolla's house, where Miss Wallace lives.[1] Rosalie is a theosophist and rather nice and comic. Met there a young Baron Stempel, who has the villa – the big one, just below the Duca, which is placarded to sell. He is from Baltic Russia, and has been

improve somewhat.

You are certainly right about WOMEN IN LOVE. It is not only your best novel but one of the best ever written. It stays with me as few literary works do and I am tempted every now and then to pick the book up and read passages in it. Everyone seems to feel the same way about it. "A tremendous book", is the general opinion. Considering the conditions and the price it has gone well too. In less than two months, up to January 1st, we sold 338 copies. Now it is beginning to move even faster. I think we must have sold close to 100 copies during January. I should not be surprised if we sold the whole edition in the not remote future, provided that no copies of the English edition find their way here. I shall do all I can to prevent them being smuggled in. If the English edition does not appear before May, we are fairly safe anyway. I am now thinking of bringing out another cheaper edition, at $10 or even $5, if possible.

But your most popular novel no doubt is THE LOST GIRL. I read it again in page proof and it held my interest and fascinated me. It is a book no other but D. H. Lawrence could write and yet it is so different from anything you did before.

THE LOST GIRL has been out only a few days. Our first printing is 3,000. The binder had a thousand copies ready towards the end of last week. In two days they were gone, with some orders unfilled. And this too, in spite of the impossibility to sell the book in advance, as it was brought out out of season and in a hurry, in order to stop the importations from England. The books were sold chiefly in New York City. Only a very small number have been shipped outside, so it is very, very encouraging. I hope the success of THE LOST GIRL is such that Mountsier will change his mind about big publishers. Six copies were forwarded to you February 3.

I sent Amy Lowell a copy of WOMEN IN LOVE as soon as it was published. Two days before Christmas she long distanced from Boston for a copy to be sent over to a friend of hers in New York.

Please write me what you are doing now. I hope all is well with you.

Yours.

[1] Rosalie Bull (d. 1922?), an Englishwoman, had founded a Theosophical Society in Taormina. Cipolla owned the Pensione Valverde. Miss Wallace has not been identified.

through it all: glum, but I like him best.[1] Bowdwin is hauling Rocca Bella about, and pressing us to go and see him at it. He is living in Diodoro! Hubrecht writes that she has hurt her knee in Christiania, cant get yet to Holland – hopes to come here in spring. – Today comes to tea Mrs Leader Williams, from *your* palace – where they *sell things* at home.[2] Very fine your palace looks, but my God, more junk, more junk. Makes me sick. She wore black brocade and gold tissue when she gave us tea – and is a withered darling of the Queen Alexandra days – goes in for a crest – and nobody calls on them – don't know why. He is glum, because nobody comes to buy. Rather liked him. They have nice things: – but junk, junk! Rosalie Bull's house is pretty and nice. – The Duca is just coming back from Maniace. – Insole is in Tunis or the Sahara. Kitson goes to Egypt on Jan. 2nd.

Did I tell you we've got such a good *oven* in our kitchen. Being Sunday, roast beef, baked potatoes, spinach, apple pie. Also I made heavenly chocolate cakes and *dropped them*, burning my finger – also exquisite rock cakes, and *forgot to put the fat in*!! And we are in for 3 tea-parties this week. But I shall call the pseudo-rock-cakes currant bread – quite good, *oppure*.[3]

Taormina is amusing, if one doesn't take it a bit seriously. I am cogitating whether to take this house for another year, or whether to retire to the wilds of Sardinia. Which?

We have fires at evening in our salotta – *very* cosy. – Diodoro seems a great success – all love it – 35 francs. But you will be trotting back here. – Hope you got the Christmas hanky sent last week.

Love. DHL

2141. To Martin Secker, 12 December 1920
Text: MS UInd; Secker 36–7.

Fontana Vecchia, *Taormina*, Sicily.
12 December 1920

Dear Secker

I have today yours of 6th Dec. in answer to my telegram.[4] I still think it is

---

[1] Stempel (1872?–1965?) is remembered in Taormina as an eccentric.

[2] Basil and Lilian Leader Williams had come to Taormina from Palermo; they were antique dealers.

[3] 'or else'.

[4] Secker had replied on 6 December 1920 to the telegram mentioned in Letter 2135, as follows (*Letters from a Publisher*, p. 9):

> Dear Lawrence,
>   Your telegram just received. There are two or three booksellers in New York who specialise in English books and like to have the first editions of English writers, to whom I have posted a

inexcusible that you send this *Lost Girl* edition to America, and a breach of faith. If the copies you send are *so few*, then how can they make it worth while to take the edge off Seltzer's market? And why, for a paltry few, create bad feeling? I confess I still feel angry – and beg to request you not to send any books to American in future, which are copyright over there – books of mine I mean, of course. Remember, any time you are not content with me, I am quite willing to dissolve the agreement between us.

I have Seltzer's edition of *Women in Love* – a fine-looking book. If you haven't a copy, and would like one, I will send you one.

About the English edition of *W. in Love*, – you know I don't want it published in London before May 1st. next. Probably that date suits you. – I don't quite see your point about a limited edition. If *The Lost Girl* sells, it is obvious it will sell *against* the reviews, not because of them. I have seen the *Observer* and the *Times Lit. Sup.* – and snap my fingers at them: the drivel of the impotent.[1] – Therefore, if you choose to bring out *Women in Love*, publicly, and to advertise it as you do *The Lost Girl*, and merely refrain from sending out review copies, that, I think, is the best way. It will give reviewers a chance to say nothing, which is best. – I don't think a private edition necessary. But I am ready to hear all you have to say.

Probably between *Women in Love* and *The Rainbow* best insert another incensorable novel – either *Aaron's Rod*, which I have left again, or *Mr Noon*, which I am doing.

Yours   D. H. Lawrence

I should like to see all the press notices. If you will send them me I will return them –

---

few copies but these are only a trifling number and cannot possibly affect Seltzer's sales. In any case I shall be posting no more but I must point out, and I think you might also point out to Seltzer, that there is nothing at all to prevent any American bookseller purchasing English books through any of the ordinary exporters or from Messrs. Simpkin, the wholesale agents.

The book is going very well and sales to date are in the neighbourhood of 2000 of which the library orders account for about half. This is all the more encouraging because so far there have been hardly any notices.

I have safely received the proofs to the end of 'Women in Love'. I will write later about your suggestion of aiming only at a limited circulation but in that case I should of course have to reduce my printing order to about 1500 at the outside and could not pay you any advance. I will go more fully into costs and let you know about the matter.

Yours sincerely

[1] The *TLS* review on 2 December 1920 was by Virginia Woolf (see Draper, ed., *Critical Heritage*, pp. 141–3); she considered that the novel lacked the distinctive originality she had come to associate with and expect of DHL. Under the heading, 'The Quest for Beauty', the *Observer* reviewer on 5 December decided that 'he who is preoccupied with beauty is doomed not to find truth'. This observation clearly annoyed DHL and he delivered a rejoinder to it in *Mr Noon* (see *The Lost Girl*, ed. Worthen, p. xlvii).

– The copy of *Hutchinsons Magazine* never came.
I wish you would send a copy of *Lost Girl* to
    Norman Douglas, c/o Thomas Cook, Via Tornabuoni, *Florence*.
He is coming back there from Mentone.

2142. To Lucy Short, [14 December 1920]
Text: MS UT; PC v. Taormina. Veduta dell' Etna; Postmark, Taormina 15 12 20;
Unpublished.

Taormina.
14 Dec.

Dear Mrs Short.
    I was so sorry to hear from Whittley that you and Capt. Short were not well
– do hope it is better now. We are jogging quietly along, with a few tea parties
here. It has rained solidly for two months, but now is fine and sunny and
warm, we have meals out of doors – not Christmassy at all.

Many good wishes –   D. H. Lawrence

2143. To Marie Hubrecht, 16 December 1920
Text: MS Hubrecht; Unpublished.

Fontana Vecchia, *Taormina*, Sicily.
16 Dec 1920

Dear Miss Hubrecht
    I had your letter from Kristiania – so sorry you have hurt your knee: and
hope it is better and that you may still get to the Witte Huis for Christmas.
The world feels dreary, I think, and one needs the cosyness of home, if there
be such a thing. Here the rain has left off for a time, thank goodness, but the
world is all green, as green as England, and unnatural for the south here: also
rather cold from Etna, who is deep in snow.
    How nice it will be if you can send my mother-in-law her velvet and cloth.
She is feeling unhappy too, like so many people.
    I am writing a sort of comic novel[1] – rather amusing, but rather scandalous.
Also I am copying from a photograph at Lorenzetti *Anacoreti nel Tebaïde* –
from the Uffizzi. It is an amusing picture, primitive, with many many little
anchorites. I enjoy doing it.
    We see a few people – Kitson, Rosalie Bull, Bowdwin – and people staying
at Diodoro. Diodoro seems to be a great success, and is nearly always quite
full: very popular. In Timeo many Danes and Scandinavians. Bowdwin is

---

[1] *Mr Noon.*

living at Diodoro, and tinkering with Rocca Bella. – The natives are all impudent and in a temper over the exchange, which is now 100, I believe. Really it isn't my fault, so why should they vent their spite on me? And prices are absurd.

It feels anything but Christmas here. I wish you were here – we might have had one jolly party at least.

Carmelo wants to go to America in the spring, and Ciccia is marrying, and wants to go with her husband Vicenzo also, leaving the baby with Grazia. But *vediam*.[1]

Frieda urges that we go to Germany for the summer and autumn. If we do, I don't think I shall come so far south for next winter. Italy becomes less and less agreeable. – An American Bonner – he is just going to New York with an opera under his arm, he once shared Rocca Bella with someone – says he would like Fontana Vecchia next year, if we give it up. Our lease ends March 9th. I can't make up my mind. But tell me, in case we *should* decide to give it up, whether you would like this house, or whether I shall tell Bonner[2] to speak to Ciccio.

The Lost Girl was sent to you. – I hope you had it and were amused. I believe it is quite a success.

I do hope you are better – Send a line to say where you are.

With many warm greetings from us both.   D. H. Lawrence

Juta is in Rome still – Insole in Cannes with the Hansards. – The Major is very ill: so is old Baroness Stempel. I rather like the young Stempel. – Kitson is going to Egypt in January – The society is much more broken and unstable than last year.

DHL

2144. To S. S. Koteliansky, 24 December 1920
Text: MS BL; PC v. Taormina – Teatro Greco; Postmark, Taormina 24 12 20; Zytaruk 215.

[Fontana Vecchia, *Taormina*, (Messina), Sicily]
24 Dec. 1920

Gorki *Reminiscences* just come – what a charming little book! – and just right, I think, *format* and matter. I shall enjoy reading it. Hope Secker has sent you *Lost Girl* as requested. Christmas here – a bit cold today, but nice. All best greetings to you all at the Cave.[3]

DHL

---

[1] 'we shall see'.   [2] Bonner] Vicenzo   [3] See p. 250 n. 1.

2145. To Emily King, 24 December 1920
Text: MS Needham; PC v. [Courtyard scene]; Postmark, Taormina 2 1 21; Unpublished.

[Fontana Vecchia, *Taormina*, (Messina), Sicily]

24 Dec 1920

My dear Pamela

Just had your letter – so thankful you got your parcel. Of course they are opening everything – though it is illegal. There were no big packets of Rowntrees choc. in yours – only 3 little packets with little plain tablets – and about ½. doz. shortbreads. So glad the watch is safe.

DHL

One doesn't pay duty on *letter* post.

2146. To Rosalind Baynes, 26 December 1920
Text: MS UN; Unpublished.

Fontana Vecchia, *Taormina*, Sicily

26 Dec 1920

Dear R[osalind]

Your letter today – Christmas over – very quietly – but wonderful sun, lovely, bright, warm as May. Hope your puddings etc. are a success. We have a huge turkey, rather to our dismay.

Sorry you think Alvina too improper for Sir Hamo[1] – We live and learn – or live without learning.

Here no news – I think of going to Sardinia in January to look at it and see if it is habitable. Will let you know. Am rather tired of Sicily. Never come to live here: people impossible.

So the divorce is *en route*!

Ask Eleanor when she is coming to Taormina – I don't want to be in Sardinia. Thank her for sending those postage stamps.

DHL

[Frieda Lawrence begins]

Dear Rosalind,

It's so beautiful here to *look at* but, oh dear the people the 'society' live in a perpetual state of 'holidaying' and it is'nt simple enough for me – And the 'common' people are never as nice as your Maria[2] and those were *so* greedy –

---

[1] 'Alvina' – considered too improper for Rosalind Baynes's father, Sir Hamo Thornycroft – is the central character in *The Lost Girl*.
[2] Unidentified.

But I wish you would have come just to *see* it – It's so *lovely* – That divorce – never mind you will be *free* to do as you like – *The Lost Girl* is selling [Lawrence interjects: Sic!] – Is Eleanor coming? We have been gay lately and have gone out a lot – and are already tired of it and are *re*tiring – Those toys I had for your children, Lawrence gave away to my chagrin, he said nothing but *iron* ones would do for them!! So I am absolved. A very happy new year to you – and the children – Wish I had seen them.

F.

2147. To Dr Anton Kippenberg, 27 December 1920
Text: MS GSArchiv; Unpublished.

Villa Fontana Vecchia, *Taormina*, Sicilia
27 December 1920

Dr Anton Kippenberg
Dear Sir

I wonder if you received my letter sent from this address in *October*, in answer to yours concerning the translation of *Sons and Lovers* and *The Rainbow*: Also if you had the play *Touch and Go*, which I sent by registered post. I have not had any acknowledgement of either, and must attribute this to the mischance of the post, rather than to any failure in courtesy on your part.

In the continued unhappy financial state of Germany, perhaps you do not wish to proceed at all with the translations. In that case will you be good enough to return the books to Fraü Baronin von Richthofen, Ludwig-Wilhelmstift, Baden-Baden.

Or if you do wish to continue at some time, and would prefer to quote me a figure in German Marks, I will willingly consider it, as I have every sympathy with Germany's fallen fortunes.

I am, dear Sir

Yours Sincerely   D. H. Lawrence

2148. To Robert Mountsier, 31 December 1920
Text: MS Smith; Unpublished.

Fontana Vecchia, *Taormina*, Sicily
31 Dec. 1920

Dear M[ountsier]
Your letter about Huebsch today.[1] In the first place, Pinker had MS. of *W*.

---

[1] Mountsier's letter of 10 December 1920 (TMSC Smith) reads as follows:

in Love for two years, and nothing happened. I concluded, naturally, Huebsch had seen it. When therefore Seltzer cabled for it, I sent it, under *complete* impression Huebsch had already rejected it, to Pinker. This being so, *how* could I promise Huebsch MS. I had already sent to Seltzer? I cabled and wrote to S. time after time, asking him to release to Huebsch, and promising to pay him back (Seltzer) his £50. advance. But I could not *force* S. to release the book, could I, after accepting £50. from him as advance? Huebsch knows the facts, all my letters will prove them – so will my letters to Seltzer: so he is a cad to call me a liar. *He*, Huebsch, always fogged me and kept me in the dark and never answered, and bePinkered me. Then he dished himself. Enough of him.

Dear Lawrence: –

At last I have seen Huebsch. The dirty, vile Jew, trying to hide his dirtiness and vileness under his publisher's cloak!

I wish I could sit down with you over a bottle of chianti and tell you the whole story, but I shall give you only the straight business, or rather the crooked business of it.

The following is the information I secured from Huebsch:

Huebsch set up and still has "any number of copies" of "Amores," "Look, We Have Come Through," "New Poems."

Huebsch imported sheets of "Twilight in Italy" and still has copies.

Huebsch imported sheets of "The Prussian Officer" and when he had sold the edition tried to arrange with Duckworth for more but found them too expensive.

Huebsch says he is going to republish "The Rainbow" when the time is propitious. I talked to him as if it were out of print, and asked him if there was a six months' clause, and he tried to make me believe that there wasn't. (Seltzer told me yesterday that Huebsch now and then provided a bookseller here and there with copies, at an increased price, I take it, for copies of the edition here have sold for $15.) I asked Huebsch if he had cut anything out of the original edition, and he said he had.

Huebsch's contract for "The Rainbow," "The Prussian Officer" and "Amores" is with Doran, with whom Pinker made the contract for you. Huebsch says he has settled with Doran to May, 1920, the statement and payment being made in July.

Huebsch makes statements to Pinker on "Look, We Have Come Through."

His contract with "New Poems" is with you direct. He says they are now working on the statements up to November. He says you owe him $83 (the equivalent of £20), against which the "New Poems" royalties will be charged. He expects little from "New Poems."

So far as business matters are concerned Huebsch has a reputation for honesty, but there is no doubt but that he is slow and slipshod. He is willing to make returns direct to you if Doran and Pinker will absolve him. He says that through the English Authors' Society you can compel Pinker to render you a complete accounting.

Now for Huebsch's nastiness: "Lawrence is a liar, and he has shown himself ungrateful. When I say 'liar,' I mean it literally." And then he undertakes to prove to me that you lied in connection with the "Women in Love" manuscript. He wastes fifteen minutes hunting for letters and reads various extracts. I point out that there wasn't one extract that he read me that could not be explained by Pinker's actions or inactions. Then he informs me that he can't find the letter he wants, a letter in which he claims you said you were sending him direct the manuscript of "Women in Love." What if you did? That doesn't justify his accusation.

As to the charge of "ungratefulness," he told me how well he had been treating you by advances and by money which he secured from several people for you.

He wrote me six months ago that *The Rainbow* was withheld from publication. There is a six-month clause in all agreements. – But you will have had the batch of agreements by now. – Duckworth said he could not find agreement with Kennerley. I'll write him that he *must*. – I hope Seltzer will get *The Rainbow* and *Prussian Officer*.

I had two cringy half-offended letters from Secker about the *Lost Girl* copies. He is a cur – but there you are. I gave it him hot each time. He is withholding *W. in Love* until May 1st. at my express wish. I told him he had already broken contract.

One must fight the little swine all the time.

I've written you lots of letters – you must have them by now.

I want to send you this by hand, by a man named Bonner, who is coming to

I could have said much to Huebsch to let him know what I thought of him, but I refrained simply because it seemed better business policy. All we want from him are "The Prussian Officer" and "The Rainbow." Has he ever written to you that "The Rainbow" was out of print? If we can get it Seltzer will issue it in an edition uniform with "Women in Love," and if he had it set by linotype he thinks he could get it out for $10 next April or May and pay $1.50 royalty per copy.

I am anxiously awaiting copies of the contracts involving "Sons and Lovers," "The Prussian Officer" and "The Rainbow." Even at that, we should have copies of all the contracts.

Under separate cover I am sending you a copy of "The New Republic" containing the "second" introduction to "Studies in Classic American Literature." It seems to me that Lippman missed your point when he took you literally. Since the "Studies" that have not been published in "The English Review" are too long for any weekly or monthly here that might print them, I am going to try to cut them, with "The New Republic" in mind. Could you write an introductory article, which would give the substance of "The Spirit of Place" (published in "The English Review") and answer Lippman without appearing to be an argumentative article, the article to serve as an introduction to the unpublished studies. If "The New Republic" or some other publication would want more, you might re-write those already printed in "The English Review." I shall write to you later this week about this matter.

So far the only money received is the $20 from "The Dial" for "Pomegranate." The check from "The New Republic" has not yet arrived.

"The New Republic" still has "The Revolutionary."

"Fanny and Annie" went to "The Century" and "The Atlantic Monthly" but were not accepted. This story, with the "Peach," "Fig" and "Grapes," I turned over to a literary agency here to see what more they could do with them than I could, if anything was possible beyond my ideas. I think the objection to "Fanny and Annie" is its "too Englishness."

Has Seltzer sent a contract for "The Lost Girl" to you? If he has, I hope you send it back through me. It is about ready to read in galley proof, and "Ciccio" has 3 C's.

In the next letter you write him ask him to make a payment of what he can to me, and I'll open an account in your name. He said the other day that if you needed any money he could make a payment, and I think it isn't a bad idea to get money when they are willing.

I think this summarizes everything for you.

The last letter received from you is dated October 18, written following your return to Taormina. The only other word from you to date (December 13) was the cable, "Very angry cabling Secker."

Let's hear something from you and Frieda. Damn these dirty publishers' details!

Yours, R.M.

New York with an opera under his arm. He is a Southerner. I shall try and get him to meet you, and tell you of Taormina – he is an old stager here. – I am a bit tired of it. We are going to look at Sardinia, and if I like that I shall move there. It is simpler, not so sophisticated and foreigner-flooded as here. But I shall let you know.

This is the last day of this unsatisfactory year. I wish you all luck for the new one. The world feels as if it were getting ready for a bigger bust.

I will write to Seltzer as you suggest. – I left off *Aaron's Rod*, and now have done ⅔ of 'Lucky Noon'. I hope to finish it in January: see no reason why I shouldn't. Probably you'll dislike it: it is peppery. I like it myself better than *Lost Girl* – much.

I wonder when we shall meet again: and where. Perhaps in Sardinia. Anyhow, let us keep our pecker up. It's no use giving in to the multitudes of little swine of this world.

Health for the new year, Amico!   D. H. Lawrence

Seltzer has *not* sent a contract for *Lost Girl*.

I'll do what I can about the *Studies* [*in Classic American Literature*] when I get the *New Republic* and Lippman's pronunciation.[1]

Hope you got *Birds Beasts and Flowers* all right. Am not sending it to England.

2149. To J. B. Pinker, 2 January 1921
Text: MS UNYB; Unpublished.

Fontana Vecchia, Taormina, Sicily
2 Jan. 1921

Dear Pinker

Huebsch is mistaken. I want to know about *The Rainbow*. He has had it withdrawn from publication for nearly a year, and I want to know if his right has lapsed. He side-tracks.

I wrote a month ago and asked you if 'The Blind Man' story had been printed in America, as I heard it had. If so, where. And if they paid. And if Harrison has paid for the story, the same one, in the *English Review*. Would you mind telling me.

Do you know anything about Mitchell Kennerley's agreement for *Sons and Lovers*? Duckworth says it must have been made through you. But surely Duckworth made it direct. I should like to know.

Thanks for your letter.

Yrs   D. H. Lawrence

[1] See p. 654 n. 1.

2150. To Thomas Seltzer, 2 January 1921
Text: MS Smith; Unpublished.

Fontana Vecchia, *Taormina*, Sicilia
2 Germaio 1921.

Dear Seltzer

Here's the New Year: all good luck to you.

I hope *Women in Love* goes satisfactorily: and shall be right glad if you can get *The Rainbow* from Huebsch. It pleases that gentleman to call me a liar: over the *Women in Love* MS. business. Hence if we can get *The Rainbow* and *Prussian Officer* from him, I shall be the *more* pleased. It is nearly a year now since he wrote me that *The Rainbow* was withheld from publication: wrote to me to Capri. He has certainly forfeited his rights. Avanti!¹

I left off *Aaron's Rod* and began 'Lucky Noon'. Have done two-thirds, and if the infernal gods don't prevent, I shall finish it this month. I get much wicked joy out of it. Probably you and the world will detest it. But it is unique. Which, from a publisher's point of view, is I know a misfortune.

I got a lame sort of apology from Secker about his *Lost Girl* being in America, and a definite pledge that no more should go from *him*.² Also a pledge that *Women in Love* shall not appear in London before May 1st. But he has all corrected proofs: so heaven knows his tricks.

It is spring here, with the mimosa in blossom and the sun so hot on the sea. I am a little tired of Taormina: flooded with foreigners, particularly Scandinavians, shabby and frowsty *Pillars of Society* they are too,³ peering with mean noses. I am going to make a little dash to Sardinia to see if I should like to live there. And if I find a place, we shall move soon. In which case I ought to have a few dollars behind me. Would it be convenient to you to give some to Mountsier for me, so that he⁴ could open an account for me in New York, and I could change a few dollars over here at an opportune moment? But not unless it suits you.

All good wishes for 1921.

Yrs   D. H. Lawrence

---

¹ 'Let's get on with it!'
² See p. 637 and n. 4.
³ *Pillars of Society* (1877), by Henrik Ibsen (1828–1906).
⁴ he] I

2151. To Ada Clarke, [14 January 1921]
Text: MS Clarke; PC v. Cagliari – Nuovo Palazzo Comunale; Postmark, Taormina 15 1 21;
Lawrence–Gelder 119.

[Fontana Vecchia, *Taormina*, (Messina), Sicily]
[14 January 1921]

We went to Sardinia to see if we liked it to live in – love it, but decide to keep
Fontana Vecchia another year. – Came back last night – find the blazer – fits
beautifully and looks so chic. I like it extremely – Say how much it cost as I
want to pay for it. – Brilliant sun, almond trees all coming into full blossom –
oranges and lemons all ripe. – Have got a funny little thing for Jack – send
tomorrow.

Love DHL

2152. To Martin Secker, [14 January 1921]
Text: MS UInd; Secker 37.

Fontana Vecchia, *Taormina*, Sicily.
14 Jan 1920

Dear Secker
Your letter of 31st. Dec.[1] Will you let me see the 'excisions or paraphrases'
you require in *Women in Love*.

---

[1] Secker had written as follows (Secker Letter-Book, UIll):

Dear Lawrence,
I have postponed writing to you until I could let you know the sales of The Lost Girl up to
the end of the year. They amount to approximately 2000 copies, 1000 of which have been taken
by the libraries. I think we may anticipate that the book will carry over the holidays and go on
selling until next year, but you can see that without the assistance of Mudie & Co., the sales will
not be very large.
It seems to me that the decision we have to come to – or rather the decision you have to come
to – about Women in Love, is whether you will aim at a free circulation, necessitating two
or three excisions or paraphrases in the text, or whether it is to be printed as it stands and to be
sold only in booksellers' shops. I am quite ready myself to fall in with either plan, but, of
course, if we have to cut out the libraries, I shall only print 1500 copies of the first edition, and
in that case, would ask you to reduce the amount of the advance to £50 instead of £100.
I am sending you a bunch of Press notices under separate cover which you might return to
me after you have gone through them. I am also posting you a copy of the magazine which I am
sorry slipped my memory.
I hope all goes well. Let me know how the new book is getting on, and when you think you
will be able to complete it. I am very anxious indeed to read it.
Yours sincerely

Thank you for the Press Cuttings, which are rather amusing. I will return them. Also many thanks for that Magazine.[1]

Have been away in Sardinia – rather fascinating. Think of going and writing a sketch book of Sardinia in the early summer.[2]

I think I may finish 'Lucky Noon' – the new novel – next month. But you'll simply hate it.

Douglas says you did not send him a copy of *The Lost Girl* to Florence. If not do post him a copy

c/o Mlle Rola, 4 rue St. Charles, *Mentone*, France.

Also please send a copy to

Mrs Réné Hansard, Cottage Naledi, Le Cannet, *Cannes*, France.

and one to

Miss Ruth Wheelock, American Consulate, Palermo.

Yours.   D. H. Lawrence

2153. To Dr Anton Kippenberg, 14 January 1921
Text: MS GSArchiv; Unpublished.

Villa Fontana Vecchia, *Taormina*, Sicilia
14 Jan. 1921

Dear Dr Kippenberg

I have your letter of 4th. January – also the Almanach and Katalog:[3] for all of which many thanks. I am glad you will go forward with the books.

I have not received any writings of yours on the *Weltsammlung*. Did you post something to me here?

Fontana Vecchia is a little villa where my wife and I live all by ourselves, just outside the village. I hope you will come and see us here, with your wife. My German is hopelessly bad, but we can get along. If you will tell me what kind of hôtel you would like I will ask for rooms for you, should you wish it. *San Domenico* is the best, and costs about 40 Lire a day: far too expensive for me. *Timeo* is the same. *Castellamare* is good, and has a German proprietress – and costs, I think, 30 to 35 Lire a day. *Naumachia* is in the corso, very pleasant, I think – and costs from 25 to 30 Lire a day: an Italian hotel: and the one I should choose. The *Bristol* too is good, and costs about the same, but is about a Kilometer out of the village. The cheapest is the *Pensione Fichera* –

---

[1] *Hutchinson's Story Magazine*, November 1920, including 'The Fox'.
[2] To be *Sea and Sardinia*, published by Seltzer on 12 December 1921.
[3] He had published *Katalog der sammlung Kippenberg* (1913) and the first *Jahrbuch der sammlung Kippenberg* (1921): these may be the works in question.

which is 20 to 25 Lire a day, and is I believe quite good. A fair number of Germans stay there. None of these prices include wine.

My wife and I are poor people. We live here and keep house for ourselves. So we know well enough what it is to be scared of hôtel prices. If you wish, I will make detailed inquiries for you. Taormina is fairly full of foreigners: very many Danes and Scandinavians. It is lovely – and very friendly. I believe you will like it.

Yours Sincerely   D. H. Lawrence

2154. To Eleanor Farjeon, 20 January 1921
Text: MS UT; Postmark, Taormina 22 1 21; Huxley 511–12.

Fontana Vecchia, Taormina, Sicilia
20 Jan 1921

Dear Eleanor

Well, perhaps you'll be glad you haven't come to Sicily. It thunders and lightens for 24 hours, and hail storms continually, till there is hail-ice thick everywhere, and it is deadly cold and horrid. Meanwhile the almond blossom is almost full out – a sea of blossom, would be, if it weren't shattered.

I should like to talk to you: but feel myself shut up and I can't come unshut just now. I don't like it.

We made a dash to Sardinia – liked the island very much – but it isn't a place to live in. No point in living there. A stray corner of Italy, rather difficult materially – to live in. I have said I will keep this house on another year. But I really don't believe I shall come back for another winter. The south is so lifeless. There's ten times more 'go' in Tuscany.

If I knew how to, I'd really join myself to the revolutionary socialists now. I think the time has come for a real struggle. That's the only thing I care for: the death struggle. I don't care for politics. But I know there *must* and *should* be a deadly revolution very soon, and I would take part in it if I knew how.

Ask R[osalind] what book she means – *The Moose*?[1] – But that disappeared with Chapel Farm Cottage.

I enclose 10 francs for those stamps. I hope it is enough. Tell me.

Let's hope we'll meet when something is doing.

DHL

When do you go back?

[1] By Agnes Herbert (1913).

2155. To Robert Mountsier, 21 January 1921
Text: MS Smith; Unpublished.

Fontana Vecchia, *Taormina*, Sicily
21 Jan 1921.

Dear M[ountsier]

Your letter of Christmas Day – a sad one – I don't know why you suddenly talk about being honest. I feel I'm not a fifth part as honest about your time and energy as you are about my ten dollars. Dear M., it will probably be years and years before we make 1,000 dollars. And you are getting less than nothing out of it. I beg and pray you, don't bother about the bits of things. Let them drift – they cost more nerve energy than they're worth. Don't bother – please please don't bother. Just do the simple straightforward things and let the others go to blazes – Kennerley and so on. Life's too short. Just do the simple things with Seltzer. I feel you bother far, far too much. I never send out a story more than twice – I *never* fret myself really about publishers. My life is too precious to me. So don't you start worrying over there. Do it just casually, so it costs you nothing. Else I can't bear it.

We came back from Sardinia – am doing a little Diary of the trip, which I shall send you. I don't want to live there. Shall stay here till May, then I don't know.

We had bad colds – I can't write you an *interview* letter yet. If you knew how I don't care about it all.

You will have seen Bonner by the time you get this, and heard all about Taormina. And I do hope you're happier, and feeling well. We'll go to the Marquesas yet.

About business. Pinker wrote rather injured by Huebsch's note. I believe Pinker to be honest. So I answered him it was about *The Rainbow* I *really* wanted to know. And I asked him about 'The Blind Man'. You see his answer.[1] The *English Review* has no right at all to make any Amer[ican] contract for 'Blind Man' – none.

---

[1] Pinker had written to DHL on 11 January 1921 (TMS Smith):

Dear Lawrence,

Thank you for your letter. When you wrote to me before about "The Blind Man" I asked the editor of the English Review to let me know whether he had used the story but I have not received a reply from him. I am writing to him again to-day and when I have the information I will let you know. I did not have a copy of the story for America so that if the story appeared there it was not placed by me.

I think the American rights in "Sons and Lovers" must have been arranged by Messrs Duckworth direct as I did not arrange it for you.

I am writing to Huebsch about "The Rainbow" and will let you know what he says in reply.

Sincerely yours,

Duckworth was in[1] the same muddle about Kennerly, Says there was no agreement – *Sons and Lovers* all arranged through letters – nothing definite – only thing to be done to put the business into hands of some legal agency. He won't do anything.

Secker is a swine – he knows I know it.

The tortoises lived in the Villa La Canovaia, where I was all September – near Florence.

I'll get a definite statement out of the Oxford Press. They wished a nom de plume – because of *schools* (it is a book a text book for secondary schools) and my *Rainbow* scandal. I shouldn't think America matters, whether it's known or not. Use your judgment.

I will swear to a paper when I am in Palermo – before an American consul. I will write to Duckworth that he is to communicate with you concerning Kennerley. Kennerley sent me a cheque for £25. with the date altered – I couldn't cash it – returned it to him – and never heard another word. That was somewhere about December 1913 or early 1914. I don't keep letters.

I am pretty sure I have Pinkers letter about Amer. rights of 'The Fox'. Anyhow he would repeat the letter. I'll do the end soon. – When I've finished *Mr. Noon* and the Trip I'll remember about long short stories.

Business bores me so. I almost think of having an *English* (only) agent once more – Pinker again – or Curtis Brown. What do you say?

I hope you'll come this spring. The almond blossom out here – but very cold. We've had bad colds. – *Lost Girl* steadily selling in London – Secker wants me to cut *W. in Love.* I won't. – I hate Huebsch since he called me a liar.

DHL

Write to Duckworth direct for anything you want
Gerald Duckworth, 3 Henrietta Street, Covent Garden, W.C.2.

2156. To J. B. Pinker, 25 January 1921
Text: MS UNYB; Unpublished.

Fontana Vecchia, *Taormina*, Sicily
25 Jan. 1921

Dear Pinker

I am trying to get my various affairs straight in America, between Huebsch, Doran, Kennerley and so on: particularly I want to settle with Huebsch about *The Rainbow*, and Kennerley about *Sons and Lovers*. Robert Mountsier is

---

[1] MS reads 'was the'.

seeing to the business for me. I should be so much obliged if you could send him

       Mr Robert Mountsier, 417 West 118 Street, New York City
an answer to the following questions.

1.   The agreement says 'the publisher shall publish the said novels on dates _ _ _ which shall not _ _ _ be later than six months from the date of delivery of each manuscript.'
Did you give Doran or Huebsch permission to delay the publication? When was the MS. delivered?

2.   – 'The publisher shall pay _ _ _ in advance and on acc. of royalties of each of the said novels the sum of £100 _ _ _ half on delivery of MS., half on date of publication.' – Were these payments so made? Please answer *particularly* for *The Rainbow*, also for *The Prussian Officer*, *Twilight in Italy*, and *Amores*.

3.   – 'Accounts shall be made up to 31st. March and 30th. Sept. – and settled in cash on or before 30th June and 31st. Sept following.'
Have the payments for the *Rainbow* (particularly) and the other books been so made?

4.   'Publishers shall not abridge, expand etc.'
Did Huebsch have your permission to cut out certain parts of *The Rainbow*? He never had mine.

(5.   Can you tell me if Duffields have any right to *The White Peacock* – or was that Duckworths show.)

I want to know whether Huebsch has (I know he has) violated any of the clauses of that three-novel contract he had through Doran and which you signed for me.

If you could send a direct letter in answer to Mountsier, and a carbon copy to me, I should be so glad. They have got me into a fine muddle there in America – play as they like – and then become insulting to me.

I am sorry to trouble you. But those Americans just let ones books die and are insulting if one speaks of it.

                         Yours Sincerely   D. H. Lawrence

2157. To Robert Mountsier, 25 January 1921
Text: MS Smith; Postmark, Taormina 26 1 21; Unpublished.

                      Fontana Vecchia. Taormina. Sicilia
                                   25 Jan 1921.

Dear M[ountsier]

Your letter Jan. 4th. today. Here an answer.

1.   I have detailed your questions to Pinker and asked him to reply to you

    direct. If he doesn't, write him direct –
    J B Pinker, Talbot House, Arundel Street, Strand. W.C.2.

2. I also wrote to Duckworth asking him to send you copies of any papers relating to *White Peacock* and *Trespasser* in America.

3. I'm only terrified of the money costings – for I have poco pochissimo – very little indeed over here.

4. Amy is a good soul. I'll tell you what she says when she writes.

5. I want you to put that Juta Portrait Sketch in front of *Birds Beasts* etc when you publish it.

6. You've got *several* life-jobs straightening my affairs over there. And your life's too good for it. – But I long to *down* the swinish Kennerleys and Huebschleys and the lot.

7. Duckworth will (I hope) answer about Duffield and *White Peacock*. I would like to have the rights: but where is the money to come from?

8. *Mr Noon* will be, I think, *most* dangerous: but humorously so. It will take me about a month still to finish – this month was lost moving about. *Aaron* will not be dangerous – if only his rod would start budding, poor dear.

9. Let us wait and see about Seltzer. If he doesn't do well by me he'll be ready to drop me.

10. Do try and get them to publish the *Studies* in the magazines – or parts of them.

11. I think the first 200 pages of *Mr Noon* might make a rather funny serial. It is an episode all by itself: a little book all to itself. And the girl in the American consulate who is typing it says: *so* like an American small town.

12. I detest the little worm Secker.

13. Last but not least – and I believe in unlucky numbers – I shall rejoice if we can have our ship and go to the South Seas and Mackenzie to hell with his channel isles.

Let us make it go. I am more than game. See if we can't do something this year of disgrace 1921. I am on the warpath.

I'll say the word, and hold up my end. But I have to wait on the 'spirit' that moves me: so don't be impatient.

Frieda says all right – not *very* enthusiastically.

I'll finish those Sardinian Snaps soon, *Mr Noon* holds me.

              From Typee under Etna
              To Typee upon Broadway.

                        D. H. Lawrence

Enclosed a darling whom I do *not* answer.

I didn't answer Mary Austin either – so boring.[1]

Sara Teasdale sent me a book of poems which I like – but I dont know her address.[2]

2158. To Beatrice Bland, 25 January 1921

Text: MS UT; PC; Postmark, Taormina 26 1 21; Unpublished.

Fontana Vecchia, *Taormina*
25 Jan. 1921.

Dear Miss Bland[3]

Are you still at Girgenti? – and are you liking it? – and are there many wild flowers? Tell me.

We went to Sardinia – such a dash and such fun: but decided we didn't want to live there: so think of staying here another year. The almond blossom is very lovely, the air all gentle perfume at the moment – and your washing on the rocks below.[4]

Greetings   D. H. Lawrence

2159. To Robert Mountsier, 27 January 1921

Text: MS Smith; Unpublished.

Fontana Vecchia, *Taormina*, Sicily
27 Jan. 1921

Dear M[ountsier]

Stock's article came last night, and I have read it.[5] It is a bit sad, like

---

[1] DHL's 'America, Listen To Your Own', in *New Republic*, 15 December 1920, was answered in the same issue by Walter Lippmann (see Roberts 339); he was answered in his turn by Mary Austin (1868–1934), American novelist and essayist.

[2] Sara Teasdale (1884–1933), American poet, may have sent DHL her most recent volume, *Flame and Shadow* (New York, 1920).

[3] Emily Beatrice Bland (1868–1951), artist, who studied at the Slade and from 1926 was a member of the New English Art Club. According to the *Times* obituary (24 January 1951), it was about 1920 that she showed a marked maturing of artistic sensibility and discrimination. She excelled both in still life and in landscape painting; she exhibited regularly at the New English Art Club, the Royal Academy and elsewhere. (DHL's postcard was addressed to Hotel des Temples, Girgenti, Sicilia.)

[4] See Letter 2175.

[5] An article by Ralph Stock (b. 1882) entitled 'The Dream Ship: The Story of a Voyage of Adventure More Than Half Around the World in a 47-foot Lifeboat' appeared in *National Geographic*, xxxix (January 1921), 1–52. It is well illustrated (43 black-and-white photographs, some full page, and one map). Stock mentions pearl hunting in the Marquesas; he sells the boat in Tonga Tabu and is 'miserable' afterwards.

everything else. But they deserve to be left sad. *Because* they wanted *finally* to have money. I detested them for going hunting pearl in Marquesas – and I despise them for selling their ship. One must be, first and foremost, clear of the money complex: even if one earns one's living.

Then, to tell the truth, I think the Dream Ship is too little. I should like a ship that has about five hands, like these Mediterranean schooners that are so lovely. And I should like at least two *uneducated* sailors. And one would have to do just a bit of trading to make a living: not to make money.

The difficulty is beginning. There are lovely sailing ships that go from Sardinia to all Mediterranean ports. I ought to break away from the land and get them to carry me about. But then I am so bad at making casual acquaintances. I must make a shot at a beginning somehow.

I would like more than anything to have a ship. Even to cruise the Mediterranean and the African shores. The point is to begin. One must begin.

I used to have a friend[1] – his father a quite rich man – who was a sailing-ship hand – had worked before the mast. I must find such another friend.

The beginning is everything. And the beginning of the beginning is the absolute *decision*. One must decide to break from the land and to break from the last deep land-connections: with society, essentially.

I[2] believe this will be the year that will decide our fortunes.

If one can get to the S. Seas, one can roam: of that I feel sure.

DHL

2160. To Francis Brett Young, 27 January 1921
Text: MS UB; cited in Jessica Brett Young, *Francis Brett Young*, p. 113.

Fontana Vecchia, *Taormina*, Sicily
27 Jan. 1921.

Dear B[rett]-Y[oung]

I was dreaming of you so hard last night – of you and Jessie BY. and Mackenzie: that we were all frenziedly straying round strange places, and parting and going three separate ways. If I had the energy I would recall particulars. To-day your letter that you are off.[3] Well, good luck. When I can afford it I shall go too. Enough of Europe: enough of Secker and Mackenzie and everything. Basta – bastissima!

[1] Unidentified (but perhaps Captain Short).
[2] I] We must see
[3] To South Africa; they sailed on the *Carnarvon Castle*.

Mackenzie invited us to a cottage on Herm. But what are the Channel Isles to me! I prefer Sicily, even.

As for Secker, less said the better. I dislike him.

Lost Girl sells merely very moderately. Has cleared her 2000, and thats about all. I don't trust Secker, however: *at all* or *in anything*. I should like to be independent of literature. The world is too full of fools.

We made a little dash to Sardinia: sailed from Palermo via Trapani to Cagliari: fun: I like Sardinia. I wanted to see if I could live there. But no. I won't make any more attempts in Europe. I shall hang on to my Fontana Vecchia till I clear out. I loved being on *the sea*.

It is very lovely here just now with Almond Blossom in clouds. And do you remember the creeper on the terrace – it is heavy with buds, nearly out once more. It puts me in mind so often of our chase round Sicily: and our little lunch here on that terrace: and the marmy American woman, who has now, thank God, gone back to her native land, taking that great blowsy, but nice (and dirty, as we found) Neapolitan maid-servant with her.

Some friends are here for the moment[1] – in Villa S. Pancrazio. The town is *full* of foreigners – many Scandinavians. We went to a little fancy-dress ball last night (not dressed – me in my same-as-ever old grey jacket: to hell with them) – and such a pitiable display of ridiculous imbecility you needn't wish to see.

Ach, that I were out of it all! But it won't be long.

Write from Africa and say what happens. Don't forget. – I have a long memory really: but can't stand showing off. I find everybody just imbecilely showing off. Lord, how nauseating and humiliating.

Best of luck to you both: from Frieda as well.

                                                            Yrs   D. H. Lawrence
I shall look for the red funnel. I do wish I had a spy-glass.

2161. To Robert Mountsier, 28 January 1921
Text: MS Smith; Unpublished.

                                                Fontana Vecchia, Taormina, Sicily
                                                            Friday 28 Jan. 1921.

Dear M[ountsier]

Your letter of Jan 5th.

Deal with Duckworth direct. It is so much quicker.

[1] Jan Juta and Alan Insole; they stayed until 30 January (Tedlock, *Lawrence MSS* 92). It was during this visit that Juta discussed with DHL the illustrations he would provide to *Sea and Sardinia*; he also painted his portrait of DHL (Nehls, ii. 86 and 466 n. 199).

Do as you like about the arrangement of *Birds Beasts* etc. Leave out that little Foreword altogether if you don't like it. Consult someone else if you like. It is not important. I won't bother to write another.

I'll tell you what Amy says. Do you never send anything to Harriet Monroe, of *Poetry*, Chicago? She likes me.

'Pomegranate', in the singular, I think.

Raughming is a Midlands dialect word for reaching over. If raughting is by any chance American, let it be raughting.

I'll tell you what Amy says. Not heard yet.

Canovaia was the villa near Florence where nearly all the poems were written – an old, well-known villa. But leave it out.

I send you four more poems: 'Snake', 'Almond Blossom', and two bare trees.[1] The title covers them.

I haven't mentioned the poems to Seltzer, I think – nor will I do so. I don't write him any *particular* business – leave all to you.

I've got a cold.

I do so hate Ralph Stock for selling his ship. Else I'd write to *him*.

Can you send this enclosed note to Sara Teasdale. She sent me her book of poems.

DHL

If Mary Austin or that man Hitchcock[2] should ask you to let them see the *Studies in Classic Amer. Lit.*, let them see the MS. – or some of it at least.

Your poem on cigars was so good. Am tempted to send it to Brookline Mass.[3]

2162. To Marie Hubrecht, 29 January 1921
Text: MS Hubrecht; Unpublished.

Fontana Vecchia, *Taormina*, Sicilia
29 Jan 1921

Dear Miss Hubrecht

Your letter yesterday – and you still in Christiania. I am so sorry you are not well. The north does not agree with you, I am sure.

We have decided to keep Fontana Vecchia another year, so shall be here if you come.

---

[1] DHL had written poems entitled 'Bare Fig-Trees' and 'Bare Almond-Trees'; he is presumably referring to both here. All four poems mentioned were collected in *Birds, Beasts and Flowers*.

[2] Perhaps the publisher Frederick Hills Hitchcock (1867–1928). He had founded the Grafton Press in 1901.

[3] i.e. to Amy Lowell who was a cigar smoker.

Juta and Insole are here this week to see the almond blossom, which is lovely. Next week Insole goes to England – en route for America and Japan. Juta goes to Rome – and in the autumn to Paris. We think to stay here till May – then perhaps to Germany. I wonder when you will come to Taormina.

I have a letter from a German painter – Werner Gotheim, München who badly wants a studio for a few weeks.[1] He is poor. If you do not think of coming for a month or more, would you let him have your studio for a moderate rent. It seems a pity to let it just stand shut up.

Bowdwin is very busy altering all the inside of Rocca Bella. It will take him at least two years more. I doubt if he will ever live there. He has gangs of workmen and is very busy.

If you are willing to let Gotheim have the studio, would you telegraph the one word *agree*.

Taormina *full* of foreigners – mostly Scandinavians – and very expensive everything is.

Yes, when I can afford it I shall go to Spain. It is the one European country that still attracts me.

I never thanked you for the Norway book. It looks fascinating – but so *cold*.

auf wiedersehen   D. H. Lawrence

2163. To S. S. Koteliansky, [31 January 1921]
Text: MS BL; PC v. Castello S. Acessio; Postmark, Taormina 1 2 21; Zytaruk 215.

[Fontana Vecchia, *Taormina*, (Messina), Sicily]
31 Jan.

Have the *Green Ring*[2] – and many thanks – read it again and find something attractive in it as I did before. – Any more news with you? Your mother? – And anything of Gertler? – Ottoline was with Mary Cannan at Monte Carlo. – Lovely summery weather here – all almond blossom. Where is Grisha! Greet everybody.   DHL

---

[1] Most likely Werner Gothein (1890–c.1960), painter, wood-engraver and lithographer who lived on Lake Constance. He was strongly influenced by Frans Masereel and specialised in subjects from Greek mythology and from circus life.
[2] See p. 421 n. 1.

2164. To Robert Mountsier, 1 February 1921
Text: MS Smith; Postmark, Taormina 1 2 21; Unpublished.

Fontana Vecchia, *Taormina*. Sicily
1 Feby. 1921

Dear M[ountsier]

I send you another flower poem – 'Hibiscus and Salvia' – which I like myself immensely.[1] Hope you will.

DHL

2165. To Robert Mountsier, [3 February 1921]
Text: MS Smith; Unpublished.

[Fontana Vecchia, *Taormina*, (Messina), Sicily]
[3 February 1921][2]

Thrasher's Farm (Old Lynell Farm)
station: *Baltic. Conn.* about 6 miles
Village: Westminster
Town: South Canterbury
County: Wynham[3] or Windsor
ask for Old Lynell Farm, next to *Dubberke* farm. Dubberke well known.

Mrs Thrasher, wife of an Amer. sculptor killed in war. She would give a lease of the farm for twenty or thirty years, free – if one worked the farm more or less.

Am writing her again.

Dear M[ountsier]

I really feel I must come to America. We can scheme better there for the South Seas. Am writing again to Mrs Thrasher to make sure.

DHL

[1] DHL recorded in his diary for 31 January 1921: 'wrote "Hibiscus & Salvia Flowers"' (Tedlock, *Lawrence MSS* 92). See Letter 2182 and n. 2.
[2] The date is established by DHL's remark in the postscript to Letter 2167.
[3] Mountsier corrected the spelling to 'Windham'.

2166. To Martin Secker, 4 February 1921
Text: MS UInd; Secker 38.

Villa Fontana Vecchia, *Taormina*, Sicily
4 Feb. 1921.

Dear Secker

Herewith the amendments to *Women in Love*.[1]

p. 111. line	6 from end.		naked lying *against* the vegetation.
p. 445 ,,	10	,, ,, .	and lived together, *sharing the same bedroom,*
p. 373 line 11		,, ,, .	Rupert's offer of *alliance*
,, ,, line 6		,, ,, .	not merely in legal marriage, but in *a new, vital activity*[2]
p. 474			for Eleonora Duse, put *the great Rachel*

I am glad you have decided to make *W. in Love* a bookshop book. If I am not awfully pinched in the early summer I will agree to the £75., but if I am real tight, shall ask you for the £100 notwithstanding.

Lost Girl sales are few. Damn them.

We went quick to Sardinia: liked it v. much: but not to go and live in. Am writing a little itinerary of the trip. Novel having a little rest, it being a bit of a strain. But end in sight.

D. H. Lawrence

---

[1] DHL was responding to Secker's letter, 28 January 1921 (Secker Letter-Book, UIll):

Dear Lawrence,

Many thanks for your letter of the other day, which I have deferred answering until I had gone through the proofs of your book once again. I have now come to the opinion that it would be far better to regard Women in Love as a book which must find its public solely through the medium of the bookshops, that is to say, that I think it is impossible to tamper with the text in order to bring it down to the Mudie-Boots level. At the same time, there are three or four passages where I think you might make verbal alterations in order to remove any possible chance of misconstruction. I am assuming that you still have a set of proofs, so that I am merely giving you the pages where the passages occur: Page 111, line 6 from end; page 445, line 10 from end, ('lost degree of intimacy'); page 372, lines 6 and 11 from end; finally, the reference to Eleanor Duse on p. 474 is, I think, actionable.

What I propose to do is to print a first edition of 1500 copies only, and, in these circumstances, I hope you will see your way to reducing the amount of the advance from £100 to £75, which will be in fact, the Royalties due if the whole of the first edition were sold. Up to date the Lost Girl has reached about 2300, but quite a half of these have gone to the libraries.

Many thanks also for your cheque in settlement of the account. The trade price of copies is 7/6, to which must be added 1/- for postage, but you must not forget that these copies count as sales, and that you will be duly credited with royalties on them. I am very anxious to hear news about the next book . . .

Yours sincerely

[2] *activity*] *happy cooperation*

2167. To Robert Mountsier, 5 February 1921
Text: MS Smith; Unpublished.

Fontana Vecchia, *Taormina*, Sicilia
5 febb. 1921.

Dear M[ountsier]

I don't know whether these two letters are much use to you – Duckworth and Pinker.[1]

Also a nice flower poem I send. 'Purple Anemones'.[2]

I feel I should really like to come to America. If ever you get a chance and an inclination, do go and look at Thrasher's farm. Why shouldn't we have a farm between us? But I am awaiting Mrs Thrasher's answer still. – Don't be horrified at the house, and the ruin. I know I could borrow £200 or £300 for a bit of a start. If we were really going to *work* it: have a cow, goats, fowls, pigs, and raise some fruit: then Vincenzo and his wife Ciccia would come to do that. He is a young Sicilian here. It might be real jolly: and a start-off for us. Say what you think.

[1] The Duckworth letter is missing; Pinker had written on 1 February 1921 (TMS Smith) as follows:

Dear Lawrence,
Thank you for your letter of the 25th ult. I will answer your questions in the order in which you have put them: –
1. Doran delayed publication of "The Rainbow" owing to the unusual nature of the book. Corrected proofs were sent to him on September 9. 1915 and two copies of the English edition were sent in order to obtain the ad interim copyright on the 30th September 1915.
2. "The Rainbow" is the only book published so far which came under the three-novel contract with Doran. With your consent Doran transferred the American publishing rights to Huebsch on a royalty basis without advance. The arrangements for the American publication of "The Prussian Officer", "Twilight in Italy" and "Amores" were subject to separate agreements and the books were not set up in America but sheets were supplied by the English publisher and bound up over there.
3. Doran has seen to the collection of royalty accounts relating to "The Rainbow" from Huebsch and the monies received have been duly paid to you.
4. Doran cabled that he could not publish "The Rainbow" in its original form and with your consent certain alterations were made. Notwithstanding these alterations Doran finally decided that he could not publish the book and it was after this that the arrangement was made by Doran with Huebsch.
5. I had nothing to do with the negotiations for the publication of "The White Peacock" with Duffield, neither did I negotiate with Kennerley for the publication of "Sons and Lovers".
I have not the various agreements here to which I can refer as I forwarded them to you in accordance with your request some time ago.
I am not sending a letter to Mr. Mountsier as I think you will like to write to him direct in view of the information given in this letter.

Sincerely yours

[2] The poem (collected in *Birds, Beasts and Flowers*) had been written the day before (Tedlock, *Lawrence MSS* 100).

And say, shall I go back to Pinker for *English* agency only?

D. H. Lawrence

I wrote you all about Thrashers farm two days ago. – Am still doing *Sardinia*. It will make a little book. Have written to Cagliari for photographs. We'll make our way somehow or other.

2168. To Thomas Seltzer, [5 February 1921]
Text: MS UT; PC v. Taormina. Veduta dell' Etna; Postmark, Letojanni 8 FEB 21; Lacy, *Seltzer* 17.

[Fontana Vecchia, *Taormina*, (Messina), Sicily]
5 Jan. 1921[1]

Had your cable about *Lost Girl*'s start today. Hope she will really go well. Am busy with *Mr Noon*. Will you send a leaflet of *W. in Love* to

Mrs Lucille Levy,[2] 5747 Westminster, *St. Louis*, Mo, USA.
Apparently she would like a copy.
Thank you so much for *Launcelot* and *Woman*.[3] Former a bit vieux jeu.

DHL

2169. To Compton Mackenzie, 7 February 1921
Text: MS UT; Mackenzie 197–8.

Villa Fontana Vecchia, *Taormina*, Sicily
7 Feb. 1921

Dear M[ackenzie]

We had your three postcards from Herm, – with much interest. I didn't answer, because you said a letter was following.

I should like awfully to come to Herm for a week or two in the early summer. Would there be anywhere where we could have a lodging? – and

[1] DHL's dating is suspect. On 4 January 1921 he left Taormina for Palermo en route to Sardinia; Seltzer would not have known his address, and therefore DHL could not have received the cable on the 5th. The postmark suggests that DHL should have written 5 February. This conjecture seems reinforced by Seltzer's letter of the same date telling DHL the exciting news about the reception of *The Lost Girl* (see Letter 2139 n. 2). This news may have been the purpose of Seltzer's cable.
[2] Unidentified.
[3] Two publications by Seltzer in 1920 under his own imprint (his partnership with Temple Scott having been dissolved): *Lancelot: A Poem* was by Edwin Arlington Robinson (1869–1935); *Woman* by Magdeleine Marx (pseudonym of Magdeleine Paz). (Originally published as *Femme*, Paris, 1919, the novel was translated by Adele Seltzer and had an introduction by Henri Barbusse.)

where my sister could come and stay with us for a fortnight?[1] They insist I should go to England, but I loathe the thought of going to England, so it might be great fun to meet in Herm. I am so wondering what it is like: if it has that Celtic fascination.

I am fighting my way through various pieces of work: and through life. It works out to a long fight, in which one doesn't emerge as much of a winner so far.

Heard from B[rett]-Y[oung] off for Jo-burg.

Hope you're well   DHL

2170. To Mary Cannan, [12 February 1921]
Text: MS Lazarus; Moore 640–1.

Fontana Vecchia, *Taormina*, Sicily.
Sat. 12 Feb.

My dear Mary

Had your letter – glad you are once more revelling in color-wash and chimney-pieces – and enjoying it. I tell you, it's all right getting it done: it's living in it afterwards that tells.

Good news about Murry's mitigated downfall. I hear he is to work for the *Nation*: from France.[2] *The Nation* said K[atherine]'s book was the best short story book that could be or had been written.[3] Spit on her for me when you see her, she's a liar out and out. As for him, I reserve my language. – I hear from London the *Athenæum* lost £5,000 a year under our friend. I know in whose pockets I should look for that £5000, if I were the Rowntrees.[4] Vermin, the pair of 'em. And beware.

I don't approve of your gambling. I hate it. It is bad for you, and playing on your worst weakness.

No particular news here. Hubrecht writes she may be coming in April. We have the key to the studio and picnic there sometimes.

Secker says *Lost Girl* has sold only 2,300: so that he owes me about £15. over my £100. And he charged me £8·10·0 for the copies he sent out for me:

[1] DHL doubtless had his sister Ada in mind. (Neither she nor DHL ever visited Mackenzie on Herm.)
[2] Murry had resigned the editorship of the *Athenæum* which was absorbed by the *Nation* in February 1921; he joined Katherine Mansfield in Menton c. 20 February 1921.
[3] Her collection, *Bliss and Other Stories*, was published in December 1920. It was reviewed very favourably in the *Athenæum* (not the *Nation*) on 21 January 1921. The anonymous reviewer admired her 'craftsmanship, her sense of construction, the precise, concise progress of her stories'.
[4] Arnold Rowntree (1872–1951) took financial responsibility for the *Athenæum* when Murry was offered the editorship in January 1919.

8/6 a copy to me.[1] – But he's going to do *Women in Love* without altering it – it is due 1st May – and sell it merely as a book-shop book. The libraries wont touch it. He offers me now £75. Onward christian soldiers!

I send you a Gilbert notice.[2] Hope he gives domestic details. It is for these only we are all pining. The Mond Mystery.

I am sending you also my famous picture, which F[rieda] reluctantly relinquishes.[3] Hope you'll like it. You can take it as a sop to Cerberus, anyhow, for now comes the demand.

I'm tired of Taormina, of Italy, of Europe. You know Mrs Thrasher offered us her farm, 4 hours from New York, 2 hours from Boston: beautiful – but all gone wild. I want to go to America: I can place my stuff so much quicker there. My plan is to go to the Thrasher farm, and write then for America. Also, if it is at all feasible, to *work* the Thrasher farm. For this purpose Vincenzo and Ciccia would come, if I asked them, for they are pining to emigrate. It is a hilly, wild farm of 90 acres, with woods also, and suitable for fruit. It has a dilapidated wooden house. But if it were feasible, I hope you would come and have a little frame house of your own and take over one branch of the work. That is what you are born for: not having flats and dibbling at Montecarlo. – This is the worst part of the thing, though. If I need £200, will you lend them me, 5% interest, to be paid back as soon as possible. I shan't ask you if I can do without. Which I hope I can. But I want you to say yes or no, so that I can count my securities.

I have nearly done a little travel-book: 'Diary of a Trip to Sardinia': which will have photographs, and which I hope, through the magazines, will make me something. But I always hope, and am always left there.

Don't take the demand for a loan seriously. It's only merely tentative, mere bounds of possibility so far – nothing at all definite. And say yes or no as you like, without a qualm, I really shan't mind. I'd a million times rather you pleased yourself than displeased yourself.

The picture is yours anyhow: whether Cerberus swallows the sop or not.

Hope all is well. – Hear H G Wells is going out to join Rebecca West. She is in Capri with Mrs Mackenzie.[4] He is in Herm, in kilts, finding his island full

---

[1] See p. 660 n. 1.

[2] Obscure reference to Cannan.

[3] The copy of the 'Lorenzetti' painting referred to in earlier letters; DHL completed it on 1 January 1921 (Tedlock, *Lawrence MSS* 91). See also Letter 2174 for a commentary on it.

[4] Rebecca West (1892–1983), novelist, journalist and critic; it was well known that she was the mother of Wells's son, Anthony West (b. 1914). (Lady) Faith Compton Mackenzie (1888–1960) m. Compton Mackenzie, 1905; later a writer of historical biographies and autobiography. (See *Times* obituary, 11 July 1960.)

of atmosphere and ghosts, and very expensive. – Réné Hansard has bought a little farm near Cannes, called The Miracle, and is going to make her fortune growing tube-roses, which aren't planted yet, and inventing miracles at the well in the fields, the well being a miracle well by repute. Time we did something absurd.

The Wrights have come to their old house near S. Domenico.[1] She is the woman of the little Arts and Crafts shop in Cheyne Row. But they're rather nice and funny, a fat old couple.

Ciccia and Vincenzo were married last Saturday, and we supplied the wine.

D. H. Lawrence

Please *do not* mention the America plan to people, especially murry-worms –

2171. To Jan Juta, [12 February 1921]
Text: MS NYPL: PC v. Cagliari – Palazzo Comunale; Unpublished.

[Fontana Vecchia, Taormina, (Messina), Sicily]
12 Feb.

Hope you got home safely – and all is well. Did you ask the Burr the questions about passports? Do let me know. Nothing further here – except I've nearly finished the *Sardinia*. Heard from Réné that she has bought a farm near Cannes, to grow tube-roses. Time we did something outrageous, I think. – The Wrights amuse me. Do you like *W. in Love*?

DHL

2172. To Marie Hubrecht, [12 February 1921]
Text: MS Anon.; Unpublished.

Fontana Vecchia, Taormina, Sicily
Saturday. 12 Feb.

Dear Miss Hubrecht

Your telegram came today, after so long. And poor Werner Gotheim in terror at the great expense of Sicily – it *is* expensive now, and not worth it – has decided to go back to Germany at once. So there it is. I have been down to the studio once or twice. It is quite dry and safe – but seems forsaken. Gotheim did not come to Taormina.

Thank you so much for troubling about that velvet. The man was mean – sent the stuff without registering or anything, and so lost it for good.

---

[1] John J. Wright was a painter; with his wife he often stayed in Taormina.

Taormina is so crowded with foreigners, mostly Scandinavians and Americans – and the prices are so ridiculous, that I am quite tired of it. Chicken now costs 24 francs a kilo.

I am doing a little travel book of Sardinia. The Scandinavians might like that to publish.

Will you come so late as April? We shall probably be leaving by the end of April or beginning of May. Would you like the house for a time if we go then? – But it is all so indefinite. Let us just leave everything till the moment, and see how it turns out. I ought to go to America about my work. I may do that in the autumn. But I dont know.

Ciccia and Vincenzo were married last Saturday, and seem quite happy.

I am glad you are safely at home again – and better – You seem not to have been at all well in Norway.

The studio is awfully nice – but it does want whitewashing. – If any other nice, responsible person should want it, shall we let it to him for the time when you don't require it at all? Werner Gotheim would have loved it.

Winter is not particularly nice here.

If there is anything I can do for you, in Taormina or elsewhere, do tell me. We'll see what the months bring.

Yours sincerely   D. H. Lawrence

Text: MS Hubrecht; Unpublished.

[Frieda Lawrence begins]

Fontana Vecchia

Dear Miss Hubrecht,

Thank you very much for troubling about my mother's stuff – I am cross with the man, he just could'nt be bothered to register it or say when he sent it, now it must be lost, 10 yds of velvet and some blue cloth, so it was mean, considering how it's just invaluable in Germany at this moment – Thank you also for beautiful photographs you sent from Norway, oh, but it looked so cold – We are going to the studio now to have tea there, the sun goes from us at 1 o'clock so it is lovely to go to the other side for a change – I feel it must be a little hard for you to come back to Taormina, with your beautiful Rocca Bella no longer your home – But I promise we will make the studio *very* nice and festive for your home coming – You must come and see us a lot and we will come to the studio. I love the Rocca Bella garden – Bowdwin seems to have a rare time chasing his workman, it's quite made a *man* of him as they say – Juta and Insole came to see us, we had a jolly dance fancy dress together and several feasts here – And a nice girl American from Palermo[1] – The young German is'nt coming – Taormina is no place for cheapness with German money – Yes, I shall hope to see you in April, and then if we go away, you must certainly have Fontana Vecchia – We *loved* the studio when Mary had it, sitting after dinner on very hot evenings on the tower – Did I tell you that Kippenberg (Inselverlag) is translating *The Rainbow* into German – I am very pleased. The Kippenbergs are coming here – I hope you are better, here the almond blossom has been a joy we were sitting in a bouquet of it – I am glad you are happy at Doorn – *The Lost Girl* was a great success but, alas, never so much monetarily in England – and it looks as if it would be one in America – We had a fascinating trip to Sardinia, Lawrence is just writing about it –

With our love   Frieda Lawrence

2173. To Robert Mountsier, 22 February 1921
Text: MS Smith; Unpublished.

Fontana Vecchia, *Taormina*, Sicily
22 Feb. 1921.

Dear M[ountsier]

Today I sent you the first part vol. 1. of *Mr Noon* registered Manuscript post. The novel will have three vols, I think. I have nearly done the second: but am having a rest from work at the moment. This first vol. is very small. You do as you like with it. I think it should serialise. For a serial, cut it and arrange it as you like. But keep an *intact* MS. for printing the *book* from, finally.

I am *not* sending this MS. to England yet: waiting for you. I have asked a friend, *Miss Barbara Low, 13 Guilford Street, W.C.1.* if she will act for me in London as you are doing in New York. I dont [want?][2] a Pinkerish agent. When Barbara answers I'll let you know, and you two can act in strict concert.

I have finished the 'Diary of a Trip to Sardinia'. It is being typed: 80,000 words, I should say. I am trying to get photographs from Cagliari. I hope to send you the MS. with photographs complete within a month's time.

Will you please send me a typescript of those additional poems I sent you for *Birds Beasts* etc, so that I can arrange the English MS. I didn't keep copies of 'Hibiscus and Salvia', and 'Almond'[3] and 'Bare Fig-Tree', and 'Purple Anemone', and 'Snake'.

And now the real business: Thrashers Farm. I hear from Mrs Thrasher today that she will be delighted if we will only occupy the farm and use it. She

[1] Ruth Wheelock.   [2] MS reads 'dont a'.   [3] 'Almond Blossom': see Letter 2177.

will give us a thirty years lease, for nothing. But the place will be ruinous. I
wrote you before, asking you to look at it.

Station: Baltic, Connecticut. – 6 miles from farm. At the Baltic livery stable
ask to[1] be taken to the Old Lynell (Lynnell) farm – the next beyond
Dubberke's mills. – Village of *Westminster*, Conn. *1 mile*. The Baltic road a
very bad one: the better roads to the farm are from *Willimantic*, Conn. – or
Plainsfield. These are the automobile roads. Also Wm Cone,[2] of South
Canterbury, Conn., will give you information. – Mrs Thrasher says it is
lovely country: and one could grow peaches.

I want you to look at it and think carefully. I want to come. I would like a
place in the country of my own. I think I can raise, by borrowing from good
friends over here, at least £400 sterling. We should try and get berths in a
cargo boat: also through friends: so hope to land in America with £300. clear.

Second point: here are Vincenzo and Ciccia, married, aged 26 and 23: he a
gardener: both ready to emigrate and pay steerage passage for themselves: but
Ital. govt. stopped issuing passports for emigrants. But that I might manage.
Would it be possible to put up a tiny frame house for these two: they are
sound workers, and I like them?

Send me a cable. If you advise not coming at all, say just *Useless*.

If you advise F[rieda][3] and my coming, and saying *nothing* to V. and C.,
wire *Alone*.

If you advise my speaking to V and C, to prepare, whilst we go first, wire
Instalments.

And if we are to come as far as possible together, all four, wire *Together*. I
am very serious about this. I want to come. I believe we could make
Thrashers Farm pay enough for Vincenzo and Ciccia, and keep us in food and
home.

If I cable you, I think it will be via Seltzer, because it costs less. So tell him.

I am sending this to Barbara Low to post. If it comes much quicker than
Italian post, put a *foreign* stamp on your letter and address me c/o her –
'please forward'. I shall warn her.

I haven't even heard yet if you have got the letter and little box I sent by
Bonner: and he left here Dec. 29th. It is too slow.

I am very keen about Thrasher's farm. Mrs T. says we should want a Ford
motor car: and that it would grow peaches: but that Wm Cone would tell us
everything.

I shall be dying to hear from you.

F. greets you.

D. H. Lawrence

[1] to] for   [2] Real estate agent (d. 1930?).   [3] F.] my

No word from Amy yet – no more American mail.

Have the *Metropolitan* published 'Wintry Peacock'?[1] If so, have you a copy.

2174. To Mary Cannan, 24 February 1921
Text: MS Lazarus; Moore 642–3.

Fontana Vecchia, *Taormina*, Sicilia
24 Feb 1921

My dear Mary

Your letter today – very exciting that we can have the money. I heard from Mrs Thrasher. She is at Pension Giraud, Via Montebello No 1. Florence. We can have the farm, though she says the house will be in ruins. I have written to a friend in New York to cable me if it is possible. And I hope we can sail about the end of May. You imagine our state, and the rage with which we make plans. We intend just to have a goat and begin to plant fruit bushes, to start. It will be a tight squeeze to get there on the funds – but we'll manage. I hope devoutly that I can earn dollars over there. Then I shall get Vincenzo and Ciccia to come, and plant peach trees, and have a couple of cows, and a Ford runabout that can take the goods to market – and make a permanent thing of it. And if we are in any sort of way, I want you to come next spring: and if you like it, you will have a little frame house of your own, and we shall be like those Anchorites in the picture, dotted about. I hope you will come prepared to take over one branch of the industry: perhaps strawberries and bees and jam: and we will make a tiny living. Mrs Thrasher says it is *lovely* country, and streams and woods on the farm. If only one had capital to start. But perhaps its more fun starting with nothing. – Anyhow I'm going to try.

What have you done with your Italian money? We might possibly use that. I shall try if I can't get a cargo boat to take us. And if it were from Italy one could pay in Liras. Anyhow I needn't change any more into Liras – and I really don't think the Italian money is worth *keeping*, with the exchange now constant at 105–106: and further drop threatened. So if you haven't transferred you might give us some Liras: at once, if you like, to save my changing the bit of English.

Your conjoined ignorance, yours and Molly Muirs,[2] on the subject of the early Christian Church is wicked. The Thebaïd is the bit of the Egyptian desert just back of Alexandria, where it is hilly and dry. In the 3rd and 4th.

---

[1] See p. 493 n. 4.
[2] A friend of Mary (and Gilbert) Cannan's since c. 1908.

Centuries many ascetic christians retired, like John the Baptist, into this desert, and they lived alone, each in his little hut of palm-boughs, or his cave. Saint Anthony was the most famous. It was out there in the Thebaïd the women tempted him. – But these anchorites were devils, really: half naked, hairy, fanatic brutes, always seeing devils and laying them to other people's score. And they used to come down into Alexandria in horrible black gangs, with great cudgels, and smash people's heads and sack the town: being moved by the Holy Spirit, of course. – But the Thebaïd is reckoned as the beginning of the monastic system, and all Lorenzetti would know would be from the pious and flowery legends of St. Anthony of Egypt and St. Mary of Egypt and the like. Did you never read Anatole France's *Thaïs?*[1] – The blue water in front of the picture is no doubt the River Nile: all imaginary, as goes without saying.

I am amused about the *Pug and the Peacock*;[2] Gilbert no doubt is doing a bit of swank.

Are those miserable Murry's still about?[3]

I will tell Mrs Thrasher. It may be she will take Fontana Vecchia from us when we go. We are corresponding about it.

I still don't think well of the gambling. It's a nasty business – and I hope to heaven you won't let it become a habit. I hope you'll lose again.

It is so cold here, we almost die. Such a demon of a wind. But we light the fire at Sundown. We have the key of the Studio, and sometimes go and make tea there, but never feel quite comfortable: there is your ghost there, and your absence. But the garden full of flowers. – Bowdwin pulling Rocca Bella to pieces inside.

If all goes well, I hope to be coming north about the beginning of April, en route for America. Do you know anything about our getting a berth in a cargo ship? – to go to America – Boston or New York? I wouldn't mind where we sail from. – I suppose I shall have to go to England to see my sisters and have some clothes. My appearance is becoming a Taormina scandal.

                                                    Love from both   DHL

---

[1] Published 1891; trans. 1902, 1909 etc.
[2] *Pugs and Peacocks*, Cannan's next novel to be published, was probably only recently completed; it appeared in July 1921.
[3] Murry and Katherine Mansfield remained in Menton until early May 1921.

2175. To Beatrice Bland, 25 February 1921
Text: MS UT; Unpublished.

Fontana Vecchia, *Taormina*, Sicily
25 Feb. 1921

Dear Miss Bland

Thank you for your letter. Yes, I always appreciate a bit of good feeling. But I'm afraid the people who say, at dinner, that I'm a genius have their revenge on me for it when they get me on paper.

Glad the pictures please you now you are in London. I'm quite sure they're good. How's the washing one?[1] They've got a real southern quality, haven't they? – There is here a Miss Beveridge – think that's how you spell her – struggling with unpaintable Taormina and having a bad time.[2] I think she can paint – in a certain one-line modern Parissy way. She's with Mr and Mrs John Wright: who have the Arts and Crafts shop in Cheyne Row:[3] such a nice odd pair, I think. Otherwise I too am rather hating Taormina, especially as it is *very* cold, with a bitter north wind, snow on Calabria, and no sun. However, I shouldn't grumble. I've finished two bits of work and I am having a bit of a holiday.

Mackenzie, who invited us to Herm, is now very doubtful of having any place where we could stay. So there we are: sempre lo stesso.[4] But let him sit on his island till his feet are cold. I guess, as you suggested Faith M[ackenzie] is glad to be rid of him.

My wife sends greetings. Hope we'll have a convivial teaparty yet. Best wishes to the work – also the woman.

Yours   D. H. Lawrence

2176. To Thomas Seltzer, 28 February 1921
Text: MS UT; Postmark, Taormina 28 2 21; Lacy, *Seltzer* 17–19.

Fontana Vecchia, *Taormina*, Sicily
28 Feb. 1921.

Dear Seltzer.

Your letter, and 6 copies of the *Lost Girl*, came yesterday. I like the look of

---

[1] No picture is known by Beatrice Bland which corresponds to the subject hinted here and in Letter 2158.
[2] Anne Millicent Beveridge (1871–1955), b. Kirkcaldy, Fife, who had lived in Paris for many years. Her paintings were exhibited at the Indépendants (1907, 1909), the Salon d'Autumne (1910), the Artistes Français (1911) and the Nationale (1912–24). For an account of her first meeting with DHL, in Sicily, see Carswell 133.
[3] Beatrice Bland herself lived in Cheyne Walk; Millicent Beveridge and two of her sisters also had a flat there.
[4] 'always the same'.

the book immensely – much better than Secker's. Am glad it started well. If only it will keep on.

I believe that *Women in Love* will sell all right. Secker definitely is not publishing[1] before 1st. May. He will hardly send copies to New York before he issues the book in London, will he?

We went to Sardinia – but decided Sicily is better. It is just possible I may come to America – but there, I have said it so often. There isn't any news from here till I make up my mind to something. It is full spring in Sicily – lovely really – and Etna deep, deep in snow.

I do hope things will go well.

Yrs   D. H. Lawrence

P.S. I do wish you could give Mountsier some dollars for me.

DHL

P.P.S. – Just come *Precipitations* and *Blind Mice* forwarded by you.[2] Many thanks. If books come for me – or letters – hand them to Mountsier will you please.

DHL

2177. To Robert Mountsier, 28 February 1921
Text: MS Smith; Unpublished.

Fontana Vecchia, Taormina, Sicily
28 Feb. 1921.

Dear M[ountsier]

I think the only help is to come to America. I have written twice about Thrasher's Farm.

Thrashers Farm

usually known as Old Lynnell Farm
next to Dubbèrkes Farm (or Dubberke's Mills)
Village Westminster – 1 mile. (Connecticut)
Station (nearest) Baltic, Conn. – 6 miles. livery stables at Baltic. – road *bad*.
Town: South Canterbury. a certain Wm Cone will give you information.
better roads approach farm from *Willimantic* and *Plainsfield* Connecticut. We can have the farm for nothing for a 30 years lease if we like. I am expecting Mrs Thrasher at Taormina shortly, to settle. I believe the place is in a ruinous state. But could F[rieda] and I live there? I don't want *anybody* to know we are coming to America. I have here a young Sicilian couple who would come and work and cost little: Vincenzo, and his wife Ciccia.

---

[1] publishing] printing
[2] *Precipitations* (New York, 1920) was a book of verse by Evelyn Scott (b. 1893); *Blind Mice* (New York, 1921), by Cyril Kay Scott, was a prose satire.

In my letter *via* Barbara Low, 13 Guilford St. W.C.1. I said to you – please cable –

Useless: if it's no go at all, and we mustn't come.

Alone: if Frieda and I are to come alone.

Instalments: if we are to arrange for Vincenzo and Ciccia to follow on.

Together: if we are all to come together – supposing I can manage it. Wire me anyhow.

A friend has offered me £200. sterling.[1] I hope to manage another £200. That is £400. on this side. And you will have some dollars from Seltzer.

There is a French line (Favre) sailing from Marseilles, Naples, Palermo, to Algiers, Azores, N. York. I hope to sail from Palermo before end of April.

I hear that there is quarantine at N. York now. But hope it won't last.

Shall I bring you some junk? Do you love it? What sort do you like? I hate it myself.

D. H. Lawrence

F. is so amused by it all.

No letter from Amy. The bitch is probably jealous of *B[irds] B[easts] and F[lower]s*.

[2][Please return with answers:]

[Do you know the date of delivery of the manuscript of *The Rainbow* to Huebsch? Did you or Pinker give Huebsch permission to delay publication or to eliminate any sections of *The Rainbow*?]

I can't remember anything at all. I never keep any letters. I sent you all Pinker's useless communications. Don't worry yourself into distraction and me into disappearance.

[Just to what extent does Pinker have an interest in the contracts which he signed for you? Does he have any legal hold of any kind on you or them, or if you ignored him entirely, could he bring legal action against you? Is he entitled to a commission in the future on the royalties?]

I believe Pinker has legal right to royalties on all agreements made by him for me: on not many books, really.

[What's your usual custom with your manuscripts? Seltzer has the one of *Women in Love*, and there is no doubt but that it has a certain value and will have a greater. He had a typewritten copy made of it – 'it cost over $100,' he told me some time ago. If you insist on its return, there's no doubt but that he

---

[1] Mary Cannan: see Letter 2180.

[2] The sections which follow within square brackets were typed by Mountsier; he left spaces for DHL's answers.

will charge you up with the copying, perhaps he already has. There's a statement due shortly. What action is going to be taken by you in this matter? I'd say get the manuscript.]

I always burn my MSS. That which Seltzer has is a typescript so scribbled over that it is horrible. For heavens sake let it go to limbo.

[Have you received any books sent on to you by Seltzer other than his own publications? Yesterday he said to me: 'Here's a book from Doran for Lawrence. Do you think I had better send it to him? I have received a number of books for him, but I think he doesn't want to be bothered with them?' He had opened the package containing this particular book from the George H. Doran Co. (But I suppose a person who opens his letters shouldn't complain!) There was a letter with said book.]

I have recd. from Seltzer today two books – *Precipitations* (Poems) by Evelyn Scott – and *Blind Mice*, by Cyril K. Scott. No letter. No other books. Ask him to hand over to you anything that comes for me – and I'll write him the same.

[Give me a full list of the English publications to which I may send poems and any stories you send me, with the names of editors where they should be addressed to editors. I'll see if I can't arrange for simultaneous publication here and in England for some of them.]

– I'm [. . .] waiting to hear from Barbara Low – if she'll agent me in London as you in N. York.

P.T.O.

Gen$^{mo.}$ = gentilissimo = most gentle (!!!)

Preg^{mo} = Pregevolissimo = most valued, most esteemed.

Your letters drive me perfectly frantic. I've written you *dozens* of letters. Oh, if only I could but keep my diary. Lately I've written twice about Thrasher's Farm. And I sent you before that poems: 'Almond Blossom' and 'Snake' etc, and 'Hibiscus and Salvia Flowers' and 'Purple Anemones'. – 3 separate letters. Hope they arrive. I shall send this letter *expressed and registered*. Yours came this morning (*Feb. 28*). (Yours of F. 8th. acknowledging Bonner's box and letter). I always answer your letters *the same day I receive them*. I do so because I can't keep count afterwards.

Act as you think well about *The White Peacock* and Duffield.

I don't mind if you open any letters.

Oh dear – curse *all* jews. But don't be too disagreeable with Poor Seltzer. He sent me 6 copies of *Lost Girl*: very nicely done, they are, much better than shoddy Secker. – I enclose Seltzers letter to me. I will answer him most circumspectly.[1]

I sent you a type copy of the First Part of my novel *Mr Noon* a week ago – on 22nd. Feb, to be exact. Hope it comes. Am awaiting typescript of 'A Trip to Sardinia': also, most anxiously, a reply from Cagliari about photographs for the same. I have received copies of 'Rex' and 'Revolutionary' and other *New Republic* poems.[2] Jane Burr wrote me to England, long ago.[3] Damn her. I am a hebrophobe. – Go gently with Benny Huebsch, the little Jew.

All answers are on this sheet. – Feel these awful non-arriving letters will send me dotty.

On the other sheet, more important, *Thrasher's Farm*.

Seltzers Sunday Afternoon with Jane Burr and the Ten Tribes sounds too ghastly to contemplate. – and I've got an Oppenheim and wife[4] coming to tea this mortal afternoon.

2178. To S. S. Koteliansky, 2 March 1921
Text: MS BL; Postmark, Taormina 3 3 21; Moore 643–4.

Fontana Vecchia, *Taormina*, Sicilia
2 Marzo 1921

My dear Kot

Well your letter was a nice little kettle of old fish. How they do but all stink! I hear the *Athenæum* lost £5,000 a year under our friend the mud-worm. But he is incorporated into the *Nation* – Nations foster such worms. I hear he is – or was – on the Riviera with K[atherine] – who is doing the last gasp touch, in order to impose on people – on Mary Cannan, that is. K. pretending to be sick of Jack; another old dodge; in order to pump the interlocutor to say things. K. also announcing that the *Rowntrees* couldn't bear *her* writing. Ah me, we have become important. Two mud-worms they are, playing into each other's long mud-bellies.

[1] So that Mountsier could see how circumspect he had been, DHL copied his letter to Seltzer as a long postscript to this letter; since the text is virtually identical to that of Letter 2176 (except that the second postscript was omitted), it has not been repeated.
[2] On 'Rex' see p. 536 n. 1; for 'The Revolutionary' see Letter 2083 n. 1; the 'other *New Republic* poems' may have included 'Humming-Bird' published by the journal on 11 May 1921.
[3] See Letter 1869.
[4] Edgar Oppenheim was not legally married.

I am tired to death of travellers. Taormina wriggles with them. But there is
a worse sort even than the british: viz, the Scandinavian. There must be at
least 600 Scandinavians in this village at present: horrible greedy Pillars of
Society escaping their taxes. No wonder Ivy Low hates Stockholm, or
wherever she is.

I get bored with people altogether of any sort. But this house is very nice,
the world is green and flowery, the sun rises bright over the sea, Etna with
heavy snow is beautiful, and there is a peculiar glamour – a sort of Greek
morning world glamour. Yet I itch to go away – and think once more of
America. But I have thought so often before. I have this house till end of
April: with option of another year. And it costs only Lit 2,500 – and is
beautiful, and alone, with much land sloping in terraces. I love my Fontana
Vecchia – et pretera nihil.[1]

I think Italy will not revolute or bolsh any more. The thing will settle down
to a permanent socialisti v. fascisti squibbing – the old Italian faction, Guelph
and Ghibelline – and so the house will come to bits. It will have no one smash,
like Russia.

And what of Russia? And dear darling England?

Remember me warmly to Sonia, Grisha, and the long, two-plaited Ghita. I
hope you are better.

                                                                                           DHL

2179. To Rosalind Baynes, 2 March 1921
Text: MS UN; Huxley 512.

                                                            Fontana Vecchia, *Taormina*, Sicily
                                                                                    2 March 1921.

Dear R[osalind]

Your letter yesterday – I don't write because nothing happens. We went to
Sardinia – it was an exciting little trip – but one couldn't live there – one
would be weary-dreary. I was very disappointed. So much so that I have been
planning to go to America. You remember Mrs Thrasher's farm – well she
still offers it. I don't know if I shall get off. I have said so often I was going. We
shall see. I have taken this house definitely till end of April – with option of
continuing the year out. But I doubt very much if we shall stay after April.
Only the house itself is so nice – just as Canovaia was nice.

We too have had hot sun and cold wind. The sun is dangerous these
months – it has a radio-chemical action on the blood which simply does for

---

[1] 'and nothing else'.

me. I avoid it. The thing is to keep *cool* – not get hot at all. Etna is looking extremely beautiful – with very heavy snow. I always wonder when she's going to burst out. I dont trust her.

Italy begins to tire me. I hear the official opinion now is that there will be no definite revolution or bolshing at all: that it is going to resolve itself into the continual faction fights between socialists and fascisti – genuine Italian Guelph and Ghibelline business, and let the world wag elsewhere. Rather dull. But the thought of England is entirely repugnant. I promised to go and see my sisters – but I can't cross the channel. No no – England is a mud-bathos.

Do the children keep all right? Is Brid[get] going to Godwin? How is he? And the divorce? Surely these are news items.

Remember me to Eleanor – Tell her to take my greetings to Joan and Bertie and the children, including the unseen.[1] I shall let you know if anything materialises in the shape of plans.

DHL

2180. To Robert Mountsier, 3 March 1921
Text: MS Smith; Postmark, Taormina 4 3 21; Unpublished.

Fontana Vecchia, *Taormina*, Sicily
3 March 1921

Dear M[ountsier]

Your letter of Feb. 15 today – enclosing the unsatisfactory *Lost Girl* agreement. *Nothing come by hand.*

Seltzer has not written me direct about agreement – only a note with clipping of *L.G.* – I leave all to you.

No word from Amy. Send her to blazes, along with her cigars.[2] She is trying to keep afloat on the gas of her own importance: hard work, considering her bulk.

I wrote Teasdale.

I *can* typewrite, but haven't a writer – and I *hate* doing it.

The poem I sent direct I asked Thayer[3] to refer to you about. It was 'Turkey Cock'.[4] He didn't like it. I shall send *nothing else* direct.

[1] Joan and Herbert Farjeon's children were Joscelyn, Annabel and Gervase.
[2] See Letter 2161 and n. 3.
[3] Thayer] him
[4] The poem, which DHL described to Harriet Monroe as 'one of [his] favorites' (23 September 1922), was published by her in *Poetry*, November 1922; it was also collected in *Birds, Beasts and Flowers*.

I have had letters from those Boni Liveright people[1] and not answered at all.

I want you to act entirely on your own discretion: quite approve of your opening the Seltzer letter. I hate Jews and I want to learn to be more *wary* of them all.

I don't want any money. I told you I had a promise of £200 from Mary Cannan, an old friend (Mrs Gilbert Cannan, separated from Gilbert; previously Mrs J M Barrie!) She will give it like a shot.

Cut the poems, and also *Mr Noon* (Vol I) as much as you like for magazines, but *not* for a book. Do you think *Tortoises* would sell as a chapbook?[2]

Pinker retains rights on all agreements made by him: unless I can get him to cancel.

I have done *nothing* with regard to English publication, leaving that till you are settled. I depend on America. I haven't heard from Barbara Low yet: Post gone bad: too many disorders here: sickening.

I don't think England will attack *W. in Love*. Secker has it ready printed. He will *incur* all the risks of prosecution – only *libel* is my damage. Seltzers 'objectionable' clause makes me hate the little stinker. Secker fixed 1st. May for *Women in Love* publication.

I am so anxious to hear of Thrasher's Farm. *Cable* me. Frieda today has a wire that her mother is very ill:[3] she'll probably be dashing off to BadenBaden in a few days. In which case I shall make all ready, and sail for America from Palermo as soon as I get your cable (if it is at all favorable) – Europe is no good. I may come from Palermo to New York by the Favre (French) line, calling Algiers and Azores. Shall cable you. You must by now have had my letters about Thrasher's farm. – Don't come to Europe. Unless you really want to – I can't get photographs of Sardinia for my 'Trip' – curse!

Try and make a bit of friends with Huebsch. I won't write him at all.

– au revoir.   D. H. Lawrence

If you think I *shouldn't* come to America at all, say *Quite useless*.

That 10% of yours, out of me, won't do you much good, alas. But we'll do more than percents. We'll make a life somehow. Thrashers Farm can be a start: the ship next. If I can get Vincenzo on the farm we can always leave it.

[1] A New York publishing house which later acquired certain publishing rights from Seltzer and reprinted some works by DHL.
[2] See Letter 2098 and n. 2.
[3] DHL wrote in his diary, 3 March 1921: 'Telegram from Else [Jaffe]: Mama schlecht Alfred sehr krank Komm. Believe it a trick' [Mother unwell Alfred very ill, come.] (Tedlock, *Lawrence MSS* 92).

2181. To Dr Anton Kippenberg, 4 March 1921
Text: MS SVerlag; Unpublished.

Fontana Vecchia, *Taormina*, Sicilia
4 Marzo 1921.

Dear Dr Kippenberg

Today I have received three volumes of the *Biblioteca Mundi* – Byron, Stendhal's *Amour*, and St. Teresa's Life.[1] The last, I am sad to say, I cant read. But probably I shall go to Spain, and so must learn Spanish. – I think they are delightful books, such lovely gift books. I feel so grateful, nowadays, for a well-printed, carefully produced book. In England they are rather shoddy, and in France and Italy always trivial.

I am very much interested in your first list: should like to see the Napoleon book particularly. In what language is the *Anthologia Hebraica*? – and the *Helvetica*? In the list of the *Bibliotheca Mundi* everything interests me except Musset and Horace. Can anybody read de Musset any more? And surely everybody who loves Horace will possess a standard edition.

The same with Homer and Dante. We have had them pushed at us so often. I can only speak for myself. But really, I don't see why you should publish again the books, old monumental classics, which have been published *ad nauseam* in every country. And who will buy Chaucer nowadays?

As for binding men together in a new spirit of Internationalism, of which you speak in your letter, alas, I doubt it is no good trying that any more. The only active internationalism is the Soviet sort, the Moscow manifestoes. And these are dead against the internationalism of the cultured spirit. For the rest, all the world is running about, and if your *Bibliotheca Mundi* is well exposed for sale in Rome and Florence and Cannes and Paris and London and New York, I am sure there will be plenty of buyers. And these buyers, I should say, will snap up *Fleurs du Mal* and Napoleon and perhaps Byron: but I doubt if they'll look at Horace or Dante or Homer. Though really, you know better than I do.

But of this I am sure, that mental internationalism has no effect on real nationalism. Nationalism, as we have it, is established upon *interest*: material interest, commercial interest, what the Italians mean when they say *interessi*. And there is a complete gulf, unacknowledged, but absolute, between *mental* interest and national or commercial interest. Mentally, we are all cosmopo-litan nowadays. But passionally, we are all jealous and greedy and rabidly national. For my part, I prefer to live abroad and to escape as far as possible

---

[1] These – together with the works such as *Anthologia Helvetica* mentioned later – all form parts of the *Bibliotheca Mundi* published by Insel-Verlag at Leipzig.

the stigma of national interest. But it is all very well. Here in Taormina, in Rome – in Cannes – nations are more suspicious, jealous, jeering and antagonistic than ever they have been. It is a kind of rabies: hate-your-neighbour madness. It is absolutely time to put away all idealism on this matter. League of Nations is as ridiculous as a poor vaudeville.[1] At the bottom of all European hearts a rabid, jealous nationalism of hate-your-neighbour is the basic feeling. Along with it goes a good deal of superficial curiosity concerning that detested neighbour or neighbours. So that people will buy books in foreign languages. The old *insular* spirit is really dead. But the old internationalism of human interest, the old philanthropic internationalism is dead or gone quite silly. In its place is a fizzing, acid internationalism of detestation and spite: not even hatred, for hate is too grand a passion: but spite, jealousy, and acid dislike. This is the thing to reckon with. It's a case of every man for himself. And when there is a mob unison – as between France and England, or between all socialists – it is now a unison founded on the lowest interests and the lowest passions of greed and spite. No getting away from that fact.

Therefore, if I was doing a *Biblioteca Mundi* I should calculate my public: and realise that they are curious about the famous but not well known books in other languages: such as Stendhal's *Amour* or some Swinburne or Whitman: – things with a slightly lurid interest. But I *can't* see anybody buying Chaucer. People don't buy books in a *good* spirit any more: at least, cosmopolitan people dont. They buy them in a perverse spirit.

My wife is coming shortly to Baden-Baden, because her mother is ill. Probably she will write to you from there.

But oh, don't trust to a new wave of idealism in Europe. I do believe, for some things, Germany is a bit of a fool's paradise now. The sooner she disillusions herself the better. There are *no* good intentions in these old countries. Everybody is grasping for commercial power and thinks to get it by squeezing somebody else's throat. And the fool who persists in idealistic blindnesses will get his throat squeezed first. – Italy is really pro-German: but is frightened. But she hates France and England deeply. The hate accumulates everywhere. It means war ahead: not love and peace.

The Italian official opinion is that there will now be *no* social revolution. Italy has gone back to her old method: split into two factions, Guelph and Ghibelline again, and is going merely to tear her own entrails. The Socialisti and the Fascisti will just tear Italy to pieces, gradually, till she falls into a

---

[1] The League of Nations – an organisation for international co-operation – was established by the victorious Allies at the Paris Peace Conference in 1919.

number of divided states again: for neither party will triumph, because neither party *wants* to triumph. – But if there is outside pressure – foreign war – they will amalgamate at once.

Well – that's what I feel about things at present. You ask me about a *Biblioteca Mundi*: well, there's the *Mundi* part of it.

I send you under a separate cover a copy of the American edition of *The Lost Girl*. I hope soon to send you a copy of *Women in Love*, sequel to *The Rainbow*.

Very many thanks for the three books.

Yours Sincerely   D. H. Lawrence[1]

2182. To J. C. Squire, 7 March 1921
Text: MS Lazarus; Moore, *Intelligent Heart* 278–9.

Fontana Vecchia, *Taormina*, Sicily
7 March 1921.

Dear Squire

Thank you for your telegram and letter. Yes, I have been insulted so many times, by little people like Murry for example, that I thought I'd best make sure.

However, it's all right.

I send you three poems. They are from a book I have just finished – called *Birds, Beasts, and Flowers*. I send you just a bit of the Flowers part.[2] The Birds and the Beasts you can see sometime, if you like.

I heard from a friend Robert Mountsier, 417 West 118 Street, New York, who is acting for me over there, that he was going to send you a copy of a little story 'Fanny[3] and Annie'. If it comes and you don't like it, don't have any qualms about returning it to me. I don't mind in the least if you send back the things I offer. But just say what it is in them you don't care for, and then I shall know another time what kind of thing to send you.

I have just got the typed MS. of a little novel *Mr Noon* – very comical I think: about 40,000 words. Also I am just finishing a little 'Diary of a Trip to Sardinia': light and sketchy. That is my stock at present.

Best of wishes   D. H. Lawrence

I guess you'll find 'Hibiscus' too long, even if you care for it at all.

[1] Attached to the MS is a German translation of DHL's letter, in another hand.
[2] DHL's diary, for 7 March 1921, reads: 'Send Hibiscus & Salvia Flowers, Purple Anemones, & Pomegranate, to Squire for London Mercury' (Tedlock, *Lawrence MSS* 92).
[3] Fanny] Fannie

2183. To Irene Whittley, 8 March 1921
Text: MS UT; Unpublished.

Fontana Vecchia, *Taormina*, Sicily
8 March 1921

Dear Mrs Whittley

Frieda should have answered your letter before. But we have been in such a state of indecision. A friend offered us a little farm in America, if we would go and live on it and work it. I made all preparations to go – and then suddenly feel I cant. Came telegrams too to say Frieda's mother very ill: so she is struggling to get away to BadenBaden, at this unpropitious hour.

So there we all are.

I know you said you might like to come to Taormina in the spring. Would you and Whittley care to come quite soon? – at Easter perhaps? If so, *do*. I shall be alone – there is plenty of room for you here in Fontana Vecchia – we can have our picnics as last year. – Also, if you are coming, you might persuade my younger sister to come with you. Do try to.

Mrs L. A. Clarke, Grosvenor Rd. Ripley, near Derby.

The fare now is about £21. return, *first class*, with sleeping car from Paris and from Rome. You *must* have a sleeper from Rome to Taormina. If you like to go from Paris to Rome Second, it is possible. But it's an awful long journey. Anyhow the costs here would be nil.

If you think of coming, let me know at once. And please, Whittley, will you do all my sister's passport business through your bank.

Frieda will probably leave tomorrow. I shall go with her to Palermo, fix up her passport, and see her on the Naples boat, then come back here.[1]

If you come, get the visas good for the return journey if possible.

I do hope Mrs Short and Captain Short are well.

Send us news of yourself, anyhow.

Taormina full of foreigners, and Rome much fuller. Impossible to get a bed there.

Do hope all is well.

Yours   D. H. Lawrence

---

[1] According to his diary (Tedlock, *Lawrence MSS* 92), DHL went to Palermo on 11th and returned on 14 March 1921.

2184. To Mary Cannan, 15 March 1921
Text: MS Lazarus; Unpublished.

Fontana Vecchia, *Taormina*, Sicilia
15 March 1921

My dear Mary

I found your letter when I came back from Palermo last night. Frieda had such disquieting news of her mother that she felt she must go. I accompanied her to Palermo and saw her off on[1] the boat. I expect she is still in Rome, doing passports. The German address is

bei Frau Baronin von Richthofen, Ludwig-Wilhelmstift, *Baden-Baden*.

I am staying here for the time being. F. may come back in about a month: or I may go for a walk with Juta and meet her in the north, end of May.

With one thing and another, I can't manage my plan. I shall have to give up this farm and America for the present. So I return your cheque, with a thousand thanks.[2] An end of this little splash. – Also the plural of mille is mila:

one thousand = mille
two thousands = due mila

I dont suppose the bank would cash the thing, mis-spelt.

It is rather rainy here – and not particularly nice being alone with the rain. I have half a mind to migrate to the studio – but probably shan't. A Scotch-woman – a Miss Beveridge – who has worked for years in Paris – is doing a portrait of me.[3] But it isn't like me. It has some resemblance of me, but is just somebody else.

Sicily looked so lovely coming back yesterday. The fields are blue with big blue anemones: and then great scarlet ones like poppies: and then two fields full of lovely pink snapdragon, big and velvety and beautiful.

I am taking on Fontana Vecchia for another year – my rent remains the same 2,000, but I agree to pay for the oven which was put in – another 400. It is very cheap.

It will be wise of you to spend your Liras in Turin or somewhere this summer. There will be another fall in the autumn. – Fancy your going to England. I don't want to go. But I've promised to meet my sisters somewhere: so am half-seas over. I do wonder how you'll like it.

As for the Murrys, I utterly disbelieve in either of them. – Juta met Ottoline and Julian in Rome.[4] Insole is on the way to Japan: everybody *in giro*: you restless too.

So many thanks for the cheque. I shall consider I have had the 4000.

DHL

[1] on] in
[2] See Letter 2170.
[3] She was due to begin on 5 March 1921 (Tedlock, *Lawrence MSS* 92).
[4] Julian Morrell (b. 1906), Lady Ottoline's daughter. See *Letters*, ii. 308.

2185. To Robert Mountsier, 15 March 1921
Text: MS Smith; Unpublished.

Fontana Vecchia, *Taormina*, Sicilia
15 March 1921

Dear M[ountsier]

Frieda is in Rome doing her passport to go to Germany to her mother, who is very ill: I am now alone in Fontana Vecchia. Don't know how long she will be away.

Circumstances one or the other have combined to make Thrashers Farm almost impossible. I don't think I can come to America this summer – or this year. And perhaps I agree with some Americans here, that this is precisely the wrong time to think of going.

However: I give it up: and am going to renew my lease of Fontana Vecchia to March 1922. It costs only 2,400 Lire the year.

In Palermo I looked at ships, and started enquiries going in the port. I saw lovely two-master Mediterranean boats. We will see what Palermo can do for us.

Come some time during the summer. One can live very cheaply in Fontana Vecchia. And we can look definitely for a ship, *if we can afford it*. I am now almost determined to borrow money from *nobody*, and not to have any sort of help from middle-classy people. Also I learn that Ralph Stock is a journalisty story-writing man: and I know I could do better by nosing round the Italian ports alone, in the summer, and picking up what chance offers. Come and nose with me.

So there we are: all my plans for farms suddenly shivered. Well, let us burn our homes and take to our ship.

I hope by now you have received *Mr Noon* Vol I, and approve of it.

I want to tell you *not* to be too humble with editors, publishers, Amys or any other stinkers with money or office. *Don't* tout my MSS. as if you were a poor man trying to sell. Don't stand a moment's impudence from them – and never be intimate with them. They are all enemies, and it is a devil's game in which we must not be losers any more. Treat them all like the dirt they are: only politely.

I have got most of the *Sardinia* MS. from the typist, but not photographs. Curse!

I think I shall finally settle with Barbara Low that she does my agenting in London.[1] So prepare her a full list of instructions about things wherein she must concur with you.

---

[1] DHL's diary-entry for 15 March 1921, 'write to Barbara Low & Mountsier' (Tedlock, *Lawrence MSS* 92), suggests that a letter may have gone to her on the same day. No correspondence between DHL and Barbara Low about her becoming his agent has been traced.

Miss Barbara Low, 13 Guilford Street. W.C.1.
Let us all fight hard for a real footing this year, and we can sweep the world.
DHL[1]

2186. To Baroness Anna von Richthofen, [16 March 1921]
Text: Frieda Lawrence, "*Not I, But the Wind . . .*", p. 119.

Fontana Vecchia, Taormina, Sicilia
16 March

Meine liebe Schwiegermutter:

Your post card came this morning. I do hope you will be feeling better. Frieda is in Rome, doing her passport. I hope by the time you have this card she will be with you. It will make her happy to nurse you and get you better. Soon you must be about walking – and then I will come to Germany and perhaps we can all go away into the Schwarzwald and have a good time. Meanwhile I sit in Fontana Vecchia, and feel the house very empty without F. Don't like it at all: but don't mind so long as you will be better.

I am having my portrait painted: hope that today will be the last sitting, as I am tired. I look quite a sweet young man, so you will feel quite pleasant when I send you a photograph. The weather is once more sunny and beautiful, the sea so blue, and the flowers falling from the creeper.

---

[1] Part of Mountsier's answer to DHL's letter has survived; dated 1 April 1921 (TMS Smith) it reads:

Dear Lawrence,
    Your letter of March 15 telling me you had decided not to come to America. This is somewhat of a let-down after the letters I have been receiving from you. I have put quite a bit of time and thought on this farm proposition, and we could have carried it through. As to what any Americans in Taormina, or anywhere else in Europe, tell you, I have only this to say that it was an opportune time.
    Your chief publishing field is here, and the nearer you are to it the better. Ship or no ship, I feel that your base should be here. We could have earned the necessary money for the farm and the ship if you had come. I didn't like the idea of your borrowing money and wrote you so.
    What gets me about the whole thing is that you came to a definite decision to come to America and put it up to me to cable you on the basis of a programme you outlined. I reached the same conclusions you had, reasoning doubtless on a different basis of facts, and here I am waiting for you to cable me your sailing date and whether or not V[incenzo] and C[iccia] are coming, when bang – everything goes for nothing because you meanwhile have come to another decision which has been influenced more or less by some Americans who do not know your affairs on this side.
    I am not writing this in a spirit of antagonism, but rather of disappointment. We must come to an understanding: Am I now to go on with a feeling that every decision you arrive at is, so far as I am concerned, to be considered as one that isn't definite at all – not that I do not think it a good idea at times to change.

I have no news as yet from F. from Rome, but hope she is managing everything easily. I am all right in Taormina: people invite me to tea and dinner all the time. But I don't want to go very badly. I am correcting the MS. of my diary of a Trip to Sardinia, which I think will amuse you. Give my love to Else. Tell me if there is anything I can send: and do get better soon.

DHL

2187. To Marie Hubrecht, 20 March 1921
Text: MS Simpson; Unpublished.

Fontana Vecchia, Taormina, Sicilia
20 March 1921

Dear Miss Hubrecht

I was pleased to hear from you again: but sorry you are not feeling all yourself, and that you won't come south this spring. The studio garden is quite beautiful, full of freezias and stocks and violets, the red montbretias dying, and the tulips. I go down quite often, because a Miss Beveridge, a Scotch woman, who has worked for years in Paris, is painting my portrait. I shall send you a photograph when it is done. I took the liberty of sitting in the studio – I thought you wouldn't mind: so there the picture is, on the easel, nearly finished. Miss Beveridge is staying with the Wrights: do you know them, an elderly couple with an old house in Piazzetta Garibaldi? Tell me you don't mind my using the studio for having my portrait painted?

Bowdwin is in a great mess at Rocca Bella: ten work-people, lime, sand, masons hammering: and nothing will ever be done. The house, furniture and books, all exposed. Really better if Carmelo put them in the studio or the little locked studio-room. You see Rocca Bella is being torn quite inside out. Bowdwin will never finish and the workpeople are very objectionable really. Don't you think of *building* at the studio while the working people are in this beastly humour. But before you come, you might like to tell Carmelo to whitewash the studio. It is very dirty.

We are rather in a fix too. Frieda had telegrams that her mother was very ill, and she must go at once. It is heart trouble. So she set off: and is, I trust, in BadenBaden today. The address is

c/o Frau Baronin von Richthofen, Ludwig-Wilhelmstift, *BadenBaden*.
I am sitting here quite alone in Fontana Vecchia – only going out to teas and luncheons. But there is a peculiar quality in Taormina society. It does not agree with me, and I am not happy in it. I am all right in Fontana Vecchia – but not out among the people here.

Juta has various plans. You must know he is very much in love with an

American girl in Rome,[1] so that that occupies him as well as his work. But I promised to do a walking-tour and a sketch-book with him. He wants me to come to Florence on the 15th. April, to spend a fortnight there with him and Mrs Hansard: then on 1st. May go to Sardinia, and there walk for three weeks, doing sketches – for a joint book, my words, his drawings. After the end of May I shall meet Frieda either in Germany or in north Italy. I would like very much to come to Doorn – but can't say anything for sure. Thank you very much indeed for the invitation. – Juta, after Sardinia, is going to Anticoli, near Rome, to work for three months. I think his *fiamma* will be in Anticoli too. In September he proposes to go to Paris, where he is seeking for a studio, and work the winter there.

This is all the news. The weather is warm and lovely. I feel you are not very happy. If there is anything I can do for you here I shall be only too pleased. Tell me I don't trespass in the studio. And let us meet *somewhere* in the early summer.

With many greetings   D. H. Lawrence

2188. To Dr David Eder, 22 March 1921
Text: MS SIU; Hobman 122–3.

Fontana Vecchia, *Taormina*, Sicilia
22 March 1921

Dear David

Barbara says you are off to Palestine again. I still think it must be better than England, and prefer it for you – though Edith hates it.

I should like to see you again. Which way are you going? I wish you called at Palermo. But I think I could dash even up to Naples or Taranto, to meet you. Wire me if it is any good.

Frieda is in BadenBaden: her mother very ill. Haven't heard if she's got there yet: last letter from Milan: but feel almost sure she has arrived all right.

Here I sit alone in Fontana Vecchia. But I know plenty of people in Taormina – none of whom I care for. The world isn't worth raging against. After all, if one can rove about a bit, why bother about humanity.

I suppose you wouldn't like me to come to Palestine for a couple of months, and do a Sketch Book of Zion. I'm sure I could make a very good one: and I have nothing much to do till June.

---

[1] Elizabeth Humes (who later provided DHL with a prototype for Lou Carrington in *St. Mawr*, 1925).

A thunder-storm here bumping and rumbling all morning. I feel the elements are in a temper too.

Say if I shall see you.

Tell Edith.

DHL

Couldn't you squeeze a few days in Sicily? Oh do! Come and see me in Fontana Vecchia.

2189. To Robert Mountsier, 22 March 1921
Text: MS Smith; Unpublished.

Fontana Vecchia, *Taormina*, Sicily
22 March 1921.

Dear Mountsier

This is coming to you via London. I am today posting *BirdsBeasts*, and *Mr Noon* I to Barbara Low, 13 Guilford Street. W.C. 1. Send her full information about each MS. Also please send her a copy of 'Bare Almond Trees', 'Bare Fig Trees', 'Almond Blossom', and 'Snake'.[1]

She will send to you a final version of 'Hibiscus and Salvia Flowers', and 'Purple Anemones': also 'The Ass'.[2]

You and she will act in strictest concert. I hope post between London and New York is not so slow.

I have got the MS. of 'Diary of a Trip to Sardinia', and will send it at the end of this week. It makes a book about 70,000 words. I still haven't managed to get Sardinia photographs: only Sicily. But I don't give up.

I am alone in Fontana Vecchia. Frieda has gone to BadenBaden to her mother. I intend to try to finish *Aaron's Rod*. But am not in a good work-mood.

My plans are: America is dead off. I have promised to walk with a man called Juta in Sardinia – or drift through the Lipari Isles and the Egadi (off Trapani) – and do another sketch-book: he is a painter. This to occupy the month of May. After May I shall meet Frieda in Germany or somewhere not too hot.

---

[1] Mountsier promptly did DHL's bidding and wrote to Barbara Low on 9 April 1921 (TMS Smith). He sent typed copies of the four poems; discussed details of arrangements for the publication of *Birds, Beasts and Flowers, Psychoanalysis and the Unconscious* and *Tortoises*; and outlined a general policy for publishing DHL's works: 'English publication of books and poems is to be determined by the American publication. For all books we will attempt to have simultaneous publication in England and the United States. The chief reason for this is that more money can be made for Lawrence through such an arrangement for publication.'

[2] The poem, 'The Ass' (collected in *Birds, Beasts and Flowers*) had been written on 2 March 1921 (Tedlock, *Lawrence MSS* 100).

A friend is enquiring about a little ship, in Palermo. Perhaps it would be better, if it were any way possible, to *hire* for three months or so, and see how we liked it. The money is the chief question. I have very little over here. How much is there in America? I might get temporary partners.

I am feeling absolutely at an end with the civilised world. It makes me sick at the stomach. It would have been a mistake to tie oneself down to a farm. But I can't quite find my direction: can't quite make up my mind in which direction to turn my nose, to try a flight.

Write to me what your plans are. Don't be discouraged by American publishers and editors. It is a fight, and it will always be a fight. So you must fight for me, there's nothing else for it. Meanwhile I am going to find some way out of this nose-tied existence. I am quite seriously going to track down a ship and *try*.

If you come to Europe, don't come till May, and then we shall know what to be doing. But we must meet before long: and I feel it must be over here. We can live very cheaply.

A friend half invited me to go to Palestine to do a book. Don't suppose anything will come of it.

If we all fight, and never give in in any sense to the *Canaille* – they are all Canaille – Dorans or Seltzers, Amys or others – then we shall get our own way. It won't take very long.

a rivederci   D. H. Lawrence

F's mother very ill.

Have removed introduction from English *Birds Beasts*.

This instant your telegram: *together hurry buy farm cost repair Thrashers impossible Noon arrived*.

But *who* will buy the farm, and with what money? I am terrified. And the Italian govt. simply won't give any emigrants passports, and America won't let them in anyhow. F. and I would have to come alone, I fear. And F. is in Germany, her mother suddenly very ill. Nevertheless, if you still wire *Come* – or write – we will have a shot at getting off in the early summer. A friend promised to try and find us a cargo boat. – If only the post were not so slow! What can one do!

2190. To J. B. Pinker, 23 March 1921
Text: MS UT; Unpublished.

Fontana Vecchia, *Taormina*, Sicilia
23 March 1921.

Dear Pinker

If you haven't yet done so, would you be so good as to write to New York to

Doran and *Huebsch* telling them that the contracts for my books have been
turned over to Robert Mountsier, 417 West 118 Street, New York City, – and
that they are authorised to deal with Mountsier in any matters regarding the
contracts.

I find that 'The Blind Man', short story, was published in the Boston
U.S.A. magazine called *The Living Age*, on August 7th. 1920. You said you
had nothing to do with this. I certainly knew nothing of it. Did Harrison do it
all on his own? And is he not going to pay for the story? It must have appeared
in *The English Review* simultaneously with the American copy.[1]

Please let me know.

                                                       Yours   D. H. Lawrence

2191. To Louis Golding, 23 March 1921
Text: MS NWU; Unpublished.

                                        Fontana Vecchia, *Taormina*, Sicilia
                                                            23 March 1921.

Dear Golding

I received *Babylon* about three days ago:[2] delay owing to your having sent it
parcel post. I have read it and was interested. I do wish it had been more
Jewish. One can hardly see any difference between your vision and[3] the
English vision. I wish you had given one the passional truth of Reb Monash's
Yidishkeit. What is there at the bottom of the soul of a Jew which makes him a
Jew? That's what I want to know. And you don't tell me. – Is it nothing but a
mechanical habit which is just collapsing? – The mother is not a bit Jewish. Is
it true? Or is there a basic consciousness of difference – radical difference
between Jew and Gentile? Is there, or isn't there? If there is, then it must be
something important indeed. And a Jewish book should be written
in terms of *difference* from the Gentile consciousness – not identity
with it. I sort of feel there is a gulf: but always hidden and bridged over, or
stated as if it were not a real thing, only a question of habit. I am tired of
sympathy and universality – I prefer the sacred and ineradicable *differences*
between men and races: the sacred gulfs. Yet even in Zionists I can't really get
at any gulf between me and them. They seem like one of us English just doing
a Zion stunt.

Are you doing another book?

                                                       Yrs   D. H. Lawrence

[1] See Letters 2137 and n. 1. and 2155 and n. 1.
[2] Golding had published his *Forward from Babylon* in November 1920. The novel concerns the
     struggle of the adolescent Philip Massel to break with Jewish tradition incarnated in his father
     Reb Monash.
[3] between your vision and] in your vision from

2192. To Eugene Saxton, 23 March 1921
Text: MS UT; Unpublished.

Villa Fontana Vecchia, *Taormina*, Sicily
23 March 1921.

Dear Sir[1]

I have your letter today. *Blind Mice* came about three weeks ago. I must say I read it with wicked amusement. It seems to me *so* true to life: so American: so unrelentingly serious: and so perfectly, spitefully, perhaps unconsciously funny. The suburban storm in a sauce-boat so darkly gloomy and intense. No, it is funny. The blind mice all prancing about as if they were Apocalyptical Beasts, symbolising the vast[2] tragedy of human fate: and only mice. Just bob-tailed mice in the end, uneasy at the rear, where the carving-knife of domestic fate has lopped off their extension of mousiness.

To tell the truth, it's a wee bit too cruel. It is like watching a mouse-tragedy – the mice in bibs and aprons and tailored suits feeling oh, so hopelessly serious. I don't like to feel quite so superior: as if I were Jove: or in the dress circle. And I can't help hating the raw posteriors in the end.

After all, Mr Scott should have had a grain of charity, and let the people off a little more gently, and placed the blame where the blame lies: not on Nanny at all, nor on the weak husband: not on these two any more than on the other two: but on American Ideal Sympathy, that superannuated and ricketty god. If tails must be cut: well, first put a bit of salt on the tail of the love-bird. It is the love stunt, the love ideal which causes the blindness and the mouseyness: ridiculous SYMPATHY, which wants to have its cake and eat it. I really prefer Nanny, who openly eats her sympathy-cake, to the daughter, who keeps it in the domestic cupboard.

This letter is for Mr Scott, not for the public. I do feel that the book leaves one in a terrible state of emotional nihilism. And I do feel it is *unjust*: the vulgar injustice of blaming Nanny: the vulgarity of the common code of virtue. An artist should relieve us by showing that it isn't the unvirtuous Nannies, but Ideal Virtue itself which is all wrong. Else we are left feeling sick, seeing a number of mice running about with bleeding posteriors, squeaking and not able to know why or to help it at all. Which is too bad. It's the God in the Machine, Holy Sympathy, which should finally have its tail sliced off by the avenging artist.

Yours Sincerely   D. H. Lawrence

---

[1] Eugene F. Saxton (1884–1943) was head of the editorial department for George H. Doran Co., the publishers of *Blind Mice* by Cyril Scott (see letter following). Saxton worked for Doran 1917–25, then went to Harpers.
[2] MS reads 'vasty'.

2193. To Cyril Scott, 23 March 1921
Text: MS UT; Unpublished.

Villa Fontana Vecchia, *Taormina*, Sicily
23 March 1921

Dear Mr Scott[1]

I wrote the enclosed letter to Mr Saxton:[2] but it is really for you and nobody else, so I send it to you. *You* may do as you like with it.

Is Evelyn Scott any relation?[3] *Blind Mice* and *Precipitations* came in one parcel. I am writing to her today.

Yours Sincerely   D. H. Lawrence

2194. To Robert Mountsier, [25 March 1921]
Text: MS Smith; Unpublished.

Fontana Vecchia, *Taormina*, Sicily
Good Friday 1921.

Dear M[ountsier]

I have two letters of yours: dated Feb. 26th. and March 4th.: the latter arrived yesterday, the former today.

1.   I think I can quite definitely say I received nothing whatever from Kennerley for *Widowing of Mrs Holroyd*. – *The Trespasser* was settled entirely through Duckworth. – I don't think I *ever* received *anything* from Kennerley, except that discredited cheque for £20. But I never kept any account: I have only my memory to depend on.

2.   I will not think of Pinker. Really I detest him. I have sent Barbara Low the MSS of *Noon* and *Birds*. But perhaps she is a bit wobbly. I am not sure. She's certainly honest. If you think better Curtis Brown, write her to that effect.[4]

3.   Write to me via Barbara Low. I plan to leave Taormina about April 15th – go to Florence for a fortnight to be measured for a suit of clothes: then do a pledged 3-week walking tour with Juta, in Sardinia or somewhere.

4.   Compton Mackenzie, Hugh Walpole, and Arnold Bennett and May Sinclair are all quite friendly to me – professedly very friendly.[5] I am

---

¹ See p. 672 n. 2.   ² See previous letter.
³ Cyril and Evelyn Scott were married in 1913.   ⁴ See Letter 2202.
⁵ Compton Mackenzie's friendship had been clearly proved; the novelists Hugh Walpole and Arnold Bennett had demonstrated their sympathy for DHL in earlier years (see *Letters,* i. 421–2; ii 136, 446 n. 4, 479 n. 3; and Letter 1924 and n. 1); and in 'The Bad Side of Books' (Edward D. McDonald, *A Bibliography of the Writings of D. H. Lawrence*, Philadelphia, 1925, p. 12) DHL coupled the novelist, May Sinclair (1863–1942), with Bennett, as raising 'a kindly protest' against the suppression of *The Rainbow*.

pretty sure Wells and Conrad and Galsworthy would all say their say: so would Sir James Barrie, unless he had a funk. Get Seltzer to ask them *quick*, before *W. in Love* is out (1st May) – and they are scared. –
5.   Curse Kennerley. But he must be made to hand over *Sons and Lovers.*
6.   (March 4th letter) – Your 'sins' (Friedas letter) are sins of omission against the almighty female, presumably, nothing to do with me. – But it was merely a figure – why are you so touchy?
7.   I wrote Pinker as requested, about Doran and Huebsch contracts.
8.   Curse *all* business affairs.
9.   Barbara Low will send you the *final* version of 'Hibiscus': use this: also a copy of 'The Ass'.

Dear M.

Here are my plans. Frieda is in BadenBaden, her mother ill. She will probably stay all summer.

I propose to leave here on April 15th.: go to Florence for ten days
    (address c/o Thomas Cook and Son, Via Tornabuoni, *Florence*)
always quite safe. Then, in month of May, walk with Juta in Sardinia or 'somewhere' (pledged to this). Then go and meet Frieda, either Germany or 'somewhere.'

I don't really think I want a farm: particularly not to buy one. Am I not right?

I don't think I want to come to the United States.

I dont think I want to keep on Fontana Vecchia. I have almost decided to give it up at end of April.

I thought of buying a small ship – but if you come, let us *hire* one for three months, and try what it's like. Shall we do that? Will you come?

This is a sort of crisis for me. I've got to come unstuck from the old life and Europe, and I can't know beforehand. So have patience. One way or another we'll fix ourselves up. I think it will be the ship.

Cooks, Florence is *always* a reliable forwarding agent.

I think I shall be seeing you over here this summer.

Tell Seltzer if I cable him, it will be for *you*: so much cheaper, his address.

                                                                    D. H. Lawrence

2195. To Evelyn Scott, [25 March 1921]
Text: MS UT; Unpublished.

                                        Villa Fontana Vecchia, *Taormina*, Sicily
                                        Good Friday 1921.

Dear Miss Scott,

Your letter came yesterday – *Precipitations* a while back.

I think the poems are good: express something genuine, not mere verbal footling. Such new genuine epithet too, real coin, not like most American bad pennies of poetry – or English bad halfpennies.

But I tell you, it scares me. Talk about 'already dead' – 'those already dead'. Gruesome business. 'Death enjoying life.'[1] There it is. I am glad you say it. It seems to me so American. But when Death doesn't lose its head – when it knows it is death – then there *must* be resurrection. England never dare face it, and so moulders. There is not resurrection for everybody.

But come, one must burst the tomb. And it needs some hard shoving: harder even than death. Resurrection isn't the soft-as-butter business we take it for.[2] It's the hardest pang of all, it strikes me. I doubt they never told us the truth about Jesus'. There's a lot lies behind that *noli me tangere*.

Here's a good-Friday tirade – and the village band howling and wallowing in lugubriousness down the Corso, in procession after the coffin of Jesus. Damn them, this is their days of days. The egg of Resurrection is addled, here.

I shall probably hate what you say of me in *The Dial*: but no matter. I look forward to the novel.[3]

D. H. Lawrence

2196. To Mary Cannan, [26 March 1921]
Text: MS Lazarus; Moore 646–7.

Taormina
Saturday[4]

My dear Mary

So nice of you to think of Frieda. Her mother is quite a nice lot better. F. was asking for your address in her last letter.

I think I shall leave here about 15th. April – call for Juta – do the walking trip, probably in Sardinia – then go to Germany. So write to the
Ludwig-Wilhelmstift, *Baden-Baden*.

---

[1] DHL is referring to the following passages in Evelyn Scott's poems: 'let us smile kindly,/ Like those already dead,/ On the warm flesh/ And the marriage bed', in 'The Tunnel', ll. 39–42, in *Precipitations*, p. 40; '[The moon] is Death enjoying Life' in 'Autumn Night', l. 16, p. 100.
[2] 'Resurrection' is the title of a section in *Precipitations*.
[3] See Letter 2242.
[4] The letter is dated with reference to Millicent Beveridge's portrait of DHL and the production of photographs of it. On 20 March, Marie Hubrecht was promised a photograph when the painting was completed; Mary Cannan receives a similar promise here; and on 31 March photographs were clearly available (see Letter 2198). 26 March therefore seems the most likely date for this letter.

I have been hating Taormina – but one hates everywhere in fits and starts. As a matter of fact everybody is so nice with me here – natives and britons and all. But it is the britons that make me tired when I go out, and the natives somehow I mistrust. However I think I shall go on with Fontana V[ecchia] another year.

I am going to send you a photograph of the portrait Miss Beveridge painted of me in the studio.

When do you think you'll be back in Cabbé?

Also I got two more copies – I had two before – of the American *de luxe* edition of *Women in Love* – 15 dollars.[1] It's a nice looking book. Probably you'll hate the inside, but I shall send you one this afternoon.

I was so disappointed for the moment about America, but now dont care.

Ottoline also left Juta in the cold. She is having her portrait painted by Eric Gill, the fat-hipped soft fellow we saw at Anticoli last year.[2] Hope I shant see her in Rome.

It has been a very wet season here – hence *very* green – but a great number of flowers. I think of this time last year. Etna is grand and white this morning – much more snow than last year – and those little blue irises everywhere – very many flowers of all sorts.

I am just going out picknicking. Friend offered to take me in motor car to Castrogiovanni. – I should like to come and see you in September. Then won't you come down here with us for a month or two – you wouldn't mind the journey if we were all together.

I doubt if I shall get to England.

Tell me all news.

Love   DHL

2197. To Robert Mountsier, [29 March 1921]
Text: MS Smith; PC v. Costumi Sardi – La trebbiatura nel Nuorese; Postmark, Taormina 30 3 21; Unpublished.

[Fontana Vecchia, *Taormina*, (Messina), Sicily]
29 March

Sent you MS. of *Sardinia* yesterday: am still struggling to get photographs,

[1] Roberts A15 (a).
[2] Eric Gill (1882–1940), stone-carver, engraver and typographer, had only recently begun to extend his drawings to portraits and studies from life. In fact he did not produce a portrait of Lady Ottoline. (Some years after her death Philip Morrell commissioned a stone plaque, based on a photograph of her, from Gill; it now hangs in Garsington Church. See Robert Speaight, *The Life of Eric Gill*, 1966, p. 159.)

and hope to succeed. I want you to do as you please with this MS. – cut it as you like, I don't care. I'll send you a second (carbon) copy tomorrow. Write me via Barbara Low. No America yet.

DHL[1]

2198. To Robert Mountsier, 31 March 1921
Text: MS Smith; Unpublished.

Fontana Vecchia, Taormina, Sicily
31 March 1921.

Dear M[ountsier]

I am sending off herewith all photographs, as far as Palermo. I still hope for Sardinian ones. – Enclosed also a photograph of a portrait of myself. It might go in front of some book of poems: or even this book, if you like. – Use what title you like for *Sardinia*:

   – A Moment of Sardinia
     A Swoop on Sardinia
     A Dash through Sardinia
     Sardinian Films or
     Film of Sicily and Sardinia
– the 'Diary' title was merely provisional.

I am sending you a second copy by this mail: also two copies of the Oxford Press history. I am still waiting to hear from Humphrey Milford exactly what he is doing with the book. Shall write immediately I hear.

I have your letter of March 16th.,[2] direct. I can't come at once: not enough money anyhow. And passports for Vincent and Ciccia almost impossible. But I think I shall give up this house, take all luggage to Florence and leave it there – and let the summer drift by before deciding further. I shall certainly leave Taormina in about 14 days time. Address me via Barbara Low, or c/o Cook, Florence.

They said in Palermo they wanted 2000 Lire per ton, for a ship. That is too much. Wait, I will go round myself.

I will get photographs of Sardinia in May, if not sooner.

Have a cold and feel stupid, so no more now.

DHL

Sending other photographs. If these are printed, please put photographers name under the reproduction:

---

[1] DHL added 'Sardinia' to the caption on the verso of the postcard.
[2] 16th.] 22nd.

Phot. von Gloeden
Phot. Grupi
Phot. Zagari
Phot Alinari
etc

Probably shall send two photographs of *Messina* next week.

Have written to an old friend in *Cornwall* about a ship: he is *very* likely to know.[1]

DHL

I have decided to pay for Fontana V[ecchia] until next Sept., and so have a place to come back to if I wish.

Have decided to write to Curtis Brown; for I *must* have a London agent *at once*.

You need not let the word Taormina appear at all in the 'Film' – the 'Diary'.

2199. To Irene Whittley, 1 April 1921
Text: MS UT; Postmark, Taormina 1 APR 21; Unpublished.

Fontana Vecchia, *Taormina*, Sicily
1 April 1921.

Dear Irene Whittley

Sorry you couldn't come just now: but glad Whittley's move to Dulwich will make him happier.

As for plans: I'm going to give up this house and leave Taormina – unless a sudden event or brain-wave changes my decision. My projects are as follows: leave Taormina with all the traps not later than April 15th.: stay a day or two in Rome: then go to Florence, and stay till about April 30th.: after which do a walking tour in Sardinia with Juta for about three weeks: then go to Germany to Frieda, and try the Black Forest. Say when Whittley will have his holidays, and which bit of this plan is any use to you. Would you like the Black Forest do you think? I suppose we shall come back to Italy for the winter: but where exactly I don't know.

You can write me
c/o Thomas Cook, Via Tornabuoni, *Florence*.

My sister won't come to Italy anyhow this spring. So sorry if she neglected to answer your letter. Thank you so much for writing her.

---

[1] The friend was Captain Short but no such letter has survived. The next letter raises the possibility that DHL used Short's daughter as an intermediary. However, he received a reply from Short himself (see Letter 2222).

Another plan. An American friend of mine is mad to get me to go shares with him in a little *ship*. It sounds crazy but isn't so *very*. A *schooner*, built for fishing, about 100 tons, and length from 100 ft to 120 ft. – with an auxiliary engine. That's the idea. I want you to ask your father to tell me if one could find such a ship, and about how much she would cost. I am serious about this, so don't laugh. It has always been my heart's desire to have a boat. And the *next* holiday we would cruise with you in the Mediterranean. Your father is just the man to nose out just what we want.

Frieda is in Baden: finds her mother rather better, but very shaky. She'll probably want to stay near her all summer. If you came to the Black Forest you could come via Paris and Nancy, or even Basle – and so get none of North Germany. The usual way is Hook of Holland, and straight down the Rhine.

Shall look for your letter in Florence.

D. H. Lawrence

2200. To Robert Mountsier, [2? April 1921]
Text: MS Smith; Unpublished.

[Fontana Vecchia, *Taormina*, (Messina), Sicily]
[2? April 1921]

[Lawrence begins][1]

This letter come this minute. If you were here we'd do this trip. I am so *afraid* of expenses. But this *tripping* we *could* do.

[Ruth Wheelock begins]

March 31.

Dear Lorenzo:

First the price, to buy 400,000 lire! Tony, the messenger at the consulate, found and brought to me a man who led me to a ship. We crawled on board and examined it all over. It is a ladder ship of 300 tons – simply thrilling. The kitchen is in a little box – a blue and white enamel stove with two holes for charcoal. The macaroni was boiling and there were lovely colourful earthenware bowls sitting about and a coffee mill. I *loved* it. Then we went into the cabin at the other end. First a wee entrance, then the dining room with an oil lamp burning and a round table, a shelf for the wine and the

---

[1] DHL hastily added a postscript at the head of the letter received from (and dated by) Ruth Wheelock, his typist for *Sea and Sardinia*, *Mr Noon*, etc.; he then sent the letter to Mountsier. Local people named in her letter are unidentified.

glasses. Then a tiny corridor with two infinitesimal staterooms on either side, smotheringly close, of course, and dirty, with two bunks in each – but the captain wouldn't give up his stateroom, so there would be room for only you and Frieda, I should think.

But, they say the postmaster insists on every boat's carrying a crew of five and the captain. So it would cost 200 lire a day to run it – too expensive to be worth while, don't you think. The price of the boat includes complete remodeling and the addition of other cabins.

They won't rent it, but I have hopes of finding a rentable one – for 20,000 lire for three months.

This ship leaves Palermo about next Thursday for Porto Empedocle, near Girgenti, and if you want to try it they would take you along for the cost of your food. They would even take two people if you wanted to take Jan with you. The trip would take from 5 to 20 days, according to weather. From Porto Empedocle they go to Ravenna and from there to Dalmatia.

Does it appeal to you as a little adventure? It *is* dirty, of course, but I wanted to tell you in case you might care to try it.

I had a card from Frieda today. She days her mother is much better – almost well.

And a letter from Jan yesterday.

My San Giovanni degli Eremiti story was turned down by the first people who even considered it because I hadn't sent photographs! I'm broken-hearted.

Hope you have the manuscript of *Sardinia*, left at the Williams' by Mrs. Dreyfus.

Greetings. Wheelock.

These ship people could get you a little yacht for 200,000 lire, but do you want anything so sophisticated? I enclose their card. If you can't come up for this trip, I could look about for another for you.

2201. To Douglas Goldring, 4 April 1921
Text: MS UCin; Postmark, Taormina 6 APR 21; Huxley 514.

Fontana Vecchia, *Taormina*, Sicily
4 April 1921

Dear Goldring

Very many thanks for your letter. I believe you're right – so I'll go to Curtis Brown. I've written to Barbara (she has various MSS by now) saying they are to be handed over. See that CB. makes a proper agreement with me. I'll stick to him if he does me square and *energetic*.

Am leaving Taormina on Saturday: going eventually to Germany, where my wife is – BadenBaden. But send me a line

c/o Thomas Cook, Piazza delle Terme, *Rome*.

I'd like to meet you if you come within reach.

Oh those babies. Poor Betty! But perhaps they'll make her happy.

I like *Women in Love* best of all my books. Glad you do too.

Wonder what your job will be like.

Yrs   D. H. Lawrence

2202. To Curtis Brown, 4 April 1921
Text: MS UT; Huxley 513–14.

Fontana Vecchia, *Taormina*, Sicilia

4th April 1921

Dear Curtis Brown[1]

Will you undertake to place my stuff? and will you let me know your terms? Do you make a fixed agreement? If so, make it for not more than five years, so that we needn't be tied to one another.

There are three pieces of MS. in hand:

1. *Birds, Beasts and Flowers (poems)* – of these two[2] poems went to Squire of the *Mercury*: viz. 'Hibiscus and Salvia Flowers' and 'Purple Anemones'. These two poems, and 'The Ass', are in handwriting. If Barbara Low has not done so, please send copies (typed) of these three poems to Robert Mountsier. – No one has seen any of these poems, save[3] Squire's two.

2. *Mr Noon (Part I)* – Try and serialise this, and for serial purposes cut as much as you like. Secker's agreement claims the book. I enclose the said agreement: it is for 5 books: but *Rainbow* makes one of the 5, and *Lost Girl* another: leaves *three*: of which here two.

3. 'Diary of a Trip to Sardinia' (provisional title). Am sending photographs of first part – hope to send other photographs shortly – of Sardinia itself. Try and sell this book to periodicals – or part of it. And I don't care how much the editors cut it.

But before you do anything definite *at all* please communicate with Robert Mountsier, 417 West 118 Street, *New York City*.

He has all my stuff in hand over there, trying to unravel a beautiful tangle of

[1] See p. 566 and n. 1.
[2] two] three
[3] save] say

publishers and agreements and Pinker. Please work absolutely in unison with Mountsier.

I wish I'd come to you ten years back: you wrote me just too late.[1] But now, don't tie me too tight – I get restive.

Am leaving Taormina on Saturday – wandering. But write
        c/o Thomas Cook, Piazza delle Terme, *Rome.*

I enclose the Oxford Press agreement. I have received 6 presentation copies of the book,[2] but have no idea what they are doing, especially as regards America. American rights are mine.

Shall I turn over to you all the back agreements? very little remains to Pinker. Or shall we only go on with what lies ahead? Let us consider.

                                    Luck to us   D. H. Lawrence

2203. To Catherine Carswell, 4 April 1921
Text: MS YU; cited in Carswell, *Adelphi* 81.

                        Fontana Vecchia, *Taormina*. Sicily.
                                    4 April 1921

My dear Catherine

Well, how are you? – I send you that history – you asked for it. Some of the chapters I think are good: first worst. Dont read it if it bores you.

I'll send you also a photograph of a portrait a Scotch woman – Millicent Beveridge – painted of me.[3] She must have been at Glasgow art school about the same time as you – has lived long in Paris.

Frieda is in BadenBaden. Her mother was very ill, so she went – about a month ago. I am leaving Taormina on Saturday – Palermo – Rome – then perhaps a walking tour in Sardinia: then I dont know: to Germany probably. Suppose we shall come back here in autumn.

What are you doing? How are things going? Where shall you be all summer. I have worked a good bit, but not finished much. Yes – a book of very free poems *Birds Beasts and Flowers*: a 'Diary of a Trip to Sardinia': and first vol. of a funny novel: but a *tiny* first vol. Quite a lot. Yet not much.

I sort of get indifferent to the world – to God and man I almost said – down here. The South cures one of caring. Very good too.

---

[1] See *Letters*, i. 482 n. 2.
[2] i.e. *Movements in European History.*
[3] The photograph presented to Catherine Carswell is reproduced as the frontispiece to Nehls, volume ii.

How is Don? What doing? And John Patrick running about and getting a
big boy. Aieee, we're getting older, Catherine. It's almost time I began to be
middle-aged and famous. Pah! There's not much spunk in the world, is there.
Neither here nor there.

Well – I hope you're going on nicely. Write if you feel like it to me
c/o Thomas Cook, Piazza delle Terme, Rome.
It will always reach me.

If only I had money I should buy a Mediterranean sailing ship that was
offered me: *so* beautiful. Then you'd cruise with me.

I'm having Curtis Brown for an agent.

Many greetings to you three   D. H. Lawrence

2204. To Martin Secker, 4 April 1921

Text: MS UInd; Postmark, Taormina 6 APR 21; Secker 38–9.

Fontana Vecchia, *Taormina*, Sicily
4 April 1921

Dear Secker

A long time since I heard from you. Hope everything goes well.

I am leaving Taormina on Saturday. My wife had to go to BadenBaden, her
mother ill. So I am alone in the house. I shall go to Palermo and Rome – then
perhaps do a walking tour in Sardinia – then to Germany.

I am going to have Curtis Brown for an agent. I am sending him three
pieces of MS

1. *Birds Beasts and Flowers* (poems in very free verse)
2. *Mr Noon* (Part 1) – *very* short indeed.
3. 'Diary of a trip to Sardinia' – about 70,000 words.

I want him to serialise if he can. Of course he will show you the MSS.

I shall try and finish *Aarons Rod* this summer, before finishing *Mr Noon II*
– which is funny, but a hair-raiser. First part innocent – *Aarons Rod* innocent.

How are you on with *Women in Love*? Are you scared of it? I don't believe
they'll fall on it. They'll hurt themselves if they do. Is it ready for 1st May?

Write me a line
c/o Thomas Cook, Piazza delle Terme, Rome.

Is Mackenzie still on Herm.

Had a p c. from Brett Young at Mozambique.

Greetings   D. H. Lawrence[1]

---

[1] See p. 708 n. 1 for Secker's reply.

2205. To Martin Secker, [15 April 1921]
Text: MS UInd; PC; Postmark, Capri 15. 4. 21; Secker 39.

Capri
15 April

Dear Secker
Will you send a copy of *The Lost Girl* to
    J. Ellingham Brooks, Villa De Angeles, *Capri*, Golfo di Napoli.
I am here for a few days only – everybody seems pretty well, but a deadness
over the place. Heaven knows what has happened everywhere. Expect a line
from you in Rome.

Yrs   D. H. Lawrence

2206. To Thomas Seltzer, 16 April 1921
Text: MS UT; Postmark, Capri 17. 4. 21; Lacy, *Seltzer* 19.

Capri
16 April 1921

Dear Seltzer
I have left Taormina for the summer. Write me a line:
    per Adr. Frau Baronin von Richthofen, Ludwig-Wilhelmstift,
                BadenBaden, *Germania*.
That is quite safe. Tell me how all things are. Send the copies of
Psychoanalysis and the Unconscious to me there: also one copy to
        Miss Elizabeth Humes, American Embassy,
            Piazza S. Bernardo, Rome.
Don't forget.

Best of wishes   D. H. Lawrence

2207. To John Clarke, [18 April 1921]
Text: PC; Lawrence–Gelder 116–17.

Capri
[18 April 1921][1]

Am staying here with friends for a few days – leave for Rome tomorrow or
Wednesday – then direct to Baden. I am planning to see you this summer. –
What about this strike?[2] The boats in the picture are being towed behind the

---

[1] In Lawrence–Gelder the date is wrongly given as 18 April 1919.
[2] A national coal strike had begun on 31 March 1921; railway and transport unions had
threatened to join the strike but, on 15 April, decided not to do so; the miners remained on
strike until 28 June.

steamer, to take off passengers into the Blue Grotto. Wish there was good news from England.

2208. To Robert Mountsier, [18 April 1921]

Text: MS Smith; PC v. Capri – veduta dal Mare; Postmark, Capri 19. 4. 21; Unpublished.

Capri.
18 April

Am here with friends for the moment: leave for Rome tomorrow – then straight to BadenBaden. Write me there
      per Adr. Frau Baronin von Richthofen,
      Ludwig-Wilhelmstift, *Baden-Baden.*
I hope you are coming over – I will meet you wherever you wish. Tell Seltzer to send everything to the Baden address.

a rivederci. DHL

2209. To Catherine Carswell, [22 April 1921]

Text: MS YU; PC v. Firenze – Piazza della Signoria con la Fontana del Nettuno; Postmark, Firenze 22. IV 1921; cited in Moore, *Poste Restante* 63.

[Florence]
22 April.

Had your letter just as I left Taormina. Tomorrow I leave here for Switzerland and Germany – joining Frieda. Send a line there
      per Adr Frau von Richthofen, Ludwig-Wilhelmstift, *BadenBaden.*
I hope to see you this summer – then we can talk plans. Splendid if you can really be free.

Greet you all. DHL

2210. To Irene Whittley, [22 April 1921]

Text: MS UT; PC v. Firenze – Piazza della Signoria con la Fontana del Nettuno; Postmark, Firenze 22. IV 1921; Unpublished.

[Florence]
22 April

I had your letter here – am leaving tomorrow for Germany. The address is:

per Adr. Frau Baronin von Richthofen, Ludwig-Wilhelmstift,
Baden-Baden, Germany.
Send us a bit of news there. I have kept on Fontana Vecchia. Would you like
to come to Taormina in Sept. or Oct? – But perhaps I'll see you in England
before then.

DHL

2211. To Curtis Brown, 22 April 1921
Text: MS UT; Huxley 515–16.

Florence.
22 April 1921

Dear Curtis Brown
I had your letter in Rome. I agree to be quite patient and fair.
The Secker agreement I enclosed with photographs to Barbara Low. I am
still struggling for photographs of Sardinia itself. – And a friend of mine, Jan
Juta, is just going to Sardinia to paint suitable illustrations for the book – in
flat colour. I want you to wait for his pictures before you publish the *book*: for
magazine publication, go ahead as you think best. The title for Sardinia book
Mountsier objected to. I suggested others: Sardinia Films, for example. – Do
please work in everything in strict conjunction with Robert Mountsier.
I agree not to send anything to any publisher direct – only to act through
you.
Go warily, but please go gently with Martin Secker.
My address will be:
per Adr. Frau Baronin von Richthofen, Ludwig-Wilhemstift,
Baden-Baden, Germany.
I shall probably be in London in July. – I am going direct to BadenBaden
now.
My English things are not very tangled – my American business was the
mess.

Good Luck.   D. H. Lawrence
Show Secker the various MSS. as soon as you conveniently can.

2212. To Martin Secker, 22 April 1921
Text: MS UInd; Secker 39.

Florence.
22 April 1921

Dear Secker
I had your letter in Rome. Have written Curtis Brown settling with him

that he shall be my agent, and asking him to show you all MSS as soon as possible. Hope everything turns out satisfactorily.

I was in Capri and caught just a glimpse of Faith Mackenzie. Tell Monty I shall probably be giroing round towards England in June and look forward to seeing him.

Write to me c/o my mother in law

Frau Baronin von Richthofen, Ludwig-Wilhelmstift,
Baden-Baden, Germany.

I am going straight there now – and it's a safe address.

Best wishes   D. H. Lawrence

2213. To John Ellingham Brooks, [28 April 1921]
Text: MS IEduc; PC v. Ruine und Dorf Eberstein bei Baden-Baden; Postmark, Baden-Baden -1. 5. 21.; Unpublished.

Ludwig-Wilhelmstift, *Baden-Baden*
28 April.

I got here two days ago – devil of a journey: feel I'm not quite there, inside my own skin. We are living just outside BBaden, with the forests just round us – and there is a northern tang in the air, and a curious stillness and emptiness – so different from the south. One suffers a bit. I ordered *Women in Love* for you – hope it will come.

Frieda greets you warmly.   DHL

2214. To Margaret King, [28 April 1921]
Text: MS Needham; PC v. Ruine und Dorf Eberstein bei Baden-Baden; Postmark, Baden-Baden -1. 5. 21.; Unpublished.

[Ludwig-Wilhelmstift, *Baden-Baden*, Germany]
28 April

I arrived here two days ago – we have come out of Baden about three miles, and are living in one of the houses you see in the picture. It is lovely country, all forests and so different from Sicily. – I find here the photograph of you and Joan and Peter:[1] very good of you, and what a big girl you are: I can't quite tell what Miss Joan is like, only that she seems a young lark: Peter is the most self-satisfied person on earth, apparently. A charming photograph, I think. – I feel very strange here – and cold – Germany seems empty and rather depressed, but enough food now – not any abundance, however. Frieda's mother almost well.

DHL

---

[1] See Letter 2117 and n. 2.

2215. To Curtis Brown, 28 April 1921
Text: MS UT; Huxley 516–17.

Ludwig-Wilhelmstift, *Baden-Baden*, Germany.
28 April 1921.

Dear Curtis Brown

I had your booklet here: and a letter from Barbara Low saying she had handed you all MSS. Expect to hear from you shortly concerning these.

Robert Mountsier is coming to Europe – arrives Paris May 10th., and is proceeding to London. He will come to see you, and you can discuss the American side with him. If he is staying in Europe no doubt he will transfer all American business to you. But that is for him to decide.

I hear from the Oxford University Press that they have published the school book of mine: *Movements in European History – nom de plume Lawrence H. Davison* – that one edition is sold out[1] – but that they have *not* succeeded in placing the book with their American representatives. American rights therefore belong to me. You may like to discuss this with Mountsier. Please show him Humphrey Milford's agreement.[2] And I will write Milford as soon as I hear from you, telling him to deal in *England* with you.

Trust things are going satisfactorily.

Yrs   D. H. Lawrence

2216. To Robert Mountsier, 28 April 1921
Text: MS Smith; Unpublished.

Ludwig-Wilhelmstift, *Baden-Baden*, Germany.
28 April 1921

Dear M[ountsier]

I got here yesterday: a big change after Italy. – Frieda's mother is much better – almost well, but much shaken. We are due to stop here all summer, but doubt if I shall stand it more than a month. We will see.

Anyhow I will meet you somewhere: not in England – Italy for preference, I think. We might even do a bit of a walk together. Write to me to the Ludwig-Wilhelmstift so that we can fix things up. You might come with us to Taormina as soon as it is cool[3] enough. – Or come here and let us walk across the Black Forest. Or let us walk down the Sud-Tirol towards Venice: something nice. – Quite soon; if you like.

---

[1] Though Oxford University Press apparently told DHL that the first edition (published in February 1921) was 'sold out', OUP records show that a second printing was not required until the year ending March 1923.
[2] DHL had signed the contract with OUP on 4 April 1920.
[3] cool] warm

Call and see Curtis Brown and *impress* him. I have written to him, accepting him as *English* agent.

Waiting to hear from you.

DHL

[Frieda Lawrence begins]

How jolly it will be if we go for a walking tour here together –

Auf Wiedersehen   F

2217. To Martin Secker, 28 April 1921
Text: MS UInd; Postmark, Baden-Baden 29. 4. 21.; Secker 40.

Ludwig-Wilhelmstift, *Baden-Baden*, Germany.
28 April 1921

Dear Secker

I got here yesterday – Germany very quiet and empty-feeling: don't know how long I shall stay, but my wife and my mother-in-law say all summer long. We will see.

Probably by now you have seen Curtis Brown and the three MSS. Hope everything goes satisfactorily.

Let me know precisely about *Women in Love*.[1] Alfred Douglas is a louse.[2] –

[1] DHL is here responding to Secker's letter of 13 April 1921 (Secker Letter-Book, UIll):

Dear Lawrence,
  Many thanks for your letter of April 4th which has just reached me. Everything goes well here, except that trade conditions are most dismal. However, I am publishing 'Women in Love', in the course of May, and I do not think there is any doubt that the book will sell well, barring accidents. You will have seen from the papers that that Alfred Douglas is on the warpath, and he is always making references to you and 'The Rainbow' and The English Review, in that scurrilous paper [*Plain English*, 1020–2] which he edits.
  I am very pleased at what you tell me about your work. I take it that 'Aaron's Rod' is the novel which you wish me to publish next. If you finish it, as you anticipate, this summer, there is no reason why it should not come out in the autumn, unless serial considerations delay it. But what is 'Mr. Noon'? In any case I look forward to seeing this, your poems, and especially the diary of your Sardinian excursion, and I hope Curtis Brown will not delay in showing them to me.
  Mackenzie is still at Herm and not likely to leave the island. He is in robust health, is out all day long, engrossed in farming, and everything is most successful. I have just come back from a fortnight's visit. He often mentions you and looks forward to seeing you on the island one day.
  Yes. We also had a postcard from Brett Young, with a picture of a very depressing hotel built of corrugated iron surrounded by a few deck-chairs, with some tropical vegetation in the background. Nobody can read 'The Black Diamond'.

Yours sincerely

[2] Lord Alfred Douglas (1870–1945) was notorious for his friendship with Oscar Wilde; his father initiated the action which led to Wilde's conviction. Editor of *Academy*, 1907–10. DHL was ambivalent about his poetry: see *Letters*, i. 107.

Seltzer is *very* anxious that no copies of your *W. in Love* shall find their way over there. Do please do your best to prevent it. If you care to delay the English publication to a more favorable moment, I have no objections. I saw Rebecca West in Florence: very angry at your refusing to give her a copy of *Lost Girl* for review. If she asks for *Women in Love*, best give it her.

I am not going to give people *Women in Love*. They can either buy it or do without it. Will you just send me *one* copy here. And the few others will you please post according to enclosed instructions.

Pay me the £100 into my bank, will you – the Law Courts branch of the L[ondon] C[ounty] W[estminster] and Parrs Bank. After this travelling I am at a low ebb, and trying to re-coup by living here for 2/6 a day. But I've got to travel again. I may be in England in July. Are you there then?

Well, best of luck to you. – If Robert Mountsier should call on you, please see him and talk over the American side with him.

Yrs   D. H. Lawrence

2218. To Robert Mountsier, 29 April 1921
Text: MS Smith; Unpublished.

Ludwig-Wilhelmstift, *Baden-Baden*, Germany
29 April 1921

Dear M[ountsier]

Your letter of 8th April here today – I knew you'd feel the change of plans rather bitterly: so did I. But somehow it was impossible. I could *not* get passports for V[incenzo] and C[iccia]: and then Ciccio wrote them from Boston that he had a grand job for them at millions of dollars: so they were all agog for it: and *that* settled my efforts on their behalf. – Then Frieda and Baden.

However, here I am in Germany, which I don't really like. I don't know what I am going to do next: I just don't know. I shall wait to hear from you, to fix up something. – The only thing about Taormina (the house is paid for till Sept.) – is that it is almost unliveably hot from July to Sept.

See Curtis Brown, 6 Henrietta St., Covent Garden – and talk about business. He wants to take over American side too: I told him that is absolutely for you to decide.

Germany is cheapest: Italy next: Sardinia also very cheap. Didn't you get my 'Diary'?

DHL

710

[*1 May 1921*]

2219. To Robert Mountsier, [1 May 1921]
Text: MS Smith; PC v. Schloss Eberstein (Murgtal.); Postmark, Baden-Baden -2. 5. 21.;
Unpublished.

[Hotel Krone, Ebersteinburg, *Baden-Baden*, Germany]
1. May.

Of course much the cheapest place is here. F[rieda] and I are in a peasant inn some three miles outside Baden, 30 Mark a day each, and very well done indeed – and lovely country. – Hotel Krone, Ebersteinburg, bei Baden Baden. Very easy for you to come here from Paris to discuss plans. And as for ships, I see such good advertisements in the Munich papers – so cheap. But those of course are boats on the Starnberg Lake. Yet if these are cheap, why not sea-boats? – The Oxford Press failed to place the *History* with their Amer[ican] representatives, so it is on our hands. – One edition sold out in England. – I don't much like Curtis Brown's tone – familiar, and a bit impertinent. Keep him in his place. Let us never give an inch to these people. – He seemed quite pleased with *Mr Noon*. Did you not get the *Sardinia* MS. before you left? And no letters with the Ludwig-Wilhelmstift address? – I am ready to make some sort of plan – almost any sort – only the farm scares me, with too much responsibility – I don't feel like pinning myself down anywhere. – Come here before you go to London. Write to me at the Ludwig-Wilhelmstift, BadenBaden. My mother-in-law is always there. But send a postcard here also to the Krone. Shall look for word about the 12th.

DHL

2220. To Mary Cannan, 2 May 1921
Text: MS Lazarus; Unpublished.

Ludwig-Wilhelmstift, *Baden-Baden*, Germany
2 May 1921.

My dear Mary
I wonder where you are: and why neither of us has had a line from you: and if you got the copy of the *de luxe* edition of *Women in Love* which I sent you from Taormina.
You see I am here in Baden: not right in the town, but with Frieda in a country inn about three miles out. The country is beautiful, Baden a lovely little town, and there are some exquisite things in the shops. Everybody is very nice with us: and we live for about 5/- a day the pair of us. Food is very good: wonderful asparagus. And for us plenty. But of course we are out in the country and the peasants have everything. The people are very nice with us:

so simple and clean: and travelling so clean and easy. If you think you might like it, come and join us. It is quite easy from Paris, or from Holland.

Frieda's mother is a good bit better: but has sudden relapses: heart very weak. We shall have to get a nurse for her. Suddenly she has broken up, after being so well for all these years – all her life – she is just seventy. Now she can't be left alone: and it is impossible for F. to go on nursing her. There must be a hired woman.

I wonder where you are – in Paris or London or where. Send a line, if this ever reaches you from Roquebrûne. I did think I might come to England. But travelling is so expensive, and the north so unfriendly. I think we shall go to Bavaria in July. Frieda's brother-in-law died last Thursday:[1] funeral today in Munich. Then from Bavaria into Austria, to Frieda's other sister: the younger, who has a place near Graz. And so back to Taormina end of September. I kept Fontana Vecchia, not knowing what else to do.

It is unlike you not to write. I hope you are having a good time, anyhow. I am trying to go on with my *Aaron's Rod* novel: but God knows if I am going to succeed.

Germany is rather depressed and *empty* feeling – the place feels half inhabited only – nobody about. Yet there are many people. The men are very silent and dim.

Shall we be seeing you this summer?

                                                                DHL

2221. To Earl Brewster, [2 May 1921]
Text: MS UT; PC v. Schwarzwälder Leben; Postmark, Baden-Baden -2. 5. 21; Earl and
Achsah Brewster, *D. H. Lawrence: Reminiscences and Correspondence* (1934), p. 20.

                                        Ludwig-Wilhelmstift. Baden Baden.
                                                                2 May

I would write a letter if there were an envelope within reach – but there isn't.[2]
My wife and I are in a country inn about 3 miles outside Baden – the forest

---

[1] Edgar Jaffe, Else's husband.
[2] The recipients of the postcard were Earl Henry Brewster (1878–1957) and his wife Achsah
Barlow Brewster (1878–1945), American painters whom DHL had met on Capri in April. The
Brewsters had lived in France and Italy since 1910; Earl Brewster's paintings had been
exhibited in Paris and Rome. They were later to publish *D. H. Lawrence: Reminiscences and
Correspondence* (1934). In May 1921 the Brewsters were planning a visit to Ceylon and
'projecting a Buddhistic pilgrimage in the autumn' (*Reminiscences*, p. 244). From 1935 they
lived in India.

around, the people very pleasant. We may stay a month or more: then to
Bavaria. I can't bear the thought of England or any further north. – I think of
you and Buddha and Mrs Beckett,[1] and measles and zigzaggy pictures.
Nirvana is all right if you get at it right. It is a sort of all-inclusive state, and
therefore includes sorrow, does *not* supersede sorrow: no such impertinence.
And *your* Nirvana is too much a one-man show: leads inevitably to navel-
contemplation. True Nirvana is a flowering tree whose roots are passion and
desire and hate and love. Your Nirvana is a cut blossom. – Pardon this on a
p.c. It is the result of the Fatherland. – Still let us see what Burma blossoms
from what roots. – Tell your wife not to paint any more Francises. Tell Mrs
Beckett I should so like to see her convent – I have never been to Assisi – but
that I feel I must consult the birds before I claim sistership with them – they
might object to my lack of feathers. Greet the child[2] and tell her to weep for
me.

D. H. Lawrence

Please write a line to the given address.

2222. To Robert Mountsier, [2 May 1921]
Text: MS Smith; Unpublished.

Ludwig-Wilhelmstift, BadenBaden, Germany
2 May.

Dear M[ountsier]

Enclosed letter from Capt. Short, our old landlord at Tregerthen. He is a
useful and wise and wary old bird. The ship sounds rather a darling: but oh,
my dear M., I am so terrified of borrowed money. However, proceed as you
think best, with my blessing. If I make money, there it is. But it isn't made
yet. – Write to Capt Short: *Capt J T Short, 15 The Terrace, St. Ives, Cornwall.*
You could go and see him if you wished. Lelant, where the ship lies, is just
next to St. Ives. – Capt. Short's daughter is in London. You might call on her
in my name:
Mrs Irene Whittley, 1. Albert Palace Mansions, Battersea Park. S.W.11.
I will forewarn her. – She is nice.

---

[1] Lucy ('Lucile') Katherine Beckett (1884–1979), daughter of the 2nd Baron Grimthorpe, had
known the Brewsters since the war years when they all lived in Rome. m. (1) Count Otto
Czernin, 1903; divorced 1920; (2) Capt. Oliver Harry Frost, 1926; divorced 1941. She
resumed her maiden name by deed poll in 1922 and had clearly done so *de facto* in 1921. 'Her'
convent to which DHL refers was the Carcere hermitage at Assisi; she appeared to believe it
was for sale.
[2] Harwood Brewster (1913–   ).

I enclose also the Oxford Press letter about the *History*.[1]

All this I send to the Librairie Terquem. – I await news of your arrival, here.

D. H. Lawrence

I asked Capt Short to write you any further particulars, to Paris.

2223. To Irene Whittley, [2 May 1921]

Text: MS UT; PC v. Ausgang aus dem oberen Ravennatal; Postmark, Baden-Baden
– 2.5.21.; Unpublished.

Ludwig-Wilhelmstift. Baden Baden.
May 2.

I had your father's letter this morning – and answer at once. My Amer[ican] friend arrives in Paris on May 10th. – from thence comes straight to England. It is chiefly his affair. I have asked your father to send a line to Paris – and then Robert Mountsier can dash off to St. Ives. He may also call on you in Battersea. I gave him your address. Do you remember him – Mountsier? He is the Amer. who stayed with us and was supposed to be the spy. – It is very beautiful here in Germany – and very very cheap – and quite friendly. Would you like to come? The Black Forest so beautiful. My mother-in-law much better, and Frieda quite happy. Send a line here and tell of your future plans.

DHL

2224. To Robert Mountsier, 6 May 1921

Text: MS Smith; Postmark, Baden-Baden -7. 5. 21.; Unpublished.

Ludwig-Wilhelmstift, *Baden-Baden*, Germany
Friday 6 May 1921

Dear M[ountsier],

I have today your letter of April 11th., saying you are sailing on Apr. 25 on the *Coronado*, for Havre.

I have written you various letters and p.c's to the Librairie Terquem. I trust you will find them all.

---

[1] The letter from G. H. Ely (TMS Smith) informed DHL that OUP had decided not to publish *Movements in European History* in USA. Included was a report from an American academic who advised against publishing the book in America on three grounds: it did not 'correspond in scope and content to any historical course' in American schools; it was 'too narrowly political' and lacked a concern for 'social and economic changes'; and its focus was too English and Protestant.

Frieda and I are at a little country inn about 3 miles outside BadenBaden:
> Hôtel Krone, Ebersteinburg, bei BadenBaden.

It is very pleasant, everything good and sufficient, and costs 30 Mark a day without extras.

My letters however go to the Ludwig-Wilhelmstift, where my mother-in-law, Frau Baronin von Richthofen, lives.

As I have told you before, I have agreed to have Curtis Brown as English agent: Curtis Brown, 6 Henrietta Street, W.C.2. He has strict injunctions to take *no* step without reference to you. – For your going to London, do as you think best, and use the money accordingly.

Now for other matters. I am terrified of borrowed money, but prepared to take risks. At the present moment I have not more than £50 in the English bank: but am asking Secker to pay in to me the £100 which he owes me on publication of *Women in Love*. I want to live on my English money, if possible, without touching the American.

Call and see Martin Secker, 5 John St., Adelphi, W.C.2 – if you go to London. Otherwise write him about[1] *The Rainbow*. He is variable.

I am working on *Aaron's Rod*, and have some hope of finishing it here, in Germany. *Mr Noon* II I leave for the winter.

I must stay in Germany at least till end of May. So I shall wait here to see you or to hear from you. From June 1st. I have no plans whatsoever – shall wait for you, to concoct them together.

The Oxford Press asked me if I'd do the letter-press to a Medici Society book of Art Pictures for Children.[2] I write asking them for terms. It need not take me more than a month. But I ought to be near a library. Of all towns, I think I would prefer Florence. That is, June and July in Florence. But I am sure of nothing. Only I will wait here till I hear from you.

I sent you Capt. Short's letter about the ship in Cornwall. Sounds perfect. But near £2000 sterling – and *then* the cost of captain etc, and stores etc. Where *is* the money to come from? If only I had it!

Today Frieda's sister and a Berlin banker. They say we should probably get, in Hamburg, a ship *much* cheaper than elsewhere: also a crew. The Italians are now *greedy*, very. Here much cheaper. I will have enquiries made in Hamburg.

Fontana Vecchia is kept on, and paid for till September. We could go there – but July and August *very hot*. But we can discuss it. I might hire a very attractive flat in Florence from a friend. We will see.

---

[1] about] if
[2] Neither the records of Oxford University Press nor those of the Medici Society Ltd. contain any mention of this enterprise.

I hope this is all explicit. Letters from here to London take only 3 or 4 days: so from Paris should be less. Write here, to the Krone, or to the Ludwig-Wilhelmstift – perhaps better *here*: or a p.c. to both.

alors, au revoir.   D. H. Lawrence

2225. To Dr Anton Kippenberg, 8 May 1921
Text: MS SVerlag; Unpublished.

Ludwig-Wilhelmstift, Baden-Baden, Germany
8 May 1921.

Dear Dr Kippenberg

I should have thanked you sooner for the books which arrived in Taormina just before I left. I was delighted with them: and the little Pandora books have such an attractive appearance, that I am sure they will sell tremendously once the world can get out of the bad temper it is in. The English people in Taormina liked them very much: but the reparation fever has got into English blood just now, so they could hardly bear to think that anything nice came out of Germany. However, I really believe this feeling will not last long. I am quite sure that booksellers in Florence, Venice, Rome, Naples, Palermo and Taormina could sell dozens of the Pandora books. I know that some hundreds of the Tauchnitz novels were sold this season in Taormina alone: a mere village. And the English people who came to see me all at once hastened to examine the books you sent me, liking them so much, for everything but their German origin. – Ah, it is so boring and stupid, this national prejudice, it wearies me. – But though everybody here is quite nice with me, I can see they don't like the fact of my Englishness. The world is all alike.

I am staying in Germany till the end of this month – then perhaps to England, or more probably back to Italy, to Florence or Venice. My wife and I intend to return to Taormina at the end of September, to the house there.

If there is anything I can do for you in Italy I shall be very pleased to do it: or in England.

I expect my novel *Women in Love*, sequel to *The Rainbow* will appear in London this month. I will have a copy posted to you. Have you any news of your translation of *The Rainbow*. Please tell me if you have.

Many thanks again for the *Biblioteca Mundi* and the Pandora books. I am so pleased to have them there in Taormina, waiting for me when I get back.

Yours Sincerely   D. H. Lawrence

2226. To Else Jaffe, 9 May 1921
Text: MS Jeffrey; Unpublished.

Ludwig-Wilhelmstift, *BadenBaden*
9 May 1921

Dear Else

A friend of ours, a boy of eighteen, studying at the London University, would very much like to find a German family with whom he could spend the holidays – all August and September. His name is Stephen Guest, a tall, thin, blond sensitive lad: I like him very much. His father is of the well-known Welsh family – the Guests: and is a writer, was a socialist, and is now a member of Parliament. You may know his name – Dr. Haden Guest.[1] The mother was a Jewess – a clever woman. She got divorced from Haden Guest and married a friend of mine, a Jew – a Dr. David Eder. The Eders were[2] the great Freudians in London: he practised as psychoanalist: and they translated Freuds *Traumdeuting*.[3] But now Eder is one of the three Commissioners for Palestine, and he and Edith Eder are in Jerusalem. – Stephen remained with his *mother* after the divorce, and lived with Eder, not with Haden Guest. Now he is more with his father, but I think likes his mother best. He is very fond of Eder, who is a very delightful man. – I like Stephen very much, and I think he is *something*. But he is really shy and rather English and diffident – introvert, as they say. He would pay 50 or 60 Mark a day. He knows a fair amount of German, I think – wants to know it well. – I wonder if you would care to have him – and let him go away with Friedel to Irschenhausen or anywhere, for the holiday time. If so, will you write to his aunt:

Miss Barbara Low, 13. Guilford Street, *London, W.C.1.*
I don't know Steffy's address at the moment.

Haden Guest by the way was one of the most energetic men on the Hungarian Relief committee.

If you can't be bothered with a stranger, you might know of some other family. – We will speak also to Alfred about it.[4]

Alfred was here one evening: but I'm afraid it was rather much for him. We shall be seeing him probably tomorrow. – Nusch's Emil returned last

---

[1] Dr Leslie Haden Haden-Guest (1877–1960) was prominent in both political and medical affairs in London; he was a Labour member of the London County Council, 1919–22; and became MP for North Southwark, 1923–7. m. (1) Edith Low, 1898, divorced 1909; (2) Muriel Carmel, 1910. He was created Baron Haden-Guest in 1950. His son, Stephen Haden Haden–Guest (1902–74), translator and editor of scientific works, succeeded to the title in 1960.

[2] were] are

[3] *Die Traumdeutung* (Leipzig, 1900) was translated by Dr David Eder under the title *On Dreams* (1914).

[4] Alfred Weber; Else was his mistress (see *Letters*, i. 413).

evening to Berlin.[1] – The Schwiegermutter is fairly well – not very. I think the best would be to find for her a real companion – some young woman who could be as it were a friend, and do the little amount of nursing required: and live in the Stift. Your mother will *never* consent to be alone: she will demand one of you all the time: and that is impossible.

I think to stay here till about 1st. June. I have promised to write the letter press for a picture book of the Medici Society. That would make it necessary to live near a library for a couple of months: in Florence for choice. So perhaps in June we shall go to Florence. Shall we pass by München, and see you for a few days?

I was glad Edgar died: better death than ignominious living on. Life had no place for him after the war. I hope you are all well and managing things easily.

Love from both   D. H. Lawrence

2227. To Curtis Brown, 12 May 1921
Text: MS UT; Unpublished.

Ludwig-Wilhelmstift, BadenBaden, Germany
12 May 1921

Dear Curtis Brown
Your letter of 5th May last evening. – If Secker wishes to publish the first part of *Mr Noon* as a separate little book, let him:[2] because the second part may be a bit startling – I have only half done it – and I shan't be able to finish it till I go back to Taormina. Cant write it here. Am having a shot at finishing another novel *Aaron's Rod* – which is $\frac{2}{3}$ done.

Tell Secker I want proofs of *Mr Noon*.

Greetings   D. H. Lawrence

But Secker must not publish before Thomas Seltzer has made all his arrangements also. We must *not* have any more clash between London and New York.

---

[1] Emil von Krug (1870–1944) whom Frieda's younger sister, Johanna, married in 1923 after divorcing her first husband.

[2] Secker's admiration for *Mr Noon* had been conveyed to Curtis Brown in a letter of 29 April 1921 (Secker Letter-Book, UIll): 'It is certainly excellent, and I fully share your enthusiasm for it. It is quite clear from the last page that it is complete as it stands, and that the author intends it to be published in a book by itself, with one sequel, possibly more, to follow later. Although its length presents certain difficulties, (it is only 25, or 30,000 words) I can undertake to make a book of it to sell at 6/-.' Despite Secker's enthusiasm the first part of *Mr Noon* was not separately published at this time.

2228. To Earl and Achsah Brewster, [15 May 1921]
Text: MS UT; Brewster, *Reminiscences*, pp. 21–6.

Ludwig-Wilhelmstift, *BadenBaden*, Germany
[15 May 1921][1]

Dear Brewster

Your letter today – Sunday – and I'll answer smack off because I prefer to do things on the spur.

    I.   Damn the Norwegian chap.[2]

   II.   We must meet before you go East.

  III. *Sons and Lovers* is supposed, *technically*, to have no construction. The world is full of technical fools.

  IV. You probably do know me better than I know you, because I don't know you – hardly at all. You Buddhistic people are dark birds, and hardly know yourselves what you build your nests of, I believe.

   V. What I mean by the eternal quality – and what you mean – I believe we should never make the two fit. But I agree quite about the *not grasping*: first because of thorns, then because it's so horrid (not sorrowful but enraging) to be grasped.

  VI. I here and now, finally and forever give up knowing anything about love, or wanting to know. I believe it doesn't exist, save as a word: a sort of wailing phoenix that is really the wind in the trees. – In fact I here and now, finally and forever leave off loving anything or everything or anybody. Basta la mossa![3]

 VII. All right, let white include all colours, if you like. – Only, white does *not* include all colours. It is only pure colourless light which includes all colours. And of even that I am doubtful. I doubt the exact sciences more than anything else – I don't know *anything* about Nirvana, and I never shall.

VIII. Does the admission of difference presuppose the possibility of superseding? When any life-creature has reached a certain – I don't mean that – I mean any vivid *being* can no more be superseded than life itself can be superseded. I consider the tiger is a *being*, a created being. If you kill all tigers still the tiger-soul continues. The mankind which kills the tiger assumes, willynilly, the tigers nature and need of

---

[1] The undated letter is clearly in response to Brewster's reply to Letter 2221. The tone suggests a speedy exchange of letters; DHL's reference to 'finishing Aaron' links the date to that of Letter 2230 ('have the end in sight'); and consequently it is conjectured that 'Sunday' was 15 May 1921.

[2] Unidentified.

[3] i.e. a word to the wise is enough.

being – Just as white America assumes, inevitably and frighteningly, the Red Indian nature – little by little. – But the point is I dont *want* the tiger superseded. Oh, may each she-tigress have seventy seven whelps, and may they all grow in strength and shine in stripes like day and night, and may each one eat at least seventy miserable featherless human birds, and lick red chops of gusto after it. Leave me my tigers, leave me spangled leopards, leave me bright cobra snakes, and I wish I had poison fangs and talons as good. I *believe* in wrath and gnashing of teeth and crunching of cowards bones. I *believe* in fear and in pain and in oh, such a lot of sorrow. As for your white Nirvana, my boy: paint stripes on it, and see how it looks. I'll bet it has a tiger's hungry sides and buzzing, disagreeable tail. Only it's like Wells' Invisible Man, it makes no show except when it's had its dinner.

IX. As for Mr Hume: Ambition, avarice, selflove, vanity, friendship, generosity, public spirit:[1] the *words* are all the same: the actuality is *so* different in each individual, as to make the statement feeble. You need only translate *generosity* into German or Russian, and you'll see that Mr Hume knew nothing about it. As for Die Liebe, Minne, l'amour, love, l'amore, Amor, and the two blessed Greek words which we pretend stand for love: look at 'em. – But I believe there is a certain life concord. But life-expressions are *so* different, it is idiocy to count them like cash. Give me *differences*.

X. Nirvana-ing is surely a state of continuing as you are. – But I know nothing about it. Rather hate it.

XI. I'll go eastward when the west pays me enough for my books to carry me there.

XII. Tell Mrs Beckett yes, to write to me, and please to invite us to look at the convent. I have a mind to – or a nose to sniff out a Franciscan rat.

XIII. I wish they had been tears.

D. H. Lawrence

PRIVATE GROUNDS   TRESPASSERS PROSECUTED
by order. Jas BUDDH.

Dear Mrs Brewster

All right, write your *own* first name as if you weren't trying to hide it: succeeding in hiding it, too. Might as well be Absalom for all I make of it.

---

[1] DHL is referring to a passage from Hume's *Enquiry concerning Human Understanding* (1748), VIII. i. 65 which he and Brewster had discussed in conversation. Brewster quotes the passage in *Reminiscences*, p. 19.

Guess old Rosalie does it for stinginess. – As for me, this is the only sheet of paper you'll get out of me this time.

Who on earth is the third lovable woman in *S. and L.*? – As for Miriam, I dreamed of her two nights ago. – But the word *love* has for me gone pop: there isn't anything any more. Not tragically, of course: but just so: quite a new sort of feeling.

Nellie Morrison is an ass who would say a pudding on a dish looked like Buddha, if only you crossed the spoon and fork in front to look like two cross-legs.[1] Your St. F[rancis] needs a good *schiaffo*,[2] and a pint of Chianti. Never ate enough.

I am finishing Aaron. And you won't like it *at all*. Instead of bringing him nearer to heaven, in leaps and bounds, he's misbehaving and putting ten fingers to his nose at everything. Damn heaven. Damn holiness. Damn Nirvana. Damn it all.

What a mercy your daughter doesn't shed a woful tear at mention of me. – I suppose I buddhistically removed her beyond sorrow: though a Punch and Judy show might have been better.

Epaphroditus is good.[3] Wish I had my Greek lexicon. What is Epaphros?

I don't want that tranquillity of heart which springs from within. Too much at my own expense. I want a bit of a good time – can't sit supping forever at these inside BadenBaden cure-springs.

Weather report. – My wife and I are in a little inn about 3 miles from Baden – among the hills, just on the edge of the Black Forest – the deep, deep green meadows, with bell flowers and big daisies, and the old black and white village scattered amongst, and amongst trees: the reddish castle ruin sticking above, out of green maples and beeches: the opening walnut-trees beside the loop of road: the great woods on the final hills, many-pointed fir-woods, and edges of flaming beech: the hills just steeply ceasing, and the wide Rhine-plain beyond, seen from the window, with a loop of river: the nice little northern, barefoot children playing, playing so childlike, not Italian adult-infant: the yellow oxen in the long wagons of grass: everybody nice, but rather spent, rather life-empty: and all so different from before the war: and so different from Taormina. Cheap too – 35 Marks a day each – 70 Mark for us two: about 6/-. Good food – good German sausages and beer, *good* Rhinewine, *good*

---

[1] Nellie Morrison, born in India, the daughter of a Scottish Presbyterian doctor, lived in Florence but was on a visit to Capri. It was she who took DHL to meet the Brewsters at Villa Quattro Venti. She had remarked that Achsah Brewster's painting of St Francis looked like DHL (*Reminiscences*, p. 24n.).

[2] 'box over the ears'.

[3] Epaphroditus was a leader of the Church of Philippi; see Philippians ii. 25–30.

whipped cream, and the first strawberries. No sausageless Nirvana: no! no!
Get a new *Cook!!* Enquire of Anna di Chiara.

Ah, the flesh-pots! We had ASPARAGUS (German the best in the world)
STRAWBERRIES and RHINEWINE and ROAST PORK[1] (dots are a
halo) – for dinner. WHAT!! did you have?

We must contrive to meet. Is that convent habitable? Couldn't we turn it
into a den of thieves, and pitch a camp there? I mean the Assisi, not the
Burmese. I may have to come to Italy – Florence – in the summer, to do a
book for the Medici Society. Not sure. But I need not stay long in Florence.
Are you staying all the summer in Capri? We'll be wandering South in
September, if we don't meet anywhere else, might meet then. But you sail in
October!! Send a line of sound practical *plotting*.

DAVID (NOT DANIEL) HERBERT (i.e. BRIGHT LORD)
LAWRENCE.

2229. To Percy Whittley, [16 May 1921]
Text: MS UT; PC; Postmark, Baden-Baden 17. 5. 21; Unpublished.

Ludwig-Wilhelmstift, *BadenBaden*
16 May

Dear Whittley

I have a friend in London – Mr Robert Mountsier, c/o American Express
Co, 6 Haymarket. W. – He is coming via Paris here. He might bring my sister.
But she hasn't got her passport. If she writes could you get her a passport
quick – and a French visa *good for a year* – and a German visa *to enter and
depart* – and if she left here via Hook of Holland, could the Dutch visa be got in
London too? – to enter Holland at Emmerich from Germany, en route for
Hook. – Perhaps this will be a nuisance to you. Don't bother if so, send her to
Cooks.

Let me know *when* you expect your holiday, and I'm sure we can plan it.
We may be in Florence till Sept. – then Taormina – or we may be in my sister-
in-laws country farm place near Salzburg, Austrian Tyrol – quite lovely,
snow mts. and lake. And in any place we could arrange for you if you like. So
keep me informed.

Are you happy in your new job.

Frieda sends best greetings.

D. H. Lawrence

With the exchange Germany and Austria are *very* cheap – 3/- or 4/- a day,
good.

---

[1] Each letter of these two words is surrounded by dots.

2230. To Martin Secker, [16 May 1921]
Text: MS UInd; Secker 40–1.

Ludwig Wilhelmstift, *BadenBaden*, Germany
16 May.

Dear Secker

I expected a reply to my Florence letter: nothing forthcoming.

Please tell me about *Women in Love*. And will you please pay the advance, or £50 of it, in to my bank Law Courts Branch of L[ondon] C[ounty] W[estminster] and P[arr]'s. Because I am afraid of overdrawing – and that, in Germany, would be very unpleasant for me. Please meet me in this matter, or I shall be angry.

I told Curtis Brown to let you go ahead with *Mr Noon*. Alternative title 'Lucky Noon'. – I have postponed finishing Part II – it will give you a fit – of laughter also, I hope. But I intend to finish it in Taormina. Here I have got *Aaron's Rod* well under weigh again, and have the end in sight. Nothing impossible in it, at all.

I *must* have proofs of *Mr Noon*. And publish if possible simultaneous with Seltzer. – Robert Mountsier arrives in London on Thursday. Please see him and talk about conjunctions.

Please write. I shall – I have told Curtis Brown to act in all ways friendlily towards you. And I know I am perfectly reasonable, till I get annoyed. But don't make me angry.

D. H. Lawrence

If you tell me anything straight out, and it is reasonable, I shall agree to it. But I am rather annoyed when, I having promised to forfeit if necessary all *Rainbow* advance, you hedge again about *Women in Love* advance.

Tell me, what are *Lost Girl's* sales.[1]

---

[1] Secker replied to DHL on 19 May 1921 (*Letters from a Publisher*, p. 13):

Dear Lawrence,

Many thanks for your letter of the 16th, to hand this morning. I had delayed answering your Florence letter for I had been hoping to let you know definite news about the date of publication of 'Women in Love'. The book was printed some time ago, in Scotland, but transport for the past month has been so difficult that it is only just now that the quires have reached my binders in London. Binders also are very slow as they prefer only to work four days a week, but I should be able to publish not later than June 10th. I have noted the names and addresses of the people who are to receive free copies and will of course send you one also. I have paid £50 into your account at the Law Courts Branch and will pay the balance on publication or in any case not later than June 10th. The sales of 'The Lost Girl' to the end of April amounted to 2591.

I am very glad to hear that I am to go ahead with 'Mr Noon' and I expect to hear from Curtis Brown in due course. When I see Robert Mountsier I will arrange publication to suit Seltzer's date. You will of course receive proofs of the work in due course.

I am very pleased also to hear that 'Aaron's Rod' is well under way again.

Yours sincerely

2231. To Robert Mountsier, [17 May 1921]
Text: MS Smith; Postmark, Baden-Baden 18. 5. 21.; Unpublished.

Ludwig-Wilhelmstift, *Baden-Baden*
Tuesday 17 May.

Dear M[ountsier]

Your letter just now. Hope this will get you Thursday or Friday. If you wire me, wire Hotel Krone, Ebersteinburg, BadenBaden.

Luggage has been *very* badly used in Italy: but terribly. Perhaps best bring it all with you. If we walk here, we can come back for it, or send it on. Germany is safe. But we'll pick it up at the frontier.

Bring cigarettes here. We can divide them and they won't bother us. But if you ship luggage, declare everything. But best bring all luggage along.

I wish you could bring my sister along – if she'd come – to stay here a week or ten days. It would so relieve me of my duty to go to England. She can travel with you via Paris–Strasburg to Baden: not far from Paris here. But to go home she had best take the direct train from Baden-Oos, over Emmerich to *Hook of Holland*: no change then. Book all but German tickets in London. – My sister is Mrs L.A. Clarke, Grosvenor Rd, *Ripley*, near Derby. I am writing to her now to tell her to communicate with you.[1] If you would like to go and see her I know she'd like it – Derby about three hours from London, Midland Railway: Ripley about 8 miles from Derby. But they could fetch you from Derby in their little 2-seater. – The only bother would be her passport. – (They might prefer to pick you up with their car in Nottingham.)

Do bring a photograph apparatus along. – We'll do a walking trip in Black Forest, and then to Florence. – I haven't heard yet about that damned picture book. The Oxford Press is doing it in conjunction with the Medici Society – and Mr. De Grey, of the Medici Society,[2] is supposed to be writing to let me know. I wish he would hurry up, because the Florence idea depends on this book.

I wanted my sister to send me a raincoat. Will you buy for me two pairs of cotton drawers for myself, for summer wear, *not* to come below the knee – cost about 3/6 a pair. That's all. My sister will or will not send the raincoat – depends how much time you give her.

I haven't kept Curtis B[rown] letters – but nothing of the least importance. He expects you.

Call and see Secker: tell him I am wondering about *Women in Love*, and

---

[1] Ada Clarke wrote to Mountsier on 26 May 1921 (MS Smith); she was unable to go to Germany; but she sent a coat for DHL and asked Mountsier to take it with him to Baden.

[2] Nigel de Grey (1886–1951) had worked for Heinemann (1907–14) at the time that *The White Peacock* was published; after war service he had recently become a director of the Medici Society Ltd. Later published *A Brief Guide to English Painting* (1933).

why he hasn't answered my letter. I want him to pay something in to my bank.

Let me know when to expect you, and I'll meet you at the station. We'll deposit luggage with my mother-in-law here in the town – Fraū Baronin von Richthofen. Prepare just *one* suitcase to come up to Ebersteinburg. I'll have you a room ready there.

Frieda's sister Else wants to see us in Munich: and her sister Johanna wants us to call at Zell-am-See, near Salzburg, in the Austrian Tyrol, where they have a property. We can do that if we go to Florence – via München and Innsbruck and Verona.

Ripley is full in the Notts-Derby coalfield. You might do an article on the Strike, if you like.[1]

Then – auf Wiedersehen   D. H. Lawrence

My sister and her husband have a tailoring business – and shop – all for miners. They know the miners well.

You have a certain number of my dollars. Use them for everything, as you think best.

The Oxford Press has sold out first edition of *History* and is printing another. The man there is G. H. Ely – Falcon Square. E.C.4. See him if it is any use to you. And if you see him collect news of the picture book.

2232. To Robert Mountsier, [17 May 1921]
Text: MS Smith; Postmark, Baden-Baden 17. 5. 21.; Unpublished.

Hotel Krone, Ebersteinburg, *BadenBaden*.
Tuesday 16 May.

Dear M[ountsier]

A post-script to this afternoon's letter. Frieda says will you bring her $2\frac{1}{2}$ yards of fine grey woollen cloth, for a light coat, velour cloth, if you can get it, light in weight: stone grey, as near in color to pattern as possible, fine light woollen cloth. Go to Marshall and Snellgrove, or Liberty: and bring enough thin silk for lining, the shop girl will tell you.

Secondly, the first part of *Aaron's Rod* was being typed by
Miss V. Monk, Grimsbury Farm, Long Lane, near Newbury, Berks.
I wrote a week ago and asked her please to post me the carbon copy only. You might ask her if she has done so: and if she hasn't, bring the whole, both type copies, *if you like*. I really think I may finish *Aaron's Rod* while I am here.

Thirdly, if my sister will come with you here – she hasn't got a passport at all. But a friend, Percy Whittley, 1. Albert Palace Mansions, Battersea Park.

---

[1] See p. 703 n. 2.

S.W.11. said he would get everything through his bank: they have a passport dept. It would be a question of[1] French visé – get one *good for a year*: and German visé – in and out journey – *Ein und Aus Reise* – and then the Dutch visé, for the frontier at Emmerich, for Hook of Holland, by the direct train Basle to Hook. Book all tickets except German, at Cooks, Ludgate Circus. – Tell her to bring only one light handbag, and *no* dutiable things. Then she can have one of your boxes of cigarettes – but open, and a few taken out.

Hope this doesn't bore you horribly. If it does, don't bother with any of it, but just come straight here when you are ready.

a rivederci   D. H. Lawrence

Don't mention Oxford Press to C[urtis] B[rown] – except *History* – not the picture book.[2]

2233. To S. S. Koteliansky, [17 May 1921]

Text: MS BL; PC v. [unknown painting of rural scene]; Postmark, Baden-Baden 19. 5. 21.; Zytaruk 217.

Ludwig-Wilhelmstift. BadenBaden.
17 May

Here have I been for three weeks, and never a word. We are in a little inn about 3 miles out of Baden – edge of Black Forest. The woods are very big and lovely – a sense of a big wide land and strong deep trees – so different from Italy.[3] Germany very quiet and numb seeming – and all the old order completely gone. It feels queer and vacant. BadenBaden hasn't really existed since 1914 – and now a mere memory. Living for us very cheap, and plenty of food here – everybody quite nice – quite nice with me – the old show gone for ever – but a bit depressing, feels so life-empty. Don't quite know how long we shall stay – shall tell you when we move. Tell Sophie Issayevna I had her letter in Taormina: so sorry about the headaches. Any news of your people? – I asked Secker to send you *Women in Love* – but don't know when he is bringing it out.

---

[1] MS reads 'question French'.
[2] This postscript was written on the verso of the envelope.
[3] Italy] England

2234. To Catherine Carswell, [17 May 1921]
Text: MS YU; PC v. Partie Im Kammbachtal; Postmark, [. . .]; cited in Carswell 144.

Ludwig-Wilhelmstift. *Baden-Baden.*

17 May

Have been here now three weeks – we have come out to a little inn, 3 miles from Baden, where we live for about 3/- a day each – minus extras. There is quite enough food again – plenty in fact – and we are very well done. The great woods, end of Black Forest, all round, with the Rhine valley and the Vosges beyond. Germany quite friendly, but a bit depressing – sort of stupefied or numbed rather than anything else. But a great sense of magnificent, spacious country. – We sent the boy some little Black Forest toys last week: hope they arrive. – Am not quite sure how long we shall stay here – my mother-in-law much better, but shaky. How is your book getting on? I feel a stranger everywhere and nowhere.

DHL

2235. To Marie Hubrecht, 17 May 1921
Text: MS UN; Unpublished.

Ludwig-Wilhelmstift, *Baden Baden*, Germany

17 May 1921.

Dear Miss Hubrecht

I had your letter last week – but waited a while to see what we are going to do. – I should so much have liked to come to Doorn: but I am so tired of travelling, and it costs so much too, that I fear I shall have to give it up. I thought perhaps of asking you if I might meet my sister at Hook, and we both stay a few days at the Witte Huis. But I won't really trouble you.

It is possible I shall have a book to write for the Medici Society, which would take me back to Florence in June – to stay for a month or six weeks. But I am not sure. Then my sister-in-law invites us to spend August and September on her place – she has a farm and villa and land near Salzburg, in the Austrian Tyrol. But I am not sure. – I did think I should go to England – but now I don't want to. So there we are.

The world really makes me tired. – Germany is very quiet. Frieda and I have come out to a little inn about three miles out of BadenBaden, with the woods all round, the edge of the Black Forest. It is very lovely – the great trees, and the great magnificent landscape, so very different from Sicily or Italy. But the life-spirit has sunk very low – life all seems numb and feeble here. There is a sense of vacancy, life-emptiness. The people are all quite nice with us: and the little children are very jolly, playing in their little northern way in the village street. Thank heaven they don't beg and clamour for soldi, like parasites of human life, as they do in Taormina. There is plenty of food again – not abundance, but plenty – and we live very cheaply owing to the exchange. But clothing and luxuries are expensive even counting the exchange: 400 mark for a hat, a man asked me – and it would not cost more than 15/-, at the most, in London.

My mother-in-law is much better – but must keep very still indeed – her heart gone wrong. She clings to us, and doesn't want us to go away. And really, one place is as good, or as bad, as another nowadays. I have got so tired of the insatiable money-avarice of the Italians, and their callous materialism. But yet one can't stay for a very long time in Germany. – I plan to go back to Taormina in September. When will you be there? I hear that the studio is now full of all your furniture. – But thank you so much for saying we could use it, the studio, while you were away.

Martin Secker is supposed to be publishing my novel *Women in Love* this month. The strike may delay him. Anyway I will have him send you a copy when it comes out.

And we will meet in the autumn in Taormina, if not before. It is so kind of you to ask us to Doorn. But sometimes my spirit fairly gives way, at the thought of travelling further.

Frieda sends her warm greetings – and hopes, as I do, that you are feeling strong and well again now we have this lovely warm weather.

Juta is in Sardinia painting illustrations for a book of travel-sketches of Sardinia, which I did in the spring. I hope all will come off well: then later we can send you the book.

With many greetings   D. H. Lawrence

2236. To S. S. Koteliansky, 27 May 1921
Text: MS BL; Postmark, Baden[-Baden] 28. 5. 21; Moore 654–5.

Ludwig-Wilhelmstift, *BadenBaden*, Germany
27 May 1921

My dear Kot

Your letter and *Tchekhov's Note-Book* today.[1] They are *charming* little books, in format and appearance, these. I have read only a bit, walking up here to Ebersteinburg through the woods. It makes me want to sneeze, like pepper in the nose. – But very many thanks for the book. –

[1] *The Note-Books of Anton Tchekhov Together with Reminiscences of Tchekhov by Maxim Gorky*, trans. Kot and Leonard Woolf, was published by the Hogarth Press in April 1921.

Secker says now he will have *Women in Love* ready for June 10th. He is not dependable. Tell me if you get the copy. I have one: dirty paper.

So the Murrain is renewing his bald youth like the vulture, is he, and stuffing himself with Oxford garbage.[1]

And how is Gertler *personally?*

Well, your letters are really bad-to-worse bulletins. So there is no end to anything.

As for me, thank God I have no news and know nobody. We are in this peasant inn at Ebersteinburg, among geese and goats and a pig – with the big Schwarzwald Woods near the door – and the wide Rhine plain beyond. One eats quite well. – Germany is queer and empty, and never a uniform save the postman. There is really no authority at all – but everything goes the same, in perfect order, because nobody wants to do anything different. Only it seems so *quiet.* The Hotel Stephanie in Baden was full of Schieber[2] for Whitsun, and the manager said they paid on an average 800 Mark a day: over £3. English. We pay 35 M. a day each, and all we want we have.

I cannot but think that Europe is having a slight reactionary swing, back to conservatism. But underneath I feel that only some sort of Bolshevism is inevitable, later.

The world at large makes me sick. I never want to think of it. Hardly ever do think of it. – We have had hot good weather – the deep woods – innumerable birds – and no people. *Alors* –

I have *nearly* finished my novel *Aarons Rod*, which I began long ago and could never bring to an end. I began it in the Mecklenburg Square days.[3] Now suddenly I had a fit of work – sitting away in the woods. And save for the last chapter, it is done. But it won't be popular.

Tell Sophie Issayevna I am so sorry she was ill. There is not much fun for her in London, I am sure. I like to feel I can drift about. – And there is something very fine about this Schwarzwald – the big straight strong trees with all their power and their indifferent proud new leaves. One forgets people. Germany seems so *empty.* And nobody seems to care any more what happens politically.

Greet Sophie Issayevna and Ghita. It will soon be two years since I left Acacia Rd and England. You were the last person I spoke to in England.

DHL

Yes, Edgar Jaffe was my brother in law. But he had gone cracked after being Bolshevist Minister of finance for Bavaria.

[1] Murry had been invited by Sir Walter Raleigh to give six lectures in Oxford during May 1921; they were subsequently published as *The Problem of Style* (Oxford, 1922).
[2] 'racketeers'.
[3] October–November 1917. See also Letter 1545 and n. 4.

2237. To Martin Secker, 27 May 1921
Text: MS UInd; Postmark, Baden[-Baden] 28. 5. 21.; Secker 41.

Ludwig-Wilhelmstift, *BadenBaden*, Germany.

27 May 1921.

Dear Secker

Your letter yesterday. Many thanks for having paid in the £50. to my bank. Now I need have no qualms.

I had the copy of *Women in Love* also three days ago.

You will be glad to hear I have as good as finished *Aaron's Rod*: that is, it is all done except the last chapter – two days work. It all came quite suddenly here. But it is a queer book: I've no idea what you or anybody will think of it. When it is typed I will let you see it. It is about as long as *Lost Girl*, I presume.

Will you get *Women in Love* out for June 10th.? Will you add two copies, please, to the list of those I asked you to send out.

1.   Mrs L.A. Clarke, Grosvenor Road, *Ripley, near Derby*.
1.   Mrs S. King, 480 Main Street, *Carlton, near Nottingham*.
Send me any news.

Yrs   D. H. Lawrence

I suppose you have seen Mountsier and talked over everything with him.

2238. To Robert Mountsier, [27 May 1921]
Text: MS Smith; PC v. Ebersteinburg; Postmark, Baden-Baden 28. 5. 21; Unpublished.

Baden.
Friday.

I had your letter today – the first from England. Did not write again, waiting to hear from you. – Of course I tremble in my shoes about the ship. But still am ready to do all I can: and you know what that is. – *Aaron* is finished, save for the last chapter. – What troubles me is the money to *carry on with*, if we ship on the high seas. – But I say nothing [. . .] more till I hear again: on tenterhooks I am. – This is a picture of the house where we are living. I make a X over my room. – Frieda is terrified of the adventure.

D. H. Lawrence

2239. To Robert Mountsier, 1 June 1921
Text: MS Smith; Unpublished.

Hotel Krone, *Ebersteinburg, BadenBaden*
1st. June 1921.

Dear M[ountsier]

My first feeling is that the *James and Edgar* isn't quite good enough. You would find there would be *enormous* expense fitting her up: and you *must* have an engine of some sort, for emergencies. We could have had a proper little yacht, all ready, for £1,500, in Palermo. The *James and Edgar* is not our ship, I fear.

Second, let us make a little money before we buy. I would rather do that. Otherwise we should feel so *very* much tied by the nose. Also let us discuss farms: though I prefer the ship. But am afraid of being too much tied to it. One must never feel doomed to anything.

Thirdly I simply don't want to come to England. I know it would only make me feel dreary: and I can't work in England.

As to plans here. I am waiting for various word of ships from Hamburg. Believe we could get what we want, by autumn, cheaper here than anywhere.

Also it is much cheaper to live here. We have all we want for 35 Mark a day, and most beautiful country. – Then F[rieda]'s sister Johanna has a villa and a farm on a little lake in Austrian Tyrol near Salzburg: with boats and fishing and shooting and snow-mountains: we can go there and stay as long as we like: I am also invited to Doorn by a Dutch friend – lady – who has a country house there: also invited to Berlin: and we could have a flat in Florence, or maybe a friend might loan a place in Assisi. We can decide in a little while.

Secker has paid £50. in to my bank, after a sharp letter from me. Now I hear from C[urtis] B[rown] that he, Secker, wants to count this little *Mr Noon* novel as not a novel, but a bit thrown in with his legal five. Also that Secker wants very much to see *Sardinia*.[1] – I think I would rather another publisher did *Sardinia*. – And I think I would rather Secker held over this *Mr Noon* Part 1. and did *Aaron's Rod* first. *Aaron* is complete. – Do you care to see Curtis B. about this? – I'll write, however, to him.

You will have had my letter about the Medici Press. The man is Nigel de Grey, Medici Press, 7 Grafton Street. W. – nr. Bond Street. – If you see Ely ask him if Oxford Press will supply me with reference books: at any rate, all they have in stock. If you see de Grey, ask him the same. I will guarantee their safe return. – And then I had better put the drafting of the agreement into CurtisB's hands, had I not? – This book will come under a *nom de plume*. – I have notes for the next vol. of the little *Psychoanalysis and Unconscious* Book: to be called Psychoanalysis and the Incest Motive.[2] Is this worth writing? Again ask CB. – Also Juta was in Sardinia all May painting illustrations for the *Sardinia* Book. I must see them soon.

---

[1] The two matters had been raised with Curtis Brown in Secker's letter of 26 May 1921 (Secker Letter-Book, UIll).
[2] Eventually called *Fantasia of the Unconscious* and published by Seltzer in October 1922.

As for drawers – just common cotton half-drawers – summer under-pants. – Don't bother about the cloth: or if you do, let shop post it to Frieda at LudwigsWilhelmstift, largely labelled Geschenk – Gift: and do you write six words in a letter saying 'Dear Frieda, I am sending you this bit of stuff as a present to make yourself a summer coat –' Then there is *no duty* to pay. An *insured* parcel is perfectly safe.

Declare 100 cigarettes. Duty is so small, comparatively: i.e. paid in Marks. If you get camera etc. stamped you'll get them out quite without trouble. I have found the German frontier *very* easy indeed – so has F. always. – If you like to leave your trunk in Paris, do so. It can be forwarded anywhere, if it is *unbreakable*, iron-fastened etc. If at all fragile, bring it with you.

Au revoir   D. H. Lawrence

Luggage can also lie at the Stift if we walk.

2240. To Curtis Brown, 1 June 1921
Text: MS UT; Unpublished.

Ludwig Wilhelmstift, *BadenBaden*, Germany.
1st June. 1921.

Dear Curtis Brown

Ask Secker if he would not rather do the normal-length novel *Aaron's Rod*, which I have just finished, before this little *Mr Noon* Part 1.[1] As soon as I have got this MS. of *Aaron's Rod* typed and looked over, I'll send it you. Then any decision regarding the little *Mr Noon* can be postponed.

What do you think about the *Sardinia* book? Is anyone else likely to put more push behind it, do you think? – Is it enough to let Secker go on with the novels? – I leave it to you. – We will be as compliant as possible with Secker with regard to novels, but perhaps with regard to other books there is no obligation. – I wish somebody would do pieces of *Sardinia* in a magazine or periodical, for the sake of the odd money, which I need.[2] It's a slow slow business waiting on royalties. – I believe *Time and Tide*, though insignificant, pays quite well. – But if you *really* think it better not to waste time on serialising, go ahead as you like. – A friend has been in Sardinia all May painting illustrations. I'll let you see them as soon as I can lay hands on them.

---

[1] Secker wrote to Curtis Brown also on 1 June 1921 (Secker Letter-Book, UIll); he had reached the same conclusion about DHL's finished and partly-finished works: 'My feeling now about "Mr. Noon" is that it would be better for Lawrence to write the remaining half next and let it succeed 'Aaron's Rod'' as the next novel under my contract. This seems to me the most straightforward course and, in the circumstances, much preferable to issuing it in two separate parts.'

[2] Selections from *Sea and Sardinia* appeared in the *Dial*, October and November 1921.

I am sure somebody else would do better than Secker with the little *Psychoanalysis* book. I have made notes for a second little vol. – following up – called Psychoanalysis and the Incest Motive. Do you think it's worth while writing it?

Glad you liked Mountsier.

D. H. Lawrence

2241. To Thomas Seltzer, 3 June 1921
Text: MS ColU; Postmark, Baden-Baden -3. 6. 21.; Delany, *DHL Review*, ii. 198.

per Adr Frau Baronin von Richthofen, Ludwig Wilhelmstift,
Baden Baden, Germany.
3 June 1921

Dear Seltzer

Today ten copies of *Psychoanalysis and the Unconscious*: beastly long title.[1] I am always so pleased when the books come from you, they *look* so nice. Whereas Secker's are so scrubby! I got a copy of his *Women in Love* the other day, and fairly spat. He brings it out on June 10th, so he says. – Many thanks for these ten copies.

I want you to tell me fairly soon if this sells enough to make it worth while my going on with the next little volume, which continues the development of the theory of the Unconscious. I have begun it, and it should be as interesting, if not more, than this first book.

I have finished *Aarons Rod*, writing away in the Black Forest here: so still, so strange, such a different Germany. Feels so empty – as if uninhabited: yet of course every house is crowded to the coal cellar. Yet it feels empty – life-empty: no young men. I like the big wideness of the landscape – we are living out in a village – the big magnificence. It seems all to have gone still and remote and far off, and I feel a bit as the Romans must have felt on the edge of the great Hercynian wood. They were so terrified of it. – Everybody is very nice – inwardly tired and very sad. Never a uniform left, and no real authority. Yet the people by themselves obey the laws, and everything works perfectly. It is strange after the impudence and disorder of Italy.

But one feels, the old order has[2] gone – Hohenzollern and Nietzsche and all. And the era of love and peace and democracy with it. There will be an era of war ahead: some sort of warfare, one knows not what. But Mars is the god before us: the real Mars, not Jesus in arms.

I expect Mountsier here next week. We shall wander about: perhaps stay

---

[1] Published by Seltzer on 10 May 1921.   [2] has] of

the summer in the Austrian Tyrol, where my sister in law still has a little estate among the mountains. Perhaps back to Florence. Mountsier wants me to go to London – but no, not England! It depresses me and makes everything feel barren.

I read Evelyn Scott's *Narrow House*. Really it is a sort of last word. After that we drop to bits, piecemeal, like lepers. – I read Magdeleine Marx's *Woman*, and didn't like it. Ugh, I detest such 'Women', and long to box their ears and jump on their straw turbans and use absolutely *low* language to the bitches. – I read Cecil Scotts *Blind Mice* – and if *only* he'd grinned, even up his sleeve, what a marvellous satire it would have made. But he never grinned. – Mountsier will write you everything.

D. H. Lawrence

I suppose you know Germany quite well. – This place will never really revive. It belongs to Turgenev and Dostoevsky and Edward VII.

Orchestra concert in Kurhaus last night – Siegfried Wagner conducted. Great men should *never* have sons. – Lichtenthaler Allee full of Schieber: ach, so ugly: and they pay 800 Mark a day in the Stephanie.

This is my Schwiegermutter's address: always a safe one.[1]

I wish you would send Evelyn Scott a copy of *P. and the Unconscious* – c/o Boni and Liveright.

DHL

2242. To Evelyn Scott, 3 June 1921
Text: MS UT; Unpublished.

Ludwig-Wilhelmstift, Baden Baden, Germany
3 June 1921.

Dear Evelyn Scott

I had your letter and your book – received both here. The book I began, and was frightened off by the butcher's meat. Am fastidious, and catholic *au fond*. But scented my hanky and started off afresh. So I read the *Narrow House* right to the kerbstone and the chimney pots.[2] Well, I think it's all vile, but true, and therefore valuable. Perhaps more a last word than D'Annunzio: a last last word. I feel it is white America's last word, before a cataclysm sets in, or a new start. Two more words, and the life-centre of all the people, and even the authoress, will have broken, and unresisted putrescence set in. It's death

---

[1] This postscript was written alongside the address at the top of the letter.

[2] *Narrow House* (Boni & Liveright, 1921) was Evelyn Scott's first novel. (It is the story of Winnie Price's marriage to Laurence Farley, the consequent displeasure of her parents and the inevitable quarrel between the two families.)

enough in all conscience. But why not kick the bottom out of the old show? Why is everybody always caring so hard about somebody else? Why not leave off? In short, why not have done with Jesus and with love, and have a shot at conscious, proud power. Why not soldiers, instead of lovers? Why not laugh, and spit in the eye of love. Really, why not laugh? As for the absolute, I have no absolute but myself. And as for visions – two a penny, three a penny, mine go cheap. Kick the posterior of creeping love, and laugh when it whimpers. Pah, it is a disease, love, and apparently you love dying of it, like so many people. I say this, the *Narrow House* made me hate the disease of love, finally for which, many thanks. Give me henceforth Mars, and a free fight.

I think *so* often, oh, what a very good satire *Blind Mice* would have made, if only C[yril] K[ay] S[cott] would have grinned up his sleeve. I still have faint hopes that he may have done. Did he? – Or is a sort of Red Indian seriousness inevitable in America?

I didn't think your *Women in Love* review in *The Dial* very sensible.[1] But there, we have different sets of values.

Why does CKS do jobs? I left off ten years ago, and my wife and I have lived on 37 dollars a month before now: and always with sang froid. I doubt if I make more than £400 per annum now – and knock about Europe as I like, and spit in the face of anybody who tries to insult me. One goes away with a woman who is somebody else's wife, but one doesn't feel wistful about it. Oh hell alive – Why don't you just spit in the eye of the world, and shit on the doorstep of the *Narrow House*? Those are the sacraments at this juncture. Oh my holy God, always *au grand sérieux* about a pound of stewing meat. *People* are like that – but why oh why should one care? Why not leave off caring? Kick, and not complain. Kick – Kick 'em. For Gods blessed sake, don't do them the honor of feeling bad about them. Tell them to shit, and see what a marvellous, startling, miraculous effect it will have on 'em.

Vale!   D. H. Lawrence

Even you are incomplete. A *Narrow House* without a watercloset!

– You should have had a Part IV, a part 222–too-too-too! – so! 'Pfui! What a cockadoodling lot! Shut 'em all up in the W.C. and make 'em describe, in definite language, how they wipe their arses, before you let 'em out.'

THE END OF THE NARROW HOUSE – Valissime!

I mean no offence: am as serious as John the Divine.

[1] Evelyn Scott's review of *Women in Love* and *The Lost Girl* appeared in the *Dial*, April 1921, under the title 'A Philosopher of the Erotic' (see Draper, ed., *Critical Heritage*, pp. 161–4). She concluded: 'Mr Lawrence, by accident a novelist, actually is the priest of an age almost intolerably self-aware. Evocative, rather than delineative, he consciously desires what all ritual infers, the release of individuality in the confusion of sense.'

I asked Seltzer to send you a copy of *Psychoanalysis and the Unconscious*. Oh what jew-jaw it will seem to you.

Tell Boney and Liveright they can say I found *The Narrow House* a damned good cure for the love-disease: a cataplasm.

INDEX

No distinction is made between a reference in the text or in a footnote.
All titles of writings by Lawrence are gathered under his name.
For localities, public buildings, etc. in London see the comprehensive entry under the place-name.
A bold numeral indicates a biographical entry in a footnote.